Gender Roles
A Sociological Perspective

4th Edition

Linda L. Lindsey
Maryville University of St. Louis

PEARSON
Prentice
Hall

Upper Saddle River, New Jersey 07458

Library of Congress Cataloging-in-Publication Data

Lindsey, Linda L.
    Gender roles : a sociological perspective / Linda L. Lindsey.—4th ed.
        p. cm.
    Includes bibliographical references and index.
    ISBN 0-13-010428-0
    1. Sex role 2. Sex role—United States. I. Title.

HQ1075.L564 2004
305.3—dc22

2004053482

Publisher: Nancy Roberts
Editorial Director: Leah Jewell
Editorial Assistant: Lee Peterson
Senior Marketing Manager: Marissa Feliberty
Marketing Assistant: Jennifer Lang
Prepress and Manufacturing Buyer: Mary Ann Gloriande
Cover Art Director: Jayne Conte
Cover Design: Koala Bear Design
Cover Photo: Gerald Bustamente/Stock Illustration Source, Inc.
Director, Image Resource Center: Melinda Reo
Manager, Rights and Permissions: Zina Arabia
Manager, Cover Visual Research and Permissions: Karen Sanatar
Manager, Visual Research: Beth Brenzel
Image Permission Coordinator: Robert Farrell
Full-Service Project Management: GGS Book Services, Atlantic Highlands

This book was set in 10/12 New Baskerville by GGS Book Services and was printed
and bound by Hamilton Printing Company. The cover was printed by Coral Graphics.

To Phil Loughlin

Pearson Education LTD.
Pearson Education Singapore, Pte. Ltd
Pearson Education, Canada, Ltd
Pearson Education–Japan
Pearson Education Australia PTY, Limited

Pearson Education North Asia Ltd
Pearson Educación de Mexico, S.A. de C.V.
Pearson Education Malaysia, Pte. Ltd
Pearson Education, Upper Saddle River, New Jersey

10 9 8 7 6 5 4 3 2 1
ISBN 0-13-010428-0

Contents

PART II Gender Roles, Marriage,
and the Family

PART III Gender Roles: Focus on Social Institutions

Preface

Interest in gender related topics continues to expand rapidly in all disciplines and sociology is no exception. This interest has led to such an explosion of theory and research on gender and how gender intersects with other social categories, such as race, social class, ethnicity, religion, age, and sexuality, that the discipline itself is being reshaped. An important ingredient of this reshaping is that the feminist paradigm has joined with functionalism, conflict theory, and symbolic interaction to become sociology's fourth major theoretical perspective. The globalization process is yet another reshaping trend—a process that fuels diversity yet makes people more connected to one another than at any other time in human history. Gender role change in our relationships, homes, workplaces, and schools is a fundamental feature of globalization. Through abundant data documenting cutting edge research on gender and theoretical applications demonstrating how this research can be interpreted differently according to various sociological theories, the 4th edition of *Gender Roles* effectively captures all these trends. This edition strongly emphasizes the junction between sociological theory and its application to gender and issues of diversity that are reverberating around the globe. Students will better understand the theory–research connection through the new critiques this edition incorporates throughout. In addition, students will be able to locate themselves when they examine material on the intersection of gender with the other social categories they occupy and as they grapple with gender issues in their everyday lives.

Since the last edition of *Gender Roles,* the rapid growth of gender related scholarship has brought with it more interpretations, more sophistication, and more complexity. The good news is that there is a wealth of material from which to choose. Students need to be introduced to the richness and complexity of scholarship on gender and the important issues emerging from this scholarship. Because only a fraction of this abundant information can be included, material for this edition had to be carefully chosen to adequately and accurately represent competing theoretical views on gender and how various groups are portrayed according to these views. Interdisciplinary work aids in these portrayals. This edition makes focused choices from the contributions of other disciplines as they impinge on the sociology of gender roles. Although the task in selecting new material and discarding old material is formidable, it is manageable when a sociological perspective directs the process. Students will find a solid sociological foundation that links the range of information presented.

Written primarily as a core text for courses variously titled Sociology of Gender, Sex and Gender, Gender Roles, or Sex Roles, this text may be used for those studying the sociology of the family, psychology of women, gender and globalization, and women's or men's studies. Although guided by a sociological perspective, those with little or no background in sociology will find the text easy to navigate. It is also an excellent review for upper division students who will have their sociological expertise reinforced early in the text. Both groups will have the requisite knowledge to tackle the more complex gender issues they will then confront. The opening chapter provides an overview of the sociological perspective, its theories, and its basic concepts. Basic concepts from women's and men's studies are also introduced. Key terms are defined and boldfaced. Students will quickly understand that these theories and concepts can be used in explaining the sometimes contradictory research on gender issues. Theoretical discussions and applications that are both meaningfully linked with research as well as critiqued reinforce this understanding.

Part I provides insights on gender roles and the development of beliefs about women and men and masculinity and femininity from the disciplines and study of biology, psychology, anthropology, language, and history. Biological and sociocultural explanations for gender development are highlighted in the wealth of new material from interdisciplinary research that exposes the myths and offers critiques of essentialist explanations for gender roles. In turn, these insights are linked back to sociological understanding of the issues being discussed. This section expands considerably on interdisciplinary research on health and sexuality and on the connection between family and workplace that impacts the well-being of men and women in their gender role performance. New data on gender issues in globalization focusing on the developing world highlighting the paid and unpaid work roles of women and men and the similarities the globe's women share as a result of these roles round out the section. The significant issues related to work–family themes set up in Part I are carried throughout the text.

The sociological perspective dominates the balance of the book. Part II focuses on marriage and the family and provides the latest research, demographic portraits, and explanations regarding gender issues in love, choosing a partner, parenting, and the changing family in a multicultural context. The impact of work on gender roles in the family is highlighted. In addition to an expanded chapter on men and masculinity, all chapters integrate new material from men's studies highlighting how traditional definitions of masculinity and men's roles are being challenged, how men are responding to these challenges, and how they are responding to the changing roles of women. Part III views gender continuity and change in the economy, education, religion, media, politics, and law and suggests future trends related to gender roles. The gendered nature of the media and the huge impact of women's entry into the labor force are accentuated as key influences impacting gender roles in the social institutions.

This text provides opportunities for students to explore a variety of gender issues and how these impact their personal, academic, and professional lives. Rapid social change collides with our attitudes and behaviors regarding gender and forces us to confront traditional ways of thinking and doing. We may eagerly pursue new directions or stubbornly resist them. In either scenario, we will make wiser decisions in our relationships, homes, schools, and workplaces when we better understand the myth and reality associated with gender.

For both women and men the topic of gender roles is definitely a controversial one. You will be confronted with ideas that reinforce as well as challenge your thinking about women and men and masculinity and femininity. An objective of this book is to raise your level of consciousness about what you take for granted concerning gender. Once you grapple with the research, confront the stereotypes, and select the theory you consider most reasonable in explaining gender issues, you will have increased your understanding of our gendered world. You will also have gained insight about the other half of humanity.

ACKNOWLEDGMENTS

The completion of the 4th edition of *Gender Roles* relied on the time and talents of many people. My longtime editor, Sharon Chambliss, and my Prentice Hall mentor, Nancy Roberts, could be called on for support, advice, and encouragement through the long process. My production editor, Donna Lee Lurker, and the staff at GGS Book Services ensured that the manuscript was clear and accurate. Gerald Van Ravenswaay did an outstanding job creating an index that will serve the needs of students doing term papers and of faculty and scholars who will find this text's extensive and up-to-date references useful for research, and Monte Abbott, my friend and colleague, did the test item file. I am indebted to those who have read and critiqued various chapters, including: Essie Manuel Rutledge, Western Illinois University; Edward J. Steffes, Salisbury State University; Mary White Stewart, University of Nevada–Reno; and Tom Kasulis, Ohio State University. Those people and places who provided research assistance and kept me supplied with the most current material have been extremely helpful. In this regard, I thank Staley Hitchcock, Ken Harris, and the East-West Center. The administration and staff at Maryville University and Washington University's Social Thought and Analysis Program provided much needed support services and leave time. I wholeheartedly thank Juanita Aycock, Keith Lovin, Ed Palm, Sandy Reeder, and Pat Zollner in this respect. I would like to thank my mom, Ruth, for the food and the love, and my friends and colleagues for the words of encouragement when deadlines loomed, time was short, and stress magnified. These include Marsha Balluff, Betty Buck, Larry Grieshaber, Cheryl Hazel, Nancy Hume, Morris Levin, Bill Nagel, and Joe Overton. The St. Louis Bread Company (Panera) in Kirkwood, as always, offers not only a vital place for outlining and proofreading, but also for respite and reenergizing. With manager Mary Klein's warmth and expertise at the center, its wonderful staff—especially Berlinda McNeal and Judy Warneke and Stella Burlacu in Webster's BreadCo—provides an inviting environment to all they serve, and they served me so very well, even as I occupied tables for long periods surrounded by mounds of paper. Finally thanks to my many BreadCo friends who cheerfully read excerpts, provided insight about gender from their own lives, and also offered ongoing and much appreciated encouragement to finish this edition. These include Louise and Bill Blade, Nancy English, Tom Loughrey, Bob Ott, Bill Reineke, Jim Lake, Tim Stickney, and Wendy and Michael Zilm. And thanks to my friend Jack Wehrle, who astutely observed that writing a book is like biting off an elephant one piece at a time. His encouragement during the digestive process was highly valued.

Linda L. Lindsey
St. Louis, Missouri

CHAPTER 1

THE SOCIOLOGY OF GENDER

Theoretical Perspectives and Feminist Frameworks

BASIC SOCIOLOGICAL CONCEPTS

Key Concepts for the Sociology of Gender
Distinguishing Sex and Gender

SOCIOLOGICAL PERSPECTIVES ON GENDER ROLES

Functionalism
Conflict Theory
Symbolic Interaction
Feminist Sociological Theory

FEMINISM AND ITS BRANCHES

Liberal Feminism
Socialist Feminism
Radical Feminism
Multicultural and Global Feminism
Ecofeminism
Backlash to Feminism

All causes, social and natural, combine to make it unlikely that women should be collectively rebellious to the power of men. They are so far in a position different from all other subject classes, that their masters require something more from them than actual service. Men do not want solely the obedience of women, they want their sentiments.

—John Stuart Mill, *The Subjection of Women* (1869)

The study of gender has emerged as one of the most important trends in the discipline of sociology in the twentieth century. The research and theory associated with studying gender issues has propelled the sociology of gender from the margins to become a central feature of the discipline. This text will document how sociologists have aided our understanding of the influence of gender in shaping our lives, our attitudes, and our behavior. This understanding is enhanced by investigating the links between sociology and other disciplines and by integrating key concepts, such as race and social class, to clarify gender relations. Sociology is interested in how human behavior is shaped by group life. Although all group life is ordered in a variety of ways, gender is a key component of the ordering. An explosion of research on gender issues now suggests that all social interactions, and the institutions in which the interactions occur, are *gendered* in some manner. Accounting for this gendering has reshaped the theoretical and empirical foundations of sociology. On the theoretical

1

side, gender awareness has modified existing sociological theory and led to the creation of a new feminist paradigm. On the empirical side, gender awareness has led to innovative research strategies and opened up new topics for sociological inquiry. We open with an examination of basic concepts and theories that lay the groundwork for our sociological journey into gender roles.

BASIC SOCIOLOGICAL CONCEPTS

All societies are structured around relatively stable patterns that establish how social interaction will be carried out. One of the most important social structures that organizes social interaction is **status**—a category or position a person occupies that is a significant determinant of how she or he will be defined and treated. We acquire statuses by achievement, through our own efforts, or by ascription, being born into them or attaining them involuntarily at some other point in the life cycle. We occupy a number of statuses simultaneously, referred to as a **status set**, such as mother, daughter, attorney, patient, employee, and passenger. Compared to achieved statuses occurring later in life, ascribed statuses are those immediately impacting virtually every aspect of our lives. The most important ascribed statuses are gender, race, and social class. A status is simply a position within a social system and should not be confused with rank or prestige. There are high-prestige statuses as well as low prestige statuses. In the United States, for example, a physician occupies a status ranked higher in prestige than a secretary. All societies categorize members by status and then rank these statuses in some fashion, thereby creating a system of **social stratification**. People whose status sets are comprised of low-ranked ascribed statuses more than high-ranked achieved statuses are near the bottom of the social stratification system and vulnerable to social stigma, prejudice, and discrimination. To date, there is no known society in which the status of female is consistently ranked higher than that of male.

A **role** is the expected behavior associated with a status. Roles are performed according to social **norms**, shared rules that guide people's behavior in specific situations. Social norms determine the privileges and responsibilities a status possesses. Females and males, mothers and fathers, and daughters and sons are all statuses with different normative role requirements attached to them. The status of mother calls for expected roles involving love, nurturing, self-sacrifice, home-making, and availability. The status of father calls for expected roles of bread-winner, disciplinarian, home technology expert, and ultimate decision maker in the household. Society allows for a degree of flexibility in acting out roles, but in times of rapid social change, acceptable role limits are often in a state of flux, producing uncertainty about what appropriate role behavior should be. People may experience *anomie*—normlessness—because traditional norms have changed but new ones have yet to be developed. For example, the most important twentieth-century trend impacting gender roles in the United Sates is the massive increase of women in the labor force. Although women from all demographic categories contributed to these numbers, mothers with preschool children led the trek from unpaid home-based roles to full-time paid employment roles. In acting out the roles of mother and employee, women are expected to be available at given times to satisfy the needs of family and workplace. Because workplaces and other social institutions have not been modified in meaningful ways to account for the new statuses women occupy, their range of acceptable role behavior is severely restricted. As a result, family and workplace roles inevitably collide and compete with one another for the mother–employee's time and attention.

Key Concepts for the Sociology of Gender

As key components of social structure, statuses and roles allow us to organize our lives in consistent, predictable ways. In combination with established norms, they prescribe our behavior and ease interaction with people who occupy different social statuses, whether we know these people or not. There is an insidious side to this kind of predictable world. When normative role behavior becomes too rigidly defined, our freedom of action is often compromised. These rigid definitions are associated with the development of **stereotypes**—oversimplified conceptions that people who occupy the same status group share certain traits in common. Although stereotypes can include positive traits, they most often consist of negative ones that are then used to justify discrimination against members of a given group. The statuses of male and female are often stereotyped according to the traits they are assumed to possess by virtue of their biological makeup. Women are stereotyped as flighty and unreliable because they possess uncontrollable raging hormones that fuel unpredictable emotional outbursts. The assignment of negative stereotypes can result in **sexism**, the belief that the status of female is inferior to the status of male. Males are not immune to the negative consequences of sexism, but females are more likely to experience it because the status sets they occupy are more stigmatized than those occupied by males. Compared to males, for example, females are more likely to occupy statuses inside and outside their homes that are associated with less power, less prestige, and less pay or no pay. Beliefs about inferiority due to biology are reinforced and then used to justify discrimination directed toward females.

Sexism is perpetuated by systems of **patriarchy**, male-dominated social structures leading to the oppression of women. Patriarchy, by definition, exhibits **androcentrism**—male-centered norms operating throughout all social institutions that become the standard to which all persons adhere. Sexism is reinforced when patriarchy and androcentrism combine to perpetuate beliefs that gender roles are biologically determined and therefore unalterable. For example, throughout the developing world beliefs about a woman's biological unsuitability for other than domestic roles have restricted opportunities for education and achieving literacy. These restrictions have made men the guardians of what has been written, disseminated, and interpreted regarding gender and the placement of men and women in society. Until recently, history has been recorded from an androcentric perspective that ignored the other half of humanity (chapter 5). This perspective has perpetuated the belief that patriarchy is an inevitable, inescapable fact of history, so struggles for gender equality are doomed to failure. Women's gain in education is associated with the power to engage in the research and scholarship offering alternatives to prevailing androcentric views. We will see that such scholarship suggests that patriarchal systems may be universal, but they are not inevitable, and that gender egalitarianism was a historical fact of life in some cultures and is a contemporary fact of life in others.

Distinguishing Sex and Gender

As gender issues have become more mainstreamed in scientific research and media reports, confusion associated with the terms *sex* and *gender* has decreased. In sociology the terms sex and gender are now fairly standardized to refer to different content areas. **Sex** refers to the biological characteristics distinguishing male and female. This definition emphasizes male and female differences in chromosomes, anatomy, hormones, reproductive systems, and other physiological components. **Gender** refers to those social, cultural, and psychological traits linked to males and females through particular social contexts. Sex makes us male or female; gender makes us *masculine* or *feminine*. Sex is an *ascribed status* because a person is born with it, but gender is an *achieved status* because it must be learned.

This relatively simple distinction masks a number of problems associated with its usage. It implies that all people can be conveniently placed into unambiguous "either-or" categories. Certainly the ascribed status of sex is less likely to be altered than the achieved status of gender. Some people believe, however, that they were born with the "wrong" body and are willing to undergo major surgery to make their gender identity consistent with their biological sex. **Sexual orientation**, the preference for sexual partners of one gender (sex) or the other, also varies. People who experience sexual pleasure with members of their own sex are likely to consider themselves masculine or feminine according to gender norms. Others are born with ambiguous sex characteristics and may be assigned one sex at birth but develop a different identity related to gender. Some cultures allow people to move freely between genders, regardless of their biological sex.

These issues will be addressed fully in chapters 2 and 3, but are mentioned here to highlight the problems of terminology. From a sociological perspective, this text is concerned with gender and how it is learned, how it changes over time, and how it varies between and within cultures. Gender can be viewed on a continuum of characteristics demonstrated by a person regardless of the person's biological sex. Adding the concept of role to either sex or gender may increase confusion in terminology. When the sociological concept of role is combined with the biological concept of sex, there is often misunderstanding about what content areas are subsumed under the resultant *sex role* label. Usage is becoming rapidly standardized, however, and most sociologists now prefer to employ the term *gender role* rather than *sex role* in their writing. **Gender roles**, therefore, are the expected attitudes and behaviors a society associates with each sex. This definition places gender squarely in the sociocultural context.

SOCIOLOGICAL PERSPECTIVES ON GENDER ROLES

Sociologists explain gender roles according to several *theoretical perspectives*, general ways of understanding social reality that guide the research process and provide a means for interpreting the data. In essence, a **theory** is an explanation. Formal theories consist of logically interrelated propositions that explain empirical events. For instance, data indicate that compared to men, women are more likely to be segregated in lower-paying jobs offering fewer opportunities for professional growth and advancement. Data also indicate that both in the United States and cross-culturally the domestic work of women performed in or near their homes is valued less than the work of men performed outside their homes. Because the issue of gender crosses many disciplines, explanations for these facts can be explained according to the theoretical perspectives of those disciplines. Biology, psychology, and anthropology all offer explanations for gender-related attitudes and behavior. Not only do these explanations differ between disciplines, but scientists within the same discipline also frequently offer competing explanations for the same data, and sociology is no exception. The best explanations are those that account for the volume and complexities of the data. As research on gender issues accelerates and more sophisticated research tools are developed, it is becoming clearer that the best explanations are also those that are both interdisciplinary and incorporate concepts related to diversity. Sociological theory will dominate this text's discussion, but we will also account for relevant interdisciplinary work and its attention to diversity issues.

Sociological perspectives on gender also vary according to the *level of analysis* at which they operate. *Macrosociological* perspectives on gender roles direct attention to data collected on large-scale social phenomena, such as labor force, educational, and political trends that are differentiated according to gender roles. *Microsociological* perspectives on gender roles direct attention to data collected in small groups and the details of gender interaction occurring, for example, between couples and in families and peer groups. Microsociological perspectives overlap a great deal with the discipline of social psychology (chapter 3). We will see that theoretical perspectives may be differentiated according to macro- and microlevel of analysis, and perspectives from each level may be more or less compatible. When theoretical perspectives can be successfully combined, they offer excellent ways to better understand gender issues from a sociological perspective.

Early sociological perspectives related to gender roles evolved from scholarship on the sociology of the family. These explanations centered on why men and women hold different roles in the family that in turn impact the roles they perform outside the family. To a large extent, this early work on the family has continued to inform current sociological thinking on gender roles. The next sections will overview the major sociological perspectives and highlight their explanations regarding the gender–family connection.

Functionalism

Functionalism, also known as structural functionalism, is a macrosociological perspective that begins with the premise that society is made up of interdependent parts, each of which contributes to the functioning of the whole society. Functionalists seek to identify the basic elements or parts of society and determine the functions these parts play in meeting basic social needs in predicable ways. Functionalists ask how any given element of social structure contributes to overall social stability, balance, and equilibrium. They assert that in the face of disruptive social change, society can be restored to equilibrium as long as built-in mechanisms of social control operate effectively and efficiently. Social control and stability are enhanced when people share beliefs and values in common. Functionalist emphasis on this *value consensus* is a major ingredient in virtually all their interpretations related to social change. Values surrounding gender roles, marriage, and the family are central to functionalist assertions regarding social equilibrium.

Preindustrial Society. Functionalists suggest that in preindustrial societies social equilibrium was maintained by assigning different tasks to men and women. Given the hunting and gathering and subsistence farming activities of most preindustrial societies, role specialization according to gender was considered a functional necessity. In their assigned hunting roles, men were frequently away from home for long periods and centered their lives around the responsibility of bringing food to the family. It was functional for women, more limited by pregnancy, childbirth, and nursing, to be assigned domestic roles near the home as gatherers and subsistence farmers and as caretakers of children and households. Children were needed to help with agricultural and domestic activities. Girls would continue these activities when boys reached the age when they were allowed to hunt with the older males. Once established, this functional division of labor was reproduced in societies throughout the globe. Women may have been farmers and food gatherers in their own right, but they were dependent on men for food and for protection. Women's dependence on men in turn produced a pattern in which male activities and roles came to be more valued than female activities and roles.

Contemporary Society. Similar principles apply to families in contemporary societies. Disruption is minimized, harmony is maximized, and families benefit when spouses assume complementary, specialized, nonoverlapping roles (Parsons and Bales, 1955; Parsons, 1966). When the husband–father takes the **instrumental role**, he is expected to maintain the physical integrity of the family by providing food and shelter and linking the family to the world outside the home. When the wife–mother takes the **expressive role**, she is expected to cement relationships and provide emotional support and nurturing activities that ensure the household runs smoothly. If too much deviation from these roles occurs, or when there is too much overlap, the family system is propelled into a state of imbalance that can threaten the survival of the family unit. Advocates of functionalist assumptions argue, for instance, that gender role ambiguity regarding instrumental and expressive roles is a major factor in divorce (Hacker, 2003).

Critique. It should be apparent that functionalism's emphasis on social equilibrium contributes to its image as an inherently conservative theoretical perspective. This image is reinforced by its difficulty in accounting for a variety of existing family systems and in not keeping pace with rapid social change moving families toward more egalitarian attitudes regarding gender roles.

Often to the dismay of the scientists who developed them, scientific theories and the research on which they are based are routinely employed to support varying ideological positions. Functionalism has been used as a justification for male dominance and gender stratification. In the United States, functional analyses were popularized in the 1950s when, weary of war, the nation latched onto a traditional and idealized version of family life and attempted to establish not just a prewar, but a pre-Depression, existence. Functionalism tends to support a white middle-class family model emphasizing the economic activities of the male household head and domestic activities of his female subordinate. Women function outside the home only as a reserve labor force, such as when their labor is needed in wartime. This model does not apply to poor women and single parents who by necessity must work outside the home to maintain the household. It may not apply to African American women who are less likely by choice to separate family and employment and who derive high levels of satisfaction from both these roles.

Research also shows that specialization of household tasks by gender in contemporary families is more dysfunctional than functional. Women relegated to family roles that they see as restrictive, for example, are unhappier in their marriages and more likely to opt out of them. Despite tension associated with multiple roles and role overlap, couples report high levels of gratification, self esteem, status security, and personally enriched lives (chapter 8). Contemporary families simply do not fit functionalist models.

To its credit, functionalism offers a reasonably sound explanation for the origin of gender roles and demonstrates the functional utility of assigning tasks on the basis of gender in subsistence economies or in regions in which large families are functional and children are needed for agricultural work. Contemporary functionalists also acknowledge that strain occurs when there is too sharp a divide between the public and private sphere (work and family), particularly for women (Johnson, 1993). They acknowledge that such a divide is artificial and dysfunctional when families need to cope with the growing interdependence called for in a global economy. Finally, neofunctionalism accounts for the multiple levels where gender relations are operative—biological, psychological, social, and cultural. A functionalist examination of their interdependence allows us to understand how female subordination and male superiority became reproduced throughout the globe.

Conflict Theory

With its assumptions about social order and social change, the macrosociological perspective of conflict theory, also referred to as social conflict theory, is in many ways a mirror image of functionalism. Unlike functionalists, who believe that social order is maintained through value consensus, conflict theorists assert that it is preserved involuntarily through the exercise of power one social class holds over another.

Marx, Engels, and Social Class. Originating from the writings of Karl Marx, (1818–1883) conflict theory is based on the assumption that society is a stage on which struggles for power and dominance are acted out. The struggles are largely between social classes competing for scarce resources, such as control over the means of production (land, factories, natural resources), and for a better distribution of all resources (money, food, material goods). Capitalism thrives on a class-based system that consolidates power in the hands of a few men of the ruling class (*bourgeoisie*), who own the farms and factories that workers (*proletariat*) depend on for their survival. The interest of the dominant class is to maintain its position of power over the subordinate class by extracting as much profit as possible from their work. Only when the workers recognize their common oppression and form a *class consciousness* can they unite and amass the resources necessary to seriously challenge the inequitable system in which they find themselves (Marx, 1964, 1967). Marxian beliefs were acted out historically in the revolution that enveloped Russia, Eastern Europe, and much of Eurasia, propelling the Soviets to power for a half a century of control over these regions.

Marx's collaborator, Friedrich Engels (1820–1895), applied these assumptions to the family and, by extension, to gender roles. He suggested that the master–slave or exploiter–exploited relationships occurring in broader society between the bourgeoisie and proletariat are translated into the household. Primitive societies were highly egalitarian because there were no surplus goods, hence no private property. People consumed what they produced. With the emergence of private property and the dawn of capitalistic institutions, Engels argued that a woman's domestic labor is "no longer counted beside the acquisition of the necessities of life by the man; the latter was everything, the former an unimportant extra." The household is an autocracy, and the supremacy of the husband is unquestioned. "The emancipation of woman will only be possible when women can take part in production on a large social scale, and domestic work no longer claims but an insignificant amount of her time" (Engels, 1942: 41–43).

Contemporary Conflict Theory. Later conflict theorists refined original Marxian assertions to reflect contemporary patterns and make conflict theory more palatable to people who desire social change that moves in the direction of egalitarianism but not through the revolutionary means outlined by classical Marxism (Dahrendorf, 1959; Collins, 1975, 1979). Modern conflict theory asserts that social structure is based on the dominance of some groups over others and that groups in society share common interests, whether its members are aware of it or not. Conflict is not simply based on class struggle and the tensions between owner and worker or employer and employee; it occurs on a much wider level and among almost all other groups. These include parents and children, husbands and wives, young and the old, sick and healthy, people of color and whites, heterosexual and gay, females and males, and any other groups that can be differentiated as minority or majority according to the level of resources they possess. The list is infinite.

Gender and the Family. Conflict theory focuses on the social placement function of the family that deposits people at birth into families who possess varying degrees of economic resources. People fortunate enough to be deposited into wealthier families will work to preserve existing inequality and the power relations in the broader society because they clearly benefit from the overall power imbalance. Social class *endogamy* (marrying within the same class) and inheritance patterns ensure that property and wealth are kept in the hands of a few powerful families. Beliefs about inequality and the power imbalance become *institutionalized*—they are accepted and persist over time as legitimate by both the privileged and the oppressed—so the notion that family wealth is deserved and that those born into poor families remain poor because they lack talent and a work ethic is perpetuated. The structural conditions that sustain poverty are ignored. When social placement operates through patriarchal and patrilineal systems, wealth is further concentrated in the hands of males and further promotes female subservience, neglect, and poverty. Contemporary conflict theorists agree with Engels by suggesting that when women gain economic strength by also being wage earners, their power inside the home is strengthened and can lead to more egalitarian arrangements.

The conflict perspective is evident in research demonstrating that household responsibilities have an effect on occupational location, work experience, and number of hours worked per week, all of which are linked to the gender gap in earnings

(Shelton and Firestone, 1989). Undesirable work will be performed disproportionately by those lacking resources to demand sharing the burden or purchasing substitutes. Because household labor is unpaid and associated with lack of power, the homemaker (wife) takes on virtually all domestic chores (Lindsey, 1996a; Riley and Kiger, 1999). The more powerful spouse performs the least amount of household work.

Critique. Conflict theory has been criticized for its overemphasis on the economic basis of inequality and its assumption that there is inevitable competition between family members. It tends to dismiss the consensus among wives and husbands regarding task allocation. In addition, paid employment is clearly not the panacea envisioned by Engels in overcoming male dominance. In the Soviet Union women had the highest levels of paid employment in the world, but retained more household responsibilities than comparable women in other countries, and earned two-thirds of the average male income. In post–Communist Russia, there is no change in women's domestic work, but women now earn less than half of men's average earnings (chapter 6). Research unanimously concludes that even in those cultures where gender equity in the workplace is increasing, employed women globally take on a "second shift" of domestic work after returning home (chapter 8).

A conspiratorial element emerges when conflict theory becomes associated with the idea that men as a group are consciously organized to keep women in subordinate positions. A number of social forces, many of them unorganized or unintended, come into play when explaining gender stratification. Functionalism's bias *against* social change might be matched with conflict theory's bias *for* social change. Compared to functionalism, however, this bias is less of a problem for conflict theory once it is stripped of some Marxian baggage. Contemporary conflict theory has made strong inroads in using social class to further clarify the gender–race–class link, suggesting that the class advantages for people of color may override the race disadvantages (Gimenez, 2001; Lareau, 2002; Misra, 2002). Most people are uncomfortable with sexism and patterns of gender stratification that harm both women and men. Women are denied opportunities to expand instrumental roles offering economic parity with men outside the home; men are denied opportunities for expanding expressive and nurturing roles inside the home. At the ideological level, sociological conflict theory has been used to support activities designed to reduce racism, economic-based disparity (classism), and sexism.

Symbolic Interaction

Symbolic interaction, also called the interactionist perspective, is at the heart of the sociological view of social interaction at the micro level. With attention to people's behavior in face-to-face social settings, symbolic interactionists explain social interaction as a dynamic process in which people continually modify their behavior as a result of the interaction itself. Herbert Blumer (1900–1987), who originated the term *symbolic interaction*, asserted that people do not respond directly to the world around them, but to the meaning they bring to it. Society, its institutions, and its social structure exist—that is, social reality is bestowed—only through human interaction (Blumer, 1969). Reality is what members agree to be reality.

People interact according to how they perceive a situation, how they understand the social encounter, and the meanings they bring to it. Another important step in the interaction process involves how they *think* other people who are part of the interaction also understand the encounter. Each person's *definition of the situation* influences others' definitions. To illustrate symbolic interaction's emphasis on the fluidity of behavior, I developed the concept of the **end point fallacy**, asserting that the negotiation of social reality is an ongoing process in which new definitions produce new behavior in a never-ending cycle. The end point fallacy is an excellent way to explain the inconsistencies between people's behavior as they move from setting to setting.

Social Construction of Reality. Symbolic interaction is a microlevel perspective, but it does take into account that social interaction is a process governed by norms that are largely determined by culture. Cultural norms offer general guidelines for role behavior, but symbolic interactionists assert that we have latitude in the way we act out our roles. The context of the interaction is usually a key determinant of role performance. What is appropriate role performance in one context may be inappropriate in another. Cultural norms are modified whenever social interaction occurs because people bring their own definitions about appropriate behavior to the interaction. These definitions shape the way people see and experience the world. Symbolic interactionists refer to this shaping process as the **social construction of reality**—the shaping of perception of reality by the subjective meanings brought to any experience or social interaction. Consistent with Herbert Blumer's view, every time social interaction occurs, people creatively construct their own understanding of it—whether "real" or not—and behave accordingly.

Doing Gender. Symbolic interactionists contend that gender does not exist objectively but emerges through a socially constructed process. People called "females" or "males" are endowed with certain traits defined as feminine or masculine. Concepts such as gender, therefore, must be found in the meanings people bring to them (Denzin, 1992, 1993). Gender emerges not as an individual attribute but something that is "accomplished" in interaction with others. People, therefore, are **doing gender** (Fenstermaker and West, 2002). In "doing" gender, symbolic interaction takes its lead from Erving Goffman (1922–1982), who developed the **dramaturgical approach** to social interaction. Goffman maintained that the best way to understand social interaction is to consider it as an enactment in a theatrical performance. Like actors on a stage, we use strategies of *impression management*, providing information and cues to others that present us in a favorable light (Goffman, 1959, 1963, 1971). Research on singles bars exemplifies these concepts. Both men and women "stalk" for partners, but they do it according to agreed-upon rules. A man, who usually comes to the bar alone, operates from a script in which he makes the first move. A woman, who is more likely to be with a female friend, must disengage herself from that friend if she is "selected" by the man. In singles bars and other places where men and women who do not know one another meet, a process of unspoken negotiation and choice based primarily on gender roles is operating (Laws and Schwartz, 1981; Rouse, 2002).

Gender roles are structured by one set of scripts designed for males and another designed for females. Although each script permits a range of behavior options, the typical result is that gender labels promote a pattern of between-sex competition, rejection, and emotional segregation. This pattern is reinforced when we routinely refer to those of the *other* sex (gender) as the *opposite* sex. Men and women label each other as opposite to who they are, then behave according to that label. The behavior serves to separate rather than connect the genders.

Doing Difference. Research on men and women in various social networks—formed at school, work, and in volunteer activities—further illustrates this process. From early childhood these groups are usually gender segregated. Gendered sub-cultures emerge that strengthen the perceptions of gender differences and erode the common ground on which intimate, status-equal friendships between the genders are formed (Ridgeway and Smith-Lovin, 1999; Migliaccio, 2003). Differences rather than similarities are much more likely to be noticed, defined, and acted on. When cross-gender social interaction occurs, such as in the workplace, it is unlikely that men and women hold statuses with similar levels of power and prestige. Once the genders are socially constructed as different, it is easier for those with more power (men) to justify inequality toward those with less power (women). Social difference is constructed into social privilege (Fenstermaker and West, 2002).

Critique. Symbolic interaction's approach to understanding gender role behavior is criticized for its overall lack of attention to macrolevel processes that often limits choice of action and prompts people to engage in gendered behavior that counters what they would prefer to do. Cultural norms may be in flux at the microlevel of social interaction, but they remain a significant structural force on behavior. In some cultures, for example, women and men are dictated by both law and custom to engage in certain occupations, enter into marriages with people they would not choose on their own, and be restricted from attending school. Larger social structures also operate at the family level to explain family dynamics. Men and women interact not only as individual family members but also according to other roles they play in society and the prestige associated with those roles. For example, a wealthy white man who holds a powerful position in a corporation does not dissolve those roles when he walks into his home. They shape his life at home, in the workplace, and in the other social institutions in which he takes part. Race, class, and gender offer a range of privileges bestowed by the broader society that also allow for a power base to be established in his home. Power and privilege can result in a patri-archal family regardless of the couple's desire for a more egalitarian arrangement.

Feminist Sociological Theory

By calling attention to the powerful impact of gender in the social ordering of our relationships (microlevel analysis) and our institutions (macrolevel analysis), the feminist theoretical perspective in sociology has emerged as a major model that has significantly reshaped the discipline. By the research it spawned, feminist soci-ological theory is not only bridging the micro-macro gap, it has also illuminated the androcentric bias in sociology and in broader society. Disagreement remains on all the elements that need to be included in feminist theory, but at a minimum, the consensus is that a theory is feminist if it can be used to challenge a status quo that is disadvantageous to women (Chafetz, 1988; Smith, 2003).

The feminist perspective provides productive avenues of collaboration with sociologists who adopt other theoretical views, especially conflict theory and symbolic interaction. The feminist perspective is compatible with conflict theory in its assertions that structured social inequality is maintained by ideologies that are frequently accepted by both the privileged and the oppressed. These ideologies are challenged only when oppressed groups gain the resources necessary to do so. Unlike conflict theory's focus on social class and the economic elements necessary to challenge the prevailing system, feminists focus on women and their ability to amass resources from a variety of sources—in their individual lives (microlevel) and through social and political means (macrolevel). Feminists work through a number of avenues to increase women's **empowerment**—the ability for women to exert control over their own destinies.

Symbolic interaction and feminist theory come together in research focusing on the unequal power relations between men and women from the point of view (definition of the situation) of women who are "ruled" by men in many settings. For example, corporate women who want to be promoted need to practice impression management based on acceptable gender role behavior of their corporate setting, but at the same time they need to maintain a sense of personal integrity. The feminist perspective accounts for ways to empower these corporate women by clarifying the relationship between the label of "feminine" (symbolic interaction) and how these women are judged by peers and by themselves.

Linking Gender, Race, and Class. One of the most important contributions of the feminist perspective to sociology is its attention to the multiple oppressions faced by people whose status sets are disadvantaged due to distinctive combinations based on their gender, race, and social class. The gender–race–class linkage in analyzing social behavior originated with African-American feminists in the 1960s who recognized that an understanding of the link between these multiple oppressions was necessary to determine how women are alike and how they are different. For example, when the issue of poverty becomes "feminized," the issue is defined primarily by gender—women are at a higher risk of being poor than men. A focus on the feminization of poverty ignores the links among race, social class, and marital status that puts certain categories of women, such as single parents, women of color, and elderly women living alone, at higher risk than others (Vartanian and McNamara, 2002; Wilson and Hardy, 2002). To explain poverty, racial and class oppression must be considered along with gender. When white, middle-class feminists focus on oppression of women, they sometimes have difficulty recognizing the privileges that come with their own race and class (Collins, 1996).

The attention to sociocultural diversity that originated with the gender–race–class link has reverberated throughout sociology and other disciplines, generating a great deal of interdisciplinary research. It has opened new academic programs in Women's Studies, Men's Studies, and Gender Studies and has increased dialogue between men and women. Feminist scholarship provides opportunities for men to view themselves as gendered beings and to make visible their concerns (Kimmel, 1996; Brod, 2003). With the gender–race–class link as a foundation, feminist researchers are identifying other sites of oppression that put people at risk both inside and outside their families, such as religion, sexual orientation, age, or disability.

Feminist Perspectives on the Family. Feminist scholars in the 1960s and 1970s viewed the traditional patriarchal family as a major site for the oppression of women. They asserted that when the patriarchal family is regarded as beneficial to social stability, it hampers the movement into egalitarian roles desired by both men and women. Feminist sociologists recognize that gendered family relations do not occur in a vacuum and that lives are helped or hurt by the resources outside the family that shape what is happening inside the family (Baca Zinn, 2000). Along with gender, for example, single-parent African-American, Latino, and Native American women are disadvantaged by race when they seek employment necessary to support their families. Lesbians must deal with a system that represses same-sex relationships when they fight for custody of their children. The growing consensus of feminists in all disciplines is that women may be doubly or triply disadvantaged by their race, class, or sexuality, but they are not helpless victims. To some degree they possess **agency**—the power to adapt and sometimes to thrive in difficult situations.

Critique. With a view of gender, marriage, and the family focusing on oppression of women, the feminist perspective tends to minimize the practical benefits of marriages. This contention is that a marriage may be patriarchal, but it also includes important economic resources and social support that women in these marriages may view as more important in their daily lives than their feelings about subordination (Waite and Gallagher, 2000). Feminist scholars also find it difficult to reconcile research suggesting that women in traditional marriages are as satisfied with their choices as women in egalitarian marriages. Finally, emphasis on human agency may minimize situations in which women's victimization is condoned by custom and ignored by law (chapters 6, 9, and 14).

A key strength of the feminist perspective is its ability to provide bridges between sociological theories and account for social diversity is all its forms. With its challenge to the patriarchal status quo and the androcentric bias inherent in much sociological research and theory, it has created dissent that may limit its acceptance by some sociologists. On the other hand, the feminist perspective may plant the seeds for building a truly integrative theory to draw together "conceptual pieces into a web of ideas that transcend patriarchal theory building" (Ollenburger and Moore, 1992:36). Feminist theory offers a powerful new perspective in sociology. Sociology will benefit from the intellectual ferment it has already created.

FEMINISM AND ITS BRANCHES

Feminist theory and its attention to diversity provide support for those organizations working to change women's inferior social position and the social, political, and economic discrimination that perpetuates it. Many of these organizations come together in networks under the umbrella of **feminism**, an inclusive worldwide movement to end sexism and sexist oppression by empowering women. Thirty years ago the women's movement faltered because it did not realistically account for how intersecting categories of oppression can divide women (chapter 14). Through efforts of feminist networks across the globe and under the leadership of the United Nations and the women's conferences they organized, many of these divides have been bridged (chapter 6).

Global social change presents new and ongoing challenges for women, so a feminist agenda addressing the needs of all women is never in a finalized form. Feminists accept the goal of ending sexism by empowering women, but there is a great deal of disagreement about how that goal is to be accomplished. Because the feminist movement *is* inclusive, it is unlikely there will ever be full agreement on identifying problems and determining strategies to address the problems. The very inclusiveness and diversity of the movement makes unity on some issues virtually impossible. Indeed, absence of complete unity is appropriate because it fuels those worldwide debates that often result in the most creative, realistic, and innovative strategies for women's empowerment. Reflecting the difficulty of adopting one agenda, the movement has tended to partition itself into several different branches according to general philosophical differences. Women and men may identify with organizations that fall under more than one branch, but feminists as individuals or in the formal groups to which they belong generally subscribe to the principles of one or another of the following branches.

Liberal Feminism

Liberal feminism, also called egalitarian or mainstream feminism, is considered the most moderate branch. It is based on the simple proposition that all people are created equal and should not be denied equality of opportunity because of gender. Because both genders benefit by the elimination of sexism, men are integrated into its ranks. Liberal feminism is based on Enlightenment beliefs of rationality, education, and the natural rights that extend to all men and women. This is articulated in John Stuart Mill's (1869/2002) *The Subjection of Women*, with his statement that "what is now called the nature of women is an eminently artificial thing—the result of forced oppression in some directions, unnatural stimulation in others." Women can work together within a pluralistic system and mobilize their constituents to effect positive and productive social change. Demands will be met if mobilization is effective and pressure is efficiently wielded (Deckard, 1983:463).

Liberal feminists believe society does not have to be completely restructured to achieve empowerment for women and to incorporate women into meaningful and equitable roles. This view tends to be adopted by professional, middle class women who place a high value on education and achievement. These women are likely to have the economic resources to better compete with men for desirable social positions and employment opportunities. Liberal feminism thus appeals to "mainstream" women who have no disagreement with the overall structure of the present social system, only that it should be nonsexist. The National Organization for Women (NOW, 2004) is the formal group representing this branch, with a statement of purpose calling for an end to restrictive gender roles that serve to diminish opportunities for both women and men (chapter 14).

Cultural Feminism. Liberal feminists may also embrace "cultural feminism" with its focus on empowering women by emphasizing the positive qualities that are associated with women's roles such as nurturing, caring, cooperation, and connectedness to others (Worell, 1996:360). The issue of how much women are alike and how much they are different is highlighted in this emphasis. Although it does not constitute a separate branch of feminism per se, the debate around the "degree of gender difference or similarity" has allowed cultural feminism to become incorporated in all the feminist branches at some level. Liberal feminists, however, are more likely to subscribe to these principles than women in other branches.

Socialist Feminism

Also referred to as Marxist feminism, socialist feminism generally adopts the Marx–Engels model described earlier that links the inferior position of women to class-based capitalism and its alignment with the patriarchal family in capitalistic societies. Socialist feminism argues that sexism and capitalism are mutually supportive. The unpaid labor of women in the home and their paid labor in a reserve labor force simultaneously serve patriarchy capitalism. Many socialist feminists—both men and women—also believe that economic and emotional dependence go hand in hand. Fearful of the loss of economic security, a husband's power over his wife is absolute. Capitalism needs to be eliminated and socialist principles adopted to both home and workplace. Sexism and economic oppression are mutually reinforcing, so a socialist revolutionary agenda is needed to change both.

Socialist feminism appeals to working class women and those who feel disenfranchised from the economic opportunities in capitalism. It has made a great deal of headway in Latin America and has served as a powerful rallying point for women in other developing nations. It is ironic that its most vivid expression occurred in the former Soviet Union, where women continued to carry the heavy burden of unpaid household labor while also functioning in the paid labor force.

Although socialist feminism is explicitly tied to Marxist theory, there are key differences between the two. Whereas Marxist theory focuses on property and economic conditions to build an ideology, socialist feminism focuses on sexuality and gender. Men and women retain interest in their own gender group, so it is unclear if the socialism being struggled for is the same for both men and women (Hartman, 1993). A humane socialist approach to feminism requires consensus on what the new society should be and would require men to renounce their privileges as men.

Radical Feminism

Radical feminism is said to have emerged when women who were working with men in the civil rights and anti–Vietnam War movements were not allowed to present their positions on the causes they were engaged in. These women became aware of their own oppression by the treatment they received from their male cohorts who insulted and ridiculed them for their views. The radical feminist model thus originated as a reaction against the theories, organizational structures, and personal styles of the male "New Left" (Donovan, 1985:141). The second wave of feminism leading to the rebirth of the women's movement in the United States in the twentieth century may be traced to the women who found themselves derided and ignored by the people they believed to be their allies. History repeated itself. The roots of American feminism in the nineteenth century are traced to the women who were denied expression of their views by the men they worked with in the anti-slavery movement. The patronizing attitudes of the men of that era provided the catalyst for women to recognize gender-based oppression and then organize to challenge it (chapter 5). A century later it happened again.

Contemporary radical feminists believe that sexism is at the core of patriarchal society and that all social institutions reflect that sexism. Whereas liberal feminists focus on the workplace, radical feminists focus on the patriarchal family as the key site of domination and oppression (Shelton and Agger, 1993). They believe that because all social institutions are so intertwined, it is virtually impossible to attack sexism in any meaningful way. Women's oppression stems from male domination, so if men are the problem, neither capitalism, nor socialism, nor any other male dominated system will solve the problem. Therefore, women must create separate institutions that are women centered – those that rely on women rather than men. Radical feminists would agree with cultural feminism in that the alternative path for women is to be different than men. A society will emerge where the female virtues of nurturance, sharing, and intuition will dominate in a woman-identified world.

Acknowledging the impossibility of removing sexism from all institutions, radical feminists work at local levels and in their neighborhoods to develop profit and not-for-profit institutions that are operated solely by women to serve other women, such as small businesses, day care facilities, counseling centers, and safe houses for women escaping domestic violence.

Reflecting more overall diversity than any of the other branches in its ranks, especially related to race and sexual orientation, these institutions vary considerably in structure, philosophy, and strategies to attain their goals. The blueprint for the women-identified society they envision is stamped on their activities that are much more individualized in other feminist branches. The conviction that male supremacy and oppression of women is the defining characteristic of a society is what unifies the disparate elements of radical feminism.

Multicultural and Global Feminism

The attention to diversity issues at the macro level is evident among feminists who organize around multicultural and global issues. This feminist branch focuses on the intersection of gender with race, class, and issues related to the colonization and exploitation of women in the developing world. Global feminism is a movement of people working for change across national boundaries. The world is interdependent and becoming more so. Global feminism contends that no woman is free until the conditions that oppress women worldwide are eliminated (Bunch, 1993:249). Multicultural feminism focuses on the specific cultural elements and historical conditions that serve to maintain women's oppression. In Latin America, for instance, military regimes have devised specific patterns of punishment and sexual enslavement for women who oppose their regimes (Bunster-Bunalto, 1993). Global feminism works to empower South Asian and Middle Eastern women who are restricted from schooling, health care, and paid employment simply because they are women.

In efforts to empower women, they do not support the idea of cultural relativism when it violates a woman's human rights, such as restricting a girl's access to education on religious grounds (chapter 6). The women who came together for the United Nations Conferences on Women are representative of this view.

Ecofeminism

Some women are drawn into feminism by environmental activism. These women are the catalysts of ecofeminism, feminism's newest branch. Ecofeminism connects the degradation and oppression of women with the degradation of the ecosystem. Drawing on earth-based spiritual imagery, ecofeminism suggests that earth's original balance was upset through patriarchal domination of the planet (Warren, 1997; Low and Tremayne, 2001). The planet can be healed and ecological harmony restored through political action emphasizing the principle of equality of all species (Bowerbank, 2001). With its holistic viewpoint and emphasis on interdependence in all its forms, ecofeminism is particularly compatible with global feminism.

All branches of feminism deal with the linkages of gender with other relevant social categories. Members of each branch and the groups they work with negotiate how gender is constructed according to their own needs and priorities (Stack, 1994). Different feminisms result from these constructions.

Backlash to Feminism

A final note is in order about why feminism is considered the "f-word." Feminism is a movement to end the oppression of women. It uses women's perceptions and experiences to devise strategies for overcoming oppression. It embraces political goals that offer gender equality. We will see throughout this text that public support for feminist goals and women's empowerment is widespread. A large majority of American women agree that feminism has altered their lives for the better. Yet many women refuse to identify themselves as feminists. Why?

Because feminism *has* empowered women, the dialogue has changed. Passivity has been replaced by open and critical debate between feminists themselves and between those who agree or disagree with feminism. This debate is stimulating, is necessary, and fuels further empowerment. As noted earlier, inclusiveness feeds disagreement. Like the branches of feminism overviewed here, feminists can agree to disagree. There are many feminisms and many themes of feminist thought. "Although we have joined a common parade, we do not all march to the same music" (Worell, 1996:361). Feminists understand and accept these distinctions, but they are presented to the public in highly distorted ways.

Media have a formidable influence in reinforcing gender role stereotypes, and the feminist stereotype is no exception. Both feminist agreement and the feminist value of disagreement are ignored or ridiculed throughout mainstream news and entertainment media. Can feminist power be projected positively and productively in an era of backlash when feminists dare to disagree with one another in public (Sylvester, 1995:943)? The media latch on to disagreements among feminists and present sound bytes giving the impressions that feminism has split into irreconcilable warring factions. This negative media attention is reinforced with news format entertainment shows suggesting that women have already achieved political parity and legal parity with men, and because feminists have nothing else to fight for, they fight among themselves. Young women appear to be receptive to these messages because self-identification for feminism decreases significantly with age (Schnittker et al., 2002).

In addition to highlighting disagreement among feminists, media depict feminists as puritanical, man-hating, obsessed with harassment and victimization, taking unfair advantage of men in the workplace, and controlling men in their homes (Wolfe, 1993b; Blackwell et al., 2003). Prime time television series portray feminists in negative and highly stereotyped ways. Jokes deriding feminists about their appearance, sexuality and love life, and how they control their children and husbands are common. Racist comments are unacceptable in the media. Sexist comments are acceptable. Young women and teens are often the targets of sexist jokes. Sexism is reinforced by the contemptuous statements about feminists routinely made by the popular and attractive characters in the shows (chapter 13). Given the power of the media to construct gender roles, it is difficult for young women and men who may identify with feminism in principle to do so in public.

The unfavorable light feminists are cast into by the media is not going unchallenged. The backlash against feminism may be a sign that goals are being reached and real power shifts are occurring. It may take another generation, however, to determine if this is the case.

The theories and concepts presented in this chapter and the visions of society that they suggest are offered as tools to be used in approaching the following chapters and the diverse array of issues related to gender roles you will be confronting. Each theoretical perspective has its own insight and explanation for any given issue. Issues are further refined when theories are used in combination with one another. As these issues are addressed, consider which perspective you believe to be the most appropriate and realistic. It is hoped that at the conclusion of this book you will have developed a perspective on gender roles that is most meaningful to you.

Summary

1. As one of the most important trends in sociology in the twentieth century, the study of gender has led to a new feminist paradigm and opened up new topics for research, especially the connection between gender, race, and social class.

2. All social interaction is gendered. Gendered social interaction is guided by status, positions people occupy, and roles, the behavior associated with a status. Sexism and discrimination result when the status and role of female and male become stereotyped.

3. Sex is the biological component of male and female, gender is the social and psychological component, and sexual orientation is the way people experience sexual pleasure. These terms are often confused.

4. Sociological explanations for gender roles are guided by four theoretical perspectives: functionalism focuses on how gender role contributes to social order or equilibrium; conflict theory focuses on the level of power associated with gender; symbolic interaction focuses on gender as socially constructed and how people "do" gender in everyday life. The feminist perspective focuses on women's empowerment and draws attention to multiple oppressions due to race, class, and gender.

5. Feminism is a worldwide movement to end sexism by empowering women. Branches of feminism include: liberal feminism, its most mainstream and inclusive branch focusing on working within the system to end sexism; cultural feminism, focusing on positive qualities of women's roles; socialist feminism, focusing on ending sexism by eliminating capitalism and adopting socialist principles; radical feminism, calling for women to create separate, women-centered social institutions; multicultural or global

feminism, working for change across national boundaries; and ecofeminism, focusing on environmental action.

6. A backlash to feminism is associated with fear of women's empowerment and media reinforcement of gender and feminist stereotypes.

Key Terms

androcentrism 3	gender 4	sexual orientation 4
agency 13	gender role 4	social construction of reality 10
doing gender 10	instrumental role 6	
dramaturgical approach 10	norms 2	social stratification 2
empowerment 12	patriarchy 3	status 2
end point fallacy 10	role 2	status set 2
expressive role 6	sex 4	stereotype 3
feminism 13	sexism 3	theory 4

Critical Thinking Questions

1. How would a functionalist, conflict theorist, symbolic interactionist, and feminist answer the following question: Why do men hold the most powerful economic and political positions across the globe? What social policies would theorists from each of these groups offer as mechanisms to make this situation more gender equitable?

2. Considering the intersection of gender, race, and class and the distinctions between the various branches of feminism, provide realistic alternatives for ways women can "celebrate" both their diversity and their unity at the same time.

3. The backlash to feminism (the "f-word") is often media based. Which sociological theory do you think best explains this backlash? Suggest strategies consistent with the theory you select to alter this perception.

GENDER DEVELOPMENT

Biology, Sexuality, and Health

CHAPTER 2

Women are biologically more suited than men to do housework because men's brains do not predispose them to notice dirt. (cited in Bing, 1999)

It must be stated that conceptual thought is exclusive to the masculine intellect. Her skull is also smaller than man's; and so, of course, is her brain.

—T. Lang, 1971 (cited in Tavris, 1996:336)

The argument used against equality between males and females is fundamentally a biological one. **Essentialism** is the belief that males and females are inherently different because of their biology and genes. This difference makes men and women "naturally" suited to fulfill certain roles regardless of their intellect, desires, expertise, or experiences. Like sociological functionalism, essentialism does not explicitly state that difference equates to inferiority, but the assumed quality or essence that makes men and women different is consistently drawn on to justify that conclusion. Although men are sometimes its targets, essentialism points to women's biological and reproductive makeup that refrains them from standing on equal ground with men.

The explosion of research on issues of sex and gender globally provides massive evidence refuting essentialist claims. Research does not discount the role of biology in gender development, but it clearly demonstrates that culture is a greater barrier to equality than biology. When desire and talent are combined with opportunity and encouragement, people can move with relative ease into the "traditional" gender role of the other. When such movement becomes widespread, gender distinctions are blurred. Decades of research have made it empirically clear that the benefits of equality for males and females alike far outweigh the disadvantages.

NATURE VERSUS NURTURE

How much of our gendered behavior is determined by nature (heredity, biology, and genes), and how much is determined by nurture, the environment or culture in which we live and learn? Sociological explanations for gender differences are rooted in the nurture side of this question. Certainly males and females are different. Patterns of differentiation include not only physiology, but also differences related to demographics, attitudes, and behavior. Are these differences significant enough to suggest that patriarchy is inevitable? Do the differences outweigh the similarities? What role does biology play in determining these differences? An examination of the research and theory generated by these questions will help shed light on the "it's only natural" argument. This argument is in fact an extension of the nature versus nurture debate. Because this chapter's focus is on biological issues, the categories of male or female will frequently be referred to as (the) "sexes."

Margaret Mead

Famed anthropologist Margaret Mead (1935/2001) was interested in exploring sex differences when she journeyed to New Guinea in the 1930s and lived with three different tribes. Among the gentle, peace-loving Arapesh, both men and women were nurturant and compliant, spending time gardening, hunting, and child rearing. The Arapesh gained immense satisfaction from these tasks, which were eagerly shared by both men and women. Arapesh children grew up to mirror these patterns and became cooperative and responsive parents themselves, with a willingness to subordinate themselves to the needs of those who were younger and weaker. Personality, Mead concluded, could not be distinguished by gender. What many societies would define as maternal behavior extended to both men and women. By contrast, the fierce Mundugumor barely tolerated children; they left them to their own devices early in life and taught them to be as hostile, competitive, and suspicious to others as their elders were. Both mothers and fathers showed little tenderness to their children, commonly using harsh physical punishment. Children quickly learned that tribal success was measured by aggression, with violence as the acceptable, expected solution to many problems. Because both males and females demonstrated these traits, the Mundugumor, like the Arapesh, did not differentiate personality in terms of gender. Even by global standards of masculinity, the

Mundugumor represented the extreme. Finally, the Tchumbuli demonstrated what would be considered a reversal of gender roles. This tribe consisted of practical, efficient, and unadorned women and passive, vain, and decorated men. Women's weaving, fishing, and trading activities provided the economic mainstay for the community; men remained close to the village and practiced dancing and art. Women enjoyed the company of other women. Men strived to gain the women's attention and affection, a situation women took with tolerance and humor. Contrary to her original belief that there are natural sex differences, Mead concluded that masculine and feminine are culturally, rather than biologically, determined.

Critique. Mead's work is an anthropological standard on gender differences and it is presented here in some detail. The gender roles she described over seventy years ago were undoubtedly as unusual then as they are today. Yet her work still challenges the "it's only natural" argument. We know today that gender roles vary within a narrower range than suggested by Mead's research. However, "her message that gender constitutes an arena of great variability in human experience has borne out under empirical evidence" (LeVine, 1990:5). In fact, no existing theory, especially those grounded in essentialism, can explain the immense variety of meanings attached to being male and female. It is precisely this variation that has led to so much research questioning biologically based beliefs regarding femininity and masculinity. As this chapter demonstrates, we can identify biological differences and similarities between female and male, but to determine how these relate to what is considered masculine and feminine the world over is exceedingly difficult.

Sociobiology

Rooted in the nature side of the debate, the field of **sociobiology** also addresses questions of sex differences in its examination of the biological roots of social behavior. Originally developing out of research based on insects (Wilson, 1975, 1978), sociobiologists argue that evolutionary theory can be used to draw conclusions about humans from studies of animals. The fundamental assertion of sociobiology is that, like other animals, humans, are structured by nature (biology) with an innate drive to ensure that their individual genes are passed on to the next generation. This is the motivating factor in all human behavior. It is as adaptive for a mother to care for her children as it is for men to be promiscuous. Each sex evolved these attributes to increase its reproductive success (Low, 2000). Sociobiologists believe that principles of evolution pointing to species survival provide the best understanding of how gendered social behaviors developed. For example, aggressiveness not only allowed humans to successfully compete with nonanimals who shared our primeval environment but also allowed males to compete between themselves for females. The same principles explain promiscuity in men. Whereas women are highly selective in choosing mating partners, men will spread their sperm as widely as possible. For sociobiologists, other behaviors rooted in natural selection include mother–infant bonding, female dominance in child care, and male dominance in virtually all positions outside the home. As an evolutionary result of natural selection, the separate, unequal worlds of male and female emerged (Udry, 2000). Contemporary gender roles, therefore, reflect this evolutionary heritage.

Critique. Sociobiology has some success in applying evolutionary theory to animal behavior, but because it is virtually impossible to test the natural selection principles on which it is based, empirical support for evolutionary links to human behavior is weak (Nielsen, 1994). Feminist scientific critiques center on the fact that sociobiology is an *androcentric* perspective that makes faulty assumptions about human behavior and disregards well-documented research about animals. For example, it ignores the fact that the female chimp is notoriously promiscuous. Sexual selection in sociobiology emphasizes competition and aggression in male chimps, but neglects the other part of the process, in which female chimps make choices among males. Female chimps can be sexually aggressive and competitive just as male chimps can be nurturing and passive (Hrdy, 1999). This could be used to argue that human females are more intelligent or more powerful in controlling human males. Also, the latest evidence now suggests that aggressiveness in primates is rare (probably less than 1 percent of all activities), with affiliated, friendly behavior, such as grooming and playing, probably a hundred times more frequent (McGinn, 2002). Sociobiologists may offer some productive leads for studying human social behavior, but leaping from animals to humans is tenuous at best. In reviewing the research on the biology of gender, developmental biologist Anne Fausto-Sterling (1992) concludes that what are often considered to be the results of biology are more likely the results of culture.

The Hormone Puzzle

The chromosomal basis of sex difference is fairly clear. Of the two types of sex chromosomes, X and Y, both sexes have at least one X chromosome. Females possess two X chromosomes whereas males have one X and one Y chromosome. It is the lack or presence of the Y chromosome that determines if a baby will be male or female. That the X chromosome has a larger genetic background than the Y chromosome is advantageous to females with their XX chromosomes. The extra X chromosome is associated with a superior immune system and lower female mortality at all stages of the life cycle. All our other chromosomes are similar in form, differing only in our individual hereditary identities.

It is when hormones are added to the sex difference equation that the boundaries between biology and culture become more blurred. There is a subtle but significant interaction between sex hormones and psychosocial factors in gendered behavior. *Hormones* are internal secretions produced by the endocrine glands that are carried by the blood throughout the body, which affect target cells in other organs. Both males and females possess the same hormones, but they differ in amounts secreted. For example, the dominant female hormone, estrogen, is produced in larger quantities by the ovaries, but in smaller quantities by the testes. The male hormone, testosterone, is produced in larger quantities by the testes and smaller quantities by the ovaries. The endocrine differences between males and females are not absolute but differ along a continuum of variation, with most males being significantly different than most females (Woldow, 1996).

We know that sex hormones have two key functions that must be considered together. They shape the development of the brain and sex organs and then determine how these organs will be activated. Because hormones provide an organization function for the body, their effects will be different for the sexes. For example, during fetal development when certain tissues are highly sensitive to hormones, the secretion of testosterone both masculinizes and defeminizes key cellular structures throughout the brain and reproductive organs. The fetus first starts to develop female organs but later masculinizes itself if it possesses a Y chromosome, under the influence of testosterone. A male may be viewed as a female transformed by testosterone—the female body form is the "default" form (Mealey, 2000:14). The processes of masculinization and the development of sex differences are continuous, "influenced by later activity of the hormones *as well as* individual experiences" (emphasis added) (McEwen, 1990:36).

Aggression. The debate on the influence of hormones in gender behavior is further complicated when studying sex differences in aggression. Research suggests that in most species, including primates, males are more aggressive than females with higher aggression in human males evident at about age two (Archer and Lloyd, 2002; Connor, 2002). Some animal studies link testosterone to increases in aggression, and in humans, correlations are found between testosterone level and criminal violence (Ellis, 1986; Browne, 2002). Overall, girls and boys are about equal in learned aggressiveness, but because it is less socially acceptable to show aggression for girls, they are more likely to suppress their anger or carry it out through verbal confrontation. Boys and young men, on the other hand, are more likely to show aggression, but carry it out in physical ways, such as through fistfights, and shouting matches coupled with pushing and shoving their (usually) male adversary (Archer et al., 1995; Cox et al., 2000; Haines, 2001). When considering aggression according to key demographic features (age, race, ethnicity) and key features of context (workplace, home, school), research spanning several decades does *not* show overall higher levels of male aggressiveness, and those that do are often not statistically significant (Frodi et al., 1977; Archer, 1991; Hatch and Forgays, 2001; Hubbard, 2001).

Although animal studies, mostly done on rats and guinea pigs, do show a clear, possibly causal, connection between androgens (male hormones) and male aggression, a wealth of research on humans simply cannot support the same claim (Björkqvist, 1994). Not only is it impossible to design studies that empirically make the causal leap from animals to people, but well designed studies on the most intelligent social animals, especially primates, cannot make the leap either (Nelson, 1995; Pavelka, 1998; De Waal and Tyack, 2003). An important longitudinal study of boys going through puberty did show the typical large increases in testosterone, but not the corresponding increases in aggression often found in nonhuman species (Halpern et al., 1994). Perhaps the most damaging argument against the aggression-hormone link is, as noted earlier, that whether males or females are more aggressive depends on the type of aggression and the situation in which it occurs (Björkqvist and Niemelä, 1992). The cultural features of the context are powerful forces in determinants of aggression. There are different standards regarding the appropriateness of aggressive behavior, and they are learned early in life. As adults, men may feel pressured to act aggressively when publicly challenged. Males and females experience anger differently, but the expression of it is associated with being male (Huesmann, 1994). Hormones shift constantly as people move in and out of various social situations. The context can determine if testosterone increases aggression or aggression increases testosterone. In competitions, testosterone levels increase in winners and decrease in losers (Archer, 1994). Sex differences in aggression are real but not very large. If there is a biological predisposition in males toward aggression, it is mediated by powerful social influences.

Motherhood. Animal studies of primates focusing on hormones released during pregnancy that allegedly fuel mother–infant bonding have been used to suggest the existence of a maternal instinct in human females. These studies assert that the female hormones of estrogen, progesterone, and prolactin biologically propel women toward motherhood. Furthermore, because they are elicited in larger amounts during pregnancy and after labor, women are driven to protect, bond, and nurture their infants from the moment of birth (Hrdy, 2000; Maestripieri, 2001). Feminist sociologist Alice Rossi (1977, 1984) argues that types of mother–infant interaction such as cradling the infant on the left so it is soothed by the "maternal heartbeat familiar in uterine life" suggest the presence of unlearned responses. She does not deny the importance of learning in parenthood, but asserts that fathering is learned but mothering is propelled by evolutionary forces. Infertile women who believe motherhood is based on a maternal instinct may view their inability to have children as inadequacy and failure (Ulrich and Weatherall, 2000).

Mothers bond, protect, and nurture their infants, but these behaviors cannot be based solely on unlearned responses. The notion of a maternal instinct is not supported by available research. Almost a century ago sociologist Leta Hollingworth (1916, reprinted 2000) discounted the maternal instinct belief and suggested that "social devices" are the impelling reasons for women to bear and rear children. Socialization of females maximizes attachment to the young, whereas for males it is minimized. Some women suffer from postpartum depression and may even reject the child. And infanticide by mothers, especially for their daughters, is all too common globally. Other women voluntarily choose to remain childless (Vissing, 2002; Sichel, 2003; Spinelli, 2003). A woman's nurturing behavior will be heightened when she is in immediate contact with her newborn, but parental love emerges within the first week of the birth through repeated exposure to the infant (Klaus and Kennell, 1983; Maccoby, 2000). The fact that the majority of women eagerly respond to their infants and readily take on the caretaking role is due to many factors.

The birth experience undoubtedly creates a more unique mother–child bond than the father–child bond, but this does not mean that hormones will make one parent better or more nurturing than the other. When new fathers take part in the birthing process, measures of infant–father bonding are as high as infant–mother bonding. If gender-typing is low, infant care can be a rewarding joint effort by parents. Consider Mead's study of the gentle Arapesh, where both sexes enjoyed childcare responsibilities. The intense interest fathers have for their newborns and their capacity for nurturance are not based on hormones.

The influence of hormones on gendered behavior is somewhat puzzling, and some research is equivocal. But there is consensus among biologists and social and behavioral scientists that sex differences in behavior involve a complex mosaic of nature and nurture. Biological inheritance and social experience are not independent of one another.

GENDERED SEXUALITY

Until fairly recently beliefs about males and females differed in regard to human sexuality and were shrouded in myth and superstition. Research on gendered sexuality has helped dispel many of these myths, but as we shall see, many others still persist.

Sigmund Freud: Anatomy Is Destiny

The impact of Sigmund Freud (1856–1939) on medicine and science has been profound. There was no systematic psychology as a discipline before Freud. He was the first to tie a specific theory of psychosexual development to a therapeutic intervention, psychoanalysis, which he founded. Although a century of research on the foundations of Freud's work has produced questions, inconsistencies, and disagreement, he remains a powerful force on the intellectual climate in many disciplines.

The fact that a boy possesses a penis and a girl does not is the dominant factor in Freud's theory of psychosexual development. Of his five stages of psychosexual development (oral, anal, phallic, latency, genital), the one that has received the most attention is the *phallic stage* as it relates to gender socialization. At ages 3 to 5, children recognize the anatomical difference between the sexes. They focus gratification on the genitals (the clitoris for the girl and the penis for the boy), and masturbation and sexual curiosity increase for both. Freud argued that girls come to believe that the penis, unlike the barely noticeable clitoris, is a symbol of power denied to them. The result is "penis envy," which culminates in a girl's wish that she could be a boy (Freud, 1962). She views her mother as inferior because she, too, does not have a penis. The girl's *libido*, or sexual energy, is transferred to the father, who becomes the love-object. Later writers called this experience the *Electra complex*. The resolution occurs when the girl's wish for a penis is replaced by the wish for a child. A male child is even more desirable because he brings the longed-for penis with him. In this way, the female child eventually learns to identify with her mother. Clitoral stimulation is abandoned for vaginal penetration, which is proclaimed as a sign of adult maturity for women.

A boy also experiences conflict during the phallic stage, when his libido is focused on his mother, and his father is the rival for his mother's affections. Freud called this experience the *Oedipus complex*. When a boy discovers that a girl does not have a penis, he develops "castration anxiety"—the fear he will be deprived of the prized organ. The psychic turmoil a boy experiences during this stage leads to the development of a strong *superego*. For Freud, conscience and morality, the very hallmarks of civilization, are produced with strong superegos. Freud believed that girls have weaker superegos because the resolution of the Electra complex occurs with envy rather than fear. Because they experience less psychic conflict than boys, personality development is tarnished. This explains why women are more envious, jealous, narcissistic, and passive than men. A boy eventually overcomes the underlying fear, identifies with his father, reduces incestuous desires for his mother, and is later ushered into psychosexual maturity. Indeed, anatomy *is* destiny for Freud.

Critique. Asserting that women cannot be fully mature unless they experience orgasm through vaginal intercourse, Freud's beliefs about the biological inadequacy of females ignore the clitoris serving a purely sexual and pleasureful function.

Physiologically orgasms are the same, regardless of how they are reached. The sexism in Freudian theory is obvious, even though its unfortunate effects concerning the idea of female inferiority exceeded the intentions of Freud himself (Millett, 1995:61). Some critics argue that his sweeping generalizations were fueled by a personal longing for greatness (Bregar, 2000). His ideas were no doubt conditioned by the Victorian society in which he lived—one that embraced strict gender differentiation based on traditional roles for men and women in a patriarchal world. Freud was severely criticized for his ideas about infantile sexuality and the psychosexual stages of development but gained quiet acceptance for his comments on the biologically inferior design of females.

Feminism and Freud. Can feminists also be Freudians? Blatant sexism notwithstanding, the answer is yes. Feminist scholars and therapists reject sexism but still find useful core elements of his theory and therapeutic techniques. It would be counterproductive, for example, to reject psychoanalysis when it is successful for women patients. Psychoanalytic feminism has emerged to analyze the construction of gender and its effects on women, including women's subordination (Mitchell, 2000). Freud provides a basis for "seeing domination as a problem not so much of human nature as of human relationships—the interaction between psyche and social life" (Benjamin 1988:5). Feminist reinterpretation of psychoanalytic theory allows the problem of domination to be viewed from this unique perspective.

Another important writer representing psychoanalytic feminism is Nancy Chodorow (1978, 2001), who integrates useful aspects of psychoanalytic and sociological theory. She posits that because in most cultures women do the child care, mothers produce daughters who then desire to mother. Mothering thus reproduces itself. Sons are produced who devalue women for these very roles. Penis envy occurs because women, even young girls, recognize the power of males, so it is natural to desire this kind of power. There is nothing inherently biologically superior about this. It is the ability of the girl to maintain identification with her mother that achieves the desirable traits of empathy and connectedness. In this sense, there is a positive resolution of the Oedipus complex, which Freud overlooked, ignored, or rejected from his male-biased view.

Disagreements between psychoanalytic feminists and between feminism in general and Freudian theory have not been resolved. Feminists are searching for an androgynous, theoretical and therapeutic model to replace the traditional, often Freudian-based, androcentric approach (Ganley, 1988). This model would encompass feminist therapy appropriate for both male and female clients. With the required reinterpretation and empirical justification, it is likely that neo-Freudian scholars will use Freud's insights for the benefit, rather than the degradation, of women.

Ambiguous Sex, Ambiguous Gender

Research on infants born with sexual anomalies helps to clarify the biological basis of sex differences. From a sociological viewpoint, it allows a rare opportunity to study the link between physiology and behavior and to understand the important distinction between biological sex and gender. Referred to as **hermaphrodites** or **intersexed**, these infants are born with both male and female sex organs or have ambiguous genitals (such as a clitoris that looks like a penis). They violate the principle of **sexual dimorphism**, the separation of the sexes into two distinct groups. Assigned one sex at birth, the child's genetic sex is often discovered later.

Depending on when the child discovers his or her genetic sex makes a crucial difference in psychological adjustment and to determine if *sex reassignment surgery* (SRS) is an option. In SRS, genitals are surgically altered so that a person changes from one biological sex to the other. Sex reassignment has a greater likelihood of success if it occurs by age three because this is the time **gender identity** is learned— an awareness that there are two sexes who behave differently, with the child beginning to develop the first sense of self (chapter 3). Once gender identity becomes stabilized, attempting to change it would be emotionally traumatic.

The decision by parents to alter the sexual organs or genitalia of their inter-sexed child to fit either the appearance of one sex or the other or to correspond to the child's male or female genetic code is controversial. The child has no choice in the decision, and the surgery may not be reversible. Current advice is to assign a sex at birth, provide appropriate information and counseling about the intersex condition as the child is growing up, and then have the mature person decide on what action to take, if any, for surgery. Any irreversible surgery must wait until children are old enough to know and say which gender they feel closer to. Timing of the surgery in conjunction with hormonal therapy is an important ingredient for the development of gender identity (Dittman, 1998; Fausto-Sterling, 2000).

Transsexuals. Unlike hermaphrodites and intersexed people, **transsexuals** are genetic males or females who psychologically believe they are members of the other gender. They feel "trapped" in the wrong bodies and may undergo SRS to "correct" the problem. Only then can their gender identity and their biological sex be consistent. Transsexuals are not homosexuals. They are newly minted males or females who desire sexual intimacy with the other gender. Their ideal lover would be a heterosexual man or woman. The reality, however, is that most heterosexuals would not choose transsexuals as lovers. Transvestites, mostly males who are sexually aroused when they dress in women's clothing, are not transsexuals. Transsexuals are rare in society. The numbers worldwide are thought to be 1 in 100,000 males and 1 in 130,000 females (cited in Miracle et al., 2003:316). In 1952 when George Jorgenson was surgically transformed in Denmark to become Christine Jorgenson, the world's most well-known transsexual was "born." The first complete transsexual surgery was performed in the United States in 1965. With sex and gender identity now consistent, transsexuals ease into their new gender role with more confidence.

The outcomes of SRS are mixed. Research from the United States in the 1970s showed overall negative results. Some transsexuals believed the surgery was a mistake, and others reported no better adjustment after than before surgery. Due to better surgical techniques and therapeutic techniques coupled with more knowledge of transsexualism and increased tolerance in society, later research reports much more positive outcomes. International data indicate that the majority of transsexuals report satisfaction with their choice of sex reassignment (Landen et al., 1998; Rachlin, 2002; Smith et al., 2002).

Does Nature Rule? A Case of Sex Reassignment. The difficulty in unraveling biological and cultural sources of sex and gender is demonstrated in the now infamous case of SRS performed in Canada over thirty years ago to one of a pair of identical male twins, Bruce and Brian. During a circumcision at eight months to correct a minor urination problem an electric current was set too high, and Baby Bruce's penis was burned off. Physicians concluded that constructing an artificial penis was possible but not promising. The twins' parents learned that Dr. John Money, one of the world's experts on gender identity, spoke of encouraging results with sex reassignment surgery for hermaphrodites. According to Money, gender identity was solely shaped by parents and environment. Although Bruce was *not* a hermaphrodite and was born with normal genitals, Dr. Money agreed to take on his case and work with the family so he could be "taught to want to be a girl." Just before his second birthday, Bruce underwent surgery to remove the remaining penile tissue. Bruce was transformed to Brenda. According to Dr. Money, by age five, the twins demonstrated almost stereotypical gender roles. Brenda was given girls' toys, wore feminine clothing, and was being prepared for a domestic life. Brother Brian was introduced to the world outside the home, with preferences for masculine toys (soldiers and trucks) and occupations (fireman and policeman) (Money and Ehrhardt, 1972; Money and Tucker, 1975). Brenda's case appeared to be successful. Or was it?

Directly countering Money's positive assessment was a follow-up of Brenda at age 13, when she seen by a new set of psychiatrists. They reported a far more difficult transformation. She rebelled almost from the start, tearing off dresses, preferring boy toys, and fighting with her brother and peers. There was nothing feminine about Brenda. She had significant emotional problems related to her new female role. Her gait was a masculine gait; she was teased by other children; she believed that boys have a better life, and that it is easier to be a boy than a girl (Diamond, 1982; Diamond and Sigmundson, 1997). In therapy sessions she was sullen, angry, and unresponsive. The next step in her transformation was to be vaginal surgery, but the mere suggestion of it induced explosive panic. At age 12 she began estrogen therapy and breasts formed. She binged ate and gained weight to cover them up.

When did Brenda learn that she was born Bruce? At age 10, in an embarrassed and fumbled attempt, her father told her that she needed surgery because a doctor "made a mistake down there." She probably knew subconsciously she was a boy, but it was only at age 14 that she was finally told the truth. Expressing immense relief, she vowed to change back to a boy and took the name David (Bruce was "too geeky"). At age 18 at a relative's wedding, he made his public debut as a boy and married in 1990. David had a rudimentary penis and testicles constructed, requiring eighteen hospital visits (Colapinto, 2000).

In the media frenzy that followed David's "coming out" as a boy, the public heard only that gender identity is a natural, inborn process. Nurture's role is given little credit in the process. Three decades after the Bruce-Brenda-David transformations, John Money still makes a strong case for the social constructionist argument (Money, 1995). Although this case may support the nature side (gender identity is inborn), there are numerous reasonable counterarguments for the nurture side (gender identity is learned), which I reported in the last editions of this text before new information was available. These arguments remain viable.

Brenda's therapy began in preadolescence, but it is doubtful that the effects of her biological sex were altered early enough to make her look more like a girl than a boy. Children fervently embrace gender roles early in life, and those, like

Brenda, who do not physically or behaviorally conform to them are the most vulnerable to rejection and ridicule by peers. Consider, too, that in the fear she would revert to masculine preferences, Brenda was being raised more rigidly to conform to stereotyped gender roles than most girls. She was being prepared for a domestic life, but if her transformation was successful, ironically, she could never fulfill the ultimate female role of biological mother. In addition, Bruce became a girl nearly two years after everyone, including twin brother Brian, treated her like a boy. Interviews with Brian showed him confused and embarrassed by Brenda's tomboy behavior, which no one accepted. Brenda was keenly aware that boys had more prestige and a "better life" than girls. Her extraordinary opportunity to revert to the male sex may have been further prompted by these beliefs. As discussed in the next chapter, gender socialization begins immediately at birth, and by age two children are marked with indelible gender stamps that may be altered but not erased. Symbolic interactionists would be interested in how friends, family, and neighbors reacted to Brenda's transformation after knowing her as Bruce for almost two years. The family even moved at one point to get away from "ghosts and doubters" (Colapinto, 2000). The media never questioned the ability of a host of players to carry out a giant pretense. Everybody may have been playing a game of science fiction—but the game of social reality was largely ignored.

Sexual Orientation

Once familiar mainly to scientists, terms describing sexual preferences are now routinely used by the public and media. Depending on how they are used and who uses them, some of these terms are contentious. As a result, discourse about homosexuality is being reshaped though new labels, often offered by the people to whom they refer (Pierce, 2001). The terms used here reflect current sociological usage, but it is likely that they, too, will be altered as this reshaping discourse proceeds.

Sexual orientation, defined earlier as preference for sexual partners of one gender or the other, is divided into the categories of heterosexual and homosexual in most Western cultures. Like gender identity, sexual orientation is not automatically granted by biological sex. *Heterosexual* is the category for people who have sexual preference for and erotic attraction to those of the other gender. *Homosexual* is the category for people who have sexual preference for and erotic attraction to those of their own gender. Homosexual males are also referred to as *gay men* and homosexual females as *lesbians.* The term *gay* is often used to include both gay men and lesbians. *Bisexual* is the category for people whose sexual orientations may shift and who are sexually responsive to either gender. Humans share the same anatomy and have the same capacity for sexual pleasure, but there is a great deal of variation in how and with whom people experience sexual pleasure. According to symbolic interactionists sexual orientation is largely a social construction built during social interaction. Like heterosexuals, both men and women who see themselves as homosexual maintain a gender identity consistent with their biological sex. They are socialized into prevailing gender roles except for their sexual orientation (Lippa and Tan, 2001; Philaretou and Allen, 2001).

This socialization helps explain why homosexuals prefer for sexual partners those men or women who fit the standards of masculinity or femininity defined by the culture (Roof, 1997; Mutchler, 2000). However, because it is accompanied by gender roles that are defined as masculine or feminine, gender identity is much more susceptible to change over time than sexual orientation. In the middle of the nineteenth century a masculine gender role was associated with employment that included elementary school teaching and clerical work. Today these same jobs are associated with a feminine gender role.

Sexual orientation, like other forms of human sexuality, is extremely varied. Research shows that the conceptual distinction between gender identity and sexual orientation is a blurry one. For example, **transgender** describes people who do not conform to culturally defined traditional gender roles associated with their sex. Transgendered people may or may not identify themselves as homosexual and may or may not choose to "pass" for the other sex in appearance (Roen, 2002). The ancient Greeks, for instance, accepted both homosexuality and heterosexuality as "natural" relationships, with no moral overtones. A man's preference for males or females was seen as a matter of taste and desire; the enjoyment of one over the other did not categorize men according to a gender preference for sexual interaction. A man who pursued males did not see himself as any different from one who pursued females. It was common for a man to change his sexual preference to women after spending his youth loving boys (Foucault, 1990; Murray, 2000). For the Greeks, gender identity existed, but sexual orientation did not. Many of these Greek males may be described as transgendered people who moved between gender roles in ways that suited their sexual preferences and lifestyles at the time.

Global Focus: Challenging Definitions of Sex and Gender

Transgendered people who perform specific social functions are found throughout the world today. In India, men known as *hijras* dress up in women's clothing and are called on to bless newborn infants. In order to become a hijra and perform this important cultural role, most of these men by choice have been emasculated—their testicles have been removed. Hijra are not homosexual. They think of themselves more as females and thus prefer heterosexual men as sexual partners. They generally live and dress as females, often in a separate subculture. In the rural areas of India where hijras practice their trade, sexual orientation and gender identity do not appear to be concerns (Nanda, 1997). Hijras are ambivalent figures in India. They are teased and mocked but also valued and esteemed (Ward, 1999). The hijras have a gender role that legitimizes their function as ritual performers. This role forms the core of their self-definition and the basis of their positive, collective self-image.

Unlike hijras, who live openly as females, some people go through life with "mixed" gender identities. The *xanith* of the Arab state of Oman are also biological males. They work as homosexual prostitutes and skilled domestic servants. Described as a "third" gender, they have male names but distinctive dress and hairstyles, unlike that of either men or women. Xanith are not men because they can interact with women and are not women because they are not restricted by purdah, the system of veiling and secluding women (cited in Lips, 2001:161). The term *transgender* may also describe the *mahus* of Tahiti. Mahus are usually young boys who adopt female gender roles early in life and eventually find jobs usually performed by women. However, there is also a female form of mahu that is shaped by influences about gays and lesbians that are coming into Tahiti. In both male and female mahu, however, the status is viewed as naturally evolving from childhood roles. They have sexual relations with those of their own sex but not with other mahus. Their preferred sexual partners, however, are those from the other gender. Mahu sexuality, therefore, is "same-sex but opposite(sic)-gender" (Elliston, 1999:238). Though Tahitians may poke fun at mahus, they are accepted members in society (Stanley, 2000).

For probably 200 years among Native Americans, the role of *berdache* existed, a title conferred on those who did not exhibit conventional gender roles. These berdache womanly men and manly women still exist in some tribes. In tribal mythology, berdache may act as mediators between men and women and between the physical and spiritual worlds (Lang, 1998; Roscoe, 1998). Native Americans refer to those who act out cross-gender roles as having "two spirits."

The hijra, xanith, mahus, and berdache are roles associated with approval and sometimes honor, rather than disdain and immorality. Like hermaphrodites, these transgendered people also violate the principle of sexual dimorphism and attest to the powerful impact of culture on both gender identity and sexual orientation.

Sexual Scripts

Sociologists emphasize how sexuality is based on prescribed roles that are acted out like other socially bestowed roles. **Sexual scripts** are shared beliefs concerning what society defines as acceptable sexual thoughts, feelings, and behaviors for each gender (Gagnon, 1990). Gender roles are connected with different sexual scripts—one considered more appropriate for males, and the other considered more appropriate for females. Sexual scripts continue to be based on beliefs that for men sex is for orgasm and physical pleasure, and for women sex is for love and the pleasure that comes from intimacy. Although people may desire more latitude—such as more emotional intimacy for men and more sexual pleasure for women—they often feel constrained by the traditional scripting of their sexuality. When both men and women accept such scripts and carry their expectations into the bedroom, gendered sexuality is being socially constructed. Beliefs about gendered sexuality contribute to sexual dysfunction and sexual violence toward women and gay men. Such beliefs also hold disadvantages for both men and women by constraining their sexual pleasure (Krahe, 2000; Wiederman, 2001). Gendered scripting illustrates that biology alone cannot explain human sexuality (Frayser, 1999). Indeed, the evidence is overwhelming that biology is a player in the sexuality game, "but it is not the only player or even captain of the team" (Schwartz and Rutter, 1998:28). Contrary to assertions of biological essentialism, sexuality is much less spontaneous than we think.

Sexual scripts may provide the routes to sexuality, but over time new paths offering new directions for sexuality can be built. It is unlikely that gendered sexuality will be eliminated entirely. However, it is likely that as gender roles become more egalitarian, the sexual lives of both men and women will be enhanced.

Patterns of Sexual Attitudes and Behavior

Until fairly recently, beliefs about human sexuality have been shrouded in myth and superstition. Major assaults on these myths and on the biological determinism in sexuality were led by the pioneering work of Alfred Kinsey and his associates (1948, 1953). Just as Freud shocked science with his assertions on sexuality, Kinsey had similar results on revealing his data on sexual behavior. He reported sexual activities far different from the supposed norms.

Gender and Orgasm. The original Kinsey data revealed that 92 percent of males and 58 percent of females used masturbation (sexual self-stimulation) to achieve orgasm. Males begin to masturbate during early adolescence. Females begin to masturbate later than men, often in their twenties and thirties. These patterns have not changed significantly since Kinsey's original research (Hunt, 1974; Laumann and Mahay, 2002).

During intercourse men are more likely to have an orgasm than women. Kinsey found that over one-third of married women never had an orgasm prior to marriage and that one-third of married women never had an orgasm. Later data show that almost 90 percent of all women experience orgasm, whether married or not, and virtually all married women (98 percent) do reach orgasm, although not with every sexual intercourse. Husbands generally would like more frequent intercourse than their wives, especially early in the marriage. Later in their married life this trend may reverse; married women report more positive perception of their sexual behavior, and men report a more positive perception of their marital life. However, for both men and women, marital satisfaction and sexual satisfaction are highly correlated. And the more frequent the sex, the higher the level of sexual satisfaction (Young et al., 2000; Trudel, 2002). If sex keeps people happy in their marriages, sexual satisfaction for both sexes is also a good predictor of divorce.

Premarital/Nonmarital Sex. Kinsey's (1953) data reported that one-fourth of unmarried women born before 1900 had experienced coitus (sexual intercourse). He found that one-third of young women reported premarital sex by age 25. Premarital sex for men was 77 percent. Today the differences between men and women in premarital sex have all but disappeared. Men may have sex earlier than women, but by the time they graduate from college virtually all men and women are sexually experienced (Kamen, 2000; Rouse, 2002). Females do have fewer sex partners than men, but they will plan for their first intercourse. About half of all teenagers ages 15 to 19 have had sexual intercourse at least once. However, people are surprised to learn that during the last decade sexual activity among teens has significantly declined (Amba and Sonenstein, 2002). What is perhaps more surprising is that the number of teenage boys reporting sexual intercourse has dramatically decreased—white, African American, and Latino alike. For girls, the rate of sexual activity has remained relatively stable. The only change to this pattern is for African-American girls, who reduced their sexual activity to levels comparable to white and Latino girls (Risman and Schwartz, 2002:18).

The overall rate of sexual risk taking among teens has also appeared to decline. Norms about gendered sexuality explain the new pattern. Although girls have increased their sexual behavior, it is still within the bonds of a romantic relationship.

A decade ago a boy was likely to have his first sexual intercourse with a pickup or casual date. Girls whose first intercourse occurred before age 16 are more likely to report that it was not voluntary. Today, boys are likely to have their first intercourse with a girlfriend (Risman and Schwartz, 2002). In a major study conducted on college students almost two decades ago, Michael Moffatt (1989) concluded that premarital sexual chastity was "almost [as] dead as the dodo."

Because most people have several sexual experiences with people whom they will not likely marry, the term "premarital" sex is inaccurate. A more accurate term to refer to these experiences is *nonmarital* sex.

Extramarital Relationships. Once called adultery but now commonly called affairs, this form of nonmarital sex takes on many forms. Extramarital relationships involve different degrees of openness and include married as well as single people. They may or may not include sexual involvement. The emotional involvement with a partner other than one's spouse can be more threatening to the marriage than sexual involvement. Despite the fact that most people claim to disapprove of affairs in any form, Kinsey's data indicated that 50 percent of males and 26 percent of females engaged in extramarital sex by age 40. Currently, estimates are that about 25 to 35 percent of men and 15 to 25 percent of women have had an extramarital affair (Norman, 1998; Treas and Giesen, 2000; Atkins and Jacobson, 2001). It is clear that although most people disapprove of affairs, a significant number engage in them.

There are problems with these data. Although later research validated Kinsey's data, the high percentage of affairs he reported was suspect. It is also clear that when respondents report their knowledge of affairs others are having, the numbers increase. In addition, the fact that divorce is less stigmatized is associated with openness to extramarital relationships. Thus it is probable that reported figures for extramarital relationships are lower than the actual numbers.

The Double Standard. The **double standard** refers to the idea that men are allowed to express themselves sexually and women are not. Because the level of nonmarital sexual behavior for males and females is now similar, does a double standard still exist? The answer is yes when considering biological sex—but no when considering gender. Data on sexual behavior have changed dramatically. It was assumed that, compared to men, women had weaker sex drives, were more difficult to arouse sexually, and became aroused less frequently. These assumptions have all been proven false (Foley and Sugrue, 2002; Leiblum, 2002). It is the clitoris, not the vagina, as Freud insisted, that is responsible for the multiple orgasms experienced by women. Prompted by feminist social scientists, new models about female sexuality from women's own voices are evolving. In stark contrast to Freudian views, they offer an understanding that sexuality for women is pleasureful, fulfilling, and desired (Kleinplatz, 2001).

Major gender differences in sexual attitudes do persist. More women than men express the belief that emotional closeness is a prerequisite for sexual intercourse. Men give sexual pleasure and conquest as the main motives. They prefer more partners over a shorter period of time than women (Buss et al., 2001; Amba and Sonenstein, 2002). Women adopt a more "person-centered" approach to sex; men adopt a more "body-centered" approach. Males are less likely to be criticized or to feel guilty about their sexual activities than females. Even with the raising of a public consciousness regarding the double standard, little has actually changed in the sexual scripts subscribed to by men and women (Allyn, 2000; Groce, 2000; Scott and Sprecher, 2000).

Such gendered attitudes are especially clear for extramarital relationships. Both genders act on their desire to have affairs, but men express a greater willingness. The idea that women are sexual beings who can and should experience sexual pleasure is relatively recent. Pleasurable sexual activities are gendered—conditioned by sexual scripts defined as acceptable for men or women. The double standard, which reinforces a woman's passivity during the heterosexual sex act, is one such script. The data on female sexuality are still viewed in light of male dominance in sexuality. Women and men both believe that her orgasm is a sign of his success as a lover.

Ironically, the disappearance of a sexual double standard may not be desirable. The absence of significant gender differences in frequency of nonmarital sexual activities, number of partners, or degree of emotional involvement with partners could trigger a lifetime of more sex with not only more people, but also more people who are less known to their partners. Given the risks to both genders related to health and sexually transmitted diseases, sexual violence, and unplanned pregnancy, the disappearance of a sexual double standard may be hazardous to your health and to society.

Sexuality in Later Life. The cultural barriers and gender norms also apply to sexuality in later life. For the elderly, an already difficult situation is made worse by a combination of age and gender-related stereotypes. As with gender, there is a sexual double standard regarding age and sexuality (McCarthy, 2001). Because it is associated with youth and virility, sexuality among the elderly has been ignored or demeaned. The elderly are perceived to be sexless. If elderly males show sexual interest, they are viewed suspiciously. Women are expected to retreat to a sexless existence after the completion of childbearing and mothering. Yet women experience more comfort and less anxiety about sex as they age, thereby increasing their desire for intercourse and sexual intimacy (Rice, 2001). On the other hand, widows significantly outnumber widowers, so options for sexual activity decline for women, despite the fact that sexual desire remains strong.

Research by two other pioneers of sexuality, William Masters and Virginia Johnson (1966, 1970), shows that when advancing age and physiological changes influence sexual ability for men, performance anxiety increases. A man's wife may believe his "failure" is a rejection of her. Men are socialized early in life to believe that they will be judged by their sexual potency and talents. As suggested earlier, when a couple accepts such beliefs, a cycle of less sex, less interest in sex, and increased emotional distance is perpetuated. The irony is that it is easier to cope with these incorrect beliefs if society assumes the elderly are not supposed to be sexually active anyway.

Research illustrates that men and women of all age groups are far less sexually different from one another than once thought (Hillman, 2000). They differ more in how they negotiate sexual activities and in the kinds of sexual relationships they seek. As pointed out by Masters and Johnson over thirty years ago, cultural barriers such as traditional gender roles inhibit sexual pleasure. The social construction of women as passive sexual beings and men as sexual conquerors can be reconstructed to make them partners in a mutually pleasurable experience.

GENDER AND HEALTH

The interplay of biology and culture is necessary to understand patterns of health and well-being related to sex and gender. Various measurement techniques have been developed to determine these patterns. The simplest measure, the **mortality rate**, is expressed as a percentage of the total number of deaths over the population size (× 1000) in a given time period, usually a year. Calculating a **morbidity rate**, the amount of disease or illness in a population, is more difficult. Although illness may have well-defined symptoms, illness itself is in part subjective. Many people do not recognize their own sickness, may recognize it but refuse to alter their behavior by taking off work or seeing a physician, or prefer to treat themselves. These patterns are particularly true for calculating levels of mental illness. As a result, morbidity rates are often based on treatment and data accuracy may be compromised.

Even with these cautions in mind, however, a clear and consistent inverse pattern emerges in comparing gender differences in mortality and morbidity. Women have higher morbidity rates but live longer than men; men have lower morbidity rates but do not live as long as women.

Till Death Do Us Part: Gender and Mortality

In the United States females can expect to outlive males on an average of 6 years. Women and men die from the same three causes—cancer, heart disease and stroke—but there are significant gender differences in their mortality rate. Mortality rates for all leading causes of death are higher for males. Death rates for most of these causes are 1.5 times those for females. Only in deaths due to diabetes do males and females reach parity. Men have been gaining on women in narrowing the mortality rate, but the age-adjusted rate for men is still over 40 percent greater than that for women (Arias et al., 2003). When race is added to the life expectancy rate (LER) profile, white males are gaining, and they reached parity with African-American females in 2000. This parity, however, was short-lived. By 2001 the gap reappeared and is expected to again widen (Figure 2.1). Overall, however, when factoring in race, ethnicity, and especially social class, which have a profound health effect, females still have a more favorable life expectancy rate than comparable males (McDonough et al., 1999; Crimmins and Sato, 2001).

Males have higher mortality rates at every stage of life. The first year of life is the most vulnerable time for both sexes, but infant mortality rates are higher for males. By the 1990s mortality data showed all three nondisease causes of death (accidents, suicides, and homicides) in the top-15 list. In suicide, for example, although women experience more depression than men and *attempt* suicide about four times more frequently, men *commit* suicide about four times more than women. Men choose more lethal means and are more likely to succeed (Anderson, 2001; Oquendo et al., 2001). Males succumb earlier to virtually all causes of mortality, with the nondisease causes showing the greatest male–female differentials (Anderson, 2001; National Center for Health Statistics, 2004).

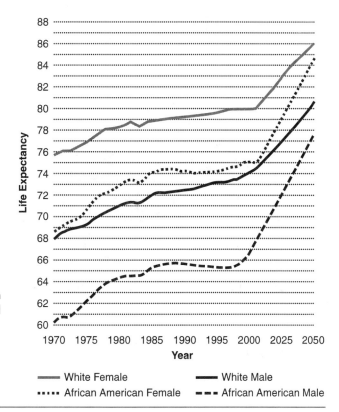

Figure 2.1 Life Expectancy at Birth in the United States by Gender and African American/White Race, 1970–2002 and Projection for 2025 and 2050.

Source: National Projections Program, U.S. Bureau of the Census, 2002; *National Vital Statistics Report* 52(3): *September 18, 2003.*

Global Patterns. The female advantage in LER holds globally as well (Table 2.1). The graying world becomes a female world. The current elderly population throughout the world is predominantly female, and it is projected to become even more so. The highest overall life expectancy is in Japan, where men can expect to live to age 77 and women to age 85. In less than a decade, many countries will have only five men to every ten women over the age of 80. In the developed world the gender gap in mortality is declining slightly. Compared to women, men are making some gains in living longer. But for both the developed and developing world, the gap favoring women widens again at the oldest age (Kinsella and Velkoff, 2001). As discussed in chapter 3, poverty combines with sex selective abortion and neglect and abandonment of female infants and girls in many parts of the world. The average global sex ratio at birth (SRB) is 105 and favors males slightly. In rural areas of China, India, and Bangladesh between 117 and 160 boys are born for every 100 girls in many regions of these three nations alone (Ghosh and Pomeroy, 2003). If a newborn is a girl, the couple tries again and again for a boy, continually increasing SRB until the desired number of sons is born (Yongping and Xizhe, 2000; *People's Daily*, 2002). Frequent pregnancy takes another toll. Of the almost 700,000 maternal deaths worldwide every year, 99 percent occur in developing countries, and most of these are preventable with primary health care intervention (Daulaire et al., 2002; UNFPA, 2004). Given this reality, the overall female advantage in mortality is astounding.

Table 2.1 Male-Female Life Expectancy Rates[*] by World Region.

	Male	Female
World Region	**63.3**	**67.6**
Africa	47.9	50.1
Asia/Middle East	65.5	67.6
Europe	70.1	78.2
Latin America/Caribbean	67.1	73.9
North America	74.5	80.1
More Developed Regions	**72.1**	**79.4**
(Australia, Europe, Japan, North America)		
Less Developed Regions	**61.7**	**65.1**
(Africa, Asia/Middle East, Latin America/Caribbean)		

[*]Projected averages, 2000–2005.

Source: U.N. Population Division, 2003. Constructed from *World Population Prospects: The 2002 Revision Population Database*. Available online: http://esa.un.org/unpp/.

In Sickness and in Health: Gender and Morbidity

Data from many sources consistently report that women have higher morbidity rates than men. Women's advantage in mortality may be offset by their disadvantage in morbidity in part because living longer reflects increased chronic illness and disability.

Men and Morbidity. Males are prone to certain physical and mental illnesses and injury categories in which women tend to be exempt. Men have lower overall acute conditions but higher prevalence of chronic conditions that are life threatening and associated with long-term disability, such as heart disease, emphysema, and atherosclerosis. Males have the highest rates of cancer at the youngest and oldest ages and are almost twice as likely to die from it than females. They are also afflicted with a range of genetic disorders much less common in females such as myopia, hemophilia, absence of central incisor teeth, juvenile glaucoma, and progressive deafness (Shinberg, 2001; National Center for Health Statistics, 2004). For mental illness, gender differences do not vary by rate, but they do vary by type. Men are more likely to suffer from personality disorders (antisocial behavior or narcissism) than women (Rosenfield et al., 2000; Sachs-Ericsson and Ciarlo, 2000). As a buffer against mental illness as well as physical illness for both genders, it is also better to be married. For men, it is much better to be married. Single men have the highest mortality and morbidity rates for both physical and mental disorders. Never married, divorced, and single men have higher rates of mental illness when compared to all marital categories of women (Simon, 2002; Sobal et al., 2003).

Gender roles also put more men in occupations that are potentially hazardous to their health, such as police and fire protection, the military, mining, and hazardous construction work. Sports-related injuries are also much higher for men than women and are associated with chronic illnesses and disabilities. Males in all age groups are more likely than comparable age females to engage in over 30 behaviors and roles that increase their risk of disease, injury, and death (Courtenay, 2000:81).

Women and Morbidity. Morbidity appears to gradually emerge in females, especially noticeable in preadolescence, where girls begin to report higher levels of asthma, migraine headaches, and psychological and eating disorders than boys, a pattern that occurs in the United States and other developed countries (Wade et al., 2002; Sweeting and West, 2003). Small gender differences in self-esteem favoring males show up during late adolescence and continue through the life course (Kling et al., 1999). As adults, women report more physical and mental disorders and use health services more than men. Anger, frustration, and depression are intensified when doctors face multiple, unexplained symptoms in their female patients (Morris, 2001). Often a physician cannot find anything physically wrong. They have more daily and transient illnesses such as colds and headaches and a higher prevalence of nonfatal chronic conditions such as arthritis, anemia, and sinusitis. Most all autoimmune disorders, such as juvenile diabetes and multiple sclerosis, are skewed toward women (Angier, 2001). Employed women and women who are identified as androgynous or less traditional in gender role orientation have better physical and psychological health. Like men, type of work is correlated to health. Professional women frequently describe their jobs as stressful, but clerical and lower-level workers are more likely to report stress-related illnesses, such as insomnia and headaches (Glenn and Feldberg, 1995). Regardless of employment status, women are more likely to suffer from depression and anxiety compared to men (Rieker and Bird, 2000).

Premenstrual Syndrome. In many cultures menstruation is viewed as a disease of women and associated with pity, suspicion, scorn, and fear. Menstruating women may be isolated and undergo ritual purification at the conclusion of their periods (Delaney et al., 1988). The medical literature has viewed this normal physiological process in two distinct ways: as a pathology that victimizes women and as a condition that dismisses a woman's physical pain as inconsequential or fabricated (Martin, 1994a). The myths associated with it have not been dispelled, even in the health care and scientific community.

Recent research on premenstrual syndrome (PMS) has challenged these myths. There are many faces of PMS that are variously defined by health professionals, researchers, and women themselves. Overall PMS is widely viewed as a blanket term for a variety of physical and psychological symptoms occurring between two days and two weeks before a menstrual period. Physical symptoms include water retention, breast tenderness, and cramping, and psychological symptoms include heightened tension, anxiety, irritability, and depression. As many as 75 percent of women in their twenties and thirties experience some premenstrual *symptoms*, but only 2 to 10 percent experience severe to disabling symptoms that may be defined as premenstrual *syndrome*—a serious psychiatric disorder (Figert, 1996; Mayo Clinic, 2002). A diagnosis of PMS is vastly different from the normal bodily changes associated with menstruation.

Correlational research has indirectly linked PMS to fluctuations in hormones, like estrogen, which are seen to influence anxiety, depression, and other behavioral changes. Research shows that hormone concentrations change prior to a woman's period, but they do so in the same manner for *all* women, regardless of a woman's symptoms. Women are more anxious or irritable because of the physical symptoms, not because of the hormones. Hormones cause the reduction of the mood-altering chemical serotonin, in turn increasing anxiety or depression. PMS, therefore, is not directly caused by hormones but by their effect on the brain. There also appears to be a nutritional connection between hormones and serotonin that impacts symptoms (Rosenfeld, 2001; Bernard, 2003). It is not only difficult to sort out the causal path for explaining PMS related to hormonal fluctuations, but also to date it is virtually impossible to separate the physical symptoms from the cultural expectations associated with menstruation. Researchers who adopt both biological and cultural strategies in their explanations will be more successful.

The whole notion of PMS is still equivocal, but the acceptance of the term by some health care professionals has aided those women who experience great physical and psychological difficulty with their periods. Prior to "legitimizing" PMS, countless women were turned away from a male-dominated health care system with vague, paternalistic assurances that it was all in their heads. On the other hand, as a term, PMS is so commonly misused in the media (a staple of comedy shows, for example) that it is now equated with *all* menstruation. It is a convenient but erroneous explanation and justification for the behavior of women. If women "have" PMS, it reinforces the myth that up to two weeks a month most adult women have impaired judgment. Thus women may be put in a double bind if they attribute changes in their behavior to PMS.

Menopause and Hormone Replacement Therapy. Misinformation and cultural stereotypes surround menopause, when menstruation permanently ceases. Up to several years before menopause, now referred to as *perimenopause*, women experience irregular menstrual cycles and often report symptoms of irritability, depression, and headaches. Some report the infamous hot flashes. Like PMS, most symptoms are not disabling. The severe distress accompanying menopause is experienced by only about 10 percent of women. Research does not support the relationship of the physical symptoms of menopause to serious depression in women. When combining the physical and psychological factors, menopause for most women is probably much easier than was puberty. Indeed, women look forward to the time when menstruation ends. Medicine, however, still largely subscribes to the maternal instinct idea and carries it over to viewing menopause as psychologically crippling because reproduction is sealed at this life stage. The reproductive cycle cannot be reversed but women can escape the fate of menopause. Many gynecologists continue to conform to beliefs advocated by Robert Wilson (1966) in his influential book *Feminine Forever* that menopause is a "disease of estrogen deficiency" treatable by hormone replacement therapy (HRT). He views menopausal women as unstable "castrates," creating untold misery in the form of alcoholism, drug addiction, and broken homes because of their estrogen starvation (cited in Fausto-Sterling, 1993:336).

Until 2002 HRT was the taken-for-granted remedy for menopause prescribed by gynecologists and readily accepted by patients, with over 6 million women in the United States taking the most commonly prescribed estrogen-progestin HRT. In the last edition of this text I reported that the jury was still out on the benefits and risks of HRT. Benefits were thought to include decreased chances for developing coronary heart disease (CHD), fewer hip fractures related to osteoporosis (bone loss), and less cognitive decline and memory loss; risks included increased potential for breast cancer and blood clots. The largest study ever conducted using a sample of 16,000 women followed for over five years confirmed that the estrogen-progestin HRT significantly increased the risks of invasive breast cancer, stroke, and blood clots. But, perhaps more stunning, it conclusively showed that HRT *raised*, not lowered, the CHD risk in healthy postmenopausal women. Women had an 81 percent increased risk of CHD in the first year after starting estrogen-progestin HRT (Manson et al., 2003). And yet another nail in HRT's coffin is the unexpected finding that HRT also *increased* the risk of women developing dementia (AARP, 2003; Shumaker, 2003). Earlier research on the role of estrogen in cognitive functioning—primarily using female rats—had been inconsistent, but HRT was widely regarded as the remedy to stem memory loss, "counteract the effects of aging and delay the onset of Alzheimer's disease" (Carpenter, 2001; Znamensky et al., 2003). Even with the latest results, some still advocate HRT in the belief it will alter the progress of Alzheimer's disease (Paley, 2003). The benefits that HRT did confirm were fewer fractures and colorectal cancers (Cauley et al., 2003). On balance, however, because the harm is much greater than the benefit, women were advised to immediately contact their physician to determine future HRT. This potential harm to research subjects and the need to get the information disseminated quickly was so imperative that the study was ended three years early (Women's Health Initiative, 2003).

From a symbolic interactionist view, even with known risks, the massive prescriptions of HRT played on the fears of aging women and loss of fertility in a society that worships youth. It also reinforced cultural views of menopause as a disease that produces psychologically unstable women. The cultural refusal to accept the realities of aging coupled with the gender stereotypes of women who are revered if they are young and fertile have compromised the health of millions of women over the last 50 years. As reported by a 56-year-old female pediatrician who is dealing with her own menopausal symptoms:

> There's an arrogance in thinking we can go on indefinitely taking hormones that our bodies aren't supposed to take anymore. (Cowley and Spingen, 2002:41).

The jury returned with a verdict of guilty for HRT. But if science is doing its job correctly, it will always report findings that will contradict previous findings. It is also clear from the HRT story that science is not immune from gender bias. Feminist health professionals call for a view of menopause as a normal developmental process and for providing women with accurate information to make educated choices concerning treatment (Jensen, 2004).

Eating Disorders. There are other serious health effects in the quest for youth and beauty, especially for females. As the Duchess of Windsor reportedly said over a half century ago, "You can never be too rich or too thin." Such beliefs translate to dramatic increases in eating disorders, especially *anorexia nervosa*, a disease of self-induced severe weight loss, primarily in young women. A variant is *bulimia*, which alternates binge eating and purging. The incidence rates of these "fear of fat" diseases have steadily increased since the 1950s, affecting about 7 million women today. They will affect 1 to 2 percent of late adolescent girls and adult women, of which 6 to 10 percent will die (Andereycken, 2003; Committee on Adolescence,

2003). During puberty, when a girl begins to worry about attractiveness, there is an average weight gain of 20 to 25 pounds. Males are not immune to weight obsession with their concerns focusing on body shape and muscularity. It is estimated that 1 million males suffer from eating disorders, up 50 percent from just a decade ago (Andersen et al., 2000; Luciano, 2001). About 10 percent of college age students—both men and women—report symptoms of eating disorders. Only 50 percent of people with eating disorders report being cured, a prognosis that has worsened over the last decade (Mehler, 2001; ANAD, 2003). In terms of race and ethnicity, African-American women and Latino women have higher rates of obesity than Asian or white women; but African-American and Asian women are more satisfied with their body weight, and Latino women are less satisfied than white women. However, increases in eating disorders with onset in adolescence are reported for females in all these groups; and new cases for adolescent boys are also rapidly increasing (Neumark-Sztainer and Hannan, 2000; NWHIC, 2003). Self-esteem is fragile during adolescence for both boys and girls of all races, and weight issues contribute to their insecurity.

Cultural beliefs are significant influences in the development of eating disorders (Miller et al., 2001). Anorexia can be described as a *culture bound syndrome* because it was first associated with norms unique to American society. The power of the Western media has extended these norms to other societies. In Fiji, for example, "big was beautiful" for girls. Television came to Fiji in 1995, and within three years a teen's risk for eating disorders doubled and there was a five-fold increase of vomiting for weight loss (Goodman, 1999). A global increase in eating disorders is also linked to increased cigarette smoking by girls who are concerned about weight gain (Lindsey, 1997; Keel and Klump, 2003). Female models and movie and television stars have gotten progressively thinner throughout this century. At size 14, today Marilyn Monroe would not easily find a job in motion pictures. Whereas male celebrities have gotten more muscular, female beauty contestants average 20 percent lower than ideal weight (Lee, 1998; Stearns, 2002).

Chronic dieting and excessive physical exercise are reinforced by other health messages publicizing the obesity epidemic in the United States. The messages are confusing and may seem contradictory—Americans are obsessed with thinness but at the same time an obesity epidemic is rapidly unfolding. The health and diet industries bolster these messages. From a conflict theory perspective, this has resulted in a form of *medicalization,* a process that legitimizes medical control over parts of a person's life (Conrad and Schneider, 1990). Combined with cosmetic surgery and unhealthy body weight norms, the social pressure for thinness now has a billion-dollar industry supporting it. This industry supports a culturally accepted belief that women's bodies are unacceptable as they are.

HIV/AIDS. Less than a decade ago discussions of acquired immunodeficiency syndrome (AIDS) focused on the high mortality rate of men with the disease. In the United States in 1992 it was the leading cause of death of men between the ages of 25 and 44, with the highest percentage among gay males. By the turn of the century AIDS was the fifth leading cause of death for women in this age range. Among African-American women it was the third leading cause. In 1992 women accounted for about 14 percent of cumulative AIDS cases; by 2002, the proportion grew to over 20 percent. Almost 40 percent of women were infected through heterosexual contact, a significant proportion of these through sex with an intravenous drug user (CDC, 2002). Globally, almost 20 million women are living with human immunodeficiency virus (HIV) and now account for over half of all cases. (Global Health Council, 2003).

In the United States and the developed world HIV infection rates have stabilized since the 1990s. AIDS mortality now focuses on HIV morbidity. Despite large HIV declines, most cases still occur in men, with almost half of new cases in African-American men. There have been significant declines in HIV over the last decade, the largest decline among white males. On the other hand, the lowest decline is for African-American females. When poverty and region are added to the equation, new infections show slower declines in inner city and poor African-American and Latino populations. Poor men and women living in the South account for a significant proportion of new cases, the largest increases occurring among women in these categories. Among U.S. women, poor, heterosexual, minority women are at greatest risk for HIV/AIDS (Hader et al., 2001; Karon et al., 2001; CDC, 2003).

In the United States the AIDS death sentence has been commuted to a life sentence with HIV, if the right combination of drug therapy and lifestyle changes occur. In the developing world an AIDS/HIV diagnosis remains a death sentence. The rapid spread of AIDS worldwide and the patterns that have been produced by this spread have transformed AIDS into a women's disease. Women worldwide are becoming infected with HIV at faster rates than men, with the number of annual cases for women now equaling or exceeding those of men, most of whom are in sub-Saharan Africa and most of whom are infected through heterosexual contact with a spouse or partner (chapter 6). The death rate is so alarming that the two century increase in life expectancy worldwide is expected to drop in 51 countries (USAID, 2002). Lower LERs associated with HIV/AIDS are already reported in sub-Saharan African regions of Kenya, Rwanda, Mali, Chad, and Niger. Because women are infected at higher rates than men, HIV may be the biggest threat to their LER advantage.

Drug Use. For both sexes the use of alcohol and other drugs, including caffeine and nicotine, is culturally acceptable. Gender differences in morbidity rates relative to these usages are still evident. More men than women use alcohol throughout their lives, and alcoholism is significantly higher among men. But women metabolize alcohol differently and suffer more from both its acute and chronic effects. For women, driving is impaired quicker, and alcohol induced liver disease and brain damage occur over a shorter period of time and after consuming less alcohol (National Institute on Alcohol Abuse and Alcoholism, 1999; Marelich et al., 2000). Fetal alcohol syndrome is linked to congenital heart defects, mental retardation, and low birth weight of infants. Alcohol is a critical factor in rape and spouse abuse, with homicide an all too frequent outcome (Jung, 2001).

Men are more likely to turn to alcohol to cope with stressful situations; women are more likely to turn to prescribed drugs. Prevalence rates for over-the-counter and prescribed drugs are double for women. Compared to men, women are almost twice as likely to receive a drug for a psychological problem, particularly narcotics and antianxiety drugs, and are twice as likely to abuse or become addicted to them (National Institute on Drug Abuse, 2002).

If women increasingly adopt the risky health behaviors of men, such as cigarette smoking and excessive alcohol consumption, gender differences in morbidity may decrease. For example, although adult men in all age groups continue to smoke and consume alcohol at significantly higher rates, gender differences are rapidly decreasing among adolescents (SAMHSA, 2002; National Center for Health Statistics, 2004). If these trends continue, mortality rates for men and women due to lung cancer, heart disease, and cirrhosis of the liver may reach parity. To date, however, even with the movement of women into such health risky behaviors, mortality rates for these causes have remained virtually unchanged (Wasserman et al., 2000; Bolego et al., 2002; Maiese, 2002).

Explaining Gendered Health Trends

Reasons for sex differences in mortality and morbidity are both biological and sociocultural. As noted earlier, females possess an additional X chromosome and protective sex hormones that are associated with a superior immune system. Because women bear and nurse children, biology offers the equipment allowing them to survive in the worst conditions, whether in childbirth or in cold, famine, or other conditions of deprivation (Brody, 1996). Women may have higher morbidity rates, but they are likely to recover from the same sicknesses that kill or disable men.

Added to this biological advantage is a gender role benefit. There are significant gender differences favoring women in their overall knowledge related to both physical and mental health, specifically related to information on sexuality and reproduction (Beier and Ackerman, 2003). Females are taught as young girls to be sensitive to their bodies, to be aware of changes in bodily states and physical processes, and to openly express their concerns to friends and their health care providers. For cancer therapies, women are also more likely to take advantage of the new directions for preventive health and self care and be diagnosed in earlier, more treatable stages. This translates to lowered mortality rates for breast and ovarian cancer. Role flexibility allows women to be less constrained in seeking help for illness and psychological distress. They maintain a larger social support network and have higher degrees of connectedness than men, allowing them to call on others for help or support in stressful times (Bullers, 2000; Allgower et al., 2001; Elliott, 2001). Men have higher degrees of separation and are less likely to seek out others for emotional reasons. In the United States and other parts of the developed world, widowers are more vulnerable to depression and suicide in part because their wives maintained the social networks that buffer psychological distress (Good et al., 2000; Antonucci et al., 2002). When men are socialized into the belief that seeking help is a sign of weakness, they may not get needed treatment for life-threatening diseases in time. At the same time, however, these very patterns contribute to higher treatment rates and bolster the claim that women are sicker, weaker, and less emotionally strong than men.

THE WOMEN'S HEALTH MOVEMENT

The women's health movement emerged as a challenge to mainstream modern medicine, which is dominated by androcentric attitudes and practices not in the best interest of much of the population it is supposed to serve (Norsigian, 1996).

The movement asserts that women must be empowered to take an active role in all phases of their health and health care. Blatantly sexist attitudes regarding the sexual inferiority of women still run rampant in this system. For example, in both the pre-Kinsey and post–Masters and Johnson eras, medical textbooks for gynecologists continue to highlight Freud's anatomy as destiny model (Scully and Bart, 2003).

Challenging Gender Bias in Research

The potential harm of an androcentric medical system to the health and well-being of women is demonstrated in many ways. Women had been virtually absent as participants in clinical trials involving drugs, medical technology, and health care options on which much of contemporary health care is based (Keville, 1993). Androcentric medicine insists that biological differences between men and women have major, inescapable health consequences, but then routinely conducts research using only male subjects. Male is the medical norm. A large, now infamous, federally funded study examining the effects of diet on breast cancer used only men as sample subjects (Tavris, 1996). Men *are* diagnosed with about 1 percent of all breast cancers, but this study added to the growing evidence that medical research is often flawed by gender bias. Research on heart disease is another notable example where the exclusion of women in clinical trials is ominous. The key study on the effect of low doses of aspirin and the risk of heart attack used over 35,000 subjects, all of them men. The reduced heart attack risk was so spectacular that the public was made aware of results even before findings were published (Steering Committee of the Physician's Health Study, 1989). Results could not be generalized to women in part because the role of estrogen needed to be considered. If this study added to knowledge about estrogen and heart disease, HRT may have been curtailed much earlier. In addition, excluding women ignored the fact that heart disease is the number one killer for both men and women. Women receive less aggressive cardiac care, are more likely to die in the hospital, and have greater risk of death from a second heart attack in the year following the first heart attack than men (St. Louis University, 1999; Radford et al, 2001; Rainer et al, 2002).

Midwives and Medicine

The loss of a couple's choice to use a midwife to help in delivering a child is another example of the adverse affects of androcentric medicine. The norm in preindustrial America was that infants would be delivered with the support of midwives who also served as role models and emotional supports and helped socialize women into the status of motherhood. By the early twentieth century, midwifery was in effect eliminated in the United States. Like menstruation and menopause, childbirth also succumbed to the process of medicalization. With medicalization gradually taking hold, the new medical establishment characterized midwives as "ignorant, meddlesome, and unscientific." Women were seen as unsuited for independent medical roles, even with evidence showing that midwives attended deliveries that were safe for both mother and child (Wertz and Wertz, 1990). Obstetrics practiced by men replaced midwifery practiced by women. Medicalization took root as the

American Medical Association gained control over all medical licensing. Until then, physicians and midwives were in direct competition for patients and fees (Rothman and Caschetta, 1995; Ratcliff, 2002).

Encouraged by the women's health movement, nurse–midwives are growing in numbers. What a midwife can and cannot do depends on the type of license and local restrictions largely controlled by physicians. An alliance is being forged by obstetricians, who deliver higher-risk babies and do more costly cesarean sections, and nurse–midwives, who are attracting those who desire a more natural birthing experience. Conflict theory suggests that midwives lost their right to practice because they encroached on the emerging medical profession (Seymour, 2000). The comeback of midwifery, tentative as it is, also can be explained by conflict theory. Midwives offer an alternative ideology—translated as an alternative view of procreation—that is gaining its own power.

Progress in Women's Health

In addressing these and other health related issues, many nongovernmental organizations (NGOs) have emerged to publicize and influence health policy. More women are entering the health care field as physicians, especially as gynecologists, hospital administrators, clinical psychologists, and other mental health therapists. Nurses are assuming more responsibility in decision making processes. The concept of a health care team tied to beliefs about preventive health care and holistic health has helped in this regard. Clinical trials with female subjects representing a diversity of racial and ethnic groups are rapidly increasing in number and will soon be normative in health research. The interplay of race and class in particular must also be accounted for to make findings applicable to a diverse population of women.

The empowerment of women as both patients and health care practitioners is also beneficial to men. Encouraged by successes of the health movement for women, a men's health movement has been spawned. This movement is helping to rewrite curricula in training health care practitioners and encourages men to understand how a masculine gender role is also hazardous to their health—from not seeking help when they are aware of symptoms to excessive engagement in sports and occupationally based behaviors that increase their risk for further illness and injury (Doyal, 2000; Forrester, 2000; Luck et al., 2000). There are encouraging signs that men are seeking preventive services. Mortality rates for prostate cancer, for example, have been positively influenced through early detection. The men's health movement may be responsible for small but noticeable reductions on this and some other male mortality related measures.

NATURE VERSUS NURTURE REVISITED: THE POLITICS OF BIOLOGY

Biologically, women are definitely not the weaker sex. Drawing from data on human sexuality, developmental biology, animal behavior, and ethnography, anthropologist Ashley Montagu (1999) makes the case that women are more valuable than men because they maintain the species during a child's crucial development stages. From a sociobiological standpoint, Montagu used the idea of adaptive strategies, asserting that women are superior, too, because they are more necessary than men. He literally turned around interpretations of women as passive beings who are sexually and biologically inferior.

Assertions about survival of the fittest favor women. Sociobiologists today need to account for the newest data showing that human evolution probably benefited more from cooperation and the agricultural and gathering activities favoring women, than competition and the hunting activities favoring men. DNA evidence now suggests that a "make love not war" scenario was probably the most productive, adaptive strategy of the earliest waves of human migration out of Africa (Fitzpatrick, 2002). And the primate studies sociobiologists are so fond of indicate that the dominant belief that animals compete with one another to gain resources and increase reproduction is a narrow and unsophisticated view of evolutionary theory (Cussins, 2000; Strum and Fedigan, 2000). Even the long held belief about baboons, the "most extreme male-dominated chest-thumping society in the primate world," is being questioned. The highly affiliated baboons, who went unstudied for decades, now show males spending time with females as lovers not fighters. As primatologist Robert Sapolsky states, "Female choice is built around male–female affiliation rather than the outcome of male-male aggression" (David, 2003:48). When viewed through the lens of gender, new interpretations of the biology-animal-human link emerge (Keller, 2000).

Let us return to our original question of nature versus nurture, of heredity versus environment, of biology versus society. All the evidence points to the impact of both in explaining sex differences. Deterministic theories that either dismiss or fail to account for biology and society are doomed as useful explanatory models in science. The problem, according to Sandra Bem (1996:11), is that there is too much of a focus on biological difference and not enough on the "institutionalized androcentrism" that transforms male–female differences into female disadvantage. Media take hold of the sex difference theme, and soon people believe that men have math and promiscuity genes and women have caring and victimization genes that predestine their gender roles. Genes are claiming more and more of social and individual life when scientific theories are used to serve prevailing ideologies regarding gender (Kaplan, 2003). Biological arguments are consistently drawn on to justify gender inequality and the continued oppression of women. Although evidence suggests that the female sex is the stronger sex biologically, we have seen that differences between the sexes (genders), both perceived and real, have been used to subordinate women. Natural superiority, if it does exist, should not be used to condone social inequality, whether it occurs for women or men.

As documented here, biologically based arguments may be ideologically embraced but not empirically sound. To understand data on health and sexuality, interdisciplinary work is encouraged and requires both sociocultural and biological knowledge (Marks, 2000). This book proceeds with the understanding that there are biologically conditioning elements differentiating the sexes. Chapter 3 shows that socialization has a massive, profound influence on the differences that do exist. As a sociologist I favor explanations for gender development and gender roles rooted in nurture and sociocultural factors. These sociological explanations account for a range of variables and imply that women and men have the potential to achieve in any direction they desire.

Summary

1. Arguments against gender equality are based on biology. Evolutionary approaches from animals and insects favored by sociobiology are often the bases. Massive evidence, including the work by Margaret Mead, refutes these arguments.

2. Sex hormones shape the development of the brain and sex organs and determine how these organs will be activated. Hormones play important roles in behavior but do not cause male aggression. The belief that there is a hormonally based motherhood instinct is not supported.

3. Sigmund Freud's theory of psychosexual development asserts that because boys have a penis and girls do not, females ultimately wish they were boys. Penis envy in females is resolved by the wish for motherhood. Freud was a sexist in his belief that anatomy was destiny. Psychoanalytic feminism rejects Freud's sexism but uses his theory to explain women's subordination not as part of human nature but of human relationships.

4. Infants born with ambiguous sex traits, referred to as hermaphrodites or intersexed, may undergo sex reassignment surgery. The infamous case of the sex reassignment of a male twin due to a circumcision accident illustrates that success with surgery largely depends on the age, the culture in which it occurs, and if the person freely chose it as an option.

5. Global research on sexual orientation and transgender indicates that they are extremely varied. Cultural beliefs about sex and gender determine how they are translated into patterns of behavior.

6. Sociologists emphasize the importance of sexual scripts in prescribing roles related to sexuality. This scripting clearly illustrates that biology alone cannot explain human sexuality and that sexuality is much less spontaneous than we think.

7. The double standard in sexual behavior and attitudes is declining, but gendered patterns still exist: Males have earlier, more frequent intercourse both before and after marriage, emphasize sexual pleasure as a motive for intercourse, and have more nonmarital and extramarital relationships than females. Traditional beliefs about gender roles inhibit sexual pleasure for both women and men.

8. Both in the United States and globally, females have higher morbidity (sickness) rates but live longer than men; men have lower morbidity rates but do not live as long as women.

9. Gender differences in disease and disability are clearly related to gender roles, especially in terms of occupations, drug use, eating disorders, and HIV/AIDS. Gender beliefs and not medical evidence related to premenstrual syndrome and hormone replacement therapy serve to harm women's physical and emotional health. Gender beliefs harms men when they do not seek help for physical or psychological problems.

10. The women's health movement has challenged androcentric medicine by calling attention to the lack of females in health-related clinical trials, by empowering women as patients, and encouraging them to become practitioners, practices that benefit men as well.

11. Both biology and culture (nature and nurture) are ingredients in explaining sex differences. Media attention to biological differences disregards how androcentrism and ideology transform these differences into female disadvantage. Women are biologically the stronger sex, but biology is used to justify gender inequality and oppression of women.

Key Terms

double standard 34	intersexed 27	sexual scripts 32
essentialism 20	morbidity rate 36	sociobiology 22
gender identity 28	mortality rate 36	transgender 31
hermaphrodite 27	sexual dimorphism 28	transsexual 28

Critical Thinking Questions

1. Based on your understanding of the research on the biological and cultural ingredients of gender, provide an empirical rationale countering the claim that gender roles are destined to be unequal.

2. Why is Freud's theory of psychosexual model considered sexist and used in reinforcing gender stereotypes? How has psychoanalytic feminism reconciled these issues to the benefit rather than the detriment of women?

3. Using research examples, demonstrate how patterns of mortality and morbidity are highly gendered and the consequences of this fact. How can a combination of conflict theory and symbolic interaction explain these patterns?

CHAPTER **3**

GENDER DEVELOPMENT:

The Socialization Process

Gender Socialization and Cultural Diversity

Culture and Socialization
Gender Socialization: The Impact of Social Class and Race

Theories of Gender Socialization

Social Learning Theory
Cognitive Development Theory
Gender Schema Theory

Agents of Socialization

The Family
Peers and Preferences
School
Television
Global Focus: Son Preference in Asia

Androgyny in Socialization

Girls play at being pretty, but boys play cars.

Boys don't clean house and girls don't get dirty.

Boys stay outside as long as they want, but girls can't.

Boys don't play hopscotch. Girls don't play rough or get sweaty.

Girls are cute and harmless and don't get as muddy as boys.

—Comments from seven- and eight-year-olds when asked "How are boys and girls different?" (cited in Freedman, 2001:142)

These comments demonstrate that as early as second grade, children have strong ideas about what boys and girls are supposed to do and be. They embrace and even celebrate smaller gender differences, in turn obscuring larger gender similarities. From the moment a girl infant is wrapped in a pink blanket and a boy infant in a blue one, gender role development begins. The colors of pink and blue are among the first indicators used by American society to distinguish female from male. As these infants grow, other cultural artifacts will ensure that this distinction remains intact. Girls will be given dolls to diaper and tiny stoves on which to cook pretend meals. Boys will construct buildings with miniature tools and wage war with toy guns and tanks. In the teen and young adult years, although both may spend their money on videos and CDs, girls buy cosmetics and clothes, and boys buy sports equipment and technical gadgets. The incredible power of gender socialization is largely responsible for such behavior. Pink and blue begin this life-long process.

GENDER SOCIALIZATION AND CULTURAL DIVERSITY

Socialization is the lifelong process by which, though social interaction, we learn our culture, develop our sense of self, and become functioning members of society. This simple definition does not do justice to the profound impact of socialization. Each generation transmits essential cultural elements to the next generation through socialization. Socialization is lifelong, with various requirements at certain age levels. **Primary socialization**, the focus of the research and theory overviewed in this chapter, begins in the family and allows the child to acquire necessary skills to fit into society, especially language learning and acceptable behavior to function effectively in a variety of social situations. **Continuing socialization** provides the basis for the varied roles an individual will fill throughout life.

Not only does socialization shape our personalities and allow us to develop our human potential, but the process also molds our beliefs and behaviors about all social groups and the individuals making up those groups. **Gender socialization** is the process by which individuals learn the cultural behavior of femininity or masculinity that is associated with the biological sex of female or male. The forces of social change have collided with gender socialization on a massive scale. To explain gender socialization in contemporary society, it is necessary to understand cultural diversity in all its forms.

Culture and Socialization

As a society's total way of life, **culture** endows us with social heritage and provides guidelines for appropriate behavior. Cultures are organized through **social institutions** that ensure the basic needs of society are met in established, predictable ways. Although it is the social institution of the family that sets the standards for the emergence of gender roles in children, the family itself is shaped by overall cultural values regarding gender. Parent–child interactions occur in a cultural context in which females have lower power and prestige than males. Beginning in infancy, parents socialize sons to express emotions differently than daughters in ways that support gender differences in power. Culturally mandated gender roles are thus reinforced (Brody, 2000). Institutions overlap in their socialization functions so that one will support and carry on the work of another. For example, the institution of the family is fundamentally responsible for a child's primary socialization, but the work continues with the institution of education when the child enters preschool or kindergarten. Other institutions include the economy, religion, government, and an evolving leisure and recreational institution with a media focus. Like cultures throughout the world, the social institutions in American culture are differentiated according to expectations and norms that form the basis of gender roles. These roles show up in the jobs men and women perform, leisure activities, dress, possessions, language, demeanor, reading material, college major, and even degree of sexual experience and pleasure. The list is virtually endless.

Cultures also provide for measures of **social control** to ensure that people more or less conform to a vast array of social norms, including those related to gender. Social control mechanisms that guarantee gender role compliance are often informal but very powerful, such as ridicule, exclusion from peers, and loss of support from family or colleagues. Both boys and girls ridicule boys who play with toys designed for girls or girls who engage in aggressive, rough-and-tumble play (Karniol and Aida, 1997). Adults who challenge workplace norms in which gender role scripts are changing—such as when men choose occupations as child care workers and women choose occupations as plumbers—also remain vulnerable until new norms are in place.

When socialization processes encourage the perpetuation of stereotyped portrayals of the genders, social control is particularly effective. Stereotypical thinking becomes insidious when individuals are damaged because they are defined in terms of assumed, negative characteristics assigned to their group. If we stereotype women as passive, an individual woman may be passed over for a job in which leadership qualities are required. Her own individual ability in terms of job leadership is not even considered due to the stereotype assigned to her entire gender. A man may be denied custody of his child on the basis of stereotypes that view men as inherently less capable of raising children than women. This example also suggests that stereotypical thinking about gender is so pervasive that the law is impacted.

It might appear that the power of socialization creates little robots molded by our culture who uncritically submit to mandated gender roles. However, to argue that the automatons of one generation produce their own carbon copies in the next ignores two important facts. First, socialization is an uneven process taking place on many fronts. We are socialized by parents, siblings, peers, teachers, media, and all other social institutions. We know of achievement-oriented women who are admired for their leadership abilities and men who are esteemed because of their effectiveness in caring for young children.

Second, we live in diverse, heterogeneous societies made up of numerous **subcultures** that share characteristics in common with the culture in which they exist, but are also distinguished from the broader culture in important ways, such as in gender patterns. In addition to gender, subcultures are differentiated according to many factors, including race, ethnicity, social class, age, or common interest. Age-based subcultures are especially important because they emerge at points in the life course that are strongly defined according to gender role norms. For example, age peers in elementary school determine criteria for prestige, which in turn impacts self-esteem, achievement motivation, and academic success. A boy defined as effeminate or a girl defined as a bully has much to lose in this regard. At the other end of the age spectrum, the elderly, too, are not immune to such rankings. Age and gender stereotypes combine against divorced or widowed elderly who would like to begin dating. They risk social disapproval through cultural stereotypes that devalue or view sexual activity for the elderly suspiciously. Elderly widows may be regarded as asexual and elderly widowers as dirty old men.

Gender Socialization: The Impact of Social Class and Race

Gender combines with social class and race as key determinants in how gender roles are enacted. There is a strong correlation between social class and parental values that impact gender. Overall, middle-class parents emphasize autonomy and working-class parents emphasize conformity in socialization. These values translate to more gender role flexibility in middle class families than in working class and low income families. Boys and girls from middle class homes are offered less stereotypical gender role choices in behavioral expectations and career development and hold more egalitarian attitudes (Tuck et al., 1994; Bumpus et al., 2001). Gender role flexibility and autonomy training for both daughters and sons are enhanced in middle class families with career oriented mothers. In such families, however, women express higher levels of support for such flexibility and autonomy than do men (Burris, 1991; Xiao, 2000). Research is less clear on what specific variable accounts for this pattern. Boys from middle class homes are more achievement oriented than girls. White middle class women are described by college students in more stereotypical ways than they describe African-American women. And families of all races who move upward in social mobility are more likely to embrace traditional gender roles. Although beliefs about gender equality appear to be embraced by African-American parents, those beliefs are mitigated by social class and mobility (Hill, 2002). It may be that the factors of race, mother's employment, and social mobility are more important than social class in determining gender attitudes. Because social class itself is multidimensional and determined by these very factors, it is difficult to sort out the direction of causation.

The specific variable of race further complicates the gender role socialization portrait. Overall, available research suggests that *in general* children from Asian-American and Latino homes are more likely to be socialized into less flexible, traditional beliefs about gender than African-American and white children. For Asian-American children, gender roles emphasize female subordination to all males and older females in a patriarchal family structure. Within three generations of immigration, however, unquestioned female subordination weakens considerably. This is especially true among Chinese, Korean, and Japanese families and is linked to upward mobility of the family and a college education for their children. As Asian-American children become more Americanized, both boys and girls begin to exhibit less traditional gender roles (Louie and Louie, 1998; Farley and Alba, 2002).

Data from Latino subcultures (Puerto Rican, Cuban-American, and Mexican-American), report that females act out gender roles that are more deferential and subordinate than are found in other racial and ethnic groups. Girls are socialized to value motherhood above all other roles (Garcia, 1991). This role is reinforced by powerful religious socialization within Latino subcultures that fosters women's subservience to men (Anzaldua, 1995). Latino children also receive socialization messages promoting *familism*, a strong value emphasizing the family and its collective needs over personal and individual needs. Familism buffers the development of hypermasculinity (*machismo*) in boys and serves as a source of prestige for girls, who take on the caring and nurturing functions associated with familism early in life (DeLeon, 1993). The impact of socialization into familism is supported by data showing that on weekends, Latino fathers are more involved with their children than either African-American or white fathers (Yeung et al., 2001).

Compared to data from other racial and ethnic groups, gender socialization information on African-American families is more extensive as well as more contradictory. On one hand, research shows that compared to children of other races, African-American children are socialized into views of gender that are less rigid and less stereotyped. African-American girls with nontraditional gender role training have high achievement motivation. Research also reports that, compared to white males, African-American males—both older children and adults—participate in housework and child care at more equitable levels (Hossain and Roopnarine, 1993; John et al., 1995). Androgyny may be evident for both African men and women.

On the other hand, evidence also suggests that African-American women encourage independence and self-reliance in their daughters but at the same time encourage them to accept other parts of a female role that are highly traditional. Compared to white parents, African-American parents express greater concern that their girls be feminine and their boys be masculine (Dugger, 1991). African-American views about gender are also mediated by setting, proportion of other races in the setting, and the setting's social class context. Young African-American girls attending a middle-income school with more whites are less assertive than if they attend a lower-income school that is predominately African American (Scott, 2000). African-American boys and girls attending an interracial or predominantly black summer camp construct gender more rigidly in the all-black setting (Moore, 2000). African-American college students attending a historically black university report that they view typical African-American men and women as androgynous but that they do not overwhelmingly view themselves as androgynous (Dade and Sloan, 2000). It is difficult to determine the extent of traditional gender role socialization in African-American children compared to children from other races.

In order to sort out findings that appear to be contradictory for African Americans, a host of variables need to be accounted for. The socialization work of African-American parents is strongly influenced by social inequalities in American society that work against beliefs about gender equity (Hill, 2002). African-American children who are already facing a difficult road because of racial discrimination may find it easier to adopt rather than challenge traditional gender roles if it means one less barrier must be overcome. Historical patterns of gender role configurations in African American subcultures also help understand the contradictions. High regard for the independence and initiative of African-American women is normative in these subcultures. In this sense, the "traditional" gender role of women is one of strength rather than weakness (chapter 8). Likewise, African-American children are socialized with a view of gender that is less polarized compared to views of white children (McAdoo 1990; Dugger, 1991). Males and females are not "opposite" human beings who have completely different expectations. Regardless of whether it is seen as androgyny or not, both men and women are encouraged to be nurturing and assertive. Research clearly suggests that masculinity and femininity are simply not theoretically useful if they continue to be polarized. The research is inconsistent only when race, class, and gender are conceptually separated and when white, middle-class standards of masculinity and femininity are applied to the African-American experience.

The concepts and research applications reviewed are important for understanding the three major theories of gender socialization: social learning, cognitive development, and gender schema theories.

THEORIES OF GENDER SOCIALIZATION

All theories of gender socialization focus on primary socialization and how children learn **gender identity**, when they become aware that the two sexes (male and female) behave differently and that different gender roles (masculine and feminine) are proper. Like socialization overall, gender socialization is mediated through a number of important elements, such as biology, personality, social interaction context, and the social institutions. Different theories give different weight to each element. As we saw in chapter 2, Freudian psychologists and sociobiologists contend that unconscious motivation and biologically driven evolutionary demands are powerful socialization forces. Sociologists, social psychologists, and many personality psychologists emphasize social interaction taking precedence over biology as the key socialization force. This focus on the context of social interaction has allowed significant interdisciplinary work between psychology and sociology in building theories of gender socialization.

Social Learning Theory

Unlike Freud's psychoanalytic approach which focuses on internal conflict in socialization, social learning theory focuses on observable behavior. For social learning theorists, socialization is based on rewards (reinforcing appropriate behavior) and punishments (extinguishing inappropriate behavior). They are concerned with the ways children model the behaviors they view in others, such as cooperation and sharing or selfishness and aggression. Imitation and modeling appear to be spontaneous in children, but through reinforcement, patterns of behavior develop that eventually become habitual.

As with other behaviors, gender roles are learned directly, through reprimands and rewards, and indirectly, through observation and imitation (Bandura and Walters, 1963; Mischel, 1966). The logic is simple. In gender socialization, different expectations lead to differential reinforcement from parents, peers, and teachers for doing either "boy" or "girl" things. Boys may be praised by peers for excelling in male sports such as football but derided for excelling in female games such as jump rope. Girls may be praised by peers for embroidering table linen but derided for preferring to play with toy soldiers rather than baby dolls. Gender identity is developed when children associate the label of boy or girl with the rewards that come with the appropriate behavior and then act out gender roles according to that perception. As parents and teachers model gender roles during the critical primary socialization years, children imitate accordingly. Continued reinforcement of the valued gender identity results. Social learning theory thus assumes that "knowledge about gender roles either precedes or is acquired at the same time as gender identity" (Intons-Peterson, 1988:40).

Gender Socialization for Boys. According to social learning theory, boys and girls are not parallel in the acquisition of gender role knowledge during the primary socialization years. Early research on gender socialization was conducted by David Lynn (1959, 1969) to account for his belief that boys encounter more difficulty on the socialization path than girls. Lynn asserted that because fathers are not as available as mothers during early childhood, boys have limited opportunities to model the same-gender parent. And when the father is home, the contact is qualitatively different from contact with the mother in terms of intimacy. Since male role models are generally scarce in early childhood, boys struggle to put together a definition of masculinity based on incomplete information. They are often told what they should not do rather than what they should do. "Don't be a sissy," and the classic, "Big boys don't cry," are examples. Girls have an easier time because of continuous contact with the mother and the relative ease of using her as a model.

Lynn further contended that it is the lack of exposure to males at an early age that leads boys to view masculinity in a stereotyped manner. For males, masculine gender roles are more inflexible than those offered to females. It is this gender role inflexibility that is a critical factor in making male socialization difficult and may explain why males express more insecurity about their gender identity. The consequences of this narrow view of masculinity are many. Male peer groups encourage the belief that aggression and toughness are virtues. Males exhibit hostility toward both females and homosexuals, and cross-gender behavior in boys ("sissies") is viewed more negatively than when it occurs in girls ("tomboys"). Women are more accepting of children who cross gender lines in their behavior (chapter 8). Men's fear of ridicule propels them to exaggerated antihomosexual and sexist remarks to ensure that others do not get "the wrong idea" concerning their masculinity (Kimmel, 1994). Although research does not confirm that modeling *per se* is responsible for gender role acquisition, it does indicate that gender-appropriate behavior is strongly associated with social approval. Although laden with uncertainty and inflexibility, boys express adamant preference for the masculine role. A boy learns that his role is the more desirable one and brings with it more self-esteem.

Gender Socialization for Girls. Other social learning theorists state that it is a mistake to conclude that the socialization path for girls is easy simply because mothers are more available to girls as models during early childhood. Even young children are bombarded by messages suggesting that higher worth, prestige, advantages, and rewards are accorded to males compared to females. Boys can readily embrace the gender roles flowing from these messages. Girls, in contrast, are offered subordinate roles that encourage deference and dependence and must model behavior that may be less socially valued. Gender expectations lead to a preference for characteristic masculine behavior (Geis, 1993). If modeling and reinforcement are compelling enticements to behavior, as social learning theory suggests, a girl would understandably become quite anxious about being encouraged to perform roles held in lower esteem. For socialization overall, girls have the advantage in gender role flexibility, but boys have the advantage of a higher prestige gender role.

Social learning theory provides the foundation for a great deal of research on socialization, especially when it is combined with a symbolic interaction perspective. In emphasizing the importance symbolic interactionists attach to role taking, this approach suggests that when children take on a variety of roles, including those related to gender, opportunities are available for behavior to be rewarded, punished, and imitated. Roles are also carefully defined to determine the relative influence of some people compared to others. Data on adolescents planning for the future, for example, show that they model parents and peers but also judge the level of influence of both in determining their plans. This research shows that they use both processes, but the judgment of the level of influence (symbolic interaction theory) is more important than the modeling (social learning theory) (Starrels and Holm, 2000). Congruent with gender socialization, same-gender parents and peers would be defined as more influential than other-gender parents and peers.

Critique. Children are not the passive recipients of rewards and punishments that social learning theorists envision. Because children routinely choose gender inconsistent behavior, the reinforcement and modeling processes are far more complex than they propose. First, children may not model same-gender parents, teachers, or peers or may choose other-gender models outside the family who offer alternatives to gender role behavior that enhance self-esteem. A girl may be rewarded for a masculine activity, such as excelling in sports, but she keeps a tight hold on other aspects of her feminine role. Second, social learning theory minimizes the importance of social change, a significant factor in gender socialization. Families are much more diverse than the stereotyped "at-home mother and outside-home father" that may be used to explain the rocky socialization paths for girls and boys. Divorce, blended families, single parenting, and an increasing number of non-resident parents who are mothers instead of fathers have created a wide range of models for gender socialization (chapter 8). Third, other statuses also vie for the attention of both child and parent during primary socialization. Age of child may be as important as gender in determining how parents behave toward their children. Finally, children experience subcultural family influences in which siblings and adults take on a range of nontraditional roles, such in single-parent families. And regardless of the different paths offered to them, both girls and boys learn to prefer their own gender and strongly endorse the roles associated with it.

Cognitive Development Theory

Cognitive development theoretical explanations for gender socialization contrast sharply with social learning theory. Jean Piaget's (1896–1980) interest in how children gradually develop intelligence, thinking, and reasoning laid the foundation for cognitive development theory. His work is consistent with symbolic interaction theory regarding his ideas that cognitive abilities are developed in stages through ongoing social interaction. Simply stated, the mind matures through interaction with the environment. Behavior depends on how a person perceives a social situation at each cognitive stage (Piaget 1950, 1954). Cognitive theory stresses a child's active role in structuring and interpreting the world.

Building on Piaget's work, Lawrence Kohlberg (1966) claimed that children learn their gender roles according to their level of cognitive development, in essence their degree of comprehension of the world. One of the first ways a child comprehends the world is by organizing reality through her or his **self**, the unique sense of identity that distinguishes each individual from all other individuals, and a highly valued part of the child's existence. Anything associated with the self becomes highly valued as well. By age three, children begin to self-identify by gender and accurately apply gender-related labels to themselves and often to others. By age six *gender constancy* is in place. A girl knows she is a girl and will remain one. Only then, Kohlberg asserts, is gender identity said to be developed. Gender identity becomes a central part of self, invested with strong emotional attachment (Martin, 2000; Martin et al., 2002). Studies on gender concepts of children ages three to five offer support for the cognitive development approach to gaining a gender identity and then using that identity to organize and label gender-related behavior. These labels form the basis for gender stereotypes and gender associated expectations (Martin and Little, 1990:1438). Thus cognitive development theory offers a good explanation for the development of gender-typing during primary socialization: When children finally figure out what gender means in their lives, they embrace that understanding in ways that create and then reinforce gender stereotypes.

Once gender identity is developed, much behavior is organized around it. Children seek models that are labeled as girl or boy and female or male and identification with the same-sex parent may occur. Although children base much of their behavior on reinforcement, cognitive theorists see a different sequence in gender socialization than do social learning theorists. This sequence is: "I am a boy, therefore I want to do boy things, therefore the opportunity to do boy things (and to gain approval for doing them) is rewarding" (Kohlberg, 1966:89). Reinforcements are important, but the child chooses behavior and roles according to the sense of self. Individual differences in gender roles are accounted for by the different experiences of children. Children may subsequently perceive these experiences based on reinforcement, so there is some consistency with social learning theory. A "social cognitive theory of gender self-regulation" integrates ideas from social learning and cognitive development theories. Gender constancy motivates children to seek out social interactions where they can learn gender appropriate behavior (Bussey and Bandura, 1992).

There is wide support for the cognitive development approach to gender role socialization. Research consistently finds that children's choices, interests, and activities—such as play, toys, and friendships—are organized according to their beliefs about gender compatibility (Caygill et al., 2002; Martin and Dinella, 2002; Monsour, 2002). Children begin to value their own gender more than the other and believe theirs is superior to the other. As children get older, they increasingly agree with adult gender role stereotypes (Egan and Perry, 2001; Liben et al., 2001). This research suggests that early in life children develop the ability to classify characteristics by gender and choose behavior according to that classification.

Critique. Like social learning, cognitive development theory cannot account for all of gender role socialization. The cognitive development model has also been criticized because it is difficult to test what comes first, gender identity or the child's understanding of gender constancy (Intons-Peterson, 1988:44). For the model to fit neatly with the stages outlined in cognitive development, gender identity must come first. To date research has been unable to confirm this sequence. In countering this criticism, cognitive theorists suggest that all that is needed for gender identity is simple, rudimentary knowledge about gender. Gender stability, where the child views the same gender role behavior over and over in a variety of contexts, will suffice even if the child does not fully comprehend gender constancy. Simple knowledge about gender stability allows children to begin to accurately label who is a girl and who is a boy. Critics still argue, however, that the acquisition of knowledge about gender stability is not as simple as cognitive development theorists describe. For children to determine patterns of gender stability, they must experience social interaction in a relatively large number of contexts. It is unlikely that this interaction will be either uniform or consistent in terms of gender. Understanding the supposedly simple idea of gender stability may be as complicated for children as understanding gender constancy.

Gender Schema Theory

Gender schema theory is a promising and important subset of cognitive development theory. **Schema** are cognitive structures used to understand the world, interpret perception, and process new information. Sandra Bem, one of the most important gender schema theorists, contends that once the child learns cultural definitions of gender, these schemas become the core around which all other information is organized (Bem, 1981, 1983). Consistent with cognitive development theory, before a schema is created to process gender-related information, children must be at the cognitive level to accurately identify gender. Schemas tell children what they can and cannot do according to their gender. Schemas affect their behavior and influence their self-esteem. A child's sense of self is linked to how closely his or her behavior matches accepted gender schemas. When a girl learns that prescriptions for femininity in her culture include being polite and being kind, these behaviors are incorporated into her emerging gender schema, and she adjusts her behavior accordingly.

As children develop gender schemas, they are increasingly used to organize their thinking. Gender schema theorists suggest that gender identity is created first, followed by in-group ("own-gender") schemas, which are more complex and detailed than out-group ("other-gender") schemas, which are developed later. In-group schemas are used by children to process new information, plan activities, and choose roles (Martin and Halverson, 1981, 1983). This helps to explain why a person's world becomes so differentiated by gender over the life course. In cultures that rigidly adhere to beliefs about gender differences, gender schemas are likely to be even more complex and elaborate for everyone. The influence of gender schemas may help explain why it is so difficult to dislodge gender stereotypical thinking once it is place during childhood.

Support for the influence of gender schemas comes from research indicating that these schemas appear to have an impact on the memory of young children (Martin and Halverson, 1983). Studies of gender-related childhood memories in adults that use a gender schema model find that men's memories are more active and women's more emotional. These may reflect actual differences between the genders in childhood experiences or may result from a process of memory selection that reflects different gender-related experiences as adults. For example, think about any recent class discussion when someone tries later to remember who made a certain comment. Ample research evidence suggests that if we misremember, it is more likely to be a within-gender mistake rather than a between-gender mistake (Cross and Markus, 1993:61). It is also easier to remember activities and people when they are gender stereotyped than when they are not. Our memories are better for information consistent with gender schemas (Burn, 1996).

Gender schemas of parents impact how they behave toward their children and, in turn, how this influences their development. Significant, positive correlations between parent and child gender schemas are consistently reported. Parents with traditional gender schemas are more likely to have children with gender-typed cognitions than parents with nontraditional schemas (Tenenbaum and Leaper, 2002). As early as age 18 months children can associate cultural symbols with gender— pictures of fire hats and hammers are associated with males and pictures of dolls and teddy bears with females (Eichstedt et al., 2002). By second grade children associate symbols of nature (less controllable, less predictable, and less rational, but more balanced, more whole, and more nurturant) with the concept of female and symbols of culture (the opposite characteristics) with the concept of male (Mullen, 1990:585). As adults, gender-based schematic processing directs people to use language according to gender role orientation (Crowley, 2001). These studies support Sandra Bem's contention that the way parents behave toward children and the way symbols are classified are directed by a gender schematic network of American cultural associations that we learn to accept.

The cultural impact on gender acquisition can be refined further using a gender schema model. Every culture contains assumptions about behavior that are contained throughout its social institutions and within the personalities of individuals. Sandra Bem (1993) refers to these as "cultural lenses." Sociologists would say these lenses consist of a society's values, beliefs, and norms. She suggests that in American culture, three gender lenses are most prominent: gender polarization (shared beliefs that females and males are different and opposite beings), biological essentialism (biology produces natural, inevitable gender roles), and androcentrism (males are superior to females). Despite massive research evidence against gender polarization and biological essentialism, the beliefs persist, and in turn are used to justify androcentrism. These beliefs become another set of gender schemas in which to organize behavior. Children accept them without recognizing that alternatives are possible. As adults they cannot envision their society (or any other for that matter) organized according to a different set of gender schemas.

The notion of cultural lenses provides a good interdisciplinary link to macrolevel sociology. Functionalists would be interested in identifying core cultural and subcultural gender lenses that influence social order and social change. Monitoring these gender cultural lenses over time can offer insight into the functional and dysfunctional consequences of gender roles for society as a whole.

Gender schema theory may be the best alternative in not only explaining how people develop gender identities but also how gender stereotypes can be modified. In certain contexts of social interaction when people are made aware of the influence of gender on their thought processes, gender schematic thinking may be reprocessed in the direction of *aschematic* or androgynous thinking (Sweeney, 2001). The key is to bring taken-for-granted notions about gender to the surface.

Finally, gender schema theory also bridges a gap between psychological and sociological approaches. It assumes that as people interact with their environments, they actively construct mental structures (schemas) to represent their awareness of the events around them (Intons-Peterson, 1988:48). Other schemas can also be identified, such as those based on age, ethnicity, or religion. These ideas are at the core of symbolic interaction theory.

Critique. As a cognitive model gender schema theory is subject to the same set of criticisms noted. There is also disagreement between gender schema theorists regarding the concept of androgyny. Bem believes that androgynous people as well as those people who possess only a few traits associated with their own sex would be more gender *aschematic.* Other theorists assert that *all* people are gender schematic, including androgynous people, because they still identify masculine and feminine traits within themselves (Markus et al., 1982). The only exception would be people who say that their traits are not largely associated with gender at all.

All these theories offer productive avenues for explanations of gender role socialization. A truly integrative model that incorporates the basic elements of each theory, however, has yet to be developed.

Moving from microlevel explanations, which are more psychologically based, we now turn to macrolevel explanations, which are more sociologically based. These sociological explanations account for "primary socializing agents," which have a critical impact on attitudes and behaviors regarding gender.

AGENTS OF SOCIALIZATION

Agents of socialization are the people, groups, and social institutions that provide the critical information needed for children to become fully functioning members of society. Functionalists point out that if these agents do not carry out their socialization tasks properly, social integration may be compromised. Conflict theorists point out that these agents offer varying degrees of power, allowing socialization advantages to some groups and disadvantages to others. These agents do not exist independently of one another and are often inconsistent in the gendered messages they send. Later chapters will be devoted to each agent, but the focus here will be on those agents that are the most influential in determining gender roles during primary socialization.

The Family

The family is by far the most significant agent of socialization. Although social change has increased family diversity and created more opportunities for children to be influenced by other social institutions, the family continues to play the pivotal role in primary socialization. The family is responsible for shaping a child's personality, emerging identity, and self-esteem. Children gain their first values and attitudes from the family, including powerful messages about gender. Learned first in the family and then reinforced by other social institutions, gender is fundamental to the shaping of all social life. Gender messages dominate and are among the best predictors of a range of later attitudes and behavior (Hill, 2001).

Do You Want a Boy or a Girl? The first thing expectant parents say in response to this question is, "We want a healthy baby." Then they state a gender preference. Preference of one gender over the other is strong. Most couples agree on their preference for male over female children, especially for a first or only child, a finding from studies conducted in the United States since the 1930s and one that holds true for most of the world (Williamson, 1976; Beal, 1994; Baunach, 2001). When surveying individuals rather than couples, however, there are important exceptions to the son-preference finding. Data on college students from two surveys conducted three years apart who were asked the question, "If you could have only one child, which one would you prefer?" indicate that 80 percent of male students in both survey years prefer a male child, showing an even stronger preference than in the earlier study. Female students, however, preferred a female child (54 percent in the first survey and 58 percent in the second) (Pooler, 1991). Reviews of more recent data from the United States and some European countries, including gender equitable Scandinavian countries, find that college women, first time pregnant women, and young adults state a daughter preference or no preference more often than a son preference (Brockmann, 2001; Marleau and Saucier, 2002).

Parity is an issue related to parental gender preferences. The ideal for couples in the United States and much of the developed world is to have two children, one boy and one girl. It is well documented that couples with two children of the same gender are more likely to try for a third child than those with one son and one daughter (Hank and Andersson, 2002). If son preference by women is indeed decreasing in the United States, it may be that they believe that raising a daughter is easier than raising a son and that daughters will be emotionally closer to them than sons (Forbes and Adams-Curtis, 2000). It may also be related to sex selection technology (SST), which increases the chances of having a child of the preferred gender. Data on attitudes toward use of SST for a firstborn child show a preference for a firstborn son (Swetkis et al., 2002). When considering the gender balance issue, couples who use SST are only slightly more likely to try for a boy if they have two girls compared to couples who try for a girl if they have two boys (ABC News, 2001). As we will see, however, the apparent decline of son preference in the developed world does not predict its decline globally.

Gender Socialization in Early Childhood. Gender-typing of infants by parents begins on the day of the child's birth. Gender of the child is one of the strongest predictors of how parents will behave toward their children, a finding that is reported globally and one that crosses racial and ethnic lines in the United States (Parke, 2002; Sidanius and Pena, 2003). Both parents are likely to describe infant sons as strong, tough, and alert and infant daughters as delicate, gentle, and awkward, regardless of the weight or length of their infants. Fathers, however, are more stereotyped in their assessments than mothers (Stern and Karraker, 1989; Beitel and Parke, 1998). With gender stereotyping evident on day one of life, it is easier to explain why parents treat their sons and daughters differently and have different expectations for what they can accomplish. Parents engage in more physical, rougher play with their infant and toddler sons, believe that girls require more help than boys, and offer more autonomy to their young sons than their young daughters (Ross and Taylor, 1989, Pomerantz and Ruble, 1998; Leaper, 2000). Gender socialization in early childhood helps boys develop "wings," which permit them to explore realms outside the home independent of adult supervision, whereas girls develop "roots," which tend to anchor them and keep them closer to home (Block, 1984). Fathers are more likely than mothers to make these distinctions and to encourage more traditional gender specific behavior in their sons (Fagot and Leinbach, 1995; Hardesty et al., 1995). Socialization by parents encourages gender appropriate norms allowing separation, independence and more risk taking for boys and connection, interdependence, and more cautious behaviors for girls.

While Dick is allowed to cross the street, use scissors, or go to a friend's house by himself, Jane must wait until she is older.

Gendered Childhood: Clothes and Toys. On leaving the hospital with their newborn, proud parents deposit their infant in a household ready to accommodate either a boy or a girl. The baby is also welcomed into the home by greeting cards from friends and family that display consistent gender stereotyped messages (Willer, 2001). Pink and pastel colored cards for darling, sweet, and adorable girls and cards in primary colors for strong, handsome, and active boys are standard. The first artifacts acquired by the infant are toys and clothes. In anticipating the arrival of the newborn, friends and relatives choose gifts that are neutral to avoid embarrassing themselves or the expectant parents by colors or toys that suggest the "wrong" gender. Teddy bears and clothing in colors other than pink or blue are safe bets. Most parents will know the sex of their baby before birth and decorate the child's room accordingly. If parents choose not to know the sex of the baby in advance, decorations for either gender will be chosen. But within weeks of the baby's arrival, the infant's room is easily recognizable as belonging to a girl or a boy. Although toys for toddlers are often gender neutral, by age two children begin to reject these toys as well as toys designed for the other gender and select those designed for their own gender. By preschool, children have a firm commitment to own-gender toys and tend to reject children playing with other-gender toys, especially if a boy is seen playing with a girl's toy (Karniol and Aida, 1997). Gender is a better predictor of toy selection than if the toy matches a child's specific interests.

Color-coded and gender-typed clothing of infants and children are widespread and taken for granted. Pink and yellow on girls are sharply contrasted by blue and red on boys. Although jeans for school and casual wear are now more common than dresses, girls' clothing is likely to be in pastels with embroidered hearts and flowers. Since pants for girls often do not have pockets, a purse becomes a necessity. Both boys and girls wear T-shirts and sweatshirts. Boys wear those that have superhero and athletic motifs, and girls wear those depicting female television characters or nature scenes. Pictures of outstanding male athletes are typically represented in nonathletic clothing for boys and sometimes for girls, but it is unusual to find female athletes depicted on clothing for girls. Halloween costumes provide a good example of gendertyping in clothing. Gender neutral costumes are rare at Halloween, with hero costumes highly favored for both boys and girls. Girl heroes are clustered around beauty queens and princesses, and boy heroes are clustered around warrior themes of masculinity, especially villains and symbols of death. Animal costumes are also favored for younger children, but these, too, are gender typed. The pink dragon is female and the blue teddy bear is male (Nelson, 2000). Gender oriented clothing and accessories provide the initial labels to ensure that children are responded to according to gendered norms. If her gender is not readily identifiable by her clothing, an infant girl of three months may have a Velcro bow attached to her bald head in case onlookers mistakenly think she is a boy.

A clothing–toy link carries a formidable force for socialization, especially true for girls who buy "fashions" for their dolls. Dolls for girls, especially Barbies, and "action figures for boys" (advertisers will never call them dolls) are standard gifts to children from parents. One study reports that virtually every girl in the United

States between ages three and ten, from all social classes and races, owns at least one Barbie™; the average girl has eight (Rogers, 1999). Not only are messages about beauty, clothing, and weight sent to girls via Barbie, but girls also learn about options in life. Barbie has held a variety of jobs, including flight attendant, ballerina, fashion model, teacher, and aerobics instructor. In one year she held three jobs: fashion designer, television reporter, and corporate executive. Things apparently didn't go well, since for the next several years she engaged in unpaid volunteer work (Urla and Swedlund, 2000:403–404).

A generation ago the male counterpart of Barbie was G.I. Joe.™ Although today G.I. Joe is sold mainly to nostalgic adult men, it was the prototype for subsequent action figures. The action figures currently sold to boys have larger body frames and show more muscles than the figures of a generation ago (Klugman, 1999; Powers, 2001). Girls equate beauty with Barbie. Boys equate handsomeness and ruggedness with heroic action figures. Messages about masculine and feminine ideals are sent to both boys and girls through these toys. Combined with an entertainment based youth culture, gendered toys are another link to lower self-esteem and the origins of eating disorders in children (Vallone, 1999; Kenway and Bullen, 2001; Grogan and Richards 2002).

Toys for girls encourage domesticity, interpersonal closeness, and a social orientation. Boys receive more categories of toys, their toys are more complex and expensive, and they foster self-reliance and problem solving. At an early age both Jane and Dick are given toys that require less imagination to use. But as they get older, they acquire toys that encourage more imagination, pretense, and role taking. Pretend play is developed earlier in girls, but by second grade, boys surpass girls in imaginative play. Girls stage one type of activity, having to do with dolls and playing house, in caretaking, domestic roles. Girls script their play around role taking in realistic settings, such as playing house. Boys script their play around more fantastic scenarios, such as superheroes (Leaper, 1994). Girls do have one advantage over boys in their toy selections. They are allowed to cross over and play with toys originally designed for boys (Raag, 1999). Playing with masculine toys in childhood is associated with later sports participation of girls (Giuliano et al., 2000). Boys, however, are not allowed to cross over and play with toys designed for girls. If boys are restricted in any way, it is in the lack of encouragement in staging activities with toys suggestive of domestic roles.

Source: © Baby Blues Partnership. Reprinted with permission of King Features Syndicate.

Both parents and children express clear preferences for gender-typed toys. These preferences reinforce the persistent gender-related messages that are sent to children through the toys (Wood et al., 2002). On your next outing to a toy store, note how shelves are categorized according to gender and how pictures on the boxes suggest how boys and girls should use the toys. Little Jane uses her tea set to give parties for her dolls in her room, whereas same-age Dick is experimenting with sports or racing trucks outside in the mud. Siblings and peers ensure that the children will play with toys or stage games in gender-specific ways. The gender-related messages, in turn, show up in differences between girls and boys in cognitive and social development in childhood as well as differences in gender roles as adults. And research continues to show that even with massive social change impacting the genders, gender-typed preferences persist and may be growing (Lueptow et al., 2001; Serbin et al., 2001).

Gendered Parenting Practices. As social learning theorists suggest, through the toys and clothes children receive during early childhood, parents send powerful messages about what is or is not gender appropriate. In turn, children come to expect that their mothers will respond to them differently than their fathers. Parenting practices thus vary not only according to the gender of the child but also the gender of the parent. By preadolescence, children expect their parents to respond to them according to traditional instrumental-expressive gender role stereotypes. They expect mothers to soothe over hurt feelings more than fathers. They expect to spend more leisure time for recreational activities with their fathers. Household chores are usually divided according to gender, but mothers are more likely than fathers to encourage both their sons and daughters to take on chores that would usually be assigned to the other gender (Cunningham, 2001; Leaper, 2002; Turnbull and Cerpendale, 2002). These patterns of gender intensification increase as children get older (Schuette, 2000). Fathers may be more traditional than mothers in their stereotypes, but both parents have strong convictions about which gender is better suited to which activities. Parents perceive the competencies of their children in such areas as math, English, and sports in regard to their child's gender, even if these influences are independent of any real differences in the children's competencies (Cote and Azar, 1997; McHale et al., 1999; Eccles et al., 2000). Children may recognize the inequity in their parent's actions, but largely accept the behavior as appropriate to their parent's gender roles. This acceptance of stereotypes is consistent with cognitive development theory by suggesting that the development of gender role identity is linked to children's perception of adult behavior.

Gender of parent does not predict level of responsiveness—both parents respond swiftly and appropriately to the demands of their children—but it does predict type of response. There are clear differences between men and women in gender role expectations concerning child rearing. Children of all ages are seen more frequently with women than men. Girls do housework with mothers, and boys do yardwork with fathers. Mothers take on caretaking roles, talk to their children, and stay closer to them than fathers. Fathers are much more involved with their sons, a pattern that increases as their sons get older. They concentrate on instrumental support and activities and engage in more rough-and-tumble play with sons than daughters. Fathers tell stories to their sons with more autonomy themes than they tell to their daughters. Mothers tend to be more supportive in the traditional, affective sense, regardless of the gender of their children (Fiese and Skillman, 2000; Gleason and Ely, 2002; Mellen, 2002).

Today's parents are much more likely to support beliefs about gender equity and feminist values than their parents. A growing new generation of feminist parents are socializing the next generation of feminist children. However, parents who are forerunners of change face some difficult obstacles. This ideological shift toward equity is more strongly supported by mothers compared to fathers. Fathers have less support for gender equity when they have sons only, but more support when they have daughters only (Warner and Steel, 1999). Some researchers argue that feminist fathers are lagging behind feminist mothers because the fathers tap into the gender differences that were part of their own socialization experiences (Myers and Booth, 2002). According to symbolic interactionists, the ideological shift in beliefs about equity cannot fully erase these early family influences. In addition, the children of feminist parents are in continuous contact with nonfeminst—often antifeminist—environments outside their homes and in the media (Sherwood and Risman, 2000: 319). As we have seen, however, socialization is a forceful element serving both gender role continuity and gender role change. As beliefs about gender equity become more widespread, the next generation of parents should socialize their children in less traditional ways than they were socialized.

Peers and Preferences

Children transfer gender role patterns established in the family when they begin to form friendships with their peers. With family gender role models as a foundation, peer influence on children's gender socialization is even more powerful. Parents initiate the first peer relationships for their children, with these often developing into later friendships chosen by the children themselves. Two- and three-year-olds delight in playing with their same-age companions, and parents are not compelled to separate them by gender at this early age. As school age approaches, however, this situation is altered dramatically.

Activities, games, and play are strongly related to gender roles and become important aspects of socialization. These are easily seen when a brother and sister play together. When Jane pressures Dick into playing house, she is the mommy and he is the daddy. Or she can convince him to be the student while she is the teacher and relishes the prospect of scolding him for his disruptive classroom behavior. On the other hand, if brother Dick coerces Jane into a game of catch, he bemoans her awkwardness and ridicules her lack of skill. What would social learning theory say about the likelihood of Jane's becoming an expert in catch? Games such as these are usually short-lived, dissolve into conflict, and are dependent on the availability of same-gender peers with whom siblings would rather play.

Games. Peer play activities socialize children in important ways. The games of boys are more complex, competitive, and rule-governed and allow for more positions to be played and a larger number of participants than games played by girls. Girls play ordered games, like hopscotch or jump rope, in groups of two or three, which take up less space, minimizes competitiveness, and tends to enhance cooperation (Lansford and Parker, 1999; Kelle, 2000). Playgrounds shape the spaces of children, and boys are offered more space for their games than girls (Gagen, 2000).

Both boys and girls play kickball, but boys play it at younger ages than girls and graduate to more competitive, physically demanding sports much sooner than girls. There are significant consequences of gender differences in games. When girls are weaned from sports and physical activities in early childhood, by adolescence they have already lost bone density, and as inferred by some research, they have turned themselves into prime candidates for early osteoporosis (Dowling, 2000). Another important early study of these effects bitterly concluded that girls' games teach meaningless mumbo-jumbo—vague generalities or pregame mutual agreements about "what we'll play"—while falsely implying that these blurry self-guides are typical of real world rules. (Harragan, 1977:49–50).

Later research does lend support to the notion that girls lose out in developing early skills related to competition. Girls may also take longer to develop the ability to take on the roles of several people at once—referred to as the *generalized other* by symbolic interactionists—which is valuable in understanding group dynamics by anticipating how others will react in a given group situation. Complex games such as team sports require this ability. Yet this learning process may have negative effects for both girls and boys. The games of young boys do provide earlier guidelines that are helpful for success later in life, such as the importance of striving for individual excellence through competition as emphasized in American culture. However, boys may be at a disadvantage because it takes them longer to learn values such as cooperation and intimacy, which are also essential to interpersonal and economic success.

Cognitive development and social learning theory highlight the importance of peers in fueling gender segregation during early childhood. Peer group influence increases throughout the school years, exerting a powerful effect on children. When children interact, positive reinforcement for the behavior of same-gender peers occurs more frequently than with other-gender peers. Boys are mocked for displaying scaredness, associating it with devalued girls' characteristics (Kyratzis, 2001). Boys are more tenacious in their gender role behavior and exhibit strong masculine preferences through preadolescence. Children prefer to interact with other children who have the same styles of play as their own (Hoffman and Powlishta, 2001). Boys interact in larger groups and have more extensive but less communal peer relationships, and girls interact in smaller groups and have peer relationships that are more intensive and more communal. Research consistently shows that early intimacy with peers carries over to higher levels of self-disclosure and trust for women, especially between best-friend pairs (Neppl and Murray, 1997. Fagot and Leve, 1998; Maccoby, 1998, 2000). The trust and openness that enhance same-gender relationships could inhibit later cross-gender friendships. Since gender boundaries are strictly monitored and enforced by peers in childhood, the worlds of male and female are further divided. Because they learn different styles of interaction, when boys and girls meet as teenagers they may do so as strangers.

In interpreting the results of research on peer enforcement of gender segregation and how behavior changes for one gender in the presence of another, researchers caution us to keep in mind that the context of the peer interaction should not be dismissed (Apostoleris, 1998). In some contexts, for example, boys of middle school age say they would support other boys who act more communally rather than individually (Hibbard & and Buhrmester, 1998). Like girls, boys also have high levels of approval for expressions of happiness rather than anger and offer sympathy and acceptance for children who have physical or learning disabilities (Ferguson et al., 2000; Hepler, 2000; Sorber, 2001).

School

Family life paves the way for the educational institution, the next major agent of continuing socialization. The intimacy and spontaneity of the family and early childhood peer groups are replaced by a school setting environment in which children are evaluated impersonally with rewards based on academic success. School will play a critical role in the lives of both parents and students for the next twelve to twenty years. We will view the gender impact of the educational institution fully in chapter 11. The intent of this section is to briefly consider its role in primary socialization. Regardless of the mission to evaluate children impersonally—by what they do rather than who they are—schools are not immune to gender role stereotyping and often serve to foster it.

Teachers who honestly believe they are treating boys and girls similarly are unaware of how they inadvertently perpetuate sexist notions. When Jane is ignored or not reprimanded for disruptive behavior, is encouraged in her verbal but not mathematical abilities, or is given textbooks showing women and girls in a narrow range of roles—or not showing them at all—gender stereotyping is encouraged, and Jane's self-confidence decreases (Tepper and Cassidy, 1999; Jacobs et al., 2002). Dick discovers his rowdiness will gain attention from his female elementary school teacher, that he can aspire to any occupation except nurse or secretary, and that he is rewarded for his athletic skills at recess. Unlike Jane, who may begrudgingly be admired by engaging in "tomboy" behavior, Dick is loath to even investigate school-related activities typical for girls, lest he be called a "sissy." A decade of research on students of all grade levels conducted by Myra and David Sadker (1994) brings this point home. Their study asked: What would it be like to become a member of the "opposite sex"? Both boys and girls prefer their own gender, but girls find the prospect intriguing and interesting and were willing to try it out for a while. As girls wrote: "I will be able to be almost anything I want" or "I will make more money now that I am a boy." Boys, on the other hand, found it appalling, disgusting, and humiliating. Comments from two sixth-grade boys suggest the intensity of these feelings: "My teachers would treat me like a little hairy pig-headed girl," and at the extreme: "If I were turned into a girl today I would kill myself" (Sadker and Sadker, 1994:83).

Functionalists emphasize the responsibility of the schools to socialize children to eventually take on positions necessary to maintain society. Schools provide experiences that offer technical competence as well as the learning of values and norms appropriate to the culture. American culture places a high regard on the values of competition, initiative, independence, and individualism, and schools are expected to advocate these values. We have already seen how these values are associated more with masculinity than femininity. Also, from a functionalist viewpoint, schools are critical ways of bringing a diverse society together through the acceptance of a common value system.

Unfortunately, many schools unwittingly socialize children into acquiring one set of values to the exclusion of the other. Stereotypical thinking assumes that in filling breadwinning roles, boys will need to be taught the value of competitiveness; in filling domestic roles, girls will need to be taught the value of nurturance. Though both are positive values and both are needed to function effectively, they are limited to, or truly accepted by, only one gender. As schools begin the task of fostering gender-fair behaviors, differential gender role socialization harmful to both girls and boys can be altered (Smith, 2000, Chick et al., 2002).

Television

Television aimed at young children is a commanding source of gender socialization. This observation is empirically justified, considering that a child may spend up to one-third of the day watching TV. Heavy television viewing is strongly associated with traditional and stereotyped gender views, a pattern that is demonstrated for all races and age groups. Children are especially vulnerable in believing that television images represent truth and reality. Television is by far the most influential of the media. Television establishes standards of behavior, provides role models, and communicates expectations about all of social life. Children use television more for role modeling—patterns found for both genders and for children of all races in the United States (Cantor et al., 2001; Murray and Mandara, 2002; Shrum, 2002; Smith and Wilson, 2002). When television images are reinforced by the other mass media, like movies, magazines, and popular songs, the impact on socialization is substantial. Chapter 13 documents how mass media portray the genders, but here we overview the influence of television programming directed at children.

Television Teaches. Strongly supportive of social learning theory, children as young as two years of age copy what they see on TV, with imitation increasing through the elementary school years (Comstock and Paik, 1991; Wood et al., 1991). Television encourages modeling. Children identify with same-gender characters. Boys identify with characters possessing physical strength and girls with those who are physically attractive (O'Reilly, 2001; Scharrer, 2001). Television is gender stereotyped. Gender role portrayals in shows that are deemed acceptable for children are highly stereotyped, especially female roles. Data from two popular shows for preschool children, *Barney & Friends* and *Teletubbies*, indicate that some changes in more flexible gender role portrayals are occurring for boys, but that traditional gender roles are reinforced for girls (Powell and Abels, 2002). Even *Sesame Street*, arguably the most popular children's show for preschool children of all time, highly underrepresents female characters—human or Muppet™—and portrays males as dominant figures (Ditsworth, 2001). In cartoons for preadolescents, male characters outnumber female characters ten to one. Females are portrayed more in family roles and are more physically attractive than male characters (Klein et al., 2000). Cartoons influence girls in their beliefs about female roles. Cartoons are usually either all male or have one or two females, often in helping or little sister relationships. Many of you may recall from your childhood the lone Smurfette™ among all the other male Smurfs™. When girls are portrayed with boys in dangerous situations, boys determine the story line and the code of values for the group. Girls are defined in relation to the boys. Television influences self-image. Implicit in Saturday morning TV is that boys are more significant persons than girls, if only by the sheer number of male characters compared to female. This is bolstered by television's consistent and stubborn portrayal of female characters existing primarily as add-ons to males (Leaper et al., 2002; Nathanson et al., 2002).

Children's television is supported by commercials aimed at products for children, mainly toys, fast food, and sugared cereal. Before television transformed the family, advertising for children's items was aimed primarily at adults. Today children are more likely than adults to actually watch the commercials. Marketing to the child consumer is a key tactic of the toy industry with age and gender linked ads designed to entice a specific niche of children. It is for this reason that, unlike overall television programming for children, commercials represent males and females as primary characters in more equal numbers (Jackson, 1994a; Buijzen and Valkenburg, 2000; Bresnahan et al., 2001). Advertisers orient children to the idea that products are waiting to be bought at local stores and that to do without them is an unfortunate hardship. Commercials are blatant in creating desires for toys encouraging domesticity in girls and high activity in boys. Samples of ads from children's advertising over the last two decades show commercials portraying males and females in traditional gender-polarized voices. In mixed-gender commercials boys and girls are shown interacting cooperatively, but in single-gender commercials girls are portrayed in stereotypical domestic settings and boys are portrayed in settings related to violence and aggression (Bird, 2000; Larson, 2001; Johnson and Young, 2002).

Parents who resist pressure from their children to buy these products or find that the products children want are unavailable are made to feel guilty, by advertisers and children alike. Remember the frantic search for limited supplies of Cabbage Patch™ dolls, Power Rangers™, and Tickle Me Elmo™ by parents who feared a disappointed child during holidays or on his or her birthday? Picture, too, the angry exchanges we have witnessed between parent and child in front of the toy, candy, or cereal displays. Parents searching for nonstereotyped toy alternatives may feel demoralized when the offer of a tea set to their son or a truck to their daughter is met with resistance. Tantalized by television, the child's desire is within reach. The desire is likely to be gender role oriented. The parent stands in between. Who is likely to give up the fight first?

Global Focus: Son Preference in Asia

Level of economic development is strongly associated with preference for sons. In regions where economic development is higher, such as in North America and Northern Europe, son preference appears to be weakening. In less developed regions, particularly throughout Asia, favoritism for sons is bolstered by the poverty of the couple, women's subordinate status, the low economic value given to the work women perform, religious beliefs, inheritance norms, and naming customs (Clark, 2000; Croll, 2000; Winkvist and Akhtar, 2000).

China. In China, where son preference is centuries old, a family name may be "lost" if there is no son to carry it on. Confucian practices related to ancestor worship, which trace the family name only through male lines, combine with marriage customs requiring newly married rural women to move into the household of their husbands and inheritance laws keeping women economically dependent on their new families. Low-income Chinese women living in mountain villages express even stronger son preference than urban women who earn cash income, because they need their sons to provide for them in old age (Li and Lavely, 2003). Women are outsiders and remain so even after marriage, and women without sons may be abandoned by their in-laws if they are unable to carry out household or farm work. The naming ceremony at the birth of a boy involves a banquet and festivities as elaborate as the family can afford. Because she loses her name at marriage, a daughter is viewed as a temporary commodity, and her naming meets with little celebration. She is not identified as an individual, but only in kin or category terms, such as "youngest daughter," "new bride," or later in life, simply as "old woman." All men worry about the quality of their names and those of their sons, but women are excluded from this discourse because, even as adults, they remain unnamed, nor do they name others (Watson, 1993:121). The Chinese proverb "Raising a daughter is like weeding another man's garden" attests to the strength of preference for sons.

Son preference is pervasive globally, but it is strongest throughout East and South Asia, in developed countries such as Taiwan, Hong Kong, and especially South Korea, which appears to have the most steadfast son preference in the world, and in developing countries such as India, Pakistan, Bangladesh, and Vietnam. It persists in rural and urban areas and among Muslims, Hindus, Buddhists, and those who do not practice institutional religions (Wang, 1998; Belanger, 2002; Das, 2002). As noted in chapter 2, a major shift favoring males in the average sex ratio at birth (SRB) has occurred throughout much of Asia. The worst SRB imbalances occur in poor, rural areas in China, India, and Bangladesh. SRB in India and Bangladesh has worsened over the last century but in China it has worsened over the last three decades, traced to the introduction of the one-child policy in 1979 (see chapter 6). Son preference has artificially inflated SRB, and the consequences of this inflation for girls are profound. These include underreporting of female births, female infanticide, neglect of female infants and girls resulting in their premature deaths, and the use of ultrasound technology leading to sex-selective abortions of female fetuses (Arnold et al., 1998; Hussain et al., 2000; Ganatra et al., 2001; Pomfret 2001). As explained by an educated 29 year old who finally gave birth to a boy after having three abortions in five years,

> I had no way to protect my baby girls because my parents-in-laws and husband want a boy to carry on their ancestral line. (*Shanghai Star*, 2002).

South Asia. In India and Bangladesh, female infanticide and neglect are associated with the economic survival of the family, which is dependent on the number of sons and the control of the number of daughters, who are regarded as financial liabilities (Sudha and Rajan, 2000). As in China, a rural woman generally moves to the village of her husband and into his household at marriage. She is expected to bring money and goods in the form of a dowry to help offset the expenses associated with her upkeep. When dowries are considered too paltry by the groom's family the bride may be tortured and poisoned by her husband or in-laws or she may commit suicide (Vindhya, 2000; Johnson and Johnson, 2001). After a long dormant period, dowry abuse is rapidly increasing among all castes in India, with estimates ranging from 5,000 to 25,000 occurrences per year. In many cases the women are doused with kerosene and set on fire, in what is supposed to look like a cooking accident (Narasimhan, 2000; Hitchcock, 2001).

In addition to the obvious human rights violations involving females, the artificially inflated SRB has other major economic and social implications. Large families, which consist mainly of girls, have higher poverty rates than small families, which consist mainly of boys. Although poverty is associated with larger families overall, it is deepened when girls face lower pay than boys if seeking employment outside the home. This economic issue collides with social repercussions of a serious bride shortage in China, India, and Korea. "Bachelor villages" are growing at alarming rates, particularly in China and India. These are populated by young, jobless unmarried men and few unmarried young women. Enticed by factory owners into low paid unskilled jobs, girls are migrating at record numbers from rural to urban areas. The irony is that these girls are more marketable than boys precisely because they can be paid less and are seen as docile employees who will not agitate for better working conditions. China alone is soon estimated to have 50 million unhappy, unmarried, men. This "surplus" restive population is being closely monitored by government authorities concerned about their potential for kindling political ferment (Heng, 2000; *Hindu*, 2003).

It may appear that because women are viewed as objects—a commodity of exchange—then the principle of scarcity would make them more valuable from a market perspective. The scarcity principle of supply and demand, which would put a premium on women, is not borne out by research (*Hindu*, 2003). In Asian cultures where the SRB is highest and gender equity the lowest, the scarcity of women is associated with selling and kidnapping of young girls and women, keeping unmarried girls cloistered in their homes, and violence and domestic abuse by husbands and fathers. Fewer girls are available to care for the daily needs of infirm mothers and grandmothers, who usually outlive fathers and grandfathers. Because boys will soon shoulder more than the traditional financial responsibilities for their elders, elder abuse by sons is likely to increase as well.

Despite overall improvements in health care, education, and employment for Asian women and the outlaw of fetal sex screening in China and its disapproval in India, Pakistan, and Bangladesh, son preference persists and has dire consequences for the well-being of females. Socialization practices regarding son preference for much of developing Asia not only remain strong, but also may be growing. And as discussed in chapter 6, when these socialization practices serve to socially and economically comprise over half the world's population, efforts at development and poverty reduction are severely undermined.

ANDROGYNY IN SOCIALIZATION

Socialization is neither consistent nor uniform. It occurs via diverse agents at the cultural and subcultural levels. Yet identifiable gender role patterns still emerge, and children are taught to behave in feminine or masculine ways. But major contradictions also arise in this process. Girls climb trees, excel in mathematics, and aspire to be surgeons and professors. These same girls are concerned about physical attractiveness, financial success, finding the right husband, and raising a family. Boys enjoy cooking, babysitting small children, and cry when they are hurt or sad. These same boys are concerned about physical attractiveness, financial success, finding the right wife, and raising a family.

The socialization theories and research overviewed in this chapter strongly support the notion that views of masculinity and femininity need to shift in the direction of gender role flexibility. These terms are not the opposite of one another. Sandra Bem's (1974) pioneering work in androgyny shows that even decades ago, large numbers of people were identified as androgynous on her widely used Bem

Sex Role Inventory (BSRI). The concept of **androgyny** refers to the integration of traits considered to be feminine with those considered to be masculine. Both men and women can score high or low on either set of traits or have a combination of them. People accept their biological sex (being male or female), have a strong sense of gender identity, but also acknowledge the benefits of gender role flexibility. Gendered behavior does not disappear, but we adapt it according to the various situations and contexts confronting us and at the same time act on our own talents and desires. Parents who are identified as androgynous are less stereotyped about masculinity and femininity and offer a wider range of behavioral and attitudinal possibilities to their children. Many of these are the forerunner parents to the feminist kids mentioned earlier.

The concept of androgyny suggests that people can be defined according to a range of gendered behavior and then classified accordingly. This in itself may be stereotypical thinking. In a revision of her earlier view, Bem (1985:222) now argues that even if we define what is masculine and feminine according to our culture and subcultures, we need to stop projecting gender into situations "irrelevant to genitalia." Men and women may be culturally defined as androgynous because they are nurturing, sensitive, and cooperative as well as assertive, ambitious, and competitive (Bem, 1993). A gender-neutral model for socialization oriented toward a range of positive traits for both females and males has yet to be developed. Until then, an androgynous model provides one alternative allowing people to accept some behaviors defined by their culture as gender inappropriate.

Androgyny does recognize that socialization into two nonoverlapping gender roles is not a productive way of meeting the demands of a rapidly changing society. Nor do such roles offer the best options for fulfilling a person's human potential. Agents of socialization must be altered to meet these demands. Consider this pronouncement as we view the role of language as another powerful agent of socialization.

Summary

1. Socialization is the process by which we learn culture and become functioning social members. Gender socialization tells us what is expected cultural behavior related to masculinity and femininity.

2. Gender role socialization in children is patterned by important cultural factors, especially race and social class. Middle class parents are more flexible than working-class parents. Children from Latino and Asian-American homes are generally socialized into less flexible gender roles than African-American and white children.

3. Three major theories of gender socialization explain how children learn gender identity, an awareness of two sexes, and the behavior associated with them. Social learning theory focuses on the rewards and punishments for acting out appropriate gender roles; cognitive development theory asserts that gender identity allows children to organize their behavior. Once they learn gender identity, they choose their behavior accordingly; gender schema theory, a subset of cognitive development theory, asserts that of all cognitive structures, or schemas, a child learns, gender is the core one around which information is organized.

4. Socialization, including gender socialization, occurs through specific agents—people, groups, social institutions—that provide children the information they need to function in society. These agents are interdependent and often send inconsistent messages. The family, the most important agent, provides the child's first values and attitudes about gender.

5. Expectant parents in the United States usually state a son preference for a first or only child. College women and first time pregnant women in the United States and Europe, however, are more likely to state a daughter preference or no preference.

6. Gender of the child is a strong predictor of how parents behave toward their children and in the selection of the toys and clothes they give to them. Boys are allowed more independence, separation, and risk-taking, and the toys they receive encourage these behaviors. Toys for girls encourage domesticity and social orientation. Girls have the advantage of playing with toys for boys, but boys cannot cross over and play with toys for girls.

7. The gender of a parent predicts gender role expectations in child rearing. Although today both mothers and fathers support beliefs about gender equity, the shift to these beliefs is much swifter for mothers.

8. Peer play activities are highly gendered. Boys play at more complex, competitive games in larger groups. The play of girls fosters cooperation, intimacy, and social skills. Peer groups monitor and enforce gender segregation.

9. Teachers are often unaware that they treat boy and girl children differently, such as encouraging more cooperation in girls and more competitiveness in boys. Gender socialization in schools often inhibits learning both these necessary skills.

10. Television teaches children about gender in highly stereotyped ways. In cartoons, male characters outnumber female ten to one. In popular and acclaimed shows males outnumber females and are in more dominant, important, and active roles. Commercials aimed at children reinforce these gender stereotypes, especially showing girls in domestic settings and boys in aggressive settings.

11. Son preference has artificially inflated the sex ratio at birth throughout Asia. In China, India, and Bangladesh son preference is associated with abortion of female fetuses and female infanticide, neglect, and abandonment.

12. Androgyny in socialization suggests that people can integrate femininity and masculinity in their personalities. Androgyny suggests that people can be classified according to gendered behavior, but socialization into nonoverlapping roles based on that behavior is harmful.

Key Terms

androgyny 73	gender socialization 51	social institutions 51
agents of socialization 61	primary socialization 51	socialization 51
culture 51	schema 59	subcultures 52
continuing socialization 51	self 57	
gender identity 55	social control 51	

Critical Thinking Questions

1. With reference to research on parental expectations for behavior, gender segregation, and peer play activities, explain patterns of gender socialization in early childhood from the perspectives of social learning and cognitive development. Which explanation better accounts for the research?

2. Through specific research examples, demonstrate how gender schema theory can help "bridge the gap" between sociological and psychological approaches to gender role socialization.

3. Based on your understanding of the theory and research on gender socialization, what suggestions would you offer to parents and teachers who want to socialize children into more androgynous and flexible gender roles? Demonstrate how your suggestions counter the negative gendered impact of agents of socialization.

CHAPTER 4

Man: An individual human; especially an adult male human
Woman: An adult female person
    — *Merriam-Webster Dictionary*, 2004

Language wields a powerful but taken for granted force in socialization. Primary socialization literally bombards children with mountains of information and learning they must absorb. This process includes learning both the verbal and nonverbal rules and complexities of their language. Language reflects culture and is shaped by it; therefore, it is fundamental to our understanding of gender. Language tells us about how the culture defines and categorizes the genders. In learning language children are taught that the genders are valued differently. However, since language socialization is a lifelong activity, we continually modify it in response to social change. As we shall see, it is the taken-for-granted part of language socialization that makes language such a powerful element in determining gender role continuity and change. For speakers of English, unless stated otherwise, everyone begins as a male. Decades of research on American English suggest that all people are male until proven female.

THE GENERIC MYTH

The English language continuously focuses attention on gender. The best example of this attention is when the word *man* is used to exclude woman and then used generically to include her. This is demonstrated when we speak of culture as *man-made* or the evolution of *mankind.* Other examples may be less clear, such as referring to a voter as the typical "man on the street" or finding "the right man for the job." Are women included as voters or workers? More often the word is used to distinguish man from woman, such as in the phrases "it's a man's world" and "this is man's work." The word is definitely ambiguous and may be subject to interpretation even within the context. Although it is unclear where women belong, it does imply that they are "part" of man. Sometimes no interpretation is necessary. At a wedding ceremony when a couple is pronounced *man and wife* , she becomes defined as his. Not only is generic language ambiguous, it is discriminatory.

It is awkward to change language to make it more precise. If *man* is supposed to refer to *woman*, then *he* is also supposed to mean *she.* Because English does not have a neutral singular pronoun, *he* is seen as the generic norm, with *she* as the exception. A doctor is he and a nurse is she. Most neutral designations are also "he" words. A consumer, employee, patient, or parent is he, despite the fact that women represent over half of these categories. Now we see that language is ambiguous, discriminatory, *and* inaccurate. The generic use of *he* is presumed to include all the *shes* it linguistically encompasses. It is quite clear from research, however, that this is not the case.

People develop masculine imagery for neutral words, a pattern firmly in place by preadolescence. The pattern cuts across race, ethnicity, and social class, but males in all these categories adopt the pattern more than females. Generics are supposed to be neutral, but children and adults report primarily male, sex-specific imagery when hearing generic terms (Conkright et al., 2000; Flaherty, 2001; Lambdin et al., 2003). People visualize male and interpret the reference as male rather than male *and* female. A research example is from an eight-year-old girl who, in reading of "The Story of the Caveman," asks how we got here without cavewomen (Richardson, 1996:421). When an encyclopedia states that "man is the highest form of life on earth" and that "his superior intelligence has enabled man to achieve things impossible for other animals, the response of a young boy is likely to be 'wow!' while the response of a girl to the same information is 'who?,' does that mean me, too?" Although some insist that the word *man* is a clear, concise, and universal reference to mean *person,* the mass of evidence is squarely against this view (Miller and Swift, 1993: 73–74).

To encourage inclusiveness and avoid sexism, several suggestions are offered in dealing with the generics issue. Many writers use he/she, she or he, s/he, or they explicitly note that both males and females are being discussed, using forms you will find throughout this book. Of these options, "they" is the most accepted. However, when the "he and she" or "she and he" alternative is used, people overestimate the rate of female pronouns—regardless of which pronoun comes first—and say the language is biased in favor of women (Madson and Hessling, 2001). Another suggestion is to offer inclusive replacements for outmoded terms. For instance, some colleges use "first year student" to replace the archaic and noninclusive use of the word *freshman.* These examples offer the least cumbersome and most accurate solutions to the generic problem, but they are also the least accepted. People tend to oppose what they perceive as invented language—an issue we will return to later.

Titles and Occupations

Linguistic sexism abounds in the usage of titles and occupations. We write "Dear Sir" or "Dear Mr. Jones," even if we are unsure of the gender of the addressee, especially if it is a business letter. After all, business*men* are considered to be the likely occupants of these positions. The same can be said for chair*men,* fore*men,* congress*men,* news*men,* and garbage*men.* Physicians, attorneys, and astronauts are men. Nurses, schoolteachers, and secretaries are women. If either gender deviates occupationally and enters a nontraditional field, we add linguistic markers to designate this remarkable fact. The media, too, are grappling with these issues and remain extraordinarily inconsistent in use of generics, as a quick read of your Sunday paper will verify. Women are referred to as chairmen or chairwomen for charitable events or are referred to as he when they are business executives and grouped with men who are also executives. The nonsexist designations would be "chair" of the event or "they" to refer to all the executives.

Children confront this usage issue in their reading material. They may assign meaning to words quite differently than what the adult assumes the child understands. Consider a child's shock on discovering that a cat burglar is not a cat at all. Children also use linguistic markers in referring to females in traditionally male roles or males in traditionally female roles. What emerges is the idea of a female scientist, lady spaceman, or male nurse. Children may need these markers when they find a mismatch between what they see and what they perceive to be true (Liben et al., 2002; Sturt, 2003). The stereotyped gender role thus remains unscathed.

When women enter predominantly male occupations, little attention is given to how they are named. A woman may become an engineer and be referred to as a female engineer, lest people mistakenly think most engineers are women. The male occupation becomes linguistically protected by invasion from females. However, when males begin to enter predominantly female occupations in greater numbers, a language shift occurs rather quickly. Although women are the majority of elementary teachers and nurses, men are rapidly entering the fields, making the use of *she* as a label a subject of controversy. It is now considered improper to refer to teachers and nurses as she when more than a token number of men enter the occupations. The same can be said for stewardesses today being called flight attendants. Females will soon become a majority of practicing pharmacists, but the generic *he* is likely to be retained in referring to them as a group. Another linguistic marker involves adding appendages or suffixes to words to show where women belong occupationally. A poet becomes a poetess, an usher becomes an usherette, and an actor becomes an actress. Women are defined as the exceptions to the male-as-norm rule. The linguistic markers are not necessary for men who already own the occupations.

Titles of address for women also reinforce the idea that women are part of men. The title of Mr. conveys the fact that the person addressed is probably an adult male. But for women, marital status is additionally conveyed in forms of address. Any time a woman fills out a form where she must check either "Miss" or "Mrs." she is conveying personal information not required of men. Miss and Mrs. are still considered the acceptable titles for women, who are defined according to their relationship with a man. This distinction historically served the purposes of providing information regarding a woman's availability, and pressure was on the single woman to think about marriage. To counter this titular sexism, Ms. was offered as an alternative to both married and unmarried women who believed that their marital status is private information they chose to convey or not.

Yet language change does not come easily. When first introduced, Ms. was ridiculed and maligned in the media as a radical, feminist invention used by women trying to cover up the shame of a divorce or not being married (Connor et al., 1986). When an opposition speaker of the New York Equal Rights Amendment (ERA) addressed Senator Karen Burstein, an ERA supporter, an agitated digression on whether to address her as Miss, Mrs., or Ms. ensued. Burstein quietly diverted the tumult by suggesting, "Perhaps it would be easier if you addressed me as Senator" (cited in Miller and Swift, 1991:109). Editors bemoaned its style, while ignoring its precision. These objections have largely disappeared, and today Ms. is a normative, standard form of address with a high level of acceptance. Revisions to the powerful *New York Times* and Associated Press style guides endorsing its use in news releases attest to this acceptance (Ehrlich and King, 1993; Crawford et al., 1998).

What's in a Name?

A simple one word answer to this question is identity. Whereas a name symbolically links us to our past and provides us a sense of self-definition, in most Western cultures girls are socialized early in life to expect the loss of their surnames upon marriage. A woman may also lose her complete name and be called someone different. Jane Smith becomes Mrs. Richard Jones. The new name and title alter the earlier identity legally, socially, and even psychologically. Mrs. Jones is now linguistically encompassed by her husband. Today the legal requirements for a woman to abandon her name at marriage have all but disappeared, but the belief that women and children should take their husbands' and fathers' surnames is strong (Johnson and Scheuble, 2002).

The change in status from single person to wife or husband carries with it other linguistic conventions. Newspaper articles often identify women of accomplishment according to their husbands' names, such as Mrs. Richard Jones, rather than Jane Jones. In dictionaries of famous people, women are typically listed with male names, even if the males did not contribute to the reasons the women are in the dictionary at all. How many of us are aware that Mrs. George Palmer Putnam is Amelia Earhart, Charlotte Brontë is Mrs. Arthur B. Nicholls, and Harriet Beecher Stowe is the sister of Henry Ward Beecher (Nilsen, 1993)?

The surname change at marriage has grave implications for women whose accomplishments are recorded under their birth ("maiden") names. These women can literally lose years of professional recognition that impact their income, tenure, notoriety, and career choices (Tescione, 1998). Contemporary strategies women use to offset such liabilities include retaining their birth name for professional purposes or hyphenating their birth and married surnames. These strategies are likely to increase because research now reports that college students have positive perceptions of *both* men and women who choose to hyphenate their names. Compared to other married women, those with hyphenated names are perceived to be friendly, well educated, and intellectually curious. Men with hyphenated names are perceived to be accommodating, nurturing, and more committed to their marriages (Forbes et al., 2002). Women students are more positive about hyphenation than men students, but the generally positive perceptions of both bodes well for future shifts to more equitable gender roles.

Another linguistic dimension involves the ordering and placement of names and titles. Husband and wife, Mr. and Mrs., and Dr. and Mrs. give prominence to men. If she is a doctor and he is not, Dr. and Mr. would not be used, and if they are both doctors, Dr. and Dr. would not be a form of address. Men own the province of placement so their names and titles come first. An exception to this ordering rule is bride and groom. Considering that her wedding is the most important event in the life of a woman, this is understandable. *Her* wedding day, the *bridal* party, *brides*maids, *bridal* path, and mother and father of the *bride* indicate the secondary status of the bride*groom* in the whole affair. His status is resurrected, however, by phrases such as "giving the bride away," indicating his new ownership of her.

Children's Names. As with occupations, children's names are chosen to ensure that people readily distinguish boys from girls. As you would expect, boys' names are ripe for the picking as girl's names but not the reverse. Popular boys' names for girls include Madison, Morgan, Taylor, Cameron, Dylan, and Bradley. It is also permissible to append a name normally given to a boy to refer to a girl, such as: Paul to Paula, Christopher to Christie, and Gene to Jean or Jeanette. Female names are easier to identify because the last letters are usually *a, e,* or *i* (Barry and Harper, 2000). A boy's name will often be used to designate girls, especially in shortened form. Pat, Lee, Dale, Chris, and Kelly are examples. But when boys' names are co-opted by girls, such as Shirley, Jody, Marion (John Wayne's given name), Ashley, and Beverley, they quickly lose their appeal for boys. As expressed by a concerned writer for a devastated boy whose name has been co-opted by girls:

> In schoolyards. . . . permanent damage is already inflicted on budding male psyches of defenseless. . . Taylors and Jodys. . . It's not like little guys have names to spare. Even before the young ladies hijacked Bradley and Glenn, there were fewer boys' names than girls. . . Girls names were more like fanciful baubles for the decorative sex. (Goldman, 2000:22)

This writer then laments that girls academically outperform boys, and girl virtues like teamwork are valorized and boy virtues like aggression are demonized. The obvious sexism in such comments bear out the taken-for-granted assumption that the superiority of boys over girls must be preserved. The equity option is ignored.

English can be very unsympathetic to women. Women are typically referred to in derogatory and debased terms that are highly sexualized. There are several hundred such sexually-related terms for women and only a handful for men. A few of the examples for females include: *broad, chick, doll, bitch, whore, babe, wench, fox, vixen, tramp,* and *slut.* When men want to insult other men, they often use these same terms. Sexually derogatory terms are used almost exclusively by men and frequently in the context of sexually-related jokes. Research shows that men who use and hear sexist jokes find them more amusing and less offensive than women, but that both men and women judge the object of the jokes or the person who is referred to in sexually derogatory terms as less intelligent and less moral (Murnen, 2000; Greenwood and Isbell, 2002). And consider the connotations of *mistress* and *madam* and the male counterparts of *master* and *lord*. Females are sexual beings and males are superior beings (Palczewski, 1998). The word *girl* suggests both child and prostitute. It would be insulting for grown men to be called boys, but we routinely refer to grown women as girls. College students take for granted the "guys-girls" distinction so that males do not have to be referred to as boys. Linguistic practice regularly implies that males are complete beings who take on adult qualities, and females are childlike and incapable but at the same time seductive and sexual, who linguistically retain these statuses throughout their lives.

Over time English words for women acquire debased or obscene references. Words such as *lady, dame, madam,* and *mistress* originally were neutral or positive designations for women (Henley, 1989:60). The masculine counterparts of *lord, baronet, sir,* and *master* escaped pejoration. Another example is the word pair *spinster/bachelor.* Which word would you select to fill in the blank?: "One attractive _____ is always invited to their parties." When a man chooses to remain unmarried he is a "confirmed" bachelor. A woman may be an "old maid." Positive terms for an adult, unmarried female are unavailable, or if available (i.e., bachelorette) are not commonly used. If women occupy a secondary position in society, stereotyped language continues to reinforce this placement.

Language frequently trivializes women. The phrases *women's work, women's place,* and *wine, women, and song* suggest this. When the word *lady* is substituted for *woman* in other contexts, implicit ridicule occurs. The nonseriousness of the "lady" designation is demonstrated by substituting it for "women" in the following organizations: National Organization for Women; Harvard Medical School Committee on the Status of Women, and Black Women's Community Development Foundation. Substitute it in the following titles: The *Subjection of Women* by John S. Mill; *The Emancipation of Women* by V. I. Lenin, and *Vindication of the Rights of Women* by Mary Wollstonecraft (Bosmajian, 1995:390). If the terms *man* and *woman* imply maturity, the term *lady* minimizes any woman's adulthood. A wife or child may be referred to as "the little lady" of the house. When the term *woman* is used in this context, an adjective often accompanies it, serving to bolster the childlike reference. Thus we have "the little woman." The male equivalent term is nonexistent. Until our linguistic consciousness is raised and such references are abandoned, women internalize a language that is belittling to them.

GENDERED LANGUAGE USAGE

We are socialized into the language of our culture and subcultures. Women and men occupy overlapping but distinctively different subcultures. Although subcultural overlap is much more apparent than even a decade ago, it is well documented that subcultures continue to be differentiated according to gendered language.

Registers

Sociolinguists use the term **register** to indicate a variety of language defined according to its use in social situations. Registers are gendered in that males and females who share the same formal language, such as English, also exhibit distinctive styles of communication, including vocabulary, grammar, sentence structure, and nonverbal communication. They are socialized into overall linguistic systems that are culturally shared but also speech communities that are subculturally separate.

Female Register. Important aspects of female register identified by researchers (Lakoff 1975; Crawford 1995; LaFrance, 2002; Weatherall, 2002; Holmes and Meyeroff, 2003) that highlight issues related to gender equity include the following:

1. Women use more qualifiers than men. These words usually hedge or soften evaluative statements: A friend is defined as "sort of" or "kind of" shy, rather than simply "shy" to soften the statement. Another qualifier is when the sentence already begins with words that make it doubtful. "This may be wrong, but. . . " is an example.
2. Women may end a sentence with a tag question. When tags are used, a question follows a statement: "I enjoyed the concert, didn't you?" or "It's a beautiful day, isn't it?" Less assertive than declaratory statements, tag questions appear as if she were asking the other person's permission to express her opinion or feelings. Use of qualifiers and tag questions may suggest that women are uncertain, tentative, or equivocal in what they are saying. They may be used as defenses against potential criticism. Consider the impact of the following statements that use both qualifiers and tag questions in the same sentences:

   I guess this is correct, don't you?
   This sort of makes sense. Does it to you?
   I kind of liked the movie. What do you think?

3. Women use more intensifiers than men. Many of these words are employed as modifiers—adjectives and adverbs—that make up many word lists used by females: "This is a divine party," "Such a darling room," or "I think croissants are absolutely heavenly" serve as examples. Men do use intensifiers, but a pattern exclusive to women is literally to intensify the intensifier by heavily emphasizing and elongating the word. In describing a fine dining experience, for example, both men and women may say "It was so wonderful," but women will draw out and accent the adverb to become "It was so-o-o-o wonderful." An emotional overtone is added to a simple declarative sentence.
4. In those areas where women carry out their most important roles, vocabulary is more complex and descriptive than men's. Women express a greater range of words for colors, textures, food, and cooking. They are able to describe complex interpersonal relationships and emotional characteristics of themselves and others using a greater variety of words and communication styles that are adapted to the setting, a pattern that is supported cross-culturally. When parents talk to their children about emotional aspects of events, women use a

greater number of "emotion" words with daughters than with sons (Cervantes and Callanan, 1998; Fivush et al., 2000).

5. Female register includes forms of speaking that are more polite and indirect. By keeping the conversation open, asking for further direction, and not imposing one's views on another, polite requests rather than forced obedience result. Women will make polite requests to others, including children ("Please answer the phone," or "Will you please answer the phone?"). Men are more likely to use imperatives (Answer the phone).

Both men and women share the same view of what is considered polite speech—by what is said and who says it.

Male Register. For both men and women, specialized vocabularies and communicative styles emerge from specialized roles and gendered expectations. Male register, like female register, contains important features that vary accordingly and have important implications for gender equity.

1. Men use a wider range of words related to mechanics, finance, technology, sports, and sex. Sexually-related words are used much more frequently by men. Males in all age groups direct derogatory sexual slang to females ("bitch," "cunt") and gay men ("fag," "prick") (Burn, 2000; Murnen, 2000; Halstead, 2001).

2. There has been a steady increase in the public use of profanity by both genders in the last 50 years, but profanity in general and sexual profanity in particular remain the province of men. Women still disguise profanity with polite words (darn, shoot) rather than the obvious stronger expletives. Men and boys use profanity more frequently, use it in more contexts, and are not judged harshly—and may be judged more positively—when using it (Macaulay 2001; O'Neil 2002; Coates 2003).

3. Because men are more likely than women to be in roles allowing them to give orders and expect compliance, features of male register include being direct, succinct, instrumental, and personal (Mulac et al., 2001). The personal feature may appear contradictory, given a man's tendency to emotionally distant himself from others. In the male register context, however, personal denotes language use that is more informal and less precise. Men in leadership positions can be relaxed, friendly, and therefore more personal with subordinates of either gender than the reverse. They can also be more direct and less polite.

4. Men talk more than women. Contrary to the stereotype of the bored man listing to the talkative woman, in mixed-gender conversations in a variety of contexts, research clearly indicates that men do the bulk of the talking. In classroom interaction at all educational levels, male students talk more and for longer periods than female students and are listened to more by teachers (Swann, 2003; Sadker and Sadker, 2004). In arguments, men talk more than women opponents and in political debate, business negotiations, or trials where expertise is an ingredient, men are offered proportionally more time to speak than women (Mattei, 1998; Kosberg and Rancer, 1999; Tannen, 2001a). However, the perception that women are more talkative than men persists. When men outspeak women by margins of two to three times longer, the men feel they did not have a fair share of conversation. This relates to the

belief that women, like children, should be seen but not heard: "Quite simply, if a woman is expected to be quiet, then any woman who opens her mouth can be accused of being talkative" (Spender, 1989:9).

5. Because men dominate women in amount of talking, it is not surprising that communication domination of women carries over to what is talked about, how topics are switched and the frequency of interruption. In conversing with women, men use interruption to indicate boredom and impatience and pave the way to a topic change. In conversing with men or with other women, when women interrupt conversations, they do so mainly to indicate interest in what is being talked about, to respond, and show support (Okamoto and Smith-Lovin, 2001; Schmid-Mast, 2001). Learned in childhood, gender role expectations regarding a man's right to dominate and structure a conversation are taken for granted by both men and women.

The Language of Friendship

Gendered registers are important contributors to conversational strategies in building friendships between the genders and within single-gender groups.

It is common to see several women in a restaurant engaged in lengthy conversation long after they have eaten, young girls intently and quietly conversing in their rooms, or teenage girls talking on the phone or via the Internet for hours. When comparing talk within same-gender groups, women talk more frequently and for longer periods of time, enjoy the conversation more, converse on a wider variety of topics, and consider coming together to "just talk," a preferable social activity (Johnson, 1996; Johnson and Aries, 1998). All these talk-related activities may suggest a great deal of "gossiping" is going on. The term is used almost exclusively to indicate a specific kind of talk engaged in by females—talk that is often viewed as negative and pointless. To the contrary, research clearly shows that in all age groups, friendships are cemented between females when experiences are shared and dissected and personal information is revealed (Goodman and O'Brien, 2000). In gossip begins friendship. Gossip allows girls and women to talk to one another in their common roles, share secrets, and support the needs of each other as well as themselves. In written form, such as e-mails, female correspondence contains a higher number of words connected to rapport and maintaining intimacy than found in male correspondence (Colley and Zazie, 2002). This dual focus on self (agency) and peers through talk and gossip for females is used to explain females' high-affiliation strategies, which in turn strengthens their friendships (Coates, 1998; Rose and Asher, 1999).

Conversation strategies of males are frequently defined as low-affiliation ones: using commands, threats, withdrawal, and evasiveness to get demands met. Adolescent boys, for example, are less concerned with the needs of who they are talking to then getting their own needs met, a pattern that carries through to adulthood (Leaper 1994; Strough and Berg, 2000). Popular girls will often modify their behavior to account for the needs of an unpopular girl. When paired with popular boys, unpopular boys often use appeasement tactics, such as smiling or offering small toys as gifts (Murphy and Faulkner, 2000). When men want to encourage or cement friendships with a few other selected males, they do activities like golf or tennis, go to football games, fish and hunt together, or play poker. These activities tend to discourage lengthy conversations but encourage time together and open up possibilities to discuss more serious matters. Whereas women use open, free-flowing conversations in bonding and appreciate self-disclosure, men often feel uncomfortable in this regard. Women tend to like both men and women who self-disclose, but men do not. Safe topics like sports and politics deter men from revealing details of their personal lives to one another. In same-gender contexts, where competition and power are minimal and efforts at bonding are ongoing, female talkativeness is higher than for males.

If gossip is defined as talking about others or oneself by revealing personal information, women may gossip more than men. Men do gossip about others and reveal personal information about the people they gossip about. But when men talk about themselves, they do so cautiously and minimize the amount of personal information revealed. There are no significant gender differences in derogatory tones of gossip. Although men gossip more about acquaintances and celebrities and women gossip more about close friends and family, gossip topics are converging. Both genders gossip about dating, sex, colleagues, and personal appearance (Clark, 1998; Pilkington, 1998; Coates, 2003). As topics converge, it is likely that male self-disclosure will increase in their gossip with other males.

Except for the greater reluctance of men to self-disclose, I would argue that any gender differences in gossip depend on which aspect of gossip is being investigated. If men "talk" and women "gossip" but are conversing on similar topics in the same manner, it is apparent that what separates the two is simply the gender stereotype associated with gossip. Gossip defines women but not men.

In mixed-gender relationships with romance as a goal, conversational strategies differ over time. At the beginning of a male–female relationship, men talk more than women, but once the relationship "takes hold," communication decreases. Women would like to talk more, men would like to talk less. As she attempts to draw him out, he appears to wordlessly resist, frequently using silence as a mechanism of control. Women fear that lack of communication indicates a failing relationship or that he has lost interest in her. Married women are more likely to identify communication as a marital problem than married men (DeFrancisco, 1998; Tannen, 2001b).

NONVERBAL COMMUNICATION

The language we verbalize expresses only one part of ourselves. Communication also occurs nonverbally, often conveying messages in a more forceful manner than if spoken. In addition to bodily movement, posture, and general demeanor, **nonverbal communication** includes eye contact, use of personal space, and touching. Overall, women are better at expressing themselves nonverbally and appear to be more accurate in understanding the nonverbal messages of others.

Facial Expressions and Eye Contact

In decoding nonverbal cues, females rely more on facial information and exhibit a greater variety of facial expressions than men do. The accurate decoding of emotions is associated with better social adjustment of children, with girls doing better than boys, a pattern found in many cultures (Hess et al., 2000; Leppänen and Hietanen, 2001). Females can correctly identify an emotion more often than males and have less difficulty distinguishing one emotion from another (Hall et al., 2000; Thayer and Johnsen, 2000:243). Although the context may explain why males and females display certain facial expressions, the nonverbal expression of smiling is clearly gender differentiated.

Photographs taken throughout the twentieth century show steady increases of both genders smiling, but women are still more likely to smile and smile more fully than men (DeSantis and Sierra, 2000; LaFrance and Hecht, 2000). At all age levels, females smile more than males, a pattern that peaks in adolescence and remains relatively constant through adulthood. As a test of this, take a look at your high school yearbook. Smiling increases for females in situations where gender-appropriate behavior is more conspicuous (being in a wedding party) or more ambiguous (entering a mixed-gender classroom for the first time). In candid and posed photographs, females not only smile more, but are more rigid in their posture, seeming to show a higher level of formality than males (Dodd et al., 1999; Hall et al., 2001; LaFrance et al., 2003). Early research explained gender differences in smiling by socialization into less powerful feminine roles that teach girls to be demure, attractive, and aiming to please. But since females still smile more than males, even when they have equal statuses, the power difference argument has lost some credibility (Henley 1977, 2002; Hall et al., 2002; LaFrance, 2002).

Boys are taught to resist displaying emotion and to mask it in facial expressions. Girls are allowed to display their emotions more openly. The notable exceptions to this pattern are fear and sadness and anger. Parents allow girls to display fear and sadness but not anger, and they allow boys to display anger but not fear and sadness (Plant et al., 2000; Garside and Klimes-Dougan, 2002). What happens, therefore, when girls get angry and boys get sad and fearful? For girls, anger may be masked by crying, which may be acceptable for children in some settings. In contexts such as the workplace, when a woman's anger results in tears, she is judged as weak. If she does not confront the aggressor, she can be exploited. If she counters the anger with a verbal barrage, she is too aggressive. Compared to men, however, women have a greater repertoire of acceptable anger coping styles and anger diffusion strategies (Guerrero and Reiter, 1998; Linden et al., 2003). For boys, anger is often expressed through sports, physical fights, or barrages of profanity, which may be acceptable for children in some settings. For adult men, overt aggression in the workplace is discouraged, but occasional outbursts of anger are often overlooked. There are few instances where males of any age can express fear and sadness by crying. The "Big boys don't cry" reprimand is frequently used by parents and teachers. Peer disapproval of crying is another effective mechanism of social control (Queenan, 2000; Vingerhoets and Scheirs, 2000). For adult men, the expression of fear and sadness by crying in a workplace setting can amount to career suicide.

Compared to research on gender differences in anger and fear, people are usually surprised by data showing that women engage in more eye contact than men. The stereotype is of a woman who modestly averts her eyes from the gaze of an adoring man. In both same-gender and other-gender conversational pairs, females of all ages look at the other person more and retain longer eye contact, a pattern found in children as young as one year old. Men have more visual dominance than women—a pattern of looking at others when speaking but looking away from them when listening (Ellyson et al., 1992; Tannen, 1994; Leeb, 2001). Eye contact may be an indication that the gazer is subordinate to the gazee. An employee is anxiously watchful of his or her boss to determine what follows next in their interaction. Superiors expect subordinates to be prepared in this regard.

An alternative interpretation is that the higher amount of eye contact is assertive, and strength rather than meekness is communicated. Direct eye contact increases perception of power, whether it comes from a man or woman (Aguinis and Henle, 2001). In countering verbal and nonverbal behaviors that may put women at a disadvantage, women may capitalize on their ability to retain eye contact to gain prestige and power. Again, the communication context must be considered.

Touch and Personal Space

Because touch can suggest a range of motives, such as affection, dominance, aggression, or sexual interest, the context of the touching is important. Men touch women more than women touch men, and women are touched more often than men overall. Subordinates are touched by superiors, such as a hand on the shoulder or pat on the back. But when female flight attendants and bartenders are pinched and poked or when a man nudges and fondles a status equal in the office, sexual over-tones cannot be dismissed. The increase in sexual harassment cases calls attention to the fact that women feel threatened by them, especially if the "toucher" is a boss or superior. Women tend to view touching as harassing when men use it to establish power (Poire et al., 1992; Snodgrass, 1992). With the glaring exception of sponta-neous displays related to sports, men seldom touch one another. It is even more rare if touching is associated with emotions such as fear, nervousness, timidity, or sadness.

Men are more protective of their personal space and guard against territorial invasions by others. In his pioneering work on personal space, anthropologist Edward Hall (1966) found that in American culture there is a sense of personal dis-tance, reserved for friends and acquaintances, that extends from about one and a half to four feet, whereas intimate distance, for intimate personal contacts, extends to 18 inches. Men invade personal space of women more than the reverse, and this invasion is more tolerated by the women. The space privilege of males is taken for granted. The next time you are on an airplane or at a movie, note the gender dif-ferences in access to the armrests. In walking or standing, women yield their space more readily than men, especially if the person who is approaching is a man. Men retreat when women come as close to them as they do to women and feel provoked if other men come as close to them as they do to women (Payne 2001). Even in their own homes, women's personal space is more limited. An office or study pri-marily used by the husband may be off limits to the rest of the family. Wives and mothers rarely "own" such space.

GLOBAL FOCUS: THE LANGUAGE OF JAPANESE WOMEN

The language of Japanese women has been recognized as a separate social dialect for at least 100 years. Its origins can be traced as far back as the eighth century. One of the most important novels in all of Japanese literature, *The Tale of Genji*, was written in 1016 by a woman, Lady Murasaki, in women's language. Although Japanese women's language today is an expression of language used in women's quarters for nearly a thousand years, it is being reconfigured in response to rapid social change in Japan (Ide and McGloin, 1990; Inoue, 2002).

Like English, Japanese female register has distinctive linguistic patterns in terms of vocabulary, topic, grammar (syntax), phonology (sound and intonation), and styles of communication. Unlike English, there are grammatical forms in Japanese used exclusively by women. There are numerous forms for which men and women use entirely different terms. Rules of grammar governing how words are combined to form sentences may also differ according to gender of the speaker. For example, the words for "box lunch," "chopsticks," and "book" differ depending on if they are spoken by a female or male (Shibamoto, 1985). Special terms of self-reference and address through different sets of first- and second-person pronouns distinguish speakers by gender. Female speakers may avoid second-person pronouns ("you") entirely. Female speech is associated with a higher and wider range of pitch than male speech, a characteristic that stereotypes Japanese women as being more emotional than Japanese men (Van Bezooijen, 1996; Ohara, 2001).

It is Japanese gender-related syntax focusing on the end of the sentence where gender differences are most evident. Choice of verb endings is particularly constrained by gender of the speaker. Women are obliged to select endings that have the effect of rendering their sentences ambiguous, indirect, tentative, and less assertive. With gender distinctions built directly into the syntax, women's speech is not derived from female applications to (supposedly) gender-neutral grammar as it is in English (Takahara, 1991:61).

One of the most consistent findings on Japanese women's speech is that it is highly formal and polite, much more so than the polite gendered varieties of other languages such as English. Japanese women, for example, rarely use profanity. Politeness is also expressed by women's use of honorific and humiliative speech much more frequently than men's use of these forms. Women use fewer interrogatives, assertions, and requests and construct them differently from men when they are used. These patterns are demonstrated in the media, in the workplace, at school, and even at home (Takahara, 1991; Ohara, 2000; Ohara and Saft, 2003). In conversations, women speak of different things than men and say things differently when they converse about the same topic. The following is an abbreviated example: (Shibamoto 1985:48–49).

FEMALE VERSION
My what a splendid garden you have here—the lawn is so nice and big. It's certainly wonderful, isn't it?
Oh no, not at all, we don't take care of it at all any more, so it simply doesn't look as nice as we would like it to.

MALE VERSION
It's a nice garden, isn't it?
Un.

When these styles of discourse are combined with the formal linguistic features of Japanese women's language, the image of a Japanese woman that emerges is one who lacks self-confidence and is timid, overly polite, formal, and tentative in her speech. The consequences of these speech forms are linked to social powerlessness in the public domain, putting women at a disadvantage when they venture into nontraditional roles outside the home. Japanese women who are in positions of authority experience linguistic conflict when they attempt to defeminize their speech (Smith, 1992). Consider the case of a midlevel manager in a Japanese corporation.

As a manager, she cannot display linguistic traits indicative of women that give the impression she is indecisive or indirect in her talk. But at the same time, she cannot be as authoritative as her male counterparts. She must not be too informal with employees she supervises or with other managers, the majority of whom are male. If she defeminizes (or masculinizes) her speech too much, she may be perceived as a threat to established business and social norms, which she has already violated by becoming a manager in the first place. In the home or workplace, Japanese language has a great impact on the way in which Japanese women live.

Despite these observations, there are indications that women are adopting linguistic strategies to deal with linguistic conflict. One method is to adopt the speech patterns that are successful in the home for use outside the home (Smith, 1992). A study on Issei women—first-generation Japanese-Americans—shows them using various linguistic devices, including silence, that "created the least conflict in order to have a cover behind which they could act and exert some modicum of power" (Von Hassel, 1993:549). Another is to defeminize speech within limits and then gradually expand the limits, creating new linguistic norms. Consistent with classic social conflict theory, when any individual woman challenges the linguistic system, the seeds for changes in female speech are sewn. A ripple effect of conflict can create needed energy to undermine traditional language that is disadvantageous to women (Reynolds, 1998). Other research suggests that social class needs to be accounted for in the speech of Japanese women. Data drawn almost exclusively from samples of middle class homemakers or part-time employees disregards the other class and occupational categories occupied by many Japanese women. These are the women who have already expanded the limits imposed on them by their language (Takano, 2000). Similar to the explosion of feminist research looking at the connections between race, class, and gender, these data call into question the notions of women's homogeneity.

A final thought is to use the politeness norm to the advantage of women. Styles of discourse in Japan stress ancient traditions of politeness for both men and women in a society where social ranking persists as a defining cultural characteristic. The language of the Japanese workplace is one that stresses cooperation, consensus, and conflict-evasive strategies, all of which reinforce the politeness norm. Japanese women are socialized into a female register allowing them to be even more proficient in politeness than men. Women in nontraditional roles, such as corporate managers, who adopt these strategies have a linguistic advantage (Lindsey 1992). "The language of women is for female speakers, but the language of courtesy is for all within the Japanese speech community" (Takahara, 1991:84).

EXPLAINING GENDERED LANGUAGE PATTERNS: DUAL-CULTURE, DOMINANCE, AND SOCIAL CONSTRUCTIONIST MODELS

Explanations for the gendered language patterns revealed in this chapter can be grouped according to what sociolinguists describe as dual-culture, dominance, and social constructionist models. Each of these models is also generally compatible with one of the three guiding perspectives in sociology and as such is associated with corresponding strengths and criticisms.

The Dual-Culture Model

The **dual-culture model** argues that the interactional styles of males and females are separate but equal. Also referred to as the difference or separate world's approach, the dual-culture model emphasizes that because childhood socialization puts boys and girls into separate subcultures, they develop different communication styles. If miscommunication occurs, it is not due to male power or unscrupulous motivations, but because of lack of cultural understanding (Crawford, 1995). Girls learn to use language to negotiate relationships and establish connections, and boys learn to use it to maintain independence and enhance status. The dual-culture model avoids women-blaming or female deficit in language.

In important ways, the dual-culture model is compatible with functionalism. Functionalists maintain that language serves to bind people to their culture and that social equilibrium is helped when one language, including its nonverbal elements, is used and accepted by everyone. Functionalists suggest, therefore, that any gender differences in language are useful for maintaining this equilibrium and minimizing confusion in communication. The research on children's use of linguistic markers when there is a mismatch between stereotyped perception and reality suggests argument. Research on problems people have in comprehending when a pronoun does not match the gender stereotype shows that confusion is created (Kennison and Trofe, 2003). From this perspective, it is better to avoid the confusion than to change the pronoun. It also implies that when people communicate in ways that reinforce traditional gender roles, there is less possibility for disrupting social patterns.

Critique. There is support for the separate tenet, but not the equal tenet, of the dual-culture model. The model overlooks the cultural context of conversation and does not consider that along with gender, people bring with them other statuses that offer varied degrees of power that influence communication (Algoe et al., 2000; Kyratzis, 2001). The multiple statuses of race, class, and gender held by all people highlight this criticism. Stereotyped beliefs about style of speech are stronger for race than gender. When race and gender are connected, white males and African-American females are much more likely to hold their conversational grounds when challenged than white females (Lindsey 1974; Smith-Lovin and Brody, 1989; Popp et al., 2003).

Research on housing suggests that rental agents have the opportunity to discriminate against people of color because they can determine race from a phone conversation (Massey and Lundy, 2001). A white woman compared to a man or woman of color has an advantage in this regard. However, social class may also be inferred from speech patterns. A poor woman of color may be more disadvantaged in her housing choices than men of any race. Whether the language differences stem from any combination of gender, race, and social class, they are not value-neutral and can lead to inequity. Separate is not equal.

The Dominance Model

Robin Lakoff's (1975) groundbreaking work was influential in the **dominance model**, arguing that gendered language is a reflection of women's subordinate status. Nancy Henley (1977) extended this hypothesis to nonverbal behaviors, including face, body movements, gaze, and interruptions. Compatible with conflict theory, the dominance model explains gendered language use according to the power differences between men and women. The structure and vocabulary of English, such as the accepted uses of male generics, have been fashioned by men, and they retain the power to name and to leave unnamed. Data on interruptions provide another example. Interruption is an attempt to dominate and control a conversation by asserting one's right to speak at the expense of another. The dominance model views men's interruption of women as the right of a superior to interrupt a subordinate. Female subordination is reinforced through their use of hedges, tag questions, and conversational cooperativeness. Learned through socialization, girls and women adopt language patterns that keep them from acting as independent or nonsubordinate agents.

Critique. Contrary to the dominance model, research suggests that differences in status do not explain gender differences in nonverbal behavior and that the gender differences persist even when men and women occupy the same status (Hall and Friedman, 1999). When verbal behavior is considered, the dominance model's emphasis on the superiority associated with male speech and the inferiority associated with female speech implies that women are victims of culturally determined speech patterns that they cannot control. Feminist reinterpretations of the dominance model emphasize research suggesting that women's power in using gendered communication patterns is to their advantage. For example, a greater amount of direct eye contact may be interpreted as assertive, with strength rather than meekness being communicated. Status equals look directly at one another. Status unequals do not. Women who want career advancement can adjust their eye contact so that they appear not quite as watchful, but still deferential, to their superior. A female executive in the boardroom adjusts her nonverbals—such as amount of eye contact—to the situation according to the image she wants to project. She is practicing impression management to highlight her (superior) executive status and deemphasize her (subordinate) gender status. Men may dominate women in arguments but women's visual behavior during the argument is more dominant.

If the language of cooperation is more beneficial than the language of competition in some contexts, then women's communication skills honed in developing friendships may offer an advantage. It is wrong to assume that women's speech is weak and tentative just because it is a woman who is doing the talking (Adams and Ware, 1995). If female register is associated with powerlessness, it occurs in a society that appears to value consensus less than competition, and connection less than independence. Linguistic patterns are reflected accordingly.

The Social Constructionist Model

By highlighting how language as a symbol shapes our perception of reality, how reality is redefined by altering language, and how interpersonal communication is negotiated, the social constructionist model is embedded in a symbolic interaction view. There is much evidence to indicate that the use of masculine generics, for example, makes it difficult to actually image women mentally. The use of male generics gives more prominence and visibility to men and contributes to women's invisibility (Spender, 1993).

The key feature of the social constructionist model is its focus on the context or setting of the conversation and on the use of impression management in interpreting gendered language. It is clear that both women and men organize their talk via gendered norms but alter it to their advantage as they move between conversational settings (Eckert and McConnell-Ginet, 2003; Reid et al., 2003). Gender differences in conversational topics are determined in part by the opportunities to express whatever interests the speakers have (West, 1994). As we move into more multicultural contexts of speaking, social constructionists alert us to be attuned to not only gender, but also to the backgrounds and cultural characteristics of all speakers. It is the flexibility and choice offered by various contexts of conversation that distinguish social construction from other models (McElhinny, 2003).

Critique. The social constructionist model's reliance on the context of conversations and the impression management individuals practice in specific contexts makes it difficult to generalize explanations for gendered language to other settings. Contrary to symbolic interaction, such nonverbal exchanges correlate with research suggesting that the harmful effects of stereotypes cannot be completely overcome with individual attempts at impression management (Riordan et al., 1994). To effectively attack such stereotypes, all social institutions at both the micro and macro levels must be part of the effort.

THE IMPACT OF LINGUISTIC SEXISM

We have seen that language subtly, and not so subtly, transmits sexist notions that are harmful to both men and women. Language influences our perceptions of what is proper, accepted, and expected. When we hear the words *man* and *he*, we conjure up male images. When *she* is associated with nurses and homemakers, men are linguistically excluded. Alternative images remain unexpressed because they remain unimagined. Language supports a powerful "nonconscious ideology" (Bem and Bem, 1970).

Research plainly shows that ambiguous interpretations of masculine generics not only bias cognitions but differentially affect the self-esteem of people who read, hear, and use them. Those who use sexist language in written form are also likely to use it in oral form. During primary socialization, boys internalize masculine generics that they apply to their expanding environment. Their own sense of well-being is linked to that environment. When girls begin to expand their environments, they have no such set of referents. They must adopt symbols that are different and separate from the symbols used to identify people in general.

Language learning also produces a double bind for women who are socialized into believing they must speak politely and refrain from "man talk." Women's language is associated with maintaining femininity. But because female register may deprecate, ignore, and stereotype women, they regularly internalize beliefs that they are lesser persons. Research on sexist remarks and jokes made by men suggests that women respect women when they confront the person who made the remark, but that men did not like being confronted. The typical responses to women who express their dislike of being the targets of profanity and degrading sexual humor are: "Can't you take a joke?" and "Don't take it personally." With the negative repercussions that come with confrontation, women may believe silence is justified

(Gallivan, 1999; Dodd et al., 2001). Language learning for girls may be the counterpart for the difficulty boys often experience in gaining a sense of their identity from incomplete information they are offered during primary socialization (chapter 3). In either case, the socialization road is not easy.

Toward Language Change

The evidence that sexist language creeps into our perceptions and does damage to both men and women is strong. Yet despite this evidence, people who would fervently work on other gender issues, such as equal pay or violence toward women, are mystified or even angry at calls to change language to make it more inclusive. Similar to the type of ridicule that came about when *Ms.* was introduced, media reports tell us that *he* is now a loaded word and that no one

> dares to show insensitivity to gender-neutral terminology in public, with people preferring to offend against rules of grammar rather than against women's sensibilities. Women should not be insulted but should remember that gender may be unrelated to sex in language. (*Economist*, 2001:20).

In this condemnation, rules of grammar are more important than how they are used against people, and women are denied any emotional response by being told how they are supposed to feel about the issue. Those who advocate for gender inclusive language are often labeled "politically correct" in the media. The label sarcastically implies that people are required to change acceptable terminology on frivolous, inconsequential, and unreasonable grounds.

Attempts to introduce language change are also resisted when changes are viewed as artificially imposed rather than naturally evolving. Examples from linguistic history counter this argument. The use of *he* as the required pronoun for referring to a single human being of indeterminate sex came into usage during the eighteenth century in England and the United States (Curzan, 2003). Formerly, *they* or *he* or *she* were considered proper choices. The use of *they* as a plural word to identify a single entity was disdained by several powerful educators and self-styled language reformers, who were able to establish *he* as the rightful substitute. In 1850 the British Parliament passed a law declaring that "in all acts, words importing the masculine gender shall be deemed and taken to include females" (Miller, 1994:268). In both instances language change occurred by fiat, not through "natural" evolution. Although the earlier usage may not have been as grammatically sound, it was certainly more accurate. It also created a great deal of interpretive problems. Today we have a term that is presumed to be both generic (he = he and she) and nongeneric (he = he). The quick acceptance of the generic rested on cultural definitions that gave males more worth than females. In order to make language gender-neutral today, it is necessary to challenge the taken-for-granted belief that males are regarded more highly than females. Such challenges are met with resistance.

On the positive side, gradual but steady progress in efforts to make language more gender equitable is occurring in written and oral forms as well as nonverbally. Recognition of the harm of sexist language is widespread. At the macro level, people are expressing more support to use inclusive language in government, schools, and media. Teachers are using exercises to highlight the impact of linguistic sexism and are selecting student reading material with inclusive language in mind. Organizations, professions, and academic disciplines are adopting inclusive language standards in their style guides, publications, and presentations (Hayes, 2000; Matthews, 2000; Butt, 2001). Media may be at the vanguard of these efforts:

> . . . to boldly go where no man has gone before.
>
> —Capt. James T. Kirk, *Star Trek*

> . . . to boldly go where no one has gone before.
>
> —Capt. Jean-Luc Picard, *Star Trek, The Next Generation*

> . . . I don't like being called "sir". . . I prefer "Captain."
>
> —Capt. Kathryn Janeway, *Star Trek, Voyager*

At the micro level, although gender differences cut across context, on many verbal and nonverbal behaviors, girls and boys are more alike than different. Gender differences in conversational topics persist but are getting smaller over time. The language of consensus and cooperation is moving into the workplace; its benefit for both employee satisfaction and company profit is increasingly recognized. Men are displaying more self-disclosing nonverbal behaviors, such as hugging another man as a greeting rather than using the mechanical handshake of the past. Media portrayals of men support this contention. Watch a night of Jay Leno or David Letterman as confirmation. Such behaviors are approved by both men and women and contribute to man's sense of well-being (Bischoping, 1993; Kolaric and Galambos, 1995).

As the world changes to accommodate newer, egalitarian gender roles, language needs to reflect the changes. There appears to be slow but steady movement in this direction.

Summary

1. Research shows that the generic use of words such as *man* and *he* is ambiguous, discriminatory, and inaccurate. Inclusive replacements are suggested to counter this usage.

2. Linguistic sexism in titles and occupations abounds. Children often use linguistic gender markers, such as lady spaceman, when they see a mismatch between what they see and what they perceive to be true.

3. Customs about names are highly gendered. At marriage women are expected to take their husbands' last names. Children's names ensure that boys and girls are distinguished. It is common for girls to take boys or append boys' names but not the reverse.

4. There are several hundred English words that refer to women in derogatory or debased and obscene ways. Over time words for women that were originally neutral acquire debased references.

5. People use language according to gendered registers. Females use a register with more qualifiers, tag questions, intensifiers, and politeness. Males use a register with more profanity, directness, and order giving. Males outtalk females and interrupt females more than females interrupt males. These patterns are largely taken for granted by both men and women.

6. Conversational strategies for females are high affiliation ones used for intimacy, rapport, and to cement friendship. Conversational strategies for males are low affiliation ones to get demands met. If romance is a factor in mixed-gender conversations, men initially outtalk women, but later men talk less and use silence as a control mechanism.

7. In nonverbal communication females rely on facial information and decode emotions much better than males, even when males display less facial expressiveness. Females smile more and are allowed to display sadness and fear but not anger. Males can display anger more, but not sadness and fear.

8. Men touch women more than women touch men, and women are touched more than men overall. Men invade the personal space of women more than the reverse. Men are provoked when other men come as close to them as they do to women.

9. The language of Japanese women is a separate social dialect that differs by vocabulary, topics, grammar, and phonology. It is so highly formal and polite that women are often defined as being timid and lacking self-confidence. However, women are adapting linguistic strategies to counter these images, especially patterns outside the home.

10. The dual-culture model of language is compatible with functionalism and asserts that the language styles of males and females are separate but equal. The dominance model is compatible with conflict theory and asserts that gendered language reflects women's subordinate status. The social constructionist model focusing on the context of conversation is compatible with symbolic interaction by showing how language shapes perception of reality.

11. Language transmits sexist notions but people often resist changing language to counter sexism. Gradual progress is being made, however, to make language more gender equitable.

Key Terms

dominance model 89   nonverbal communication   register 81
dual-culture model 89   84

Critical Thinking Questions

1. With reference to the gender patterns of generics, titles, naming, derogation, and registers, demonstrate how language is a potent agent of gender role socialization. Which sociological theory do you think best accounts for these patterns? Justify your choice.

2. Explain how both gendered verbal and nonverbal language cement relationships between women but inhibit close relationships between men. How can gender socialization provide more opportunities for crossing the linguistic boundaries important for bringing men and women together?

3. How can sociological and linguistic perspectives (dominance, dual culture, social constructionist) combine to explain gendered verbal and nonverbal language?

WESTERN HISTORY AND THE CREATION OF GENDER ROLES

CHAPTER 5

Men have had every advantage of us telling their own story. Education has been theirs in so much higher a degree; the pen has been in their hands.

—Jane Austen, *Persuasion*, 1818

Echoing Jane Austen's sentiments, in 1801 an anonymous author wrote in the *Female Advocate*, an American publication: "Why ought the one half of mankind, to vault and lord it over the other?" Reflecting an egalitarian model far ahead of its time, these writers identified a critical need to explore the other half of humankind. Distinguished historian Gerda Lerner extends this message to contemporary scholars. She suggests that the recognition that women had been denied their own history "came to many of us as a staggering flash of insight, which altered our consciousness irretrievably" (Lerner, 1996:8). This insight reverberated throughout the academy, and as a result, the field of women's history rapidly expanded.

It is impossible to understand the present without reference to the past. Historians say that they search for a "usable past," for a record that will clarify and give meaning to the present (Carlson, 1990:81). In order to explain the differential status of women and men in contemporary society, it is necessary to examine the impact of powerful historical forces creating gendered attitudes. Only recently has scholarly work started to scrutinize the past with the goal of uncovering the hidden elements of a woman's history. As we shall see, such a history is vastly different from centuries of discourse that highlighted the proper roles of women in society.

These discourses date back to the earliest writings of the Greek philosophers and center on debates about women's place, women's souls, and women's suitability for domestic functions. Writings of this type were used, and often continue to be used, to justify a patriarchal status quo. What is clear is that the centuries of debate on "women's themes" do not constitute a women's history. As pioneer women's historian Mary Ritter Beard asserts, in the 2,500 years history has been written, most male writers overlooked the histories of females. In historical writing, the whole of human experience has been dominated by the political, economic, and military exploits of an elite, powerful group of men. Through the historical glimpses in this chapter, we will find that throughout history women have assumed a multitude of critical domestic and extradomestic roles, many of which were previously ignored or relegated to inconsequential historical footnotes.

PLACING WOMEN IN HISTORY

The revitalized women's movement of the 1960s provided the catalyst for the independent field of women's history to emerge. Although there is general agreement as to what is *not* women's history, scholars do not agree on what the approach, content, and boundaries of the field should or must include. There is broad consensus, however, that because women and men experience the world around them in qualitatively different ways, the starting point must be on those very experiences. Women's history asks why women have a profoundly different historical experience than men.

Because women have essentially been left out of historical writing the first attempts at reclaiming their historical place centered on combing the chronicles for appropriate figures to demonstrate that female notables of similar authority and ability to males existed. If there was Peter the Great, there was also Katherine the Great. Referred to as **compensatory history**, this approach chronicles the lives of exceptional, even deviant, women and does not provide much information about the impact of women's activities to society in general. Another track is **contribution history**, documenting women's contributions to specific social movements. Their activities, however, are judged not only by their effects on the movement but also by standards defined by men. Lerner suggests that we can certainly take pride in the achievements of notable women, but these kinds of histories do not describe the experience of the masses of women who still remain invisible to the historical record.

Both compensatory and contribution history parallel historical standards that, until recently, also ignored society's nonelites—the men and women of classes and races defined as marginal to society. Such groups are now being historically rediscovered, with the notion that an inclusive approach to the past must account for their lives and cultures. The "usual way of doing history is incomplete" and since "the male world is the point of reference for traditional history females become peripheral" (Carlson,1990:79). A balanced history makes visible women and other marginalized groups and, in turn, affirms their identity.

The Gender, Race, and Class Link in History

Another critical factor in approaching history is the inevitable gender/ race/class link. If a women's history emerges from the notion of patriarchy and the dynamics leading to the power of men over women, it glosses over the power relations between women due to social class and race. Despite the fact that the relation of gender to power is the foundation of women's history, African-American women historians are reluctant to use a gender based male/female dichotomy that falsely homogenizes women. Finding it impossible to separate gender, race, and class, this perspective cautions us that claims to a homogeneous womanhood remain unconfirmed for women of different races, regions, socioeconomic backgrounds, and sexual orientations. Related to this is the concern that when the historical experiences of women of color become chronicled, they may be acknowledged according to race, yet within another dichotomy—people of color versus white. Other elements, however, are still missing. A multicultural framework also should be adopted because it explores simultaneously the interplay of many races and cultures and provides what may be the only way to organize a truly inclusive history of women (Ruiz and DuBois, 1994). As women's history becomes both more sophisticated and mainstreamed, feminist scholars must account for all these dimensions.

Historical Themes about Women

It is impossible to provide a full historical reckoning of women's history in this chapter. The intent here is to offer an overview of key historical periods important in influencing attitudes and subsequent behavior concerning the genders. The focus of this chapter is Western society and the paths that lead to the gender roles of American women and men. This history will illustrate the impact of **misogyny**, the disdain and hatred of women, that propels their oppression. This reflects the first of two important themes of women's history to be overviewed. The first is the theme of patriarchy, and it relates to the power of men over women and the subjection and victimization of women. This theme is central to all feminist scholarship on women, regardless of discipline.

Countering the women as victim approach, the second theme explores the resistance of women to patriarchy, focusing on stories of courage, survival, and achievement. This alternative view indicates that although women's history is still unfolding, it has issued a formidable challenge to traditional thinking on gender roles. Feminist historical scholarship has challenged gendered dichotomies, not only related race and class, but also to nature versus nurture, work versus family, and private versus public spheres of men and women (Bock, 2003). Similar to feminist scholarship in sociology, this theme reflects interdisciplinary elements in the field of *social history*. This field employs theories and methods of sociology to understand the linkage between social and historical patterns. I suggest an additional dichotomy— unicultural versus multicultural. This dichotomy reflects the second theme and considers how gender—race—class links to other cultural components, such as region and religion. Culture is used in the broadest sense to highlight diversity and to provide for more inclusiveness in women's historical record. Many of these cultural components will be explored from a global perspective in chapter 6.

This approach has several objectives. First, the roots of patriarchy will be discovered in a format that is manageable. Second, misconceptions about the roles of women and attitudes toward these roles will become evident. These misconceptions are often at the root of current debates about gender and social change. Third, it is a history of "most women," a massive group whose contributions to their societies and whose response to the multiple oppressions they faced have been historically ignored. This is the perspective of social history, in that it addresses social change by connecting larger social structures with everyday life and experiences (Elliott, 1994:45). Finally, this overview has a consciousness-raising objective. A discovery of an alternative historical account allows us to become aware of our culturally determined prejudices and stereotypes. *Her* story allows for a balance to the historical record.

CLASSICAL SOCIETIES

The foundation of Western culture is ultimately traced to the Greek and Roman societies of classical antiquity. Western civilization is rooted in the literature, art, philosophy, politics, and religion of a time that extends from the Bronze Age (about 3000 to 1200 B.C.W.) through the reign of Justinian (565 C.E.). The period between 800 B.C.E. and 600 C.E. witnessed spectacular achievements for humanity. With the achievements came ideological convictions that persist in modified form today. The dark side of classical societies was laced with war, slavery, deadly competitions, and a brutal existence for much of the population. Inhabiting another portion of this cordoned-off world was democracy, literacy, grace, and beauty. These opposites serve as a framework from which to view the role of women. Like the societies themselves, the evidence concerning women's roles is also contradictory. This contradictory evidence must be viewed in light of the fact that no authentic historical voice of classical woman survived into the Renaissance (Spongberg, 2002). What we know about women and gender relationships in these societies is almost entirely from sources written by men.

The Glory That Was Greece

The Greek view of women varies according to the time and place involved. Greek literature is replete with references to the matriarchal society of Amazons. Though shrouded in mystery, Greek mythology saw the Amazons as female warriors, capable with a bow, who had little need of men except as sexual partners. Greek heroes were sent to the distant land on the border of the barbarian world to test their strength against the Amazons. Because the Amazons invariably lost and eventually were raped by, or married to, the heroes sent to defeat them, some feminist historians suggest these myths reinforce historical ideas that patriarchy is inevitable. Too much evidence exists to dismiss the stories outright (Kleinbaum, 1990). We know that throughout Asia Minor and the Mediterranean during this period there are innumerable references to physically strong women who were leaders and soldiers. The admiration for the skills of these warrior women is used to support the belief that ancient Greek women were held in higher esteem than women of later times.

Partnership. Archaeological material from the Neolithic to the Early Bronze Age period immediately predating the birth of Greek civilization provides substantial evidence of matrilineal inheritance, the sexual freedom of women, the goddess as supreme deity, and the power of priestesses and queens (Gimbutas, 1991). Some contend that these ancient societies show neither matriarchy nor patriarchy as the norm. In this view, the inference that if women have high status, then men must inevitably have low status does not necessarily follow. A generally egalitarian or partnership society is also possible.

The egalitarian zenith was reached in the goddess-worshipping culture of Minoan Crete. It is defined by cultural historians as a high civilization because of its art, social complexity, peaceful prosperity, and degree of technological sophistication. The social structure of Minoan Crete conformed to a partnership model, with a key part of that partnership a free and equal sexual relationship between men and women (Eisler, 1988, 1995). At the birth of civilization women enjoyed more freedom, including sexual freedom, and less restraint on their modesty. Interaction and unity rather than separation and isolation were the gender norms of the time (Stikker, 2002). Analysis of the mythology of such cultures pointing to the absence of warfare, private property, class structure, violence, and rape would support this kind of model (Judd, 1990). Referred to as the Golden Age, the mythology bolsters the view of a society where stratification based on gender was largely unknown. Evidence from the Amazonian myths through to Minoan Crete does not necessarily suggest that matriarchy existed, but it does suggest plausible alternatives to patriarchy. Claims about women's power in prehistory remain contentious (Eller, 2000). Some claim that that patriarchy is inevitable today because it was inevitable throughout history. Regardless of historical accuracy, however, images of women in powerful, respected roles, and of men and women working together as partners prove empowering to all women (Lane and Wurts, 1998).

Over time, a matrilineal system tracing descent from the female line was replaced by a patrilineal system. As documented in chapter 12, the goddesses who dominated the ancient world lost their central position as gods were added to religious imagery. The earlier maternal religion lost its ascendance as patriarchal theology was grafted onto it. Patriarchy eventually prevailed. Patriarchy did not completely dislodge the revered goddess from later Greek mythology. Religion was the main realm where the women of ancient Greece maintained a degree of power and prestige.

Oppression. The Amazon legends and goddess images helped perpetuate the idea that Greece revered women. But except for religion, most of the Greek world saw women as inferior in political, social, and legal realms. Plato called for girls to be educated in the same manner as boys with equal opportunities open to them to become rulers, believing that a superior woman was better than an inferior man. In the *Republic* he stated, "There is not one of those pursuits by which the city is ordered which belongs to women as women, or to men as men; but natural aptitudes are equally distributed in both kinds of creatures." Alongside his supposed enlightened image of women, however, is Plato's disdain and antipathy of women. In championing the democratic state, Plato was a pragmatist as well as a misogynist. He believed an inferior class of uneducated women might work against the principles of democracy, so he appeared to champion the emancipation of women. Women may "naturally participate in all occupations," Plato continues, "but in all women are weaker than men." Women were excluded from his academy and no women speak in his dialogues. Indeed, women's sexual nature could distract men from reason and pursuit of knowledge so men and women must exist in separate worlds. In the end Plato's emancipated women were likely to be illiterate, isolated, and oppressed.

It is Aristotle who is more representative of the Greek view of women. In *Politics,* Aristotle explicitly stated that a husband should rule over his wife and children. If slaves are naturally meant to be ruled by free men, then women are naturally meant to be ruled by men. Otherwise, the natural order would be violated:

> Man is full in movement, creative in politics, business and culture. Woman, on the other hand, is passive. She stays at home, as is her nature. She is matter, waiting to be formed by the active male principle.

Because the active elements of nature are on a higher level than the passive, they are more divine. This may be why Aristotle believed women's souls were impotent and in need of supervision.

Athens. The women of Athens can be described as chattels. At one point in Greek history, even a wife's childbearing responsibilities could be taken over by concubines, further lowering a wife's already subordinate status. Divorce was rare but possible. As a group, women were classified as minors, along with children and slaves. Aristotle speaks of a propertyless man who could not afford slaves but who could use his wife or children in their place. Husbands and male kin literally held the power of life and death over women. Some upper-class women enjoyed privileges associated with wealth and were left to their own devices while their husbands were away at war or serving the state. Considering the plight of most women of the time, these women achieved a measure of independence in their households only because of the absence of their husbands for lengthy periods. But Athenian repression of women was so strong, wealth could not compensate for the disadvantages of gender. From a conflict perspective, the class position of a citizen woman belonging to the highest class is determined by her gender, "by the fact that she belonged to the *class* of women" (De St. Croix, 1993:148). Her male relatives could be property owners, but she was devoid of property rights. As a woman, therefore, her class position was greatly inferior. In Marxian terms, women were an exploited class, regardless of the socioeconomic class to which they belonged.

Athenian society did not tolerate women in public places except at funerals and all-female festivals, so for the most part they remained secluded in their homes. Mourning was ritualized, and women could not express their grief in public or at the funerals they were allowed to attend (Loraux, 1998). Athenian households were segregated as well. Women had special quarters that were designed to restrict freedom of movement and to keep close supervision over their sexual activities. Supervision was so strong that evidence suggests Athens established a formal police force to monitor and protect the chastity of women (Keuls, 1993).

The few women who did become successful in this world of men were of two groups. One group consisted of those women who practiced political intrigue behind the scenes to help elevate their sons or husbands to positions of power. The second group were the *hetairai,* high-level courtesans whose wit, charm, and talent men admired. When pederasty was in vogue, men sought boys or other young men for their sexual and intellectual pleasure. It was common for a man to change his sexual preference to women after spending his youth loving boys. By the fourth century B.C.E. Athenian men "rediscovered" women, but not their wives, because they had no desire to become family men. The uneducated wives could not compete with the social skills and cultural knowledge exhibited by either the hetairai, thoroughly trained for their work since they were girls, or the sexually experienced, educated males frolicked with earlier in life (Murray, 2000). Throughout much of history, courtesans had a better life than wives.

Sparta. The subordinate position of Athenian women extended to most of the Greek world. When comparing Athens to Sparta, some differences can be ascertained. Sparta practiced male infanticide when newborns were deemed unfit enough to become warriors. Whether girls were killed is unclear. Regardless, it cannot be said that male infanticide indicated a higher regard for females in Sparta. It is significant only to the extent that Spartan society was organized around the ever present threat of war and strongly influenced the roles of Spartan women (Cartledge, 2003). If Athenian men were separated from their wives by war, the situation was magnified in Sparta. Spartan men were either at war or preparing for it. Army life effectively separated husband and wife until he reached the age of 30. These years of separation, marked by infrequent visits by their husbands, allowed wives to develop their own talents and capabilities that would have been impossible in Athens.

While the men were away, the women enjoyed a certain amount of freedom. Although the woman's responsibility was to bear male children who would become warriors, girls were also to be physically fit. Gymnastic training to promote both fitness and beauty was encouraged. Compared to women in Athens, young unmarried Spartan women enjoyed a higher degree of freedom. Euripides, an Athenian, commented on this scandalous state of affairs:

> The daughters of Sparta are never at home! They mingle with the young men in wrestling matches, their clothes cast off, their hips all naked. It's shameful! (Cited in Miles, 1989:31)

In addition to physical activities, citizen women were expected to manage the household and all the associated properties. Women retained control of their dowries and were able to inherit property. In comparison to Athens, the free women of Sparta had more privileges, if only because they were left alone much of the time. But in the context of the period as a whole, the vast majority of women existed in a legal and social world that viewed them in terms of their fathers, brothers, and husbands. Subordination and suppression of women was the rule.

The Grandeur That Was Rome

The founding of Rome by Romulus, traditionally dated at 753 B.C.E., led to an empire that lasted until it was finally overrun by invading Germanic tribes in the fifth century C.E. The Roman Empire evolved and adapted to the political, social, and cultural forces of the times and in turn influenced these very forces. Changes in gender roles mirrored the fortunes and woes of the empire. The prerogatives of women in later Rome contrasted sharply with the rights of women in the early days of the republic. It is true that women remained subservient to men and cannot be portrayed separately from the men who dominated and controlled them. But compared to the Greeks, Roman women achieved an astonishing amount of freedom.

Early Rome granted the eldest man in a family, the **pater familias**, absolute power over all family members, male and female alike. His authority could extend to death sentences for errant family members and selling his children into slavery to recoup the economic losses of a family. Daughters remained under the authority of a pater familias throughout their lives, but sons could be emancipated after his death. Even after marriage, the father or uncle or brother still had the status of pater familias for women, which meant the husbands could exercise only a limited amount of control over wives.

The absolute authority of the pater familias may have helped women in the long run. The right of guardianship brought with it a great deal of responsibility. A daughter's dowry, training, and education had to be considered early in life. If she married into a family with uncertain financial assets, the possibility existed that she and her new family could become a continued economic liability. The pater familias exercised extreme caution in ensuring the appropriate match for the women under his guardianship. This system allowed for total power of the pater familias, but it also caused a great burden for that very power to be maintained. By the first century C.E., legislation was passed that allowed a freewoman to be emancipated from a male guardian if she bore three children. The roles of childbearer and mother were primary, but they allowed for a measure of independence later in life. Like Sparta, Rome was always involved in warfare, and a declining birth rate was alarming. The abandonment of the pater familias rule functioned to decrease the economic burden women caused for the family. Emancipation in exchange for babies was an additional latent function.

Compared to the Greeks, Romans recognized a wider role for women. In the civic realm Romans acknowledged women's productive role in the origins of the state and offered select women citizenship. Religious life still retained vestiges of goddess worship, and women shared in the supervision of the religious cult of the household. The comparative power women held in the religious life of the empire is reflected in the highly revered *Vestal Virgins,* who symbolized society's economic and moral well being. Though open only to a select few, these women took on roles of great public importance. Roman women in general, however, knew that their lives would be carried out as wives and mothers. But wives also carried out the business of the family while their husbands were on military duty. These roles gradually extended so that it became common for women to buy and sell property as well as inherit it and participate in the broader economic life of the society (Gimbutas, 1991).

Their expertise was both praised and criticized, especially as women amassed fortunes in their own names. The necessity for economic decision making led to a much less secluded lifestyle. The Greeks would have been astounded to see women in public roles and seated with men at dinner parties. Although most women remained illiterate, including upper class women who had the most independence, women had greater opportunities for learning and were taught to cultivate music, art, and dancing. These women challenged a system where they were chained to their husbands or fathers. Roman women were eventually granted the right to divorce.

Freedom is relative. Roman society allowed a few women of higher social standing privileges unheard of in Greek society. Religion was the one area where women exercised much control, but with few exceptions, religious dominance did not expand into other realms. The abhorrent misogynistic texts of the poet Juvenal are more representative of beliefs about women (McLeod, 1991). Agreeing with Aristotle and Plato, these texts warn men that women are dangerous and distracting. Women may have been important in the establishment of the Roman state, but women's evil is also represented as a cause for the decline of the Roman Empire. The emancipated woman was a rarity even in Roman times. That a sexual double standard existed is unquestionable. Women may have been more visible, but they were definitely not autonomous. Rome was a brutal, slave-based society in which a dominator model of male control over women and the control of "superior" men over "inferior men" regulated all existence at all levels, whether personal, familial, national, or international (Eisler, 1995:123). When compared to almost any free males in Rome, the most assertive, independent, and visible women were still in bondage to men.

THE MIDDLE AGES

When the Roman emperor Constantine reigned (306 and 337 C.E.), the empire was already in the throes of disintegration. Constantine's decision to wed the empire to Christianity was politically astute because Christianity seemed to offer an integrative force in a period where the empire's decline was accelerating. Constantine's foresight on the impact of Christianity was remarkable. He did not envision, however, that the collapse of Rome itself would be instrumental in allowing Christianity to gain a firm grip on Europe that lasted throughout the Middle Ages. The Renaissance and feudalism combined did not radically diminish this powerful hold. Christianity profoundly influenced the role of women. Compared to the preclassical era, women's status in the classical era markedly deteriorated. This already bleak situation was considerably worsened when Christianity dominated Europe during the Middle Ages.

Christianity

To its credit, the Church, in the form of a few monasteries and abbeys, became the repository of Greek and Roman knowledge that surely would have been lost during the sacking, looting, and general chaos following the disintegration of the Roman Empire. The decline of a literate population left reading, writing, and education as a whole in the hands of the Church. The power of literacy and the lack of literate critics permitted the Church to become the irreproachable source of knowledge and interpretation in all realms. The Church's view of life was seen as absolute.

If certain sentiments of the early Church had persisted, Christianity might not have taken on such misogynous overtones. Extending from Jewish tradition, the belief in the spiritual equality of the genders offered new visions of and to women. The ministry of Jesus included women in prominent roles, demonstrating spiritual equality in the steadfastly patriarchal society of the time (chapter 12). Also, the Church recognized that women provided valuable charitable, evangelistic, and teaching services that were advantages to the fledgling institution. Some positions of leadership in the church hierarchy were open to women and served as models for women who might choose a religious life. The convent also served as a useful occupation for some women, particularly of the upper classes, who were unsuited for marriage. It also provided a place of education for selected girls. Whereas the convent may have offered opportunities for women, the measure of independence that they achieved in becoming nuns was viewed with suspicion. Education for nuns eroded, and with more restrictions put on women's ownership of land, it was increasingly difficult to found new convents. Existing ones later came under the management of male friars. Distrust of the independent woman in Catholic Europe served to strip nuns of their autonomy, and in Protestant Europe women were left without an acceptable alternative to marriage (Weitz, 1995).

Misogyny eventually dominated as the Church came to rely heavily on the writings of those who adopted a traditional view of women. With Old Testament restrictions on women elevated, women remained excluded from the covenant community. Biblical interpretations consistent with a cultural belief of the inferiority of women and placing the blame squarely on Eve for the fall of humanity became the unquestioned norm.

Christianity also changed the attitudes about marriage and divorce. Unlike in classical society, marriage could not be dissolved. Because divorce was unobtainable, women may have benefited if only for the fact that they could not be easily abandoned for whatever transgressions, real or imagined, their husbands attributed to them. Whereas childlessness was grounds for marital dissolution throughout history, even this was no longer an acceptable cause. However undesirable the marriage, the marriage was inviolable in the eyes of the Church.

With the medieval Church as a backdrop, misogyny during the late Middle Ages created an outgrowth for one of the most brutal periods of history concerning women—the time of the witch hunts. It was the woman who deviated from gendered norms who generated the greatest distrust. If she remained unmarried, was married but childless, was regarded as sexually provocative, or was too independent or too powerful, she could be denounced as a witch (Ankarloo et al., 2002; Briggs, 2002). Women who were not economically dependent on men—husbands, fathers, or brothers—may have been higher in social class, but like their sisters in classical societies, their gender class dominated all other statuses. Money and power condemned rather than protected them from the witch hunts. The power of the Church was directly related to the poverty of the people. Women who survived economically in their paid roles as healer, midwife, and counselor were particular targets of the witch hunts. Such women were admired for their expertise and sought out by the communities in which they practiced their professions. They were transformed into witches who symbolized evil and the wrath of God (Barstow, 1994).

Female power was on trial but so was the fear of female sexuality, reinforced by Christian theology's view that sexual passion in women is irrational and potentially chaotic (Reineke, 1995). The vast majority the victims of the European witch hunts were women. It displayed an eruption of misogyny that remains unparalleled in Western history. Accused of sexual impurity and in order to appease God's anger, thousands of women were burned as witches, confessing to anything their tormentors suggested. Although confession meant death at the stake, the horrible tortures used to extract confessions were impossible to endure. It was common for women to publicly confess to such absurdities as eating the hearts of unbaptized babies and, the most used condemning confession, having intercourse with the devil (Stephens, 2002). God and the devil are enemies, and the methods of the devil worked well on weak women with evil temperaments, so burning the witch upheld righteousness and morality and claimed a victory over Satan (Kramer and Sprenger, 2000). It cannot be denied that the medieval church's attitudes about women played a prominent role in sanctioning the witch craze.

Feudalism

The feudal system was adapted to the ongoing threat of war. Serfs and their families were protected by lords, who in turn expected their serfs to fight when called upon. All serfs owed their lives to the lord of the manor, and the wives of serfs owed their lives to their husbands. The lack of respect for serfs in general and their wives in particular is indicated by a custom that allowed the lord to test the virginity of the serf's new bride on their wedding night.

Women of noble standing fared somewhat better in that they were valued for their role in extending the power of the family lineage through arranged marriages, though here, too, the lord of the manor had to grant permission for any marriage. An unmarried noblewoman was a property worth guarding, her virginity a marketable commodity, assuring the legitimacy of a male heir. Her marriage united two houses, perpetuated a lineage, and expanded the economic fortunes of both families.

At marriage the bride would be given in exchange for a dowry of money or jewelry, and in some places, the custom required her to kneel in front of her husband-to-be to symbolize his power over her. As her husband was controlled by the lord of the estate, she was to be controlled by her lord and husband. Whether serf or noble, feudal wives had much in common.

The Renaissance

The last 300 years of medieval Europe, which included the Renaissance and Reformation, were years of ferment and change that inevitably extended into the women's realms. Although more control by male religious orders was established, convents were often viewed as the sanctuaries where women could write on religious subjects, as well as be poets and dramatists. Educated aristocratic women became patrons of literature and art, many of them as authors in their own right. Notably in Italy and France, these noblewomen set the standard for patrons of the arts for the centuries to follow (Skinner, 2001). A few literate women of noble blood were accorded a certain amount of prestige for their accomplishments. But other forces were at work that kept traditional images of women from being seriously challenged.

Martin Luther and the Reformation. With the Reformation came the startling notion that a church hierarchy may actually exclude people from worship. Preaching a theology of liberation from a Church he indicted as too restrictive,

Martin Luther advocated opening Christianity to everyone on the basis of faith alone. Critical of Aquinas's view that a woman was imperfect, in essence a botched male, Luther argued that those who accused her of this are in themselves monsters and should recognize that she, too, is a creature made by God. Many women embraced Luther's justification by faith principle, but some paid a heavy price as a result. For example, Ann Boleyn was beheaded in England in her effort to introduce Protestantism; Jane Grey and Anne Askew, both who dared to criticize the Catholic mass, were tortured and executed (Zahl, 2001). The degree to which the first women embraced Protestantism for personal, political, or social justice convictions is unclear. The Reformation did appear to offer an opportunity to present different interpretations of Christianity highlighting men and women's spiritual equality that would elevate the position of women.

This was not to be the case. Luther himself presents a paradox. Women may not be "botched males," but he still believed they were inferior to men. Though woman is a "beautiful handiwork of God," she does "not equal the dignity and glory of the male" (quoted in Maclean, 1980:10). Theological statements of the time abound with themes of superior man and inferior woman. Women bear the greater burden for original sin because of Eve's seduction by Satan. God's natural order assigns women functions related to procreation, wifely duties, and companionship to men. Upsetting the natural order, such as a woman's adultery, justified her being stoned to death, but the sentence did not extend to an unfaithful husband (Karant-Nunn and Wiesner-Hanks, 2003; Mattox, 2003; Peters, 2003). As the Reformation reverberated throughout the Western world, no dramatic changes relative to the Christian image of women occurred.

The Renaissance generated the rebirth of art, literature, and music in a world that was rapidly being transformed by commerce, communication, and the growth of cities. As a force in people's lives, Christianity now competed with others, especially education. Literacy expanded to more men and some women, opening up intellectual life that had been closed to most except clergy and nobility. Women made some economic headway by working in shops or producing products in the home for sale or trade. As money replaced barter systems and manufacturing increased, a new class of citizens emerged who were not dependent on either agriculture or a feudal lord for protection.

Like other periods in history, the Renaissance presents contradictory evidence about women. The question of whether women had a Renaissance depends on the answer to other questions: Which women? Where were they located? What was their social class? Historians have scoured the 100 years (1580–1680) of this Golden Age for records of female notables, and hundreds have been discovered or rediscovered (Wiesner-Hanks, 2001; Spongberg, 2002). These records provide abundant testimonies to the intellect, talent, and stature of women poets, artists, artisans, and musicians.

Although they provide an image of the past that is affirming to women, they remain, as always, a witness to extraordinary rather than ordinary women of the day. Social history provides a more inclusive view, and from this several plausible conclusions can be drawn. The Renaissance witnessed women in more diverse roles. Many women, particularly lower-class women, migrated to the expanding cities and were employed as servants, barmaids, fishmongers, textile workers, and peat carriers, to name a few. More educated women established themselves as actresses and midwives. Although a woman was protected from financial destitution by marriage, a surplus of women in European cities such as Amsterdam may have made marriage unattainable, but less disastrous, if she was employed. Prostitution also burgeoned during this period (Kloek et al., 1994). Compared to wives and unmarried women (spinsters), widows in England enjoyed the most freedom because they could inherit property and were free to continue their husbands' businesses (Prior, 1994). But misogyny continued to govern Europe. Women who ventured outside prescribed gender roles found themselves in precarious positions, both socially and economically.

THE AMERICAN EXPERIENCE

Women's history and American social history are fundamentally intertwined, a productive association for the growth of both areas. Because social history focuses on previously neglected groups, such as minorities and the working classes, women are brought in as part of that cohort. Until recently, the interest in women was largely confined to issues related to the attainment of legal rights, such as the suffrage movement. Only in the last few decades has women's history in the United States come into its own. This new women's history issues three challenges: to reexamine gendered social relations, to reconstruct historical generalizations, and to reconfigure historical narrative (De Hart and Kerber, 2003). Similar to the new sociological paradigm based on the infusion of feminist theory, these challenges from women's history are laying the foundation for a paradigm shift in history.

The First American Women

As a prelude to this paradigm shift, women's history is bringing to the surface a range of taken-for-granted assumptions about women in America. Although it is obvious that the first American women were Native American women, this fact has been virtually ignored by historians. In those instances when it was not ignored, stereotyped and inaccurate portrayals based on European, Christian, patriarchal beliefs prevailed.

Prior to colonization, in the fifteenth and sixteenth centuries, at least 2,000 Native American languages existed. Given such tribal diversity, it is certainly difficult to generalize about the status of Native American women as a group. The archeological and historical record, the latter based mainly on diaries, letters, and some ethnographic descriptions from the period, does allow some reliable conclusions, especially for coastal and Midwestern tribes, such as the Seneca of western New York, the Algonquins distributed along the Atlantic coast, and a number of Iroquoian tribes scattered throughout the territories east of the Mississippi River.

Accounts of American Indian women during this period can be interpreted in many ways, and much of this is dependent on their particular tribe. A missionary view of American Indian women on the Eastern shores during the 1600s saw them as beasts of burden, slaves, and "poor creatures who endure all the misfortunes of life" (Riley, 1995). This led to the stereotypical and derisive "squaw" image that was perpetuated by zealous missionaries, who generally saw Native Americans as primitive savages (Fischer, 2002). This image contrasts sharply with the historical record.

Gender Role Balance. The old tribal systems were characterized by complementarity, balance, and functional separation of gender roles. Although gender segregation was the norm in most spheres of life, it provided women a great deal of autonomy, especially given the value placed on women's economic, political, and artistic skills (Kuhlmann, 1996). The success of the system depended on balanced and harmonious functioning of the whole. The work of both men and women was viewed as functionally necessary to survival, so even if a leadership hierarchy existed related to leadership, one group would not be valued or, more importantly, devalued in comparison to the other. In sociology this would be recognized as the ideal functionalist model, void of judgments that define inferiority or superiority based on the tasks performed. Many tribal units were matrilineal and matrilocal, a man living in the home belonging to his wife's family. Women were farmers and retained control over their agricultural products, feeding hungry settlers with their surpluses and influencing warfare and trade with the settlers through the power to distribute economic resources (Jensen, 1994; Perdue, 1994; Van Kirk, 2001). About 1600, the constitution of the Iroquois Confederation guaranteed women the sole right to regulate war and peace.

They were also tribal leaders, many who represented gynocratic systems based on egalitarianism, reciprocity, and complementarity. Venerated for their wisdom, women were sought as advisers and as arbitrators in tribal disputes (Trigger, 2001; Fur, 2002). The Iroquoian gynocracy was referred to as a "petticoat government" by John Adair (Allen, 1995). Among Virginia Indians, women often held the highest authority in their tribes and were recognized as such by white colonists. As noted by one historian, "the English, fresh from the reign of Elizabeth I (1558–1603), knew a queen when they saw one" (Lebsock, 1990). A European perspective based on patriarchal assumptions would, of course, envision systems using hierarchal imagery. The notion of gynocratic egalitarianism is consistent with a new angle of vision for women's history: "Only when women's vision is equal with men's vision, do we perceive the true relations of the whole and the inner connectedness of the parts" (Lerner, 1995:20).

Another significant source of authority and status for native American women was through their roles as religious leaders and healers, creating a most powerful entity when roles of shaman and war leader coincided (Joe and Miller, 1994; Woloch, 1994). Spiritual role assignments were so important that in some tribes the gods were women (Daly, 1994). In North American creation myths, women are the mediators between the supernatural and earthly worlds. Men and women sought spiritual understanding through individual quests for vision. Again, the worlds of men and women were rigidly separated. Fasting and seclusion were part of a woman's spiritual quest. Menstruating women were believed to be so powerful that they could drain the spiritual power men required for hunting. Women would withdraw to menstrual huts outside of the villages during thus time. Is this interpreted as taboo and banishment? Women probably welcomed the respite and saw it as an opportunity for meditation, spiritual growth, and the enjoyment of the company of other women (Evans, 2000). The balanced and cooperative functionalist system represented by these practices would serve to enhance gender solidarity.

Colonization and Christianity. Colonization and its accompanying Christianity were the most disruptive forces of ancient tribal patterns and, by extension, the status of women (Miller, 2002). The Iroquois Confederacy provided an image to the Europeans for a self-ruling inclusive democracy. But female participation in a democracy that was economically based on matrilineal–matrilocal clans was mystifying to them. With increased European contact, women were gradually stripped of tribal political power and economic assets, becoming more defined, hence confined, by their domestic roles. They began to look more and more like their subordinated European sisters. Christianity further eroded their powerful religious roles. The impact of Christianity on Native American women continues to be debated among historians. There is evidence from the writings of Father Le Jeune in 1633 about the tribes living on the St. Lawrence River that women were the major obstacles to tribal conversion. They resisted being baptized and allowing their children to be educated at mission schools run by Catholic Jesuits. The women were accused of being independent and not obeying their husbands, and under Jesuit influence, the men believed that the women were the cause of their misfortunes and kept the demons among them (Devans, 1996:25). This indicates that women were acutely aware that conversion to Christianity brought with it severe role restrictions.

On the other hand, New England and Puritan missionaries, specifically the Quakers, had greater success in converting women. If change was gradual and the Indians could retain key cultural elements, the belief was they would willingly accept the Christian message. This Christian Gospel did not obliterate native culture but "offered membership in God's tribe" and attracted women by "honoring their traditional tasks and rewarding their special abilities" (Rhonda, 1996). Their culture could remain simultaneously Christian and Indian. Although historians disagree on the extent of Native American women's resistance to Christianity, most scholars now accept the fact that these women had a high standing in precontact societies.

The Colonial Era

The first white settlers in America were searching for a religious freedom that had been denied expression in the Old World. The Puritans sought to practice a brand of Christianity unencumbered by bureaucratic or doctrinal traditions that they believed hampered the expression of humanity's devotion to God. As with the Reformation, religious change was advocated, but the Puritans felt such change was impossible, given the political and theological climate of England and the Old World. In challenging the old order, however, the Puritans retained traditional beliefs about women.

Gendered Puritan Life. The Christian assumption of male superiority carried easily into the New World. Males were subordinate to God as females were subordinate to males. Puritan settlements such as the Massachusetts Bay Colony extracted a high degree of religious conformity considered necessary to the well-being and survival of the community. The Puritan community existed on the basis of obedience to the civil and moral law of the Old Testament as defined by the clergy. Social harmony and order were praised; any deviation from what these clerics sanctioned was a threat to the entire social fabric (Carlson, 1990:92). What complicated this picture was that Puritanism placed spiritual power in the individual. Cultivating women's spiritual autonomy and religious development was encouraged, but only within the confines of a rigid patriarchal family structure. In 1637 Anne Hutchinson was banished from Massachusetts Bay for criticizing the minister's sermons, holding separate meetings for men and women who were of similar mind, and as indicated by documents from her trial, for challenging gender roles by not fulfilling her ordained womanly role.

Along with the threat of banishment, the convenient accusation of witchcraft kept potentially ambitious women in tow. An epidemic of witchcraft persecutions ravaged the Puritan colonies, fueled by images of independent and disobedient women who defied authority. The infamous Salem witch trials of 1690 to 1693 occurred when a few adolescent girls and young women accused hundreds of older women of bewitching them. Invariably the older women were viewed as aggressive and threatening, out of character with the submissive women who knew their proper place in the Puritan community. Considering that this community was strictly organized around hierarchy and order, it was easy to condemn people who did not accept biologically ordained places in this order (Hill, 2000). Family relationships of many accused witches were marked by conflict. Women were brought to court for witchcraft for "railing" at their husbands or "speaking harsh things" against them (Demos, 1996:59). Perhaps more important, there was an economic rationale to witchcraft. Many women condemned as witches had no male heirs in their immediate families and could potentially inherit larger portions of their fathers' or husbands' estates. These women were "aberrations in a society designed to keep property in the hands of men" (Karlsen, 2004). An inheritance could produce more economically independent women. Being burned as a witch was a convenient way to rid the colony of its aberrations, foil challenges to gender norms, and maintain the desired social order.

Because religion extended to all areas of life and only men could be citizens, women were denied any public expression. When married, colonial women entered a legal status known as *civil death*. Based on English Common Law the marital union meant that she could not vote, own property, sue or be sued, administer estates, sign contracts, or keep her children in the event of divorce. She had some control over property she brought to the marriage and could inherit property at the death of her husband but could not sell it. Marriage was sacrosanct, but divorce was possible, particularly in cases of adultery or desertion. These arrangements ensured family harmony and prevented the community from taking over the responsibility of destitute women. The community was divided into public and domestic spheres. Though women had essential tasks in the domestic area, Puritan men still controlled both spheres.

The other side of the picture saw Puritan men being required not only to provide for the economic and physical needs of the family, but also to love their wives. The revolutionary idea that love and marriage must be connected was historically significant because until this time marriage was simply seen as an economic necessity (chapter 7). If the couple happened to love one another, so much the better. The ideal family was patriarchal, and marriage, although based on love, fit into a family power structure that required a wife's obedience to her husband.

Puritan women were also valued because they were so scarce. Most settlers were male, and because many colonies were literally wiped out by disease or starvation, the colonists knew that it was vital to repopulate or see their religious visions doomed. Besides providing domestic services and children, women were deemed essential to build a foundation for a stable social order. Though wives were valuable, when it came to starvation, patriarchy prevailed, as the following excerpt from a Jamestown, Virginia, historical record documents.

> And one amongst the rest did kill his wife, powdered (salted) her, and had eaten part of her before it was known, for which he was executed, as he well deserved. Now whether she was better roasted, boiled, or cabonadoed (grilled), I know not, but of such a dish as powdered wife I never heard of. (quoted in Frey and Morton, 1986:40)

Women were important for their economic productivity within the family. Family survival, hence community survival, was tied to the efforts of both men and women. But planting gardens, weaving, canning, and candle and soap making contributed to the family's economic fortunes, and these tasks were largely confined to women (Applebaum, 1998; Branson, 2001). Subsistence living was the rule, but surplus products could be bartered or sold. The family was the basic social unit for the colonists, and women were integral to its well-being.

A Golden Age for Colonial Women? Historians are at odds about the prestige of women during this period. Because there were far fewer immigrant women than men, and women were considered valuable, this leads some to suggest that the colonial period was a golden age for women. Although the colonists came to the New World with patriarchal ideas, adapting to the harshness of the environment required the modification of many beliefs. Strict adherence to gender roles was impossible for survival. Women were economically productive and of necessity had to have expanded roles. Outside the home women could be found engaging in merchant, trading, and crafts functions. And although English Common Law intruded into the colonies, it was often circumvented.

If a golden age existed, it had clearly declined by the late eighteenth century. The family lost its centrality as the economic unit in society, to be replaced by a wider marketplace dominated by men. Women's work was once again confined to activities that were not income producing. Colonial women became more dependent on their families for how their lives were defined. The American economy did not allow many opportunities for women to be wage earners, and resistance increased for women, who out of necessity, more than desire, sought work in enterprises outside the family realm. The crucial element, however, is that Puritan ideology was based on the assumption of female inferiority and subordination, which was never really questioned throughout the colonial period. The colonial environment was a modified version of Old World notions about women. The thesis that between the seventeenth and nineteenth centuries a status decline occurred for women from a golden age (in the colonial period) is still contested (Lewis, 2002; Hoff, 2003; Norton, 2003). Although there may not have been a golden age, political participation and education enhanced women's autonomy during the Revolutionary era. These changes kindled public discourse on women's roles that served as a catalyst for later gender role change.

The Victorians: True Womanhood

The struggle for survival faced by the colonists gradually diminished as they prospered on farms and in shops. As judged by economic contributions to the family, a woman's productive role lessened, and she became occupied with solely domestic tasks, such as housekeeping and child rearing. By the nineteenth century her world had changed considerably. Victorian examples of womanhood made their way into magazines and novels directed toward women. Despite an undercurrent of liberal feminism that was fermenting during this period, periodicals targeted to middle-class women presented them with the ideology of domestic femininity (Cantor, 1993). More and more women achieved literacy, and what they read admonished them to subscribe to the cult of **True Womanhood** and the cardinal virtues of piety, purity, submissiveness, and domesticity. The Victorian middle class home was to be a bastion of morality, and women were glorified in the pulpit and in print as the high priestess of the home (Plante 1997, 35). These were the standards on which society would judge them and which they would judge themselves.

Tied completely to her family, the middle class woman found herself with time on her hands, a luxury not shared by her colonial sisters. The reality of idleness was transformed into gentility, an ideal for which many families strived. This gentility was accompanied by attitudes that put women on pedestals that literally made them out of reach. Women were to be protected from the harshness of the world outside the home. Protection translated to repression. Victorian femininity was equated with sexual, social, and political repression. The doctrine of separate spheres for the activities of women and men became firmly entrenched in the American consciousness.

The strength of the True Womanhood cult was generally effective in silencing many voices of feminism that were being heard in Europe and America during the Victorian era. From pulpits throughout America, women were told that happiness and power could be found in their own homes, with society being disrupted if they chose to listen to voices calling them to other spheres. Supposedly, a woman did have a choice to define her rights and roles either inside or outside the home, as attested to by the Rev. Mr. Stearns:

> Yours is to determine whether the beautiful order of society. . . shall continue as it has been (or whether) society shall break up and become a chaos of disjointed and unsightly elements. (Welter, 1996:122)

The Victorian era conjures up images of rigidity and repression that cannot be denied, but explorations into women's history are providing alternative views. Karen Lystra (1989) demonstrates that middle-class Victorian America exhibited marked sexual expression and erotic intensity through the private correspondence of lovers. Her analysis of this intimate correspondence from the perspective of Victorian social conventions is sociologically a symbolic interaction approach. Romantic love and sexual expression flourished at a time when public prudery was the norm. Though hidden, this intimate reality is also culturally significant. "The system of ideas and behavior commonly referred to as romantic love provided one significant means of integrating private and public worlds" (Lystra, 1989:6).

Because one's true self was disclosed in this correspondence, it can be argued that women gained a sense of mastery not allowed in other parts of their lives.

Other historical research confirms that women exercised active control in adapting conditions of their domestic, sexual, and intellectual lives to meet their personal needs and to work toward the social justice causes they embraced (Thompson, 1999; Passet, 2003). Although the patriarchal family remained firmly entrenched and basic gender inequities intruded into domestic life, Victorian women were able to achieve a modicum of autonomy. Gender role segregation produced gender solidarity, which was nurtured by the emotional segregation of men and women. This allowed for the existence of a female world in which a supportive, intimate network of female friendships and intimacy could grow. This secretive world created an autonomous female culture serving to empower women (Smith-Rosenberg, 1996). Contemporary functionalism would suggest that a focus on the rigidity associated with the Victorian era and the True Woman model overlooks the latent functions these very patterns served for women.

Frontier Life

Idleness was impossible on the frontier. Victorian America extolled the gentility and supposed frailness of middle class women. Frontier society would have been disdainful of these very traits. As with the colonial era, women were valued for their work both inside and outside the home. During the early frontier expansion, women were scarce, yet colonial society never seriously questioned the notion of woman's inferiority; hence, her relative status remains unclear. Through the hardship and deprivation of frontier life combined with less adherence to religious proscriptions concerning gender, it is evident that the pioneer woman achieved a higher degree of freedom and respect unlike in previous periods of America's brief history.

The frontier experience began with the grueling trip west, which often took six months to complete. Faced with the deprivation of the trail, surviving the trip meant that the normal gender division of labor was suspended, with both women and older children filling expanded roles. Rather than viewing the situation as an opportunity for male–female equality, diaries from these women suggest that they saw themselves as invaders of a male domain. Although few women who emigrated west on the Oregon or Overland Trails came from the northeastern middle classes where the cult of True Womanhood reached its zenith, they were not immune to it either. In the journey west, women and men maintained separate worlds of existence as much as possible. Women created a specific female culture based on their roles of mother, healer, and nurse. Compared to men, however, trail life precluded sustained interaction and deep attachments to other women (Faragher, 1996:207). Whereas men used the trip to fulfill dreams of "camaraderie, action and achievement," many women found the experience lonely and isolating.

Life on the trail and later settlement in the West threw their domestic roles in a state of disarray, but women appeared reluctant to redefine their boundaries to create anything but a temporary alteration of affairs. Although women often shared work and had overlapping functions with their fathers and husbands, gender remained the key variable in determining their duties and interests and kept them focused on their domestic lives.

It is not safe to conclude, however, that frontier women were passive. They exhibited a spirit of nonconformity, adventure, and extraordinary adaptation. Frontier settlements saw the necessity of woman's labor not being confined to the home. The Homestead Act of 1862 propelled women to own and establish farms independently of fathers or husbands or to maintain their farms as widows (Lindgren, 1996). Child rearing was often left to siblings as wives worked in the fields. Subsistence farming required that as many goods as possible be produced and consumed within the home. Women took the major responsibility in this area. Isolated farms, prairie loneliness, and the daily harshness of frontier living generated the understanding that men and women, wives and husbands, depended on one another for physical and emotional survival. Both prior to and after the Civil War, African-American men and women also trekked west, carving out new lives on frontier farms they purchased. In their struggle to eke out new lives on remote farms dotting the western landscape, African-American women and white women shared much in common (Jeffrey, 1998). These experiences served to elevate the status of women. Popular images of women as saints in sunbonnets, madonnas of the prairies, and pioneer mothers abounded during the era of westward expansion as well as accounts of the deprivation, ardor, and premature aging associated with frontier life (Riley, 1995). Diaries and letters of pioneer women demonstrate that Victorian domesticity and compliance existed side by side with new roles, ultimately challenging this compliance.

Accounts of women who emigrated to the Kansas frontier during the latter part of the nineteenth century provide testimony to these critical roles. In her diary a daughter recalls the birth of her brother on a day when her father was away. Her mother was alone with two babies, no neighbors, and no doctor, when the stork arrived.

> So my brave mother got the baby clothes together on a chair by the bed, water and scissors. . . drew a bucket of fresh water from a sixty-foot well; made some bread-and-butter sandwiches; set out some milk for the babies. . . .So at about noon the stork left a fine baby boy. . . .My mother, having fainted a number of times in her attempt to dress the baby, had succeeded at last; and when my father came in he found a very uncomfortable but brave and thankful mother, thankful that he had returned home with the precious wood, and that she and the baby were alright. (cited in Stratton, 1981:87)

Such accounts are characteristic rather than exceptional. They speak of women who, with their families, endured prairie fires, locusts, droughts, disease, and the ever-present loneliness. Most did not return to their homes in the East, but accepted their new life with stoicism and a hope for making their own farm an economic success. Through hundreds of excerpts from diaries, letters, and oral histories, a number of writers have provided a picture of matter of fact women who adapted to and thrived in their frontier existence.

The intent is not to idealize the brutal existence many pioneer women confronted. It is only to point out that adversity was apparently an important ingredient in bringing men and women together more equitably on the frontier, even if the participants themselves did not acknowledge the altered gender roles.

Industrialization

An interesting incongruity in American history is that as the cult of domesticity gained ascendance, the first mass movement of white women into industrial employment was also occurring. From the founding of the United States, women have always participated in the world of paid labor and were not completely circumscribed by their domestic roles. When teachers or shopkeepers or planters or traders were needed and men were unavailable, women were encouraged to fill these roles. Industrial expansion during the nineteenth century required an entirely new class of workers. Faced with a shortage of males who continued to farm, industrialists convinced women that, although they were too weak for agriculture, work in the mills could suit their temperaments, was good for them, and was good for the nation. For the less marriageable, factory work saved them from pauperism. The Civil War and its aftermath accelerated the need for women in industry. Thousands of women and many children answered the call.

By the latter part of the century, the shift from an agricultural to an urban industrialized economy in the nation was accelerating. New definitions of work recognized that the family was no longer a critical unit of production and that work was to be performed for wages at other locations outside home and farm. By the turn of the century, agriculture required less than 10 percent of America's labor power, with 20 percent of all women in the United States over the age 16 employed outside the home (Balanoff, 1990:611). These women were young, single, or the wives and daughters of working-class families, whose income was necessary to keep the family out of poverty. Married women worked only out of dire necessity, often driven into the labor market by widowhood.

It was the middle class married woman who was expected to devote her time and talents to the emotional well-being of the family. This was happening at the very time when labor-saving products and appliances began to be introduced to the home. By 1900, the realization that housework and child care were no longer a full-time occupation led to more leisure, boredom, and restlessness for women who were, however, discouraged from seeking paid employment outside the home. This led to two important results. First, many middle class women became involved in social reform work, including the growing feminist movement. Second, the already existing schism between working-class and middle class women widened. As we shall see, to date this schism has not been completely mended.

Working class women were confronted with different issues. Industrial growth increasingly demanded an abundance of cheap labor and looked to poorer women and immigrants to take on this load. The rapidly urbanizing eastern states accommodated the flood of immigrants who settled in areas close to the factories, mines, and mills in which they worked, often creating a ghettolike atmosphere that cut them off from wider society. By the beginning of the twentieth century, 25 percent of unmarried immigrant women worked outside the home in comparison to 15 percent of native-born women, with immigrant women overrepresented in unskilled labor activities (Banner, 1984:61). African American women worked on farms and as domestics because factory labor was, for the most part, closed to them in the North. In the South, an oversupply of African American female labor made their position worse.

The working conditions faced were appalling, even by the standards of the day. Unsanitary conditions, no rest breaks, rules against sitting down, fifty-five hour, six-day workweeks, and grueling, rote tasks were characteristic. In combination with an unsafe environment in which machines had no safety guards and buildings were poorly ventilated and lacked fire escapes, it is understandable why job-related injuries and deaths skyrocketed. In 1911, the Triangle Shirtwaist Company in New York caught fire, killing 146 workers, many of them women. Doors were kept locked so that workers could be inspected before they left for possible possession of company merchandise, and what fire escapes were available were in need of repair and buckled under the pressure of those fleeing the fire (Stein, 2001). The owners of the factory, accused of locking the doors, were tried on manslaughter charges but acquitted. Civil suits brought by relatives of 23 victims ended with payments of $75 to each family (Kaufman, 1999).

The garment industry was notorious in its treatment of lower-level workers. A system of subcontracting finishing work to people, primarily immigrant women, became common. Women would work in what came to be called sweatshops, in basements and workrooms of low-rent tenement apartments, thereby saving the company much in the way of production costs (Banner, 1984:67). What made an already dismal situation worse was that it was necessary for workers to purchase their own equipment, which would then require years of arduous labor to pay off.

When men and women were employed in the same factories, women took less prestigious jobs and were paid less. Men resisted being employed with women in the same job. The fact that the genders were segregated by type of activity led to a stratification system that justified the lower wages paid to women. Women rarely resisted the system because they moved in and out of the labor force at the discretion of others. Because both women and their employers viewed employment as temporary, gender segregation of jobs not only perpetuated low wages but also kept women out of training programs and demands for job-related benefits (Kemp, 1994:157). The nineteenth-century roots of gender typing in jobs has carried over to contemporary debates about comparable worth (chapters 10 and 14).

The Union Movement. The Triangle fire also ignited massive protest over the scandalous conditions under which people worked, generated much sympathy nationally, and created a ripe atmosphere for unions to flourish (Von Drehle, 2003). The major growth period occurred from the 1870s through World War I. Union activist Mary Harris ("Mother") Jones reported on the horrendous plight of women and children in industry,

> condemned to slave daily in the washroom (of breweries) in wet shoes, and wet clothes . . . in the vile smell of sour beer, lifting cases . . . weighing from 100 to 150 pounds.

In 1881 the **Knights of Labor** was opened for women and African Americans calling for equal pay for equal work. In 1885, 2,500 women members of the Knights of Labor endured a six-month strike marked by violence in Yonkers, New York, at a mill where they worked as carpet weavers. The International Ladies' Garment Workers Union (ILGWU) gained recognition in many shops as a result of a strike that lasted through the winter of 1909 and involved 20,000 mostly female shirtwaist workers (Wolensky et al., 2002). With the support of the Women's Trade Union League and public outrage from the Triangle fire, legislation was passed requiring more stringent safety and inspection codes for factories.

Compared to the union movement involving men, women's attempts to unionize were not nearly as successful. Union efforts were not supported by a broad spectrum of people, including the police and courts. Many unions still refused to admit women, and even with an official policy urging equal pay to women, the most powerful union, the American Federation of Labor (AFL), was unwilling to exert the pressure necessary for its affiliates to conform to the rule. The AFL was also becoming a union of skilled crafts workers made up exclusively of men, and there was fear that the success of the union would be diluted if it took on the numerous women still in the ranks of the unskilled. Originally welcoming women as members, a period of economic recession saw members of the Knights of Labor competing with one another for scarce jobs. In 1895, only 5 percent of all union members were female, and by 1900 only 3 percent of all women who worked in factories were unionized. The ILGWU had become the third largest affiliate of the AFL by 1913, and it did capitalize on the power that was being wielded by the AFL itself. But because men and women were segregated by job, the unions representing women had less success. Unionization was obstructed by men's fears of job competition and the tenacious belief that women's place was in the home (Kessler Harris, 1991). By 1900, women represented half the membership of unions in five industries (women's clothing, gloves, hats, shirtwaist and laundry, and tobacco), and they earned about half of what men earned; African-American women earned half of what was earned by white women.

The characteristics of the female labor force also made unionization efforts difficult. Work for women was unstable, temporary, and subject to economic ups and downs. In jobs performed by both genders, men were given preference in slack periods and women were laid off. Young women worked until marriage, which was the preferred exit out of the factories and into a middle-class lifestyle. Although they did provide opportunities for women to develop leadership skills and agendas representing their own interests, unions of women workers tended to be small, more isolated, and financially weak. Overall, unions were most helpful to women when they were allowed to join with men.

Women advance more in the labor force during periods of growth as well as in periods of war. During the Civil War women served as nurses, clerks, and copyists and produced uniforms and munitions. World War I also saw an expansion of job opportunities both in Britain and the United States. Government campaigns to rally support for war, its supply needs, and women's labor force participation have been seen throughout American history. World War I was also the first war where women in America and Europe were actively recruited for military service. After the war British women who had worked in engineering; on buses, railways, and trams; in the services; and in government offices were dismissed and expected to return home. Those who persisted on jobs were often labeled as hussies or as women who stole men's jobs (Beddoe, 1989:3). Such statements were also echoed in the United States. Public support for the war effort made the transition to the labor force easier for women who, if they had a choice, had not considered working outside the home. In most instances women were summarily dismissed after the men returned.

Although women who ventured outside the home were caught in conflicting roles, it is apparent that both industrialization and war were the catalysts for creating the "new woman" of the 1920s. Lamenting the demise of the True Woman, her new counterpart was both hailed and damned as she strove for equality with men. She "entered the 1920s with high expectations, ready for challenge and for choice" (Brown, 1987:30–31,47). The flapper era saw a loosening of sexual and social restraint. Searching for independence from parents and excitement from one another, working women migrated to cities, seeking each other out in the crowded boarding houses in which they lived. These furnished rooms created new peer-oriented subcultures where women charted sexual terrain that other women later followed (Meyerowitz, 1990:150). While retaining a separate political sphere from men, many of these new women worked for social and legal change. Prosperity, hope, and the formation of an identity that included extradomestic activities led many of these women to pursue feminist causes.

The Depression. In less than a decade, much of this hope was dashed. The rule that scarce jobs should go to men first continued through the Depression. Job segregation and the belief that there was women's work and men's work ironically protected the jobs of women employed as waitresses, domestics, or clerks. Rather than accepting the loss of prestige that would be associated with doing a "woman's" job, some men abandoned their families because they were no longer breadwinners. In those instances in which a job was not defined completely in gender terms, such as teacher, it was rare to see a woman either obtain it or keep it if a man could be employed instead.

In general, industrialization saw women make steady headway in the world of paid employment. Older attitudes about women's functions in the family continued to compete with the needs of an expanding economy. But the precedent for women working outside the home gained strength and was nurtured by gradual public acceptance for newer roles. Once the industrial era established this trend, World War II provided the most important catalyst for expanding employment options.

World War II

Throughout history, war has been latently functional for social change that otherwise might not have occurred or would have occurred at a much slower pace. War suspends notions of what is considered typical or conventional and throws people into novel situations, which in turn sensitize them to an awareness of potential never dreamed possible. In addition to the impacts documented here, for example, World War II gave women the only opportunity in U.S. history to play professional baseball (Corey, 2003). Novel situations occur both on and off the actual battlefield.

As this chapter documents, by choice and necessity women have consistently taken on expanded roles in wartime. Considering, too, that the history of the world has been marked by frequent and prolonged periods of war, the roles women assumed during wartime were essential for social stability. Usually these newer roles have been short-lived, with the prewar social order swiftly reestablished when the men returned home. Although this was indeed the case with World War II, it is also true that this particular war profoundly influenced American women in unprecedented ways. The liberating effects of the war effort not only endured but also had powerful consequences for the next generation of women. The impact was seen most in the areas of employment and family.

Demand for Women's Labor. When America officially entered the war in 1941 government leaders quickly recognized that victory depended on the total commitment of the nation. One task of the Office of War Information (OWI) was to monitor public opinion to determine the degree of commitment and willingness to sacrifice for the war. Accustomed to men taking the lead in both politics and war, women were less enthusiastic about the war and less receptive to military themes and national and international events regarding the war than were men (Campbell, 1984:6–7). Because women were socialized into values related to domesticity, the war was more remote for them. Within a few months of Pearl Harbor, when patriotism was at its height, a concerted national policy to fully mobilize the civilian population in the war effort was initiated. Much of this policy was focused on women.

The powerful War Production Board (WPC) and War Manpower Commission (WMC) were set up to convert to a wartime economy, coordinate labor for the various sectors of the economy, and allocate workers for both war and civilian production. The booming wartime economy ended the Depression almost overnight. It soon became apparent to these agencies that the war machine required uninterrupted production schedules through an increased labor supply. Women were essential in filling the roles in the war production industry as the men were called into military service. An efficient propaganda program was put into effect that prompted women to respond to the employment needs of a nation at war.

The battle abroad could only be won if women would recognize their patriotic duty to become employed on the home front. After the Depression years, the higher pay and better working conditions offered in the war industry found many women eagerly seeking work in all areas. When jobs became available again, women were first hired in positions in which women had previously worked, as clerks or semiskilled laborers in factories producing uniforms or foodstuffs. The higher pay for work in defense plants enticed many women to apply for jobs, but they found themselves rebuffed.

At first defense employers were reluctant to hire women, even if it meant paying men overtime or creating shortages in production. And when plants were converted from civilian to war production, thousands of women lost their jobs and were replaced by men. Women were likely to be excluded from government training programs, although there was official acknowledgment that women could be efficient and versatile employees. If implemented over a long period, such a policy would have had disastrous consequences for the war effort.

As labor shortages reached crisis proportions job training for women and opportunities in almost all phases of defense work soared. Within six months after Pearl Harbor, employers indicated a willingness to hire women in a variety of semiskilled, professional, and managerial jobs. OWI was responsible for selling the war to women and created images of defense work as exciting, glamorous, and economically rewarding. Campaigns appealed to patriotism and guilt for slacking off when the war effort needed women. "Rosie the Riveter," popularized through a wartime song, became the new home front heroine. She represented the millions of women who worked at munitions plants, foundries, and quarries as lumberjacks, shipbuilders, and plumbers (Hill, 1997). OWI met with success in recruitment for the civilian labor force as well as for induction into the armed services. Women's corps of all branches of the military were formed during World War II, and by January 1944, over 100,000 women joined. The employment of women reached its wartime peak in July 1944, when 19 million women were employed, an increase of over 5 million from 1941.

Women's Diversity in the Labor Force. Once the gender barrier eroded, women's opportunities in the war industry flourished, with less concern about age, marital status, and race. However, preferences were still given to women who were white, single, and younger. The war allowed African American women access to employment in defense plants, which significantly decreased their reliance on agricultural and domestic labor. Employment prospects for both African American men and women were increased by defense contracts, which contained clauses prohibiting racial discrimination. However, some companies refused to hire African American women throughout the war. Labor shortages increased their numbers, but they were hired for the lowest-level jobs and, unless they were protected by a union, were paid less than either white women or African American men. The mixed feelings of this situation—patriotism and pride along with disenchantment—are poignantly expressed by an African American woman who worked in a defense plant.

> I'm not fooling myself about this war. Victory won't mean victory for Democracy—yet. But that will come later . . . maybe a hundred years later. But doing my share today, I'm keeping a place for some brown woman tomorrow. (Johnson, 1943/1996)

As the war continued and the demand for defense workers grew, the demographic balance of the female labor force shifted considerably so that both older and married women were recruited, with some industries reporting an even division between single and married workers. Near the end of the war married women outnumbered single women in the labor force.

What about the Children? The new encouragement for married women to enter the labor force challenged a society that firmly believed that a mother's place was at home with her children (Langley and Fox, 1998). By the close of the war, 32 percent of women who worked in the major defense centers had children under the age of 14. Day care centers, foster home programs, and other variations of child care were developed throughout the country. By suggesting that defense production was tied to provisions for child care, day care services increased dramatically. The Federal Works Agency administered a program that, at its height, enrolled 130,000 children in over 3,000 centers.

Rather than viewing such options as a menace to children and an indictment for their mothers, such provisions were praised for allowing mothers of younger children to enter the work force where they were sorely needed. The lure the government used was to assure mothers that their children would be well looked after. Overall, day care centers were not that abundant and were used by relatively few employed mothers, with most relying on friends and relatives for child care. Some women remained suspicious of organized day care and preferred to remain unemployed rather than believe the media campaigns. The key issue here is that when women were needed for industry, innovative strategies were developed to help them in their quest for adequate day care. Also, the suspension of traditional beliefs combined with an effective media and government propaganda program allowed a nation to view day care, at least for a time, as a virtuous and acceptable choice (Streitmatter, 1997). Mothers were working in defense plants in unprecedented numbers, but their children were not regarded as being socially, physically, or psychologically at risk as a result.

The earlier reluctance to employ any women, especially married women, for the heavy industry of war was replaced by an understanding that women could and should shoulder more of the responsibility for the war effort. But a paradox remained. The men were doing battle overseas to protect the cherished values of home and family, and yet these very values were potentially being threatened by the kinds of roles in which women found themselves. To get around this problem, another propaganda campaign suggested that women were in it only "for the duration," and they would reassume their domestic duties after the war, gladly giving up their jobs to the returning men. This would supposedly alleviate any problems of joblessness for the men. Of course, female unemployment was never an issue. Devotion to country meant the sacrifice of temporarily becoming employed for pay, with the home held up as where women would and should want to be. And to a great extent, this belief was accepted by both men and women after the war.

Peacetime. The ideal for which the war was fought—nation and family—remained unshaken. Romantic visions of resumed, postwar lives as wives and mothers abounded during the war, alongside the images of capable women working in defense plants. Hovering in the wings during the war years, the cult of the home made a triumphant comeback to entice even the most reluctant women out of the labor force. For some women who remained in the labor force, a return to prewar job segregation caused mobilization and protest. But with no fully articulated class consciousness or feminist movement to bolster them, they had no real basis for a sustained challenge to the system (Milkman, 2003).

The conversion to a peacetime economy was accelerated with soaring marriage and birth rates. Labor saving devices and technological innovations were introduced that revolutionized housekeeping but did not allow for a lessening of a woman's domestic responsibilities. Whereas the wartime media appealed to a woman's efficiency in the home to keep her productive in the defense plants, propaganda after the war concentrated on homemaking roles (Mathis, 1994) and higher standards of excellence for them. In addition, wives were made responsible for the psychological adjustment their husbands had to undergo with the return to civilian life. This meant that her needs were to be subordinated to his. Women were cautioned to be sensitive, responsive, and above all feminine because this was what civilian life meant for men.

It is clear that the new roles for women created during the war existed alongside traditional beliefs concerning their primary domestic duties. The view that World War II represented a watershed for gender role change is shared by several historians, whereas others argue that continuity and persistence of gender roles was the reality (Campbell, 1984; Kaledin, 1984; O'Neill, 1989). The women themselves were divided in their postwar plans. Although many enjoyed the work, they saw it as temporary and only for the duration of the war. Many women who gained a sense of independence from their wartime jobs were bitter when postwar cutbacks forced them out of the labor force. Single women, war widows, and those who had to support themselves anyway had no choice but to continue to work. The loss of pay and respect during the postwar years weighed heavily on many women.

The Postwar Era to the Millennium

This discussion about the impact of World War II takes us into the postwar era and the massive reentrance of women into the labor force over the next half century. This labor force trend is the foundation for much of the material in this text. Debates continue about the level of impact, but it is impossible to ignore the liberating effects of World War II on women. The war itself contributed to broad social changes in American society. The seeds of social change were planted during the war and took root in an atmosphere of economic growth. Recovery from the Depression, narrowing the gender wage gap, and urban expansion profoundly affected both women and men. Home and family remained integral to women's aspirations, but a doctrine of the spheres that had effectively separated women from any other outside existence was doomed after the war. The roots of the sociocultural trends of the 1950s and 1960s can be traced to the war years. World War II was a key catalyst in the emergence of the global economy that profoundly and irrevocably altered gender roles in all social institutions. We will see in subsequent chapters that the global economy at the millennium is linked to both advantages and disadvantages for women and their families worldwide.

Attitudes do not change as quickly as behavior. Efforts that sought to restrict the nondomestic roles and activities of women in the postwar years relied on beliefs about biological determinism that were difficult to reject. Throughout history we have seen scores of women who have successfully broadened narrow role definitions. But World War II provided models for gender role change on such a grand scale that women's accomplishments could not be conveniently relegated to a forgotten footnote in history. Contemporary women and men must contend with beliefs about biological destiny and assumptions about the proper place of the genders in their separate spheres. These beliefs bolster gendered norms and restrict opportunities for both women and men. Attitudes will inevitably erode in the face of massive evidence that contradicts these assumptions. The progress made by women during the war, coupled with rapid postwar social and economic changes, provided the framework for the reemergence of the women's movement in the United States.

THE WOMEN'S MOVEMENT

In the new code of laws . . . I desire you would remember the ladies and be more generous and favorable to them than your ancestors. (Abigail Adams, March 31, 1776)

Abigail Adams wrote to her husband John when he was attending the Second Continental Congress and cautioned him that if the ladies were ignored and denied the rights for which the Revolutionary War was being fought, they would eventually create a revolution of their own. She believed that women could not be bound by laws that they had no hand in creating. Abigail Adams persisted in her quest with additional letters to her husband and her friends. To John Adams she also wrote:

> That your sex is naturally tyrannical is a truth so thoroughly established as to admit of no dispute; but such of you as wish to be happy, willingly give up the harsh title of master for the more tender and endearing one of friend. Then put it out of the power of the vicious and the lawless to use us with cruelty and indignity and impunity . . . so whilst you are proclaiming peace and good will to men, emancipation for all nations, you insist on retaining an absolute power over wives. But you must remember that arbitrary power is like most other things which are hard, very liable to be broken.

John Adams, later to become the nation's second president, dismissed these warnings while helping to draft humanistic documents that proclaimed that all men are created equal. As he wrote to Abigail, "As to your extraordinary Code of Laws, I cannot but laugh. . . . We know better than to repeal our masculine system." For the Founding *Fathers*, the business at hand was to build the infrastructure for an enduring democracy. That this democracy denied basic rights to females, as well as to blacks, was overlooked by most. The challenges that did emerge from a few individuals, even from such influential women as Abigail Adams, did not provide the momentum for any kind of organized protest. Although Abigail Adams did accurately predict that women would themselves ferment another revolution, it took another half century before it would be actualized at all in America.

Two other events served as important ingredients for the rise of feminism and the beginnings of a women's movement in the United States. The French Revolution's ideals of liberty and equality inspired the *Declaration of the Rights of Man* in 1789. A reply by Olympe de Gouges came two years later with the *Declaration of the Rights of Woman,* where she declared that "woman is born free and her rights are the same as those of man" and that "the law be an expression of the general will" and "all citizens, men and women alike" should participate formulating such law (Bock, 2002). For the first time, humanistic standards were explicitly applied to both genders. More importantly, the democratic fervor that was sweeping France and influencing other parts of Europe and England created an atmosphere in which such radical writings were at least considered. It is likely that had such a work appeared first in America, it would have been rejected, dismissed, and buried.

Second, in 1792, English writer and activist Mary Wollstonecraft (1759–1797) wrote what was to become the bible of the feminist movement, *A Vindication of the Rights of Woman.* In this remarkable work, Wollstonecraft argued that ideals of equality should be applied to both genders, and that it is only in bodily strength that a man has a natural superiority over a woman. As she writes:

> Not only the virtue but the knowledge of the two sexes should be the same in nature, if not in degree, and that women, considered not only as moral, but rational creatures, ought to endeavor to acquire human virtues (or perfections) by the same means as men, instead of being educated like a fanciful kind of half being.

She maintained that women must strengthen their minds, become friends to their husbands, and not be dependent on them. When women are kept ignorant and passive, not only do their children suffer but also society as a whole will be weakened. In advocating full partnership with men, Wollstonecraft explicitly called for a "revolution in female manners" to make women part of the human species by reforming themselves and then the world:

> Let women share the rights and she will emulate the virtues of man; for she must grow more perfect when emancipated. . . . (Excerpts from Wollstonecraft, 1792/1970)

The Early Movement: 1830 to 1890

The Industrial Revolution radically reorganized of the process of production. By the 1830s, women found themselves working for low wages in factories under dismal conditions. When manufacturing altered home production of items such as soap, bread, candles, and clothing, middle-class women lost much economic power. Whereas factory women used unions as vehicles for organized protest, middle-class women realized that their aims could best be met through opportunities for higher education and political rights. In both instances, these women had different class-based ambitions and used divergent strategies to meet their needs. But unique to American history, they organized into their respective groups as women meeting the needs of women.

The issue of economics generated the stimulus for working-class and middle-class women to first organize. But the major catalyst for the women's movement was ostensibly humanistic in orientation and provided an outlet for mostly middle class women who had the time and money to participate in a social cause. It was only during the latter suffrage movement that more women of both classes joined together for a common goal. Before suffrage became the rallying point for women, slavery was the issue. When Wollstonecraft was calling for the emancipation of women, many women were already playing a critical role in the abolitionist movement.

It soon became apparent to the women who worked in the antislavery movement that they were not on the same political level as the male abolitionists. Women abolitionists were often not allowed to make public speeches, and with the formation of the American Anti-Slavery Society in 1833, they were denied the right to sign its *Declaration of Purposes*. When the World Anti-Slavery Convention met in London in 1840, women members of the American delegation, including Lucretia Mott and Elizabeth Cady Stanton, had to sit in the galleries and could not participate in any of the proceedings. They became painfully conscious of the fact that slavery had to do with gender as well as race.

The Seneca Falls Convention. Women abolitionists began to speak more openly about women's rights to the extent that their male comrades feared the anti-slavery issue would be weakened. As progressive as the abolitionist movement was, the inherent sexism of the day served to divide and alienate its members. While continuing their work for antislavery, women were also now more vocal about legislative reforms related to family rights, divorce, women's property, and temperance issues and how they affected home and society. Recognizing that the inferior status of women needed to be urgently addressed, in 1848 the **Seneca Falls Convention** was held in upstate New York, an event hailed as the birth of the women's movement in the United States.

The Seneca Falls Convention approved a *Declaration of Sentiments* modeled after the Declaration of Independence, which listed the forms of discrimination women had to endure and which they vowed to eliminate. Examples from the declaration demonstrate the continuities of the past and present concerns of women (Ritchie and Ronald, 2001).

1. We hold these truths to be self-evident: that all men and women are created equal; that they are endowed by their Creator with certain inalienable rights; that among these are life, liberty and the pursuit of happiness.
2. The history of mankind is a history of repeated injuries and usurpations on the part of man toward woman, having in direct object the establishment of an absolute tyranny over her.
3. He has compelled her to submit to laws, in the formation of which she has no voice.
4. He has made her, if married, in the eye of the law, civilly dead.
5. He has monopolized nearly all the profitable employments, and from those she is permitted to follow, she receives but a scanty remuneration. He closes against her all the avenues to wealth and distinction that he considers most honorable to himself. As a teacher of theology, medicine or law, she is not known.
6. He has endeavored, in every way he could, to destroy her confidence in her own powers, to lessen her self-respect, and to make her willing to lead a dependent and abject life.

This listing of the discriminatory practices against women was accepted by the convention as well as eleven of the twelve resolutions aimed at ending such practices. Whereas it was agreed that women had to submit to laws they did not help create, there was not unanimous agreement about whether they should seek the vote. History has given the Seneca Falls meeting the distinction of originating the suffrage movement, but the suffrage resolution was passed only by a small majority. Although the early women's movement has become synonymous with suffrage, this was the very issue that initially split its supporters. Perhaps difficult to understand by today's standards, many women believed that equality was possible without the vote.

The following years saw conventions for women's rights being held throughout the North and West. Because abolition was part of its platform, the movement itself never spread to the South before the Civil War. During the war, activities on the behalf of women per se were dormant, but they emerged in earnest soon after. Even with no national agenda, disagreements on strategy, and run by a few women who had the strength and spare time to work for its causes, the movement grew in strength. Several outstanding women and their unique talents are credited for this growth: Lucy Stone, the movement's most gifted orator; Elizabeth Cady Stanton, philosopher and program writer; and Susan B. Anthony, the organizing genius (Clift, 2003; Million, 2003). They spoke on social, economic, and legal issues affecting women and pressed for reforms in such areas as education, wages, organized labor, child welfare, and inheritance.

As the movement grew, so did its opponents. First as abolitionists, then as feminists, and always as women, the movement was despised and ridiculed by many. Suffrage women were accused of being unnatural, masculine, and female sexual inverts who would doom America to sociobiological disaster (Behling, 2001). By the standards of the day, what were seen as militant methods fueled opposition. The ever-present verbal abuse at women's rallies along with the threat of mob violence caused some supporters to advocate less militancy and to downgrade the importance of the vote. The ranks of the movement were divided so that by the end of the Civil War, it was split into two factions.

Although both factions agreed on the need to get the vote, they were split on questions related to ideology and strategy. In 1869 two organizations were formed. Susan B. Anthony and Elizabeth Cady Stanton founded the National Woman Suffrage Association (NWSA). NWSA did not admit men, was considered militant in tactics, focused on issues that were controversial such as husband–wife relations, and worked for the vote to achieve other rights for women. Enfranchisement, then, was seen as a means to a greater end.

The second organization, the American Woman Suffrage Association (AWSA), led by Lucy Stone and Julia Howe, was more moderate in character, attracting many middle- and upper-class women. Concentrating on making the suffrage question more mainstream, the AWSA refrained from addressing issues thought to be controversial, such as marriage and religion. The primary goal of AWSA was to work within each state to achieve the vote. Wyoming was the first state to grant the vote to women, doing so in 1869, for a pragmatic rather than strictly democratic reason. Women were scarce in the territory, and it was felt that the right to vote would encourage more migrants to the area. Wyoming was almost not granted statehood because Southern congressmen argued that the states did not have the right to grant suffrage. Because the legislature was elected with women's votes, supporters for statehood asserted that Wyoming "will remain out of the Union for a hundred years rather than come in without the women." By a small margin Wyoming was admitted to the Union in 1890.

AWSA strategies eventually brought in many proponents to the movement, with suffrage gaining the respectability it needed to attract a broader base of support. In the meantime, NWSA increasingly turned its attention to suffrage and campaigned for political and legal rights. In 1890, the two groups merged to form the **National American Woman Suffrage Association** (NAWSA). One unfortunate consequence of the merger and the gain in "respectability" was that the organization became isolated from the plight of black women, immigrant women, and working-class women in general. African-American women worked diligently in the suffrage movement but were acutely aware that a double standard existed for black and white women suffragists. Black suffragists called on their white sisters in the movement to "put aside their prejudices and allow black women, burdened by both sexism and racism, to gain political equality" (Terborg-Penn, 1991:133). Their words were largely unheeded. The exclusion of these potential allies at the turn of the century impacted the movement for the next half century. It took another half century before the schism was narrowed considerably.

The Nineteenth Amendment

The next thirty years saw renewed energies for passage of a suffrage amendment, though NAWSA actually accomplished very little. Strategies deemed as too radical were disavowed, militant members were expelled, conservatism set in, and a crisis in leadership occurred. Some of the expelled faction joined a group founded by militant suffragist Alice Paul in 1913 (Butler, 2002). Embracing the tactics of the more militant English suffrage movement, Paul headed the Congressional Union, later known as the Woman's Party, and used mass demonstrations to bring the constitutional amendment to America's public consciousness. In the meantime, Carrie Chapman Catt became president of NAWSA and in 1915 began a rigorous suffrage campaign. NAWSA continued distributing leaflets, lobbying, and speaking to numerous influential organizations. Woman's Party members held rallies, went on hunger strikes, and used other unorthodox, and definitely unfeminine, means. Although the tactics varied, the common goal was passage of a suffrage amendment that had been introduced and defeated in every session of Congress since 1878.

By the end of World War I, giving the vote to women had widespread support. In 1919 the Nineteenth Amendment was passed by margins of 304 to 90 in the House and 56 to 25 in the Senate. But the struggle would not be over until two-thirds of the states ratified it. On August 26, 1920, by only two votes, the amendment was ratified in Tennessee, making the Nineteenth Amendment part of the U.S. Constitution.

The Contemporary Movement

Once the right to vote was gained, feminism literally died in the United States for the next 40 years. The end of the arduous campaign resulting in ratification of the Nineteenth Amendment found some feminists insisting that broader social reforms, rather than narrower feminist goals, were now necessary, because they believed political equality had been achieved. Others, including Alice Paul, called for passage of the Equal Rights Amendment (ERA), which would prohibit all forms of discrimination against women. The ERA was first introduced in Congress in 1923, but even by this time the unity of support for a specific cause had been dissolved. Coupled with the Depression and a conservative national mood, most activism for women's issues was abandoned. It was not until after World War II that the women's movement emerged again on a national scale. The reawakening of feminism was encouraged by three major events. First, President John Kennedy established the Commission on the Status of Women in 1961. The Commission issued a report documenting the inferior position of women in the United States and set up a citizen's advisory council and state commissions to deal with the problems addressed in the report. Second, in 1963 Betty Friedan published her landmark work, *The Feminine Mystique*. In this book, Friedan argued that women were given no road to fulfillment other than wife and mother. They had no identity apart from their families, found themselves unhappy, and could not even name their problem. Despite restrictive roles and a society that condoned and applauded such restrictions, women were beginning to voice their unhappiness. "It is no longer possible to ignore that voice, to dismiss the desperation of so many American women" (Friedan, 1963:21). The second-class status of women, which was pointed to in the Kennedy report, was bolstered by Friedan's assertions and research.

National Organization for Women. The third event heralding the return of feminism was the founding of the **National Organization for Women** (NOW) in 1966, with Betty Friedan serving as its first president. These events are not in isolation from one another. Many of the women first met when they worked on state commissions set up after the Kennedy report. They were also unhappy with the progress being made on their recommendations and felt that a separate effort to deal with issues related to women was important. The creation of NOW can be viewed as an indirect result of the Commission on the Status of Women.

It is important to remember that NOW was formed during the turbulent 1960s, an era of heightened political activism and social consciousness. The drive to organize women occurred during a time when African Americans, Native Americans, Latinos, poor people, students, and anti–Vietnam War activists were also competing for public attention through mass demonstrations for their respective causes. In comparison to many of the organizations spawned as a result of these causes, including other women's groups, NOW was, and is, more moderate in its approach. Perhaps NOW's ability to survive into the twenty-first century as a viable organization can be tied to its mainstream emphasis.

White, college-educated, middle-class women were attracted to NOW and became the base for its original growth. The disadvantage was that a top-down structure was created, and this in itself tended to limit diversity. NOW remains hierarchically organized with a national body and formal constitution, but its local chapters are more autonomous and have aided its growth and diversity. In the decades since its founding, NOW's membership has expanded considerably, bringing in more nonprofessional and younger women and women of color. This is vital to the ultimate success of feminism in America. A feminist consciousness among African-American women, for example, can only be nurtured through a framework that addresses the ideology of racism in America (Higginbotham, 2003). The organization has also become more controversial, adopting a more flamboyant style.

In 1967 the first NOW national conference adopted a Bill of Rights that included support for the adoption of an Equal Rights Amendment to the Constitution, women's full right to work at all types of jobs, maternity leave rights, and the right of women to control their reproductive lives. As suggested by these goals, NOW has a wide orientation in terms of areas of interest affecting women, but with a focus on political tactics to achieve these goals. Using a traditional organizational format, other groups were also founded during the 1960s and 1970s and have more specialized interest areas but with a similar focus on tactics. Thus, in addition to NOW, the moderate branch of the movement generated the Women's Equity Action League (WEAL), which seeks to enact legislation that is not as gender specific, and the National Women's Political Caucus (NWPC), which promotes women as candidates for public office.

The second branch of the movement consisted of a more diverse array of women and still remains more radical in orientation. Many shunned the structure of organizations like NOW, believing that such a formal hierarchy could inhibit individual expression. This branch was made up of younger women and women who had been involved with the other social movements of the time, especially the civil rights movement. Unlike NOW, some groups excluded men from their ranks, others worked solely for reproductive rights, and many came together simply under the banner of sisterhood for the purpose of consciousness raising and dialogue (Freeman, 1995). Attitude change at one level can help serve broader social change later. Whatever issue spawned such groups, solidarity with other women is a critical byproduct.

The two broad branches of the movement that developed in the 1960s are still evident today, although there is some overlap in membership. The belief in passage of the Equal Rights Amendment (ERA) is what all factions can agree on, and they have worked for this effort to varying degrees with a variety of approaches. The political impact of ERA will be discussed in chapter 14. ERA's importance in this context involves keeping the movement alive and serving as a unifying force. As judged by the failure to gain the necessary two-thirds of the states for ratification before the legal deadline expired, the movement has not been successful. But considering that NOW was able to lobby to extend the 1979 deadline by three years, an unprecedented move by Congress, it was obvious that the movement was still a viable force in the 1980s. Until its ratification, ERA will continue to be a focus of activity for the movement. After ratification, concern will likely shift to issues relating to its enforcement.

Other activities remain on the agenda for the women's movement, many of which are international in scope. On both the national and global levels, this movement has impacted millions of women and men worldwide. Although much of this discussion relates to issues that have been divisive for the women's movement in the United States, divisiveness is being bridged. The next chapter demonstrates that the diversity of women worldwide is more conducive than detrimental for a strong global feminist movement.

Summary

1. Women's history emerged to uncover the hidden elements of the other half of humankind, which had been ignored by male historians writing about the exploits of a few powerful, elite men. The first compensatory and contribution histories focused on exceptional women. Today women's history accounts for the race, class, and gender links. Historical themes include misogyny and women and victims but also the resistance women have used against patriarchy.

2. Predating Greek civilization, Minoan Crete may have been a partnership society with a matrilineal system, Amazon legends, Goddess worship, and high gender egalitarianism.

3. Illustrated by the writings of Plato and Aristotle, later Greek society relegated women to inferior legal and social status. Described as chattels, in Athens the vast majority of women were segregated and restricted. A few high-level courtesans and wealthy women exercised some privileges. Women in Sparta were expected to be physically fit and manage households when the men were at war.

4. Roman women had more freedom. Vestiges of goddess worship remained, and women had important religious roles. Selected women could become citizens, some amassed fortunes in their own names. But even the most independent and wealthy women were in bondage to men.

5. During the Middle Ages Christianity enveloped Europe, and the misogyny of the Church carried over to the lives of women. The most notable misogyny occurred with witch burning. The Renaissance and Reformation offered some women the opportunity for literacy and to become patrons of the arts and saw women in more diverse roles overall. But Luther's image of women generally coincided with earlier views, and misogyny continued to govern Europe.

6. The first American women were Native American women from gynocratic tribal systems based on gender reciprocity and balance, often holding important leadership roles. With colonization and Christianity, women's high standing was largely lost.

7. Colonial white women in the Puritan era lived under Christian views imported from Europe. Some scholars argue that because women were scarce and had vital economically productive roles in the household, they enjoyed a measure of prestige and that this era was a golden age for women.

8. The Victorian era saw the rise of True Womanhood—telling women to be pious, pure, and submissive. Despite these messages middle-class women exercised some control over their lives to meet both personal needs and social activities.

9. Frontier women were valued for their work in and outside their homes. They lived adverse lives, but adapted and often thrived on their frontier farms.

10. Industrialization opened up employment to women from all walks of life. The appalling working conditions and the Triangle fire that killed 146 mostly women workers helped spark the union movement. The Knights of Labor was opened for women and African Americans. Women's attempts to unionize were not as successful as men's. Gains in pay and employment for women were lost with the Depression.

11. World War II opened up employment for women. The demand for female labor led to higher paying defense jobs and acceptance of married women and women of all races and classes in the workplace. The cult of the home emerged after the war. But World War II altered gender roles, and the next half century saw increased opportunities for women.

12. Several yardsticks mark the Women's Movement and rise of feminism: The publication of *The Vindication of the Rights of Women* in 1792; the denial of women to sign the *Declaration of Purposes* of the Anti-Slavery Society in 1833 or speak at the World Anti-Slavery Convention in 1840; the Women's Rights Convention in Seneca Falls, New York in 1848; the passage of the Nineteenth Amendment in 1920; establishing the Commission on the Status of Women by President Kennedy in 1961; the publication of the *Feminist Mystique* by Betty Friedan in 1963; and the formation of the National Organization for Women in 1966. All factions of the movement today agree that the Equal Rights Amendment should be passed.

Key Terms

compensatory history 96

contribution history 96

Knights of Labor 116

misogyny 97

National American Woman Suffrage Association 126

National Organization for Women 128

pater familias 102

Seneca Falls Convention 125

True Womanhood 112

Critical Thinking Questions

1. With the intersection of race, class, and gender as a framework, demonstrate through specific historical examples how the theme of misogyny and women as victims exists alongside themes related to women's resistance to subjugation and women in esteemed and powerful roles.

2. Considering the historical record, demonstrate how periods of gain and loss for women tend to offset one another. Overall, what historical events provided the opportunities to sustain gain in gender equality?

3. Based on your knowledge of gender and history, and with specific references to feminism in the United States, what suggestions would you offer to contemporary feminists who are working for the passage of the Equal Rights Amendment?

CHAPTER **6**

Development, if not engendered, is endangered.

—United Nations Development Program

GLOBAL PERSPECTIVES ON GENDER

Israel

Religion, Family, and Employment
Jewish Feminism

The Muslim World

Islamization: Iran and Afghanistan
The Arab Middle East
North Africa: Female Genital Mutilation
To Veil or Not to Veil

Scandinavia: Norway and Sweden

Social change has been a central concern of sociology since its existence as a distinct discipline. To understand the profound gender impact of social change, we need to review two other change-related processes—globalization and development. **Globalization**, the vision of the world as a single social space in which diverse societies borrow, learn, and compete against one another, and **development**, programs designed to upgrade the standard of living of the world's poor in ways that allow them to sustain themselves. This chapter focuses on gender issues in **developing nations**, also referred to as the *developing world*, the United Nations designation for those less developed countries with poverty-level incomes per capita. Most of these nations are in Africa, Asia, Latin America, the Caribbean, and the South Pacific. As we will discover, globalization and development go hand in hand, and as beneficial as they appear on the surface, they differentially impact men and women in profound ways. Globalization may connect people but it does not necessarily unite them.

The gender issues selected for review here may be seen as flashpoints identified by activists, scholars, researchers, and feminists across the globe that serve as culturally defined gender markers on a given nation or region. Even with such a limited focus, the task is formidable. This chapter is written with the caution that generalizations are necessary and countless exceptions exist. However, a chapter objective is to illustrate the degree to which patterns of life and living throughout the world are highly gendered and that women share a great deal in common as a result of these patterns. More than any other of the globe's institutions, the United Nations has allowed for many of these issues to be assessed.

THE UNITED NATIONS CONFERENCES ON WOMEN

In its Charter of 1945, the United Nations (UN) announced its commitment to the equality of women and men. The year 1975 was declared International Women's Year, and the next decade was declared as the UN Decade for Women. Official conferences to work on a global agenda of women's issues were held in Mexico City in 1975, Copenhagen in 1980, Nairobi in 1985, and Beijing in 1995. Under the banner of "equality, development and peace," each conference assessed the progress of commitments made on behalf of women by various nations.

Alongside each official UN conference ran a parallel one, a forum consisting of hundreds of **nongovernmental organizations (NGOs)**—privately funded nonprofit groups concerned with relief and development and advocacy for the poor—that brought women from all over the world and all walks of life together. These grassroots organizations represented a wide diversity of opinions and agendas. Inclusiveness brings dissent, and the conferences were marked by political, religious, and economic factionalism, which, unfortunately, became media highlights. A concerted effort by conservative groups to discredit and interrupt the proceedings also occurred. Many women attending the NGO Forum in Copenhagen were discouraged by the friction that appeared to separate rather than unify them. Some women felt that the Copenhagen conference became politicized because the focus was on issues such as the class–race intersection highlighted by women in the developing world, detracting from what they shared in common as women. They left the forum, however, with a better understanding that feminism must raise issues relevant to women in both the developed and developing countries, and with a greater acceptance of diverse perspectives and priorities. By Nairobi, then, much of the friction dissipated as dialogue opened and consensus was reached on key issues. A central change from Copenhagen was the "widespread recognition that political issues are women's issues, and that the women's movement is fundamentally a political movement" (Cagatay et al., 1989:468).

The gains in political astuteness were clearly evident a decade later. In 1995 the international women's movement took center stage when Beijing, China hosted the largest UN conference in history. With an attendance estimated at 50,000, Beijing was historic not only in terms of numbers, but also because the woman's agenda moved from the margin to the center of global debate.

The Legacy of Beijing: A Personal Perspective

It is not surprising that in covering the largest gathering of women in history, international media attention focused on controversy and conflict rather than the more pervasive atmosphere of unity and support that emerged from the conference. The Beijing gathering and the parallel NGO Forum in nearby Huairou represent landmark developments in global understanding and cooperation among women of the world.

As addressed in a number of sessions at the conference, women represent a glaring blind spot for the media. News outlets in many countries, including the United States, too often approach women's issues with stereotypes, misconceptions, and biased data. And when addressing a public believed to relish controversy, the seeds for reinforcing these stereotypes continue to be sewn. Yet the truly remarkable events in Beijing managed to alter this trend.

Even while attending the conference, many of us were acutely aware that the international media were dwelling on issues that generated the most controversy, especially religious fundamentalism, with frequent staged demonstrations by those representing conservative groups. The Iranian delegation of fully veiled women and their male "escorts," for example, provided the media much camera time. Their efforts were met by what I would describe as "bemused toleration." The international media would willingly toddle behind with cameras and microphones and report on the nightly news that religious fundamentalism was tearing the conference apart.

This could not be further from the truth. Although religious fundamentalism was certainly one of many controversial topics, the NGO Forum was remarkable in its ability to bring women of all faiths to engage in dialogue over matters that impacted their daily lives—including issues of reproduction, parenting, domestic violence, and health and well-being—all of which have religious overtones. Many workshops brought together women representing diverse religious and spiritual traditions. When politics, religion, and cultural tradition were met head on, as between Palestinian and Israeli women or between African, Muslim, and other women who did and did not accept veiling or female genital mutilation (discussed later), toleration and understanding emerged in an atmosphere of open dialogue. What became clear, however, is that the die is cast against religious fundamentalism when religion is used to restrict women's human rights. In a presentation I gave on this topic, I argued that religious fundamentalism can be recast so that it becomes liberating rather than restrictive and used as a weapon against sexism and for empowerment (Lindsey, 1995).

The norm of the NGO Forum sessions was to ensure that everyone had the opportunity to voice opinions, and in most cases there was not complete unity. Although such inclusiveness may be at the root of controversy when people "agree to disagree," the stage is set for a better understanding of the issues and more toleration of dissenting opinion.

What is the legacy of Beijing? I speak from the perspective of attending the gatherings in Copenhagen and Nairobi as well as Beijing. The previous conferences were more divisive, but also smaller, less inclusive, and with fewer women on the organizing bodies or official delegations. Although the Beijing conference was racked with negative international media attention, Chinese obstructionism, logistical nightmares, and inadequate facilities, the ability and perseverance of the women who attended and worked to get the Platform of Action adopted were nothing short of spectacular. As Hillary Rodham Clinton stated in her address to the Forum, "NGOs are where the action is." With thousands of NGOs as watchdogs, governments are monitored for the pledges made to women and their families through the ratified UN document. This document addressed twelve critical areas of concern, including education, health, and employment and outlined action steps to be taken in implementing objectives. The number one issue was women's poverty. Action steps for this issue included calling for gender-sensitive economic policies, placing economic value on women's unpaid work, and increasing education and training programs for poor women.

After overviewing gender roles from a global perspective, it will become clear that Beijing served as a watershed for the women's movement worldwide. Even with the inevitable backlash with which any movement for social change must contend, the women's movement has been successful in sending its message throughout the world. This message is that women's inferior status will no longer be ignored, that women's rights are human rights, and that nations will be held accountable for their progress, or lack thereof, in ending gender inequality. The numerous follow-up conferences, seminars, and workshops held since Beijing are vehicles NGOs use to measure progress and ensure accountability. The gathering of women in Beijing attests to the recognition that women's empowerment is beneficial to everyone, and that, despite misconceptions in the media and still with a long and rocky path ahead, global sisterhood is emerging as an undeniable sociopolitical reality.

WOMEN IN DEVELOPMENT

The United Nations has spearheaded major efforts to reduce the gender gap in human capability—areas such as literacy, access to health care, job training, and family planning. Women in the developing world are the most restricted in almost all important areas of human capability. The good news is that since 1985 the gap in education and health has been cut in half. The bad news is that patterns of gender inequality continue to have dire consequences on the lives of women and girls. As reported by the United Nations (UNDP, 2003; UNFPA, 2004) and the World Bank (2003), and verified by NGOs across the globe, these patterns include the following:

1. Seventy percent of the 1.3 billion people worldwide who live in abject poverty (living on less than one dollar a day) are women and girls.
2. Almost two-thirds of the 854 million illiterate adults worldwide are women.
3. If the unpaid work women perform—such as subsistence farming and domestic labor—was counted in economic terms, the world's gross domestic product would increase by almost one-third.
4. Women grow three-quarters of the world's food but receive less than 10 percent of agricultural assistance. Eighty percent of Africa's food is grown and processed by women.
5. Eighty percent of the world's 50 million uprooted people or "official" refugees are women and children.
6. In virtually every sub-Saharan African nation, women constitute over half of all cases of HIV/AIDS.
7. Ninety percent of all countries have organizations that promote the advancement of women, but women make up about 10 percent of the world's legislative seats.

Overall, the underlying cause of the inequality of women is that their roles are primarily domestic (mother, wife, homemaker), and although these are vital to the well-being of society, they are undervalued and unpaid. Other social institutions, especially the economy, reinforce the existing inequality.

The Impact of Development on Women

Fueled by globalization, the role and status of women in the process of economic development has emerged as a major global social issue. Beginning with Ester Boserup's (1970) pioneering study on women in development (WID), the argument that development has an adverse effect on women, often leading to further impoverishment, marginalization, and exploitation, is well documented (Lindsey, 1996b; Kurian, 2000; Rai, 2002). This pattern indicates that development serves to erode women's overall well-being, undermines their authority often within their own households, and leads to a more disadvantaged status. The path to negative development outcomes for women is a deceptively simple one. As development proceeds, women are denied access to productive sources and new technologies, which then "serves to lower their relative, if not absolute, productivity" (Norris,

1992:183). In societies characterized by powerful patriarchal institutions, men and women rarely share equally the limited resources available to families, a situation that deteriorates with development.

The hardest hit are rural women whose nondomestic work consists of subsistence farming. Even though they were not landowners, before cash crop farming, Latin American and African women for several centuries managed farms and retained control over their produce. Colonialism and subsequent agricultural development projects introduced technology and cash-crop farming, which undermined farming practices and virtually eliminated the traditional economic resources available to women. Subsistence farming is vital to the livelihood of a family. But because subsistence agriculture is defined as domestic work and there is no cash exchanged and no surplus for profit in the marketplace, it is not considered "productive" in traditional economic definitions of labor (Waring, 1988; SIGI, 2001). Development programs typically rely on standard international economic definitions, which exclude the majority of work women perform, such as child care, domestic labor, and subsistence farming.

In addition to farming, development policies have also ignored the gender implications of other labor-force activities. At the family level, the *trickle-down model* is supposed to operate. Policies are designed to upgrade the economic standards of families by concentrating on the assumed male head of household, who is the breadwinner, with his dependent wife in the homemaker role. Development programs often assume that by improving employment of men, the whole family would benefit. The problem with this assumption is that it is based on an urban, middle class model that fails to acknowledge the varied productive roles of women, especially rural women. As a result, women's work remains undercounted, undervalued, and underpaid (Staudt, 1998).

Men often migrate to cities in search of paid work, leaving women with loss of help in remaining subsistence activities. Paid employment available to rural women usually consists of low-paid domestic work or work on commercial farms. Others are recruited for work in the assembling and light-manufacturing plants that multinational corporations are building on the fringes of urban areas in less-developed countries. Multinational corporations favor young women, most between the ages of thirteen and twenty-five, for their willingness to work for low wages in substandard conditions and their presumed docility that keeps them from challenging the conditions. Others migrate overseas to join the massive ranks of domestic workers employed in the households of the world's wealthy. Overall, development planners have failed to account for the various ways that women and their families are impacted by the global economy and the supposed economic benefits that come with it (Moghadam, 1999; Cagatay, 2001).

On the positive side, the correlation between women's impoverishment and development is no longer ignored. Propelled by the international women's movement, strong women-oriented NGOs and the Beijing Platform of Action gender analysis in development planning have moved from the fringes to the center. All development projects funded through the United Nations and World Bank must now do a gender analysis at the planning stages to determine how the project may differentially impact the lives of women and men.

A Model of Women in Development

A sociologically informed model of women in development (WID) can offer planners useful leads to help explain, understand, and then design appropriate development projects. The following elements should be included in any WID model (Lindsey, 1995). First, the model must be informed by sociological theory and take into account the global stratification system that keeps the developing world in an economically dependent position. Capitalism and colonialism intertwine to determine the economic structures that ultimately shape the subordination of women. Second, it must account for the forces of globalization and market-driven economic development that, paradoxically, may serve to both empower and disempower women (Lindsey, 2004). Third, because the strength of sociological theory for development planning is only as useful as how it is translated into practice, sound methodology must be employed with a feedback loop to further nurture and refine theory. The theory–practice link is necessary for both sociology and those who use sociology in development planning. Fieldwork and policy inform one another and contribute to new ways of employing social science concepts in real-world applications. As envisioned by sociology's founders, a "sociology of usefulness" is encouraged (Deutscher and Lindsey, 2005). Fourth, it should be interdisciplinary in scope and capitalize on the rich conceptual and empirical work throughout the social sciences that informs different segments of the development process. Sociologists, economists, and anthropologists need to talk to one another, to practitioners who work in development, and most important, to the community that will be impacted by development decisions.

Fifth, a WID model should adopt a feminist perspective emphasizing women's empowerment. When combined with sociological theory, this would be subsumed under a broad conflict theoretical approach because it issues a challenge to the patriarchal status quo. Women's empowerment and gender equity are clearly associated with an enhanced quality of life for women, their families, and their communities.

Development projects that neglect gender analysis and ignore broader definitions of production are both unrealistic and unsuccessful. Gender disparities are being increasingly recognized for what they are, "unacceptable injustices and serious constraints to the achievement of sustainable people-centered development" (SIDA, 1995). The focus here has been on the agricultural role of women, but all the daily child care and household production activities should also be included. These productive activities are necessary for family survival in much of the world. This livelihood must be protected, extended, or realistically evaluated and modified. At a minimum it must be acknowledged.

RUSSIA

The collapse of the Soviet Union was heralded with the belief that a true democratization of the world would begin. Former Soviet Premier Mikhail Gorbachev's policies of *glasnost* ("openness") combined with *perestroika* ("restructuring") were to be the key elements to transform the Soviet Union into a democratic nation with a free-market economy. Gorbachev's vision of a more democratized, capitalistic Soviet Union was not to be. The USSR rapidly crumbled into independent nation states, most which did embrace capitalistic ideals but restructured themselves according to an array of political models intertwining elements of both socialism and democracy. Russia, the largest and most economically and politically influential of the former Soviet republics, continues to exhibit the woes rather than the benefits of a transitional economy. The number of Russians economically enhanced in the transition is to date not offset by the vast majority whose quality of life deteriorated during the same period. Poverty deepens, unemployment increases, subsidies for health and welfare are slashed or eliminated, and economic development is stalled and discontent rises (Khasbulatova and Egorov, 2002). With the collapse of an infrastructure that ensured a level of social support to its population, Russia may now be likened to some developing world nations in quality of life indicators.

Comparable to women in developing nations, Russian women have been further marginalized by the combined effects of globalization and the transition to a free-market economy (Dawson, 2002). The impact of these processes reverberated throughout most of the other post-Soviet republics. In Azerbaijan, for example, educational and health care subsidies were drastically cut and public sector jobs, which disproportionately employed women, were eliminated. Loss of paid employment propelled women into poverty, and simultaneously, loss of subsidies for child care and elder care increased their caregiving responsibilities. In the past decade Azerbaijan dropped from 71 to 90 in the UN Development Index (Najafizadeh, 2003). Although women's advocacy organizations have emerged to fill some of the gaps left by the ravages of transition, it remains to be seen how long it will take before the benefits of the capitalism–democracy–development link are realized for women.

The Soviet Legacy

The former Soviet constitution stated: "Women and men have equal rights." One of the first mandates of the 1917 Lenin regime was to upgrade women's position in the new society by abolishing all forms of discrimination against women inherent in tsarist Russia. Women were to have full equality in educational and employment opportunities, family and property rights, and competition for administrative offices. Over the next half century women secured about half the positions as deputies in state legislatures and were well represented in the trade unions. Regardless of the formal commitment since the founding of the USSR, however, the most influential national political positions were essentially devoid of women. The old adage of "the higher the position, the fewer the women" readily applied to the equality-conscious former Soviet Union. As a result, the rhetoric of equality served to mask women's continued oppression (Mamonova, 1994).

Employment

In terms of paid labor, the Soviet Union had a larger percentage of women in the labor force than any other industrial society. Women's hours were regulated and so-called protective labor laws were instituted during the Soviet Union's industrial expansion. In no country in the world did women constitute such a significant part of the working class in so short a time (Ilic, 1999; Goldman, 2002). In today's Russia paid employment is virtually universal for women. Although Russian women have high representations in law, medicine, and engineering as well as in the skilled trades, they are overrepresented in low-paying and menial jobs, are underrepresented in managerial jobs, and hold the least prestigious specialties within professions such as medicine (Harden, 2001; Riska, 2001). Most are engaged in industrial or manual work, and this is despite negligible gender differences in education. The official doctrine of equal pay for equal work exists, but women make less money than men, even in the professions and even if more highly qualified than men. Under the communists, the average female worker earned two-thirds of the average male income, but the postcommunist erosion continues for women. Women now not only earn less than half of what men average, but in the rapidly changing transitional economy it is likely that the plateau in the wage gap has still not been reached (Brainerd, 2000). The pay gap is larger for professional women who are in feminized jobs, such as teaching, nursing, and social work—occupations considered an extension of women's natural aptitude for caregiving (Iarskaia and Iarskaia-Smirnova, 2002). In the transitional economy white-collar, professional, and technologically-oriented jobs are growing in prestige and garnering higher salaries. But with women already entrenched in unskilled jobs, in feminized professional jobs, and within a gender-based system of job segregation, for the foreseeable future, they will reap fewer benefits.

Gender inequity in the labor force persists when considering unemployment as well. Economic restructuring, the need to move workers out of heavy industry and create a service sector, and the call for a reduced government bureaucracy have taken a heavy toll on women. Female unemployment has reached an all-time high, and at the same time unemployment benefits have considerably eroded. In examining this trend, a paradox unfolds. Women who have lost their jobs are likely to be professionals, technical specialists, managers, and white-collar workers who would seem to be the most marketable in a new service-oriented economy. Professionals make up the ranks of the employed, the majority of whom are women. Of the manual workers who are the unemployed, the numbers of men and women are roughly equal. Women are competing with men for those better jobs with better working conditions. Women who cannot withstand the competition from men are ousted precisely from specialized jobs because men are "not interested in competing with women for manual or heavy jobs or for work which is injurious to health" (Khotkina, 1994:101). In this instance, gender equity in education has worked as a detriment against being employed in the very jobs for which they have been trained and where they could contribute to what Russia desires in terms of economic growth.

The inequity between men and women is most evident in agricultural production. During the Soviet reign women did almost all the labor associated with private agricultural plots when they were made available (Dodge and Feshbach, 1992). During the grueling transition period to a free-market economy, women may see opportunities to both produce food for their families and receive a profit for excess production. In line with worldwide trends, subsistence farming for pre- and post-Soviet women has been beneficial. It remains to be seen if these women will have a repeat of the experiences of women in the developing world where a move to cash crops translates to severe loss of economic opportunity.

The Collision of Family and Employment. The glaring disparity between men and women in labor force activities can be explained by a unique combination of ideological factors. Family barriers that impose a double burden on women, in turn hindering career advancement, remain formidable. As in the West, men have not taken on anywhere near an equal share of domestic duties when their wives, sisters, and mothers are also in the paid labor force. The situation is particularly acute for women who suffer most from the second shift of household labor following work outside the home. On the average husbands have 30 hours more free time per week than wives. Both rural and urban women report a slight decrease in work hours outside the home but a sharp increase in work hours inside the home (Karakhanova, 2003). Women are torn by how to deal with *peregruzhenost* (overburdening). Heightened by the chaos generated by the collapse of the state-controlled economy, traditional views of family roles, coupled with a chronic labor shortage in rural areas, serve to maintain this situation.

The dilemma faced by the Russian government is that there is alarm over a falling birth rate and the increased preference for smaller families but a need for the cheaper labor of women who can be hired part time or as temporary workers. Professional women are being pushed out of the labor force and manual workers are still in demand. The economy could not withstand a mass exodus of women from the ranks of paid labor. But measures to encourage high levels of national productivity by providing for the health and well-being of the mother and her child—such as day care facilities, prenatal and pediatric health care, and pregnancy leaves—are usually not provided in private enterprises, especially if women are hired on a part-time basis. Men are preferred as employees in part because they do not demand such fringe benefits. Another confounding factor is that although Russian couples do not want large families, available and affordable birth control options are limited. Abortion is costly but abortion rates are very high. Official figures show that for every one birth there are two abortions in Russia. This ratio does not capture the number of illegal abortions, estimated to be as high as eight abortions for every birth (Bodrova, 2002). Russia's pronatalist call has fallen on deaf ears because the government is unwilling to subsidize birth control options, and over half of all Russian men and women are against suggestions to ban abortions.

Marriage and Family

Despite the fact that women take on virtually all domestic responsibilities, the prospect of marriage and children, albeit a small family, is increasing in priority, especially among rural women. Women are more preoccupied with romance and appear to accept the far from egalitarian arrangement that will likely emerge after marriage. Regardless of occupation, Russian women are more family oriented than men and continue to place a high value on child-rearing activities. Family, children, and social order continue to be the highest values for women, with the importance of paid work declining significantly as a value (Goodwin and Emelyanova, 1995; Karakhanova, 2003). They may be agricultural workers, professionals, or clerks, but their main concern is to be married and raise a family.

The falling birth rate and the view that the family is disintegrating have prompted authorities to promote the image of women as homemakers. Unlike during the Soviet era, women who strive for equality with men in the workplace are caricatured as masculine and blamed for family related social problems such as divorce, teen pregnancy, drug abuse, and juvenile delinquency (Boyko, 2002; Dement'eva, 2001). Although women are also needed in the labor force and as income earners for their families, there is still no reprieve from social disapproval. Officials openly state that women take good jobs away from deserving men. Media routinely run stories stating that both women and the workplace suffer when women work outside the home. In fact, the tendency toward bolstering gender stereotypes is increasing, fueled by media images reinforcing these beliefs. Women lament the lost masculinity of contemporary men and men reproach women for their lack of femininity (Lipovskaya, 1994; Clements et al., 2002).

Support or Backlash to Feminism?

The emerging picture suggests that in the transition period women face a number of difficult issues. The restructured economy ushered in by perestroika has intensified sexual inequality, but glasnost at least opened discussion on the plight of women, particularly rural women. The democratic trend sparked by glasnost played an important role in publicizing the benefits of a women's movement and has since evolved into publications, research, and media information regarding women's rights and increased inequality. Glasnost rekindled a hidden but viable feminist spirit that the Soviet Union had driven underground. There is agreement that women have been manipulated throughout Russian history and must now hear their own voices and that a democratic society must concern itself with gender equity in a meaningful way (Hesli et al., 2001). Some local governments have responded to these voices and are seeking women's help in formulating strategies for gender development in areas related to violence, reproductive health, media, and political decision making (Boustany, 2002).

On the other hand, the revival of feminism appears to be waning at the dawn of the new millennium. The feminist movement in Russia suffers from a lack of leadership because the feminists of the Soviet era have not been replaced by younger women. The failure of Russian bred NGOs to become organizationally viable and financially sustainable and the lack of political representation further contribute to the movement's inertia (Golosov, 2001; Zdravomyslova, 2002). Another factor that does not bode well for the movement is that it appears easier to mobilize activists and advocates for Russian women outside Russia than inside Russia (Sperling et al., 2001). Democratization ushers in civil activism but most Russians—both men and women—remain suspicious of feminists who, for example, parade the glories of full-time employment for women who also take on all domestic chores. Feminists are seen, therefore, as modeling Soviet style expectations about women's roles (Sperling, 1999; Conze, 2001). Because the Soviets *imposed* gender egalitarianism—whether it was to be objectively viable or not—by decree from the central government, feminism in Russia has been unable to shed the image that it is not so different from communist ideology.

As disheartening as it sounds to Western feminists, many Russian women would agree with the words of a woman who, although very poor, has the luxury of being a stay-at-home wife. "Women will never win in the fight within the establishment for power. Why should I try when I can achieve so much more at home?" (Tavernise, 2003:4). Research shows that women retain management even when they define themselves as housewives (Clarke, 2002). Contrary to Marxian assertions, the life of toil inside the home for no pay is eagerly embraced by women who toiled for pay outside the home. Another woman, a psychologist, suggests "The principal function of a women's movement in this country would be to quiet our women down (and) make them more capable of reassuring their men" (Gray, 1991:307). This is not incompatible with what many women see as the future for Russia. Their ability to cope has sustained them through the catastrophes of pre- and post-Soviet history. As put by one woman, "We'd like bigger apartments. We'd like more women in the legislatures. We'd like men to treat us better. But we can wait. We're used to it" (Clements, 1994:143). Glasnost paved the way to openly debate critical problems faced by women but government and popular mobilization answers to the problems have not been forthcoming. The ironic twist to democratization in Russia, in the short term at least, is the eroding of women's rights.

CHINA

Even before the revolution elevating Mao Tse Tung to head of the new People's Republic of China, the Chinese Communist Party (CCP) recognized that women were valuable allies in building socialism. In order for the peasant revolution to maintain its momentum during the construction of a new regime, it was believed that women's issues must be given priority. Because women were inextricably bound to an ancient, oppressive, and seemingly immutable family structure, this area was given highest priority. Priorities, however, are mediated with more immediate goals in mind, specifically economic development. For the CCP, as long as women's rights and economic development conveniently coincide, they remain a government priority.

Similar to the ideology of the former Soviet Union, the Chinese government's goal to increase labor force participation proceeded with the argument that if women gain in the economic sphere, they will also gain in the family. Whereas Karl Marx articulated the structure of classical social conflict theory, it was Friedrich Engels who carried this approach specifically to the family (chapter 1). For Engels, the family is the basic source of women's oppression. The patriarchal family is a microcosm of a larger, oppressive capitalistic society. By this reasoning, therefore, once women expand their roles outside the family to become economically productive in the new socialist system, servility to men will cease. Popularized as the "liberation through labor" ideal, the improvement of the economic status of women continues as the foundation for achieving gender equality. Family reform would inevitably follow.

Reform and the Chinese Family

The record of Chinese family reform since the revolution is mixed. The traditional Chinese family was based on Confucian principles that gave complete authority to males. The family was patriarchal, patrilineal, and patrilocal. In Confucian classic writings, females are seen as naturally inferior, unintelligent, jealous, indiscreet, narrow-minded, and seductive to innocent males (chapter 12). Given these views, it is not surprising that women's lives were severely restricted and that laws would reflect these values. A woman's marriage was arranged; she could not normally inherit property, would move into her husband's household at marriage, and had to survive under the unquestioned authority of her husband, his father, and his grandfather, as well as other assorted male relatives. A female hierarchy also existed. Her mother-in-law exercised strict control, and she could beat or sell her daughter-in-law for disobedience or for running away. The bride occupied the lowest rung in the domestic hierarchy of the traditional Chinese family.

Footbinding. Running at all was impossible for those women who endured the technique of footbinding, which could reduce a foot to as small as three inches. Dating to the early part of the twelfth century, this crippling procedure was more extreme for women from the upper classes who did not have to work in manual labor or in the fields. Besides becoming a status symbol and a prerequisite for marriage among the upper classes, footbinding ensured that women remained passive and under the control of men. Indeed, for the family and hence Confucian society to function smoothly, the subordination of women was required, and practices such as footbinding helped ensure this.

Marriage. The Marriage Law of 1950 abolished many of the practices that had oppressed women in the traditional Chinese family. The fundamental principle on which the new law was based was free-choice marriage. It was expected that this would lay the foundation for releasing women from their abysmal existence in feudal marriage and alter the belief that for thousands of years regarded men as superior to women. Not only did both genders gain equal rights to divorce, but also marriages had to be monogamous; bigamy and other forms of plural marriage, as well as concubinage, were abolished. Also eliminated were child betrothal, bride prices, and any restrictions placed on the remarriage of widows.

Again with women's rights in mind, in 1980 a sweeping new law was passed to update the older law. The 1980 law specified that husband and wife hold equal legal statuses in the home and both have the freedom to engage in paid work, to study, and to participate in social activities. Neither party is allowed to restrain or interfere with the other. It is clear that the 1980 law bolstered the rights of women—especially urban women—in their homes, but most notable in rural areas, lack of enthusiasm for some provisions and minimal efforts of enforcement hampered progress. In the next two decades China witnessed alarming increases in domestic violence, child abandonment, a quadrupled divorce rate and large increases in poverty rates of divorced women. After years of legislative debate, amendments to the 1980 law were passed in 2001 that again are largely efforts to protect women's rights in their families. Adultery and cohabitation were outlawed, and property division in divorce was extended to include all property gained in a marriage, including salary, profits, and inheritance. Bigamy and forced marriage were already illegal, but ancient concubinage practices make the new law difficult to enforce (chapter 7).

By abolishing many of the blatant abuses existing in the feudal Chinese family, these marriage laws have been beneficial to women. But these successes must be tempered with the cultural realities of an ancient patriarchal society as well as other official policies that have undermined gender equality. For example, although about three-fourths of marriages are free-choice marriages it is still difficult to provide the conditions for young people to meet and develop relationships. Cultural restrictions on girls' activities combined with lack of privacy make reliance on arranged meetings and matchmakers acceptable alternatives. It is difficult to determine the extent to which these alternatives are freely chosen, regardless of the marriage laws. The law stresses "mutual responsibility and faithfulness in marriage," but it is exceedingly difficult to define, measure, and enforce this provision (Gittings, 2001). Despite the massive campaigns to create marriages and families based on egalitarian principles, the ideals envisioned in the new marriage law are far from the reality. Second wives are typical for wealthier men and jeopardize the families of all the unions. Kin customs pervade, and parents of potential partners still wield much authority in arranging marriages. A patrilocal extended family structure in rural areas continues to put new brides at a disadvantage and reinforces the preference for sons. Parents know that daughters are only temporary commodities. Ancient Chinese proverbs such as "Raising a daughter is like weeding another man's field," continue to be quoted and attest to the strength of the preference for sons.

The One-Child Policy

As noted in chapter 3, the extent of ancient traditions that put a premium on sons and devalue daughters has taken a more ominous turn. Government policy has focused on upgrading the status of women. They simultaneously introduced a stringent campaign to reduce population growth. These two goals have disastrously collided with one another. In 1978, the central government initiated the one-child policy. Whereas China had other programs to curb its rate of population growth, the one-child policy is unique in that enforcement is more uniform, with severe consequences for noncompliance. Massive public campaigns make prospective parents aware of the incentives or penalties related to the policy. The program of incentives has become standardized throughout most of China.

Couples receive one-child certificates which entitle them and their child to an annual cash subsidy. For subsequent children, an "excess child levy" is imposed as compensation for the extra burden placed on the state in educating and feeding the extra children. What makes these sanctions more punitive is that rewards for the single child must be returned with the birth of the second. If an employed woman with a one-child certificate gets pregnant again, she is encouraged to have an abortion. If she refuses she would lose her bonus, be left out of the next wage increase, and suffer scorn by her coworkers. Male sterilization is no option because it is seen to "weaken" men. The baby is inside her body so she is to blame (Wolf, 1993:349).

The policy has affected poorer urban families more than their rural counterparts. Although some rural areas show a decline in the birth rate, farm families have the ability to produce their own food in private plots for subsistence and profit, and "excess" children can be pressed into agricultural labor. Peasant communities recognize that enforcement of the one-child law is weaker in rural areas and often welcome two or three children per couple. If sanctions are applied, they are not nearly as detrimental when compared to the smaller urban family.

Son Preference. Regardless of location, the one-child policy has reinforced the preference for sons. Strong vestiges of ancestor worship exist throughout China. Many believe that they exist only by virtue of ancestors and live on in the spirit world at their own deaths. Ancestors are powerful and could bless or curse a family, so offerings and prayers must be bestowed frequently. A woman could gain ancestral status only through her husband and sons. Without male descendants she could have no afterlife. Chinese women who trace their family trees back three thousand years cannot find any women on them. Dismal indeed were the prospects of a wife who conceived no male children or who remained unmarried or a childless widow.

With one child as the option, that child had better be a male. Female infanticide has been practiced in China for centuries, but it diminished considerably in the decades after the Chinese revolution in 1949. Egalitarian ideology, large numbers of international adoptions of unwanted girls, outlawing of sex screening, and improvements in health care notwithstanding, incidents of female infanticide and deaths of girls through neglect continue to climb. It is a case of unintended effects of public policy and the limits of government coercion. In a culture that prides itself on large families, the one-child program is likely to be the most unpopular policy in contemporary China.

On the other hand, the latent functions of a one-child policy include reducing the significance of patrilineal heritage and encouraging women to make nontraditional career choices (Hong, 1987:317). And regardless of one-child policy strictures, Chinese couples increasingly say they desire only one child, many believing that future generations of women will be better off when the one child is a girl (Greenhalgh, 2001; Merli and Smith, 2002). In the long run the one-child policy may improve the status of women and make daughters more valued overall.

Enforcement of the one-child policy appears to be eroding among the rising middle class in urban areas like Shanghai and the exploding cities in Guangdong Province. Those couples who do desire more than one child are now wealthy enough to adequately provide for them, from obtaining high quality housing to sending them to private schools. Since they do not rely on government subsidies to survive and if they feel reasonably confident that they will not be criminalized, they can conveniently disregard the one-child agenda. Couples desiring more than one child are increasingly from urban areas and are also likely to be part of the highly educated, skilled, elite needed for the continued fueling of China's economy. Thus it is probable that their second child or third will be quietly ignored by the local authorities.

The long-term consequences of the one-child policy are unknown, but it is clear that at present the one-child policy has dire consequences for females. The jury is still out on its ultimate gendered consequences.

To Get Rich Is Glorious

Change is on the horizon. Under the banner of Chinese-style capitalism, the slogan "To get rich is glorious" has been eagerly embraced throughout China. Market-driven economic development is already influencing family life in both urban and rural areas. The massive entry of women into the paid labor force is one of the most consequential socioeconomic transformations in late twentieth-century China (Cartier, 2001). The impact of these initiatives at the household level is profound. In rural China, where women are valued for their domestic work, female employment rates are historically lower. Coupled with relaxed restrictions on migration, however, opportunities for off-farm income are rapidly accelerating.

Women's employment soared in historically unprecedented ways, many finding jobs near their villages or others migrating to the mushrooming global factories in China's Special Economic Zones (SEZs). As hosts to foreign investment firms, SEZs are a major engine driving market socialism—Chinese style capitalism—where the profit motive thrives unfettered. Others migrate as couples, the more educated among them bypassing factories for higher paying service and technical jobs (Xu, 2000; Fan and Li, 2002).

The Paradox of Women and Economic Development

It appears that state policy and economic reform are mutually supportive and foster both gender equality and women's economic integrity. Support for this contention is strong. Women's new activities in both rural and urban areas have significantly increased household income. This income is directly linked to improvement on important measures of health and well-being, including literacy, life expectancy, infant mortality, fertility, and maternal mortality. The increase in rural income is eroding woman's rural poverty. When women carry on farm work because husbands and children migrate, the expense may be offset by higher levels of household decision-making power (Mathews and Nee, 2000; DeBrau et al., 2002). Women welcome market-driven reforms that offer flexibility to on-farm work and the increased opportunities for off-farm employment, both of which help elevate their household status. Women report more confidence, independence, and freedom from patriarchal and parental control over their lives (Zhang, 1999). For urban working couples, women have more freedom to orchestrate job shifts according to their own educational and professional priorities (Zhou and Moen, 2001). The prediction that when globalization fuels market liberalization, gender inequity will increase and women's disadvantage will increase is not necessarily borne out by research in both rural and urban areas (Rozelle et al., 2002:21).

These trends are impressive. However, it also appears that China is not that different from the "classic" pattern documenting the downside of globalization and development for women. Globalization widens gender disparities in state sectors that hired more women, and they are the first to be laid off when market liberalization is ushered in (Roy, 2000; Lee, 2002). In areas where family-based rather than communal-based agriculture is now normative, farming shifts to older, less educated women (Wang, 2000). Despite greater overall household income, these women experience sharp increases in domestic responsibilities. Economic viability is weakened and future earnings compromised because when family members migrate, not only must additional help be hired, but also girls often drop out of school to work on the farm. Although women are expected to work outside the home, they work in gender differentiated jobs and are paid less than men. And when rural women do work for pay, the gender disparity in income is even greater. Although the government is officially committed to women's equality, it has not devised legal or administrative mechanisms to enforce it in the workplace. Women remain in transient, low-paying, and subordinate jobs.

China's WID paradox has several key dimensions. First, women's employment has skyrocketed at the same time as massive increases in unemployment for both men and women. Second, there are major gains in household income, especially in rural households, but women gain less than men, and in female-headed households there is an overall net loss. Third, essentialist beliefs about the proper place of women are reemerging. The belief that employment and family life are incompatible for women encourages them to return to hearth and home, and the problem of unemployment is "solved." At the same time, they hear other messages that they are needed in the labor force (Lindsey, 2004).

In addition to the fact that China is not a democracy, its enviable position as the world's largest market allows it to navigate its development course with apparently more freedom than its developing world neighbors. More data are needed to resolve the paradox. It remains uncertain if women in China will be culturally permitted to share in the "to get rich is glorious" mandate.

INDIA

As with other developing nations, India is confronting challenges that threaten its economic and political stability. At the one-billion mark, after China, it is the world's most populous nation. Considering the staggering problems related to population growth, land and food shortage, unemployment, and a growing disparity between poverty and wealth, India must look to all segments of its very heterogeneous society for solutions. Opportunities for women are a major factor in the solution of many of these problems, but economic planners have barely acknowledged this reality.

The Religious–Political Heritage

India is similar to Western nations in that its history and religious heritage reflect inconsistencies regarding the role of women. Goddess images, important female religious occupations, and critical economic roles for women in the pre-Vedic and Vedic eras (2500 to 300 B.C.E.) demonstrate a modicum of prestige for large numbers of women. Coupled with technological changes that excluded women, the ascendance of Hinduism gradually eroded this prestige and sent more women into a chattel-like existence. Indian women share a religious legacy with Western women. Their freedom and status are severely compromised when religion gains an institutional foothold (chapter 12).

By the beginning of the first century, India had gone through a period of decentralization of the authority of the various Indian states. High-caste Brahmin scholars were powerful enough to interpret the ancient *Smitris* (laws). By this time the *Laws of Manu* enveloped India and demonstrated the extent to which the position of women had deteriorated. Manu made a woman completely dependent on a man (husband, father, or son). Manu also forbade widow remarriage and reduced a widow's status to such a lowly extreme that the ritual of burning widows (*satis*) steadily took hold (chapter 12). The Laws of Manu not only demonstrated "the polarized male perception of the female" but were also used to both legitimize gender inequality and protect the interests of the ruling Brahmin class (Mitter, 1991:87).

The Social Reform Movement

By the nineteenth century, new ideas concerning the status of women began to emerge in India, and the roots of a reform movement took shape. Blatant aspects of the inhumane treatment of women were attacked, such as child marriage, lack of property rights, harsh purdah conditions, and the dismal condition of widows. Reformists were most successful when they accounted for the religious proscriptions embedded in these customs. They believed that regardless of caste or religion, such customs were responsible for the condition of women. Through education and literacy, however, women would make better wives and mothers. Although the position of some women may have been elevated by these strategies, reformists accepted the belief that a woman's life was restricted to her family life. Today the vast majority of rural and lower-caste women remain untouched by the reforms. Divorced, widowed, and single women are in peril when they have no source of male support in their families but cannot be employed for pay outside their homes. Cultural beliefs about women and marriage and the patriarchal organization of the Indian joint (extended) family impose huge economic hardships on women.

The Gandhis and Nehru. Serious questioning of women's roles came with Mahatma Gandhi, who believed that women were not only essential to India's quest for independence, but also that social justice demanded their equality. Given the nationalist sentiment and the charisma of Gandhi, women of all castes and regions flocked to the independence movement, assuming leadership roles and participating in all manners of political dissent (Desai, 2001; Sarkar, 2001). Jawaharlal Nehru shared Gandhi's vision. As India's first prime minister, and against much opposition, Nehru pushed through legislation giving women the rights of inheritance, divorce, and voting. But as with the reforms a century before, the effect was minimal for the majority of women. A strong women's movement in India worked for gender equality 30 years before independence. But its effectiveness was curtailed by agendas set by British colonialists and Indian nationalists who supported women only when their interests happened to coincide. Patriarchal bias held on in the postindependence era, and the contributions of women were not only forgotten, but women become victims in further conflicts (Anjum, 2000). The overall effect was, and to a large extent continues to be, that the vast majority of Indian women have not seen the effects of a woman's movement on their daily lives.

The Nehru factor in Indian politics has been played out politically since independence. Nehru's daughter, Indira Gandhi, succeeded to the post of prime minister in 1966 largely because she was a member of the Nehru dynasty and because her party believed they could control her. Her skill and strength proved them wrong. She was politically astute, using her gender as an asset rather than a liability. She identified herself as a member of the oppressed but also appealed to those looking for a mother-goddess figure, so imbued in the Hindu tradition (cited in D'Souza and Natarajan, 1986:373). Until her assassination Indira Gandhi ruled with an authoritarian hand for sixteen years.

The Gender Gap in Human Development

Though Indira Gandhi certainly served as a symbol for women who aspired to other than traditional roles, it must be said that her own commitment to elevating the position of women in India is far from realized. Over half of India's adult population is illiterate, but among males illiteracy is about 32 percent and among females it is 55 percent. Whereas 59 percent of boys continue to the secondary school level, only 40 percent of girls continue (USAID, 2003). Education translates to paid employment. When compared to the masses of unskilled female laborers in India, most of whom work in agriculture, professional women comprise only a tiny minority. Although there has been an expansion of female employment in general, this has not offset the decrease in the employment of unskilled women. The most important statistic related to gender and paid work is that 96 percent of women work in the **informal sector**, the economic activities of people who work as subsistence farmers, landless agricultural laborers, street vendors, or day workers. Many are employed in village and cottage industries (Lakhani, 2002). Much informal sector work is undocumented because services and goods rather than cash income is often the exchange basis. The United Nations' Human Development Index (HDI) is a composite measure of a nation's achievement in three categories related to health, education, and employment. India's rank of 127 out of 175 countries is directly linked to the fact that women and girls represent the largest proportion of the population living in absolute poverty (UNDP, 2003).

Health. Regarding health and reproduction, and despite development efforts, mortality rates have increased and life expectancy rates have decreased in some regions. Similar to China, the sex ratio in India is declining. Son preference contributes to higher mortality rates for females than males, with female infants less likely to receive the necessities for survival in poverty-ridden households. The neglect of girls is also linked to a strong, continuing dowry tradition in India. In highly stratified societies such as India, dowries, like other property, are a means of social mobility where men use rights over women to compete for social status. Although recent evidence suggests that girls and boys may be reaching parity in health and nutrition (Mishra et al., 2004), the harmful consequences of dowry and son preference on females discussed in chapter 3 have not been eradicated.

Frequent and excessive childbearing also severely compromises the health of women despite the fact that Indian women have knowledge of family planning and want to limit the number of children. In addition to strong cultural beliefs about a man's right to have frequent and unprotected sex on demand with his wife, women remain unaware of methods enabling them to space births, with less than 10 percent using any spacing method. The most widely used method of contraception is female sterilization, with one-fourth of married women unaware of male sterilization as a modern contraception device (UNDP, 2003). The inability to space births is correlated with both maternal mortality and infant mortality. When a mother dies in childbirth, it is also likely that her infant will die soon thereafter.

The increased mortality rate for females in India is also linked to the explosion of HIV. Ten percent of the world's HIV-positive population is in India, and women are infected at faster rates than men (Heine, 2003). India's increasing infection rates were first linked to the sex workers in the hundreds of villages off the major highways servicing truck drivers and men in neighboring villages. In these locales girls are socialized early to put on makeup and go out to earn money to support the family. Girls are clean and well fed, and boys are not. But their HIV rate is staggering, and many of them report that they have never even seen a condom (*Asia-Pacific Population and Policy*, 1995).

HIV is no longer restricted to high risk groups such as sex workers or drug users. The virus is on the rise in rural areas and among all castes. Research suggests that in three of India's largest states, three out of four rural women have not even heard of HIV/AIDS (OneWorld, 2003). These are the women who are infected by their husbands but cannot refrain from sex with them. Can poor women insist their husbands wear condoms? "Yes, in an ideal world, but in India most women are forced to treat their husbands like God" (Sify, 2003). Sex workers also have limited choices regarding their sexual partners. Even if they have knowledge about the disease, a fatalistic attitude about their lives persists. "What can we do?" asks one young woman. "We have to earn a living. The choice is dying of AIDS or dying of starvation" (Roy, 1994).

Feminism in an Indian Context

The disheartening Human Development Index does not go unnoticed by officials at all levels of government. A revitalized feminist movement led by strong NGOs has promoted serious governmental attention in efforts to put the principles of development and democracy into practice. The central government has taken its first steps to combat the negative impact of a restructured economy on poor women and those in the informal sector. Violence against women, especially dowry-murder, is also a priority. The Indian women's movement has made strides in public awareness to domestic violence and is a watch guard to ensure that laws are passed and enforced rather than passed and ignored (*India News*, 2001; Rudd, 2001). A five-year plan that specifically addresses the issues of excessive female mortality and low literacy rates of women was recently adopted. Programs designed to combine traditional and modern medicine in a way that is acceptable to the rural population are underway. Efforts to combat AIDS through education and awareness that account for traditional beliefs and cultural practices will be more successful.

Through their efforts on social and welfare measures, women's organizations are increasingly being drawn into the political process, with political parties beginning to recognize the importance of the women's vote. Training is a component of this process as well. Outreach programs for poor, marginalized producer women are enhancing their empowerment and self-reliance. Family-owned microenterprises in India are more productive when women have joint decision making with men. At the community level, they are starting to participate and influence decisions in local self-governing bodies and for the first time are exerting their voting rights at all levels. Organizations such as SEWA (Self-Employed Women's Association) are trade unions successfully representing poor, self-employed women who comprise the huge invisible labor force of India. With SEWA's advocacy, many of these women have seen enough of an income increase to move out of abject poverty.

As successful as these efforts may be, the feminist movement in India is constrained by some of the same issues faced by feminism worldwide. The movement has been unable to expand its diversity and attract rural women or to effectively mentor poor women as grassroots leaders. NGOs that make up the movement continue to be led and controlled by women from elite castes. Whereas the activists working for independence in the early twentieth century were able to create a sense of sisterhood that transcended caste and cultural boundaries, the contemporary movement has been unable to replay that achievement.

The feminist movement in India proceeds through a loose network of NGOs that must pursue different agendas in advocating for various constituencies and who in turn garner varying degrees of media attention and government support. A key factor preventing them from speaking in a unified voice is how to portray the brutal reality of life faced by millions of Indian women but also refrain from a victimization discourse that tends to dismiss the subversive tactics women routinely use to resist oppression. New strategies to address the everyday experiences of women (microlevel analysis) and to account for conditions of change due to globalization and the emerging political economy (macrolevel analysis) are necessary for feminism to be a tool for achieving a more inclusive, gender equitable social order in India (John, 2001; Mehrotra, 2002). Fueled by feminists in India and supported by the international NGO network, a concerted government effort is necessary to even begin to approach Mahatma Gandhi's vision of an inclusive society. Indian women are beginning to challenge the rigid cultural codes of their country.

JAPAN

When comparing gender role patterns in Japan to other developed nations, we immediately confront a series of contradictions. During World War II, Japanese and American women had much in common in that both assumed major responsibility for the functioning of the domestic economy, yet were denied leadership positions in the government and industries that relied on their services.

The Occupation

After Japan's surrender in 1945, Occupation forces were determined to establish policies supporting the emergence of a democratic system compatible with a Japanese cultural climate. Japan's remarkable advances in economic growth, health, higher education, and overall prosperity attest to the spectacular success of the experiment in guided social change introduced during the Occupation. In congruence with this, major shifts in attitudes occurred regarding equality of human relationships, particularly those involving women and men (Suzuki, 1991:246). It can be argued that the single largest beneficiary of this experiment was the Japanese woman.

Occupation policy was also dictated by the provisions of the Potsdam Declaration, July 26, 1945, which mandated that democratic tendencies among the Japanese people be strengthened and that freedom of speech, religion, and respect for the fundamental human rights be ensured. With the enactment of the new Showa Constitution on May 3, 1947, five articles provided for rights of women. Included are the assurances of equality under the law with no discrimination because of race, creed, sex, social status, or family origin; universal adult suffrage; equal education based on ability (women could be admitted to national universities); permission for women to run for public office; and marriage based on a couple's mutual consent. Although legal guarantees are only valid through stringent enforcement, Japanese women in 1947 in essence had greater rights than American women because their new constitution explicitly provided for gender equality. A similar statement of equality is embodied in the Equal Rights Amendment to the United States Constitution, but this has yet to be passed.

Gender Equity and Public Policy

The legal assurances of equality had their greatest impact on Japanese employment practices beginning with the Occupation. Laws were enacted that guaranteed women protection from long work hours, as well as pregnancy and menstrual leave, and emphasized that a new Japan required the strong support of women as the producers and socializers of the next generation (White, 1991). It is obvious today that such laws serve to inhibit women's advancement and stereotype women as less physically capable than men. Yet it took 30 years before the disparity was acknowledged. The Equal Employment Opportunity Law (EEOL), passed in 1986, calls for equal pay and other improvements in hiring and working conditions. Unfortunately, without viable enforcement provisions, many employers simply do not adhere to the law. Others believe the failure of the law is due to the principle of Japanese *gradualism,* which companies use to block unpopular initiatives by invoking cultural norms emphasizing social order over the potential disorder produced by policy enactment (Knapp, 1999). Gradualism can take so long that, without continued advocacy, a policy will never be enacted. Although some changes have occurred in terms of overt discrimination and public consciousness and support for activism relating to women in the labor force have increased, the law remains weak and can neither prevent gender-based personnel policies nor tackle the monumental problems of indirect discrimination (Gelb, 2000).

A more recent governmental approach to gender issues is the creation of the Gender Equality Bureau, a Cabinet level council created in 1994 and upgraded by an act of the Japanese Diet in 1997. Envisioned as a policy to take a stand on women's issues well into the twenty-first century and with new receptiveness to feminist input, this council produced a Basic Plan for Gender Equality in 1999. Like EEOL, however, the Plan's enactment is seriously hampered by competing views about traditional values related to women's place in society and by lack of funds to oversee the reforms needed (Osawa, 2000). The Bureau continues to be directed by all male high-level officials who seek input from the few women holding political office in Japan, by NGOs, and through UN initiatives on gender equity. Men thus hold virtually all the decision-making power about gender equity in Japan.

To its credit, support for elements of the Plan is evident. Issues related to human rights and violence against women, gender equality training for teachers, closing the (already narrow) gender gap in education, and on the global level, funding programs aiding women in the developing world have met with fairly high levels of public enthusiasm (Gender Equality Bureau, 2003). On the other hand, key provisions of the Plan related to gender equality at home, at work, and in the community reveal large and persistent attitude gaps between women and men, between the married and unmarried, and between homemakers and employed women. Men talk about the economic burden of marriage, and women talk about the difficulty of harmonizing home and family life. Employed women and homemakers report being overburdened with household responsibilities and caregiving to elderly parents-in-law (almost 100 percent of caregivers in Japan are women) (Ogawa et al., 2003). Highly educated women serve tea or are secretaries to male superiors with less education or training. Regardless of these differences, however, cultural values about the proper roles of men and women in Japan remain largely intact. Another dilemma is that Japan will soon face a huge labor shortage, but rather than violating a cultural norm of providing equal opportunities for women, the government is willing to violate another taboo—encouraging large-scale immigration from foreign men to fill Japan's labor shortage (French, 2001a).

Despite decades of litigation, gender discrimination in recruitment, employment, and pay remains intact, and lack of opportunities for women outside their homes persists. Women have equal rights but, in addition to discrimination, negative attitudes about ambitious, rebellious women who do not conform to social norms are rampant (White, 2001:152) The Plan established Gender Equality Week and other annual campaigns to raise awareness of gender issues, but awareness of equality does not match Japan's massive inequality.

Work and Family: A Nondilemma

The cultural belief that women in the labor force are temporary commodities until marriage is so taken for granted that the issue of a work–family collision may be viewed as a "nondilemma." Japanese couples certainly discuss the issue and may express regrets with how it is played out in their lives. Married women know that the roles of wife and mother will limit their employment opportunities, but the issue is almost always resolved in favor of home over workplace. As woman often point out, a "guillotine falls on their careers on their wedding day" (Off-Centre, 2001).

Like women throughout the world, women in the Japanese labor force are constrained by restrictive and stereotyped gender roles. Though they make up almost half the work force, they are concentrated in lower-level jobs with poorer working conditions and insecure long-term prospects, and with a wage gap of 65 percent, they earn far less than comparable males (Broadbent, 2001; Gender Equality Bureau, 2003). The gender education gap is rapidly closing, but women are virtually excluded from management positions in most Japanese firms. The flexibility associated with female employment makes it easy to hire or fire women, keeps women as part of a peripheral labor force, and excludes them from the fringe benefits associated with permanent jobs, such as the potential for lifetime employment which is reserved for selected male employees (Broadbent, 2002a). As a result of the highly competitive global economy, women's labor is becoming casualized, pushing women into even more "nonregular" jobs (Bishop, 2000).

Japanese women entering paid employment do so largely as reentry employees after child rearing. They are likely to be middle aged women who are concentrated in part-time or temporary employment and who take lower-level jobs not commensurate with their education. They face discrimination due to a combination of gender, age, and family status factors. (Weathers, 2001). Many of these women would choose to be in full-time, permanent positions but face systemic cultural barriers limiting their access and locking them into a secondary labor market (Broadbent 2002b; Yu, 2002). The large number of reentry women bolsters the belief that women should not be hired or trained for permanent positions because they will inevitably leave their jobs when they get married (less likely today) or when they become mothers (highly likely today). Whether by choice or circumstance, this pattern continues unabated for women and the gendered division of labor remains universal and unchallenged.

Marriage and the Family

It is said that Japanese women walk with their feet pointing to the inside, toward *uchi* (home). The pull toward home and any perceived incompatibility between home and family life are so powerful that the uchi-pointing path is the only realistic one for the vast majority of Japanese women (Hirao, 2001; Bueno, 2002). Girls are socialized into traditional gender role values early in life. High school continues to drive their preparation to become full-time homemakers even as they tackle the courses preparing them for the difficult university entrance exams. Girls express ambivalence about the gender paths laid out before them and are aware of the stereotyped messages they receive, but like women throughout Japan, they know they will be full-time homemakers for at least a portion of their lives (Shikakura and Hougham, 2000; Nishimura, 2001).

In comparison to other industrialized nations, Japan is also unusual in that both women's labor force activity and fertility declined in the latter half of the twentieth century. The more common global pattern is that a lower fertility rate, especially for highly educated women, is associated with higher labor force participation. At 1.38 in 2003, Japan has the lowest fertility rate in the world. This trend reflects the demand that educated women can offer the one or two children they have the highest quality home environment.

Given powerful cultural beliefs that a woman's goal in life is to bear children, this trend is not surprising. Motherhood remains the essence of a woman's social and personal identity. A women's role is ranked as mother first and wife second. Employment is not even considered in the ranking hierarchy. This expectation is so strong that it is virtually impossible for employed women with preschoolers to escape social judgment if anything is amiss at home when she is at work (Kashiwagi and Hasuka, 2000). A mother is solely responsible for her child's well-being. The principle of segregation into different spheres puts a greater burden on her when compared to her American counterpart. Those few professional women who do remain in their jobs may compensate by employing substitute housewives or relying on their mothers who live with or near them. Such an arrangement provides no assurances of equality on the job nor does it eradicate role overload. But it does allow some measure of occupational success for women who refuse to give up the domestic sphere of mother and wife.

Demography and Family Change. Demographic shifts are impacting marriage and the family in Japan. Besides the world's lowest fertility rate, Japan has the happy distinction of having the world's highest life expectancy rate. By 2030 Japan will have the largest percent of the oldest old (those 85 and older) in the world. Women are marrying later and waiting longer to have children, preferring instead to embark on university education offering them more options for employment (Retherford et al., 2001; Raymo, 2003).

Delayed marriages for women, who still marry at younger ages than men, has created a huge number of bachelors. In Tokyo alone over 40 percent of men in their early thirties are bachelors who live with their parents. Young people who continue to live with their parents when they are employed full time and have finished their education are derisively referred to as "parasite singles" or "spongers" (Hayashi, 2003). Representing yet another Japanese contradiction, despite the fact that men are not seen as possessing domestic skills necessary to survive on their own, male parasite singles are more disparaged than females. They may lament a bride short-age, but they are in no hurry to prove to a potential spouse that they will participate in housework or child care. The vast majority of husbands do not engage in any domestic work in meaningful ways (Gender Equality Bureau, 2003). In their defense, however, many of these men will fill the ranks of the "salarymen"—compa-ny men who are expected to spend 10 to 14 hours a day on and off the job with their colleagues. These are the men held responsible for Japan's success in the global economy. Whereas a woman garners social disapproval from perceived neglect of her children, a man garners it from perceived neglect of his job.

After centuries of arranged marriages, love matches took hold in Japan by the 1970s. Romance is sought by young women and men, but it is increasingly difficult to find once they leave school and enter a highly gender segregated labor force largely comprised of full-time married men and part-time married women. The shortage of eligible brides is reflected in the emergence of matchmakers and Japanese date clubs which unlike singles bars, do not serve alcohol and allow cou-ples to size each other up across smoked glass dividers (French, 2001b). "Groom schools," where men learn to polish their social skills to attract women into matri-mony, offer other options. Unlike in the United States, this is a facet of an expand-ing marriage industry catering primarily to men and one in which women retain a high degree of power in the process of mate selection (Nagao, 1993).

Another contradiction presents itself when considering the role of women in the Japanese family. Postwar changes concerning women saw laws that no longer regarded them as incompetent. Parental consent was abolished as a condition for marriage beyond a certain age, divorce by mutual consent was possible, and in a divorce, property would now be divided between husband and wife. It would appear, therefore, that such laws were to augment the wife's lowly status in the fam-ily. Herein lies the paradox. On the one hand Japanese women are depicted as pow-erless, relegated to domestic drudgery; buffeted by the demands of her husband, her child's school, and her in-laws; and expected to be humble and submissive. But this stands in opposition to a strong tradition of decision making in the family to the extent that the Japanese housewife is viewed as being in full control of domes-tic life with almost unlimited autonomy (Iwao, 1993).

To shed light on this paradox, it is likely that most women fall between on a submissiveness–assertiveness continuum, but that there is gradual, steady move-ment toward the assertiveness pole. Women hold highly specialized roles in the domestic sphere and are inferior to men on measures related to esteem, power, honor, privilege, and authority. Thus women as a group are defined by the princi-ples of domesticity, seclusion, and inferiority, although individual women can be placed at some point along a continuum for each element (Lebra, 1984:2). If infe-riority is assigned to women in certain spheres, it is balanced somewhat by the pow-ers of their domestic role. Overall, the long-held view of the submissive Japanese woman is challenged by research showing that women are active agents in con-structing and reconstructing their identities in positive ways in their family and are influential players in its decision making (Liddle and Nakajima, 2000).

Motherhood. Being a Japanese woman is synonymous with motherhood (Jolivet, 1997). Mothers are revered, almost idealized, by their children and the mother–child bond is viewed as an almost sacred dyad (Notter, 2002). With such strong mother–child attachments and concern that the mother–child role may be compromised, children in Japan are reared for more dependence and less autonomy than American children, a socialization factor contributing to the parasite single syndrome noted earlier. From a functionalist view, the more dependent the child, the more indispensable the mother. Husbands, too, assume a childlike dependence on their wives. Patriarchy exists outside the home, but a husband who does household work deprives his wife of domestic matriarchy. Nowhere is domestic matriarchy more evident than in how household expenses are divided. Although it is expected that the husband is the provider, the wife maintains full control over the financial management of the household. Paradoxically, his authority is demonstrated when he hands over his paycheck to her. In this sense patriarchy and matriarchy are reciprocal. Earning the money is his responsibility. Managing the money is hers.

A Japanese Woman's Profile

Given all these contradictions, how can the contemporary Japanese woman be portrayed? Surveys suggest that the portrait is of a person who values family life and will sacrifice for it, who is unwilling to divorce even in an unsatisfactory marriage, who believes she is discriminated against in both society as well as in the family, but who is also proud of her decision-making family role, especially in financial matters. She is also more egalitarian and more individualistic in her role values than women were in the 1970s but does not openly identify with feminist values calling for gender equality in broader society (Akita, 2000; Yamaguchi, 2000; Ezawa, 2003). She is likely to have worked outside the home until her first child was born and then to have returned to the labor force when the oldest child entered high school. In her homemaker role, she is a professional and enjoys the status associated with being a "good wife and wise mother" (Hendry, 1993). Mariko, a forty-four year old, middle class Tokyo suburban woman with three children, two part-time jobs, and a disengaged husband, exemplifies this pattern. The moving ethnographic case study of Mariko provides us insight into the life of a Japanese woman.

> It was a Japanese life, a woman's life, no worse and no better than so many others, a life spent largely in reaction to children, to a husband, to sick parents. Even on a good day Mariko knew how hard it was to get out in front of her life, to do the few things she wanted to do, to feel a sense of accomplishment, to have fun

> . . . . Her children were getting older and would soon be gone, just in time, it seemed, for her to turn around and be a parent to her parents (Bumiller, 1995:289).

As women achieve higher levels of education the principle of seclusion into separate domestic and occupational spheres will also be weakened. It is unlikely, however, that these women will disavow what they perceive as their basic domestic responsibilities.

Women in Japan have been vital in bringing their country to economic prominence in the world, in achieving a high standard of living, and in amassing the globe's best overall health record. Coupled with media images of modernity, legal reform paved the way for challenges to the ancient patriarchal model in Japan.

These reforms helped prompt limited, but increased support for gender equity in the home and workplace and more involvement from both parents in child rearing (Makita and Ida, 2001; Bassani, 2003; Sato, 2003). Reform has proceeded through elements of feminist activism linking different women's and citizen groups under a common banner. Compared to the women's movements in other countries, however, mass-based feminism in Japan is still at an embryonic stage. As young women assess the opportunity costs of marriage, social norms propelling them into early marriage and social disapproval for singlehood are eroding (MacKellar and Horlacher, 2000). Women are demanding expanded roles and greater autonomy for those roles, more than men at this point see (Tanifuji, 1995). Rising expectations and the wish to improve one's lot in life will provide the basis for reforms aimed at equalizing the positions of women and men.

LATIN AMERICA

Latin America exhibits a great deal of diversity in terms of ecology, politics, and culture, but common features can be identified, including a rigid class structure, the prevalence of Catholicism, and a colonial heritage from Spain and Portugal that help to define the region. Latin American women also demonstrate both diversity and common features that unite and divide them. Although there has been a marked improvement in the overall situation of Latin American women, a gender gap in all human development indicators persists.

The Gender Divide

As discussed in chapter 8, the socialization of men and women in Latino cultures hinges on the concepts of *machismo* and *marianismo,* which are viewed as mutually exclusive beliefs separating the genders. Because machismo emphasizes virility, sexual prowess, and the ideological and physical control of women, it is associated with legitimating violence against women as well as compromised physical and mental health among men. Its long-term ideological effect reproduces male privilege throughout all social institutions. Machismo allows for male dominance in the household and is invoked to restrict socioeconomic, sexual, and other lifestyle choices of women. Reinforced by teachings of the Roman Catholic Church, marianismo is associated with glorification and spiritual verification of motherhood, a stoic acceptance of one's earthly lot, and the endurance of an unhappy marriage. Unlike men, the moral superiority of women maintains that hardship is suffered in silence. It has evolved as a nearly universal model of behavior for Latin American women.

These rigid images are more likely to be embraced by the *mestizos*—people of mixed Indian and Spanish descent. Before the Spanish conquest there was apparently more egalitarianism and role complementarity between men and women. The conquistadors brought views of women stemming from Old World religious and feudal attitudes that allowed marianismo and machismo to eventually become entrenched in the New World. Although this ideology survives today, research on Guatemalan wives suggests that women's behavior is not merely a response to machismo but also a survival strategy emerging from female economic, political, and social dependence on men (Ehlers, 1993). From a conflict perspective, gender relations shift with the material conditions of women's lives.

On the other hand, cracks in the gender divide are evident. Women who achieve higher levels of education and work in well-paying jobs are less likely to embrace marianismo ideology, trends identified in Brazil, Costa Rica, and Chili. Research on men in Nicaragua finds them coming together to form groups such as the Association of Men Against Violence which challenge machismo ideology. In "unlearning" machismo, they improve well-being for both themselves and all the women in their lives and "reclaim the human dimension of their beings." Indeed, in postrevolutionary Nicaragua the unlearning of machismo is truly revolutionary (Welsh, 2001:190).

Family Planning. Discourses on issues surrounding family planning and reproduction provide other indications of a potential machismo–marianismo crack. NGO initiatives resulting from the UN Beijing conference include persuading governments to review family planning and birth control issues. Both politically and culturally, Latin America remains solidly linked to the Catholic Church. In Chile, for example, the close relationship between the state and the Catholic Church has greatly impacted women's lives and thwarted widespread efforts at family planning (Willmott, 2002). In contrast, Peru has collided with the Vatican in policies to disseminate birth control material and to ensure that women have counseling to achieve their desires with respect to birth spacing. Although women and their families will certainly benefit from this, it is also in response to the doubling of Peru's population since 1960, about half of whom live in extreme poverty, and a fertility rate of 6.2 among women with little or no education. Despite the Church's stubbornness, Peru's family planning policies have been generally successful. In 1990 the fertility rate was 4.1, and in 2000 it was estimated to be 3.1. It is expected to drop to 2.3 by 2020 (McDevitt, 1999). The appointment of women to top level cabinet posts in Peru provides more political clout to implement state-supported family planning efforts.

Nicaragua has followed suit with government policy now stating that reproductive health, sex education, and services in family planning will be available to women. While continuing to condemn abortion to prevent pregnancy and for population control, Nicaragua recognizes a woman's right to decide when and how frequently she will have children. These positions have been advocated despite the Church's insistence that it is sinful to practice any form of birth control other than the rhythm method. Political influence for Latin American women has previously been exercised mostly within informal settings and in regard to accepted cultural norms that have not seriously challenged gender role differentiation. The influence of feminist NGOs is altering this pattern. Even in conservative Chile feminist discourse on human rights related to reproductive and sexual rights is being heard and is unleashing the potential for policy changes on issues of birth control (Willmott, 2002).

Latin American Women, Globalization, and Development

Research also confirms the link between the erosion of women's position with globalization and development strategies that harm rather than help women. Structural adjustment programs (SAPs) designed to increase foreign investment eliminated some jobs in the private sector but many more in the public sector, which employed more women. As a group women shoulder the brunt of the SAPs. In Mexico and Costa Rica, for example, SAPs increased levels of female unemployment, malnutrition, poor health, and illiteracy. Women's empowerment was severely compromised—impoverishment and disempowerment go hand in hand (Anastaskos, 2002).

In the agricultural sector, the forces of globalization remove subsistence farming as an economically productive activity of women. A family's economic degradation accelerates when males enter external labor markets and receive cash income. Women are often abandoned by men and enter into fragile and temporary alliances with other men for the same reasons they originally wed—for money and children (Ehlers, 1993:319). Thus in addition to religion and the survival of feudal attitudes, economic factors remain important in explaining the inferior position of women in Latin American cultures. Except for certain regions, most notably in Brazil and Argentina, Latin America remains underdeveloped after almost 500 years of European colonization, the establishment of independent republics in the nineteenth century, and the elimination of dictatorships and communist regimes in the twentieth century. Underdevelopment can be approached through *dependency theory,* which looks at the unequal relationships between Latin America and world markets. Dependency theory can be used to explain how processes of change have specifically affected women in Latin America. Unequal opportunities due to fluctuations in world markets negatively influence the region anyway, but the effects on women are disastrous.

The transformation from subsistence farming to commercial agriculture hastens this process. Both psychologically and monetarily, women lose ground as a result. When women take nonagricultural jobs, their economic returns are very low. In the expanding industrial centers, work is segmented by gender, and women work in low-paying, nonunion, dead-end jobs. Development issues are also intricately tied to the innumerable economic crises and political transitions that have occurred in Latin America. Not only are women and children the most vulnerable when the subsistence economy erodes, but also in response to debt burdens, governments cut welfare budgets first. State policy and agricultural reform are not gender neutral but indeed serve to diminish the status of rural women.

Feminist Agendas

Latin American women have not been passive observers to these economic events and continue to engage in collective action to ensure their survival. In contrast to women's movements in other parts of the developing world, the Latin American movement has been much more successful in consensus building and developing a feminist agenda embraced by women from a wide variety of backgrounds (Friedman, 2002; Vargas, 2002). Large numbers of peasant women, for example, are grassroots leaders, core organizers, and mentors for the next generation of leaders from their villages. In coalition with international NGOs, Latino feminists actively participated in those struggles leading to the establishment of democratic regimes throughout Central and South America (Luciak, 2001). This organizational legacy provided strength in numbers and the political shrewdness to challenge economic and social policies deemed detrimental to women. Feminist voices are heard when states prioritize reforms and when questions about gender-based discrimination are addressed. Unlike women in India, who are hindered in gender equity by peasant reform movements, such tactics by Latin American women allow them to become more politically astute and to form both a class and gender consciousness.

The Class–Gender Link. The plight of the majority of Latin American women who are in poverty is contrasted sharply with upper- and upper-middle-class women who are employed in professional occupations or who are part of the elite leisure class. Career women are supported by their husbands, parents, and other institutionalized devices that allow them to combine professional and family roles. The irony here is that professional success is to a large extent dependent on the hiring of domestic help. Domestics provide services that help to blunt the impact of a career on the family. Domestic servants in Latin America—many of whom migrate from other countries to these jobs—represent the majority of female wage earners. There is considerable disagreement about whether working as a servant provides a channel for upward mobility or whether it reinforces a rigid stratification system based on class (Pappas-Deluca, 1999; Radcliffe, 1999). Although data on the role of globalization in the lives of domestic servants and their employers are needed to help resolve the issue, it is a prime example of the intersection of class and gender and the difficulty of separating their relative influence in explaining the role and status of Latin American women.

Feminist scholars and political activists in Latin America also have yet to resolve the issue of whether class or gender is the overarching issue that serves to perpetuate the low status of women. Over two decades ago consensus emerged among Latin American feminists that both categories are valid. Women's liberation reinforces class struggle. In sociological terms, this is congruent with a strong conflict theory orientation within the socialist/Marxist branch of feminism asserting that patriarchy influences women to uphold a system that perpetuates their inferior position. Only when class and gender barriers are simultaneously assaulted can equality for all people be realized.

ISRAEL

Issues of gender equality have been salient in Israel since its new beginning as an independent nation. We are aware of impressive experiments partly challenging traditional forms of gender stratification, such as in the military and on the kibbutz. The rise of Golda Meier to the highest political position in the fledgling state is another often-cited instance in how far women can progress. Legislatively, women in Israel have achieved what women in the United States continue to fight for, such as paid maternity leave and equal opportunities with men in education and employment. What is the success of these experiments?

Despite impressive gains and the internalization of an egalitarian gender role ideology, feminists contend that gender equality in Israel is illusory and the system that informally serves to limit the choices of women remains intact. The military, for example, is often displayed as the height of gender egalitarianism because Jewish Israeli women have been conscripted since the state was founded.

Despite conscription, however, the Israeli Defense Force (IDE) is probably the most gendered of all social institutions in Israel. Women are exempt if they marry, get pregnant or declare that they are religiously observant. They are excluded from military role IDE jobs that allow for promotion and higher pay. IDE jobs are strongly gender segregated. The majority of women soldiers are secretaries, clerks, or health personnel (Frankfort-Nachmias, 2001:135). Similar to the military in other countries, the IDE functions as a rite of passage into male adulthood and identity and ultimately shapes the discourse leading to beliefs perpetuating gender inequality in other parts of society (Klein, 2002).

Myths of gender equality in the Jewish state are traced to socialist egalitarian rhetoric before the modern founding of Israel (Swirski and Safir, 1991). Alongside the egalitarian ideal and ideology favoring increased status for women, the thrust of Israeli public policy serves to reinforce traditional gender roles. This thrust is related to three key institutions: religion, family, and government, all of which are intertwined and all of which are tied to fundamental concerns about national security.

Religion, Family, and Employment

Israeli society is organized around the principle of the family as the dominant institution and the family as the cradle of Jewish heritage. As such, the Jewish family is tied to ancient religious traditions, which are unquestionably patriarchal in nature. The family is what defines the woman's role. Israel is neither a religious nor a secular state, but rabbinical courts have jurisdiction over matters of marriage and divorce, and their interpretations tend to favor Judaism's most traditional branch—that of Orthodox Judaism (Graetz, 2003). Women in all branches, however, are expected to be in charge of domestic functions and prepare their households for religious observances. These roles in turn free men to study, to teach, to be breadwinners, and to be more fully engaged in the religious life of the community. A woman may contribute to her community's social and economic life, and she may see the division of household tasks as unfair, but religious ideology takes precedence over gender ideology in most Jewish Israeli Families (Blumen, 2002).

Kibbutzim. It may seem contradictory that a patriarchal family structure reinforced by seemingly immutable religious beliefs could give rise to a gender egalitarian experiment in collectivization, the kibbutz. Dating from a century ago the *kibbutz* is an Israeli agricultural collective in which children are raised together in an arrangement that allows parents to become full participants in the economic life of the community. Initially designed as a radical departure from the traditional gender division of labor in the family, the kibbutz represented an effort at eliminating distinctions between the work of men and the work of women.

It is the child-centered approach to cooperative living that distinguishes the kibbutz from other communes worldwide. Until about 1970, kibbutzim (plural form) were characterized by collectivization in family and work life that minimized gender role differences and maximized instrumental and expressive role sharing. In the spirit of communal socialization, between one and two months after birth, infants were moved to a children's house, where they spent the next twelve years of their lives living with their peers. The Sabbath was reserved for children and their parents to spend time together, but teachers and nurses were responsible for the daily socialization of children. Although children did not live with their biological parents, the parents were still critical to their development. Children identify with them and derive security, love, and affection from them. Ideally, such an arrangement would free both parents from child-care responsibilities which would in turn allow them to work for the betterment of the community as a whole. Again, based on the principle of gender equality, it is assumed that there is no substantial differentiation between the roles performed by women and men.

These principles, however, have not been sustained. Raising children communally increased women's dissatisfaction with kibbutz life and distanced men from their children. Some men reported the same feelings of dissatisfaction. Research shows, for example, that men's satisfaction with fatherhood increases significantly when children sleep at home rather than with their peers (Lev-Wiesel, 2000). The "child-centered" approach is being gradually replaced by the "family centered" approach—"nuclear like" in structure—with children raised by their parents and living at home. Regardless of this change, however, women are still more likely to leave the kibbutz than men. Second and third generation kibbutzim children are abandoning the kibbutz in favor of urban living and nuclear families. The loss of agricultural profit has fueled outmigration of young people and further undermined the strong egalitarian ideology of the traditional kibbutz (Gavron, 2000). In addition, once financial stability and numbers sufficient for kibbutz survival were assured, gender stratification and segregated jobs accelerated. Today women function almost exclusively as child-care workers, nurses, teachers, and kitchen workers.

Although it is uncertain what the kibbutz family will look like in the future, kibbutzim members are equipping themselves with the social and economic tools to bolster community survival (Mort and Brenner, 2000). The change in kibbutzim from relationships based on cooperation, community, and equality are also traced to a stronger emphasis of market relationships and how to survive in the global economy. As in other counties, the market approach to life has a negative impact on women in Israel (Palgi, 2003). Overall, however, the legacy of equalitarianism in the kibbutz has not vanished and it is likely that the legacy will be evident in emerging kibbutzim forms.

Education. Although the gender gap in Israeli education is small and higher education for both females and males is encouraged and normative, education and religion work together to influence beliefs about marriage and the family in Israel's youth. Religious schools inculcate a religious-based conception of womanhood that is shaped by both divine law and the male world (Rapoport et al., 1995). Education, however, is a powerful factor in moderating the views of Jewish women when women have the authority to interpret scripture. Women have increased their numbers in seminaries and being ordained as rabbis in all branches of Judaism except Orthodox.

The Workplace. Across the globe, increases in education and smaller family size fuel women's employment and offer them alternatives to domestic roles. When women venture into the workplace they face gender gaps in earning, higher rates of unemployment and underemployment, and occupational gender segregation regardless of their job level. They also face the effects of globalization. They risk the loss of public sector jobs but face the less pay and more pay discrimination in existing private sector jobs. When conflict arises between family and employment, unless in dire circumstances, employment is rejected to deal with family responsibilities. Israel is no exception to these patterns (Kulik, 2000; Yaish and Kraus, 2003). Despite the Equal Opportunity Law passed by the Knesset in 1988 prohibiting discrimination in advertising, training, promotion, and severance pay and later provisions prohibiting sexual harassment and unequal fringe benefits, these patterns persist. Laws are ineffective if enforcement is lax and women do not challenge the discrimination they routinely experience (Kraus, 2002). Most important is that women continue to be viewed—and often view themselves—as wives and mothers first and much further down on the ranking scale, as secondary breadwinners.

Jewish Feminism

Public policy overall has not significantly helped with the burdens women must face in carrying out their roles and the contradictions they face within these roles. To counter ancient traditionalism which hampers gender equity, the policy-making process must be used to translate the needs of women into effective and culturally acceptable legislation.

The feminist movement in Israel is clearly the vanguard to do this necessary translation, but lack of unity among Jewish women has hampered its goals. Feminism was imported to Israel from the West in the 1970s and like in the West, its agenda was shaped by the leadership of educated professional women. For two decades the movement remained dominated by Ashkenazi women—largely white, European-oriented and solidly middle class (Freedman, 2003). Feminist conferences held during the 1990s were marked by considerable dissent from Jewish women of color and working class women representing women from Mizrahi, Palestinian, Bedouin, Asian, and Ethiopian backgrounds. Mizrahi women, whose heritage is traced to Arab North Africa, the Middle East, and East Asia, led the rallying cry that signaled hidden, deep divisions within Jewish feminism (Motzafi-Haller, 2000, 2001). They asserted that feminism as constructed by Ashkenazim could not possibly speak for the diversity of women in Israel. They accused feminism of tokenism, and of ignoring the plight of poor and marginalized Jewish and non-Jewish women. This accusation led to the formation of a separate branch of feminism. This new branch appears to be growing in stature, but it remains ideologically and strategically separate from mainstream feminist organizations (Dahan-Kalev, 2003:108).

Feminists in Israel imported feminism from the West, but they have been less successful than their Western sisters in dealing with the contentious, fundamental connections between race, class, ethnicity, and gender that hinder efforts for feminist progress among all groups. Considering these divisions, a universalist feminist agenda in Israel, at least in the near future, appears illusory (Dahan-Kalev, 2001).

THE MUSLIM WORLD

The Muslim world represents conflicting images and attitudes to Westerners. On the one hand, the oil-rich nations have created better living standards and enhanced educational and job opportunities for their inhabitants. On the other hand, as

Islamic nations, efforts at development occur within unique socioreligious frameworks that Westerners view with curiosity and suspicion, which were both heightened with the 9/11 terrorist attacks in 2001. Nowhere do these conflicting images emerge more forcefully than when viewing women in Islamic cultures.

Given the stereotypes surrounding Islam, it is surprising for many to discover that Islam first developed as both a new religion and as a movement toward social reform and legal change specifically aimed at challenging and ultimately changing the lowly status of women (chapter 12). The letter and the spirit of the law are different matters. Reforms are possible only in the context of a culture's willingness to undergo change and endure stressful transitions. This has simply not been the case in Arab, South Asian, and African cultures dominated by Islam. Regardless of the position of women in the pre-Islamic world, the Qur'an continues to be drawn on as a moral rationale for restricting women. A resurgence of religious fundamentalism has bolstered Qur'anic interpretations endorsing the inferior status of women. Islamic legal reform does have many advocates, and they can provide evidence from the Qur'an for upgrading rather than degrading the position of women. But reform has barely kept up with fundamentalist resurgence.

Islamization: Iran and Afghanistan

This resurgence is fueled by **countermodernization**, or antimodernization—a social movement that either resists modernization or promotes ways to neutralize its effects. Throughout much of the Muslim world, countermodernization takes the form of **Islamization**, a religious fundamentalist movement seeking a return to an idealized version of Islam as a remedy against corrupt Western values. With Islamization, religion and state are inseparable, and all laws governing public and private life have a religious basis. Islamization is replayed in South Asia (Pakistan and Bangladesh), in the Middle East (Saudi Arabia and Iraq), and North Africa (Egypt and Sudan). Until the Taliban takeover of Afghanistan in 1996, its most virulent expression worldwide was the Iranian revolution that propelled Khomeini to power after the overthrow of the Shah of Iran in 1979. As elsewhere in the Muslim world, in both Afghanistan and Iran, Islamic authorities ("mullahs") have long played an influential role in all aspects of social life. Countermodernization is selective, with certain ideas and technologies being accepted whereas others are rejected. Iran and Afghanistan are the extreme versions of this movement, but powerful elements can be found in most Arab cultures as well as in other Islamic societies, such as Pakistan, Bangladesh, and Sudan (Lindsey, 1984, 1988; Hashmi, 2000). When countermodernization and Islamization are combined, women are likely to be its victims rather than its beneficiaries.

Islamization in Afghanistan, for example, targeted women as key vehicles to restore Islamic identity when they returned to their primary domestic roles. Islam is invoked to deny reproductive choice, educational opportunity, and paid employment. With gender apartheid taking effect, Islamization under the Taliban banned women from employment and schools for girls and hospitals serving women closed, lest women come into contact with men to whom they are not related. Women were executed for adultery and prostitution, often defined as simply being seen with a nonkin male. Beheading, amputation, shooting, and public beating occurred for religious infractions such as clothing not sufficiently covering a woman's entire body, for illegally teaching girls to read and write, and for going out in public alone—even if completely veiled (Lindsey, 2002). The Taliban decreed out of existence even the minimal rights women and girls gained as Afghanistan began the process of economic development during the Soviet era.

In Taliban-controlled Afghanistan the search for a social formula that would protect traditions under Islamic law while dealing with the inevitable demand for change was resolved in favor of an extreme form of countermodernization.

The Shah and Khomeini. With a better infrastructure, Islamization in Persian Iran was (and is) not as extreme in its treatment of women. Women receive medical care in facilities designed for them and girls are in gender segregated schools. However, women in Iran remain under the strict control of their fathers or husbands, are restricted from a variety of paid employment, and must answer to Islamic authorities for violations of dress and traditional gender roles, most related to marriage, family, and motherhood.

The case of Iran provides the best example of how countermodernization can serve to restrict women. What is startling about the overthrow of the Shah of Iran in 1979 and the establishment of the Islamic regime under the Ayatollah Khomeini is that women were a major force in propelling the Ayatollah to power. As sentiment against the exploitation under the Shah grew, women became more politically active and took to the streets in mass anti-Shah demonstrations. At a time when the veil was becoming a remnant of the past, women embraced it as a symbol of solidarity against the Shah. The images of veiled women protesting in mass demonstrations shocked many. It seemed to contradict the liberal view of women which was supposedly a hallmark of the Shah's regime.

Actually, the veil served several purposes. It prevented the easy identification of the protesters which could make them targets of the secret police, and it was a symbolic gesture halting the modernization and Westernization of Iran. When that identity is linked to women, by restoring the veil as the Islamic marker, broader social identity is also restored (El Guindi, 1999). Many women saw the veil as a symbol of solidarity, which was to be discarded or worn at will after the fall of the Shah. These women believed that the new leadership would reward them for their sacrifices and militant support and that religious leaders would support rights for women, such as expanded educational and employment options and the granting of more self-determination in their domestic roles.

Khomeini's position during the anti-Shah movement increased women's support for him. His views on women were vague at times but straightforward at others. He opposed the idea of women-as-objects and saw a woman as a man's equal: "She and he are free to choose their lives and their occupations." He stated that the "Shah's regime has destroyed the freedom of women as well as men" (cited in Sanasarian, 1982:117). The new republic would not oppress women, according to Khomeini. Less than a month after the ousting of the Shah, illusions of equality were shattered. Legislation was enacted to alter gender relations so they would not resemble anything like those existing in the West (Najmabadi, 2000). Gender segregation in all parts of public life intensified when the Islamic Republic emphasized that the family was rooted in motherhood, the highly praised and most precious role of women, and that male and female roles are separate and distinctive (Kazemzadeh, 2002). The minimum legal age for girls to marry was lowered from 18 to 13 and then to 9. An extreme example of loss of freedom is physical brutality and loss of life. Women have been executed for adultery and prostitution and beaten for improper dress. No longer was the veil a symbol of militant solidarity. In the eyes of many Iranian women, it has become a symbol of oppression.

With Khomeini's blueprint, the next regime systematically undermined the freedom of women. Religious righteousness originally compelled both men and women to work in overthrowing the Shah. Once this succeeded, women were literally pushed out of public life and into the home. It is likely that many women would have embraced domestic roles anyway, but the new regimes severely circumscribed all other options (Mir-Hossein, 2001).

Toward Reform. Attempts at reform, however, have not been silenced. Both Khomeini and the Taliban are gone but Islamization continues—but it is taking a different, less extreme course. Excessive countermodernization can never be sustained. Despite efforts to maintain the fervor of Islamization, a liberalizing current is coursing through Iranian life. Iran is quietly making overtures to investors and Western leaders that should help reopen its doors to the world. For the first time in decades, women are venturing back into workplaces and job training programs. Because women do have the right to run for public office in Iran, they have gained several parliamentary seats. Prompted by the potential political clout of Iranian women, religious intellectuals are debating, albeit reluctantly, how the "woman question" can be addressed in the Iranian context (Farhi, 2001; Moghadam, 2002). Although economic reasons, which are acceptable, rather than feminist reasons, which are unacceptable, are cited for these changes, it is clear that women on the whole can benefit. Feminists in Iran are divided by degree of support for Islamic principles and how their highly praised roles as wives and mothers can be used to their benefit (Gheytanchi, 2001; Povey, 2001). These divisions do not bode well for seeking reform with a unified voice, but the fact that feminism is even minimally resurgent in Iran signals a reopening of dialogue between women and between women and the state.

Fueled by massive international aid, NGOs are creating an infrastructure in Afghanistan that includes schools for girls and reproductive health services for women. Although the swift demise of the Taliban in Afghanistan occurred because of the repercussions of the 9/11 terrorist attacks, it is clear that their extreme version of Islamic countermodernization—condemned by Muslims throughout the world—would have eventually dislodged them from power (Lindsey, 2002).

The Arab Middle East

Iran and Afghanistan are at one end of a continuum regarding Muslim women. Other Muslim countries must be considered in light of their own traditions, beliefs, and interpretations of Islam regarding women. Some feminist scholars contend that there are no effective models for women's liberation that can appeal to Muslim women. They are either too Western or too pre-Islamic (Fernea, 1998). Others say that Islamic societies are based on such rigid definitions of family that tampering with these definitions brings fear that social chaos will result. Strongly functionalist in orientation, traditional male–female and master–slave relationships existing in Islamic nations are therefore accepted (Mernissi, 1987:174).

On the other hand, Islam regards women as potentially powerful and aggressive—images empowering to women. In their quest for modernization, women are embracing but also testing traditional norms. In Saudi Arabia women run investment firms, manage shops, and are employed in hospitals. Most businesses are still gender segregated, but opportunities for employment for educated women are offered. They see themselves as pioneers who ignore rules in the hope that women's roles can be reshaped. As one women stated, "The worst thing you can do in the Arab world is ask for permission. It will always be no" (Boustany, 1994). By stretching the limits of male-dominated Saudi society, they endure public criticism, but believe that change will eventually come. In Egypt an elite strata of middle class professional women have overcome societal pressures and religious taboos to attain success outside the home. Influences on them are both modern—Western capitalism and socialist egalitarian ideology—and traditional—the images of formidable females such as Queen Nefertiti and the Prophet Muhammad's strong-willed wife Khadija (Murphy, 1993).

In Arab cultures as diverse as Jordan, Saudi Arabia, Kuwait, and Palestine, the status of women is being influenced by gains in health, literacy, and political reform. Even with the severe separatist policies against women in Saudi Arabia, two Gulf Wars provided opportunities to see women as competent, successful, and esteemed in a variety of roles—as soldiers, journalists, diplomats, politicians, and aid workers. As we have seen throughout history, war is latently functional for altering perceptions of women.

North Africa: Female Genital Mutilation

The extent of women's liberation in the Arab Muslim world is debatable and must be approached according to the political and social structure within each society. Islam is not uniform across Muslim societies, so women's roles in those societies cannot be approached simply by viewing laws and interpretations of religious texts (Kandiyoti, 1991). However, these societies are linked in their views of women by certain cultural practices. Although the veil may be a symbol of oppression from a feminist viewpoint, other customs suggest an even more frightening reality. It is the practice of female genital mutilation that has stirred global debate.

Female genital mutilation (FGM) refers to a variety of genital operations designed to reduce or eliminate a girl's sexual pleasure and ensure her virginity. If virginity is safeguarded, then she is marriageable. Otherwise, she can be condemned, living as an outcast. Sometimes she is murdered. FGM is practiced thoughout North Africa, in parts of the Middle East and in some sub-Saharan regions. The total number of living females who have undergone FGM ranges from 80 to 100 million, including 4 or 5 million children as young as age 4. It is practiced by the wealthy and the poor and in rural and urban areas. Although most girls who undergo the procedure are Muslim, it is also practiced by Coptic Christians and those who adhere to tribal religions (UNICEF, 2003). FGM's past is untraceable. It predates Islam, although some Islamic cultures justify it today on religious grounds.

Referred to incorrectly as female circumcision, FGM is not at all equivalent to the far less radical procedure of male circumcision. FGM ranges from a partial clitoridectomy to full removal of the clitoris, a woman's most erotically sensitive organ. In its more extreme form, practiced in Egypt, Somalia, Sudan, and some parts of Ethiopia, FGM removes the clitoris and then the vagina is sewn almost completely shut, leaving an opening just large enough to release urine and menstrual blood. The effects of these mutilations are many, ranging from psychological trauma, to hemorrhage, blood poisoning, painful intercourse, lack of sexual pleasure, and death from infections or complications during childbirth. The vagina is cut open again on the woman's wedding night, an experience reflected by the following lines in a poem by a Somalian woman:

> And if I speak of my wedding night; I had expected caresses. Sweet kisses. Hugging and love. No. Never! Awaiting me was pain. Suffering and sadness.
>
> I lay in my wedding bed, groaning like a wounded animal, a victim of feminine pain.
>
> At dawn ridicule awaited me. My mother announced: Yes, she is a virgin. (Muse, 2000)

As brutal as it is, the practice continues. With the elimination of sexual pleasure, virginity is more likely to be ensured before marriage and chastity after marriage. It forms a core cultural identity of many traditional people. Interviews with rural Egyptian women suggest that many do not see FGM as an infringement on their rights. In their segregationist world, they accept the view that "the pleasures of sex are reserved for men, and the dignity of childbirth and motherhood for women" (Zenie-Ziegler, 1988:95). Women who were forced to undergo the painful procedure are often its strongest advocates.

Three UN Conferences on Women have taken up the FGM issue. In 1980 African delegates argued that FGM was essential to guarantee a girl's marriage. Delegates from Western cultures, appalled by FGM, thought it should be eliminated and were accused of interfering with hallowed cultural traditions. Dialogue remained open, and five years later the issue was discussed with much less confrontation. A decade later consensus was reached that FGM was a human rights violation. Egypt, Nigeria, and Ghana have banned the practice. The United States may grant asylum to a girl returning to a country practicing FGM. Previously women feared that daughters could not be married without being "circumcised." When entire villages do not allow their girls to undergo the procedure, men must look for marriage partners elsewhere or marry uncircumcised women. Women's empowerment now suggests the latter.

It is unfair to regard FGM as the defining characteristic of an entire region, but it calls attention to the issue of cultural change through women's empowerment. The controversy also illustrates symbolic interaction's "definition of the situation" in two ways. First, what used to be referred to as female circumcision has been renamed female genital mutilation. The former name suggests something mild or benign. The latter name clearly does not. Second, the movement against FGM has been redefined as a defense of human rights rather than as cultural interference (Ibhawoh, 2000). The new definition of the situation is fast becoming the reality, so that in the last decade all major international bodies and governments have committed to its suppression. Cultural beliefs regarding women remain strong, however, and despite laws to the contrary, the practice continues in many areas.

To Veil or Not to Veil

Thirty years of debate have allowed for broad consensus on the elimination of FGM. This section ends with another contentious issue—one been debated for over two centuries in various contexts—that remains far from settled. The issue of veiling (*hijab*) in purdah-system gender segregated societies has produced two strands of feminist thought on the topic: one strand condemns it as oppressive and the other reframes it as liberating and a sign of resistance. A middle view suggests that veiling is neither liberating nor oppressive. From this perspective, any power relations that emerge from veiling must be considered in light of the context in which it occurs (Chatty, 2000; Franks, 2001). Power relations, therefore, are transitory as behavioral contexts change. Critics of veiling are accused of denying the integrity of Islamic culture and the agency of Muslim women (Mojab, 1998). Given these debates, Western feminists now tend to shy away from either indicting or celebrating veiling because of charges of both cultural interference and either misunderstanding or disregarding the link between gender, religion, ethnicity, and politics (Lindsey, 2002).

SCANDINAVIA: NORWAY AND SWEDEN

When compared to gender roles in the developing world and the gendered nature of its poverty, the Scandinavian countries of Northern Europe stand in sharp contrast. By every measure of overall human development as well as those used to assess equality between men and women, all the Scandinavian nations are consistently ranked the highest (Eisler et al., 1995; UNDP, 2003). Norway and Sweden in particular provide the global standard for gender egalitarian models.

Norway has essentially reached its goal of political parity with 40 percent of its legislative seats held by women. At 41, Grö Harlem Brundtland ascended to prime minister of Norway, holding the seat for many years. Under her leadership Norwegian society became synonymous with social democracy and elevated gender, health, and environmental issues to the highest levels. In the last two decades, women candidates for prime minister outnumbered men. This demonstrates the clear association between political power and gender equality. Women have clout when they are represented by other women in the legislative bodies of their nations.

Norway represents sociological understanding that gender permeates our lives in countless ways and that decisions that on the surface appear to be gender neutral have a different impact on women than on men. Their goal is to mainstream the gender perspective into all public activities. This does not mean that attention is exclusively directed toward women. The goal is equality and the gender perspective promotes it. As viewed by the Norwegian government, "the long-term objective is that the gender perspective shall be an automatic reflex and influence all important decisions" (Mainstreaming, 1995). In order to understand how the structure of social institutions and everyday life are influenced by gender, all public servants acquire knowledge of the gender perspective.

Norway acknowledges that gender roles will not be eliminated, and there is no attempt to do so. Women and men have different priorities and organize their lives differently, such as through job preferences, consumer patterns, and leisure activities. Such differences, however, should not be grounds for unequal access to social benefits and economic resources. The gender perspective ensures that the different behaviors and aspirations of women and men will be equally favored in the organization and governing of Norway. For example, parental leave for new fathers has been in existence for over two decades. A high priority on the political agenda is to make it easier for parents with young children to combine family with work responsibilities outside the home. As we shall see in the next two chapters, this is probably the key issue impacting American men and women and their families.

Like Norway, Sweden's trend toward gender equality has been advanced with legislative changes and an increased number of women in elective office, where Sweden also has about 45 percent women in legislative seats. But Sweden is unique in that egalitarian principles emphasize gender role change in males. Sweden has gone farther than any other government in stipulating that economic support and daily care and nurturing of children is the equal responsibility of both parents. Swedes believe that men have great stakes in gender equality, and more examples need to be set "before men at large become the good partners for modern feminism and before women become partners in men's search beyond the old traditional role" (Carllson, 1995:8).

Compared to most of the world, particularly the developing world, gender equity programs in Norway and Sweden are highly advanced. Financial outlay for these programs is considerable and therefore contentious. The level of support and cost for social and welfare benefits Norway and Sweden provide to their citizens are extraordinary from an American perspective. Although these benefits have translated into overall well-being and an enhanced quality of life, it is unclear if this path will continue in the same manner (Bergqvist and Nyberg, 2002). Like benefits associated with health care, gender equity initiatives will be scrutinized carefully to determine their cost effectiveness. It is doubtful that either nation will retreat from efforts aimed at reducing gender disparity, but the reduction of funds for these efforts is a real possibility. Regardless, Norway and Sweden still stand as powerful role models in the move toward global gender equality.

Summary

1. Globalization and development affect men and women in profoundly different ways. Bringing together policymakers, government leaders, and NGOs, the United Nations convened four major conferences to assess this impact. The 1995 UN Conference on Women was a watershed for the women's movement and for women's rights worldwide.

2. Development serves to hurt women when they are denied access to technology, subsistence farms are sold, men abandon families to seek work elsewhere, women's unpaid labor is uncounted, and trickle-down economic models are employed.

3. A model of women in development needs to account for five elements: sociological theory and global stratification, the impact of market-driven economic development, a theory-practice feedback loop, interdisciplinary work, and a feminist perspective emphasizing women's empowerment.

4. Russian women have lost economic and political power with the collapse of the Soviet Union. In its transitional economy women have lost jobs, their pay has declined and they have sharply increased work hours in their homes. The importance of paid work has declined, and the importance of family and social order has increased for women. Feminism and women's rights have eroded.

5. The People's Republic of China ushered in reform for women. Footbinding, concubinage, and child betrothal were abolished, free-choice marriage was instituted, and women had equal rights to divorce. Cultural barriers undermine these reforms. The one-child policy reinforced ancient son preference, but in the long run the policy may make daughters more valued. Research on Chinese women under market-driven development shows a paradox—women report both gains and losses in their homes and in their workplaces. More data are needed to resolve the paradox.

6. Women's progress in India is eroded by strict interpretations of Hinduism. In the twentieth century social reform gave women rights to inherit, vote, and divorce. The gender gap in human development related to education, literacy, and employment in India is huge. Female neglect and HIV/AIDS are rising due to son preference and a woman's lack of control over sexual intercourse. India has a strong feminist movement, but it is constrained by lack of diversity, disagreement on a common agenda, and difficulty of attracting poor and rural women to its ranks.

7. Gender roles in Japan are highly paradoxical. Japanese women benefited from post-war social reforms, including equal pay, improvement in hiring and working conditions, and access to higher education. Reform is hampered by Japanese gradualism, traditional views of women, women's abandonment of career at marriage, and motherhood as the essence of a woman's social and personal identity. Women have high levels of power and decision making in their households.

8. Machismo–marianismo ideology in Latin America serves as a powerful gender divide. The level of power of the Catholic Church explains the mixed success of family planning, sex education, and reproductive health throughout Latino cultures. Globalization and the shift from subsistence to commercial farming have hurt women. A strong and inclusive, politically astute Latin American feminist movement is being heard by government leaders. Debate continues on whether class or gender is the key factor in women's low status.

9. Israeli women have achieved equal rights and opportunities by law, but other polices related to religion, family, and government reinforce traditional gender roles. In most families religious ideology takes precedence over gender ideology. The egalitarian ideology of the kibbutz is also eroding. Jewish feminism is strong but divided between middle class women and women of color and working class women. This division has hindered feminist progress for all groups.

10. In most of the Muslim world the Qur'an is interpreted by men and used as the moral rationale to restrict women. Fundamentalist resurgence through Islamization has fueled countermodernization movements, with Iran under Khomeini and Afghanistan under the Taliban as the most extreme examples. Some reform is evident in Iran with women reentering the workplace and holding government office. In Afghanistan both schools for girls and reproductive health services for women have been opened by NGOs. In Arab cultures, even with extreme separatist policies, women are seeing gains in health, literacy, and political reform.

11. Female genital mutilation is practiced in the Middle East but mostly in North and sub-Saharan Africa. With the belief that a girl cannot be married unless she undergoes FGM, the brutal practice continues despite laws to the contrary. By defining it as a human rights violation, international efforts to combat it may be more successful.

12. The issue of veiling remains contentious among Muslim women and among feminist scholars. Some see veiling as oppressive, whereas others see it as liberating and a sign of resistance and the integrity of Islamic culture.

13. Scandinavia has the highest global human development rank and the highest gender equality. In Norway the gender perspective is central to all government decisions. In Sweden gender equity is advanced by concentrating on changing men's roles. Social and welfare benefits serving gender equity initiatives may suffer if costs rise too quickly.

Key Terms

countermodernization 164

developing nations 132

development 132

female genital mutilation (FGM) 167

globalization 132

informal sector 149

Islamization 164

nongovernmental organization (NGO) 133

Critical Thinking Questions

1. Discuss the factors that erode the status of women during the process of development. Demonstrate how these factors can be accounted for in a model of women in development that is useful for policy makers working to make development a success.

2. Identify the key cultural, political, and religious barriers that impede women's progress in Russia, China, Japan, India, Israel, and Latin America. Of these six nations/regions, select the two you believe will be most successful in overcoming these barriers and provide the rationale for this selection.

3. Considering the profound consequences of Islamization and controversial practices such as female genital mutilation and veiling customs for women in the Muslim world, what advice would you give to NGOs and feminists both inside and outside Muslim nations working to elevate the status of women? Make sure you account for the role of religion in this advice.

Someday my prince will come.

—Cinderella

The story of Cinderella promotes love and marriage as an escape from a world of drudgery and lack of fulfillment into one of enchantment and "living happily ever after." Indeed, the term *Cinderella story* has now come to symbolize the lives of those few fortunate and beautiful women who have gone from rags to riches when the right prince comes along. The 1949 Disney version of *Cinderella* is still alive and well. By the 1990s, instead of a cartoon prince we had Richard Gere carrying Debra Winger and Julia Roberts away from their preprincess existences as factory worker in *An Officer and a Gentleman* and as prostitute in *Pretty Woman*. The millennium Cinderella is Annette Bening, the highly educated (and beautiful) career woman who is swept off her feet by Michael Douglas, portraying the most powerful man in the world, in *The American President*. These movies suggest "modern" themes related to open sexuality, alternative lifestyles, and women's roles outside the home but at the same time "traditional" themes related to stereotypes about the power of love to overcome all obstacles and propel them into the marriages that will fulfill all their dreams. This chapter examines the myth and reality associated with such media images.

LOVE

Americans are so accustomed to viewing love and marriage as inseparable that it is rather startling to realize they have been paired only since the nineteenth century in the United States. Romantic love as an ideal existed in Europe and throughout Asia centuries ago, but it was not regarded as a basis for marriage. The poets and philosophers who sang the praises of courtly love during the European feudal era elevated love to something unattainable in marriage. The ladies of the court would bestow gifts, blessings, and an occasional kiss on suitors who would do battle or endure hardships for such prizes. Love was unseemly, feared for the sexual passion it might produce, and so was discouraged. Courtly love games were reserved for the aristocracy and excluded the vast majority of the population who did not have the luxury of playing at romance. Personal fulfillment and compatibility of the couple were irrelevant.

Linking Love and Marriage

Marriage, on the other hand, was the mundane but necessary alternative to the enchantment of feudal romance. Although the aristocracy glorified romantic ideals, their marriage decisions were based on rational rather than romantic goals. Marriage was an economic obligation that affected power, property, and privilege. From a functionalist perspective, without the assurance of marriage which produced legitimate heirs, the entire stratification system might be threatened. Passionate love could not serve as a realistic alternative for choosing a mate.

The Puritan era in the United States ushered in the revolutionary idea that love and marriage should be tied together. This was a radical departure from early church teachings, which warned men that even looking on their wives with lust made them sinners. In the new ideal, if love was not the reason for marriage, it was expected to flourish later. Parental control over approval of marriage partners remained the norm, but the belief that love should play a part in the process became etched into the fledgling American consciousness. Today the idea of love as a factor in assessing a marriage partner is gaining worldwide popularity, but initially it was a phenomenon uniquely associated with the United States.

Dramatic social change also eroded the separation of love and marriage. A political climate receptive to egalitarian attitudes was bolstered by the leveling effects of the Industrial Revolution, serving to decrease class stratification and the segregation of the genders. Consistent with a conflict perspective, as women moved into the world of paid employment their economic power increased. Social change combined with economic assets enhanced choices for both genders, but particularly for women. By the 1890s couples began to be influenced by the idea that marriages could be *companionate*—those based on romantic love—beliefs about gender equality, and an emphasis on balancing individual needs with family needs. Responsibilities that had formerly been under the control of one or the other spouse began to be shared.

Love as a basis for marriage will be strengthened in those societies where beliefs about gender equality are fostered and women and men can express their sexuality more openly (De Munck and Korotayev, 1999). Women's improved economic position, opportunities for youth to interact without being under the constant surveillance of parents, and increased time for leisure allowed notions of romantic love to blossom. By the beginning of the twentieth century love, marriage, and the belief that a spouse should be freely chosen had become inextricably bound.

Friends and Lovers

"Love is three-quarters dream and one-quarter reality—but problems rise when you fall in love with the dream and not the reality" (cited in Fulghum, 1997:19).

Defining Love. Because love is such a complex emotion and so difficult to define to everyone's satisfaction, it is easy to understand why it is encumbered with folklore, superstition, and myth. Love is extolled for its virtue and damned for its jealousy. Euphoria, joy, depression, restlessness, anger, and fear are all words used to describe love.

The love for a friend, sibling, parent, or child is certainly different from the feelings accompanying romantic love and the strong passion it stimulates. Nonetheless, distinguishing between the varieties of love is exceedingly complicated. The distinction between romantic love and other varieties of love includes what the ancient Greeks viewed as *eros,* or the physical, sexual component of love; *agape,* its spiritual and altruistic component; *philos,* the love of deep and enduring friendships; and *nomos,* subjugation of the will and allegiance to the love object, metaphorically as to God (Hendrick and Hendrick, 1992). Although romantic love ideally includes all these components, agape and philos also indicate other kinds of love relationships, such as the love between friends or siblings and parents and children. What is interesting is that the sexual dimension of eros is the key component distinguishing romantic love from friendship, but is also its most selfish aspect. The need for sexual gratification may counter the altruism idealized in beliefs about romance. As we shall see, this is an important element in female and male views of love.

Distinguishing Love and Friendship. As noted earlier, various love components overlap in friends, families, and lovers. Like with lovers, the profile for good friends and best friends includes acceptance, trust, respect, open communication, mutual assistance, and understanding. Perhaps most evident in adolescent peer groups, friends, like lovers, are the champions of one another and advocate their friendship by loyalty and sanctions against those who speak or act harshly against them (Baxter et al., 2001; Canary and Dainton, 2003). If these good friends, best friends, or other friends become lovers, the sexual passion dimension is added to the profile.

Same-Gender Friends. When asked who are their nonromantic best or close friends, both men and women identify someone of their own gender. Early socialization emphasizes patterns of gender segregation that carry through to adulthood (chapter 3). Compared to males, females report higher levels of intimacy, spontaneity, and openness with their same-gender friends, a pattern that crosscuts race and age (Granger, 2002; Siwatu, 2003). Males are more competitive and less open with their same-gender friends and are more likely than women to identify someone of the other gender as among their best or close friends. This is also consistent with gender role socialization patterns that promote instrumental and goal-oriented friendships for males and expressive and emotion-centered friendships for females (Duck and Wright, 1993). From a symbolic interaction perspective, same-gender friendships are enhanced and stabilized when each party accepts the role definitions attached to gender.

Friendships for both men and women are important for emotional and social well-being, but women appear to capitalize on them more than men. Females of all ages who maintain friendships with other women report being less lonely and depressed, but paradoxically, they also report romantic liaisons with males as simultaneously euphoric and depressive (Joyner and Udry, 2000; Knickmeyer et al., 2002). Women's friendships with other women are at risk if they believe their friends are sexually promiscuous or are their romantic rivals (Bleske and Shackelford, 2001). From a feminist perspective, beliefs about male power in love and mate selection encroach in friendships between women.

Other-Gender Friends. Same-gender friends may be more stable and emotionally supportive because the passion dimension lurks behind other-gender friendships. Enduring other-gender close friends are endangered if liking turns into loving. Men perceive that sex with their women friends is beneficial to the friendship, whereas women perceive it as more detrimental, beliefs that distort the friendship balance (Afifi and Fulkner, 2000; Bleske and Buss, 2000; Monsour, 2002). Media images showing other-gender friendships doomed by romance reinforce these patterns. In the classic movie *When Harry Met Sally*, Billy Crystal (Harry), "proves his own point that men and women can't be continuing friends" because he marries Sally at the end of the movie (West et al., 1996). In the reverse but rarer direction, *Seinfeld's* Elaine and Jerry move from a romantic to a platonic relationship. It is difficult to return to being friends after having been lovers, particularly if one partner is in another romantic relationship. Consider, too, the friendship-love-friendship-love scenarios in the television series *Friends*. If the name of the series is supposed to imply that other-gender roommates and neighbors can maintain ongoing platonic and intimate relationships, it certainly was difficult for this group of "friends." In *Will & Grace*, it is Will's homosexuality that allows them to remain best friends. Some surveys do report that close other-gender friendships can weather the gender storms invading them (Monsour et al., 1994). However, in addition to the loving-liking difficulty, these storms also include gender beliefs fostering hierarchy rather than egalitarianism that create the path for the demise of the friendship (McWilliams and Howard, 1993; Messman et al., 2000). The potential for rewarding and enduring other-gender friendships is limited by formidable gender barriers.

Gendered Love and Love Myths

It is clear that our ideas about love are dependent on whom we are considering as the object or target of our affection, whether a spouse, sex partner, sibling, child, best friend, or parent. Friendship and romantic love are distinguished by more than passionate sexual desire. Compared to friends and family members, lovers have heightened enjoyment for each other's company, are preoccupied with thoughts about the lover, are fascinated by all that the lover says or does and want to frequently communicate with their lover. According to Robert Sternberg (1988), love is a triangle formed by three interlocking elements: intimacy, passion, and commitment. Through open communication, intimacy brings with it emotional warmth and bonding. Physiological arousal and sexual desire are part of the passion component, where feelings of romance take precedence. Commitment involves the choice to continue and maintain the love relationship. All relationships undergo change and transformation, so each vertex of the triangle will not be equal, but if there is too much mismatch between the components, the prediction is that the relationship will fail. Research confirms that males and females differ in levels of satisfaction and skill for each of the three elements of the triangle. Mismatches are associated with loss of passion, unrequited and obsessive love, and depression (Patford, 2000; Regan, 2000; Engel et al., 2002). Because gender role socialization makes it difficult to maintain relatively equal vertexes, the joy and awe associated with romantic love may be compromised.

Regardless of its definition, romantic love is idealized in the United States. Americans are bombarded with romantic stimuli throughout their lives which serve to reinforce these idealizations. The most complicated of emotions has produced a range of myths that demonstrate how we romanticize love. To the extent that these myths carry over into beliefs and behaviors related to gender roles, marriage, and the family, romanticization can have dire consequences.

1. **Love Conquers All.** The "all" that is supposedly conquered in this myth involves the inevitable problems and obstacles of daily living. By idealizing the love-object, problems are even more difficult to solve. Total agreement with another person's views on life and love is impossible. Romantic love is certainly paradoxical. Idealization requires remoteness to be maintained, but intimacy evaporates remoteness. One's partner cannot fulfill all needs and make all problems disappear.

2. **Love Is Blind.** This myth asserts that true love dissolves social boundaries and anyone can potentially become the romantic love object. The belief that "it doesn't matter, as long as I love her/him" fuels this myth. As we will see, mate selection and the love that it allegedly encompasses is not a random process but one that is highly structured. We are socialized to fall in love at certain times in our lives and with certain categories of people. Particularly for people in Western cultures, the faith in romance is quite high. But love is conditioned by a number of social and demographic variables that exert a tremendous influence on us.

3. **Love at First Sight.** Because falling in love is a rational process, it counters the belief that people fall in love at first sight. Physical attractiveness is certainly a critical variable during the first encounter and provides the initial impression. Until verbal interaction occurs, information comes indirectly from the person's overall appearance. The "love at first sight" myth is bolstered by what psychologists refer to as the *halo effect*—people who are attractive are assumed to possess more desirable qualities than those who are less attractive. Beauty and good looks are associated with other positive characteristics, such as goodness, competence, warmth, and sensitivity (Eagly et al., 1991; Perkins and Lerner, 1995; Ruscher, 2001). Initial attraction based on appearance is more

important in chance encounters such as on airplanes or at one-time events. The love at first sight myth works against women because they are judged more strictly on level of attractiveness, especially related to body weight. But because love requires ongoing, sustained interaction, attractiveness issues tend to fade in the long run. As a prerequisite to love, interpersonal attraction is enhanced by the *mere exposure* effect—being frequently exposed to a person increases liking for that person. Familiarity does not breed contempt, it breeds liking. This explains why college dormitories are major marriage markets where love can flourish. It also explains why the adage "Absence makes the heart grow fonder" is incorrect. Its opposite, "Out of sight, out of mind," is the empirical reality.

Many of these points come together in the (unfortunate) comments of a seventeen-year-old male when asked on a survey: "What do you look for in a girl?" (Minton, 1997:17):

> There is no ideal height or weight but . . . .most guys want as much of a girl's weight in her chest. . . .Girls should surround themselves with beautiful people. Guys will come over to flirt with the pretty girls, and get acquainted with you, too.

4. **Women Are the Romantic Sex (Gender).** Women are thought to be the starry-eyed romantics who fall in love quickly. This belief is associated with stereotypes about women's emotionality that consume them when they fall in love. Research shatters this myth. Men express a higher level of romantic love than women and fall in love earlier and harder than women. Men also score higher on romantic idealization of love. Overall, men are found to be more idealistic and romantic and women to be more cautious and pragmatic in attitudes about love and romance (Burns, 2002; Sprecher and Toro-Morn, 2002; Cobb et al., 2003).

   However, when women *do* decide to fall in love, they exceed men in levels of emotion and euphoria. Women are defined as the experts who will work harder and sacrifice more to maintain the relationship and keep the romance alive (Burns, 2000; Medora et al., 2002). In Robert Sternberg's (1988) theory of love, women attach greater importance to the commitment vertex of the triangle. For women, the rational behavior eventually leads to the romantic idealism characterizing love in America. It is at the passionate first stage of love where men are more romantic.

5. **No Sex Without Love.** Both men and women express the *attitude* that love is a prerequisite for sex, but their *behavior* suggests otherwise. The vast majority of people engage in nonmarital sex, and many enjoy sex solely for its physical pleasure (see chapter 2). Notwithstanding the research that the most satisfying sexual experiences are with spouses and committed partners because love attributes such as caring and commitment characterize the relationship, "permissiveness without affection" is fast becoming a sexual standard. However, women are less likely to agree with the standard and are judged more strictly when they engage in any nonmarital sex, whether with a lover or acquaintance. Women are now less likely to endorse beliefs about sacrifice and submissiveness in a sexual relationship, but they are also more likely to engage in nonmarital sex when they hear love messages, even if these are not

marriage messages (Mongeau et al., 1994; Frey and Hojjat, 1998; Kamen, 2003). The double standard still operates.

6. **The Opposite of Love is Hate.** Given the difficulty of defining love in all its dimensions, the final myth is perhaps easier to understand. If indeed there *is* an opposite to love, it is not hate, but indifference.

Gender and Styles of Romance. The openness and sharing that most would agree are important components of love serve to separate women and men in the later stages of love and marriage. Gender role socialization commands that masculinity be associated with lack of vulnerability. One becomes vulnerable through self-disclosure; therefore, to love fully is to self-disclose fully. Men have higher levels of openness, communication, and self-disclosure than women at the beginning of relationship. They use more direct, open, and active strategies to initiate a romantic relationship (Clark et al., 1999). As the relationship continues, even into marriage, men tend to retreat in communication and responsiveness, but women expect more of both. Women become resentful and irritated when men appear unwilling to express thoughts and feelings. Men in all racial categories are less likely than women to regard emotional satisfaction as an important ingredient in preserving a marriage (Sprecher and Toro-Morn, 2002). For heterosexual married couples, cohabitants, and dating partners, it is the man's behavior that sets the direction for the level of intimacy in the relationship that in turn predicts level of satisfaction and adjustment to the relationship for both partners.

Explanations for this change of behavior center on a man's discomfort and vulnerability in exposing himself to the emotionality and intimacy demanded in ongoing romantic or other close relationships. Men may be blamed because they do not have the skills of emotional expression and self-disclosure that women have honed throughout their lives. Because romantic love is so identified with the expressive dimension and self-disclosure in which women are supposedly more skilled, we tend to disregard the instrumental dimension and physical aspects that men prefer. Rather than talking, men demonstrate love when they "do" masculine things for a wife or lover, such as repair the car or clean out the gutters. Men also put more emphasis on the eros/sexual component that is the distinctive marker of romantic love. But because love is so idealized for its agape/altruistic quality, even its key sexual marker is played down (Worobey, 2001; Chung et al., 2002; Kroska, 2003). Men are thus viewed as incompetent at loving. A male deficit model defining women as "relationship experts" has led to an incomplete and overly feminized perspective of love (Cancian, 2003).

Critique. It is clear that males and females are socialized into different attitudes and behaviors regarding romantic love and that the idealism associated with romantic love serves to weaken women's endorsement for its sexual component. But the claim that men do not have the skill for the effective communication necessary to satisfy both partners in the relationship is not justified. Because gender scripts call for men to be the initiators of a romantic relationship, they demonstrate these skills at the beginning of a relationship when they need to entice women into dating. Women give high marks to men who talk about goals, reveal otherwise private beliefs and attitudes, and disclose personal weaknesses to their potential partner. If men have good communication at one point, it does not suddenly disappear later. According to symbolic interaction and conflict theory, men have the skill to communicate, but the will to do so may be constrained by gender scripts suggesting that they can retain power in a relationship by determining what is left unsaid rather than said.

Androgynous Love. Regardless of which gender is more skilled at communicating, for relationships to become more loving, the rejection of polarized gender views of love seen necessary. Androgynous love may integrate masculine (instrumental) and feminine (expressive) styles (Cancian, 2003). If love and loving are gender typed, androgyny should overcome the imposed limitations. Research does reveal that highly masculine or highly feminine gender roles—both of which suggest gender inequality—are not conducive to expressing or experiencing love and negatively affect intimacy (Rodman et al., 2001).

The idea of androgynous love provides an escape from traditional gender typing, where love and loving become compromised. Remember, however, that androgyny itself assumes the existence of gender stereotyped roles. A proposed "alternative path model" agrees that men and women differ in interaction styles, but it does not presume men are lacking in either emotional depth or a desire for intimacy. The paths for men and women are different, but equally valid (Wood, 1994:183). This type of model may help us better understand the complex emotion of love.

Traditional gender roles jeopardize love and loving and the marriages on which they are founded. A woman's relationship script calls for a passive role eventually allowing her to exchange sex for commitment. A man's relationship script calls for an active role allowing for sexual conquest. Women's enjoyment of sex and their agency in sexual relations are compromised by these scripts. Both scripts are in the throes of change, and some research indicates that women's and men's conceptions of love are now more similar than in the past (Fehr and Broughton, 2001; Cate et al., 2002). The courtship game, however, continues to function according to gender role stereotypes (Brown and Amatea, 2000; Jones, 2000). Moving toward an androgynous love ideal may overcome some gender barriers. Loving relationships that endure the harshness of the "unromantic" world may result.

MATE SELECTION

Americans as well as people in other Western cultures strongly adhere to beliefs about the necessity of romantic love as the basis for mate selection and would disdain practices common in other parts of the world where the selection of a spouse is in the hand of marriage brokers, parents, or other relatives. Even for Americans, however, love may be idealistic but prior to making a marriage commitment, a prospective mate is dissected and evaluated on those qualifications important for a marriage. Like the love that propels a couple toward marriage, gender differences abound in the process of mate selection.

The Marriage Gradient

Sociological research documents the impact of **homogamy**, becoming attracted to and marrying someone similar to yourself. If romantic love was the sole basis for mate selection, coupling would occur by chance; instead, homogamy results in **assortive mating**, coupling based on similarity. Assortive mating assumes that people who are culturally similar to one another have more opportunities to meet those similar to themselves than more dissimilar to themselves (Kalmijn and Flap, 2001). College, for example, is a powerful marriage market where people meet, date, fall in love, and marry. Mating requires meeting. Parents send children to certain colleges with the expectation that they will not only receive an excellent education but they will also meet potential partners from similar backgrounds. To test predictions about homogamy, count the number of seniors you know who are engaged.

Demographic characteristics such age, race, social class, and religion are among the first elements that demonstrate this structure and are of enormous importance in mate selection (Curtis and Ellison, 2002; Jepsen and Jepsen, 2002). Though considered *nonaffective* in nature, that is, not tied to the emotional expressiveness and highly charged passion love entails, these variables predict mate selection and marital stability more that the prized notion of romantic love. It is these nonaffective elements that help to determine with whom we will likely fall in love. Romantic love is tempered by a market approach to mate selection. This results in a process that appears to be radically different from the ideology surrounding it.

Whereas homogamy is the mate selection norm, it is filtered by the **marriage gradient**, in which women tend to marry men of higher socioeconomic status (SES), the conventional practice used by women for upward mobility. Although this practice is weaker today, data still clearly support that "marrying up" is the path many women choose to bolster economic security. The marriage gradient is functional for women who prefer well-educated men who have the earning capacity necessary to support a family. Women place greater value than men on the instrumental qualities of a prospective mate. Decades of research attest that this continues to be true, even for college educated women who expect high paying jobs and who say they want to combine career and marriage (Melton and Lindsey, 1987; Philpot, 2001; Abowitz, 2002).

In addition to any SES differences between men and women at marriage, the marriage gradient also predicts some dissimilarity between marriage partners related to age, race, and attractiveness, all of which demonstrate the highly gendered mate selection process.

Age. The critical variable influencing mate selection is age. Most people marry others within a few years of their own ages. If there is an age difference, the man is usually older than the woman. Traditional gender expectations dictated that men must gain the requisite education and job skills necessary to support a family, thus keeping them out of marriage longer than women, who are socialized primarily for domestic roles. Since the 1950s there has been a gradual increase in the marriage age for both genders. With women now representing over half of all college students and half of the labor force, traditional gender roles are being altered significantly. The median age at first marriage is now higher for women than at any time since 1900 and is approaching that of men (Table 7.1). In later or remarriages, age differences are likely to be greater, but usually favoring the same younger woman–older man pattern.

However, a minitrend has appeared that indicates that younger man–older woman marriage is becoming more acceptable, most common among the elderly. Generally, elderly widows are at a disadvantage for a homogamous remarriage

Table 7.1 Median Age at First Marriage, by Gender for Selected Years

Year	Men	Women
1890	26.1	22.0
1900	25.9	21.9
1910	25.1	21.6
1920	24.6	21.2
1930	24.3	21.3
1940	24.3	21.5
1950	22.8	20.3
1960	22.8	20.3
1970	23.2	20.8
1980	24.7	22.0
1990	26.1	23.9
1995	26.9	24.5
1998	26.7	25.0
2000	26.8	25.1
2002	26.9	25.3

Source: U.S. Census Bureau, *Annual Demographic Supplement to the March 2002 Current Population Survey, Current Population Reports, Series P20-547*

because men marry younger women at all life stages and women outlive men by about seven years. New role models for women, success in economic spheres, divorce and remarriage, the marriage squeeze (discussed later), and less constraint from family and society will likely accelerate the pattern for all but the youngest women.

Race. Of all demographic variables, homogamy is strongest for race. Between 1970 and 2000, interracial marriages tripled. In Hawaii, almost half of all marriages are interracial (Fu and Heaton, 2000). Because the U.S. Census now allows an option of multiple racial responses, it is certain that the numbers of interracial marriages will surge. Marking off more than one racial category provides a more accurate picture of diversity in the United States but also a more complex one, especially when determining interracial marriages. We can still conclude, however, that interracial marriages are relatively rare, accounting for about 3 percent of all marriages. Of these, less than 1 percent are African-American–white marriages, with about 70 percent of these consisting of a white wife and an African-American husband.

When comparing race and class in these marriages, the data generally support homogamy in SES (Kalmijn, 1998; Root, 2001). However, when differences do occur, the woman's SES is usually lower than the man's, a pattern that cuts across all races. The marriage gradient serves to compensate the wife for her lower SES and the husband for his status as a racial minority (Blackwell and Lichter, 2000). Both partners marry "up" in this sense. When African Americans and whites are attracted to one another, the reasons are generally the same as for couples of the same race—they share similar interests, values, and background (Brown, 2000; Yancey, 2002).

The majority of interracial marriages, the other 2 percent, are between whites and nonblacks, the most typical pattern being Native American or Asian woman of

Japanese, Filipino, or Korean descent marrying white men. For Asians, gender role beliefs help explain these patterns, but in a paradoxical way. More acculturated Asian-American women seek marriage to men who are more egalitarian and hold less traditional views of women. White men seek Asian-American women for the opposite reason. They may desire a stereotyped Asian female—"good at house-keeping, service oriented, willing to stay at home, and sexy" (Kitano and Daniels, 1995:188). Although both may get what they want initially, patterns of acculturation toward egalitarian gender roles predict more marital satisfaction among Asian-American women than among white men.

Attractiveness. The importance both men and women attach to physical attractiveness in mate selection has increased considerably over the last several decades (Buss et al., 2001). Although men are now like women in that they add a woman's economic prospects to their marriage partner shopping list, men continue to place a higher value on attractiveness than women. (Stewart et al., 2000; Schmitt, 2002; Sprecher and Regan, 2002). For a quick confirmation of this fact, pick up any newspaper devoted to ads for dating partners. Men's are more likely to mention that they are looking for "beautiful and slender" women or those who have proper "weight in proportion to height." Women are more likely to mention that they are looking for men who are affluent and successful as well as caring and warm. Women also seek long term relationships with high levels of interpersonal understanding (Cicerello and Sheehan, 1995; Fetto, 2000). Male preoccupation with physical attractiveness cuts across race and social class. Because men value it more than women and it is the first trait they notice when checking out possible dating partners, physical attractiveness is an important factor in explaining why men fall in love sooner than women.

The Marriage Squeeze

Age at marriage is also affected by the proportion of women and men who are available. When there is an unbalanced ratio of marriage-age women to marriage-age men, a **marriage squeeze** exists, in which one gender has a more limited pool of potential marriage partners. Most people marry in their midtwenties, and men marry women who are a few years younger than themselves. After World War II the birthrate increased considerably (the "baby boom" era). There were more women born in 1950 than men born in 1940. By the 1980s there was a shortage of marriageable men. Because of the steep decline in birthrates in the 1960s and 1970s, men in their midtwenties faced a shortage of women.

If younger men are caught in a current marriage squeeze, the same is true for women at midlife. The trends of women marrying men two to three years older than themselves combined with higher male mortality rates and economic independence for women help explain this. Although the proportion of single women at the prime marrying age is steadily increasing, widows make up a large portion of the single-women-living-alone category.

Perhaps for the first time in modern society, women are caught in a paradox that both restricts and enlarges their choices for marriage. They are restricted in the number of acceptable partners precisely because of their own successes outside the confines of domestic life. The marriage squeeze has little to do with women's willingness to marry men who are dissimilar to them. Strong cultural meanings of marriage and forces of attraction propelling people into marriage are more important factors. Women, like men, want to eventually marry. But women today are less likely to marry simply for financial security. This flexibility narrows the range of partners when these women are seriously thinking about marriage. Many may opt for remaining single because they do not want to settle or settle down with the single men who are left. The marriage gradient results in two categories of those who may be squeezed out of the marriage market: highly educated, economically successful women and poorly educated, lower SES men.

African American Women. When considering demographic trends related to race, age, and education, the marriage squeeze is acute for African American women as a subgroup. We saw in chapter 2 that for both race and sex, life expectancy rates are lowest for African American males. African American women outnumber men at age 18; for whites it is age 32. It is estimated that there are now eight African American men for every ten African American women. These women are also more likely to be college educated; for every ten college educated African American women, there are fewer than two comparably educated men. African American women outnumber employed African American men in every age category by two to one. Although African American–white marriages are infrequent, they are increasing, including the pattern of African American men marrying white women (Crowder and Tolnay, 2000). African American men who marry women of other races are also likely to be highly educated. Highly educated African American women are less likely to racially intermarry (as are highly educated white men).

These patterns significantly restrict the field of eligible partners for African American women. As a result, in comparison with white women, African American women are more likely to marry men who are older, are of a lower educational level, and have been previously married. If African American women select mates of their own race who are otherwise significantly different than themselves, this lack of homogamy predicts a negative impact on marital stability and happiness (Heaton and Jacobson, 2000).

The marriage squeeze may be responsible for the hard choices men and women of all races must make in today's marriage market. Demographic trends help us better understand these choices, but they do not tell us why some people are more acceptable partners for marriage than others. Eligibility in the marriage market is determined by strong gender, race, and age norms regarding what is "appropriate" to marry—norms that direct us toward some people and away from others. The marriage squeeze itself is a by-product of these influences. As these norms are altered, the marriage squeeze also fluctuates. In this sense, a symbolic interaction views the marriage squeeze not as an objectively determined demographic process, but as a socially constructed one.

Sociological Perspectives on Mate Selection

Theoretical perspectives in sociology offer competing explanations for mate selection and the marriage gradient. According to the functionalist perspective, traditional gender socialization—expressive roles for women and instrumental roles for men—contribute to social stability. An attractive woman may have more of an advantage in "marrying up," but she, her family, and society as a whole will benefit. According to conflict theory, men do not need to be as attractive because they possess greater economic power and prestige in society than women. Once economic power is in place outside the home, men will use it to maintain dominance within the home. In extending conflict theory, the feminist perspective suggests that when excluded from power, women become objects of exchange. The marriage gradient in mate selection serves to reduce women to objects based on appearance while disregarding their other statuses such as personal accomplishments and occupational success. Symbolic interactionists assert that the marriage gradient may produce a self-fulfilling prophecy—women may come to view themselves the way they are viewed by men—merely as objects of exchange based on varying degrees of beauty.

GENDER ROLES IN MARRIAGE AND THE FAMILY

Marriage and the families that are legitimated by it are both idealized and frightening for couples on the way to the altar. Images of loving couples with contented children coexist with those of abandonment, divorce, and domestic violence. Regardless of perception or reality, the vast majority of people will marry. Shifts in gender roles have altered our views of traditional marriage and families and prompted the emergence of a variety of lifestyles for those seeking alternatives to these traditional views. Marriage is emotionally and economically beneficial to both men and women. As this section documents, gender roles are critical mediators of the benefits.

Theoretical Perspectives on Marriage and the Family

Sociologists find it easier to describe what families *do* than what they *are*. Families carry out vital services to family members and society as a whole within a variety of structures. In many regions of the developing world, large families are functional for subsistence agriculture and to produce goods for family use or for sale or exchange when surpluses are available. As long as it can feed itself, a larger family unit of production provides an economic advantage. Because women are responsible for feeding the family, subsistence farming is a domestic role and is assigned to women in these parts of the world. In the developed world, the family has been transformed from a unit of *production* to one of *consumption*. *Extended families,* consisting of parents, dependent children, and other relatives, usually of at least three generations living in the same household, are typical in rural areas throughout the world. In urban areas, larger families are at an economic disadvantage because families consume but do not produce goods. Thus **nuclear families**, consisting of wife, husband, and their dependent children who live apart from other relatives in their own residence, are more typical globally in urban areas.

Because the conventional definition is too limited to encompass the structural diversity of households in the United States, especially those without marriage partners, a more inclusive definition is needed. The U.S. Census Bureau now uses the term *family* to describe a group of two or more persons related by blood, marriage, or adoption who reside together. A *subfamily* consists of a married couple and their children *or* one parent with one or more never married children under 18 living in a household. The term *subfamily,* then, combines the "traditional" nuclear family with other family forms. Finally, notice that all varieties of families are not the same as households. A **household** is a person or group of people who occupy a housing unit. There are family households, nonfamily households, and households made up of both family and nonfamily members. All these definitions emphasize family structure, but tell us nothing about how the family is organized according to functions.

Families have been profoundly altered by industrialization and urbanization, the two key elements of the process of modernization. In this sense, gender role change in families is a by-product of modernization. Family change over the last century was fueled by women entering the labor force, but women entering the labor force was fueled by the forces of modernization. The contemporary reality is that the "traditional" nuclear family is but one of many variations related to family structure *and* family function (Figures 7.1 and 7.2). These distinctions may appear to be overly academic, but how marriage and family are defined provokes a great deal of controversy and influences the lives of many people when definitions are translated into public policy. As we will see, most of the controversy surrounds gender role change related to family function.

All theoretical perspectives in sociology recognize that families are pivotal in carrying out vital functions for family members and society as a whole. There is also general agreement that the functions can be carried out within a variety of marital and nonmarital family structures found across the globe. However, sociologists disagree about the benefits and liabilities to the family and society that are associated with gender role change.

Functionalism. Functionalism argues that marriage and eventual parenting are good for society and the individual couple. Marriage and the family provide social benefits, including regulation of sexual behavior, socialization of the children, economic cooperation, safety and protection, and an environment in which love

---

Figure 7.1 Types of Households in the United States.

Source: McFalls, 2003. Population Reference Bureau, Washington, D.C.

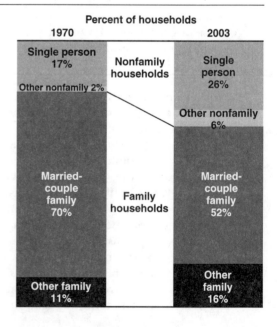

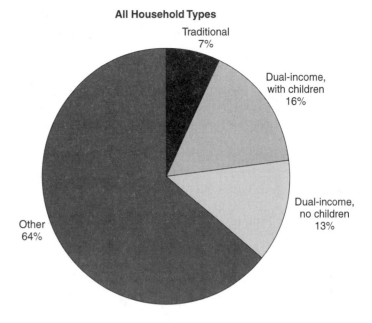

All Household Types

Traditional 7%

Dual-income, with children 16%

Dual-income, no children 13%

Other 64%

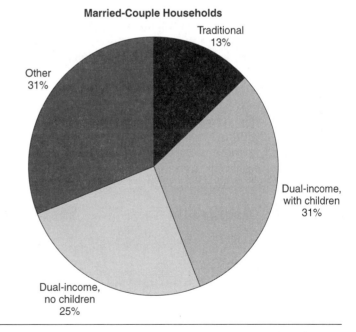

Married-Couple Households

Traditional 13%

Other 31%

Dual-income, with children 31%

Dual-income, no children 25%

Figure 7.2 U.S. Households by Type*, Dual Income, and Children Present.

*Traditional households include married couple households with children where only the husband is in the labor force.

Source: AmeriStat Analysis of the 2002 *Current Population Survey* (March Supplement). Population Reference Bureau, Washington, D.C.

and commitment can be freely expressed. Married couples benefit from ongoing companionship and ego support that combat depression and bolster emotional well-being. Families provide *social capital* to members. This includes a family's resources, such as in level of education, income, housing, and material goods and emphasizes the social placement function of families in the larger social stratification system.

The functionalist perspective highlights these family tasks as vital for social stability. If the institution of the family is ineffective in carrying out requisite social "duties," and other institutions have not picked up the slack, social equilibrium will be compromised. From the functionalist perspective, the socialization of children into nonoverlapping and accepted social roles—instrumental for boys and expressive for girls—is central to social stability. Gender role change and ambiguity of roles are disruptive to family harmony. If one partner takes on the roles typically prescribed for the other, marital dissent and family disruption result. If too many families are disrupted by such change, broader social harmony is threatened. Functionalists favor a nuclear family model that functions with a wage-earning husband, who has final power over household decisions, and a dependent wife and children. This model becomes the ideal to which all families should adhere.

Critique. The problem with the functionalist view is that change is inevitable, so what is considered to be traditional changes over time. Although the traditional model is believed to be the historical and contemporary U.S. norm, it emerged only a century ago and was associated with white, middle and upper class families. Throughout the nineteenth century, poor women, especially immigrants and their children, worked in sweatshops or at home doing piecework. Nostalgia is expressed for a family form that was never the American norm and is far from the norm today (Coontz, 1992, 1997). Functionalist snapshots of families taken at different times in history show that the model for the "traditional" family varies over time. At one time, the multigenerational family living in the same household was believed to be the U.S. norm in the early twentieth century. This belief was perpetuated by television shows such as *The Waltons,* which depicted a three-generation farm family surviving the Depression by hard work, faith, and devotion to family. A "new" traditional family emerged in the 1950s and has served as the ideal ever since, when television gave us *Leave It to Beaver* (The Cleavers—Ward, June, Wally, and the Beaver) and *Father Knows Best.* These shows portrayed a patriarchal family model with a breadwinning husband, a breadbaking homemaker mother, and their at-home children. At the millennium the Cleavers have disappeared, and alternative families and households are emerging on television. These may become the "traditional" families of the future.

Conflict Theory. Conflict theory focuses on the social placement function of the family in preserving existing inequality and power relations in the broader society. Social capital provided by wealthier families is maximized through marriages that ensure its safekeeping within their own social class. According to conflict theory, when social placement operates through patriarchal and patrilineal systems, wealth is further concentrated in the hands of males, which promotes female subservience, neglect, and poverty. When applied to the household, conflict theory argues that married couples and other family members possess differing amounts of resources and will defend their individual interests and resources to maximize their power base in the home. A husband's power base is maximized by the economic leverage that comes with his earnings. When women gain economic strength by being a wage earner, conflict theorists assert that her power inside the home is also strengthened. More egalitarian household arrangements result.

Critique. With its focus on control of economic resources in the family and the jealous guarding of family property both between and within families, conflict theory has been criticized for disregarding the cooperation and agreement that are also part of family life. Family members are highly altruistic, and kin and nonkin networks offer major sources of support to families in a variety of ways—even when their own well-being is compromised. As we will see, a paycheck for women does not guarantee egalitarian roles in their homes.

Feminist Perspective. Feminist scholars in the 1960s and 1970s viewed the traditional patriarchal family as a major site for the oppression of women. Feminists expressed concern that when the patriarchal family is viewed as beneficial to social stability, it hampers the movement into egalitarian roles desired by both men and women. They also argued that the idealized view of the family did not account for the varied experiences of women whose daily lives were lived out in multiple family forms. Since the 1980s the feminist perspective broadened considerably to include not just gender, but race, class, and sexuality as other avenues of oppression to women in the family. Feminists recognize that gendered family relations do not occur in a vacuum and that lives are helped or hurt by the resources outside the family that shape what is happening inside the family (Baca Zinn, 2000). Along with gender, for example, single-parent African American, Latino, and Native American women are disadvantaged by race when they seek employment necessary to support their families. Lesbians must deal with a system that represses same-sex relationships when they fight for custody of their children. However, feminists suggest that women may be doubly or triply disadvantaged by their race, class, or sexuality, but they are not helpless victims—they possess agency—the power to adapt and even thrive in difficult situations.

Critique. With a view of marriage and the family focusing on oppression of women, feminists tend to minimize the practical benefits of marriage, including economic resources and social support (Simon, 2000; Sweeney, 2002). Feminist scholars also find it difficult to reconcile research suggesting that women in traditional marriages are as satisfied with their choices as women in egalitarian marriages. Finally, the acceptance of all forms of family diversity that highlight informal power and human agency may disregard situations such as domestic abuse, where both law and custom sustain women's victimization (Umberson et al., 1998).

Symbolic Interaction. Symbolic interactionists suggest that there are many subjective meanings attached to what a family is "supposed" to be and what its members are "supposed" to do. But in our daily lives we adapt these beliefs to fit our own definitions and accommodate our own needs. As we saw from the census classifications, the definition of a family is not written in stone. It shifts with the broader social changes going on outside the family itself. These shifts show up in how people are labeled. The offspring of unmarried women are less likely to be referred as "illegitimate," for example. Symbolic interactionists also focus on how couples take on family roles that become traditionally gendered, even when they desire egalitarian marriages. The definitions of what a man and women are supposed to do in the home are powerful and are reinforced every time we carry out our family roles.

However, because family members can negotiate these definitions, over time the roles may change to what a couple desires rather than what they currently have.

Research on marital satisfaction also demonstrates the importance of perception of marriage and family roles. The majority of married couples say they are happy in their marriages, but males express higher levels of happiness than females (Thornton and Young-DeMarco, 2001; Stets and Hammons, 2002). A key factor in marital satisfaction is the extent to which a couple agrees on expectations regarding traditional gender roles. Marital quality decreases when a couple holds divergent views, such as how spending decisions should be made or how children should be disciplined. When wives adopt less traditional gender role attitudes (I'll decide how to spend my own income; women need time away from their families), the couple's perceived marital quality goes down. When husbands adopt less traditional attitudes (I'll do the ironing; a woman should be President) it goes up. Marriages with the lowest evaluation of marital satisfaction are those with a traditional husband and a nontraditional wife. Regardless of how traditional or nontraditional they may be, martial satisfaction will be the highest when gender role attitudes and behavior are congruent (Guilbert et al., 2000; Roehling and Bultman, 2002; Amato et al., 2003). Symbolic interactionists suggest that when a couple brings ideals related to gender roles into their marriages they will continually negotiate them to maximize martial satisfaction for both partners.

Critique. Symbolic interaction's microlevel perspective tends to minimize the importance of larger social structures in explaining family dynamics. Men and women interact not only as individual family members but also according to other roles they play in society and the prestige associated with those roles. For example, a wealthy white man who holds a powerful position in a corporation does not dissolve those roles when he walks into his home. They shape his life at home, in the workplace, and in the other social institutions in which he takes part. Race, class, and gender offer a range of privileges bestowed by the broader society that also allows for a power base to be established in his home. Power and privilege foster a patriarchal family regardless of the couple's desire for a more egalitarian arrangement.

Gender and the Family Values Debate

Sociological perspectives on gender roles in marriage and the family are implicit in the highly politicized "family values" movement that fluctuates according to media focus and election year. The theme of the movement is that new family forms and alternative lifestyles are breaking down the family and creating social havoc—children are neglected, illegitimacy rates soar, and divorce is rampant. Although there are some variations of the theme, its underlying message is that a return to the traditional family will solve these social woes. Led by the New Right linkage of conservative politicians and fundamentalist Christian churches, "family restorationists" often use sociological evidence to support their claims. They are united around the idealization of the traditional, patriarchal nuclear family (Cohen and Katzenstein, 1991). They suggest that males are disempowered in companionate marriages that emphasize equality and balancing individual needs with family needs. Such marriages and families, they believe, undermine traditional values of self-sacrifice and family commitment. The welfare state steps in to take over what should be family responsibilities (Popenoe, 2003). Gender role change led by women who sought roles outside their home usurped men from their positions of dominance. When men return to their positions as unchallenged head of the family, both families and society will benefit.

Regardless of the structural changes in the American family, arguments in defending the idealized model advocated by family restorationists are pervasive. At the extreme we have Phyllis Schlafly (2003), who continues to maintain that feminists are responsible for social havoc because they encourage women to challenge patriarchy. She argues that feminism and women who work outside the home take jobs from males, create male wimps, encourage sexuality outside the sanctity of marriage, sabotage family stability, and undermine motherhood. Not as extreme, but the same derisive tone typifies those who believe that it is impossible for women to successfully balance career and family. They assert, too, that men do not desire career oriented women. As one writer comments, men are tired of "leathery career women," and although they do not fear them, they "prefer the other kind" (Davidson, 1988:102). Apparently the "other kind" either are not leathery or do not have careers. Family restorationists argue that such conflicts are resolved when women return to their domestic responsibilities.

There are major shortcomings in the family restorationist model centered on several key points. First, the model ignores the reality of social change related to gender roles. Restorationists consider traditional families in modern societies to be "in decline," regardless of the extent of change over time or between specified points in time (Houseknecht and Sastry, 1996:727). There are all kinds of "new" traditional families depending on the time frame used. How a family is defined has changed and will continue to change over time. The demand of the restorationists is for a family ideal that has never been normative and is rarer today than ever, due as much to economic necessity as to feminist progress (Schwartz and Rutter, 1998:43). Second, many women with children who are divorced or single parents or caretakers of other family members do not have the option of being a full-time homemaker. If they receive public assistance, recent welfare legislation requires them to be in the workplace. Data show that divorce was increasing even before women's widespread entrance into the labor force. Third, the link between family change and child well-being is far more equivocal and complex than the across-the-board negative effects family restorationists emphasize (Coltrane, 1997; Cherlin, 1999). As we will see, egalitarian marriages and alternative family structures are lifestyles they condemn, but they can enhance rather than limit a child's well-being. Finally, American couples increasingly desire gender role egalitarianism in their marriages, in direct opposition to the patriarchal family model advocated by restorationists.

With media influence and ongoing legal and political challenges to extending the rights of the married to the nonmarried, the issue of "what is a family" will be kept before the public. Gender roles in marriage, families, and other kin and nonkin partnerships will continue to evolve as they face the challenges of an increasingly diverse society.

Housewives

The image of the housewife is bombarded with contradictions. The term *housewife* is used here instead of *homemaker* to specifically indicate it is a female rather than a male who is carrying out the role. On the one hand, the traditional housewife role is associated with fulfillment of the American dream for women. It is seen as the height of a woman's aspirations, a deliberate choice that gives her the maximum amount of pride and satisfaction. In overseeing her home, she can be expressive, creative, and autonomous. A classic study of London housewives found that even if women felt that housework itself was not very gratifying, they were generally happy as housewives (Oakley, 1974). More recent data suggest that women may express satisfaction in what they are doing as housewives and mothers, but they feel it is a devalued position overall. This belief is important given research that women in all household situations do more housework than men, but that the gender gap is widest for married women (Pittman et al., 2001; Hoelter, 2002).

Housewife Status. When housewives express the belief that their position is a devalued one, they focus on the intense time demands that are essential to the job but that are taken for granted by their husbands, family, and society. A woman must be continually on call to the needs of her family while her own needs are minimized or ignored (Dempsey, 2001; Phipps, 2001). The more she sacrifices for her family the more she becomes securely bound to it and the more she is blamed for family related problems. For example, children in full-time homemaker families are perceived by their fathers as less disciplined and able to manipulate their mothers than children in homes where mothers are employed (Baker et al., 2003). In addition, a housewife's time demands have not decreased, despite the wonders of microwaves and coffeemakers and the conveniences of dry cleaners and fast food. When her domestic roles include all that is related to child care, there are enormous increases in time demands. Baking brownies for an elementary school party is part of the housework and cooking time, but added to this is the time spent at the party itself. At the societal level, a conflict perspective explains the most important reason for the devaluation of the housewife role: It is not a paid role. Women carry out vital services to their families and society but receive no remuneration, a point we will return to in chapter 10.

The full-time homemaker is caught in a struggle to positively affirm her role at a time when women are completing college and entering professional careers at record rates, and are marrying later and delaying childbirth. She takes pride in her domestic work, and like the London housewives studied three decades ago, she derives a measure of satisfaction from this work. Her well-being is conditioned by how her role is socially defined in and outside of her family and how she perceives the fairness of her duties. Those whose spouse and children affirm her household work express more satisfaction with housewifery. Homemakers who have support from family, friends, and organizations important in their lives, such as a church or volunteer group, help counteract the boredom and loneliness they may experience and are also higher in marital satisfaction (Jalilvand, 2000; Grote et al., 2002; Mirowsky and Ross, 2003).

A related issue is how patriarchy functions to undermine all women, whether they are homemakers or work for pay. The homemaker role may be devalued, but it is the very role women are expected to enthusiastically embrace. A woman who works outside the home is held accountable for anything that may be construed as going awry in her family due to her commitments as an employee. From a feminist view, patriarchy inserts a wedge of suspicion and accusation between full-time homemakers and women who work outside the home. Rather than considering the gendered factors that encourage dependency for the homemaker and guilt for women who work for pay, feminists are viewed as the causes of the devalued position of housewife. The broader patriarchal economic and marital arrangements that encourage the devaluation are ignored.

The housewife role is obviously an ambiguous one. The label of housewife is gradually being replaced by the inclusive label of *homemaker*—the person responsible for the "the making of a home." From a symbolic interaction perspective, such a label change plants the seeds for revised definitions affirming the importance of home-based roles for women and men.

The Issue of Housework

As we see throughout this text, there is a research boom on the impact of women's paid labor force activities on all social institutions. At the household level a great deal of this research focuses on the impact of wives' employment on the division of household labor. For American couples, who does what housework and how much each family member does is one of the most contentious issues families must resolve. The manner in which the housework issue is resolved has an enormous impact on family lifestyle, gender socialization of the children, and marital satisfaction of the couple.

Global Trends. The gender gap in housework is a global phenomenon. Throughout the world, regardless of whether women are full-time housewives or employed outside the home, they shoulder the primary responsibility for housework (Batalova and Cohen, 2002). Cross-national comparisons show that countries with higher levels of gender egalitarian attitudes translate to men taking more responsibility for domestic labor, including cleaning, cooking, shopping, and child care. In industrialized countries, Swedish men and Hungarian women do the most housework and Japanese men and Russian women do the least. The United Nations and the World Bank report that in both the developed and developing world, women's literacy, business ownership, technological training, and paid employment increase the likelihood that men spend more time and women spend less time on domestic responsibilities (United Nations Development Program, 2004; World Bank, 2003). Since 1965 American men have increased their share of housework by about one-third and women have decreased their share by over 10 percent (ISR, 2002). A key point to understand, however, is that the increase in the proportion of his tasks is not offset by the decrease in hers. It is exceedingly difficult for a woman who works 40 hours a week outside the home to add another 40 or 50 inside. This gives no respite from work, whether it is paid or unpaid. For households in the United States as well as globally, the nonessential tasks wives leave uncompleted are not likely to be completed by husbands and children.

Dual Earners. Research on dual-earner couples in the United States usually starts with the logical assumption that a married woman's labor force activity translates into more equitable domestic role sharing with her spouse. Studies conducted since the 1960s indicate that husbands feel obligated to take on a substantially larger share of the housework when their wives are also working outside the home. When these attitudes are matched with actual behavior, however, this has not occurred. Both homemakers and employed wives spend as much as 50 percent more time on household chores than their husbands. For dual-earner couples where both partners are employed full time, over four decades of research find that a husband's contribution to domestic work has increased gradually over time but remains very small in proportion to that of his wife (Blood and Wolfe, 1960; Geerkin and Gove, 1983; Press and Townsley, 1998; Walzer, 2001). Like dual-earner couples worldwide, the decline in her household labor is largely accounted for by her increased labor force participation and other demographic factors such as marrying later, having fewer children, and having them later (Bianchi et al., 2000; Helms-Erikson, 2001).

The increased household tasks that husbands *are* doing favor traditionally male chores compared to traditionally female chores. Lawn care, house repairs, plumbing and electrical work, and automobile maintenance are the household tasks that husbands assume. Tasks for men are usually related to time-limited or seasonal projects, such as arranging for car repairs or mowing the lawn and shoveling snow. When child care is involved, fathers are increasing their recreational time with children more than in the past. Ongoing daily tasks such as laundry, cleaning, cooking, and child maintenance (as distinct from child care) are the household tasks that wives assume. Parents and children do share some domestic responsibilities more equitably, such as pet care, grocery shopping, and buying recreational goods and items for the home. But the gendered division of household labor tends to be reproduced when children are assigned household tasks, although daughters are more likely to take on tasks that sons perform than the reverse. When young sons take on routine housework normally assigned to daughters, they are likely to participate in such housework as they get older. Daughters take on more household responsibilities than sons when their mothers are employed in demanding work situations (Crouter et al., 2001; Cunningham, 2001). Gendered household tasks are further reduced if dual-earner families have only sons or only daughters.

Subcultural Variations. Household task sharing in dual-earner families is also mediated by the subculture of the family related to their race, ethnicity, social class, and religious involvement. Middle class wives may be able to afford paid help, but they maintain the responsibility for organizing paid child care, investigating day care options, and hiring and monitoring nannies or other domestic helpers. These ongoing activities may not significantly decrease their total hours of domestic labor. Mothers of all social classes have more difficulty balancing work and family roles, but professional couples have more control over how these roles can be balanced (Duxbury and Higgins, 1994). Adding race and ethnicity to the picture, compared to white men, African American, Mexican American, and Puerto Rican men in dual-earner families take on a greater share of housework and child care tasks. Asian American men take on the least amount overall. Dual-earning couples who express high degrees of religiosity also show more household and child care tasks assigned to wives (Ellison and Bartkowski, 2002). These tasks take up a greater amount of her in-home labor time if she is employed in a nonprofessional job.

For dual-earning couples of all races, because men's increased share of domestic responsibilities are taken up by recreational time with children and male chores, women perceive the household division of labor as unjust. Wives are less concerned about the *total* time they spend in housework compared to their husbands than about the type of tasks that are accomplished. They point out that men do not equitably share the mundane, routine home and child maintenance tasks that neither partner prefers to do (Baxter, 2000; Stohs, 2000). Women clearly are aware that when a man "helps out" his wife in the home on traditionally masculine tasks, it is not an indication of true task sharing. Women employed full time for pay walk into their homes after work and begin what sociologists now refer to as a **second shift** of unpaid work (Hochschild, 2003). This second shift leads into third shift of caregiving for those women who simultaneously care for their children and frail parents, grandparents, or other friends and relatives (see chapter 10).

A cultural lag between liberal attitudes about fairer task sharing in housework and how the housework is actually accomplished indicates persistent gender inequity. According to men, wives have such high standards for housework that whatever they do is not good enough. The perception of unfairness that women harbor about household task sharing decreases marital happiness and increases the likelihood that they will end the marriage (Pittman et al., 2001; Frisco and Williams, 2003). There are many reasons for husbands to get more involved in housework. They have happier marriages, better physical health, less anxiety, and even better sex lives than men who don't (Coltrane, 1996; Bird, 1999; Shelton, 2000). "Chore wars" remain the thorn in the side of dual-earner couples and compromise egalitarianism for both men and women (Thornton and Lasswell, 1997). The reality is that the old adage "Men may work from sun to sun, but women's work is never done" holds true.

Extramarital Relationships

Americans express high levels of intolerance for sexual infidelity involving married partners but frequently engage in the infidelity they denounce (NORC, 2002). In chapter 2 we saw that at the high end of the range, over one-third of married men and one-fourth of married women have had an extramarital relationship. Even these estimates are suspect because single women and men are involved with married women and men, but figures usually only give the married estimates. Today these relationships are referred to as "affairs," and they show myriad forms. Arrangements are extremely varied, involve different degrees of openness, and include married as well as single people. Many extramarital relationships are more open, with the spouse and other friends aware of the relationship. In this sense, the label of affair is erroneous with its implication of secrecy. Depending on how an extramarital relationship is defined, a sexual component may or may not be part of it, although the potential is certainly there. Some couples regard these affairs as a "spousal alternative" (South and Lloyd, 1995). Job mobility and career related travel for both men and women, more time away from home, more permissive sexual values, and greater sexual opportunities are linked to the higher likelihood of sexual infidelity among both married and cohabiting couples (Treas and Giesen, 2000).

According to early groundbreaking research on extramarital relationships, it is because Americans are unrealistic about love and the ability of a spouse to satisfy all sexual and emotional needs that prompts an affair (Atwater, 1982). This research suggested that it is impossible for one person to supply all of another's emotional, social, and sexual needs. Although affairs are destructive in some marriages, they offer the need for growth, variety, or an antidote for boredom that may enhance other marriages. The married women who were the focus of the research did not live vicariously through their extramarital partners and evolved their own "script of female-centered sexuality." Because women reported that the least satisfactory area of their marriage had to do with expressiveness and communication, they believed that relationships with their husbands actually improved as a result of emotional needs being met outside the marriage. As one woman stated: "Since I have this second relationship ongoing, I have been able to draw my husband out more and get him to talk more" (Atwater, 1982:75). Like the married women in this study, later research on single women in liaisons with married men confirms that they "experience greater control over their sexuality because they feel freer to repudiate their sexual repressions, to abstain, to have safe sex, and to explore their sexual preferences" (Richardson, 1988:368). Sexual openness leads to openness in communication and the willingness for both parties to express vulnerability to someone they can trust (Wolfe, 1993a).

Gender Differences. As would be expected, men and women differ as to their desires and expectations in extramarital relationships. Although men and women may eventually act on their desire to have an affair, men express a greater willingness to pursue them and will plan for them accordingly (Seal et al., 1994; Drake and McCabe, 2000). In this sense, there is less of a gap between what men say and actually do compared to what women say and actually do. Sexual excitement is a stronger rationale for men to pursue such relationships than it is for women. Married women report that their affairs are less for sexual fulfillment and more for emotional support and companionship. Men report the reverse (Atkins et al., 2001). The frequent reason men give for having sex outside marriage is the sexual rejection by their wives and at the same time the boring nature of repeated sex with the same person. Men who eventually seek out reasons for their boredom or lack of sexual closeness with their wives are happier in the long run than those who continue a pattern of interim affairs (Hite, 1994; Levine, 1998). A study of London men who "keep mistresses" finds that they conceive of their behavior as honorable rather than antisocial, governed by a code of conduct and gentlemanly etiquette (Nelson, 1993). Given these significant gender differences, it is surprising to find that men and women converge in agreement about a key issue regarding extramarital affairs. For both heterosexual and homosexual adults, both men and women express more concern about *emotional* infidelity than *sexual* infidelity (Harris, 2002). Because this research asked about hypothetical infidelity, more data are needed to determine if this signals a trend in which nonmarital sexuality is now so normative that what it means to be married is now largely focused on emotional commitment.

Single Women. Affairs between single women and married men demonstrate a gendered double standard. Although they are primarily secret relationships that appear to protect both parties, the woman's reputation is more threatened by exposure of the affair, with fewer penalties accruing for her married counterpart. A single man is also more likely to be absolved of an affair compared to his married counterpart. Female adulterers are treated more harshly than male adulterers, both socially and legally (Batten, 1992:90). We have the "other woman," but where is the "other man"?

With the marriage squeeze operating for professional women, more single women are opting for relationships with married men. Many of these women have no desire to marry their extramarital partner or anyone else. Rather than the other women and mistresses of the past, these "second" women have a different agenda. They want to finish their education and build their careers. Others want to recover from divorce and explore their sexuality (Richardson, 1986:24). However, if she does desire to eventually marry, her relationship with the married man will effectively keep her out of the marriage market. By having her needs met by him, she does not avail herself of opportunities to meet other men. This is especially true for younger single women with low-paying, uninteresting jobs who enjoy the material benefits a successful married man can bring to the relationship. The feeling of power that may have prompted the relationship can also lead to powerlessness for women who get caught up in a relationship in which each partner is there to gratify the internal longings of the other (Tuch, 2000). These women end up staying in a relationship that decreases rather than increases their autonomy and independence.

If the relationship is discovered, there are huge costs to the single woman and the wife, who both bear the larger burden of the infidelity. Certainly the marriage will be threatened. The unaware wife also can experience stages of grief that are akin to the loss of a loved one through death (Boekhout et al., 2000).

It is likely that there will be more second women in the future, some who are satisfied in their relationships but others who invest too much and end up with a great deal of pain that is not easily, if ever, overcome. Despite the adventure, sexual freedom, and independence from the entanglements of an exclusive relationship, feminists contend that affairs lead to distrust between women as well as reinforce beliefs about male power and privilege. In the long run, women may have more to lose than to gain by extramarital relationships.

Global Focus: The Second Wives of Hong Kong Men

Every Friday evening the first class compartments in trains between Hong Kong and Mainland China are filled to capacity with Hong Kong men toting well-appointed suitcases filled with exotic food, luxury household products, and designer clothing. These men will spend the weekend with their "second wives" across the border in Shenzhen. Sometimes referred to as "China's Tijuana," Shenzhen was decreed a Special Economic Zone in 1980 where capitalism is allowed to thrive unfettered. The result, according to one journalist, is that Shenzhen is a city of "laissez-faire business and institutionalized lust" (Perry, 2001). Thousands of women from impoverished areas migrate to Shenzhen in search of love and money. Hong Kong men flock to Shenzhen for the same two reasons (Fan and Huang, 1998; So, 2001). Shenzhen offers extraordinary business opportunities for men enthusiastically pursuing China's mandate that "to get rich is glorious" (Pomfret, 2002). They find young, attractive, and eager Mainland women willing to exchange love for the chance to become the second wife of a rich man. For the most part the second wives are in stable relationships and are provided apartments, gifts, and generous monthly allowances to support themselves and the children that they often have with their "husbands" from Hong Kong.

Why does a man want a second wife? From his perspective she is affordable and available. She gives him what he regards as "needed" psychological and sexual release when he is away from home. And because a new family is established and provided for by the liaison, he justifies the union as legitimate. Peer pressure also plays a role. The "good boys" (*houdzai*) are teased by other men and told that the first wife (*silai*) is getting old, dull, dumb, and losing her feminine qualities. Why does a woman agree to be a second wife? From her perspective, a second wife is far superior to being a sex worker or having a passionate but brief extramarital affair. Even if she is "less than" a wife, she is "more than" a mistress. More important, compared to her impoverished life before she migrated to Shenzhen, he offers her higher status, stable income, and upward mobility. Her children could become Hong Kong citizens. When he dies she may inherit half his wealth, with the other half going to his legal wife across the border. From the mass media's perspective, men are seldom blamed for their cross-border lives. *Funglau*—sexual potency and activity—is at work, and men succumb to seduction by Mainland women. It is the *first* wife who is at fault—she needs to be retrained to serve her husband better (Daswani, 1999; Perry, 2001).

As mentioned in chapter 6, although bigamy is illegal, the concubine heritage is centuries old. Like the generations of concubines before her, a second wife is not legally married but retains a normative social role. Given the large number of philandering men from Hong Kong who have second wives and families in Mainland China, the new marriage law provides stricter regulations regarding the rights of the women and children from these unions. Although first wives now have some legal recourse, it is costly and embarrassing to track down the "second" families, prove bigamy, and sue their husbands.

To date the new marriage law has not met with much success—either legally or culturally—in cracking down on Hong Kong's philandering husbands (Lindsey and Beach, 2004:201). Poor women throughout China migrate in search of a better life through marriage to men who are even marginally better off than themselves. If it means becoming a second wife, their children may escape a life of poverty. Although it is clear that the marriages and families of Hong Kong's first wives are jeopardized, the second family counterparts across the border may be in peril if her husband "succumbs to seduction" again. The law has been unable to deal with cultural beliefs that implicitly condone the behavior of these men.

GENDER ROLES IN EMERGING MARRIAGES AND LIFESTYLES

Rapid social change has significantly altered coupling in all its forms. How gender roles are enacted in these arrangements is a key feature in explaining why some couples stay committed to one another and why others do not.

Egalitarian Marriage

The alternative to the traditional family is one in which the marriage, and hence the family, is egalitarian in both structure and function. Since the 1960s there has been a substantial, consistent trend endorsing gender equality in families (Thornton and Young-DeMarco, 2001). In an **egalitarian marriage**, partners share decision making and assign family roles based on talent and choice, rather than on traditional beliefs about gender. She may enjoy lawn care, he may enjoy cooking, and together they do gardening chores they both enjoy. The undesirable chores, such as cleaning or laundry, are equitably distributed. It is sharing of the domestic chores that creates the most difficulty for the egalitarian couple, because they, too, have been socialized into a world of traditional marriage and family patterns in which gender roles continue to intrude.

Scandinavia. The Scandinavian countries, specifically Norway and Sweden, consistently rank the highest in all measures of human development, including gender role egalitarianism and public policies designed to translate it to the family (chapter 6). Parental leave for new fathers and programs to bolster women's economic status outside the home and men's child-rearing functions in the home have enhanced egalitarian marriages. As in the United States, Scandinavian men adopt more egalitarian attitudes about the division of labor in child rearing than they actually practice, but public policy will continue to support the objective of gender equity (Wennemo, 2001). In Scandinavia and the United States egalitarian attitudes about career and child rearing are increasing, but for marriages to be truly egalitarian husbands need to participate fully in housework.

Instead of ranking husband over wife, egalitarian marriage means that a partnership pattern emerges, one that is strongly associated with paid employment for wives and an effective work-family balance for the couple. This pattern suggests that when wives contribute financially to the family, their decision-making powers are enhanced and traditional assumptions about feminine duties in the household are challenged (Gilbert and Walker, 2001; Zimmerman et al., 2003). Perceived imbalance in decision making lowers marital satisfaction for both husband and wife and bolsters the patriarchal nature of marriage (Knudson-Martin and Mahoney, 1998; Rogers and Amato, 2000). Egalitarian marriage fosters better communication and sharing. It may be described as a *peer marriage* which builds on a strong, empathic friendship between spouses (Schwartz, 1994). Because the couple is less bound by gender role beliefs about a husband's dominance and a wife's passivity, conflict is likely. Conflict may be a perceived but expected cost of the open communication encouraged in egalitarian marriages (Burleson and Denton, 1997; Schwartz, 2002).

Children also benefit from egalitarianism because parents share the joy and burden of child rearing more equitably, and the needs of the couple are balanced with the needs of their children. The two sets of needs cannot be separated. This balance is very important to women who are happy in their egalitarian marriages but who must deal with the ongoing concern that their "mothering" is compromised. The egalitarian family helps women openly talk about both the rewards and the turmoil of motherhood that are hidden behind embedded beliefs about motherhood. As suggested by Susan Maushart's (1999:3) research, egalitarianism "unmasks" motherhood. She states that the mask of motherhood is revealed in cultural values glorifying the ideal of motherhood, but takes for granted the work of motherhood and in debates about child care that pass judgments on "what's best for the child," as if the child's needs were separable from those of the mother, father, and siblings.

Despite the household task overload women face, the trend toward egalitarian marriages is unlikely to slow down (Fan and Marini, 2000). Even highly traditional marriages and families show more companionate qualities than those of a generation ago. They, too, cannot remain isolated from social change. We have seen that marital satisfaction, gender equity, and communication are enhanced when men and women are partners, when women engage in satisfying employment, and when men get involved in housework (Hoffman and Kloska, 1995; Risman and Johnson-Summerfield, 2001). As society becomes more gender equitable, marriages will become more egalitarian.

Commuter Marriage

The dual-location couple is not new. Men and women who serve in the armed forces, for example, have homes maintained by their spouses thousands of miles away and see them during leaves determined by the military. Economic recession, company mergers and buyouts, and job loss requiring relocation also foster dual-location arrangements of a couple. Almost all of the home-maintainers, however, are women. What is new is a dual-career couple evolving into a dual-location couple for reasons of the wife's, rather than the husband's career. Historically, the common pattern is for the woman, literally, to follow her man from city to city as he advances up the career ladder. Her own career, if she has one, is expected to be secondary to his. Today many couples who are firmly committed to their marriages also have wives who are unwilling to abdicate their careers if a move is required. To maintain both martial and career commitments, marriages with commuter wives are growing in number. These marriages generally consist of highly educated, well paid spouses who are managers, executives, and in professional careers, who see one another on weekends or less frequently and who may continue these arrangements for several years. These patterns apply to white and African-American couples, although in the latter, wives are more likely to be in professional careers than husbands (Franklin and Ramage, 1999; Jackson et al., 2000; Rhodes, 2002).

Commuter marriages help overcome the unhappiness and stress that wives express when they put their careers on hold earlier in the marriage. Earlier career subordination on the part of the wife leads to unhappiness and stress that the eventual commuter marriage helps overcome. Research suggests that despite the inconveniences, constant travel, and missing being with the family, commuter wives willingly make their treks because of immense career satisfaction that they find healthy for themselves and their marriages. A key component of the success of commuter marriages is that husbands express high support for their commuting wives. Couples say they have quality time when they are together, communicate better, and enjoy the independence (Coolidge, 1997). The following comments by commuter wives, one a public relations manager and the other a university professor, sum up their orientation to career and marriage:

> I know I don't want to do this (commuting) for years. But at this point I don't feel I want to give up my job, which I adore, and I don't want to give up my home. (Coolidge, 1997)

> This is the best job I've ever had. I love it! I'm so grateful to my family for the chance to do this. What a great way to continue my career. (Harris et al., 2002)

The career advantages of a commuter marriage may be offset by disadvantages related to the considerable stress of living in two locations with little overall time together. Self-sufficiency and independence are enhanced, but loss of emotional support and dissatisfaction with the couple's marriage and family life increase. Strains are also associated with increased costs for maintaining two residences that may not be balanced by two incomes (Seifert, 2000). Couples in commuter marriages have less stress if they have been married longer before the dual-location arrangement began. Older couples, those whose children are already launched and those where one spouse is already established and successful in his/her career, also appear to fare better in a commuter marriage (Bunker et al., 1992; Rhodes, 2002).

It may be difficult to resolve the logistical and emotional strains of a commuter marriage. But the marriage itself is unlikely to be sustained if the career ascendancy on the part of a husband leads to the career subordination of his wife. The guilt and regret commuter couples feel when they are not together are often due to the fact they accept two standards that are not easy to reconcile: the standard that career success applies to both husband and wife and the standard that family success applies to wife but not husband. Both standards are based on traditional gender role beliefs that invade even this highly nontraditional form of marriage.

Cohabitation

Until relatively recently, *cohabitation*—an unmarried couple living together—was cause for condemnation. As increasing numbers of people choose cohabitation as their preferred lifestyle, whether they intend to marry later or not, this is no longer the case. Social support for cohabiting couples does vary, however. Peers and friends are more accepting than parents and relatives. Although parents may not openly express discomfort with the arrangement, they usually breathe a sigh of relief if the couple decides to marry. Increased support for cohabitation may account for the dramatic increase of cohabitants and the slight decrease in the marriage rate (Lipke, 2000).

The number of cohabiting couples has soared from about half a million in 1970 to almost 4 million couples today, representing close to 4 percent of all households in the United States. These households are highly varied and include college students, who report it as preparation for marriage, persons over age 65, who cohabit for financial and emotional security, and couples with children present, this last group representing close to half of cohabitant households. The U.S. Census Bureau admits that these are probably conservative numbers because people may be reluctant to report themselves as "cohabiting" and may call themselves roommates. In addition, these figures do not include gay and lesbian couples who, to date, are legally exempt from marriage in most states (see later discussion). The U.S. Census Bureau considers cohabiters as *POSSLQs*—"People of the Opposite Sex (sic) Sharing Living Quarters" (Casper and Cohen, 2000). Almost half of people in their twenties and thirties have cohabited. Today, half of all couples married since 1985 have lived together at some point before marriage (Fields and Casper, 2001). Cohabitation is now so normative that it is an accepted stage between marriage and dating. However, as a *stage*, it is highly unlikely that it will replace marriage as the preferred lifestyle.

Gender Differences. Although it would be reasonable to think that cohabitants are more egalitarian than married couples, the striking gender differences in cohabiting couples challenge this logic. Unlike married couples, cohabiting couples are less homogamous. Women tend to be younger, have higher levels of education, and earn more money than their partners (Fields and Casper, 2001). Males also express less commitment to the relationship than females (Brown and Booth, 1997). Women tend to view the relationship as temporary and leading to marriage. Men tend to view it as temporary but not leading to marriage. If children are involved, marriage is the more likely outcome. Men who have previously cohabited prefer to date, move in with, and marry women who have not previously cohabited (Wu, 1995; Elizabeth, 2000; Smock, 2000).

Issues of housework and money also signal the gender divide between cohabitants. Cohabiting women spend less time on housework than married women. But married and cohabiting women do more housework than married and cohabiting males, and like married women in traditional households, cohabiting women tend to accept the responsibility (Ciabattari, 2002). Compared to women in cohabitating households, women in egalitarian marriages would consider the larger housework burden as unfair. In household finances, money is rarely pooled, which has the advantage of financial independence, but the couple gives precedence to the man's career over the woman's. This is critical when taking into account data indicating that cohabiting women view themselves as independent, competitive, and managerial. Thus if the relationship dissolves, women are more likely to cite infringement on personal freedom as a reason (Macklin, 1988:68). Gender norms about housework and finances persist in cohabitant households.

Contrary to popular belief, cohabitation is not a good screening device for a later successful marriage. Research concludes that cohabitants who marry have lower marital satisfaction, adjustment, and commitment to marriage than noncohabitants and, perhaps more significant, have divorce rates that are equal to or higher than noncohabitants. Compared to married couples, cohabiting couples earn less, and as we have seen, money is a key predictor of marital stability (Bauman, 1999; Jabusch, 2000). Both male and female cohabitants who break up are likely to cohabit again, setting up a cycle in which one failed relationship may predispose them to another one. Living together lessens total commitment—the door to leave is always open.

Considering these findings, it is somewhat surprising to witness the increasing population of cohabitants. Perhaps they are drawn to the idealism that is inherent in an arrangement that, on the surface at least, offers more benefits than liabilities. But the benefits appear to erode as cohabiting time increases. Playing house and keeping house are fundamentally different.

Singlehood

Nonfamily households have grown rapidly since 1960, and that increase is largely due to the growth of one-person households. About one-fourth of all nonfamily households are now one person (see Figure 7.1). Women living alone represent over half (58 percent) of these households and include widowed, divorced, and single people. In 1900 only one in ten adults was unmarried; today it is almost one in four (Caplow et al., 2001; U.S. Bureau of the Census, 2004). The vast majority of both genders marry, but the percent of never-married people, especially women, continues to increase. The availability of eligible partners and the marriage squeeze do not account for this trend. Market conditions offering either mate surpluses or deficits will not propel women to marry men who do not offer what they can achieve without being married (Lichter and Landale, 1995).

Historically, failure to marry was due to supposed personal or social deficiencies. For women the stigma was, "She was never asked," and for men, "He's probably gay." Bolstered by the women's movement and gay rights activism, today these stigmas have largely disappeared. Many young people no longer view marriage as necessarily better than remaining single, with the result that the number of single people reporting that they are "very happy" has increased steadily for almost three decades (NORC, 2002). College students in particular say that although they plan to marry, it is not in their near future. Finishing college and getting a good job are more important, so for now they favor a lifestyle free of long term commitments (Levine and Cureton, 1998).

Gender Differences. Highly educated, financially independent women are likely candidates for choosing singlehood. For every age category, the higher a woman's income, the lower the rate of marriage. These women express a sense of control in their lives that is offered by remaining single (Lloyd and South, 1996; Clements, 1998; Edwards, 2000). Men are also choosing singlehood at increasing rates. For men, singlehood frees them from financial burdens associated with their instrumental role (Nakosteen and Zimmer, 1997). There are no significant gender or race differences in terms of what is liked or disliked about being single. Professional African-American women report that they are very aware of the advantages and disadvantages of singlehood, but describe their lives as satisfying and meaningful (Fuller, 2001). Both men and women of all races enjoy its mobility, freedom, and social options. But they must deal with loneliness, the uncertainties of dating, and the pressure to marry from family and friends. Despite many new options available for parenthood, women who want to be biological mothers feel acute distress by their single status. Being single in a "couples" world brings added pressures, and many singles, particularly men, report higher levels of emotional distress than married people (Phillips, 1999; Cole, 2000; Lewis, 2001).

Gender Stereotypes. As the initiators of marriage proposals, men are thought to seek out attractive, desirable women and leave the unattractive, undesirable in the unasked category. She is the lonely spinster; he is the carefree bachelor who must be wary of single women interested in matrimony. The image of a man snagged into marriage by a woman in hot pursuit has been a popular one. The media perpetrate images of women doomed to singlehood and childlessness by a marriage squeeze that leaves them desperate as their biological motherhood clocks are ticking away, a stereotype we will explore in the next chapter. Susan Faludi (1996) points to media accounts that paint women responsible for their own misery because they failed to marry before their biological clocks stopped ticking. The man shortage is "a moral comeuppance for independent-minded women who expected too much." The media condemn these women for sins of greed and pride. Single men, on the other hand, emerge unscathed by such accounts.

These are stereotypes that are simply untrue. Women singles express high levels of self-confidence and happiness in choosing a lifestyle that "flies in the face of conventional social beliefs" (Barile, 2001). We have seen that it is better for men to be married than to remain single. They are healthier, happier, and live longer if they marry. Women seem to get along better without men than vice versa. And compared to single men, single women are happier and more satisfied with their lives. Even George Gilder, the avowed champion of traditional, patriarchal marriage, laments the single status for men. "Unless he can marry, he is often destined to a Hobbesean life—solitary, poor, nasty, brutish and short" (Gilder, 1974:31).

As the current generations of never-married people age, it is likely that many will remain unmarried. Contemporary singlehood represents opportunities for happiness for a significant subset of the population who may reject marriage and any permanent and/or exclusive sexual relationship.

Summary

1. Love and marriage were linked during the Puritan era. Love includes components of sex (eros), altruism (agape), friendship (philos), and allegiance (nomos). Sexual passion distinguishes love and friendship.

2. Best friends are usually of one's own gender. Other-gender friends are endangered if liking turns to loving and if gender role beliefs intrude. Love is also seen as a triangle of intimacy, passion, and commitment.

3. Romantic love is idealized and produces many myths. These include: love conquers all, live is blind, love at first sight, women are the romantic gender; sex should not occur without love, and the opposite of live is hate.

4. Men are more open and communicative at the beginning of a relationship and show love by doing things for their lover. The male deficit model of love ignores men's skill at communication and self-disclosure early in a relationship. Androgynous love can integrate masculine and feminine qualities.

5. Mate selection is highly structured and based on homogamy. People choose partners based on age, SES, race, and attractiveness. African-American women are caught in marriage squeeze when the marriageable men of their own race are less educated and less economically successful.

6. Functionalists regard traditional expressive and instrumental gender roles as socially beneficial in mate selection. Conflict theorists say men do not have to be attractive but only economically successful. Feminists say women have less power and are objects of exchange in a marriage market. Symbolic integrationists say women may accept the view of themselves as objects of exchange.

7. Gender role change in families is a product of modernization. Functionalism regards marriage as aiding social stability, which gender role change can disrupt. The functionalist ideal family form of employed husband with his dependent wife and children is recent in history and pertains to white, middle-class families. Conflict theory asserts when wealth is concentrated in the hands of males at the household level, it leads to women's subservience. She can gain power by becoming a wage earner. Feminists contend that race, class, and sexuality are also avenues of oppression to women in their families. Symbolic interactionists emphasize how people take on traditional gender roles despite beliefs about egalitarianism.

8. In the family values debate, family restorationists believe that society will be better off when women stay home and men are unchallenged heads of the family. Their model ignores that families have changed over time, many women must be employed for their families to survive, children are not harmed when their mothers work, and couples increasingly desire egalitarian gender roles.

9. Housewives may express satisfaction in their roles but feel devalued. Patriarchy undermines bridges between homemakers and employed women. Whether employed full time or not, married women across the globe do the majority of the housework.

10. Extramarital relationships are increasing. Married women say affairs are less for sex and more for emotional support; married men report the reverse. Single women and unaware wives have more liabilities if the affair is discovered.

11. Wealthy Hong Kong men often have "second wives" in Mainland China. New marriage laws to counter this trend have been largely ineffective.

12. Household chores and imbalance in decision making create the most difficulty for egalitarian couples. Egalitarian marriages are desired and are correlated with paid employment for wives, better communication, and task sharing.

13. Commuter (dual-location) married couples are committed to their marriages and to both their careers. Couples must reconcile gender standards related to career and family success.

14. The number of cohabiting couples continues to increase. Males are less committed to the relationship than females. Couples who have cohabited have equal or higher divorce rates than noncohabitants.

15. The number of people remaining single is increasing. Highly educated, financially secure women are more likely to choose singlehood and report high self-confidence and happiness. Women who want to be biological mothers express distress at being single.

Key Terms

assortive mating 180

egalitarian marriage 198

homogamy 180

household 186

marriage gradient 181

marriage squeeze 183

nuclear families 185

second shift 195

Critical Thinking Questions

1. Using research evidence, argue for or against the following statement: We are socialized to fall in love with only certain people, therefore the notion of romantic love is a myth.

2. Construct an ideal family form and marital relationship from the perspectives of functionalism and conflict theory. Account for how marital success and happiness are determined in this idealized construction.

3. What are the gender factors working against the contentment of full-time homemakers, equalitarian marriages, commuter marriages, and cohabiting couples? How can these factors be modified to make these household forms more successful?

GENDER AND FAMILY RELATIONS

CHAPTER 8

Desire for a feminine destiny—husband, home and children—and the enchantment of love are not always easy to reconcile with the will to succeed.

—Simone DeBeauvoir,
The Second Sex (1953)

The great majority of people globally will eventually become parents. Like those from many other cultures, Americans are propelled into parenthood by the gendered processes of love, cohabitation, and marriage that prime the couple for their new roles as mothers and fathers. Parenthood is both structured by gender beliefs and produces powerful gender outcomes. These gender beliefs are so completely embedded in family practices that the differences and inequalities they produce are largely taken for granted. As we saw in the previous chapters challenges to taken-for-granted definitions about the family provoke highly contentious debates. These debates have profound consequences when one or another definition is used to determine public policy on a variety of family-related issues, including divorce, child custody, and benefits for single parents, cohabiting couples, and partners in gay and lesbian families and their children. Political rhetoric usually focuses on perceived undesirable effects of altering the traditional family structure to accommodate social change occurring outside the family, such as the massive entry of women into the paid labor force. Other views celebrate family diversity, flexibility, and the creation of new roles for all family members in response to social change. Gender-based parental roles are called into question as alternative definitions of the family emerge. We will see in this chapter that narrow views of gender severely restrict opportunities for exploration and growth for both children and their parents.

THE PARENTHOOD TRANSITION

The transition from the marital dyad to the family triad is a significant one. The first child brings numerous changes that affect the marriage and alter the lifestyle of the couple. New parents report that enormous joy is tempered with increased marital tension. To say that parenthood is filled with uncertainty is an understatement. Parenting is based on skills that need to be learned but cannot be effectively accomplished, if at all, until after the child is born. Socialization for parenthood is based on one's own family experiences, dealing with others' children, formal classes, folklore, and reading child-care and parenting manuals. Whatever the degree of preparation, new parents discover that the anticipation of what it means to be a parent is far different from the reality. Gender is a key factor in accounting for this anticipation gap. Parenthood brings different experiences and consequences for mothers compared to fathers.

Until recently sociological writing on the transition to parenthood focused on parenthood as crisis, highlighting the uncertainty—even shock—encountered by first-time parents (Belsky and Kelly, 1994). The strains of parenthood can be overwhelming, and the demands alter the quality as well as quantity of the marital relationship. More energy is spent on children-related issues than on marriage-related ones. When couples nurture their children but not their marital relationship, the risk for divorce is heightened. Traditional gender roles also drive a wedge between the new parents. When women take on the full demands of infant care, men tend to retreat to their breadwinning roles and find themselves distanced from both wife and newborn (Baldwin, 1995; Cox et al., 1999). The crisis of parenthood is eased when gender roles are more flexible and couples make a determined effort to enhance closeness.

Parenthood as crisis has been modified with the emerging view that it is a normal developmental stage to which new parents gradually become accustomed. The major shifts in lifestyle associated with tension and undesirable role change are more than offset by the joy and gratification the child brings to the new parents (Feeney, 2001).

Obviously, parenthood will alter marital roles and create new family roles. Whether the parenthood transition is seen as a crisis, a stage in normal development, or something in between depends on how a family changes to meet the parenting challenge. This change will be largely dependent on beliefs regarding gender roles. The labels *husband* and *wife* suggest different realities; the same can be said for motherhood and fatherhood.

Motherhood

The belief that a woman's ultimate fulfillment will be in her role as a mother is socialized into girls very early in life. The **motherhood mandate** issues a command to females of all ages instructing them that motherhood demands selfless devotion to children and a subordination of one's own life to the needs of children and family. Although it means halting many other activities she may feel personally worthwhile, the mandate assumes that a woman willingly submits herself first to her child-rearing responsibilities. The power of this mandate instills guilt in women with small children who work outside the home, regardless of whether they are employed because they "want to be" (employment is personally rewarding) or they "have to be" (they need the money).

The Motherhood Mandate. Although American culture idealizes the motherhood role, the actual support new mothers receive varies considerably. If women are socialized into believing that becoming a good mother is easily achieved, they are severely jolted by parenting responsibilities. The tension and strain experienced by first-time mothers can be perceived as personal failure, in turn lessening their motivation to seek help. The notion of a maternal instinct is not empirically supported (chapter 2), but the view that the mother's role "comes naturally" stubbornly persists. The motherhood mandate combines with a mystique surrounding motherhood that states it is made up of the qualities mentioned here (Hoffnung, 1995:167).

1. Ultimate fulfillment as a woman is achieved by becoming a mother.
2. The body of work assigned to mother's caring for child, home, and husband fits together in a noncontradictory manner.
3. To be a good mother, a woman must like being a mother as well as all the work that goes with motherhood.
4. A woman's intense, exclusive devotion to mothering is good for her children.

A consequence of the motherhood mandate is that children who suffer from later psychological problems tend to blame their mothers. This is linked to the trend of the "professionalization" of motherhood and the pressures it puts on women's performance as mothers (Woollet and Phoenix, 1993:216). Women are expected to seek out the latest information offering guidance in fulfilling their roles as mothers. Room mothers and cookie bakers make way for soccer moms and van pool drivers. It is often a no-win situation for mothers. If she works outside the home and her children have emotional or behavioral problems she is at fault as a neglectful parent. If she is the primary caretaker in a traditional homemaker role and her children experience problems, she is at fault because she was rigid, overprotective, and domineering. She may take on martyrlike qualities and instill guilt in her children for being less than perfect. She either does too little or too much for them. Although she delights in her child's development, she loses support for her own development, and her own sense of self can be diminished (Platts, 2000; Ostrowiak, 2001). In either instance she can incur social disapproval, family resentment, and in the most painful circumstances, a loss of self-worth.

Functionalism. In emphasizing that the motherhood mandate is essential for social equilibrium, functionalists would support these qualities. Mothers are both the biological reproducers and the social reproducers. As the primary socializers of children, they provide the necessary ingredients for maintenance, productivity, and continuity of society. If socialization does not instill girls with the motherhood mandate, and the mystique associated with it, goals of the broader society may be compromised. Functionalism assumes that the traditional division of labor of nonoverlapping gender roles within a patriarchal family is the most efficient and least contentious arrangement. Implicit in the view is that if something "goes wrong" with the children, it is the mother's fault. She takes the responsibility, the blame, and ultimately the guilt for child-rearing functions (Garey and Arendell, 2001).

Functionalism points to the responsibilities associated with motherhood. But rights accrue as well. The motherhood mandate is in tandem with the motherhood mystique which is a glorification of the role. Child rearing brings joy and pride for a child's accomplishments, for which mothers take a great deal of credit. It is apparent, nonetheless, that mothers are more likely to share the credit for what goes right, but assume the burden of blame for what goes wrong.

There is no argument that the family is the critical institution for socialization. Contemporary functionalists recognize that there are social benefits when women, including those with school-age children, work outside the home. They assert that family maintenance today hinges on the incomes of employed mothers and that women need to be encouraged to pursue the same work as men to garner the higher income associated with that work. In this sense, workplace equality enhances family and society. However, equality applies only to the world outside the home, and even there women are never far from family responsibilities (Oakley, 1993:199). Inside the home is a different reality. With the acceptance of the motherhood mandate by both parents and children, functionalists have difficulty transferring beliefs about gender equity to the home and explaining how women are supposed to be equal and different at the same time.

An often overlooked fact about the motherhood mandate/mystique is that it is recent in the United States. By the middle of the nineteenth century, a frontier economy based on subsistence farming required women to carry a multitude of productive roles. In her role hierarchy, a woman's child rearing function was less important for family survival than her farm and household related money raising activities (chapter 5). It is only since the beginning of the twentieth century that the notion of having children for purely psychological reasons became firmly ingrained on the American consciousness.

Conflict Theory. Conflict theorists focus on the motherhood mandate as contributing to the social powerlessness experienced by women in their household and extradomestic roles. Because a woman's earnings from paid employment alter the power relations within the family, men will evoke the motherhood mandate to ensure that women concentrate their energies on domestic roles. Women are handicapped in career growth and personal achievement when child and family responsibilities from which men are absolved compromise their well-being and workplace productivity (Wharton and Erickson, 1995:289). The choices wives make regarding child rearing weaken their bargaining power at home and on the job and reinforce economic dependence on their husbands. As discussed in chapter 10, in the workplace this translates to lower salaries and sagging careers. At home it translates to shouldering the bulk of child-care tasks. From a conflict perspective, not until as many men as women truly want to stay home with the children can women hope to achieve real economic parity.

Challenging the Motherhood Mandate. An acceptance of the motherhood mystique precludes much individual growth for women. By this definition, motherhood is the key worthwhile role that overrides all others. The obvious problems and contradictions emanating from the mystique are conveniently overlooked. Can women feel good about themselves as mothers if they also seek other roles?

One answer lies in the demographics of motherhood which have changed significantly since the 1950s. As women achieved career and educational goals, marriage and motherhood were delayed. The median age at first marriage for both women and men has steadily risen over the last three decades. The decline of the fertility rate since World War II is linked to higher levels of education, rising wages, and the opportunity costs of child rearing for women. This explains why so many women in their 30s and 40s are now having children for the first time. It also supports the idea that motherhood remains a central goal. Most women are unwilling to give up biological parenthood but opt for smaller families than in their parents' generation. Because career oriented women are also unwilling to give up either motherhood or professional roles, they are adapting their beliefs about family and parenting accordingly.

Young women assume that motherhood, as the mystique suggests, gives them a sense of personal fulfillment. But unlike their mothers and grandmothers, they are also challenging the idea that motherhood is the necessary ingredient for making them "complete." Motherhood is a role most seek, but it must be complemented with other personally fulfilling roles to ensure their wholeness as human beings (Bartholet and Draper, 1994). More and more women are carving out new role constellations that may or may not include motherhood. This is especially true for younger professional women, who already demonstrate higher rates of childlessness than older professional women. These women may be either less confident or more realistic in their ability to successfully carry out roles associated with motherhood and still have a satisfying career. If this is indeed the case, it may indicate a further weakening of the motherhood mandate.

Feminism. The acceptance of feminist values by a larger proportion of women also affects notions about motherhood. Women who hold traditional gender role orientations desire larger families when compared to nontraditional women. Traditional women are also likely to express higher levels of religiosity and have lower levels of educational attainment. College women who subjectively identify with feminism are less interested in motherhood or intend to delay marriage and motherhood until after they are established in their careers. However, feminism and motherhood are compatible. Feminists who intend to become mothers or those who already have children are realistic about the gendered pitfalls of mothering but also believe that motherhood offers opportunities for assertiveness, learning and mastering new skills, and ensuring that feminist principles are passed to the next generation of sons and daughters (Baker, 2000; O'Reilly, 2000; Howitz, 2001). The old view of motherhood is unacceptable because paid work has become so important to the identities of mothers. They firmly believe that simply being home all day does not automatically qualify one as a good mother and that children can be loved, nurtured, and cherished without sacrificing their mothers' sense of self (Peters, 1997).

The motherhood mandate is itself being redefined to fit the lifestyles of contemporary women. This redefinition links the perspectives of symbolic interaction and feminism. The qualities we associate with motherhood can be more widely shared by both men and women in a variety of family contexts. It is expected that like other gender roles, qualities associated with motherhood will continue to change as we experience more diversity in our families and workplaces (McDaniel, 1996).

Fatherhood

American fathers are viewed as peripheral in nurturing and child care compared to mothers. Unlike America's colonial American ancestors who expected the father to provide for both the economic needs and spiritual education of his children with the less literate mother as his able assistant (Vinovskis, 1986:188), the contemporary father is cast primarily into the breadwinning role.

Public policy and legislation regarding custody of children, child support, welfare, definitions of desertion, and child neglect reinforce the emphasis on the father's role as the economic provider for the family. Increases in divorce and cohabitation have undermined father–child relationships, and nonresident fathers are increasingly absent from their children's' lives (Cabrera et al., 2000). To get women off welfare, efforts are embedded in public policy to find unwed, divorced, and married fathers who deserted their families. Some agencies provide support services to these fathers to encourage more active, emotional involvement with their children, but it is largely the economic responsibility that is targeted (Bartfield, 2003).

The fact that fathers do take their breadwinning role very seriously does not diminish the interests or love they have for their families. Like women, men also see raising a family as a key life goal, with strong evidence that the quality of family relations and social connections are higher for fathers than nonfathers and associated with better psychological health and well-being (Eggebeen and Knoester, 2001). Compared to nonfathers, contemporary dads exhibit two models of fatherhood: the "good-provider model," encouraging them to work more hours, and the "involved-father model," encouraging them to work less hours (Kaufman and Uhlenberg, 2000). The models may seem contradictory, but they suggest that men regard the fatherhood role as a significant one.

New Fathers. As first-time parents, men adapt more easily to the rigors of fatherhood than women do to motherhood, and husbands can predict with more success than their wives what kind of parents they are likely to be. In the transition to parenthood, personal goals of husbands do not change substantially, and husbands are less ambivalent about parenting responsibilities (Salmela-Aro et al., 2000; Simpson et al., 2003). Fathers see themselves as less competent than mothers in dealing with daily child care. They internalize strong beliefs about their paternal responsibility, but largely surrender actual responsibility for child care to their wives. A father's level of engagement, accessibility, and responsibility are a fraction of the mother's. A father's time is spent more on recreational activities with their children than with their ongoing physical upkeep (Snarey, 1993, Sanderson and Thompson,

2002; Renk et al., 2003). When asked about involvement with their children, fathers respond with answers such as, "They have to put in some time with the kids"—a technically present but functionally absent father (LaRossa et al., 1991:313).

Children's Development. Because the prime directive for fathers is to provide for the economic support of their families, in comparison to mothers, the father's effect on the development of their children is often overlooked. Chapter 3 demonstrated that parental influence on childhood socialization is critical. Mothers accept the major responsibility in socialization of their children, but fathers send important early messages, especially regarding gender roles. These messages are powerful in part because fathers have reduced contact and quality of interaction with their children. Compared to mothers, fathers expect their adolescent sons to conform to gender roles much more than their adolescent daughters. Fathers are more likely to take into account a child's gender when they mete out chores, affection, discipline, and privileges. Fathers are likely to use harsher discipline on sons in the belief it enhances a son's masculinity. Increased parent–child conflict during adolescence is typical, but conflict is heightened for fathers compared to mothers and for sons compared to daughters. Such gender preferences predict a decline in attachment adolescent sons have for their fathers (Buist et al., 2002; Kurtz, 2002; Tucker et al., 2003). Fathers who are less traditional and stereotyped in their gender role beliefs have sons who match their fathers in this regard. This suggests that when fathers change, sons will follow.

Traditional fatherhood may not bring the same profound personal and marital changes that mothers experience, but research reveals that fathers can and do form strong bonds with their young children and are successfully taking on childcare tasks and nurturing roles more than fathers in the past. Success can be measured in various ways. Fathers who are more actively involved in the care of their preschoolers produce grade-schoolers with fewer problems; fathers who are highly involved in parenting and have positive, open communication with their daughters about dating and sexuality produce responsible daughters whose sexual decision making is responsible and less sexually permissive (Bowling and Werner-Wilson, 2000; Fingerson, 2000; Aldous and Mulligan, 2002).

Fathers who are successful in parenting provide the care and emotional warmth that may seem contradictory to the patriarchal yet good-provider family role. Notions of fatherhood are gradually changing, and fathers are now encouraged to develop those nurturing qualities that will make them better fathers as well as better partners. Egalitarian parenting clearly benefits children and enhances marital satisfaction.

A Fatherhood Mandate. Continued gender role stereotyping severely limits options for fathers to explore new roles. Conflict theory and the feminist perspective would argue that the motherhood mandate is a barrier to gender equity. But the opposite is true for a fatherhood mandate. Young men have not adopted a fatherhood mandate allowing them to move in the direction of androgynous, flexible gender roles. Functionalists would also support a fatherhood mandate that moves beyond the provider role so fathers can effectively meet the challenges of social change and the new family processes that emerge as a result. After the terrorist attacks on September 11 in New York City, for example, children sought protection, safety, and security from both parents, but particularly from fathers (Warren, 2001). Those fathers who listened to their children and responded to them with warmth and compassion began to carve out a tentative fatherhood mandate combining instrumental and expressive roles. The involved-father model appears to be gaining in prominence and, as discussed on chapter 9, it may signal a crack in a masculine ethic that deters men from meaningful parent–child relationships.

Voluntary Childlessness

The motherhood mandate may be weakening, but couples who choose not to have children must still contend with a prochild social message. Data indicate that childless marriages are steadily increasing and that more women of childbearing age will not have children. It is unlikely, however, that this signals a revolution against a pronatalist ideology or that cultural definitions of femininity equaling sexual reproduction are going to be altered any time soon (Hird and Abshoff, 2000). Media are replete with stories of women who "successfully" challenge their biological clocks to have children before it is too late. A billion dollar fertility and adoption industry has mushroomed to meet this challenge. The belief that couples should have children is so strong that those who choose not to do so, especially the women, continue to be denigrated, often regarded as incomplete and selfish (Gillespie, 2000; Meyers, 2002).

Married couples who are voluntarily child free might be viewed with a combination of pity, scorn, or suspicion. Married women who do not mother children are thought to live a childless existence. These are stereotyped views that are fundamentally different from empirical reality. Voluntarily childless couples express similar levels of marital happiness as couples with children, with voluntarily childless married women significantly higher than married mothers in this regard (Abbey et al., 1994). Women who are childless also do not lead childless lives. They choose not be mothers, but children are central to their lives and provide them with a sense of generativity that compares favorably to biological mothers (Joseph, 2001; Letherby, 2002). They take on a variety of meaningful child-related responsibilities through their networks of kin, friends, voluntary organizations, and employment.

Although couples continue to view parenthood as desirable, the increased number of voluntarily childless couples implies that, along with the weakening of the motherhood mandate, there is also less pressure to conform to traditional family norms regarding parenthood. As a fulfilling alternative to rearing children, support for those couples who choose to remain childless is growing.

PARENTS AS DUAL EARNERS

The massive entry of women into the paid labor force during the twentieth century has significantly impacted the structure and function of families in the United States. Paid employment benefits women socially and psychologically, especially when they work in positions that they find challenging, rewarding, and personally meaningful. Their marriages and sense of well-being appear to be enhanced, and shared decision making increases marital satisfaction for both wife and husband (Deutsch, 1999; Han and Moen, 2001; O'Keefe, 2002). As suggested in the last chapter, dual-earning couples are more likely to have egalitarian marriages than those with a wife as full-time homemaker. The cost for women involves maintaining responsibilities at home and for the children when husbands do not share household and child-care chores on anywhere near an equal basis. Multiple roles of employed women also include other caregiving demands, such as caring for infirm parents, which may compromise the benefits of employment and overall life satisfaction (chapter 10). In general, however, the evidence from dual-earner families shows that women are enriched by their labor force activities.

The dual-earner family is now the normative family. There are more dual-earning nuclear families with children present than one-earner nuclear families with children present. The largest overall increase is in families with preschoolers. Because women are traditionally responsible for child care, particularly in the preschool years, all eyes turn to them when questions arise as to how children are affected when both parents work outside the home. It is the wives rather than their husbands who reap society's disapproval if children suffer when both parents are simultaneously in the labor force. Disregarding the gendered claim that women should be largely responsible for socialization of their children, how accurate is the "suffering children" theme?

Children of Employed Women

If parents are happy and the family is enhanced by a dual-earning family structure, this should logically carry over to the children. Not so, states writer David Gelernter (1996), who maintains that the "MOTHERHOOD REVOLUTION" that propelled married mothers into the labor force "has been a disaster for our children." Day care is not the answer to the needs of the dual-earning couple because the child is not provided with a sustained one-to-one relationship with a primary caregiver that is essential to her or his healthy emotional development. A person caring for a child out of love will do it better than if doing it for pay. If parents, especially mothers, are not filled with remorse and guilt by this stage, he suggests that parents, especially the *white, married* couples he targets, have an obligation to find some other way of coping than care by paid strangers (italics mine). Implicit in this is that most other options that do not involve mothers staying home are either deemed unrealistic by working parents or dismissed as unacceptable. In addition, he ignores the same conclusions of damaged kids for women of color or single-parent women. Apparently it is acceptable for their children to have surrogate care. These claims follow the footsteps of earlier commentators, one who claimed that

> Invariably the parent who is obliged. . . . to grapple with the choice between home and office is the woman; no matter how unfettered by convention any of us purports to be, no matter how vividly we might wish it to be otherwise. . . . (Stein, 1987:62)

Apparently both men and women are condemned by unalterable roles, "no matter how vividly we might wish it to be otherwise."

The Child Care Issue. The contention from these writers is that a generation denied love when they were children will potentially create havoc as adults and do untold damage to the social structure, an argument echoed by the family restorationists mentioned in the previous chapter. Parents are abandoning their children to day care so they can selfishly pursue their own careers, which in later years will harm the next generation of *their* children. Is the evidence sufficient to warrant such a conclusion?

One major source of information is often overlooked in debates on this issue. When women were desperately needed during World War II to work in defense plants, they were recruited by the thousands in propaganda campaigns designed to alleviate their anxiety and guilt about leaving their children with others (chapter 5). Creative approaches to day care became the norm of the day. Day care centers grew because the war industry needed women who could not rely on relatives or other care options for their children. Any potential negative and long-term consequences on these children were ignored. After the war traditional attitudes prevailed and women were expected to return home and be full-time housewives and mothers. They were not guilty of being neglectful mothers during the war, but if they chose to continue to work outside the home afterward, the guilt returned. The script that employed mothers are "bad" mothers returned with a vengeance.

A half century after World War II, there is near consensus by developmental psychologists that surrogate child care is not the major risk factor in the lives of children of dual-earner couples (Burchinal et al., 2000; Colwell et al., 2001). The key problem comes if it is poor quality care. Fortunately for married, white collar and professional women, many employers now provide benefit packages offering high quality care options. The same cannot be said for single-parent women, who are more likely to rely on informal and less costly, less convenient and less desirable options of lower quality. When employed mothers prefer one type of child care option but end up with a less desirable option, they experience more stress both on and off the job (Henley and Lyons, 2000; Hattery, 2001; Riley and Glass, 2002). On the other hand, an enriched group child care experience can stimulate the development of infants and preschoolers. Moral development and prosocial behavior can be enhanced (Honig, 2002; NICHD, 2002). Poor children or those from troubled families may have resources and support in their child-care centers that are absent in their home environments. Low income mothers who gain entrance into good quality subsidized child care are able to maintain steady employment and spend half as much income on child care (Brooks, 2002). Their satisfaction with child care carries over to the well-being of their children.

Children's Time with Parents. There are no significant differences in the home environment or development of children with employed mothers than those mothers who are not employed. Dual earners build in "quality" parent–child time. For example, in homes where mothers are employed, both parents spend more time on homework and reading with their children than in homes where a mother is not employed. This pattern is associated with higher grades and fewer behavior problems for their children (Zick et al., 2001:25). Early in life children do express that they would like their mothers to be at home more and are concerned about the confusion, rush, and scheduling headaches that are the inevitable effects of job, school, and recreational demands. Nonetheless, children's appreciation for their employed mothers' accomplishments grows over time (Hoffman, 2000; Dorfman, 2001; Moen, 2003). Fueled by media stereotypes and the guilt messages received from a variety of sources, parents agonize over decisions to use surrogate care in order for a mother to return to paid employment. Compared to the parents, however, as they get older children are more likely to perceive more advantages than disadvantages to these very arrangements (Heaven and McCluskey-Fawcett, 2001)!

Adolescents. The adverse effect of maternal employment would be expected to show up during adolescence, because this is often a stress-filled time for families. Again, research does not warrant this conclusion. Adolescents from dual-career families, especially daughters, appreciate the jobs their mothers have, often want to follow in their professional footsteps, and not surprisingly have less traditional gender role attitudes than children from single-earner homes (Hoffman and Youngblade, 1999; Kinelski et al., 2002). Adolescents and adults reflecting on the effect of their mother's paid employment when they were children viewed their family lifestyle positively and reported high degrees of parental closeness, supportiveness, and interest in their personal problems (Gambone et al., 2002).

Thirty years of research data on the effects of the dual-earner family on children does not support the suffering child or abandoned child theme. Employed mothers do not neglect their children nor are the children jeopardized by maternal employment. The benefits of growing up in a dual-earning family are bolstered by longitudinal research on children of all races who were followed over a 14-year period that compared them according to whether their mothers worked outside the home or not. The results show that on measurements of self-esteem, academic achievement, language development, and behavior problems in both family types, children are not harmed in their development. This study is important because the results applied to mothers who worked outside the home when their children were babies and preschoolers (Harvey, 1999). To the relief of egalitarian couples, results such as these continue to be confirmed. Motherhood and working for pay do not harm children—to the contrary, they often improve children's social and intellectual development (Chira, 1998; Perry-Jenkins et al., 2000). Employed mothers enrich the human capital of their families.

FAMILIES IN MULTICULTURAL PERSPECTIVE

The multicultural heritage of the United States is reflected in its families. Because this heritage is linked to race and ethnicity, minority families are impacted by the same disadvantages that affect them in parts of society. To account for gender patterns in these families, the multiple risks and experiences from their unique cultural histories must be considered as well. Keep in mind, however, that white and European American families also vary in social class, cultural history, and other variables that impact gender roles in their families. Although not profiled in this section, they should not be considered the default, normative family in the United States.

African American Families

Contrary to stereotypes, there are two parents present in over half of African American families, and over half of the fathers in these families work full time (Center on Budget and Policy Priorities, 2001; U.S. Bureau of the Census, 2004. Data from the turn of the century (1910) reveal that African American households were less likely to be nuclear and more likely to be headed by women, a pattern that persists today (Morgan et al., 1993). The half of African American households that does not have two parents present is those headed by single parents, about 90 percent of whom are single-parent women (U.S. Bureau of the Census, 2001: Adapted from Table no. 58). Compared to European Americans, African American family life cycles are marked by less formal marriages, parenthood earlier in marriage, later and less likelihood of remarriage, and a higher divorce rate (Lichter and Graefe, 2001; Manning, 2001; National Center for Health Statistics, 2002). Over three-fourths of African American children are likely to live part of their life in a female-headed household, often with a female grandparent. The households are likely to consist of both kin and nonkin. The key factors in the development of these patterns are the impact of slavery and economic oppression rooted in discrimination that led to the underemployment of African American men. These factors have had a profound impact on gender roles in African American families.

Compared to all other racial groups, African American females have had a much longer legacy of paid employment essential to the stability and survival of their families. This legacy fueled the variety of family and household structures African American families exhibit. Paid employment is central to African American women's mothering and to their family experience. It is the most important reason for the greater degree of role sharing by wives and husbands and has strengthened African American families in several fundamental ways. First, families demonstrate a strong willingness to absorb others into kin structures by creating a network of **fictive kin**, where friends "become" family. African Americans tend to define the boundaries of their families with more flexibility than in families of other races, so distant kin become primary kin, and close friends and neighbors become fictive kin (Johnson, 1999). Fictive kin bring an array of exchange and support that benefits all household members. In turn, children are offered a diversity of parenting models that are seen as enriching children with a more multifaceted form of nurturing (Dill, 1994; Hasell and Scanzoni, 2000). Employed mothers who are the family's breadwinners can turn to fictive kin for child care needs.

Second, for working class and middle class married couples, family structures are likely to be egalitarian in which roles are complementary and husband and wife are dual earners in stable employment (Staples, 1997). Egalitarian arrangements are bolstered by middle class African American women who work outside the home by choice rather than economic necessity and who do not view their roles as wife-mother and wage earner as mutually exclusive (Higginbotham, 2000). Research by sociologist Burt Landry (2000) argues that these women were practicing an egalitarian lifestyle decades before it was even envisioned by white couples. Third, African American husbands appear to be more willing than white husbands to take more responsibility for child rearing and adapt themselves and the household to the needs of their employed wives (Hofferth, 2003). This last pattern is interesting because African American working class and lower class men tend to hold traditional ideas about gender roles (John and Shelton, 1997). More data are needed to determine if it is race, social class, or a combination of both that accounts for the pattern.

The Myth of Black Matriarchy. The paid work of African American women has been a necessary and constructive adaptation to the reality of economic and social inequality in the United States. Yet this very strength has been viewed as a weakness inherent in these families. An early and influential report purporting to explain the poverty of African American families in the United States by Daniel Moynihan (1965) intimated that a *black matriarchy* exists in which decision making and other family powers and responsibilities rest with women rather than men. By this way of thinking African American men are emasculated, stripped of authority, and driven from the family under an aura of self-defeat. The family is left with fewer defenses against poverty, delinquency, and illegitimacy. The notion of a black matriarchy gained support with the rapid increase of African American female-headed households.

The Moynihan report and its bequest of black matriarchy also serve as reminders of the connection between sexism and racism. The report was attacked in a large part because black (*sic*) men were usurped of their rightful place as family head. To untangle the pathology surrounding the black family, the father must be returned as the dominant person in the household. Assertive and independent women can wreak havoc on both the family and the race. Black women apparently do not suffer the same humiliation as black men and "neither feel nor need what other human beings do either emotionally or materially" (Smith, 1995:157). According to Anthony Giddings (1993:252).

> The Moynihan Report was not so much racist as it was sexist. Although it can't be held responsible for the intense Black male chauvinism of the period, it certainly didn't discourage it, and the report helped shape Black attitudes.

Such views may suggest a self-fulfilling prophecy. The demographic reality of African American households and the household structures that accommodated the legacy of economic oppression, challenges the notion of black matriarchy. However, this has done untold damage by creating and reinforcing stereotypes of superhuman women and weak and absent men, who are then blamed for the circumstances in which they find themselves. Many African American men may have internalized its assumptions, which in turn create tension between the genders.

Multiple Risks of Race, Class, and Gender. Despite their occupational and educational gains, African American women have the lowest earnings of both genders and all races. African American women must carry the double burden of their minority group status. Few would argue that these women are exploited by virtue of both race and gender. If she is a single parent, the prospects of decent wages to maintain her family above the poverty level are severely reduced. This is intensified by the kind of jobs they typically have. Although women of all races earn less than men overall, the likelihood of poverty is significantly higher for women in occupations dominated by African American women and lower in occupations dominated by white women (Catanzarite and Ortiz, 1995). This is despite a strong commitment to employment and socialization messages to girls emphasizing self-reliance, independence, and resourcefulness (Collins, 1993).

While African American women are worse off economically and face the double-minority burden, African American men must contend with a double bind of their own. African American men, like other men in the United States, are socialized into instrumental family roles that tie masculinity with being a good provider and father. This standard for masculinity is accepted by African American men, but opportunities for carrying it out are restricted. An *Afrocentric* view suggests that models are provided for people who cannot obtain them in a "culturally oppressive and race-conscious society" (Langley, 1994:242). Masculinity must then be affirmed in other ways. African American males, for example, take on a variety of masculine roles used as coping behavior that is referred to as "cool pose" (Majors and Billson, 1992). Reflecting a symbolic interaction perspective, cool pose is used by African American males to create and manage their self-presentation to others. For the coping styles of inner-city youth living in poverty who grow up on the streets, it is associated with "violent behavior, on the streets and at home, to sexual promiscuity and to problems at school" (Majors et al., 1994:251).

Compulsive masculinity related to cool pose takes its toll on the family. Data indicate that low-income, single African American mothers who are parenting boys have higher levels of depressive symptoms, more negative perceptions of children, especially boys, and that there is a poorer quality overall home environment (Jackson, 1994b; Mott, 1994). For married couples, the number of teenagers is negatively related to marital happiness (Ball, 1993). If these teenagers are boys, tension increases, and family life suffers as a result.

In addition, the African American community is not immune to other stereotypes concerning black male–black female relationships. African American men often perceive that black women have more opportunity and are held responsible for the status of black men. Tension may be heightened because African American women now have higher levels of education than black men and are outpacing men in gains of professional occupations. As pointed out earlier, the marriage squeeze is more acute for African American women searching for same-race men of comparable age and educational levels. Increased joblessness and higher death rates from violent crime, disease, and poor health care (chapter 2) deplete the pool of marriageable black males in absolute numbers and render those who are available as less desirable to marry. Besides contributing to the increase in interracial marriages, many childless women who remain single shoulder a greater share of family responsibilities and are more vulnerable to poverty and all its consequences. Stereotyping increases during periods of economic uncertainty. The high unemployment rates of black men may counter the legacy of role flexibility and egalitarianism evident in many African American families. It appears that it is the economic position of men that will significantly determine the course of many African American families and how gender roles will be enacted.

Latino Families

For the first time in U.S. history, there are now slightly more people who identify themselves as Latino or Hispanic (12.5 percent) than who identify themselves as black or African American (12.3 percent), making them the largest minority in the nation (Grieco and Cassidy, 2001). There are significant cultural and historical differences between Latinos, such as economic well-being and number of generations in the United States, that are important determinants of gender roles in their families. The three largest subgroups are Mexican Americans, Puerto Ricans, and Cuban Americans. Although all three groups suffer the economic burdens of minority status, poverty is most acute for Puerto Ricans and least acute for Cuban Americans.

Although Mexican Americans hover near the poverty line as a group, there are wide variations in overall economic status. Latinos share a heritage of Spanish colonialism and, through this, a solid connection to the Catholic Church. Several fundamental values related to gender and the family link these diverse groups. First, family relations are characterized by respect and honor. Second is the notion of **familism**, a strong cultural value emphasizing the family and its collective needs over personal and individual needs and any other groups to which a family member belongs. Familism creates strong bonds between nuclear and extended family members in terms of support, loyalty, and solidarity (Magana, 1999). These bonds ensure that family members will remain intimately connected to one another throughout their lives.

Third, and the most important element related to gender roles and the family, is that there is a strong adherence to patriarchal gender roles in a well-defined system of mutually exclusive beliefs that separate men and women; these roles are found throughout all social classes in Latino cultures. Derived from the Spanish word *macho* ("male"), the man's role is associated with **machismo**, seen to include virility, sexual prowess, and the physical and ideological control of women. The woman's role is associated with **marianismo** (from the Virgin Mary's name, Maria), seen to include the beliefs of spiritual and moral superiority of women over men, the glorification of motherhood, and the acceptance of a difficult marriage. Women are expected to have an infinite capacity for sacrifice in their role as mothers and to be submissive to the demands of the men in their family (Stevens, 2000).

The beliefs that support marianismo remain strong, but changes in what were once entrenched patriarchal gender roles in the family are appearing. Higher education for both males and females in Latino subcultures is associated with more gender role flexibility in the home and a loosening of stereotyped beliefs about humble women and aggressive men (Mirande, 1997; McLloyd et al., 2000). Factors such as socioeconomic status and degree of acculturation affect how these values are translated into the home.

Puerto Rican Families. By far research on gender and the family in Latino subcultures centers on the link between employment and home for women and their families. Puerto Ricans have the lowest income of any Latino group, and it is the critical gender-family link that explains this fact. Almost half of all Puerto Rican households are headed by women, and only half of Puerto Rican women are high school graduates. Women have been employed in low-paying jobs, such as light manufacturing, and these are shrinking in numbers as manufacturers move their operations to Asia, where even lower paid female workers are hired. (Zambrana, 1994). Families are often divided with children being raised by grandparents in Puerto Rico and husbands migrating back and forth between the island and New York in search for employment. Marriages are fragile, but marianismo and the stigma of divorce keep many couples legally married but separated. About half of all heterosexual couples form "consensual unions," different from cohabitation, that are recognized as informal marriage (Manning and Landale, 1996). Births to unmarried Puerto Rican women have soared over the last three decades, today comprising over 60 percent of all their births in the United States (Ventura and Bachrach, 2000). Women who have recently migrated to the United States, especially those who are partners in middle and working class married couples, strive to maintain a continuity of family life. Better educated women are more likely to value both career and family roles. Traditional gender roles are common, but in families with dual-earner couples, some erosion of the double standard is evident (Toro-Morn, 1995).

Mirroring the marianismo–machismo duality, Judith Ortiz Cofer (1995: 204–205) writes of her experiences growing up in a Puerto Rican community in New Jersey.

> As a girl I was kept under strict surveillance, since virtue and modesty were, by cultural equation, the same as family honor. . . . But it was a conflicting message girls got, since Puerto Rican mothers also encouraged their daughters to look and act like women. . . . The extended family and church structure could provide a young woman with a circle of safety; if a man "wronged" a girl, everyone would close in to save her family honor.

She asserts that her education gave her stronger footing to survive this kind of duality in mainstream culture and saved her from the harsher forms of racial and ethnic prejudice.

Familism may buffer girls from the "harshness" of the outside world, but it does not adequately prepare them for the role conflict they will inevitably face when they enter it as wives, mothers, and employed workers.

Mexican American Families. Mexican American (Chicana) women also confront gender roles tied to ideology surrounding marianismo–machismo and familism, factors that keep divorce rates low. The nuclear family is embedded in a network of kin who maintain intergenerational ties by passing on cultural traditions and serving as social and economic support (Dietz, 1995). Early research interpreted machismo as a male defense against the adversity of racial discrimination and poverty. The authoritarian and belittling world faced daily by Mexican American laborers is reproduced in the home, so men are bolstered when women are "kept their place." Notice how the concepts of machismo and black matriarchy can be used to justify the same conclusion and then used to perpetuate gender inequality.

The subordination of women to men in families is evident, but more recent research is challenging the model of the all-dominant and controlling male. Families are not as patriarchal as had been assumed, and there is a trend toward gender equity. Couples do report that the spheres of men and women are still separated, but that they share child rearing and household tasks. Joint decision making is becoming normative, especially when women are employed outside the home. Extended family ties are also weakening. Although families may receive less child care support from older kin, there is also less chance that the children's caretakers will bolster cultural norms emphasizing male dominance (Chillman, 1995).

Children born in the U.S. are moving up economically and in educational attainment. Compared to their parents, traditional patterns have been altered significantly. There is less poverty and higher levels of education. Men and women are entering college at increasing rates and are being trained for better paying jobs. On the negative side, Chicana women are still likely to be employed in occupations segregated by gender and offering little job mobility—both of which function to keep income levels low (Segura, 1994). Teen pregnancy rates are declining overall, but more Mexican American women are becoming single parents, and they have overtaken African Americans in teen birth rates (Amba and Sonenstein, 2002; Flanigan, 2001). The risks of class, race, ethnicity, and gender will determine if the economic prosperity of second generation Mexican Americans can be sustained.

Cuban American Families. Cuban Americans enjoy the highest standard of living of all Latino groups. Immigrants in the 1960s were highly educated, many drawn from Cuba's professional ranks. Even though women were not likely to be in the labor force, education for middle and upper class women was encouraged and helped bolster the prestige of the family. The world of politics and business was reserved for men (Chillman, 1995). The double standard of sexual morality lives on in the Cuban American subculture. Parents want their daughters to be educated but also to remain virginal, uncorrupted, and sequestered. Later immigrants were poorer, families more fragile and prone to breakup, and women in the workplace more common, a trend that continues today. However, Cuban American families are demographically more similar to European Americans. Compared with other Latino subgroups, these families have fewer children, are economically stronger, and are more likely to be headed by a married couple (U.S. Bureau of the Census, 2004). Married couples with higher levels of education are less traditional and are slowly moving toward more gender equitable family roles (Jimenez-Vasquez, 1995). Unlike European Americans, Cuban American families are more likely to be extended and children are expected to live with their parents until they get married. The elderly in these families offer child care services and in turn expect to be taken care of as they become more feeble (DeGenova, 1997). The increased number of Cuban American women in the work force is associated with child care by elderly kin. More egalitarian family and work roles are in line with the future expectations of Cuban American girls. As they become more acculturated, younger women are less likely to accept restrictions based on gender.

Asian American Families

Asian Americans are the fastest growing of America's racial minorities. Their numbers are increased by immigration rather than increases in the resident population. Asian Americans, primarily Chinese, Japanese, and Filipino, have the highest number of married couples and the lowest divorce rate of all other racial minorities at a number similar to whites. Even more so than Latino families, Asian Americans exhibit striking cultural diversity. In religion, for example, Koreans are predominantly Protestant Christians, Filipinos are Catholic, Japanese are Shinto and Buddhist, Pakistanis are Muslims, and Indians are Hindu. Religion has a powerful influence on beliefs about gender that are carried into the family (chapter 12).

Asian American families, however, do share several patterns that have important gender implications. Gender roles emanate from the originating Asian cultures and function within collectivistic kinship traditions in which personal needs are sacrificed to family needs. Extended families are normative, and children are socialized to be obedient in the family and loyal to parents and elders. Obedience is played out by marriages that are commonly arranged by kin rather than left solely to the devices of the couple (Fuligni et al., 1999; Rastogi and Wampler, 1999; Chen et al., 2001; Lee and Liu, 2001). These family traditions emphasize female subordination to all males and older females in a patriarchal family structure.

The extent to which these patterns occur is linked to length of residence in the United States. Recent arrivals are strongly connected to their ethnic community, for example, which provides social support and jobs in family businesses. Chinese and Koreans in particular appear to benefit from community ties—they have high levels of education for both females and males and enjoy relatively fast upward mobility (Ishii-Kuntz, 1997). Although still quite low, the divorce rate and the number of female-headed households are steadily increasing among all Asian American groups. When children become more "Americanized," intergenerational conflict increases, with boys more likely to challenge restrictions imposed by their male elders than girls (Kitano and Daniels, 1995; Jain and Belsky, 1997). Among Chinese Americans children will gladly provide economic help for their parents but resist their parent's advice on personal matters such as who they choose as friends or dates. Traditional expectations for marriage are eroding, and emerging norms are now emphasizing choice of partners based on romantic love. Whereas arranged marriages have not disappeared among Chinese Americans, formal arrangements have been replaced by "strong suggestions" from parents and elders, which children are at least expected to investigate. And as you would expect, boys are less likely to take their parents' suggestions for investigating a possible marriage partner than are girls.

Native American Families

Native Americans comprise less than 1 percent of the U.S. population and include those reporting American Indian and Alaskan (Eskimo and Aleut) origin. Native Americans are rapidly being assimilated into majority culture, and intermarriage rates have soared. It is estimated that nineteen out of twenty Native Americans are related to someone of a different racial group (Goldstein, 1999). At the same time, resurgent cultural pride has fueled tribal diversity and contributed to a rise in the number of people claiming Native American origin. Nonetheless, Native Americans share some key patterns related to gender roles in family life.

About one-third of Native American households are female headed; most of these are in poverty. The remaining two-thirds are made up primarily of married couples. These households are at risk for social problems related to their poverty status, such as unemployment, dropping out of high school, illiteracy, and alcoholism. Historic as well as present governmental policy is fundamentally responsible for the current economic plight of Native American populations (U.S. Commission on Human Rights, 2000).

Colonialism, which was accompanied by Christianity, altered ancient tribal patterns drastically, particularly those related to gender roles in the family. Women's power and prestige varied by tribe, but historical evidence indicates that women lost status with colonialization. Many tribal units were *matrilineal*, the family name is traced through the mother's line, and *matrilocal*, a couple moved into the bride's home at marriage. Although gender segregation was the norm, complementarity, balance, and gynocratic (female-centered) egalitarianism also existed both in the home and outside it. Women held important political, religious, and other extra-domestic roles (Kuhlmann, 1996). With increased European contact, women were gradually stripped of these roles. In order to assimilate native people, the U.S. government first sought to obliterate ancient traditions—a policy that become known as "cultural genocide." Altered family patterns were its first manifestation, and a highly egalitarian family structure changed to a patriarchal one (Harjo, 1993).

However, cultural genocide did not succeed. Although ancient tribal customs were altered, they were not eradicated, and they continue to reinforce family strength and stability. Women retain spiritual, economic, and leadership roles offering prestige and power in their families and communities (Joe and Miller, 1994; Cheshire, 2001). For those who live off the reservation, these roles contribute to more equally shared household and parenting responsibilities (Hossain, 2001). Unlike other racial, ethnic, and religious groups, a return to cultural traditions among Native Americans may signal more, rather than less, egalitarianism.

DIVORCE

An enduring marriage is not necessarily a successful one. Because Americans say romantic love is the primary reason for marriage, "falling out of love" becomes a reason for divorce. The two variables that in combination most consistently predict divorce are age and social class. Teenage marriages of couples from lower socioeconomic groups are the most likely to dissolve, probably within the first five years. For teenage couples who start out with less education, fewer economic resources, and less emotional maturity, the idealization of love quickly fades when confronted with the stark reality of married life. Teenage husbands lose the idealization quicker than teenage wives (Sassler and Schoen, 1999; Rank, 2000). Though subject to historical anomalies like the Depression and World War II, the divorce rate has steadily increased throughout the last century; it rose rapidly during the 1970s, peaked in the early 1980s, and has modestly decreased since 1990.

Depending on which standard for calculating divorce rates is used, the future of marriage in the United States as well as for its individual couples appears rather bleak. When comparing the number of divorces to the number of new marriages, it is fair to say that half will end in divorce. The problem with this comparison is that it does not account for how long a couple was married, so it may inflate the failure rate of new marriages. It is more revealing to look at annual divorces per 1000 married women (half of a married couple), which is at about 20. This indicates a less discouraging four-in-ten marriage failure rate. By all measures, the divorce rate is rising throughout the world, but the United States remains near the top, with one of the world's highest rates (Divorce, 2002).

Gender and Adjustment in Divorce

Divorce has profound social, psychological, and economic effects on the divorcing couple and their families. Accumulating research shows that divorce is strongly gendered—in how it is carried out and in its differential impact on women and men.

Gender Role Beliefs and Emotional Well-Being.   Although it is difficult to separate economic from noneconomic factors, women tend to adjust better to divorce than men. Yet both men and women who are nontraditional in their gender role orientation adjust better than those who are traditional. Androgynous men and assertive, independent women are better at reconciling themselves to divorce than the aggressive men and passive women associated with more conventional gender role perspectives. Women who have a closer match to traditional masculine attitudes and behavior have higher levels of self-esteem and independence and opt out of unsatisfactory marriages at a faster rate (Hackstaff, 1999; Simon and Marcussen, 1999; Zimmer, 2001). African American women also appear to fare better—have higher levels of personal mastery over their situation—compared to white women. (McKelvey and McKenry, 2000). Because enhanced self-concept and independence are the very qualities beneficial for psychological health and coping skills, the woman who rejects traditional gender roles would be better off should she find herself facing dissolution of her marriage. Men who adjust better to divorce are already connected to a new partner and may be able to quickly reestablish their preferred gender role pattern, whether it is a traditional one or not. Former wives and husbands appear to adjust better when they attribute the cause of the divorce to the relationship itself rather than to themselves or each other (Oygard and Hardeng, 2001; Amato and Previti, 2003). In this sense, they leave the marriage with a more intact sense of self that serves as bolsters as they face a postmarried future.

Age. Younger people are better at rebuilding their lives after a divorce, and the spouse who first sought the divorce adjusts to it more readily. Women are more likely to initiate a divorce than men, and younger women do so at higher rates than both older men and women. Women under age 40 report that divorces lead to a wider range of growth options and enhance their well-being over the long run. Older women suffer greater psychological trauma in divorce and may be more likely to stay in an unhappy marriage until a new partner is on the horizon (Esterberg et al., 1994; Sweeney, 2002).

Employment. Because women today are likely to be employed, they may have the financial latitude to end unhappy marriages. Her level of financial freedom is also related to who has more authority in the family. Although an employed wife contributes to her happiness and well-being, when her income begins to match her husband's income, his sense of well-being is lowered, especially if his share of household work is low compared to hers (Hiedemann et al., 1998; Rogers and DeBoer, 2001). The most dissatisfied couples are those in which wives want joint decision making and household task sharing by husbands whereas husbands prefer a more traditional, patriarchal style of family functioning—a pattern that holds for couples of all races (Lawson and Thompson, 1999; Kroska, 2000; Stohs, 2000). Shifts in gender role ideology help explain why today's women are now more likely than their mothers and grandmothers to initiate divorce.

The Impact of Gendered Law in Divorce

Divorce is no longer a legally difficult process. The legal ease of ending a marriage is linked to the rise of *no-fault divorce*, which allows one spouse to divorce the other without placing blame on either. Divorce is readily available to those who want it, such as women in abusive marriages, older men hoping to remarry younger women, and young couples who married quickly and confronted marital conflict just as quickly (Glenn, 1997; Rodgers et al., 1999). No-fault divorces are now the most common type of divorce in the United States.

Custody. When a divorce involves children, mothers gain custody about 90 percent of the time, usually without further legal action by fathers (Gordon, 1998). Although all states have gender-neutral child custody laws, custody is still likely to be granted to the mother, the preferred pattern for mothers and fathers (Stamps, 2002). Most often fathers give in to the mother's demand for full custody without further legal action. Women must now take on an array of roles they previously shared. Even if she is working outside the home, the divorce increases financial obligations, child care, and household responsibilities. Conflicts at work involving children can intensify and create a greater sense of insecurity.

For those divorced mothers who recognize that they simply do not have the financial capability to adequately provide for their children, the decision may be to give up custody. The belief that children—especially young children—should stay with their mothers is pervasive. Unlike a noncustodial father, a mother who voluntarily gives up custody is stigmatized, often viewed as abandoning her children. She may relinquish custody out of love, knowing that her ex-husband is financially in a better position to offer them what she cannot. Reinforced by social stigma, contact with her children may also be reduced, and guilt can continue for years (Rhoades, 2002).

Fathers are now more likely to gain full custody in contested divorces. Custody revisionists have begun to challenge the maternal preference argument, citing the best-interest-of-the-child standard (BICS) (Krauss and Sales, 2000). Fathers can be favored over mothers because they are financially better off. The courts do not award alimony to women capable of earning a living, so divorce requires women to give up any thought about staying a homemaker, if that was her predivorce existence. Earning a living can jeopardize her chances of gaining custody, especially if she has young children. Not only does the father make more money, but if he remarries, he has the possibility of another full-time caretaker. Although uncontrollable economic factors are the key reasons most mothers lose custody battles, they are cast into the stigmatized role of unfit parents. The case for fathers' rights is more of a case against mothers and that "instead of admitting the systematic discrimination which debilitates their ex-wives and families after divorce, they claim that the reverse is true, that women are the privileged ones in divorce" (Crean, 1993:514). Gender-neutral standards are supposedly in effect to ensure parity in divorce and child custody decisions, but gender stereotyping works against this in both principle and practice.

To deal with problems associated with child custody, *joint custody* arrangements—where parents share decisions related to their children, including how much time children will spend in the home of each parent—have skyrocketed. Joint custody is now the most prevalent court ordered divorce arrangement. Coparenting occurs in a variety of contexts, from simply sharing day-to-day decisions about children with their ex-spouses, to actually moving children, and sometimes parents, to different homes on a rotating basis. There are vigorous debates on the effects of such arrangements on children. Joint custody fathers are more involved in their children's lives, have increased contact with them, and actively participate in shared decision making regarding their children. Complicated scheduling is a downside, but less strain is reported than if one carries the full burden of parental responsibilities (Kurdek and

Kennedy, 2001; Bauserman, 2002). Joint custody may also be agreed on during a divorce mediation process in which parents meet with an impartial third party to reach mutually acceptable agreements (Taylor, 2002). A critical point is the degree of parental cooperation. If channels of communication remain open and children are not used as pawns, a joint-custody arrangement may be a constructive option. If parental cooperation fails, joint custody serves to increase conflict between parents. The quality of the coparenting relationship is the key factor in how a child adjusts to divorce (Morris and West, 2001; Turkat, 2002).

Joint custody fathers have a better record at maintaining contact with their children and supporting them financially. But as equitable as the arrangements may seem on paper, women are less able to take on the greater economic burden that is clearly associated with joint custody.

Divorce and Poverty. Although women appear to fare better than men in the psychological trauma of divorce, the economic consequences are often disastrous for women in the United States as well as globally (Weitzman and Maclean, 1992). For both African American and white women, divorce increases a woman's financial burdens in two important ways. First, child support payments do not match expenses of maintaining the family, and second, women are expected to work outside the home but their salaries are low, a situation compounded by both race and gender discrimination (Kurtz, 1995; Smock et al., 1999; Molina, 2000). Older women, housewives, and those reentering the labor force after a long absence are in an extremely precarious position. They are at a distinct disadvantage in the job market at the exact time when they need an adequate income to support the family.

No-fault divorce makes a bad economic situation worse for women when courts mandate an equal division of assets, such as the family home and savings. Coupled with no-fault divorce, joint custody puts women at great financial risk. Most women do not have the economic resources to coparent on an equal basis with their ex-husbands.

Misconceptions abound about women who are "set up" for a life of leisure by their wealthy ex-husbands. Actually, court ordered alimony—"maintenance"—is awarded to only a small percentage of women and in amounts so low that they barely match welfare or Social Security. The issue of what is awarded is related to the issue of what can be collected. Just over half of all custodial mothers are awarded child support, half of these mothers actually receive it from nonresidential fathers, and only 25 percent receive the full amount. When child support enforcement cases make it to the courts and support is reordered, less than one-fourth of men actually pay (Turestsky, 1999). The amount of unpaid child support is staggering. Over 11 million families are owed support, forcing 10 million children into welfare. In half of divorced families, by two years after the divorce there is no contact with the nonresidential parent, usually the father (Sorenson and Zibman, 2000). These fathers report feeling less competent and less satisfied in their parental role (Minton and Pasley, 1996), a factor that may help explain emotional and financial distancing from their children.

The severe economic consequences of divorce are played out among women of all races. Although young minority men are not well off economically, their post-divorce financial situation tends to be better than that of their ex-wives. Some data now show that a man's standard of living increases about 10 to 15 percent following a divorce; other data show that it decreases by about the same percent (Gordon, 1998; McManus and DiPrete, 2001). For women, however, although declines in their postdivorce income are less than in years past, data still show only decreases, and at losses much greater than men's postdivorce income. A loss of half the family income is typical (Amato, 2001; Josephson, 1997; McKeever and Wolfinger, 2001). Divorce is a principal reason for the high poverty rate of single-parent women and their dependent children, a factor contributing to what we identify in chapter 13 as the *feminization of poverty*. The risk of poverty for children living with single-parent mothers dramatically increased between the 1970s and 1990s because of many of these trends. The feminization and the *juvenilization* of poverty go hand in hand (Bianchi, 1999).

To ease the problem and help get divorced women off public assistance, states are more vigilant in enforcing child custody orders. Such enforcement may be responsible for the decreased income of divorced men noted earlier. But the benefits of getting men to live up to their financial obligations may be greater when men are nurtured in their identities as fathers by meaningful welfare reform programs. In addition, the men who have been slipping out of their children's lives can be brought back, especially poor men. Welfare programs that work on issues to reconnect poor, absent fathers to their children may be more successful than programs that criminalize fathers when they do not or cannot pay (Curran and Abrams, 2000). Changes in divorce law may also help with a women's postdivorce income loss. States could retain the no-fault option while recognizing that men and women enter divorce with very different levels of economic vulnerability.

Remarriage. Although the United States has the world's highest divorce rate in the developed world, it also has the world's highest remarriage rate. Almost three-fourths of divorced people remarry, and now almost one-half of all marriages are remarriages (Kim and Cole, 2000; Bramlett and Mosher, 2001). The marriage–divorce–remarriage pattern is called **serial monogamy**. Remarriages are the primary reasons for the formation of a **blended family**, in which children from parents' prior relationships are brought together in a new family. This new form of kinship affects half of children in the United States today, and by 2005 almost half of families with children will be blended families (Bold, 2001).

About 75 percent of divorced men remarry and about 66 percent of divorced women remarry. The large majority of men usually remarry within five years of their divorce. Most divorced men with children are free from sole custody and economically better off than their ex-wives, allowing for greater latitude in the remarriage market. Men have an age advantage as well. There is more acceptance of the older man–younger woman pattern than the reverse. A ten-year age difference favoring men is common in remarriages. About three-fourths of divorced women remarry within ten years of their divorce. If they were age 25 of younger at their divorce, their likelihood of remarrying is even higher (81 percent). Women who are poorly educated are most likely to remarry. Their remarriage chances decrease if they have dependent children because they represent a financial liability for men. Financially independent women are attractive to men for remarriage, but these women have less to gain in a remarriage, especially if they do not want to raise children

(Coleman et al., 2000; Sweeney, 2002b). When adding race to the remarriage picture, African American women are the least likely to remarry and white women the most likely. Latino women fall in between (Bramlett and Mosher, 2001).

These different remarriage rates are best explained by the influence of race, class, and gender in combination. Among women of all races, marriage and remarriage offer opportunities for economic stability. They seek potential married partners who offer work stability—the possibility of staying employed. But low-income African American single mothers report that respectability and control in their lives is more important. Low-income white single mothers mention trust and domestic violence as more important. The meaning of marriage differs for these women. Many believe that marriage will make their lives more difficult and hence choose to remain single. (Edin, 2000a; 2000b). Remarriage for these women appears to have at least as many costs as benefits.

SINGLE-PARENT FAMILIES

High divorce rates coupled with greater tolerance and acceptance of the children of unwed parents have led to a dramatic increase in the number of single-parent families. Since 1950 the number of single-parent families has doubled. In 1950, 7 percent of families were headed by single parents. This figure skyrocked to 27 percent a half century later, with single-parent mothers outnumbering single-parent fathers four to one (Bianchi and Casper, 2001; Simmons and O'Neill, 2001). The staggering statistic today is that half of U.S. children will live part of their life in a single-parent household before age 18. When accounting for race, about 40 percent of African American children live in families headed by women, compared to one-fifth Latino, 15 percent Asian, and 12 percent white children. For all races, African American children are most likely to live with a female grandparent (Office of Child Support Enforcement, 2000; Population Reference Bureau, 2002). Because media tend to focus on "illegitimacy rates" of single-parent mothers, people often forget that single parents include divorced parents. But the increase of joint custody arrangements and fathers gaining sole custody are more than offset by the rapid increase of never married women with children. About half of all single parents are divorced; the other half have never been married. The divorced half of single-parent mothers appears to fare better than their never married counterparts—they probably finished high school, live in their own homes, and have higher incomes (O'Connell, 1997). If children from divorced homes are living with their fathers the median family income is over one-third higher than if they live with their mothers. Overall, median family income is almost four times less in single-parent families compared to husband-wife families (U.S. Bureau of the Census, 2004).

Mothers and the Single-Parent Household

In mother or grandmother headed single-parent families, economic vulnerability is a way of life. Not only are female-headed families the fastest growing type of family in the United States, but also the odds that it is in poverty approach one in two. Almost half of all poor children in the United States live in families headed by women, and median income is an astonishing four times lower than in husband–wife families (Costello et al., 2002). When race is factored in, the poverty rate of single-mother families for white, African American, and Latino families is 22.5 percent, 39.2 percent, and 38.8 percent, respectively (National Center for Children in Poverty, 2000).

Many factors contribute to this situation. We know that child support, alimony, and joint custody are not the financial salvation for these women. Neither are welfare payments in a restrictive system, which may contribute to, rather than deter, the cycle of poverty (Christensen, 2001; Porter, 2001). Because women are more likely than men to be undereducated and engaged in menial or low-paying jobs, if employed at all, their income is far from adequate to meet the needs of the family. The financial burdens of the single-parent family headed by a woman who is divorced, never married, or was cohabiting fuel the feminization of poverty. The distinctive character of a woman's poverty is that she has the economic responsibility for children.

Financial uncertainty heightens the physical and emotional demands on single-parent women. Compared with married couples, they rely more on children for housework, have fewer social supports, and raise children who are also more likely to become single parents. Single mothers report higher rates of depression and lower levels of self-esteem than married mothers, especially if they were teenage mothers and did not graduate from high school—a pattern found in both the United States and Canada (Davies et al., 1997; Solomon and Liefeld, 1998; Sarlo, 2000). In African American households, daughters raised by single-parent mothers have lower levels of educational achievement than those raised in single-father households (Alderman-Swain and Battle, 2000). Money is the key factor in this pattern. Not only do women who are more financially secure adjust better to single parenting, but their children also tend to have better educational outcomes and fewer behavioral problems than in intact families marked by high levels of conflict (Winkler, 1993). Overall, many of these women experience chronic life strain, which impacts their physical, social, and psychological well-being.

Fathers and the Single-Parent Household

As single parents, men face a situation far different from that of women. Nearly 15 percent of all single-parent households are headed by a man, and about 4 percent of children live with their fathers only. These numbers are expected to increase in the next decade as more fathers gain sole or joint custody of their children (Center on Budget and Policy Priorities, 2001). Fathers are usually better educated, occupy higher level occupations, and continue their careers after becoming single parents. Remember, too, that financial strength is a key reason why fathers are increasingly awarded sole custody when they request it. Like single mothers, single fathers report problems balancing work and family. Single fathers who cope successfully have more flexible work situations and support networks. For child care and household tasks, single fathers appear to adapt well, perceive themselves as competent, share tasks with their children, and do not rely on outside help to a great extent. When they became single fathers, they set out to learn new tasks and domestic skills. Fathers who are more involved with housework before the divorce make a smoother transition to their new domestic roles. After divorce, single-parent mothers do less housework; fathers do more (Greif, 1995; Pasley and Minton, 2001). When fathers take on the role as the "primary" parent, they report close ties to their children and high levels of family satisfaction. But they still must deal with gender role stereotyping that assumes they cannot be as competent parents as women.

GENDER PATTERNS IN GAY AND LESBIAN FAMILIES

As society's most conservative institution, the family is highly resistant to change. Political debate concerning definitions of the family is also linked to antigay campaigns focusing on homosexuality as the enemy of the patriarchal family and the American way of life. Gay and lesbian (LGBT) families do exhibit characteristics in opposition to the structure and behavior patterns of the patriarchal family. As we will see, this seems more to the credit of these families than to their detriment.

Same-Sex Marriage

In 1995 Utah became the first state to expressly prohibit same-sex marriages. In 1996 Hawaii became the first state to legalize same-sex marriage but reversed the ruling two years later. In 2004 a San Francisco judge began issuing marriage licenses to same-sex couples. Some Massachusetts judges began following. A firestorm of controversy ensued as other states grappled with how to deal with the huge influx of same-sex couples demanding marriage licenses. To thwart these same-sex couples some politicians are calling for a "marriage amendment" to the Constitution, defining a marriage only in terms of a union between a man and woman. As a way of sidestepping the definition of a marriage, many states are following Vermont's lead, which in 2000 allowed same-sex couples to enter civil unions. Although Vermont's statute refers to *marriage* as a union between a man and women, **civil union** is a new legal classification entitling same-sex couples to the rights and responsibilities available to married partners, such as inheriting a partner's estate and filing joint tax returns. If these states uphold same-sex marriages, reciprocity with other states is the key issue. As of this writing, the highly contentious politics revolving around sacrosanct definitions of marriage and the family indicate that the matter is unlikely to be resolved soon.

The European Union is confronting the same issue. By the 1990s same sex marriages were legal in Denmark, Norway, and Sweden, but in all three countries same-sex couples still do not enjoy the complete range of marriage benefits heterosexual married couples receive. In 2001 the Netherlands approved a bill to legally recognize same-sex marriages and same-sex adoptions. It is the first country in the world with full marriage rights for gay and lesbian couples (Eskridge and Hunter, 2001). Reciprocity is expected between member countries. In the United States the fallout from any legal recognition of same-sex unions is far from over. A "federal marriage amendment" to the Constitution, making some headway in Congress, would define marriage strictly between a man and woman and could invalidate legal protections for all unmarried couples, regardless of whether or not the couple is homosexual (Gerstmann, 2003). However, the patriarchal values that are often upheld in the court are being challenged in the workplace, in the unions, and in the schools by all those who support couples who choose more nontraditional family structures and lifestyles related to sexual orientation, nonpatriarchal parenting, gender roles, or cohabitation (Mackinnon, 2003).

Children, Egalitarianism, and Gender Roles

The 2000 U.S. Census reported over 600,000 LGBT families, divided almost equally between gay male and lesbian families. Gay men and lesbians who form families and stepfamilies tend to incorporate a network of kin and nonkin relationships including friends, lovers, former lovers, coparents, children, and adopted children. These families are organized by ideologies of love, social support, flexibility, and rational choice. (Lynch and Murray, 2000; Erera and Fredriksen, 2001; Joos, 2003). Notice how this structure is similar to the fictive kin and familism evident in African American and Latino families. Although research is still limited, data suggest that LGBT families with children are highly child focused and that children raised in these homes are no more likely to have difficult emotional problems related to their family life than children raised in heterosexual homes (Kozik-Rosabel, 2000; Drucker, 2001; Barrett, 2001; Clark, 2002; Tasker, 2002). Perhaps out of concern for the stigma attached to homosexuality, gay and lesbian parents closely monitor their children in all facets of their development, including emotional health, peer influences, and school progress. When problems arise, they are likely to seek the support and counseling services that are now more widely available in the rapidly growing field of lesbian and gay psychology (Coyle and Kitzinger, 2002).

An early literature review of the scarce research on LGBT families found that homosexual couples exhibited more equality in their household arrangements than did heterosexual couples (Maccoby and Jacklin, 1974). This conclusion of more egalitarianism was confirmed in the first comprehensive study that compared homosexual and heterosexual couples (Blumstein and Schwartz, 1983) as well as research that followed. These studies generally affirmed that the stereotypical image of a gay relationship in which one partner is in the dominant "active" male role and the other in the subservient passive "female" role is a myth. The egalitarian pattern tends to occur for both lesbians and gay men, although lesbians are more successful in maintaining it over the long term (Huston and Schwartz, 1996; Kurdek, 1998; Erera and Fredriksen, 2001).

Recent research, however, does challenge some aspects of this egalitarianism. The research does *not* confirm the dominant–passive stereotype but it does suggest, for example, that like heterosexual couples, in *lesbigay* couples one partner takes on more domestic responsibilities and that domestic work is hidden and devalued (Carrington, 1999; Hagewen, 2002). In addition, the monogamy that gay men value is harder to achieve. Mirroring gender role norms in the wider society, gay men also value sexual prowess and, like heterosexual men, fall prey to its power as a defining mark of masculinity. On the other hand, like heterosexual women, lesbians view sexual prowess as less important than emotional commitment, particularly in the beginning stages of a relationship. Lesbian couples frequently adopt a peer-friendship bond that later culminates into a sexual one as physical closeness grows and the relationship progresses (Garnets, 1996; Sutton, 1999; Glazer and Dreschler, 2001).

Egalitarianism may be more evident in lesbigay families, but traditional gender roles have not been eradicated.

The debate about levels of egalitarianism in lesbigay couples has implications for the same-sex marriage issue. If same-sex couples are more egalitarian, would legally recognized marriage make them less so? From a feminist perspective, marriage is more likely to be patriarchal than egalitarian, so legally married same-sex couples may succumb to patriarchal family lifestyles (Stiers, 2000).

Lesbian Mothers

Whether it is referred to as a civil union or a marriage, legal acceptance does not mean social acceptance. We have already seen that in divorce mothers usually gain custody of children. With lesbians, however, this is less likely. Some women hide their lesbian identity to win custody and then live in constant fear of being exposed by their husbands and having the courts reverse the decision (Antoniuk, 1999). Others who are granted custody after bitter court battles may endure continual harassment from their ex-husbands or their own relatives and friends. Some mothers fear their children will be traumatized by a publicized custody fight and voluntarily accede to their husbands' demands (Arnup, 1999; Duran-Ayintug and Causey, 2001). As women, lesbians may be less stigmatized than gay men when they raise children with their partners. But because their "mainstream" motherhood identity exists alongside their stigmatized lesbian identity, they walk a fine line between the two. How they negotiate these two identities can make a difference in the emotional well-being of themselves and their families (Hequembourg and Farrell, 2001; Wilkinson, 2002).

Gay Fathers

Just as lesbian mothers can lose the opportunity of raising their children, gay fathers are even more likely to be denied custody. About 20 to 30 percent of gay men have been married at least once, and many of these are natural fathers. Gay fathers can find that visiting their children is so discouraged that they may be reluctant to subject themselves and their children to the turmoil that visits or attempted visits may bring. If their children remain unaware of their father's gay identity, the gay fathers live compartmentalized existences that compromise their emotional well-being and, like lesbian mothers, fear that their gay identity will be exposed and their children traumatized (Bozett, 1987; Warwick and Aggleton, 2002). Being gay may not be compatible with traditional marriage and the family, but it is compatible with fathering (Gottlieb, 2003; McGarry, 2003). For publicly gay fathers who do have custody of their children, research shows positive histories for these families. Problems in rearing children exist, but once men productively resolve their gay identity issues, gay fathers appear to be comparable to single heterosexual fathers who have custody of their children (Miller, 1992; Bigner, 1999; Eisold, 2001).

Alternative family forms involving gay men and heterosexual women are also evolving. Some gay men maintain liaisons with heterosexual women with whom they may have children. Women who desire children without the confines of marriage may choose to have a child with a gay man with whom she may or may not be emotionally attached, who then provides help with parenting and financial support.

There is no legal obligation, they do not live together, and the child is "hers." In this way, desires on both sides are met. Success with such an arrangement varies considerably, but it is likely that more couples will choose this new family form to accommodate their distinctive life goals in a rapidly changing society. This new form adds to the increasing diversity of nontraditional family and household arrangements.

Overall, a growing number of gay men and lesbians have gained custody, brought their biological children into an "openly" lesbigay home, adopted children, and live in permanent households with their homosexual partners and their children. Gay and lesbian families tend to be child centered, egalitarian, financially well off, and with parents who have levels of psychological health comparable to heterosexual parents (Nelson, 1999; Sullivan, 2000; Malley and McCann, 2002). These families face hostility and suspicion with society's stereotypes about homosexuality as well as idealized notions about families and the manner gender roles should be carried out in their families (Ryan, 2000). Even with legal recognition, rights may still be denied. Interpretations of family law usually work against gays and lesbians by defining them as unfit to raise children (Hertz, 1998; Mackinnon, 2003). Debates about how well children are socialized in gay and lesbian families can only be resolved when more children are permanently raised in these homes and same-sex marriages or civil unions become more normative.

Summary

1. The transition to parenthood is seen as both a crisis and normal development stage. The motherhood mandate makes parenthood more stressful for women. The motherhood mandate is supported by functionalism for its socialization benefit to children; conflict theory challenges this view because it ignores individual growth for mothers; feminists are redefining motherhood to fit the new lifestyles of women who desire career and children.

2. Fatherhood is tied to the good-provider role but the involved-father role is gaining in importance for men. Fathers are taking on more child-care and nurturing tasks than in the past. An emerging fatherhood mandate would combine instrumental and expressive roles.

3. Voluntarily child-free married couples express similar levels of marital satisfaction as couples with children.

4. Dual-earning families are now the norm. Children of employed women are not harmed by their employment and neither are children who are in high quality day care. When mothers work for pay, social and intellectual development of children is often improved.

5. Underemployment of men and employment for women in African American families is typical. Working class and middle class couples are likely to be in dual-earner, egalitarian family roles. African American husbands adapt themselves to their employed wives more than white husbands. Multiple oppressions of race and gender keep earnings low for African American women. African American men who cannot affirm their masculinity with provider roles may do so with "cool pose."

6. Gender roles in Latino families are tied to economic well-being, number of generations in the United States, and which subgroup they represent. Half of Puerto Rican families are headed by women who hold low-paying jobs. Machismo ideology serves to subordinate Mexican American women. Compared to other Latino families, Cuban Americans have fewer children, are economically better off, and are headed

by a married couple with a college educated wife. For all Latino subgroups, trends to gender equity are growing.

7. Asian American families are also diverse and share gender patterns from their originating Asian cultures. Overall women are subordinate to all males and older females in a patriarchal family structure. Traditional expectations for arranged marriages are eroding.

8. One-third of Native American households are headed by women and likely to be in poverty. The U.S. practice of cultural genocide altered but did not erase tribal customs related to family strength and stability and women's leadership roles. A return to cultural traditions signals more not less gender egalitarianism.

9. Women tend to adjust better to divorce than men, especially those who were nontraditional in their gender roles, those who are younger and those who had the financial latitude to end an unhappy marriage. Mothers usually gain custody in a divorce, but joint custody is becoming more common. Many women are propelled into poverty after a divorce. Remarriage rates for both men and women are high, but men have an age and income advantage for remarriage.

10. Single-parent families headed by women are likely to be in poverty. Mothers report high levels of depression and low self-esteem. Single-parent families headed by men are likely to be finically secure, have flexible work and support networks.

11. Gay and lesbian families are child focused and show high levels of egalitarianism. Lesbian mothers walk a line between mainstream motherhood and stigmatized lesbian identity. Gay fathers who resolve gay identity issues are comparable to single heterosexual fathers who have custody.

Key Terms

blended family 228	fictive kin 217	motherhood mandate 208
civil union 231	machismo 220	serial monogamy 228
familism 220	marianismo 220	

Critical Thinking Questions

1. Demonstrate how gender ideology permeates beliefs about motherhood and fatherhood in the United States and creates a paradox for parents. Document the benefits and/or liabilities of this ideology on couples and their children. As a result of this evaluation, what conclusions do you draw about the relationship between gender beliefs and parenthood and the likelihood of a productive resolution of this paradox?

2. Compare African-American, Latino, and Asian-American families in terms of gender socialization of children and the influence of the multiple oppressions of race, gender, and social class. Based on this comparison, determine the prospects for movement toward more gender equity in these families.

3. Identify the similarities and differences between homosexual and gay and lesbian couples in terms of their family arrangements, gender roles, and child rearing. Demonstrate how functionalism, conflict theory, and symbolic interaction account for these patterns. How does the feminist perspective provide an overarching framework that incorporates all three theories?

Wait, I've just heard how we're talking—
Only thirty million! Only thirty million
human beings killed instantly? Silence fell
upon the room. Nobody said a word.
They didn't even look at me. It was awful.
I felt like a woman.

—Recollection of a male physicist
when working with colleagues on
counterforce attack models.
(Cited in Cohen, 2003)

Men are regarded as superior to women. Whereas women wage uphill battles for
economic, political, and social equality, men wield the power that will greatly determine the outcome of the fight. All roles are made up of both rights and responsibilities, but both men and women perceive the rights and privileges of the male role
as enviable, desirable, and well worth the responsibilities associated with the role.
Men have careers; women have jobs. Men are breadwinners; women are bread
bakers. Men are sexual leaders; women are sexual followers. A man's home is his

castle. Father knows best. Is this the true story? The male mystique is based on a rigid set of expectations that, as we shall see, few men can attain. The social and psychological consequences of striving for the impossible plus the impractical can be devastating. We shall see that the role that appears to offer so many rewards also has its deadly side. In discovering more about this role, we will realize that a men's liberation movement is not a contradiction in terms.

HISTORICAL NOTES AND MASCULINE MARKERS

Images of masculinity are often confusing and contradictory. Over a half century of media heroes show men as courageous, competent, and always in control, such as Clint Eastwood, Tom Cruise, Russell Crowe, and Matt Damon and the enduring images of Sylvester Stallone's Rocky and Rambo. These images exist side by side with fallible antiheroes such as Dustin Hoffman, Jack Nicholson, Robin Williams, and Tom Hanks. Women praise the sensitive man who can admit to his vulnerability yet admire the toughness of the man who refuses to bend in the face of overwhelming odds. Most men fall short when attempting to satisfy both standards. History provides some insights into how this situation arose.

Patriarchy and History

Patriarchy is tied to male dominance, a theme in Western and Eastern civilization. It is a theme that remains accepted, unquestioned, and taken for granted. Using a Western civilization perspective, James Doyle (1995) categorized the male role in terms of five historical periods, ranging from the Graeco-Roman era to the eighteenth century (see Table 9.1). Except for the standard of "spiritual male," contemporary views of masculinity continue to be based on these historical models. The fundamental features of a male ideal that persist after two centuries attest to the stubborn rigidity of a definition that defies even global social change.

Table 9.1 Five Historical Male-Role Ideals

Ideal	Source(s)	Major Features
Epic Male	Epic sagas of Greece and Rome (800–100 B.C.)	Action, physical strength, courage, loyalty, and beginning of patriarcy.
Spiritual Male	Teachings of Jesus Christ, early church fathers, and monastic tradition (400–1000 A.D.)	Self renunciation, restrained sexual activity, antifeminine and antihomosexual attitudes, and strong partiarchal system.
Chivalric Male	Feudalism and chivalric code of honor (twelfth-century social system)	Self-sacrifice, courage, physical strength, honor and service to the lady, and primogeniture.
Renaissance Male	Sixteenth-century social system	Rationality, intellectual endeavors, and self-exploration.
Bourgeois Male	Eighteeth-century social system	Success in business, status, and worldy manners.

Source: Doyle, 1995:27.

With patriarchy already firmly entrenched, the peculiarities of American history tightened its hold. From the Puritans to the frontier era to the Civil War and World War I, the value of individualism was propelled as the hallmark of the United States. Not only did Americanism and individualism soon become inseparable as key masculine markers, but also the line between nationality and masculinity was blurred. Virtually unlimited opportunities beckoned men into farming, politics, business, or whatever their imagination sought. The fact that men of color and women were largely excluded from these opportunities was overlooked in the quest for individual success. The "lone man against the world" remained a powerful image throughout the early period of preindustrial expansion (Gerson, 1993). Nothing could stand in the way of dedicated American males setting out to achieve their objectives. Initially these objectives related to material success through hard work and physical endurance, with intellectual skills coming in second. Success based on material wealth and getting ahead were, and are, integral to American validation of masculinity.

War and Soldiering. Masculinity was also validated by soldiering. War historically is associated with idealized rhetoric of virtue and glory, but ignores its destruction and sheer horror. There are secret attractions for war: "the delight in seeing, the delight in comradeship and the delight in destruction" (Gray, 1992:25). Functionalism views war as a way to integrate society by bringing former rivals and other disparate elements together as comrades in arms to confront a common enemy. In both World Wars military training was seen as the way to build the manhood of the nation. Women served men as nurses, clerical help, or during World War II, builders of war equipment. Women were considered helpmates to the men who fought the real battles. War and the preparation for war encourage men to the highest levels of masculinity. Several forms of masculinity are interfaced in war— physical violence, heroic independence, risk taking, dominance, and competition. War becomes the supreme guideline for defining masculinity (Braudy, 2003).

The Depression. The American version of masculinity was assaulted during the Depression. The loss of jobs and daily economic uncertainty for those fortunate enough to have jobs during this time trampled the self-esteem of men accustomed to their role of breadwinner. The fact that men throughout the nation faced similar circumstances offered little assurance. Many blamed themselves for their inability to get or retain a steady job. When their wives were able to find work outside the home, their emasculation may have been complete. This kind of male self-indictment reverberated throughout the United States. Beyond the economic results of a high jobless rate, the psychological toll was also sadly demonstrated. Many men became estranged from their families; others coped by deserting them. Alcoholism, mental illness, and suicide increased. Contrary to the image of the American man as invincible and able to overcome any obstacle, men and women alike recognized how vulnerable they really were.

Vietnam and the Gulf Wars. Although the Depression could offer insights into how impractical masculinity ideals had become, this was not to be the case. World War II helped bring the nation out of the Depression and revitalized traditional images of masculinity. The harshness of the Depression added luster to these images. Even considering that Korea and Vietnam were not the victories Americans had learned to expect, beliefs about war as a proving ground for manhood continued. A "cult of toughness" emerged to sway public opinion in favor of escalating the war in Vietnam (Fasteau, 1974). America, like its fighting men, was tough. Politicians cultivated this image of toughness, but the battle carnage, the rising body count of young draftees, and the untenable political situation in Asia served to fuel protest against the war. The first young men who burned draft cards or sought asylum in Canada or Sweden were viewed as cowards and sissies, afraid to face the test of war. As the protesters grew in number and the war became increasingly unpopular, more potential draftees joined in the antiwar movement. Comments about bravery and cowardice were not wiped out, merely driven underground for a time.

Here was another opportunity to challenge what it means to be a man. War, at least as embodied in Vietnam, was not the answer. But the cult of toughness reasserted itself in the 1980s. The Reagan era was predicated on a show of toughness and not backing down. During his presidential campaign, George Bush was able to successfully demonstrate that deriding labels such as "wimp" did not in any way characterize him. Like Reagan, he was a "man's man." Indeed, the height of both his credibility and popularity during his four years as president came with Operation Desert Storm. George W. Bush also sought to continue this toughness and manliness legacy to bolster support for the aftermath of the Iraq war that, like Vietnam, became increasingly unpopular as the body count rose. The image of the President in his commander-and-chief role sharply improved sagging approval ratings when he landed an airplane on a carrier. Global media coverage of the staged event spotlighted Americanized masculinity norms—courage, individualism, toughness, and especially, independence. The world may not support Iraq (or Vietnam), but the United States, like its president, will not yield. Politicians believe that this image must be maintained at all costs. To do otherwise is "unmanly." Masculinity is almost synonymous with toughness. And behind this assumed toughness lurks aggression.

The Depression, Vietnam War, Gulf War, and war in Iraq did not alter the image of masculinity. In fact, I would argue that after periods when assaults on traditional masculine ideals are at their heights, the old definitions reemerge with a greater tenacity. This was clearly the case during the Gulf War, where the Vietnam "syndrome" was "kicked out." Analysis of the gendered imagery of the Gulf War suggests that the character model summoned by the president, his advisers, and mass media reflected a strong need to "gender" the moral discourse of war to "reaffirm the dominant, masculine identity of America as the world's one remaining superpower" (McBride, 1995:45). Although media now routinely talk about "the men and women" troops serving the nation, there is no hint that the women are any less masculine than the men.

Sports

Men no longer rely on war for validating masculinity. Whether as athletic competitor or spectator, sports have unquestionably emerged to fill this need. Sports build character and comradeship, provide heroes and role models, and offer stories of courage and the overcoming of adversity. Fathers are powerful socializing agents for introducing their children to sports, especially their sons. Children learn early in life to associate sports with males (James, 2001). The intellectual aspects of masculinity have not kept up with the physical aspects where sports are concerned. Bill Gates may be one of the richest men on the globe, but he is less of a role model than Michael Jordan. A billion-dollar industry flourishes on contests where winning can literally call for the obliteration of the athlete. Boxing, race car driving, football, hockey, skiing, diving, and gymnastics often brutalize competitors. Sport is an area where boys learn that pain is more important than pleasure (Sabo, 2004). Bodies and emotions are injured, but they are hidden or ignored in the name of competition, efficiency, teamsmanship, and of course, winning.

Brutalized Bodies. Men are not immune to the issues of weight and body image usually considered the province of women. The enormous pressure males feel early in life to achieve athletically is linked with psychological obsession and brutalized bodies. If brutalization is the price for winning friends and carving out one's place in the male pecking order, then so be it. The quest for the perfect body that is the idealized requirement for athletic success in males leads to steroid abuse, eating disorders, and overexercising that injures rather than strengthens the body (Harrison et al., 2000; Watson, 2000). In-depth interviews with former and current adult male athletes indicate that potential and actual injury are framed as masculinizing experiences and reinforce highly valued notions of masculinity (Young et al., 1994). With sport as such an intense masculine marker, it offers self-esteem for some but crippling insecurity for others. Consider, for example, the case of men with physical disabilities:

> Paralytic disability constitutes emasculation. . . . and the weakening and atrophy of the body threaten all the cultural values of masculinity: strength, activeness, speed, stamina, and fortitude. (Gerschick and Miller, 2004:349).

Sports Violence. Other than the military, sport is the only social institution that condones violence in achieving a goal. Deliberate fouls in basketball, high sticking in hockey, late hits in football, and the taken-for-granted intentional injuries in rugby are frequently overlooked by referees and applauded by spectators. As social learning theory suggests, if sports violence on the playing field is associated with admiration, respect, money, and media attention, sports violence off the field is likely. Much of that violence is directed toward women. College athletes in contact sports are significantly more likely to be involved in all forms of aggressive behavior but especially sexual assaults, partner battering, rape, and date rape. Consider, for example, Mike Tyson, O. J. Simpson, and Kobe Bryant. Sports heroes have figured so prominently in violence toward women that efforts are being made to provide young athletes with messages that do not equate male strength with dominance over women (Media Awareness Network, 2003). Scandals involving payoffs and kickbacks to athletes and college programs and coverage of rape trials of sports figures do not dampen the thirst for sports. Sports remain one of the most powerful markers of masculinity. The physical and mental stamina required of modern athletes allow men who are not themselves athletes to validate their own masculinity, if only in a vicarious manner.

ON MASCULINITY

Definitions of masculinity have remained remarkably consistent over time. All sociological perspectives on masculinity highlight how masculine role ideals embodied in the historical standards have been adapted to the lives of contemporary men. Although the definitions may be consistent, as a result of these adaptations, masculinity is enacted in myriad ways.

Hegemonic Masculinity

It is somewhat paradoxical, given the consistent definitions, but masculinity can be viewed as fragmented and uneven and at the same time tenacious and steadfast. The notion of **hegemonic masculinity** makes this paradox more understandable. This notion asserts that a number of competing masculinities are enacted according to particular places (contexts) and particular times. The characteristics of masculinity that become the idealized norm are those acted out by the most powerful men, likely to be those who are white, middle class, and heterosexual. In this process all other masculine styles are rendered inadequate and inferior (Beynon, 2002:16). Hegemonic masculinity harms men in subordinate statuses (men of color, poor men, nonheterosexuals) because it narrows their options to choose other enactments of masculinity. It also harms women because it positions masculinity in opposition to women—masculinity is superior to femininity, men are superior to women (Gardiner, 2002). The paradox is resolved when it is understood that not only "being a male" but "being male" can be interpreted differently in different circumstances (Cornwall and Lindisfarne, 1994:37).

The key is to recognize who has the power in a given situation to determine what is a dominant masculinity and what is a subordinate one. Hegemonic masculinity of the white, middle class and heterosexual variety is not only the dominant form but also, in relation to women, *is* masculinity.

Masculinity's Norms

Hegemonic masculinity shows us that there are a number of ways masculinity (manliness) can be successfully acted out. These different enactments can be subsumed under several norms that serve as masculinity's norms. Some of these standards were identified as "rules" of masculinity by psychologist Robert Brannon (1976) near the height of the women's movement. I have adapted and enlarged his five rules by two more to incorporate recent research on masculinity and serve as a framework for approaching a variety of issues concerning masculine gender roles. As we will see, these informal rules are now the institutionalized norms (also referred to as standards, markers, or themes) that have strengthened over the decades since they were formulated.

Antifeminine Norm (No Sissy Stuff). This powerful norm stigmatizes all stereotyped feminine characteristics and the qualities associated with them, including openness and vulnerability. It is closely tied to every other norm of masculinity. Males are socialized to adamantly reject all that is viewed as feminine. Women and anything perceived as feminine are less valued than men and anything perceived as masculine. Acceptance of the antifemininity norm and the traditional scripts it includes is associated with many undesirable consequences.

Interpersonal Relations. Beliefs about feminine behavior disallow many men from revealing insecurities and vulnerabilities to others who could help them cope with difficult life situations. Restraints in emotional openness are associated with suicide, Type A behavior, heart disease, and stress related conditions diseases such as ulcers, stroke, back pain, and tension headaches. Concealing emotions also inhibit the development of the repertoire of interpersonal skills essential for successful relationships in all areas of life. Intimate friendships between males are discouraged, and intimate friendships between females are blocked by messages that tell men they will be judged negatively if they exhibit "too" much emotion or sensitivity. They believe emotional expression drives others away rather than bringing them closer.

Boys learn quickly from their peers that gestures of intimacy with other males are discouraged and that expressions of femininity, verbally or nonverbally, are not tolerated. Male role models—fathers, teachers, and brothers—provide the cues and the sanctions to ensure compliance on the part of the young boy (Strikwerda and May, 2000).

The culturally inbred antifemininity norm keeps teenage boys in particular from expressing feelings toward other boys on pain of being ridiculed as sissies at best or fags at worst (see later discussion).

To bolster their formative masculinity, boys strictly segregate themselves from girls in school. This segregation means that intimacy with boys must be achieved in other culturally acceptable ways. Throughout childhood and into adult life, male camaraderie occurs in male-only secret clubs, fraternal organizations, the military, sports teams, or the neighborhood bar. Although men are taught that too much intimacy among males is forbidden, the human desire for informal interaction is powerful. The separate groups allow men to act out this human need in safety and according to masculinity's antifeminine norm, otherwise people would be suspicious of such close male interaction. Men rarely talk about friendship in these groups. "Instead we hear about something called male bonding, as if all possible nonsexual connection between men is rooted in some crude instinctual impulse," and even this is viewed as something either "terribly juvenile or possibly dangerous" (Letich, 1991:85). The antifemininity norm blocks the expression of the deepest feelings of affection between men.

Men may be guaranteed sociocultural superiority over women, but at the enormous expense of remaining psychologically defensive and insecure (Chodorow, 1993:60). Males of all ages are more likely to express feelings of uncertainty and anxiety to females, but the healthiest men are those who have an array of both male and female friends with whom they feel comfortable in expressing their emotions and concerns. Overall, men's endorsement of the antifemininity norm's quest for invulnerability has the opposite effect: It makes them more vulnerable than less vulnerable.

Success Norm (The Big Wheel). The second theme of the "Big Wheel" suggests that men are driven to succeed at all costs. Men need to be looked up to, and prestige is associated with the belief that money makes the man. Manliness is tied to career success and the ability to provide for a family in his breadwinner role. The positive "good provider" role is salient in this norm, but it comes with more than an economic price. Men feel compelled to emulate other men, and in doing so, families become display cases for masculine success. Because prestige is gained from their work outside rather than inside the home, competency as a parent is less important than competency in the world of paid labor. It is expected that the wives, children, colleagues, and peers of these men judge them accordingly. As the Depression pointed out, self-esteem is assaulted with the loss of a job. We saw earlier that unemployment for men is correlated with an array of risks to emotional well-being. Men are told that ensuring the family's financial security is their top priority in life, a message that eclipses every other role.

Gendered Occupations. In the workplace men are threatened by women's competence and their entry into traditional masculine occupations, thereby kindling controversy about what constitutes a "man's" job. Blue-collar men express the most hostility, but the resistance comes from men in the professions as well. Consistent with both the antifemininity and success norms, they may believe that their jobs will be tainted by femininity and regarded as less manly. Men who succeed in feminine jobs are frequently viewed as less competent than those who succeed in masculine jobs. An influx of women in an occupation decreases its attractiveness to men. Males who do work in predominantly female fields may be viewed as less competent by those outside the job, but they have more advantages than females in these fields (chapter 10). From a symbolic interaction view, a labeling cycle producing a self-fulfilling prophecy occurs: The job is "feminized," men desert it, working conditions deteriorate, and pay decreases. The job is resegregated, going from almost all men to almost all women. Success at a job where women are doing essentially the same work can be demeaning for men who favor conventional gender roles. Males are bound to a concept of masculinity that assumes they will dominate women occupationally and that they will enact a strong breadwinning role, with their self-esteem tied to both. Females reinforce these beliefs by viewing men as success objects.

In the bleak economic times at the start of the new millennium men flocked to female jobs, as nurses, caseworkers, elementary and preschool school teachers, and even as nannies. Men report that even with lowered pay, working with children and in caregiving roles offers flexibility, satisfaction, and a belief that they are "making a difference." However, masculinity's stubborn success norm erodes these beliefs. If men feel others view them as lacking ambition or being deficient in their provider role, they may wait out the economic downturn in female jobs but jump back into higher paying, more prestigious male jobs when conditions improve (Cullen, 2003).

Men also face confusion when they are challenged by the reality of a new economy that has transformed the traditional provider role for men. Dual-earner couples are not the exception but the norm. Although beliefs in egalitarianism in the workplace are being expressed much more than in the past by both men and women, a retrenchment favoring the conventional norm of male superiority in terms of the success norm remains. When wives work outside the home, both spouses—but particularly husbands—are reluctant to define her as on equal footing in the provider role. Conflict theory suggests that one reason married men embrace the breadwinner role is that it entitles them to privileges in the home, including less housework, more time for leisure and recreation, and more services provided to him by wife and children.

Intellectual Success. In addition to economic success, males are expected to demonstrate intellectual superiority over women. The feminist movement ushered in the idea that intellectual companionship between the genders is possible and preferable. With a few modifications, however, traditional beliefs still hold. Men now expect that their wives will be wage earners, and they express admiration for their wives' careers. But they also believe that the bulk of child care and household responsibilities should rest with a wife and that her career should be interrupted if these responsibilities are jeopardized. Men also believe that a husband should outearn his wife and that her career success is less important than his. Men are threatened by female coworkers who are promoted over them, and husbands are threatened by wives who equal or excel them occupationally. Young men have lower self-esteem if they see their wives as "winning" over them occupationally. Research on gender-related attitudes of men finds a reemphasis on work roles for men and maternal roles for women. Men's attitudes are strongly influenced by the social and historical period in which they live as much as they are by personal experiences. This suggests that cultural mandates for the "Big Wheel" image of masculinity remain entrenched.

Toughness Norm (Sturdy Oak). The "Sturdy Oak" norm of masculinity tells men to be tough, confident, self-reliant, and independent. He must express confidence in his ability to carry out tasks that appear insurmountable. He must do so with a sense of stoicism that shows he is in command of the situation. Antifeminine elements intrude here by implying that compliance and submissiveness are the negative qualities that the "Sturdy Oak" male disdains. The harried husband of the Dagwood Bumstead, Al Bundy, or Homer Simpson variety possesses such qualities. The opposite of the "Sturdy Oak" is the "wimp." Linked to the antifeminine norm is the disheartening finding that the rise of the "wimp" is associated with men who relate to their wives and children in sensitive and understanding ways (Cose, 1995:93).

Aggression Norm (Give 'Em Hell). The aura of daring, aggression, and unbending will in the face of adversity is another marker of manliness. We have seen that manliness as connected to aggression has been central throughout history, and the "Give 'Em Hell" theme endures today. Boys learn early that turning the other cheek is less respected than fighting one's way out of a difficult situation, especially if bullied. Media reinforce these images by aiming stories at youngsters glorifying war, violence, and revenge in the name of a good cause, one that is often defined ambiguously or personally, showing that war is comprised of guts and glory on the battlefield of honor. The title of hero is readily bestowed on those who come out on top through physical means. Diplomats who quietly work behind the scenes hammering out vital peace agreements are less likely to command public admiration than frontline soldiers. President Jimmy Carter, who pursued a diplomatic solution to the Iran hostage situation, was seen as soft for his refusal to use military channels. The ill-fated rescue attempt was a way to escape some of this pressure.

It can be argued that aggression, even war, is necessary at times. Functionalists emphasize that by socializing boys into masculinity with the aura of violence and aggression surrounding it, the soldier role, which they may eventually assume, will be easier to accept. In this view, the aggressive masculinity needed in wartime is latently functional. Such views are again linked to the antifemininity norm. Toughness, the repression of empathy, and less concern for moral issues are deemed essential if the goal is winning. In the name of political necessity the human cost of war is cast aside (Gerson, 1993:32). The problem with this view is that aggression and masculinity become inextricably linked and carry over into the nonwar existence of men. A soldiering mentality is maladaptive in a man's daily life, but he hauls its baggage as surely as a battlefield pack.

School Violence. The deadly influence of the three masculinity norms—antifemininity, toughness, and aggression—is plainly evident in a decade of school violence resulting in the death and injury of students and teachers in small cities and suburbs across the United States. Toxic masculinity is a critical factor in understanding this violence, but one that is ignored by almost all media accounts and many professional ones. Reporters, educators, parents, and scholars refer to the perpetrators as "violent youths," "isolated adolescents," "lonely teenagers," and "unhappy students" and rarely mention the fact that all the killers are boys. Many of these boys were considered good students but identified as passive, alienated, and ostracized or shamed by their peers—especially the schools' "popular" clique. They were called nerds, wimps, and sissies and targeted for homosexual slurs. The Columbine killers were also addicted to a diet of extremely violent video games, such as *Doom* and *Quake*, specifically designed with adolescent boys in mind. Research suggests that isolation and humiliation by peers were likely triggers for the violence. Regardless of race and social class, antisocial behavior is one result of low self-esteem and is the single best predictor of later aggression (Kerr and Nelson, 2002). All these patterns have traceable links to the way masculinity is defined and acted on by men and boys.

Sexual Prowess Norm (Macho Man). The theme of sexuality permeates the macho man norm. In this image, men are primarily sexual beings living and having ongoing heightened interests in sexuality in all its forms. In the sexualized world they create and function in, men are judged according to their sexual ability and sexual conquest. Male sexual identity, according to John Stoltenberg (1995:68), is experienced only in "sensation and action, in feeling and doing, in eroticism and ethics." Sexual harassment is a case in point. Male sexualized identify is so taken for granted that men's ogling, touching, or sexual remarks or jokes are dismissed as harmless fun rather than as sexual domination or exploitation. Men are mystified or angered when they are accused of harassment because they view it as normal gendered interaction (Quinn, 2002).

This sexual identity is reinforced by essentialist beliefs that masculinity is biologically rather than socially constructed. An impotent man is cast into a stigmatized, demeaned category because the term is used to describe more than just his penis. Media depict a man's sexual performance as a way to confirm his masculinity, with success in sex linked to success in life (Lehman, 2004). Mostly used as a front, boys develop stories and routines documenting their sexual escapades and describing successful pickup ploys. Among white male adolescents, friends are often chosen on the basis of sexual activity rather than sexual activity being influenced by friends' behavior (Miller et al., 1993:61). As boys mature and strive to be "masculine," they soon understand that credibility and bonding are achieved with male peers through sexual talk laced with aggressive overtones and sexist joking, with girls and women as their unflattering targets (Curry, 2004). When men rely on sexuality to define masculinity, their vulnerability will inevitably increase. They gain a measure of respect for sexual talk and bravado of the locker room, but at the same time they understand that they can never live up to the sexualized selves they present to others. And they are well aware of the disastrous consequences if they acted on the aggression in their sexual talk. In the pursuit of the illusion of masculinity, one set of vulnerabilities is exchanged for another.

Tenderness Masculinity (Sensitive Guy). The cultural construction of masculinity encompasses a series of inflexible elements. They stay as defining characteristics despite evidence attesting to their negative consequences for men as well as women. For a time it was thought that the older labels were on the decline and that sensitivity and openness could be added to the accepted male role. Whereas the sensitive guy image is one that resonates with men and women seeking more partnering roles, it is a masculinity that remains subordinate to all the others. Masculinity defined by tenderness, emotional expression, warmth, and sensitivity can be better described as an emerging norm rather than as a current norm. When images of tender masculinity make their way into the media, they are undermined by the more normative images. Think of Arnold Schwarzenegger in *True Lies* and *Kindergarten Cop* to understand how tender masculinity is subverted to the other types. As another example, the characterization of a heterosexual man as an exploitive sexual animal exists alongside a man as a competent lover who is striving to create pleasure for his partner (Gross, 1992:429). The latter more "sensitive" view is not particularly progressive or egalitarian if masculinity is still associated with control. The male takes charge of sexual activity and decides the sequence, the pace, the positions, and how best to stimulate his partner. Women may want to lead or communicate other needs. This can be difficult for a goal-oriented male, who has not been socialized into thinking he "might also gain pleasure from being receptive to his partner in the sexual sphere" (Rabinowitz and Cochran, 1994:98). Whenever the "crisis of masculinity" becomes a media focus, it is usually because women are outperforming men in traditionally male spheres, and men are not being assertive enough to retain or regain their positions of dominance. Their lack of assertiveness is associated with being too nice, too tender, or too sensitive. In other words, they are wimps.

Masculine images have a contradictory quality that may seem confusing to men. Men are presented with alternative images that challenge the traditional version of a male mystique. In accepting these revised images as legitimate and offering more benefit than liability, men could rally behind new definitions of masculinity. The tenderness option is one that is sought by men and women as individuals. But when men come together in groups, the older images of masculinity surface and the newer images are subverted. Both genders adhere to quite rigid views of masculinity. Men are threatened by changes in definitions of masculinity, regardless of the virtual impossibility of meeting the traditional standards. Men's roles have not kept pace with the changes in women's roles. The evidence is clear that the attitudes toward masculinity have served to hamper those men seeking to free themselves from restrictive male stereotypes. The majority of men, however, are on no such quest.

On an optimistic note, new masculinities like the tenderness option—however small the breakthrough may be—are emerging that emphasize the development of a deeper awareness of the mutuality of the two genders. This awareness needs to be taught to children. Stunned by escalating school violence, for example, educators are adopting socialization practices emphasizing nurturance and nonviolent means of resolving conflict. By accepting attitudes that have been traditionally labeled as feminine, tenderness masculinity is necessary for the development of full human potential.

Social change has influenced the behavior of men in their masculine roles, whether it is acknowledged or not. But cultural lag remains: Attitudes have not caught up with the behavior change that is evident. As far as masculinity is concerned, the disheartening overall conclusion is that the more things change, the more they remain the same.

HOMOPHOBIA

The world is primarily based on **heterosexism**—people view relationships only in heterosexual terms and in doing so, other sexual orientations are denigrated. Reflecting the taken-for-granted view that the world is *heterosexist*, at various times in history homosexuality was a sin, a disease, a crime, a mental illness, an immoral choice, an alternative lifestyle, and a health threat (Rupp, 1999).

To be masculine means more than being *non*feminine, it means *anti*feminine. A taken-for-granted heterosexist view fuels **homophobia**, the fear and intolerance of homosexuals (gay men and lesbians) and homosexuality. Homophobia is identified by researchers as such an integral part of heterosexual masculinity that being a man means *not* being a homosexual (Badinter, 1995:115). The logical extension from this definition is that homophobia in men translates to the fear of other men. Data from the United States, Britain, and Australia suggest that homophobia is learned early and reinforced through the media, peer interaction at school, and later in the workplace (Clum, 2002; Keller, 2002). In the United States, *most* teenage males express high levels of homophobia. More positive media images may temper these beliefs as they get older, but they are not likely to be erased (Plummer, 1999; Thurlow, 2001).

The Demography of Homophobia

People with higher levels of homophobia are also likely to be heterosexual, elderly, not college educated, living in the South, and religiously, sexually, and politically conservative. They also tend to be more authoritarian and hold rigid, highly traditional views of masculinity and femininity. Homophobia is also correlated with sexism and racism (Lienemann, 1998; Basow and Johnson, 2000; Cohler and Galatzer-Levy, 2000). Homophobia is lessened when people have gay friends or associates and if they believe that homosexuality is due to biology (Kantor, 1998; Hegarty, 2002). Homophobia translates to stigma, depression, and fear in the lives of gay men. Homophobia and violence against homosexuals are all too common occurrences (Mason, 2002).

The Risks of Race and Ethnicity. When the minority status of "homosexual" is added to an already disadvantaged position due to race or ethnicity, stigma for gay men increases. Those disadvantages may be higher *within* their own subcultures, African-American gay and bisexual men, for example, may be at higher risk for violence and HIV infection because they need to maintain a facade of heterosexuality and adhere to heterosexist masculinity norms in their homophobic subcultures. Although secrecy may protect them against violence, it does not protect them against HIV risk. Risky sexual behavior is associated with the sexual prowess masculinity norm that works against all men, but especially gay men (Lichtenstein, 2000; Constantine-Simms, 2001). Among Latinos, a similar scenario is played out and impacts both homosexual and heterosexual men and women. Throughout Latino cultures in North and South America, Latino males are expected to be dominant, tough, and fiercely competitive with other males. This exaggerated *machismo* masculinity is displayed more frequently in poor and working class neighborhoods. Unprotected sex with multiple partners is proof of virility and masculinity, and therefore *not* homosexuality. Young Latinos are aware of the dangers, but cultural norms about manhood and homosexuality continue (Schifter and Madrigal, 2000). Although homophobia in Latino communities is very strong and male-to-male sexual liaisons are kept secret, they may be accepted as transitory until marriage because they say a sexual outlet is needed. A gay identity, however, is not acceptable (Diaz et al., 2001).

Among Asian Americans, especially in Chinese communities, gender roles and images of masculinity are extremely rigid. Gay Chinese Americans express high levels of anguish not only because they were socialized for strong family ties, but because their families trace their heritage only through male offspring. An only son who is gay may end the family. Though it is difficult to generalize about levels of homophobia within different racial and ethnic groups, it is clear that gay men must contend with another layer of minority status that will undoubtedly impact their lives.

Gender. Over time homophobia has declined significantly for most demographic categories. Today there is more support for extending the same rights related to employment and military service to all people, regardless of sexual orientation (Andryszewski, 2000). Any state allowing legal marriages for gay couples attests to this decline as well. Media representations of gay men are becoming mainstream and popular and are portraying positive, affirmative friendships between gay and straight men (Think *Will and Grace* and *Queer Eye for the Straight Guy*). Overall, the population of young adults can be described as somewhere between tolerant and accepting of homosexuals (NORC, 2000).

Gender differences in level of acceptance of homosexuality are the single most important contradiction to the trend. Males may be less homophobic than in the past, but they have been slower to change than other groups. The homophobic gap between men and women may actually be widening.

Masculinity and Homophobic Labels

The feminine labels that boys use in name-calling denigrate other boys precisely because the word is associated with a devalued group—females. As reported by a man reflecting on homophobia in high school, the most popular insult/name that is used over and over again by male jocks is simply "girl."

> If a male student was annoying, they called him "girl." If he made a mistake during some athletic event, he was called "girl." Sometimes "girl" was used to challenge boys to do their masculine best (don't let us down, girl). (Hopkins, 1992:111)

When stereotypes about femininity and homosexuality collide, boys then combine two devalued groups (females and gay men) in using their denigrating labels. These labels range from sissy, wimp, and pussy to homo, fag, or cocksucker. Rap icon Eminem routinely uses homophobic labels in his repertoire as a slur less against a man's sexuality, but more on his gender. He states that calling someone a faggot is the "lowest degrading thing that you can say to a man" (cited in Kimmel, 2004:570).

Boys distance themselves from any behavior suggestive of these labels. They are reluctant to challenge the inconsistencies and stereotypes associated with their usage because, just by doing so, they may be threatened themselves with the label of homosexual. As adults, men still fear these labels. "Men devalue homosexuality then use this norm of homophobia to control other men in their male roles" (Lehne, 1992:389). Homophobia among men is related to the enactment of heightened levels of masculinity to dispel any notion that they may be viewed as feminine, hence homosexual (Zeichner et al., 2002).

Gay Men. Homophobia also takes its toll on gay men who undergo the same socialization processes as heterosexual men. Gay relationships, whether they are sexual or not, demonstrate the impact of socialization into masculinity standards and the homophobia of the standards. For example, in gay subcultures throughout the world a powerful gay machismo element is evident. Exaggerated masculinity takes the form of dress (leather, motorcycle regalia, military uniforms), rough language, and risky, sometimes violent sexual encounters. Gay machismo presents an image of masculinity that gay men have been taught as the proper one. Sexual potency, power, and control (macho man) are its central characteristics. When gay men adopt the heterosexist masculine standard, however, their reality is distorted because he is still gay and open to the rejection and homophobia existing in the broader society.

Gay men must contend with their own feelings of self-worth in a society that labels them as deviant. The message gays receive from the heterosexist world is that "I am straight, correct, normal, and good. You are abnormal, wrong, deviant, and bad" (Garfinkel, 1985:167). By internalizing the negative labels of the dominant group, minorities such as gay men may learn to accept the stereotyped, pejorative view of themselves. The other side of homophobia is its counterpart in gay men: self-loathing and the guilt and shame associated with their sexual orientation (Shidlo, 1994).

Gay Rights. The emergence of a gay rights movement has helped gay men to affirm positive identities and the right to sexual self-determination (Clendinen and Nagourney, 1999). In this manner, both individual and political agendas are being met. Patterned after the women's movement, one faction is working to escape the bonds of a sexist culture in which they recognize the common oppression and levels of discrimination they share with women. They are working to cast aside restrictive role playing that distances them from other men. In the gay community's long-standing critique of stereotyped masculinity, the larger men's movement has learned from gay rights' activists that men need to be more emotionally open to other men as well as to women (Williams and Doyle, 1994).

On the other hand, a significant number of gay men recognize that because women and gay men are both subordinate in society, it may be better to capitalize on their advantage of being male—regardless of how it undermines women. From this "male advantage" view, a gay male executive moving up the corporate ladder can wield power over any competing female. As conflict theory suggests, males are higher in the stratification system than females. Males are socialized into accepting the masculinity norms described earlier—whether they are gay or not.

MASCULINITY AND FATHERHOOD

Can men have it all? This phrase is usually connected to women who want to combine a career with marriage and children. Femininity norms have been flexible enough to accommodate women with such aspirations. Masculinity norms have not. The success and toughness norms dictate that men take on the responsibilities of parenthood primarily through their breadwinning roles.

Like women, men envision the American Dream as in terms of successful marriage, satisfying career, contented spouse, and happy children. Idealism notwithstanding, men willingly abdicate the daily household and child care responsibilities to their wives. Masculine images of success tied to career priorities do not allow the latitude necessary for the degree of family commitment many men desire. Contrary to belief, men do not "have it all."

Images of Fatherhood

Fatherhood means more than paternity. The word *fathering* is associated with sexual and biological connotations. The word *mothering* is associated with nurturance. The biological father who takes his provider role seriously has met the necessary criterion for masculinity. This narrow outlook disregards, even belittles, those men who want to expand their parenting roles. In families where men are househusbands and women take on the provider role, the couple is still unsettled if women cede control of parenting to men because both believe parenting is the mother's "natural" right (Ornstein, 1998). Even in househusband arrangements, complete role reversal is rare. Beliefs about essentialism and men as success objects combine to legitimize the exclusion of men from more meaningful participation in the lives of their children and devastate fathers who avidly desire these very roles.

The demeaning stereotypes of bumbling men who do not know how to hold a baby, soothe a sobbing child, or buy groceries persevere and serve to lower the skill level men need to succeed in domestic roles. Some men use the bumbling father stereotype as a strategy to get out of performing certain tasks:

> Getting the kids dressed—these buttons are so tiny—I can't do tiny buttons. Poor kids, they are always getting dressed backwards.
> When the kids hear daddy's going to make dinner they'd rather eat out. (Deutsch, 2004:470).

These men belittle their own efforts and at the same time praise their wives for succeeding where they have failed. This self-effacement functions to maintain the traditional gendered division of labor in the household.

Regardless of whether he is "playing stupid" to get out of household work, masculinity's antifemininity norm bolsters his behavior. Men who freely choose to take care of their own children as househusbands, take on equal partnering with their dual-earning or full-time homemaker wives, or take care of others' children in careers like early childhood education are suspect in their masculinity.

Socialization. Although fathers traditionally have fewer expectations built into their roles as far as socialization of the children is concerned, the child nurturing roles they do take on are extremely important. Strong father–infant attachment and involvement of fathers with their young children are linked to a child's personality adjustment, positive peer relationships, level of self-esteem, and overall sense of well-being (Lamb, 2002a; Palkovitz, 2002; Parke et al., 2002). Fathers are the key figures in preventing the connection between violence and masculinity to be acted out by their sons (Pope and Englar-Carlson, 2001). Regardless of race or social class, in homes where fathers are absent or gone much of the time, children are at greater risk for maladaptive psychological, social and development outcomes (Harris, 2002; Lamb, 2002b). Increases in divorce and cohabitation are thought to undermine already fragile father–child relationships, reinforce masculinity norms about men's economic roles, and increase women's domination in child socialization (Goldscheider, 2000).

Decades of research on the aspirations fathers hold for their children remain remarkably consistent. In all socioeconomic classes fathers are stricter in gender-typed intentions of their children than mothers, and they give sons less latitude than daughters in experimenting with different gender role definitions. Fathers now believe that both their sons and daughters need to go to college, but that the college should provide a different option for sons. Fathers continue to pay close attention to the potential for their sons to be breadwinners and good providers but believe their daughters can use a degree "to fall back on." Whereas these patterns are more pronounced among working class men compared to men in middle and upper classes, gender stereotypes surrounding masculinity norms invade socialization practices by fathers in all social classes (chapter 3).

Parents as Partners

To make parenthood a true partnership for a couple, fathers and children need to be brought closer together. Research suggests this is what is highly desired by fathers, but as we saw in chapter 8, it is eroded by images of masculinity that underscore the "good provider" image (success) of fathers to the neglect of a fledgling "involved-father" model. Fathers want to embrace new role definitions that rank nurturing equal to or higher than breadwinning but feel blocked by broader masculinity norms bolstering their advantage in the workplace but disadvantage at home (Gearing et al., 2001; Risman, 2001).

Fathers mention repeatedly that they want to be role models, teachers, companions, and playmates to their children. As stated by a 31-year-old retail manager:

> I think the most important responsibility is that of nurturing the child. . . . it's important for fathers to be with a child as much as mothers. . . . they ought to try to make it possible, even if it means giving up something. (Cohen, 1993:12)

A father's participation in family life is enhanced when expanded role definitions are accepted on all fronts. Wives, children, other kin, friends, and coworkers can be supportive of men who take on a variety of not just child maintenance but also childrearing responsibilities. Family-supportive workplace policies that allow flextime and paternity leave serve nurturing purposes as well. After his daughter was born with health problems, one father reported on his paternity leave experience where he took off two months and was part time for six months.

> I was just extremely fortunate to have the flexibility. I'm sure my co-workers would rather have had me back but I didn't get any pressure . . . (but). . . . I tried to keep up with what was going on . . . so there was kind of a self-regulating pressure. (Cooper, 2004:274)

Like the tenderness masculinity that is gradually emerging, these comments suggest that men are in transition to gender role change. Involved fathers, for example, are not quite on equal par with provider-fathers. When paternity leave options are available, few fathers avail themselves of these opportunities. Because paternity leave options are unpaid, many fathers cannot afford the time off work. The more common reason, however, is that employers and coworkers believe that men who take paternity leave are less serious about their careers. Corporate women who take time off from their careers for child related responsibilities are frequently slotted into less demanding and less lucrative "mommy track" positions. A comparable "daddy track" for men may be destined for those who choose paternity leave. The rigidity of a masculinity image equating success in fatherhood only in economic terms again intrudes.

Men in the Delivery Room. Another partnering mechanism is a father's inclusion in the childbirth experience—from training to be a labor coach and pre-parenting classes to the delivery room itself. An expectant father in a Lamaze class he attended with twelve pregnant couples in their thirties jokes about how women control the class and the entire moral discourse of the subject of childbirth (Brown, 1994). But there is also an underlying fear in the message he conveys. He is frightened by the physical pain his wife will endure and by the isolation he feels during his wife's pregnancy. Being present at childbirth offers a new father an incredibly powerful bond to his infant and to his wife or partner. After sharing in the birth of the child, the marriage is likely to be stronger, particularly if the father is highly involved in later child care.

The doors are open for contemporary expectant fathers who only a few decades ago were totally removed from the birthing process. Fathers were relegated to waiting rooms where they nervously paced until the doctor brought news of the birth. Some hospitals still discourage fathers from remaining with their wives throughout the birth process, upholding older images of men as appendages who get in the way. At childbirth, men are constrained by a double standard built into their role. They are encouraged today to actively participate, but at the same time they are seen as outsiders. Expectant mothers are cast into positive, normative roles but there are no corresponding roles for expectant fathers. Except for his laughable nervousness, his fears are not addressed. Fear of his wife's death during childbirth and anxiety over new parenting roles and family responsibilities are major concerns of expectant fathers but are rarely discussed. With attention tuned to motherhood, the major transition to fatherhood is overlooked. When natural fears experienced by expectant fathers are discussed openly and unashamedly with their spouses, relationships are deepened. The therapeutic and medical communities must be aware of their own stereotypes in working with expectant fathers. The evidence is clear that benefits will be realized for the marriage and for later parenting when this occurs.

Divorce

Divorced fathers who would like to be actively involved with their children must contend with restrictions on parenting tied to masculine gender roles that interfere with responsible parenting. Fathers who feel cut off from their children after a divorce have heightened levels of anxiety, depression, and stress. The bleak statistics on child support payments by fathers is well documented (chapter 10). Joint custody may be less economically advantageous for ex-wives, but it increases contact and self-esteem for ex-husbands. Those fathers who absent themselves from their children after divorce and fail to pay child support often report that they were treated unfairly in the divorce settlement. Investigation of postdivorce father absence found that men engage in a "masculinist discourse of divorce" as a legitimate strategy to control and punish their ex-wives (Arendell, 1992:565). These regrettable practices suggest that fathers may be "locked in" by a system shaped by gendered ideology that discourages positive postdivorce relationships for the ex-spouses and their children.

MEN AT MIDDLE AGE AND IN LATER LIFE

Sociological perspectives on the **life course** highlight the process of *continuing socialization* in the roles people play over a lifetime and the ages associated with those roles. The varied paths of the life course are shaped by individual experiences as well as broader social change, particularly related to gender.

Retirement

The transition to retirement requires major adjustments in all segments of life. It restructures daily living, alters family relationships and spending patterns, and produces psychological stress. Yet retirement has become such a part of life's expectations, if financial security is ensured, workers prefer early retirement. The provider role script and success and sturdy oak norms associated with masculinity sharpen an already strong American work ethic from which identity and self-esteem are gained. The psychological investment and normative expectations in the world of paid employment for men predict that they would have a more difficult time with retirement than women. Available data, however, suggest that retirement satisfaction is based on the same factors for women and men. Like men, career women anticipate retiring at an earlier age, but they use the resulting free time differently. Women restructure their domestic lives that were constrained because of employment and spend more time with family and on home related activities. Men take on more extradomestic roles and activities, but many of these activities are done with family members rather than friends or former coworkers (Choi, 2001; Barer, 2002; Kim and Moen, 2002). Gender is less of a predictor of life satisfaction at retirement than are income and health. Both male and female workers are less satisfied if poor health forced them to retire or if deficient economic resources forced them to remain on the job.

Midlife as Crisis

Do men have a midlife crisis? Health care professionals continue to debate the question in light of a configuration of physical and emotional symptoms that emerge for many men between the ages of 45 and 55. Variously referred to as the male climeractic, male menopause, or midlife crisis, men may present symptoms of night fears, drenching sweats and chills, and depression. The psychological and social turmoil associated with these symptoms are linked to hormonal changes, such as a sharp drop in testosterone level for a few men and a slow but gradual change with considerable hormonal variation for most men (Fischman, 2001). Unlike women, where there are noticeable changes heralding the cessation of menses, in normal aging for men, the changes are subtle. Older men retain their interest in sex, but the performance of their sex organs becomes less predictable. Gender scripts linking masculinity to sexual performance create a fear of impotence, which may come true not because of hormones but because of the fear itself (the massive sales of drugs that enhance the sexual performance of men may be linked to this fear). Thus biological changes must be seen in the light of the social and psychological factors embedded in masculinity norms.

Some professionals suggest that these symptoms are a normal part of the aging process and although initially alarming, they are not debilitating. The appearance of symptoms prompts many men to engage in a review of their lives, make choices, and alter life paths. Others suggest that this stage is neither normal nor healthy and that it produces psychological turmoil for men who make unwise decisions that are maladaptive for themselves and their families. This latter view asserts that men at midlife become acutely aware of their own mortality and, in reviewing their accomplishments, focus on what they have not done rather than what they have done. Unmet goals founded on masculinity's success scripts create turmoil for the midlife man who is then said to be in crisis.

Families at Midlife. For women, the depression that supposedly occurs when the last child is launched, or moves away from home, is referred to as the *empty nest syndrome*. Research shows, however, that the empty nest syndrome is largely a myth.

Contrary to the stereotype, most women experience an upturn in life satisfaction and psychological well-being when children are launched (West, 2000; Dennerstein et al., 2002). Most women look to the empty nest stage of life as offering opportunities to engage in activities that might have been put on hold during child raising. They generally seek expanded roles in a society increasingly receptive to women like themselves, who are venturing outside the traditional confines of the home.

Men may have a more difficult time with the empty nest than women. Some evidence suggests that men's increased depression at midlife is linked to their regrets about career priorities that distanced themselves from their children. A positive life course path to recapture the lost parenting experience prompts many men to turn to grandchildren. Grandchildren provide a sense of biological continuity, emotional self-fulfillment, and a way for men to be free of the competition, arguments, and power struggles they experienced in their workplaces and when raising their own children. The stereotype of a grandfather as a stern, aloof, family patriarch counters the reality that grandparenting brings the generations together and offers men rewarding and emotionally enriching experiences.

As implied by the satisfaction men express as grandparents, men at midlife often begin to reintegrate the masculine and feminine traits that were separate for most of a their lives. Traditional masculinity is tempered by a more well-rounded personality, which accounts for his roles of husband, father, and breadwinner. Carol Gilligan (1982a, 1982b) suggests that women approach midlife differently than men. Men are seeking greater interdependence at old age, whereas women are seeking greater autonomy. At this stage men become more nurturant and women more independent. Her capability of standing apart from him may help relieve him of the burden of responsibility he feels he has carried for the family. It is interesting that the woman who grows in assertiveness and independence provides the best source of support for a man in this phase of life. Each spouse may begin to loosen the bonds of restrictive gender roles as they make the transition from middle to old age.

Widowhood

Compared to widows, widowers are much more likely to remarry, thus among the elderly the large majority of widows reside alone. Although most older adults return to earlier levels of physical and emotional health within two years after the loss of their spouse, social isolation and loneliness are frequent outcomes of widowhood. The surviving spouse is at higher risk for physical illness and even death (Carr, 2001). If a caregiver–spouse dies, the already debilitated surviving spouse is left in an even more dependent and vulnerable position. Suicide rates among the elderly have increased since the 1980s, and they remain the highest for all age groups. But men account for 84 percent of all suicides, and white males in their 80s have the highest suicide rates of all races and both genders (National Strategy for Suicide Prevention, 2001). Suicide attempts by younger people (those under age 35) are likely to fail; suicide attempts rarely fail for the elderly, and the failure rate is smallest for elderly males.

Widows. Although the death of a spouse has a profound and devastating effect on the surviving partner, becoming a widow is a qualitatively different experience than becoming a widower. Older women are more likely to form their identity around marriage, so losing a spouse literally means loss of a central life role. Widows are likely to experience a sudden decrease in standard of living, and for working-class women, widowhood can quickly result in poverty. Isolation increases and support networks decrease (Hungerford, 2001). These are worsened if the couple has moved away from her family for his career advancement. If a widow feels emotionally secure enough to venture into dating, prospects for male companionship and remarriage are limited.

On the other hand, widows are guided by many others with whom they can share experiences, memories, and activities. Due to their numbers alone, a variety of productive roles have been carved out for widows. Because married women know that widowhood is probable, they may begin to actually mentally rehearse it through *anticipatory socialization*. Their role choices may not be completely clear but most widows cope with the crisis reasonably well, adapt as necessary, and productively map out the rest of their lives in ways that contribute to their well-being.

Widowers. The role of widower is much more vague than that of widow. At first glance, it would seem that adjustment is difficult because men lose their most important source of emotional support and probably their major, if not their only, confidant. Wives typically take responsibility for maintaining the couple's social calendar and network of friendships. Masculinity norms earlier in life prevented interpersonal skill building. Lacking the strategies for either preserving or reestablishing intimate relationships widowers find themselves with reduced social contacts. Traditional norms of masculinity may intrude again, preventing them from talking out their grief with others (Doka and Martin, 2001). Retirement increases social isolation. Widowhood intensifies it. The net result is a loss of significant personal relationships. Older men are also less likely to be prepared for the everyday domestic responsibilities necessary for taking care of themselves. When ongoing relationships and customary responsibilities are shattered, *anomie* (normlessness) can follow. This pattern helps explain the high suicide rate of elderly males.

On the other hand, marriage prospects remain bright for widowers, with many embarrassed by all the attention they receive from widows who want to "do" things for them. In addition to the numbers of women of their own age or younger who are available to widowers as potential dating and mating partners, men are better off financially to actually support another spouse. Finally, men may have a stronger need to be remarried, so they quickly move through the dating stage to make remarriage a reality (Moore and Stratton, 2002). Overall, adjustment to widowhood may be different for men and women, but it remains unclear as to which gender fares better.

GENDERED VIOLENCE

It is abundantly evident that the acceptance of traditional masculine gender roles in a patriarchal society is closely connected with escalating violence toward women. Virtually all masculinity norms (antifemininity, toughness, self-reliance, aggression, and sexual conquest) reinforce this fact. Some of these norms are functional in societies such as the United States that value individualism and economic achievement through competition. But in other contexts these norms are highly maladaptive and dysfunctional, most vividly documented in overall patterns of male violence, specifically violence against women. When men are granted permission to subordinate women in patriarchal societies, sexual terrorism is a common result. Sexual terrorism includes nonviolent sexual intimidation, threat of violence, and overt violence (Sheffield, 1995:3).

Rape

The threat of sexual terrorism and rape is so pervasive that firsthand experience is not needed to instill its fear in women. Representations of rape in the media serve to legitimize male aggression and reinforce gender stereotypes. Media lessons from coverage of the Kennedy Smith and Mike Tyson rape trials, for example, provided a disciplinary function to women. Rape fear is heightened, and women's freedom of movement is restricted.

Recent press coverage has moved away from earlier reporting that exaggerated a woman's helplessness and her inability to fight back. In light of research that there are four rape attempts for every one completed, women are being taught self-defense tactics and ways to avoid being raped (Bureau of Justice Statistics, 2002). The burden of responsibility, however, still falls on women to always protect themselves, to always be on the alert, and to always avoid places perceived to increase vulnerability. Because the general social norm is that male prerogative takes precedence the antirape strategy is to change the woman rather than change the situation that creates the problem. Fear of rape shapes women's lives and curtails their freedom (Hirschmann, 2003).

The staggering statistic is that one-forth of females are victims of sexual assault involving rape or attempted rape (Rennison, 2001). Women do commit rape, but it is quite rare and is thought to account for less than one-half of 1 percent of cases. When males *are* raped the perpetrator is another male (National Center for Victims of Crime, 1997). Considering that definitions, perceptions, and legal standards vary considerably between states and between municipalities, between victim and perpetrator and according to context of occurrence, official figures on rape are probably underestimated. In addition, women who report a rape are likely to be demeaned and can be accused of false reporting. The reality is that false reports of rape are small (estimated between 2 and 7 percent) and much less than false reports of other crimes (Uniform Crime Reports, 2002). Sensationalist media coverage on rape involving famous men contributes to her *secondary victimization* as she relives the rape again. Today most municipalities incorporate counseling and more humane approaches in questioning victims of rape, and many courts will no longer allow the sexual history of the victim as part of the proceedings. Unfortunately, the victim herself is still often treated like the criminal.

In the 1960s and 1970s it was estimated that only 5 to 10 percent of all rapes were reported. The reporting of rapes has steadily increased, but even today less than one-third of all rapes are reported (Bureau of Justice Statistics, 2003).

Profile of the Rapist. Until recently, rape was viewed as a crime committed by a few demented men of lower intelligence who have uncontrollable sexual impulses. These few psychotic men cannot be responsible for these staggering rape statistics. The reality is that there is no consistent personality type that reliably distinguishes rapists from men who commit other crimes and from men who do not commit other crimes. In addition, men are not psychotic at the time of the rape. Given the difficulty of getting accurate statistics of rape, the profile of the so-called typical rapist is a sketchy one. Rape is a crime perpetrated by a wide spectrum of men, but they do share some key characteristics (Flowers, 2001; Holmes and Holmes, 2002; Osman, 2003):

1. He appears to have a high need for dominance and a low need for nurturance.
2. He deals with his perceived inadequacies by aggression and the sexual control of women.
3. He is socially insecure and interpersonally isolated.
4. He is likely to accept rape myths and justifies his behavior accordingly so that his victim is made to seem culpable (see Table 9.1).
5. Sexual violence is used as a means of revenge or punishment, sometimes to specific women but more often to women in general, who he holds responsible for his sexual problems.
6. He presents rape in what he believes to be socially acceptable terms, and his aggression is often followed by expressions of remorse.

The following comments by convicted rapists serve as examples of this profile:

> Rape gave me the power to do what I wanted to do without feeling I had to please a partner . . . I felt in control, dominant.

> I have never felt that much anger before . . . The rape was for revenge. I didn't have an orgasm. She was there to get my hostile feelings off on.

> Rape is a man's right. If a woman doesn't want to give it, the man should take it. Women have no right to say no. (Scully and Marolla, 1990; Scully, 1993).

When men from all walks of life are presented with information about the motives of a rapist, they express disdain and horror about the victimization and anger that all men are tainted because a few men rape. Other men remain mystified about the motives of a rapist, as reported by a file clerk who heard about a woman who was beaten, raped, and hospitalized:

> That's beyond me. I can't understand why somebody would do that. If I were going to rape a girl I wouldn't hurt her. I might *restrain* her, but I wouldn't *hurt* her. (Beneke, 2004:411)

It is not difficult to understand why this profile is a sketchy one. It can fit many men.

Rape on College Campus. In the United States and Canada between 25 and 35 percent of college women report a rape or attempted rape. The typical pattern reported by college women is that rape and pressured intercourse occur through the use of physical force, drugs, alcohol, and psychological intimidation (Elliott and Brantley, 1997; DeKeseredy and Schwartz, 1998; Ottens, 2001).

Date or acquaintance rape is a fact of life on college campuses. About half of college men have engaged in some form of sexual aggression on a date; between one-fourth and one-half of college women report being sexually victimized (Johnson and Sigler, 2000; Bureau of Justice Statistics, 2003). Despite these high numbers, when victim and offender know one another and alcohol is involved, the incident is less likely to be reported to school officials or the police and even less likely to gain a criminal conviction (Cowan, 2000a; Shook et al., 2000). Date rape is also associated with alcohol for both victim and perpetrator, the belief that men are entitled to sex after initiating and paying for the date, fraternity parties, and length of time the couple has been dating (Abbey et al., 1998; Binder, 2001; Basile, 2002). The so-called date rape drugs—colorless, odorless pills slipped into a drink causing a victim's sleepiness and vulnerability—are used to plan a rape and are widespread on college campuses (Zorza, 2001). And despite substantial empirical evidence to the contrary, male college students are more likely to accept the rape myths than female college students (Cowan, 2000b; Van Wie and Gross, 2001).

Pornography and Rape. Because of its link to sexual aggression, pornography has come under a great deal of scientific and legal scrutiny. Pornography can be categorized according to two major factors—degree of depiction of sexual acts and depictions of aggression in these acts. Hard-core pornography usually depicts genitalia openly and shows sex acts that are aggressive and violent. Women are uniformly the objects of the violence, and it is rare to see men portrayed in this manner. In experimental research, sexually suggestive but nonviolent soft-core pornography appears to have no direct effect on sex crimes or attitudes toward rape. However, aggressive sexual stimuli or hard-core pornography showing rape scenes heightens sexual arousal, increases acceptance of rape myths, desensitizes viewers to violent sexual acts, and leads them to see rape victims as less injured and less worthy (Milburn et al, 2000; Sharp and Joslyn, 2001). Although it is still unclear if the arousal actually leads to later aggression, one study showed that almost one-third of women who were sexually abused and/or raped reported that their abuser used pornography, and 12 percent said it was imitated during the abusive incident (Bergen and Boyle, 2000).

The issue of what constitutes pornography and whether it should be illegal is hotly debated (MacKay, 2001). One side of the debate focuses on pornography as implicitly condoning the victimization of women, arguing that sexual violence against women is increasing and pornography fuels the desensitization to sexual violence and rape. Video pornographic images are certainly more powerful than photos. But consider the implications of a cartoon in *Hustler* (a pornographic magazine) that shows two "plain looking" women jogging through a park together and one says to the other, "The trouble with rapists is that they're never around when you need them" (cited in Russell, 1998).

The other side contends that pornography may actually reduce sex crimes by providing a nonharmful release of sexual tension. Proponents of this view do not deny the association of pornography with women's degradation, but assert that campaigns against it obscure more urgent needs of women and denies income for women who are pornographic models and actresses. There is concern in both camps that banning pornography amounts to censorship in a free society. All factions do agree, however, that child pornography should be censored, and there is also some consensus on the necessity of legally distinguishing pornography according to its degree of violent imagery.

People may not agree on the definition of pornography, and the empirical evidence of a causal link between pornography and sexual violence is debatable. This lack of agreement, however, does not justify ignoring the social issues surrounding pornography's role in socialization into masculinity and in reinforcing gender stereotypes. The effects of pornography will continue to be scientifically scrutinized to bolster or refute the claims of one side or the other in the debate.

Masculinity and Rape. Rape is behavior learned by men through interaction with others and is consistent in critical ways with socialization into masculinity norms related to antifemininity, toughness, sexual prowess, and aggression (Palmer, 2001). Coupled with patriarchal beliefs about domination, these norms blend insecure and destructive masculinity with violence and sexuality, with rape as the end logic (Herbert, 2002).

Feminists and conflict theorists contend that power and patriarchy combine to spur rape and increasing sexual violence. Media representations often legitimize male aggression and reinforce gender stereotypes, especially in college life. Movies such as the classic *Animal House* serve to legitimate and dismiss men's sexual "antics," even if the behavior is a criminal offense that clearly harms women. Patriarchal norms that culturally condone relationships putting men in dominant and aggressive roles and women in passive and submissive ones are widely accepted (Anderson and Swainson, 2001). On a global scale, patriarchal norms regarding women as the sexual and economic property of men not only dismiss rape but often have few legal protections for its victims. In the United States some states still do not have laws against marital rape, and legal standards in many places still treat rape not as a *personal* crime but as a *property* offense. Sex is seen as part of the marriage agreement, whether the wife wants it or not. Both genders are socialized with these standards in mind. This view allows the victim to be blamed and in turn justifies the crime (Morry and Winkler, 2001).

Domestic Violence and Battered Women

The dramatic increase in domestic violence makes the family home one of the most lethal environments in the United States. Intimate partner violence against women make up about one-fifth of all nonfatal violent crimes experienced by women. Although it cuts across all demographic groups, wife battering is more prevalent in families with low income and unemployment, isolation from kin and community, and alcohol use (Gelles and Straus, 1995; Bureau of Justice Statistics, 2003; Wexler, 2003). When race is factored in, African American women are twice as likely than white women to experience more violence and more severe violence (Neff et al., 1995; Richie and Kanuha, 2000).

Privacy of the family, the reluctance of the police to get involved in family disputes, lack of consistent legal standards, and accepted masculinity norms make it difficult to get accurate statistics on all forms of family violence and abuse. Statistics on child abuse are more accurate because hospitals now are on the front line in investigations of possible cases. Wife battering is the most underreported of *all* crimes, and underreporting is linked with the persistent belief that wife beating is either not improper or a part of normal marriage (Buzawa and Buzawa, 2003).

Domestic violence encompasses a wide array of physical, sexual, and emotional abuse. Marital rape and wife beating have been commonplace throughout history, but until the mid-twentieth century, a husband's right to a wife's body was considered both personal privilege and amounted to legal right. Standards from English Common Law transported to the United States generally supported a man's right to beat his wife, even for such infringements as talking back to him. The infamous **rule of thumb** allowed a husband to beat his wife with a stick no bigger than his thumb.

Marital rape laws now exist in most states but vary considerably. A man may be prosecuted if there is obvious and sustained physical injury, the couple had separated or filed for divorce, or if his wife is physically or mentally incapacitated. He may be exempt if she fails to report it to the police within a specified period of time, if the couple is not legally married, or if there is a hint that she consented to intercourse (Bergen, 1996; Keilitz, 2002). The vast majority of women raped by their spouses or partners do not report it, especially if no weapon was used or no physical injury was sustained (Bureau of Justice Statistics, 2002).

The following overview suggests the extent and lethality of gendered domestic violence (Marshall and Holtzworth-Munroe, 2002; Bureau of Justice Statistics, 2003; Williams, 2003; Dobash et al., 2004).

1. Over one-third of all women are victims of some type of sexual coercion with a husband or partner in their lifetime.
2. Domestic abuse is the leading cause of injury to women in the United States.
3. Both men and women assault one another in marriage, and mutual abuse is more common than either alone. However, a man's physical strength makes the consequences to a woman much more lethal.
4. One-third of all women who are murdered die at the hands of husbands or boyfriends.
5. Half of all homeless women and children are fleeing domestic violence.
6. Most family homicides are preceded by at least one call to the police for a domestic disturbance, often weeks before the murder.

Why Doesn't She Leave? When battering becomes public, many express disbelief as to why women remain in abusive households. Referred to as **battered women's syndrome**, abused women often have a poor self-image, which contributes to their feelings of powerlessness and dependence. They may believe they are responsible for the violence against them and attempt to alter their behavior to conform to their husbands' expectations. Expressions of remorse by the batterer lead to a short-lived honeymoon period, followed by recurrence of the abuse, with the likelihood of its increasing in severity (Stahly, 2004). A pattern of *learned helplessness* emerges for these women: the beatings are endured, they feel guilty about them, and they are unlikely to confide to others about the situation (Arias and Pape, 2001; Mechanic et al., 2002). Other battered women, especially those with small children, stay because they are financially trapped and economically dependent. They fear for the lives of themselves and their children if go to a shelter but are forced to return home (Shostack, 2001). A woman is also at risk for increased violence if she threatens to leave, files for divorce, or calls the police, although attacks will most likely continue if she stays (Albrecht, 2001). To add insult to injury (literally), insurance companies can deny coverage to battered women because of their dangerous lifestyle (Shen, 1995).

When abused women retaliate and kill their attackers, the courts are reluctant to use self-defense or battered women's syndrome as justifications for acquittal (Leonard, 2002). Many women do leave abusive husbands and partners, however, especially when they receive social support and legal help. Antistalking laws enacted to protect celebrities from deranged fans have been successfully used to protect battered women. More enlightened police responses to domestic violence calls, shelters for women and children, crisis hot lines, and self-defense classes also help (Roberts and Kurst-Swanger, 2002). The murder of Nicole Brown Simpson elevated the issue of domestic violence to the public consciousness with clear evidence she had been battered by her former husband, football star O. J. Simpson. In reflecting on the Simpson trial, Brent Staples (1995) reminds us that battering happens not just in Hollywood but everywhere, and that "the country has as many shelters for neglected dogs and cats as for bloodied and fearful wives."

Sociological Perspectives. According to the functionalist perspective, the social organization of family life, with its intimacy and intensity of relationships, lays the groundwork for family violence. The functionalist perspective, however, does not hold up to cross-cultural evidence in cultures where domestic violence and rape are rare (Sanday, 2000). Feminist and conflict theorists argue that wife battering has not gained as much attention as child abuse, for example, because it remains subtly condoned by a social system that is inconsistent in enforcing the law (Dalton and Schnieder, 2000). From these perspectives, the element of power offers the best explanation for all forms of family violence, rape, and partner battering. Violence is most common in societies where men hold power over the women and children in their families and least common in societies with high levels of gender equity. In all societies, egalitarian families have the lowest rates of domestic violence. The greater the power gap between partners, the greater the risk of violence against women (Whaley, 2001). The underlying issue in almost all cases where men batter women is his perception that his position of dominance is threatened. He protects his masculinity and retaliates based on this perceived threat.

THE MEN'S MOVEMENT IN THE UNITED STATES

Change cannot occur in a vacuum. As women take on new roles or expand old ones, changes inevitably occur for men, some of which they eagerly support, others that they find unpalatable. The movement for male liberation originated on college campuses in the 1970s as a positive response to the feminist movement. Support for feminist causes and their involvement with feminist women as husbands, partners, and friends encouraged these men to reflect on how rigid conceptions about masculinity influenced their own self-image and their behavior toward other men. They were well aware, for example, that men who reject sexual bravado and oppressive behavior toward women are targets for ridicule and exclusion by other men and that definitions of masculinity disallowing expressions of vulnerability, nurturing, and caring undermined their overall well-being.

National Organization of Men Against Sexism

These men eventually formed the **National Organization of Men Against Sexism** (see NOMAS, 2000) and have organized yearly conferences on themes related to parenting, sexism, violence against women, sexuality, sexual orientation, and friendship. This branch of the men's movement works on male liberation by consciousness-raising related to the negative effects of striving for power and the disabling effects of unyielding masculinity. A key concern is how they can change a system in which violence against women is institutionalized. To this end, they have established counseling resources and support centers such as RAVEN (Rape and Violence End Now) and ALIVE (Alternatives for Living in Violent Environments) for men dealing with issues of masculinity and violence and for women seeking to escape violent relationships. NOMAS remains a viable presence on college campuses throughout the United States, attracting to their ranks students in a variety of disciplines and men who are clergy, educators, and in the helping professions. Overall, however, NOMAS has not attracted working-class men and men of color from outside the student population. Neither has it attracted other professional men, particularly those representing the corporate, legal, or administrative elite.

Mythopoetic Men

The lack of public awareness of the first men's movement is revealed in how media publicized later men's movements. In 1990 media attention focused on poet Robert Bly's (1990) belief that men are caught in a toxic masculinity that demands efficiency, competition, and an emotional distance that separates them from one another. Rooted in a competitive work environment that keeps fathers absent from their families, Bly contends that boys turn to women to meet emotional needs. Using myths, art, and poetry as vehicles to access inner emotions, men must unearth and celebrate their lost natural birthright of righteous anger and primordial masculinity, which can be regained only in communion with men (Barton, 2000). Communication between men is encouraged, but the "soft male" who is out of touch with his masculinity and turns to women as authority figures as substitutes for absent or distant fathers is denounced. Through symbolic wounding and healing rituals at weekend retreats, men become aware of their animal instincts and come to embrace their full masculinity (Wilson and Mankowski, 2000). The media were so swept away with Bly's ability to bring these men together, his following was referred to as *the* men's movement, and they erroneously reported it as the first social movement stemming from a general malaise of men (Adler, 1991:47). Currently it is referred to as the *mythopoetic* branch of the men's movement. The retreats are few and less attended, but its healing techniques are used by psychotherapists who believe that many men can be helped when they rediscover and repair the damage caused by father deprivation. Unlike the profeminist NOMAS movement, which argues against men's privilege, the mythopoetic movement is promasculinist and seeks to heal men's pain by distancing them from women. The men attracted to the mythopoetic ranks tend to be powerful, straight, middle class, and white (Morton, 2000). Working-class men and men of color are virtually nonexistent.

African American Men

Another branch of the men's movement focuses on the African American male experience. Research shows that African American males tend to construct definitions of masculinity in direct opposition to Euro-American male models (Harris et al., 1994). Feeling blocked in achieving masculine goals offered by mainstream society, these men may initially adopt the dominant hegemonic views of masculinity. Their values change, however, as they get older and recognize that the dominant model is deficient in light of the race and class cultural configurations of African American men (Hunter and Davis, 1994). The 1997 "Million Man March" in Washington, D.C., organized by controversial Black Muslim leader Louis Farrakhan, was an effort to bring together African American men in support of one another and to offer positive role models to young people and their communities. Depending on the source of the evaluation, the effort got mixed reviews (Gabbidon, 2001). The media spotlighted positive role models, but the luster was tarnished by its antiwoman thrust and heavy infusion of patriarchy (West, 1999). Although all the national and international women's conferences welcomed men, the Million Man March did not invite women to join. And Farrakhan later applauded Iran for setting a shining example to the world on behalf of democratic principles. Iran's unquestionably brutal record regarding both women and democracy intensified any existing schism between men and women.

Promise Keepers

The newest branch of the men's movement, the *Promise Keepers*, is by far the largest, drawing over two million men to large stadium events and small group meetings in the 1990s. Founded by Bill McCartney, former head football coach of the University of Colorado, Promise Keepers (PK) is an evangelical Christian organization dedicated to reestablishing male responsibility in the family and overcoming racial divisions. Media coverage of PK has been so positive that some research suggests it is less like news and more like advertising (Claussen, 2000). Similar to both the mythopoetic and African American branches, PK sees the fatherless home as the source of America's problems. It is different, however, in that its foundation appears to resonate with many more men. To become a Promise Keeper, a man must pledge his commitment to seven "promises," including honoring Jesus Christ, practicing spiritual and sexual purity, and building strong marriages and families. PK is also founded on the goal to reconnect men to their families and to take back family leadership that "sissified men" abdicated, leaving women to fill the vacuum of leadership. As one PK leader suggests, men should not *ask* for their role back but are urged to *take* it back (Healey, 2000:221). Although PK has distanced itself from political affiliation and its members are not in complete agreement with its gender ideology, it goals for asserting Christianity into home and society strongly parallel the agenda of the political right wing and the New Christian Right (Quicke and Robinson, 2000). This political avoidance but religious thrust has attracted many middle and upper class Protestant men to become involved with the movement (Lockhart, 2000).

Critique: Looking Toward the Future

All branches of the men's movement believe women will be the ultimate beneficiaries of their agendas. All the branches expect NOMAS share a promasculinist stance that support traditional, nonoverlapping gender roles and largely exclude women from their ranks except as volunteers. In general, media have given high approval ratings to PK but have virtually ignored criticisms that the ultimate effect will be to subjugate women. Promise Keepers' leaders say that women need not be threatened, because in the kingdom "there is no male or female." Feminists point out, however, that patriarchy and not partnership is the logical outcome. PK would agree.

Feminist men and women support men coming together in exclusive male groups for healing and sharing, but the promasculinist themes in all but NOMAS propose that women are responsible for the problems of men. Blaming serves to undermine dialogue, reinforce sexism, and distance men and women from one another.

Do these gatherings of men suggest that a mass-based men's movement—whether profeminist or promasculinist—has occurred? Three decades of evidence suggest that it has not. Although these are referred to as "branches" of a larger movement, there is virtually no overlap in membership, ideology, or goals. The first three do share prosmasculinist ideology but not in a way that would unite them under a common banner. Because of the small groups that come together outside the large stadium events, PK would be predicted as the most viable of the organizations. However, members and finances have fallen considerably since its 1996 peak, and unity is being eroded by differing beliefs about masculinity, evangelism, and religious inclusiveness (ecumenism). PK's racial unification goal has made little progress because it has failed to attract a significant number of men of color to its ranks.. And it is difficult to assess the effects of McCartney's admission that he had been unfaithful to his wife (Reynolds and Reynolds, 2000; Lundskow, 2002).

NOMAS has not received the publicity or attracted the numbers of the other three groups, but after thirty years it is still convening conferences and drawing together men who are supportive of partnering roles with women and who challenge masculinity norms. In college campuses across the country young men are dialoging with one another, sowing the seeds for a new generation of potential supporters. Latino men are gathering in small groups and discussing how the concept of machismo has harmed them and relationships with the women in their lives (Mena, 2000; Stasio, 2001). It remains to be seen if the other three groups will be as successful as NOMAS over the long run. The women's movement has touched the lives of millions of women; the same cannot be said for the men's movement.

Summary

1. Patriarchy and male domination dominate history. Historically, idealized masculinity is validated by war. The loss of employment during the Depression assaulted masculinity, but subsequent wars revitalized idealized older images. Sports is the contemporary way men use to validate masculinity.

2. Hegemonic masculinity offers versions of masculinity norms that vary by time and content. These norms include: antifeminist, success, toughness, aggression, sexual prowess, and tenderness.

3. Homophobia, the fear and intolerance of homosexuals, is fueled by the antifeminine norm. Minority gay men are at higher risk of oppression and homophobia. Tolerance of gay men and lesbians is increasing; however, women are more tolerant than men.

4. The gay rights movement has helped men positively affirm their gay identity. One faction believes they share a common oppression with women; another faction believes it is better to capitalize on their advantage of being male, even if women are undermined.

5. Images of fatherhood are contradictory. The antifeminine norm and socialization for economic roles separate men from their children. Fathers desire roles that increase nurturing and involvement with their children. A father's inclusion in the childbirth experience and acknowledging his fears are examples.

6. Gender is less of a predictor of retirement satisfaction than are income and health. Most older men are concerned about sexual performance as they age, but few experience

a midlife crisis. Whereas the empty nest syndrome is a myth for women, men whose careers distanced them from children can have difficulty at this life stage. Grandfathering is particularly satisfying for men.

7. Roles for widows and widowers differ greatly, and data are unclear as to which gender fares better in these roles. Elderly widowers are more likely to remarry and have the highest risk for suicide of all age groups.

8. Traditional masculine gender roles are connected to increased violence against women. Media coverage heightens rape fears in women. Rape is perpetrated by a wide spectrum of men. Rapists do tend to have high needs for dominance, are isolated from others, use rape as revenge, and present rape in socially acceptable terms. Half of college men use some form of sexual aggression on a date; up to half of college women report sexual victimization.

9. Pornography as an influence in rape continues to be debated. There is agreement about its link to women's degradation and oppression. Hard core pornography increases acceptance of rape myths and desensitizes viewers about violent sexual acts. Debates revolving around definitions of pornography, censorship, and the loss of income for women portrayed in pornography are unresolved.

10. Until the last half century marital rape and wife beating were seen as a husband's right. Marital rape laws exist but vary greatly in interpretation. Few women report marital rape.

11. Domestic abuse is the leading cause of injury to U.S. women and one-third of murdered women are killed by husbands or boyfriends. Battered women's syndrome, learned helplessness, fear of retaliation, and economic dependence keep women in abusive relationships.

12. The men's movement in the United States is spearheaded by several groups, including: National Organization of Men against Sexism (NOMAS), the mythopoetic branch, African American men (Million Man March), and Promise Keepers. NOMAS is profeminist; all the others are promasculinist. NOMAS appears to be the most enduring.

Key Terms

battered women's syndrome 261	heterosexism 247	National Organization of Men Against Sexism 262
hegemonic masculinity 241	homophobia 247	rule of thumb 261
	life course 253	

Critical Thinking Questions

1. Identify the contemporary norms associated with hegemonic masculinity and document the consequences of these norms for men and their families and their relationships with women. What is the impact of gender socialization on reinforcing or challenging these norms?

2. Considering issues related to rape inside and outside marriage, domestic abuse, and pornography, what suggestions would you offer to policy makers seeking to reduce men's violence toward women? In your suggestions, account for legal issues related to men's rights and censorship and for the factors that may prevent women from escaping abusive relationships.

3. Compare the various "men's movements" in terms of their goals with specific reference to gender ideology, attitudes about masculinity, and gender roles in religion. Document the success of these movements according to their goals and prospects for longevity and sustained challenges to men's roles.

CHAPTER **10**

GENDER, WORK, AND THE WORKPLACE

From all I am able to gather, the girls make good wives. There is nothing in clerical training that detracts from the finest womanly qualities, and men have outgrown their admiration for feminine helplessness and have come to look upon independence as something worth having.

—On women clerks in New York, 1891, by Clara Lanza (Cited in Norton and Alexander, 1996a:288)

"A woman's place is in the home!" Although this may express a nostalgic preference, historically it was never the norm and is not the current norm in the United States or globally. Women's unrelenting global march into the labor force in the twentieth century is associated with significant changes in the family and the workplace. Employed women are socially measured according to how their paid labor outside the home impacts their unpaid labor in the home but their employers measure them in the reverse—how their home-based labor impacts the manner in which they carry out their jobs. Sociologists are interested in the type of work men and women perform and why it is differentially valued. As we will see, the standards that women are expected to live up to in the home and the workplace routinely collide, and the choices they make relative to these standards are linked to all levels of economic disparity between men and women.

HISTORICAL OVERVIEW

Throughout history, women have made major economic contributions to their societies and families through their labor. Archeological evidence from prehistory through to the written evidence of history clearly discounts the "nonworking" woman or "female frailty" myths that supposedly kept women from engaging in demanding work. Even today women grow and process over half the world's food, and in the developing world, women's subsistence agricultural activities are essential to feed their families (chapter 6). To explain the world of work for women, sociologists focus on four major types of production in which women have traditionally engaged: producing goods or services for consumption within the household, producing goods or services at home for sale or exchange elsewhere (cottage industry), care giving and volunteer work, and working for wages.

The Home as the Workplace

Women's work roles have been traditionally closely tied to the home. For over a century the United States had a family based agricultural economy that required the services of all family members for a farm household to survive. Older children took care of their younger siblings so men and women could work together in the fields. In addition to cash crops, most family farms had gardens cultivated by women producing the family's food and allowing surpluses to be packaged for sale or exchange. Women produced cloth from raw material, soap, shoes, candles, and most other consumable items required for their households. In wealthier homes in the seventeenth and eighteen centuries female slave labor and paid female domestic servants produced most necessary items for their employers' households. In nonfarm households and family owned businesses colonial women functioned as paid and unpaid workers as innkeepers, shopkeepers, crafts workers, nurses, printers, teachers, and child care providers. In more remote areas, women also acted as dentists, physicians, and pharmacists. Married women were more likely to engage in home-related work activities, whereas widows and single women were more likely to work outside the home as paid employees (Baxandall and Gordon, 1999; Goldin, 2000).

The Industrial Revolution. The Industrial Revolution indeed revolutionized the work worlds of men and women. First men and then women flocked from farms to factories as wage laborers in the burgeoning industrializing economy that desperately needed their services. With the advent of the water-powered textile factory in 1789, the Industrial Revolution made remarkable strides. Women and female children continued to be the producers of cloth, but now in the factory rather than at home. As exemplified by the famous Lowell Mills in Massachusetts, female employment in textile mills also reflected the lack of available male labor, which was still needed on the farm (Dublin, 1996). Many of the other products women traditionally produced at home gradually switched to factory manufacturing. The transition of America and Western Europe from agrarian societies to urban industrial societies took about 150 years. When the family was transformed from a unit of production to a unit of consumption, a dramatic shift occurred in attitudes and norms surrounding the work roles of women.

By the end of the nineteenth century, Victorian norms ascended to define middle class women as physically and mentally incapable of working in factory settings. The consequences of the myth of "feminine frailty" in the workplace that emerged during this era have not been eradicated. Among its negative effects, the myth created a class-based wedge between homemakers and women who either by choice or necessity worked outside the home. Different from the young women who had a semisequestered status during the Lowell era, later women factory workers were drawn from the ranks of recent immigrants, young girls from rural areas and mining towns who helped support their families, and widows with no other means of support (Stepenoff, 1999). Their high illiteracy rates and farm backgrounds planted the seeds for stereotypes linking poor women as capable only for the physical labor required in factories. When paid work was available, these women did have one competitive advantage: They were white. In times of work surplus but worker shortage, women of color were employable in factories at lower wages and less desirable jobs than white women. Except as domestic workers and restaurant help, paid employment for women of color remained limited. Men of color who migrated off farms into the rapidly growing urban areas were employable as unskilled laborers in construction, dockhands, and other jobs requiring arduous physical labor. White women still had the advantage in factory work, especially textile production, over men of color. Service jobs demanded by an industrializing economy were open for white women with some education. The latter were deemed less frail than the robust factory women, but both groups garnered public disapproval for roles that put them in the public sphere outside the home.

In the western migration woman were valued for their nondomestic work and also expected to engage in it. For those who were literally tied to the home with child-care responsibilities, "homework" was an option, especially among poor immigrants. Mostly consisting of piecework, it was dependent on the whims of bosses and swings of a seasonal market and encouraged the exploitation of its dominantly female workers (Daniels, 1993). The current ideology was that women's place was at home and, as exploitative as it was, "homework" allowed the ideology to be bolstered. However, most of these other groups, through necessity, were working outside the home. During the late nineteenth century the middle class homemaker was the enviable standard to which women aspired. Poor women who worked outside the home were often demonized as unfit mothers who were neglecting their families (Broder, 2002). The statuses of full-time homemaker and employed woman have shifted considerably over time, but as we have seen, it is the homemaker status that continues to serves as the standard by which women are judged.

War and Jobs. In the nineteenth century women were establishing control in several occupational categories, including nursing and elementary school teaching. Although women began to enter the teaching profession by the beginning of the nineteenth century, the Civil War transformed teaching from a male to female profession. Women were able to retain their teaching jobs after the war not only because of the shortage of men, but because they could be paid less than the men they replaced. Rather than celebrating the care ethic that women brought to the profession—one that contrasted sharply with the physical discipline and harshness of male teachers of the time—teaching swiftly became viewed as an extension of motherhood. Women's biological qualities offered an advantage that required no special skill base (Johnson and Reed, 2002). Historians of education trace the female takeover of teaching to the loss of pay and prestige that continue to plague the profession today (Edwards, 2002). Like teaching, clerical work was originally a male occupation. The invention of the typewriter in 1873 brought with it an increase in the number of clerical jobs and increase of female employment in those jobs. Between 1870 and 1900, the number of clerical jobs increased 8 times, whereas female employment increased 340 times, and by the late 1920s, over half of all clerical workers were female (Glenn and Feldberg, 1995). Also like teaching, as women increasingly took over the male clerical positions, there was a marked decrease in the status and wages of these positions.

The shortage of males in the labor force during the two World Wars again set the stage for the next wave of job opportunities open to women. During each war women replaced men in both factories and offices. World War I mainly reshuffled existing female workers into new areas rather than increasing overall participation rates and after the war women generally retreated back into their homes. As we saw in chapter 5, the situation was different after World War II. Women were expected to return to hearth and home, but large numbers did not. They did lose the more lucrative industrial jobs, but a new trend developed—married women began entering the labor force in greater numbers—a trend that heralded major repercussions for all areas of American society.

BALANCING MULTIPLE WORK AND FAMILY ROLES

Social change and the specialization of social functions that it brings inevitably create more role responsibilities for both men and women. Demographic changes account for many of these new or altered roles, such as increased numbers of dual-earner families, later marriages, fewer children, increased life expectancy, and geographic mobility shifting employees across a nation and across the globe. For example, men who marry later are bringing a greater range of domestic skills into their marriages than the previous generation of men. Increased life expectancy has created an active and healthy elderly population that is staying in the workplace longer and, especially among the poor, is taking on more child care responsibilities to aid their own children. The substantial increase of the oldest old, those age 80 years and older, however, are at heightened risk for dependence and needed caretaking. Job shifts that require a change of location for the family add to new role patterns in contemporary families. Whereas multiple roles are increasing for both genders, family responsibilities and unpaid work in the home remain fundamentally part of a woman's role configuration, regardless of whether she is a paid employee. But because the large majority of women are also wage earners, compared to men, their enactment of the multiple roles is substantially different.

Employment and Health

Paid employment is a major determinant of good physical and mental health for men and women. In the United States and other societies where people are socialized into a strong work ethic, satisfying work enhances health, life satisfaction, and well-being (Theorell, 2001). The impact of work is seen in Sigmund Freud's answer to the question of what "normal" people should do well. For Freud, it is "to love and to work." In other words, good psychological functioning emphasizes both one's work and one's family. The ideal is to create an environment where work and family are not opposed to one another.

Achieving this ideal is becoming more difficult, especially for women, whether in a dual-earner marriage or as a single parent. On one hand, a rewarding job in general and a rewarding career in particular has beneficial effects for women's overall well-being (Simon, 2000; Nelson and Burke, 2002). Work is not the brutal psychological jungle popularized in media accounts, and a rewarding career actually shields a woman against pressures encountered at home. Contrary to what we might expect, multiple roles that include marriage, children, and satisfying work are associated with better health, enhanced self-esteem, and lower rates of depression. A satisfying career is optimized when the marriage is egalitarian and domestic responsibilities are shared by one's spouse (Pugliesi, 1995; Mirowsky et al., 2000). Even with the multiple roles experienced by all marital categories of employed women, they are the healthiest and feel better about themselves than full-time homemakers (Barnett, 1997; MacDermid et al., 1997; Matthews and Powers, 2002). Balance at home and work is also important. When women perceive that their family and paid work roles offer opportunities for autonomy and increased decision making, well-being is enhanced (Sachs-Ericsson and Ciarlo, 2000; Griffin et al., 2002; Schieman, 2003). These studies support the "role accumulation" hypothesis, which highlights the positive outcome of occupying multiple roles for women.

On the other hand, the mental health advantages of multiple roles are fewer for women compared to men, in part because work and family hold different meanings for men and women (Gilbert and Rader, 2001). Women expect that their family roles will carry over to their jobs. Wives and new mothers have more role balance but experience more job stress compared to husbands and new fathers (Etaugh, 2001; Marks et al., 2001). The "role overload" hypothesis suggests that employment and the second shift work of family and child care roles put women into two full-time jobs, which may contribute to psychological problems (Steil, 1995; Hattery, 2001). Women with children in all marital and employment categories report more health problems than women without children. Traced in part to the financial vulnerability linked to the roles, the homemaker role by itself or the worker and single-parent roles in combination appear to be the most stressful and associated with poorer health (Lasswell, 2002; Nelson et al., 2002; Gabe, 2003). Role overload, finally, can be linked to the unique stressors women face in the workplace, including gender discrimination, sexual harassment and stereotyping (Shrier, 2002).

Caregiving

Evaluation of multiple work and family roles must also account for caregiving to other than one's own children. The second shift of a woman's unpaid work is rapidly turning into a third shift for many homemakers and employed women who must care for the elderly who are part of their lives. (Gerstel, 2000). A spouse is the first to provide care for his or her ailing partner. Because men become physically dependent and need extended care earlier in life than women, an elderly wife is much more likely to be the caregiver of her husband (Greenberg, 2001). The next level of responsibility falls to adult children. For the poorer elderly, the next level is the network of extended family and kin.

Although type of care and patterns of caregiving in families vary greatly, women are the primary caregivers to elderly parents, whether they are daughters or daughters-in-law (Abel, 2001). They have been called the **sandwich generation** because they are caught between caring for the older and younger generations at the same time. Many of these women are middle age, in the work force, and still have children at home. Love, commitment, and responsibility describe caregivers. Other words to describe caregiving are guilt, burden, depression, and strain. Assistance to the elderly produces higher levels of caregiver strain and work interference than when providing assistance to younger adults. The stress of the elder-care role for women is associated with compromises in both physical health and psychological well-being and is worsened for poor women who care for young children and parents with greater impairment at the same time (Stephens et al., 2001). Employed women report higher levels of job stress as their parents or grandparents become more and debilitated and when one elderly parent can no longer take care of the other. Time away from spouse and children can negatively affect their marriages, and guilt is produced when caregiving results in less affection to the parent. (Rossi, 2001; Shannon, 2001).

Yet caregiving also provides opportunities to grow together to explore reciprocal relationship needs of elderly parents and their adult children in their final years. Gratification and positive psychological outcomes, too, are reported by female caregivers (Moen et al., 1995; Bould, 2001).

Unpaid Work

Second and third shift work associated with household tasks and caregiving is unpaid work done primarily by women. Until recently economists have basically ignored the bulk of the productive work women perform because it is unpaid work (Beneria, 1998, 2001). All work makes an economic contribution, but the unpaid work activities related to the home have been marginalized in economic rendering of production. In addition to the goods and services provided by the unpaid work of women discussed earlier, economic contributions include managing household resources, creating and maintaining the future labor force (children), and serving as an auxiliary labor force. A mother's work "creates enormous material benefits" but receives no material recognition, such as Social Security (Crittenden, 2001). In the United States the estimated yearly cost at the going rate for services women provide for free—cooking, cleaning, shopping, child care, chauffeuring, repairing, psychological and therapeutic services, and sickness care—would cost $50,000. At the global level, if the work of women was added to the world's economy, it would expand by one-third (chapter 6).

Money and Mental Health. The better psychological health of an employed woman compared to a full-time homemaker is certainly associated with the income each receives. Dual-earning couples share spending decisions more equally than in singe-earner couples (Lindsey, 1996c). When the husband is the sole wage earner, those wages are distributed in a variety of ways. Some wives receive their husband's paychecks and determine how the money will be apportioned; other wives receive "allowances" from their husbands that go toward household expenses. Regardless of how they determine the way the money will be spent, she has not "earned" it in the same way he has.

This perception contributes to the burden of dependency experienced by many housewives. A husband's economic leverage in the household is conducive to his wife's dependency. To a great extent, his paycheck becomes the controlling factor in her life. Many women who do not work outside the home find themselves in conflict-ridden, psychologically debilitating marriages but see no alternative but to remain where they are. Financial and psychological dependency go hand in hand. On the other hand, family dynamics change when a wife brings a paycheck into the home or when she outearns her husband (Sefton, 2001). Husbands are often originally threatened by the earning capability of their wives but later may express relief that the financial burden of the household is now a joint responsibility.

Summary. Although it is complicated to sort out all these variables, we can conclude that multiple family and work roles are most beneficial for women emotionally, physically, and economically when they maintain a sense of autonomy in these roles, have shared decision making with their husbands, and perceive support in their homes by their partners or spouses and in their workplaces by their employers and coworkers (Erdwins et al., 2001; Greenglass, 2002). If these conditions are met, research on multiple roles points to the benefits associated with the role accumulation hypothesis rather than the liabilities associated with the role overload hypothesis.

GENDERED INSTITUTIONS IN CHOICE OF WORK

Societies (cultures) are organized via *social institutions* to ensure that social needs are met in predictable ways (chapter 3). Social institutions are highly interdependent. It is difficult to separate out the impact of the various institutions on gender roles as related to work because the interaction effects are both complicated and powerful. The focus here will be on the family and the economy, the latter of which includes waged work in the workplace. Economic effects reverberate throughout all the social institutions. Institutions are highly interdependent, but sociologists generally agree that the economy is the key catalyst for shaping changes experienced in all other social institutions.

The Impact of Family on Workplace

The transition from an agricultural to an industrialized economy profoundly altered the work roles of men and women and enlarged any existing gender gap between home and workplace. The outset of the transition for women led them from unpaid work on the farm to unpaid work in the family. Men were firmly established in their earner roles when women began to be tracked into the labor force in large numbers. These new female entrants quickly collided with cultural beliefs that viewed women disdainfully, suspiciously, or hostilely when they ventured out of their homes into paid employment. The instrumental-expressive schism that followed women into the workplace over a half century ago has not been eradicated.

Socialization. The family is the key force in gender socialization and primes children for later social roles, including the choices they make regarding work. The family can be further subdivided into two broad categories that differentially impact these choices. The first category, the **family of orientation**, is the family in which one grows up. In this first family a child gains a sense of self and a set of relative benefits based on the *social capital* the family offers to a child, such as material resources, housing, and education. Social capital is translated into opportunity structures for children. Because parents may be unable or unwilling to provide the same opportunity structures for all their children, social capital for boys is leveraged differently than social capital for girls. As discussed in chapter 3, children receive gendered messages from parents related to, among others, clothing, toys, chores, dating, autonomy, and education. Children match these messages to attitudes about later job options. When fathers talk to their sons about the joys of caring for others and mothers talk to their daughters about the wonders of discovery and then actually see their dad as a preschool teacher or nurse and their mom as an engineer or scientist, then the seeds are planted for their children to select these job options.

The trend toward egalitarian marriages is challenging the gender messages children receive in the family of orientation that limit their horizons about the work they will pursue in later life. Despite widespread messages about egalitarian gender roles, however, other agents of socialization counter them. The reality is that messages for girls continue to be focused on home and family taking precedence over paid work and for boys that paid work takes precedence over family. Because most contemporary young women desire a combination of family and career roles, the message that they hear is how to juggle, balance, and deal with these roles. Young men also expect to carry out both sets of roles, but they do not receive the "juggling" message received by young women. Their message is not how they will balance family and work but how they will pay for family through work.

The second category, the **family of procreation**, is the family established when one marries or establishes a long-term partnership. Because each partner brings a unique set of socialization experiences to this family and each has already lived through a generation of social change, this second family is more directly influenced by broader sociocultural factors regarding gender. When children arrive, both men and women face a new set of family contingencies that impacts roles in and out of the home. The family of procreation focuses on *continuing socialization*, as first time parents learn the requisite skills in their struggle with the demands of raising children. There is little preparation for these roles, so the process appears to be one of trial and error, all the time influenced by the gender models of the family of orientation. Parents must reconcile personal desires for fulfillment and economic obligations to maintain the home, decisions that impact their children's quality of life. Although these factors impact parents' work-related issues, men do not do not have to face the struggle to "be employed or not be employed" as women do. Most partners opt for a dual-earning status before children arrive, and most women continue some level of paid work after they arrive. These decisions not only affect what happens to home based roles, but also what happens to work roles.

The Child Care Crisis. Although the dual-earner family is the American norm, there is research agreement that higher educational attainment for women and husbands who are supportive of their wives' employment are significantly more likely to have wives working outside the home, and these homes are likely to be child centered and egalitarian in both structure and function (see chapter 7 and chapter 8). Yet even in egalitarian marriages, wives spend significantly more time on child care and household tasks than husbands (Coltrane, 2003). The U.S. Bureau of the Census (2004) shows that almost two-thirds of all married women with children under the age of 6 are in the labor force. Wives also take the lead in organizing child care arrangements for preschoolers and after school activities for older children. When a child is sick, when there is an unexpected early dismissal from school, or when a day care crisis arises, women are much more likely than men to accommodate their job schedule to resolve the problem. It is the child care issue that is of overriding importance in determining when and if a woman returns to paid work after the birth of her child. The United States is in a continuing child care crisis that is only minimally addressed in public policy.

Increased demands for child care come at a time when the supply of domestic help is shrinking, grandmothers (probable caretakers) are returning to the labor force, state budgets offering subsidized child care vouchers have been slashed, and funding for preschool and after school programs parents rely on heavily have been eliminated or, if retained, are made unaffordable. As more women with young children are joining the labor force, both out of desire and need, the child care crisis must be addressed. This problem looms larger for single parents or women receiving public assistance who are required to work or be in work training programs to preserve benefits. It is an issue that affects all working women and their families, regardless of ability to pay for adequate care. Child care issues have a major spillover effect on the career achievement of women. As one professional woman reports, five moves in six months with three children and her husband away on business trips left her with little choice but to put her career on hold until her children were older (Samuels, 1999:10).

> . . . I started thinking about the space in my life where work used to fit . . . I felt like my son does digging on a beach . . . the incoming tide always brings sand, filling the opening as quickly as he can excavate. For me the reservoir is the opportunity to work, while the tide is my family and life, filling the space as quickly as I can dig.

Married with Children: The Demography of Career Achievement. Career achievement is also impacted by a host of other family related variables including martial status, age at marriage, age at childbirth, and professional status when married. Women who marry after they have completed their education and began to ascend a career ladder bring more resources to their marriages and reduce the likelihood that their husbands expect them to give up their careers. Smaller family size and age of children also correlate with paid employment. The percentage of employed mothers decreases rapidly for families with five children or more and with at least two children under age 6. Compared to single women, married women have higher rates of interrupted job mobility—often to accommodate a career move for their husbands. These rates increase significantly for married women with children who stall careers or forgo them altogether to raise children. Both groups of married women are likely to return to paid employment, but in less satisfying work situations and lower paying jobs, rather than more satisfying and higher paying careers.

Opportunity structures in families encouraging a daughter's education have high payoffs in the workplace. The more education a woman has attained, the greater the likelihood that she will engage in paid employment. Conversely, the lower the educational attainment, the more likely a woman is a full-time homemaker. This pattern challenges the myth that those who have the choice would prefer exclusive domestic roles. By virtue of her education, she is the least likely to be financially dependent and the most likely to work outside the home. The combined impact of low education and a full-time homemaker role can have devastating financial consequences in the event of divorce or death of a spouse. Research on women who in the 1950s followed the "June Cleaver" stay-at-home model of marriage and motherhood with financial dependence on their husbands or sporadic work in low-paid jobs offering few benefits finds a significant number of them living in poverty or near poverty conditions in their retirement years (Olson, 2003).

Career versus Job. Although all employed women have *jobs*, they do not necessarily have meaningful *careers*. Jobs interfere with family in a different way than careers (Blair-Loy, 2003). A career orientation is associated with men and women in the professions who have a high degree of commitment, personal sacrifice, and a planned developmental sequence (career path). In addition to the family factors noted earlier, career orientation for married women is compromised when a wife's career is viewed as less important than her husband's career. For example, she will relocate for his career ascendance but his relocation for hers is unlikely. When he outearns her—a high likelihood in dual career couples—his career takes on more importance and will be nurtured to gain higher income returns.

The success stories of women who "have it all"—great marriages, wonderful children, rewarding careers—are replete. Women are in a second wave of progress, moving up the corporate ladder or advancing through their own business enterprises. They have found ways to favorably reconcile problems between career and family, such as purchasing services allowing for career mobility, telecommuting from home, or finding employment offering flexible work time (Wharton, 1994; Duncan et al., 1999; Rosen and Korabik, 2002). These women, however, are the exception to the rule. The rule is that women may combine work (jobs) and marriage successfully, but they are severely compromised in their quest for career ascendance by marital and family obligations and traditional beliefs about his breadwinning role compared to hers. Their careers are either put on hold, change directions, or abruptly end.

Employers are well aware of these trends. Highly educated women have greater leverage in the workplace because they are viewed as having higher commitment to their jobs. It is illegal for employers to overtly use marital status or age of children in hiring, but such decisions are routinely made covertly. Even married women with children who are in professional careers are often considered a liability because employers believe they will favor family over workplace when the inevitable juggling act occurs. For women, marriage may send a signal that she has a different set of priorities. As sexist as it is, an employer often interprets marriage and children as making a woman less reliable, dedicated, and permanent. Postponing children increases lifetime earnings for women. A key consequence of family related factors on career is that a single break in employment has immediate, adverse effects, which translates to lower wages and job status (Fermlee, 1995; Hewlett, 2002). Women in management, for example, are often tracked into two distinct groups: those with a career and family and those with only a career. The former may be "mommy track" women who will not be subject to the same set of demands as other career-only corporate women (Spiller, 1993). Businesses justify this track by arguing that their investment in women managers is lost when careers are interrupted by family concerns. When they return to the corporate world, the dues they pay go beyond catching up on seniority or retooling their skill base. They are treated virtually as beginners. For those who scale back even one day a week, that one day keeps them behind in their careers in terms of salary, title, and responsibility (Jacobs, 1994). For women planning to "have it all," timing is everything (Hudson, 2003:C3).

Married men, on the other hand, are considered more of an asset if they are married with children. Employers view a man as more stable and committed to his job and job location if he has children in school and he and his family are involved in a range of community-based activities and organizations. From an employer view, another important criterion in judging the potential for the success of his male employee is that that he has "wifely support" for demanding work roles. The vast majority of the top corporate executives in the United States are not only married men but also have

> stay-at-home wives ever ready to journey with them and be at their sides in public. (For) corporate executives . . . she planned the dinner parties, kept house in fitting style and . . . kept pace with his rising social requirements. The duties of running a corporation are so varied and relentless that no rational man tries them solo if he can split them with a wife. (Walsh, 2001:3)

A reading of these trends may make it appear that an employer is justified about hiring preferences for married men with children over married women with or without children. Often overlooked factors, however, are that there are no significant gender differences in job commitment, loyalty to firm, leadership effectiveness, and most important, number of jobs over time held by professional men and women (Vanewater and Stewart, 1997; Powell and Graves, 2003; U.S. Bureau of the Census, 2004). Any reading of the demographics of career achievement needs to account for the gender stereotypes that lurk behind differential hiring practices and promotion for men and women.

Economic Trends and the Family

Economic trends filtering down to the family reinforce the employment choices of men and women. Women are welcomed into the labor force during times of need, such as war, during periods of economic growth, such as the Industrial Revolution, and in transitions to new economic forms, such as the shift from advanced machine technology in a manufacturing economy to the information technology demanded in a knowledge based service economy. During these times women function as a reserve labor pool to be called on or discarded as needs change. Therefore, women could not rely on stable employment. Today's postindustrial era, however, requires workers with an education and skill base women are now more likely to possess. In this sense, women are catching up to men in opportunities for more stable employment.

Postindustrial societies are also unprecedented in their consumption orientation and target services and products to market niches based on household characteristics. The United States is a consumer society and the majority of consumption is done by women as they carry out their family roles related to daily household spending. Employed women have less time but more money available for consumption; the American economic system has responded to this reality. The retailing sector, in particular, caters to employed women by lengthening times they are open, by locating near homes and new housing developments, through the use of mail catalogs, and increasingly, through the Web marketplace. Although the family exerts counterpressures for women in these consumer roles, they emerge overall in a position of strength. The resources offered by stable employment combined with the traditional role of overseeing the daily household spending, make employed women a formable economic force. Conflict theorists suggest that these combined roles offer them advantages that translate to more power in their families and the workplace.

The Legal System

Propelled by the equality goals of the women's movement and minority rights movement, an array of legal and political decisions have had a major impact on gender patterns of employment and women's work roles. Discussed in detail in chapter 14, the following is an overview of some of these key legislative actions. The Equal Pay Act (EPA), passed in 1963, is the first federal legislation that addressed the issue of equal pay for men and women. It allows for differences in pay based only on a nondiscriminatory seniority system, a merit-based system, or "piecework" basis. Although originally designed with minority men in mind, the most important legal prohibition against gender discrimination in employment is **Title VII of the 1964 Civil Rights Act**. Although the language is not gender neutral, the following two key provisions impacting women make discrimination and occupational segregation illegal.

1. To fail or refuse to hire or to discharge any individual, or otherwise discriminate against any individual with respect to his compensation, terms, conditions, or privileges of employment, because of such individual's race, color, religion, sex or national origin; or
2. To limit, segregate, or classify his employees in any way which would deprive or tend to deprive any individual of employment opportunities or otherwise adversely affect his status as an employee, because of such individual's race, color, religion, sex or national origin. (Civil Rights Act of 1964)

In 1972 Executive Orders extended the provisions of the Civil Rights Act legislation to all federal contracts. Title IX of the 1972 Educational Amendments further extended them to all educational programs or activities receiving federal funding. EPA and Title VII of the Civil Rights Act have allowed the "equal work for equal pay" doctrine to resound throughout the American economy, and it is difficult to formally circumvent them. However, both laws are vulnerable to the gendering of occupations and the informal systems that evolve in the workplace.

Recognizing the realities of a continuing gender and race wage gap, the legal approach was altered from simply barring discrimination to preferential treatment through **affirmative action** to women and minorities underrepresented in certain job categories. Affirmative action has had more positive effects for women entering professions (although not for women already there) and management positions. However, with the decline in skilled trade jobs and the limited number of women in these and other blue-collar categories, most employed women have not benefited from the job integration policy. The positive effect of affirmative action has not reached the bulk of women who work in lower level jobs and has not redressed continuing wage inequalities that still exist 40 years after these critical legislative efforts (Badgett and Lim, 2001; Wolf-Devine, 2002). And as we will see in chapter 14, because affirmative action is intimately but erroneously linked in the public eye with quotas and reverse discrimination, it is on the political chopping block and may not survive in a viable form.

    Comparable worth is another strategy that carves a rocky path through legislative and judicial processes, and like affirmative action, the evidence is mixed in terms of its success (Hattiangadi, 2000). Comparable worth aims to upgrade the wage scales for jobs that employ large numbers of women. Because comparable worth arguments were successfully used in Washington and California when it was documented that women received far less pay in comparable jobs, such as police and fire dispatching, most states have taken some legislative action to deal with broadly based pay inequity.

    The judicial thrust has been generally the same as the legislative by emphasizing that employers cannot discriminate on the basis of gender if a woman meets the necessary qualifications. Working with the Equal Employment Opportunity Commission (EEOC), the judiciary oversees the thousands of gender discrimination cases that have arisen since the 1960s. A landmark case demonstrates the importance of these actions. The 1971 unanimous Supreme Court decision in *Reed v. Reed* ruled that an Idaho law giving males preference over females in selecting administrators of an estate was in violation of the Fourteenth Amendment. This was the first time the Court ruled that an arbitrary discrimination law against women was unconstitutional.

    Political and legal mandates have helped remove barriers that unfairly limit or circumscribe women's potential employment choices. They cannot focus on the individual decision-making process that is viewed as the personal province of a woman and her family. However, the atmosphere has changed considerably over the years and should be expected to continue changing. The advocacy of the 1970s has given way to the entrenchment of the 1980s and the backlash of the 1990s. A renewed commitment to fairness is needed to take the earlier accomplishments into the twenty-first century.

WOMEN IN THE LABOR FORCE

The most important economic trend in the twentieth century was the dramatic and consistent increase in the labor force participation of all categories of women (Table 10.1). Over 60 percent of all women 16 years and over are in the labor force, and the participation rate of married women with children has tripled since 1960. Female single parents (single, divorced, separated, or widowed) participate in even greater proportions: over 75 percent in 2003, up from 64 percent just since 1965. Women are more likely than men to be working part time (under 35 hours per week), and many of these women are in the single-parent ranks. The percent of middle age (45–64) college-educated women in their peak earnings years has gradually

Table 10.1 Characteristics of Women in the Labor Force, Selected Years.

Status	1970	1975	1980	1985	1990	1995	2002
Total employed women 16+	43.3	46.3	51.5	54.5	57.5	58.9	59.6
Total unemployed women 16+	5.9	9.3	7.4	7.4	6.4	5.6	5.6
Total employed men 16+	79.7	77.9	77.4	76.3	76.1	76.7	74.1
Total unemployed men 16+	4.4	7.9	6.9	7.0	5.6	5.6	5.9
Female employment by age							
16 to 19	44.0	49.1	52.9	52.1	51.8	52.2	51.3[b]
20 to 24	57.5	64.1	68.9	71.8	71.6	70.3	73.3[b]
25 to 34	45.0	54.9	65.5	70.9	73.6	74.9	76.3[b]
35 to 44	51.1	55.8	65.5	71.8	76.5	77.2	77.3[b]
45 to 54	54.4	54.6	59.9	64.4	71.2	74.4	76.8[b]
55 to 64	43.0	40.9	41.3	42.0	45.3	49.2	51.8[b]
65+	9.7	8.2	8.1	7.3	8.7	8.8	9.4[b]
Female employment by marital status							
Single	56.8	59.8	64.4	66.6	66.9	66.7[a]	69.0[b]
Married with spouse	40.5	44.3	49.8	52.8	58.4	60.7[a]	61.3[b]
Other	40.3	40.1	43.6	45.1	47.2	47.5[a]	49.4[b]

[a]1994 data
[b]2000 data

Sources: U.S. Census Bureau, *Statistical Abstract of the United States*, 1991, 1995, 1998, 2001; *Employment and Earnings*. Bureau of Labor Statistics, Employment status annual averages household data, 2003.

increased since 1970 and shows a record of stable employment but lower earnings than men with comparable education. As women's paid work has increased, the U.S. Bureau of the Census (2004) shows men's labor force participation consistently declining, from a high of about 87 percent in 1947 to 74.7 percent in 2000 and projected to decrease another 1 percent by 2008. If these trends continue, the proportion of women in the labor force will approach that of men.

Gender-Typing in Occupational Distribution

As would be expected, women are not equally distributed throughout the occupational structure. Although women make up almost half of top-level managerial and professional occupations and require requisite educational credentials even at the entry level, the jobs they hold are occupationally segregated. For example, the professional category includes accountants, architects, and engineers, who are mostly male, and teachers, nurses, and social workers, who are mostly female. Although all these occupations require high levels of education, the female occupations are far lower in degree of pay, prestige, authority, and other job-related reward criteria.

Occupational segregation by gender bolsters **gender-typing**—when the majority of the occupation are those of one gender, it becomes a normative expectation and in turn the job is associated with less pay and prestige. Sometimes referred to as the "devaluation thesis," gender-typing translates to a wage penalty for people working in occupations that are dominated by females (England et al., 2000). Gender-typing extends to the way a job is perceived. Nursing, social work, and teaching are "engendered" as feminine professions linked with caring and nurturing. Nursing, in particular, is attempting to increase its professional status by challenging the jurisdictional boundaries that have been determined by physicians (Manley, 1995). As a female-dominated profession, nursing, until recently, has been in virtual servitude to the male-dominated profession of medicine. Upgrading the profession as a whole has challenged both the gender based and occupationally based hierarchy of medicine and health care.

These professions provide other illustrative examples of what happens when men enter predominately female occupations. In tracing the trajectories of males in female-dominated occupations, although men face some disadvantages, they have more advantages than women in these jobs. In such jobs males are likely to hold the higher positions. They differentiate themselves from the devalued female work they do by dominating "that which is female." Males who cross over into nursing, social work, elementary school teaching, and librarianship face some prejudice from those outside the professions, but have clear advantages inside them. Both men and women employed in nontraditional occupations (as defined by gender), face discrimination, but the forms and consequences are different for males in female professions than the reverse. Both genders perceive that men are given fair, even preferential, treatment in hiring and promotion, are accepted by supervisors and colleagues, and are integrated into the subculture of the workplace. The subtle mechanisms that enhance a man's position in these professions are referred to as the *glass escalator effect.* (Williams, 2003). Men take their gender privileges with them to female occupations and experience upward mobility as a result. Thus even when the occupation is designated female, most women are subordinate to males who hold the most powerful supervisory and high-paying positions. This phenomenon is referred to as *hierarchical segregation* and is a strategy that further prevents women from earning equal pay and/or exercising equal power with males.

Women in the Professions. Women have significantly increased their numbers in the elite professions such as law, medicine, and university teaching. About one-third of physicians and lawyers and one-half of college professors are women, and it is expected that women will represent half of these professions within the next decade. Although these gains are impressive, gender-typing is pervasive. Women are clustered in the overcrowded, less prestigious specialties that are considered more appropriate for women in male-dominated professions (Bagilhole, 2002). In medicine, for example, women constitute large proportions of pediatricians, psychiatrists, and public health physicians. Female lawyers are more likely to specialize in domestic law rather than more lucrative corporate law, and despite enrollment of women in top law schools at 40 percent in 1985 and over 50 percent at the millennium, only 15 percent have attained law partnerships (Catalyst, 2002). Women engineers make up only 10 percent of the total, and they are more likely to specialize in chemical and environmental engineering and work in manufacturing and less likely to be aerospace and civil engineering and work in consulting or service firms. The salaries of women in all science and engineering fields are lower than their male counterparts with similar levels of experience. The dramatic increase of women throughout professional and managerial jobs is impressive, but as long as they are excluded from networks offering the highest career mobility, they remain marginal and invisible (Kaufman, 1995:302). The overall result of these trends for professional women is less pay, less, prestige, and less authority.

White Collar Women. Within white collar occupations, women are clustered in clerical and retail sales positions. Office jobs in particular exhibit strong patterns of gender-typing that are hierarchically arranged. There are three separate groups: the female clerical staff (secretaries and data entry clerks), the male managerial staff (vice-presidents, sales and product managers), and the mixed-gender technical staff (computer programmers and systems analysts). Clerical is a female hierarchy, consisting of lower level "pink collar" jobs, but where the highest-level female supervisor reports to a male superior. Management is a male hierarchy with some lower-level female supervisors. Technical has lower-ranked jobs filled by both men and women but higher-ranked jobs are almost exclusively men (Glenn and Feldberg, 1995:264).

Blue Collar Women. Women are most underrepresented in blue collar, transportation, and nonfarm labor areas. Barriers have been legally lifted for women to pursue the skilled, elite blue collar trades to become plumbers, electricians, machinists, carpenters, and craftspeople. However, they have not done so to any great degree. For those women who do enter the skilled trades, they remain in the female-dominant ones, such as dressmaker and electronic equipment assemblers. The resistance to women in the blue collar trades remains strong. Even among lower level semiskilled operative jobs, which can be learned quickly, women are underrepresented in those that are unionized. They have made their greatest strides in public sector operative jobs such as letter carrier and bus driver, where their numbers have doubled since 1980. But they are virtually invisible in the higher paying skilled trades. Over 90 percent of precision production, craft, and repair occupations are held by men (Spraggins, 2003). The majority of women who hold blue collar jobs perform those that require few skills, have poor working conditions, have high fluctuations in employment, and command low pay. In the hierarchy of the lower level blue collar jobs (as distinct from the elite trades), men still receive more job-related rewards than women (Hesse-Biber and Carter, 2000; Byrd, 2001).

Gender-typing of occupations is an integral part of the U.S. economic system, though it violates one of capitalism's basic premises—obtaining the best person for the particular job—especially as it acts to limit or channel women's choice of jobs. Gender-typing links occupational roles with gender roles and tends to designate female occupations, such as nursing and social work, as those involving nurturing, helping, and high levels of empathy. Conversely, occupations associated with detachment, leadership, and outspokenness, like medicine and politics, are designated as masculine. Although gender-typing is generally universal throughout the occupations, some jobs have changed their gender distribution, such as pharmacy and realty, and are now female dominated. And we have already seen that teaching and secretarial work were transformed from male to female. These patterns are important in countering the argument that gender-typing is based on the "naturalness" of one gender or another being suited for a given occupation.

The Wage Gap

As measured by median annual earnings of full-time employees, women earn less than men, a global pattern that holds across all racial and ethnic groups and throughout occupations. The United States and Canada have the highest wage gap (about 75 percent) and the Scandinavian countries the lowest (between 80 and

90 percent), with Iceland the lowest, at a remarkable 94 percent (United Nations Development Program, 2004). The wage gap has profound consequences. If both men and women were paid equally more than half of low income households in the United States would be lifted over the poverty line.

The gender wage gap has been a persistent economic fact in the United States since records have been available. When factoring in race, although white women earn slightly more on the average than women of color, men of all races still out earn women (Center for Policy Alternatives, 2002; Hicks, 2002; U.S. Bureau of the Census, 2004). The gender gap in earnings also continues to hold when age, occupation, seniority, and region are added to the picture (CPS, 2001; SBA, 2001; Spraggins, 2001). The strong emphasis that Americans put on talent and achievement to pay off in the workplace cannot explain why at all educational levels males still outearn females and why the gap generally increases at the higher educational levels. In 2000, male college graduates on the average earned $25,855 more than female college graduates (Lindsey and Beach, 2004:53). The wage gap inherited early in a woman's life on the job follows her into retirement. For full-time employed women approaching retirement age, the gender gap in pension wealth is huge. Median pension wealth is over three-fourths greater for men than women, a situation contributing to poverty of women at old age (Johnson et al., 1999).

With some historical exceptions, the wage gap has gradually narrowed over time in the United States. In the last century those exceptions were the Depression, World War II, and periods of economic recession that hit women harder than men. Between 1967 and 1974, for example, the gap widened from 62 percent to less than 61 percent. In 1980 a woman employed full time earned about 65 cents for every dollar a man employed full time earned; that figure now hovers at 75 cents. Although the narrowing of the wage gap by 10 cents may be a sign of progress, the bad news is that women's relative gains came largely because men are earning less (Boushey, 2001; Nussbaum, 2002).

In addition to the effects of gender-typing through occupational segregation, sociological explanations for the wage gap center on the gender link to cultural and economic features unique to the United States.

Triple Jeopardy: Gender, Race, and Social Class. Occupational distribution of minority women reflects changes in the labor force as well as gender inequality. After World War II, large numbers of African American women moved into government white collar and clerical jobs and the lowest level private sector jobs, such as data entry or filing clerks. Wage levels of minority women are less that those of men of the same group. African American, Asian American, and white women earn two-thirds to four-fifths of what men earn, with the greatest disparity occurring between white men and white women. Rooted in a tradition valuing economic opportunities for women, African American middle class women moved into the professions earlier than white women. Like white women, they are steered into traditionally female occupations, but they have an added race liability. Concentrated in the public sector, such as teaching and social work, there is less discrimination but also less pay (Higginbotham, 2002). Although white women are also segregated in female-dominated professions, they are represented throughout the private sector where pay is higher.

The Human Capital Model. Capitalism is played out in the United States according to strongly held economic convictions related to the **human capital model**. According to this view, the gender gap in wages is due to personal, individual choices in matters of education, childbirth and childrearing decisions, and occupation. If women choose to interrupt schooling or careers for marriage and family reasons, experience and productivity are compromised and wages are lower. In support of this model, because women now demonstrate less discontinuous work patterns than in the past, their wages have increased, and the wage gap is decreased (Metz et al., 2001; Mennino and Brayfield, 2002). In addition, the human capital model is consistent with the law of supply and demand. Women can be paid less because they choose occupations and work schedules, such as part-time employment, offering more flexibility that make fewer demands on their family responsibilities (Aronson, 1999; Gutner, 2002). In this supply side argument, these are the very jobs that have an abundance of workers who can be paid less (Tam, 1997). If there is artificial intervention to make jobs equitable in terms of wages, such as setting quotas for certain jobs for men and women, the law of supply and demand will be violated (Becker, 1994). The human capital model is consistent with functionalism in its argument that interventions will risk economic equilibrium in a social system founded on capitalism and will therefore do more harm than good.

Symbolic Interaction and Conflict Theory. These two sociological theories in combination offer good explanations for the wage gap and center on two factors: the power relationships between men and women in all work settings and definitions of masculinity and femininity that are carried into the workplace. Their combined view suggests that men exercise power in the workplace to maintain their wage advantage. A good example is a protégé system, in which an already powerful member serves as a sponsor for entry and upward movement of a novice. An effective "old boy system" keeps power in the hands of a few men. This system also operates on norms that support cultural notions of masculinity and femininity that often bar women from meaningful participation in informal work groups. Women will not be accepted if they are "too masculine" but are taken less seriously if they are "too feminine." Mentors and role models are essential for upward corporate mobility (Reeves, 2000; Bannerjee, 2001; Mattis, 2001). Until women's networks include people of high rank, the corporate advancement of women will be stalled.

Summary. Although there are merits to each of these explanations, there is broad consensus that the gender gap is clearly linked to three factors:

1. The work women do, regardless of content, skill, or functional necessity, is less valued overall than the work men do.
2. The higher the number of women in the occupation, the lower the wages; the converse is true for male-dominated occupations. One-third of the wage gap is correlated with gender segregation.
3. Regardless of the law, gender discrimination in the workplace endures.

Research concludes that men are paid more than women for what they do largely because they are men (Burt, 1998; England et al., 2000; Hesse-Biber, 2000). Women's patterns of employment are different from men's, but for equal work there is not equal pay.

Corporate Women

As women have increased their rate of labor force participation, they are also bringing in the education and expertise that make them excellent prospects for management level positions. Education and expertise brought by women to their careers have translated to two important but paradoxical trends. They are steadily increasing their share of management positions in corporations, and they are starting their own businesses at record levels. Understanding how gender plays out at the corporate level helps explain these seemingly opposing trends.

Corporate Barriers. Women have made great strides in corporate advancements to middle management positions, but have stalled in their ascendance to upper management. To increase female representation in upper management in the 1980s many businesses originally adopted a strategy in the addition of one woman to their corporate board of directors (Kesner, 1988). But because the vast majority of business promotion ladders were, and still are, gender segregated, there were few women to draw from. In tracking gender patterns on corporate boards for the last 25 years, women's representation has shown very little improvement. Today only 4.5 percent of corporate officers of the most powerful *Fortune 500* companies are women, up from 4.3 percent a decade ago. In viewing research on these trends, the Feminist Research Center (2000) states that "the rate of increase has been so slow that parity with men on corporate boards will not be achieved until the year 2116."

The Glass Ceiling. Studies conclude that for women at all ranks, but particularly women managers, many barriers to upward mobility exist, including role conflict, gender stereotypes, lack of mentors, insufficient feedback and training, and isolation. Under Title VII of the 1964 Civil Rights Act, sexual harassment in the workplace is also illegal, but women throughout corporate America report that it continues to be pervasive. Issues of double standards of competence and isolation from powerful networks remain a thorn in the side for corporate women. For example, high echelon professional women in many occupations are likely to be judged differently than men in terms of their work performance, even when all characteristics except gender are the same (Steinpreis, 1999; Foschi, 2000). Others report that they are denied entrance into the informal networks that allow them to understand the intricacies of the power structure that are the keys to corporate survival. Encouraged to specialize in a small area of the corporate enterprise, women find themselves in networks that lack diversity and control and are removed from understanding the broader workings of the system. With job functions also specialized via gender, a kind of corporate purdah emerges (Lindsey, 1992).

Women continue to report gender discrimination as the most frequent barrier to their advancement, a pattern found in the United States, Britain, and Australia (Stewart, 1998; Liff and Ward, 2001; Metz and Tharenou, 2001). In the elite ranks of some of the most powerful companies, regardless of legal prohibitions, "old style" gender bias emerges that effectively thwarts a woman's move up the corporate ladder (Antilla, 1995).

Many of these patterns converge in a pattern now commonly referred to as the **glass ceiling**, describing women's failure to rise to senior level positions because of invisible and artificial barriers constructed by male management. Although lateral movement is possible, women are not able to advance hierarchically. It may be unintentional, but executives hire and promote by the "white male model" and image their recruits in terms of this ideal standard (Stuart, 1992; Wirth, 2001). All women, all men of color, and many men who do not display the aggressiveness also associated with this model cannot measure up. Whether the gender discrimination inherent in the glass ceiling is intentional or not, the effect is the same: Women are excluded from the ranks of upper management.

Toward Corporate Success. In cooperation with private enterprise, the federal government initiated a number of programs to counter the glass ceiling and provide incentives for businesses to encourage the upward track and thwart the mommy track agenda imposed on corporate women. Many programs focus on offering flexibility for women who are juggling career and family responsibilities. These family friendly policies have also benefited men who may apply for leave or flexible work schedules on the same basis as women (Kelly, 1999; Mennino and Brayfield, 2002).

These initiatives are laudable, but there are criticisms. They appear to be more beneficial for women moving from middle to upper management in companies that are already female friendly or who offer products and services geared to a female market. They may also be in the nation's top 1,000 companies but not in the golden *Fortune 500*. And perhaps more important, they discount the experiences of high level women, single or married, with or without children, who followed their career path as passionately, competitively, and diligently as comparable corporate men but still could not crack the glass ceiling. This suggests that unless the "old style" gender bias mentioned earlier is explicitly targeted, not only will barriers to advancement remain, but qualified women will also desert the ranks of corporations to go out on their own.

Women as Business Owners

And indeed, they are going out on their own. Entrepreneurial women find small business formation an alternative to management positions in large organizations. Research consistently demonstrates that the number one reason women desert corporations is that they are denied access to the higher level management positions and the decision-making power they believe they fully deserved (Rosener, 1995; Korn/Ferry International, 2002). If they cannot achieve a larger role in running a company they will start their own company. Five times more women started small businesses in the 1990s compared to men. Women owned sole proprietorships are increasing at triple the rate of those owned by men; more than four-fifths of all women-owned businesses are sole proprietorships, and of all sole proprietorships, 37 percent are operated by women (SBA, 2001).

The businesses women own may be grouped into two general categories. The first is a business enterprise developed around traditional areas of female work, such as services and retail trades. For example, women have businesses that do housecleaning, catering, closet organizing, and child care or they have small boutiques and stores offering specialty items and household products geared to women. They are situated in peripheral economic niches that do not seriously compete with more powerful small companies owned by men. Women tend to be in competition more with other women in similar businesses than men. Women-owned businesses also tend to be concentrated in industries with low-volume sales that lack access to capital and government contracts and that are often in need of more management expertise. Similar to others who are self-employed, she is less likely to have health insurance. However, women view these small businesses as a way to be creative, gain autonomy and flexibility, and balance career with family responsibilities. They put in longer hours but express enjoyment of their work. They are associated with high commitments of time and energy, but also with a great deal of personal satisfaction (Jones, 2000; Pollak, 2001; Bond, 2003).

A second category of women as business owners is comprised of those who encountered the glass ceiling as middle managers and jumped into their own businesses before their corporate clock ran out—those who astutely recognized the amount of career time needed to successfully build a new business. They are the stockbrokers, banking executives, and financial mangers who capitalize on the expertise, insights, and corporate experiences gained from their previous employer. The message that this group of women in sending is that companies will ultimately lose if they continue to limit the talent and ambition of their female employees. If women leave a company to start their own businesses or jump to another company, former employees will be competitors. As one female executive of a top global assets management firm suggests to women who feel thwarted in job advancement,

> If you're at a firm that's not interested in creating a culture where you can grow, cut out of there fast . . . find a place that wants you. (Ligos, 2001)

Corporate America is now accounting for the research confirming that the loss of female talent is bad for business. There is a definite trend heralding a strong career commitment for women. But their commitment and loyalty to their companies are compromised in a climate that continues to define and rank them according to their domestic rather than occupational roles and is suspicious of women who choose to do otherwise. Overall, the cultural stereotyping of women remains a formidable barrier.

Companies are also acknowledging that profit and diversity go hand in hand. As one executive suggests, "Boards are not social agencies, and it is not their job to create cultural diversity." But it is their job to create profit for shareholders, and diverse boards generate higher returns (Biggins, 1999). As a result, companies are now more enthusiastic about seeking ways to shatter the glass ceiling and retain rather than thwart the upward mobility of their female executives (Abelson, 1999; Kelly, 1999; Meyerson and Fletcher, 2000). In the organizational sense, the term *male corporate America* is redundant. Diversity is no longer a choice but a necessity for companies to be successful. It remains to be seen, however, if corporate women will gain parity with men—before 2116.

Gendered Management Styles: The Partnership Alternative

Despite past barriers to success, some research now suggests that a woman's socialization pattern may offer an advantage to modern corporations. In sharp contrast to the traditional corporate hierarchy, women tend to develop "weblike" leadership structures, relying on skills and attitudes valuable to a workplace in which innovation and creativity are demanded but where an authoritarian chain of command is obsolete (Helgesen, 1990:37). The woman's web extends to roles outside the corporation. Women bring interpersonal skills gained outside the organization back into the organization. They tend to form friendships in their workplace that extend outside the workplace and endure even after leaving a job. In contrast, men give up significant parts of their private lives for corporate success in traditional business hierarchies, a situation detrimental to themselves, their families, and their employers (Gerstel and McGonagle, 1999; Faludi, 2000). For companies more receptive to alternative visions of corporate life, the distinctive management styles of women are encouraged. Women managers tend to adopt styles compatible with overall gender socialization patterns of females, such as encouraging participation, mentoring, sharing power and information, and interacting with all levels of employees.

These are the very patterns that traditionally have been the hallmark of Japanese Style Management (JSM). JSM encourages a sense of community in the firms in which employees work, an interest in employees' lives outside the office, consensus building, socioemotional bonding between employees and between management and labor, and a flattened management structure that is more egalitarian than hierarchical (Ohtsu, 2002). Principles of JSM are compatible with American gender role socialization patterns for females (Lindsey, 1992, 1998). JSM also fits with partnership models emerging in innovative corporations that emphasize linking rather than ranking, interactive and participative leadership styles, teamwork, and sharing (Eisler and Loye, 1990; Graham, 2003).

Critique. Partnership models appear to work best in smaller firms or where collaboration on projects is necessary for success such as in drug research and engineering firms dealing with computer technology. JSM is being reevaluated given Japan's ongoing economic woes (Jackson, 2003). Most important, a problem may arise when the "celebration" of the female advantage in the workplace leads to increased stereotyping and a reaffirmation of the differences between women and men. The image of women as nurturers who smooth over problems may be as stereotypical as the image of men who create the problems. On the positive side, with workplaces becoming increasingly multicultural, businesses today recognize that "difference" does not mean better or worse or stronger or weaker.

A partnership model is associated with a revision of the standard definition of "success" that acknowledges the critical role that parenthood plays in the life of any employee.

Today's employees are more willing to trade compensation for quality of work life. When conflicts between work and family are resolved in favor of the job, it is usually—and initially—to the detriment of the worker and his or her family. But the detrimental effect carries over to the employer and to society. Talented women often opt out of high level positions not because of their lack or competitiveness or dedication but because of the brutality associated with the corporate climb that is the antithesis of the partnership model. What is the potential effect of a new success model?

> Sanity, balance, and a new definition of success . . . just might be contagious. And instead of women being forced to act like men, men are being freed to act like women. Because women are more willing to leave (corporations), men

are more willing to leave, too . . . . It is about a door opened . . . by women that could usher in a new environment for us all. (Belkin, 2003:86).

The door is only cracked open. A paradigm shift is needed for a partnership approach to be institutionalized as a new workplace norm. Companies adopting a partnership approach can benefit by recognizing that employee job satisfaction is critically linked to quality of life—both on and off the job.

GLOBAL FOCUS: MICROENTERPRISE AND WOMEN

Propelled by nongovernmental organizations (NGOs) advocating for the world's poor, the *informal sector* of the global economy has been made more visible (chapter 6). Because large-scale development projects have largely ignored the informal sector where most of the poorest of the poor work and reside, **microenterprise programs** to address their needs have arisen. These programs consist of core segments of income-earning manufacturing or agricultural activities located in or around the household. Microenterprise is linked to the buzzword in the development assistance community, **microcredit** or microenterprise lending, where groups of four or five borrowers receive small loans at commercial interest rates to start or expand small businesses and open their first savings accounts (Khandker, 1999). Peer lending is the most important feature of microcredit so a group assumes responsibility for each other's loans: If one fails, they all fail (Conlin, 1999; Anderson et al., 2002)

Microcredit began twenty-five years ago when economic professor Muhammad Yunus founded the Grameen ("village") bank of Bangladesh and extended credit to people too poor to quality for loans at other banks. The first microcredit lending came from his own pocket. He lent $26 to a group of 42 workers who bought materials for a day's work weaving chairs and making pots. At the end of the first day as independent business owners they sold their wares, made a profit, and soon repaid the loan. The 62 cents per worker from the $26 loan began the microcredit movement (Yunus and Jolis, 1999). The Grameen program was astonishingly successful. Not only did 97 percent repay their loans at a 20 percent interest rate but their microenterprises also became sustainable and allowed their families to survive. The large majority of the workers in these successful microenterprise programs were women.

Women and Microcredit

Microcredit works better for the very poor because the very poor are usually women. Muhammad Yunus noticed very early that women used profits from microenterprise activities to feed their children and build their businesses, whereas men spent profits on electronics and personal goods. A growing body of research suggests that when women have disposable income, it is used in ways to sustain their family's long-term needs, such as nutrition, health care, and education. In addition, data on Grameen Bank borrowers show women's loan repayment rates above 98 percent. Because social and economic benefits are much greater when money is loaned to women, the Grameen Bank decided to concentrate on them. Almost two and one-half million Grameen borrowers in Bangladesh are women, compared to about 125,000 men (*Grameen Dialogue*, 1999; Mahal & Lindgren, 2002). The successes of Grameen in Bangladesh have been replayed with microcredit schemes targeted to women in Peru, Philippines, Bolivia, and other parts of the developing world (Gow, 2000; Navajas et al., 2000; Ypeij, 2000). It has been adapted to in the United States in development efforts in agricultural areas of the South and in poor inner city neighborhoods in the Midwest and Northeast. Microcredit is particularly effective in the developing world because they are likely to have collectivistic cultures. In addition it capitalizes on gender socialization patterns that build cooperative networks among women from early in life.

Critique. Lending money to women through microcredit it not without a downside. Some research indicates that when women are lent money, men often gain control of the funds making loan repayment difficult. These women do repay their loans but often under intense pressure from their peers and bank workers, who may threaten public humiliation for failure to pay. Challenging cultural and religious norms about women's traditional roles may also increase household tension, and in turn domestic violence may escalate (Rahman, 1999). However, other research suggests that microcredit lending does offer women a major step to empowerment, cultural obstacles can be overcome, and women and their families, including the men, benefit as a result (Hays-Mitchell, 1999). As Grameen Bank founder Yunus notes:

> . . . . each individual is very important. *She* alone can influence the lives of others within communities, nations within and beyond her own time. We need to build enabling environments to discover the limits of our potential. (Adapted from *Countdown 2005*, 1997:2) (Italics mine)

Summary

1. The increase of women in the labor force is linked to major changes in home and workplace. Employers are interested in how a woman's home life affects her workplace life.

2. Women have always held economically productive work roles connected to their homes. The Industrial Revolution opened paid work for women but by the Victorian era middle class women retreated to their homes. War encourages women to enter the labor force and has altered the gender composition of some fields, such as clerical work and teaching.

3. Employment is a major determinant of good health for both men and women. Multiple roles for women—the role accumulation view—including job, marriage, and children, have major health and emotional benefits. The role overload view argues that psychological problems occur when women are put into two full-time jobs. Poor, single-parent women are at most risk from role overload. Women in the sandwich generation who care for others are under added stress. Benefits of multiple roles outweigh liabilities.

4. Women make enormous contributions to the economy and families by their unpaid labor. When a woman has a paycheck of her own family dynamics change.

5. Both socialization into the family of orientation and family of procreation influence workplace roles. Girls hear messages about juggling family and employment that boys

do not hear. Even in egalitarian marriages wives spend much more time on child care and household tasks than husbands.

6. Career achievement for women is severely compromised by these tasks. Employers see women with children as a liability and often informally cast them into a mommy track in the workplace. Married men with children are seen as an asset. Gender stereotypes remain key factors in hiring and promotion.

7. The Equal Pay Act and Title VII of the 1964 Civil Rights Act, affirmative action, and comparable worth have helped gender equity in the workplace and reduced blatant workplace discrimination. Backlash against some of these provisions is occurring.

8. Women make up half of the professions but are distributed in those with less pay, power, and prestige, such as nursing and teaching for women and engineers and architects for men. Occupational segregation and gender typing go hand in hand. Men in female-dominated fields have more advantages than women in male-dominated fields. Women are segregated in the lower prestige specialties of elite fields such as medicine and law.

9. Women in white collar jobs are clustered in clerical or in retail sales with male managers. Blue collar women are largely absent from the skilled elite, such as electrician, carpenter, and plumber. Most blue collar women are in low level semiskilled jobs.

10. Men of all races outearn women regardless of age, occupation, seniority, and region. Gender, race, and class intersect to lower the wages of women or color. The human capital model, consistent with functionalism, explains the gender wage gap due to individual choices in education and family decisions. Conflict theory and symbolic interaction explain it according to the power relations between men and women and cultural norms about masculine and feminine jobs.

11. Corporate women's advancement to top management stops when women hit the glass ceiling—the invisible barrier constructed by male management. Women who are thwarted in corporations may start their own businesses. Women owned businesses are in two categories: traditional areas of female work in peripheral economic niches that compete with other women and high level managers competing with former employers.

12. Women's socialization may offer an advantage to modern corporations in that their management styles are compatible with partnership and consensus approaches. These approaches are linked to the success of Japanese firms. Celebrating the female advantage, however, may increase gender stereotyping.

13. Microcredit peer lending programs to very poor women in the developing world to start their own businesses are highly successful. If cultural obstacles are removed, these programs offer women a major step in empowerment.

Key Terms

affirmative action 278	glass ceiling 285	sandwich generation 272
comparable worth 279	human capital model 284	Title VII of the 1964 Civil Rights Act 278
family of orientation 273	microcredit 289	
family of procreation 274	microenterprise programs 289	
gender-typing 280		

Critical Thinking Questions

1. How do gender-typing in jobs and the gender wage gap violate assumptions about the economic system in the United States and the values associated with it? Evaluate policy approaches in this chapter in level of success in addressing these issues. Based on this

evaluation, offer policy strategies that would be successful in minimizing gender-typing and the wage gap.

2. As an employer interested in maximizing the potential of your female employees, what benefit packages would you offer and what management tactics would you use? Demonstrate how these devices will also serve as advantages to your male employees.

3. Document the influence of women's unpaid work on their families, their jobs, and their societies according to functionalism and conflict theory and then determine whether and/or how public policy should address the unpaid work issue. Which framework provides the better foundation for policy? Justify your selection.

CHAPTER 11

EDUCATION AND GENDER ROLE CHANGE

Why should girls be learn'd and wise?
Books only serve to spoil their eyes.
The studious eye but faintly twinkles
And reading paves the way to wrinkles
—John Trumbull, 1890s
(Cited in Kerber, 1988)

A century ago the image that women were emotional beings whose minds destined them to failure in all but minimal educational enterprises was pervasive. As satirical as it is, this poem demonstrates the turn of the century notion that beauty was a more important asset to a woman than her brain. Yet one of the hallmarks of the twentieth century has been the stellar educational achievement of women.

Compared to other social institutions, education is probably the most equitable. Like other countries in the developed world, the United States is oriented to *credentialism*—an individual's qualifications for a job or social position is based on completion of some aspect of formal education. A college degree is the key credential for the most prestigious and financially rewarding positions. Parents are concerned about quality of teaching, curriculum, information technology, and the range of opportunities schools can provide. For them, the issue of equity often focuses on amount of public funds reserved for their school district. Certainly they want the best education possible for their children. Many of these concerned parents would be dismayed if they discovered that their sons and daughters experience the educational process quite differently—even when seated in the same classroom. Education is a sorting process designed to benefit society and all students, but as this chapter will demonstrate, gendered schooling brings benefits for some students and liabilities for others. In the most equitable of America's social institutions, the gender of the child becomes a key determinant of his or her educational experience. Gender differences in education have persisted throughout history and persist in other parts of the world.

A BRIEF LESSON IN HISTORY

The history of Western civilization demonstrates that education in general, and literacy in particular, was reserved for the elite. Until about the eighteenth century the vast majority of all people—both men and women—were excluded from any formal learning. During the classical Greek and Roman era (dating from about the first century C.E.), the sons of the wealthy, and selected young men in other social classes, were taught reading, writing, and mathematics necessary for the economic, political, and military functioning of their homes and society. Certain upper-class women were educated in the arts and learned poetry and music to entertain household guests. This tradition continued into the Middle Ages and served to reinforce the image of women as sources of diversion from a tedious world.

Christianity enveloped Europe during the Middle Ages and established a stronghold over all social institutions (chapter 5). Because literacy was considered necessary for a religious calling, convent schools arose to teach women who would become nuns. The few other wealthy women who attended these schools became part of a system in which learning was designed to produce socially proper behavior and ensure sexual purity. Functionalists suggest that even the mediocre education of this era supported social values that a woman's duty was to her husband or, if entering the convent, to the church. With the church's social and political domination, the family served to reinforce the religious values of a woman's piety, purity, and devotion to hearth and home. By the seventeenth century, however, even these few educational opportunities for women in convents deteriorated, fueled by the fear that communities of educated, semi-independent women might prove dangerous to absolute church authority. Whereas many convents worked to preserve their intellectual traditions, Latin ceased to be taught. Nuns were rendered powerless in church decisions affecting them (Weitz, 1995). Thus despite the rise of universities in the twelfth and thirteenth centuries and the profound impact of the Renaissance, education was aimed at the sons of nobility and the emerging bourgeoisie, who would engage in business, become scholars and clerics, or enter the professions of law and medicine.

The Enlightenment

The first rumblings of equality of education for both genders and all classes came with the Enlightenment. It was during this period that Jean-Jacques Rousseau published *Emile* (1762), a book that was destined to become one of the most influential works in the history of education. In describing a man, Emile, and a woman, Sophie, who would be Emile's wife, Rousseau suggested that men and women are inherently different in abilities. A man must be schooled or trained according to his natural talents and encouraged to cultivate his mind and spirit without restraint or coercion. A woman, however, is passive and weak and should be humbly submissive, accepting a man's judgment in all matters. Rousseau would not deny literacy to women, but he believed a woman's schooling should be practically oriented because intellectual pursuits could wreak havoc on her naturally weak temperament. Education for women must correspond to the roles they freely choose, those of wife and mother. Women have power over men because they have power over men's hearts. Men have power over women because they provide for women's economic upkeep. Women gain more from their dependence on men and less from education (Green, 1995:79). Rousseau justified gender inequality because he believed that the patriarchal family was a necessary precondition for modern society, founded on a woman's acceptance of her subservience to a man. Education for women, therefore, was impractical, unwise, and detrimental to social stability.

Progressive Education

Considered radical at that time, Rousseau's discourses on the education of boys laid the foundation for the twentieth-century movement known as Progressive Education. His views on women were not as controversial because they reflected widespread convictions about a woman's nature and thus were used to justify continued gender inequality. Because the Progressive Education movement championed the idea of civic egalitarianism, the so-called leveling effects of the Enlightenment were directed at glaring social class differences. This discussion also demonstrates how gender and class can be discussed together yet remain analytically distinct. Unlike Marx and Engels, Rousseau's defense of civic egalitarianism is weakened because he did not account for the interdependent relationship between gender and class that perpetuates women's subordination. For sociological theory, an interesting contradiction results. Sounding like Marx and conflict theorists, Rousseau advocated social change that would increase class equality. But the final outcome was decidedly functionalist, in support of a patriarchal family considered to be the moral structure on which social order rests. Social order, therefore, could be undermined if women were educated.

Other voices were also heard during the eighteenth century that called for gender equality in education. In France the Marquis de Condorcet declared that government should provide education for all people, and that it had a duty to instruct both boys and girls in common. Equality and justice demanded it. Madame de Lambert advised women to study Latin, philosophy, and science to bolster their resources because the other roads to success were closed to them. She bitterly lamented that women have but "coquetry and the miserable function of pleasing" as their wealth (Greard, 1893). The true spirit of the Enlightenment emerged in the late nineteenth century in Europe and the United States as policies advocating free and compulsory education for *all* children were adopted. In the United States these principles were strengthened a half century later during the civil rights movement when the issue of equality of opportunity, especially in education, was seriously debated.

Americans wholeheartedly embrace the belief that education is the key to success and the vehicle for social mobility. Equality in education is assumed during the school years. Yet when the female kindergarten teacher first removes Dick's mittens and helps Jane off with her coat, by virtue of gender alone, their long educational journey will contain essential differences.

THE PROCESS OF EDUCATION

When children enter the classroom, earlier gender role patterns follow them (chapter 3). These patterns are reinforced and reproduced throughout all educational levels and at all types of educational institutions. As documented in this section, gendered educational patterns are grounded on both the formal curriculum—such as textbooks, course requirements, grading scales, and standardized tests—as well as the powerful **hidden curriculum**, consisting of all the informal and unwritten norms that serve to control students, including expectations about gender.

Kindergarten

Preschool is rapidly becoming normative and introduces children to their first educational expectations. Research clearly documents that gender segregation occurs swiftly in preschool and that it is reinforced by teacher expectations, play and game activities, types of toys, and desires of the children themselves. The transition to more formal learning begins with kindergarten and these preset patterns. In kindergarten Jane gains approval from peers, parents, and teachers for her quiet demeanor and studiousness.

The kindergarten classroom is often an extension of familiar household surroundings. Kindergarten allows for the gradual structuring of the child's day so that ample time is set aside for play activities. Both boys and girls enjoy the time reserved for playing with the variety of toys and games available, many of which they have at home or have seen on television.

When play period begins, girls rush off to the minikitchen reserved for them. Here Jane can pretend to cook, set the table, and clean with miniature household devices that are constructed for her small hands. This miniature house comes complete with dolls on which she can hone domestic skills. Because the doll corner is not designed for vibrant, rough-and-tumble play, Jane may be less restricted if she is wearing a dress or sandals. Girls are princesses, brides, and mothers in this part of the kindergarten world, fantasies that are easily accomplished by the way the classroom is structured (Davies, 1989; Kuznets, 1999). But Jane also enjoys wearing jeans and tennis shoes. This clothing does not prevent her from running with the other children and climbing on equipment in the playground. Girls may envy the boys as they display more power and freedom in their play behavior, but that envy is tempered by the teacher's obvious disapproval of the boys' boisterous classroom behavior. Although Jane may occasionally exchange the domestic roles of the doll corner for kickball and action oriented fantasy games during recess, the pull to the doll corner as a representation of home and babies is powerful and reigns supreme throughout kindergarten. Jane rarely plays with the boys and prefers playing house or, when outdoors, jumping rope with a few friends.

Kindergarten continues a process of self-selected gender segregation that increases during the school years. Gender is a better predictor of choice of playmates than is race (Haynes, 2001; Hoffman and Powlishta, 2001). Gender segregated play groups during kindergarten have powerful socialization outcomes.

Children are acquiring distinctive interaction skills that can hamper cross-gender relationships later in life.

Meanwhile, Dick enters kindergarten more unprepared for the experience than Jane. His higher level of physical activity is incompatible with the sedate atmosphere of school. He soon is aware that his teacher approves of the quieter children—and the quieter children are usually the girls. Rather than gaining the teacher's attention by copying the girls and being labeled a sissy by the boys, he plays games that are physically vibrant and selects toys that reinforce these activities (Thorne, 1993, 2002). When Dick is expected to engage in quieter activities such as art, he chooses to draw gender stereotyped pictures—such as those depicting outdoor scenes associated with fighting, building, and demolishing. Gender preferences in art emerge during preschool, much earlier than previously thought (Boyatzis and Eades, 1999). Dick discovers that the teacher pays attention to the children who are more disruptive—and the more disruptive children are usually the boys. He may also feel it is better to be reprimanded than ignored.

Physical space in the early childhood classroom is highly gendered (Martin, 1998). When boys venture into the doll corner, they use the area differently than the girls. Domestic play is accepted and tolerated if it is not disruptive. But when the boys use the area for nondomestic games, such as those based on fighting and destruction, conflict is a usual outcome. They invent "warrior narratives" to structure their play—games involving good and bad, pirates and police—and alter the domestic artifacts to fit their needs (Jordan and Cowan, 1995). The teacher, who encourages free and imaginative play otherwise, will not allow such activities in the classroom and consigns boys to the playground.

Dick and his friends favor trucks, action figures, and building blocks as toys. Girls, too, enjoy building things. A girl may wander over and attempt to join in the louder and seemingly more interesting activities of the boys. She is likely to be discouraged from long-term participation, however, by their rough-and-tumble play and the very spiritedness of the activities to which she was originally attracted. In places outside school, these activities reward boys for being independent, active, and assertive. Masculinity norms are enforced even in early childhood education (Keenan et al., 1999; Reid, 1999). School norms, however, call for docility and passivity, a realm in which girls feel more at ease. It is understandable that boys often find their first school experiences unsettling. Begun in kindergarten, this gendered pattern continues in elementary school.

Elementary School

For girls, elementary school is a vehicle for achievement. They receive higher grades than boys, and they exceed boys in most areas of verbal ability, reading, and mathematics. Teachers also put a premium on being good and being tidy, which may account for fewer negative comments given to girls. High achievement coupled with low criticism would appear to be an ideal learning environment. Yet the message that is communicated to girls very early in their education is that they are less important than boys.

Jane and the Gendered Curriculum. Compared to boys, girls are called on less, have less overall interaction with teachers, and get less criticism but also receive less instructional time. When teachers criticize boys for inadequate academic work, they suggest that it is lack of effort rather than intelligence that is the cause (Helwig et al., 2001; Burnett, 2002; Fredricks and Eccles, 2002). Research demonstrates that elementary school teaches boys that problems are challenges to overcome; it often teaches girls that failure is beyond their control. Although teachers maintain that they do not treat girls and boys differently, aggressive boys and dependent girls gain their attention (Sadker and Sadker, 1994; Strauss, 2000). As symbolic interactionists suggest, a self-fulfilling prophecy may be set into motion if girls internalize the notion that they have less intellectual ability, in turn discouraging them from tackling more difficult courses.

Although curricular material is more egalitarian today, stereotyped gender portrayals are prevalent and send the message that girls are less important than boys. Over thirty years of research on such material demonstrates that girls are depicted much less frequently than boys and depicted in marginalized, insignificant roles. For example, children's books may show girls as brave, but still needing rescue. Boys do interesting and exciting things; girls do not (Orenstein 1997; Evans and Davies 2000; Levstik 2001).

Gender stereotyping in education has received national attention. It would be expected, therefore, that current instructional materials reflect more realistic and expanded roles for both women and men. The research evidence is mixed. Children continue to read books with characters in traditional gender roles. Women and girls are portrayed as dependent, cooperative, submissive, and nurturing, whereas men and boys are seen as independent, creative, aggressive, competitive, and assertive. Research on textbooks that teach reading, social studies, and even mathematics demonstrate that less importance is attached to girls—especially girls of color—by number of female characters represented and the stereotyped roles they play. On the other hand, numbers and types of female characters have increased, and less stereotyped portrayals are evident. Girls are now more likely to be shown in activities outside the home and in the world of paid work. They are more frequently depicted in sports, although primarily in traditional female sports, such as gymnastics and ice skating (Grossman and Grossman, 1994; Odeon, 1997; AAUW, 1999). Although gender parity has not been reached, strides toward more realistic female portrayals are being made.

Dick and the Gendered Curriculum. Boys are experiencing elementary school quite differently. They do not easily adjust to a classroom environment that emphasizes quietness and inactivity, teachers reprimand them more, and they receive lower grades. Yet when boys learn that more effort and less disruptive classroom behavior will remedy this, their self-esteem is protected. Teachers talk to them more about the subject matter, listen more to their complaints and questions, and praise them most for their intellectual competence. Despite classroom protocol, boys shout out answers to questions, whether right or wrong, and get attention. Girls raise their hands and get ignored (Halberstam, 1994; Sadker and Sadker, 2002).

The textbooks boys read in elementary school are replete with male characters doing interesting and exciting things, both in occupational and recreational activities, such as sports. They see active and resourceful adult males who are jobholders and boys their own age who build, create, and discover, as well as protect and rescue girls. They often marry the females (princesses) they rescue, even if they know nothing about them except that they are beautiful (Temple, 1993). Men are scientists, firefighters, and police officers. They are involved in a variety of sports activities. Males are also cast into father roles, but these roles are given less coverage and less importance than breadwinner/career depictions. Joint father–children activities are rarely portrayed, including those involving father–son. In contrast to mothers, males have a separate life and identity. Newer textbooks do show boys in some nontradtional roles, such as babysitters, and many characters engaging in more emotional, relationship building language than in the past (Tepper and Wright, 1999). The gendered curriculum bias for boys is that Dick is bound to expectations of high achievement for career roles. The fact that he will also be a husband and father is disregarded.

In all these roles Dick is taught to be strong and tough. Except for anger, other emotional displays such as outward signs of fear, hardship, and sorrow are disapproved. According to children's author Mem Fox (1993:86), boys need permission to cry and to talk about their feelings. With this goal in mind, she wrote *Tough Boris* about a pirate who is massive, greedy, tough, and scary,

> . . . but when his parrot died, he cried and cried.
> All pirates cry, and so do I.

She hopes that if a father could read such a story aloud to his son (or daughter) it might develop into a real conversation about expressing emotions. Although Dick may find some aspects of elementary school frustrating and confusing, curricular materials confirm his expected masculine role and serve to strengthen his identity as eventual wage earner.

Overall, research on the impact of gender-typed curricular materials concludes that gender role attitudes of students at all elementary school grade levels are compromised. Instructional materials that perpetuate gender role stereotyping in turn reinforce gender-typed beliefs, with children in the younger grades being the most susceptible. On the other hand, when material depicts girls and boys and women and men in roles and situations in which gender equity rather than gender stratification is evident, less gender-typed attitudes can result (Marshall et al., 1999).

High School

Intellectual achievement and superior grades in elementary school do not predict academic success in high school. Whereas in elementary school girls are confident and assertive, they leave adolescence with a poorer self-image, with the sharpest drop in self-esteem occurring between elementary and middle school (Prettyman, 1998). On the other hand, boys experience consistent gains in self-confidence, and they believe they are good at a lot of things. As measured by standardized tests, by high school, scholastic achievement for girls tends to decline in reading and writing, but especially in mathematics, where boys are beginning to excel (Osborne, 2001).

Gender and Mathematics. The finding that girls do not do as well in math as boys has been seized on to conclude that there are biologically based sex differences in analytic ability. The biology argument in explaining gender differences in math and science has used everything from chromosomes, hormones, brain organization, and genetic codes to explain the slight male edge (Casey et al., 1992; Halpern, 2000). In terms of spatial ability, no gene has been identified that traces the ability from mother to son, and researchers are skeptical that such a "complex ability as spatial reasoning could possibly rest in a single gene" (McLoughlin, 1988:55). Biology cannot be completely discounted because mathematics and spatial tests are related, and there are gender differences in rate of development.

With better measurement techniques, gender similarities rather than gender differences in mathematics are rapidly emerging (Hyde and Kling, 2001). Because even the small gender differences in mathematics are steadily decreasing, researchers lean toward the counterargument that sociocultural factors propel boys but deter girls in mathematics (Bevan, 2001; Orenstein, 2001). When verbal processes are used in math questions, girls outperform boys. When spatial–visual processes are used, boys outperform girls. Although boys do better on multiple-choice items and girls do better on extended response items, even these differences are slight (Robinson et al., 1999; Beller and Gafni, 2000; Gallagher et al., 2000; Zhang and Manon, 2000). When the number of math courses taken is controlled for and female teachers and other role models are available for girls, gender differences in math performance are not significant (Henderson, 2001; Quaiser-Pohl and Lehmann, 2002). Girls who do poorly in math courses in high school have heightened math anxiety, believe they are not smart enough to succeed in math, and are less likely to take the additional courses they need for certain college majors (Gilbert, 1996; Chan, 2000; Rouxel, 2000). After graduation, for example, many girls do not have the prerequisites for majoring in science, engineering, or other subjects where a strong math-based competency is required. Any existing male–female difference in math and science is best explained by *gender* factors, due to culture, rather than *sex* factors, due to biology.

Race and Social Class. Research reveals that race and social class are better predictors for math and academic performance than is gender. White, middle class children of both genders outperform children of other races and children from lower and working class backgrounds (Rendon and Hope, 1995; Hall et al., 1999; Porter, 1999). In academic achievement overall, Britain has been successful in significantly narrowing the gender educational gap, but seemingly insurmountable social class inequalities persist (Arnot et al., 1999; Plummer, 2000). In the United States, a backlash to the attention paid to the gender gap in education has been launched, suggesting that the shortchanged group is not females, but males. Statistics showing higher graduation rates and college attendance for girls are used to support this contention (Table 11.1). Under the guise of helping girls, this argument contends that males are penalized simply for engaging in boy-type masculine behaviors (Sommers, 2000). African-American and Latino males are particularly vulnerable, pointing to data that males may be at the academic top compared to females, but more males, especially African-American males, are also at the academic bottom, a pattern that continues in college. Boys as a group are more likely than girls to be labeled as impaired and in special education classes (Kleinfeld, 1998). On the other hand, research consistently shows that females spend more time studying and doing homework than boys and boys spend more time watching

Table 11.1 Educational Attainment by Race and Gender, Selected Years.

| | White | | African American | | Hispanic* | |
Year	Male	Female	Male	Female	Male	Female
Completed 4 Years of High School or More						
1965	50.2	52.2	25.8	28.4	(NA)	(NA)
1975	65.0	64.1	41.6	43.3	39.5	36.7
1985	76.0	75.1	58.4	60.8	48.5	47.4
1995	83.0	83.0	73.4	74.1	52.9	53.8
2002	83.0	84.2	71.4	73.7	52.0	55.1
Completed 4 Years of College or More						
1965	12.7	7.3	4.9	4.5	(NA)	(NA)
1975	18.4	11.0	6.7	6.2	8.3	4.6
1985	24.0	16.3	11.2	11.0	9.7	7.3
1995	27.2	21.0	13.6	12.9	10.1	8.4
2002	27.4	24.4	13.1	14.8	8.6	8.9

NA-Not Available.
*Persons of Hispanic (Latino) origin may be of any race.
Source: Adapted from PPL-169 Table 1a, U.S. Census Bureau, Population Division, 2003.

television, partying and exercising than girls (Fletcher, 2002). Although it is easy to counter the argument that boys are shortchanged in school, the race–gender link is more pervasive in part because it is more politically divisive. Even if schools are doing a better job in addressing gender inequality, to argue that race is a more important oppression than gender only serves to pit one minority group against another (Bank, 1999). By implying that boys would or should be doing better than girls also devalues the achievement of girls. Scientific research may be able to eventually sort out the complexities between race, class, and gender in explaining school performance, but it is likely that a political agenda will determine which group, if any, is shortchanged overall.

Gender Diversity: Race, Self-Esteem, and Academic Achievement. Academic success in math and science is strongly related to level of self-esteem among high school girls. When a high school girl enjoys math, she also feels good about herself and her schoolwork, sees herself as important, and feels better about her family relationships. The sharp drop in self-esteem girls experience by the time they enter high school is even more pronounced for Latino girls who start out with the highest levels of self-esteem for all races and end with the highest school dropout rates (Guin and Vincent, 2000; Benjet and Hernandez-Guzman, 2001; Canedy, 2001). Many Latino girls perceive few benefits from a high school diploma because they do not associate high school graduation with economic opportunities. As one Mexican-American girl stated, "I can get the same job without graduating from high school. You don't need a diploma to work at Burger King" (Dietrich, 1998:98). However, when Latino girls perceive liberal attitudes toward women, have female role models who are married and hold down well-paying jobs, and have parents who support educational goals, academic achievement rises (Segura, 1998; Romo, 1998; Canedy, 2001).

African American girls retain higher levels of self-esteem compared to white girls, but positive feelings about their teachers and their academic work drop significantly (Orenstein, 1994; Daniel, 1999). African American girls receive the same messages other girls receive in high school—that girls are less important than boys. But African-American girls tend to retain their sense of self-esteem despite negative messages from teachers and other adult authority figures. They resolve inner conflict in favor of positive beliefs about themselves, even while rejecting the educational system. School achievement may be hampered but, bolstered by racial pride and supportive parents, self-esteem is undamaged. They listen to their own voices rather than accepting devaluing judgments from others (Brown and Gilligan, 1992; Gilligan et al., 1995).

Girls of color in high school appear to be caught in an achievement paradox (Mickelson, 1990). They clearly understand the reality of racism and know that education will not translate to the economic rewards whites with the same educational backgrounds receive. However, Jeanne Weiler's research on "at-risk" female students attending an alternative high school in New York suggests that young girls of color value academic achievement as the best route to improve their chances for better economic futures. The achievement paradox is implied by a Puerto Rican girl:

> I'll either get a job or go to college. Well, this is really what I want to do after I get out of high school. I'm gonna go into the army and I'll get the G.I. bill for college. . . (Weiler, 2000:76).

Another interesting fact about this research is that girls of color attach more importance to further schooling than do white girls; the latter view economic security in terms of their attachment to men. Weiler speculates that whereas the alternative high school provides feminist messages about the necessity of education for career goals, white girls appear to internalize the louder gender message that marriage is the better economic guarantee. Minority girls are more likely to come from families in which women are major earners. Working class white girls see more employed men in their families, hence their identities revolve around exclusive marriage and family roles where they will be economically dependent on men. Weiler's research offers important insight into the connections between race and class in explaining patterns of female educational achievement in high school.

Gendered Tracking and Vocational Education. High school girls of all races are more often tracked into academic courses like English and vocational courses like word processing and home economics. Contrary to popular belief, more girls graduate from high school than boys, and more girls are enrolled in vocational education courses than boys. Girls are likely to need proof of competency for even basic clerical work, and this proof usually comes in the form of a high school diploma. Higher female enrollment in vocational education courses is consistent with data showing more men entering college full time immediately after graduation. (National Center for Educational Statistics, 2003). Women take courses in which they can be employed right out of high school. The overwhelming majority of students in courses geared to retail sales, health assistance, and secretarial and other office occupations are female. Most vocational programs for girls, however, are still dominated by teaching household skills, mirroring the cultural assumption—but not the economic reality—that working outside the home is optional for women. The myth of female dependence on males for income is not a benign one. When young women graduate from high school with severely restricted career options, it translates to poor economic outcomes that are worsened by divorce and single parenthood (chapter 8). Overall, high school vocational education for girls is geared to the noncollege bound who either marry or wind up in low-paying, dead-end jobs.

College for young middle class women is now the norm, with most entering right after high school. Young working-class women, however, may not see college as a realistic or desirable option. Marriage looms as the alternative, and obtaining a marketable vocational skill is important until they marry. Vocational education has historically been committed to the less powerful of society, whether they are women, the working poor, or other skilled laborers (Conroy, 1998; Kincheloe, 1999). When supported by federal legislation, vocational education provides training in a variety of fields offered as options to both genders. Improving gender equity in vocational education empowers all students. But a remaining problem is that gender equity is hampered by gender codes in the high school hidden curriculum that keep boys and girls from venturing off traditional paths in vocational programs.

The Boy or Girl Hidden Curriculum. The confusion of elementary school for boys begins to evaporate as their independence is now rewarded more often. Dick's grades have improved, and he is able to demonstrate his talents in courses (shop and automobile mechanics) and sports (wrestling and football) specifically designed for boys (Eder and Kinney, 1995; Newberger, 1999). Dick sees college in his future but for his males friends who are not going to college, high school vocational education courses will help prepare them for jobs in printing, carpentry, engineering technology, and computer science. Unlike courses for girls, vocational education options for boys will have higher economic returns after high school.

Although enrollment by girls in courses traditionally designed for boys is exploding, boys are less likely to take courses associated with feminine activities. When course titles do not reflect the feminine content, boys enroll more freely. For instance, Bachelor Living and Home Mechanics allows boys to gain basic household skills without the stigma of taking a "girls'" course. Changing the title of a course to entice male enrollment may be pandering and again serves to devalue courses that females have taken all along, but it offers boys needed skills in practical domestic areas, such as cooking, basic home maintenance, and household organization.

Vocational education tracking is reinforced by other school mechanisms that help perpetuate the gendered system. For example, both genders take the same academic courses such as history, but like in elementary school, these courses demonstrate that "boys do" and "girls don't." In history books, when women are mentioned, it is usually in the context of a traditional role—Betsy Ross for sewing and Florence Nightingale for nursing—or of becoming notable because of marriage to famous men—from Jackie Kennedy to Ivana Trump. Few women are portrayed, and those who are conform to a definite stereotypical image of what women are supposed to be. The content of history courses in college is beginning to reflect newer ideas about diversity in general and women in particular (see chapter 5), but this trend is lagging in high schools. Controversial men are portrayed. Potentially controversial women are omitted. Generally college texts continue to reinforce gendered messages of earlier schooling. Research on marriage and family text-books over several decades show more photos of women in less stereotyped roles, but photos with traditional messages still dominate (Low and Sherrard, 1999).

The standardized achievement and career interest tests taken by high school students also maintain a consistent androcentric bias, from the content to the pronouns used. Although standardized tests continue to be evaluated in terms of gender bias, to date, they are not balanced in this regard. These tests are then administered by counselors, who may not be as gender sensitive in vocational and college planning. Gender bias by counselors is a problem that can affect students' attitudes to career selection, choice of major, or even willingness to pursue a college education. Other staffing patterns demonstrate to students and community alike that males are the leaders. The male high school principal reports to the male school superintendent who regularly meets with predominantly male school board members. Even among lower level school staff a gender hierarchy exists, with female cafeteria workers ranked lower than male janitors.

Acknowledging the insidious nature of all these latent but powerful gender tracking mechanisms, demands for intervention strategies are widespread. Programs funded through the 1995 Gender Equity Education Act are designed to raise the gender consciousness of both men and women teachers and counselors, to encourage girls in math and science and boys in home economics, and to better serve the educational needs of girls. These programs also help educators understand how their own cultural beliefs influence their work with students. A follow-up report indicates that public schools are making progress toward better gender equity (AAUW, 1999). This report reiterates what has long been known—academic standards are compromised for all students unless equity is in place. It is in high school athletics where a great deal of progress is reported, but where many obstacles to gender equity remain.

Athletics and Masculinity. High school coaches reigning over victorious basketball and football teams garner a great deal of honor and respect. Male achievement on the playing fields of high schools across the United States is invariably associated with community and school pride. How does this achievement affect the boys who strive to become members of the coveted teams? Whereas attractiveness and popularity with boys are linked to prestige for girls, athletic success provides the same function for boys (Suitor and Carter, 1999). From early childhood, boys receive powerful messages that athletic accomplishments are important keys for success in life. Because of the billion dollar sports-media connection, these messages are in fact stronger than at any other time in history. Boys not only see the financial rewards and personal glory associated with sports, but also the athletes themselves usually emerge unscathed and even more lustrous by the injuries, fights, and general mayhem that occur on and off the football field, basketball court, or ice rink.

Sport demonstrates the importance of competition and allows participants to gain in confidence, concentration, and courage, all traits associated with successful American males (chapter 9). In addition to these functions of sport, relationships with coaches and other players socialize boys to defer to a more powerful male status hierarchy, accept pain, and denigrate women. Football in particular is a sport that perpetuates patriarchy as well as male privilege through bonding relationships with figures more dominant than themselves, especially coaches (Sabo and Panepinto, 2001). Boys who cannot withstand the physical or emotional demands of athletics may feel inadequate and unpopular. Athletic failure is associated with a loss of self-confidence in boys, especially if a boy gauges himself by athletic prowess and cannot measure up to his peers or reach his personal goal in the athletic hierarchy (Messner, 1995). By these values, academic achievement is no real substitute for athletic rewards. In more extreme cases, he may begin to doubt his masculinity and harbor resentment toward women. A masculine gender identity is formed and polished by sports. But this identity may be tarnished if a boy engages in coeducational sports, especially if a girl can outperform a boy in the same athletic competition. Such a belief not only discourages coed teams but provides ammunition that implicitly deprecates those activities where girls can succeed at an equal or better level than boys.

The importance attached to high school athletics can be measured by the financial and organizational support given to male compared to female sports. At all levels of education, boys' teams have better equipment and facilities, more space for practice and competition, and higher paid coaches than comparable girls' teams (chapter 14). Both boys' and girls' teams are likely to be administered by men. Successful high school teams are routinely scrutinized by highly paid scouts representing major college and professional teams. It is understandable that athletics are viewed as a road to success for high school males. This is a gilded road for those boys who intend to pursue college through an athletic scholarship.

Higher Education

If high school has done its job well, the best and the brightest students will pursue a college education. Since World War II, there has been a steady increase of both men and women attending college. Women are now enrolled in greater numbers than men, due in part to enrollments of women over age 35 who attend part time. Many of these women are single parents who know that a degree will provide more financial security for themselves and their children. Other women see education as enhancing later life career choices. Ideally, college should be the key educational institution that evaluates students solely on criteria related to academic achievement and the potential for success. But the lessons of elementary school and high school are not easily forgotten.

Gender, Love, and Achievement in College. Although both men and women undergraduates are strongly career oriented, traditional values intrude as the inescapable career–family confrontation resurfaces for college women. There is pressure to find a partner and simultaneously work toward career goals. College women may also struggle with the issue of financial dependency on their husbands when family roles interrupt career roles. Females highlight career goals for immediate ambitions, but when thinking about motherhood, career salience decreases significantly (Moya et al., 2000; Stone and McKee, 2000). In college as in high school, girls' popularity is associated with how popular they are with boys. In tracing the experiences of even high-achieving college women, research suggests it is difficult to resist the "culture of romance" that serves to lower their ambition and academic achievement. Romantic ideals often propel young women into marriage and childbearing earlier than they intended and change their career direction, which impacts them throughout their lives (Holland and Eisenhart, 1990; Ranson, 1998; Fishel, 2000). Propelled by gendered expectations, the notorious peer pressure of high school transfers with relative ease to the college campus. If the future is uncertain because of gender role conflict, the present becomes more anxiety ridden. Achievement for college women may be the first victim of such conflict.

Male students remain more consistent with a career orientation when projecting their future plans compared to female students. Men's career motives are less influenced by gender ideology than women's. College men, however, are also not immune to gender role changes regarding love and romance, which put some in a double bind. Men value intelligence, competence, and originality in their female classmates much more than in the past, yet many are unable to relinquish the internalized norm of male superiority. This norm makes it difficult for true egalitarian relationships to be established.

The Gendered College Classroom.   Although both qualified women and men are likely to be admitted to college, once admitted, men find that academic life exemplifies a male mode of performance. The values of competition, individualism, and aggressive classroom debates are stronger than in high school. College men quickly learn the value of catching the attention of faculty who will be instrumental for later graduate work. Men's self-esteem continues to improve and soon outpaces their women classmates.

Women entering college experience a small, but measurable drop in self-esteem. In addition to the career–family conflict many college women experience, self-esteem is threatened by their belief that the campus climate is a "chillier" one for them (Sandler, 2004). Women discover early that they receive less faculty encouragement for their work and will be listened to less and interrupted more than their male classmates—patterns that promote lower expectations for achievement. Over one-third of women report gender discrimination in their treatment in and outside the classroom by instructors, administrators, and classmates. The impact of this perception is greater in the second and third year of college compared to the first year. This chilly climate can negatively affect a woman's personal and intellectual development (Fox, 1995; Association of American Colleges & Universities, 1999).

Major and Career Paths.   College women may find it easier to choose the well-traveled gender road of majoring in the arts and humanities. Almost half of women who enter college with science-related interests switch to other majors. The math-gender link described earlier comes into play. Insufficient precollege preparation in math and science, few female role models, and lack of peers in the field are key factors in explaining this switch (Beyer 1999; Abouchedid and Nasser, 2000; Correll, 2001). However, women earn slightly more than half of all doctorates in fields other than science and engineering. Gains in professional degrees have been steady; about one-half of law degrees and one-third of medical degrees are awarded to women. Considering that opportunities for women to pursue higher education are relatively recent, these numbers are impressive.

But compared to women, men are distributed in a wider variety of majors. Men dominate areas such as mathematics, the physical sciences, and architecture. These majors lead to jobs in expanding, more lucrative fields such as engineering, biomedical technology, and computer science. Women are concentrated in nursing, literature, home economics, social work, education, and library science. Female-dominated fields are associated with less pay and more competition for fewer job slots (chapter 10). For the behavioral sciences, about three-fourths of psychology B.A.s are awarded to women. Sociology, on the other hand, is one of the few majors with relative gender equality in numbers of B.A.s awarded (U.S. Bureau of the Census, 2004).

Over the past twenty years, differences between men and women in college majors in arts and sciences and engineering have not decreased. The gender gap in math and all sciences expect biology slightly increased. Men dominate the most influential fields where graduate work is required and are at the top of the prestige hierarchy within them. In medicine, men are surgeons and women are pediatricians. Men practice international law and women practice family law. Female nurses are in clinical roles, male nurses are in administrative roles. Gender parity in number of math and science courses is close, and gender differences in grades and SAT scores are negligible, but the gender gap in major remains. The gender effects of the college experience account for much of this gap (Turner and Bowen, 1999). The culmination of college or graduate school, whether as holder of B.A., M.D., or Ph.D., is also the culmination of a lifetime of attitudes and behaviors regarding gender.

Graduate School. For both women and men psychological roadblocks emerging at the undergraduate level are intensified in graduate and professional education as competition for grades and grants increase. Besides dealing with increasing career–motherhood pressures, women must also cope with pervasive patterns of subtle gender bias existing in many graduate departments. Both men and women prefer faculty mentors of their own gender, but the ratio of more male to female faculty may not allow for these preferences to be realized for female students.

In addition, women graduate students spend less time with faculty as role models and mentors—especially male faculty—and are less relaxed when they do (Gumbiner, 1998; Schroeder and Mynatt, 1999). Compared to female law students, for example, males report greater opportunities for, and a greater degree of comfort with, formal and informal interaction with faculty. Restricted mentoring opportunities because of gender in college and graduate school have a major impact on later careers.

Academic careers blossom through a protégé system that matches a talented graduate student with a recognized, established faculty member. Partly due to the mentoring problem mentioned earlier, women often find they are not suitable as protégés. Although not overtly discriminatory, these pervasive patterns keep both faculty and graduate student males in control of the powerful subculture of graduate school. Mary Frank Fox (1995:229) demonstrates how this subculture operates on the professional level by quoting a Berkeley student.

> Have I been overtly discriminated against? Probably no. Have I been encouraged, congratulated, received recognition, gotten a friendly hello, a solicitous "can I help you out?" The answer is no. Being a woman here just makes you

tougher, work harder, and hope that if you get a 4.0 GPA someone will say "You're good."

Academic Women. Female faculty are important for women students as both role models and mentors. Research shows that women's progress in academia is not inevitable, and more significant, past progress is being eroded. Where does the academic path lead for women Ph.D.s? Most are in two- and four-year state colleges, usually satellite campuses, with heavy teaching loads and committee responsibilities. They are clustered in less prestigious schools and in less powerful fields. They hold most adjunct and part-time faculty positions. If full time, they are instructors and assistant professors. Women constitute about one-fifth of full professors, but about half of all assistant professors (Glazer-Raymo, 1999; National Center for Education Statistics, 2003). The pattern repeats itself throughout academia—the higher the rank, the fewer the women.

When tenure decisions are made, years of subtle discrimination may become manifest. Tenure explains the low number of female full professors. Approximately three-fourths of men on the faculties of four-year colleges have tenure compared to less than half of women, a pattern holding for two decades (National Center for Education Statistics, 2003). Women are denied tenure often because they have fewer publications in lesser-known journals, devote a greater amount of their time to teaching, and engage in more unpaid professional service than their male colleagues (Association of American Colleges & Universities, 1995:3). Already tough higher education careers are tougher for females compared to males (Gerdes, 2003).

Research also shows that gender stereotypes form the basis of evaluating faculty performance. Faculty women are evaluated differently than men by students, colleagues, and administrators. They are expected to be nice as well as competent, maintain a pleasant classroom atmosphere, be more responsive to students with personal needs, be overly accessible to students outside class, and engage students using a variety of learning styles. Faculty in disciplines seen as nontraditional for their gender have more leeway than those in traditional gender fields. Women are judged more harshly when they deviate from the gender-imposed model of a caring professor (Statham et al., 1991; Chamberlin and Hickey, 2000; Bleakley, 2002). Both men and women faculty adopt stereotyped gender role images, a pattern that intrudes on peer evaluation and the informal network in which female faculty are first assessed (Gallant and Cross, 1993; Street et al., 1995). Besides the clear inequity of such patterns, it is a sad comment on college education that good teaching, where women excel, is often not the basis for the reward of tenure.

At the most prestigious colleges, women faculty often find themselves pulled away from career goals by the same challenges faced by other bright, ambitious women—the multiple demands of family and the university. Given the extremely competitive academic marketplace, Jane must make the difficult decision to uproot her life to seek employment elsewhere or find part-time work at other local colleges. The latter course will be her likely choice, especially if she has children and an employed spouse. She will remain in academia but in a marginal position, often as an "academic gypsy" migrating between part-time or temporary jobs, with little hope of advancement, influence, or tenure.

GENDER ISSUES IN EDUCATION

Gender bias in education documented here is associated with patterns that restrict options for both male and female students and faculty. Widespread sexual harassment in schools is another such restriction. Single-gender education has been offered as a strategy for dealing with sexual harassment as well as other gender-based restrictions in schools. This section will assess evidence suggesting that single-gender education is either better or worse than coeducation.

Single-Gender Education

Liabilities for female students are altered when women outnumber men in high school and college classrooms or when female faculty represent a larger proportion of overall faculty, especially in math and science. When academic experiences in single-gender and coeducational institutions are compared on measures of scholarship, academic aspirations, attitudes toward studies, leadership, and self-confidence, the research is favorable for single-gender education. (Miller-Bernal, 1991; Campbell and Sanders, 2002; Riordan, 2002). Although these benefits are demonstrated for both males and females in single-gender schools, the benefits to white and minority females as well as minority males appear to be greater. For females overall, single-gender education is linked to later academic and career success.

Other research demonstrates that women from single-gender high schools are more likely to attend better colleges. Women from single-gender colleges outperform women who attend coed colleges, and they are more likely to attend graduate or professional school (Lee and Marks, 1990; Fox-Genovese, 1995). Women's colleges offer particularly hospitable environments for minority and nontraditional-age students (Association of American Colleges & Universities, 1995). Among high school students, African-American and Latino females have higher leadership scores and a higher perception of environmental control (e.g., a student's belief that she can overcome external obstacles) than their counterparts in coed schools (Riordan, 1994). An experiment comparing talented high school girls enrolled in an advanced calculus-based physics course designated "for girls only" with girls in a coed section of the same class supports the environmental control idea. Compared to girls in the coed section, which was dominated by boys, the girls-only section showed higher levels of problem solving and analytical performance, higher enrollment in later advanced classes, and an increase in overall self-confidence. The girls' section was taught by a man using female-friendly pedagogical techniques, including teamwork in problem solving, peer learning, and employing many practical applications of physics. The classroom subculture of the girls' section is described as one of special rapport between students, taking responsibility for each other's learning, and ensuring that success is measured not just as an individual accomplishment but a group accomplishment as well (IMSA, 1995).

Females who make a transition the other way—from a single-gender to a coeducational educational environment—indicate they experience a "clash of cultures" and report discomfort and dissatisfaction with the coed format (Sadovnik and Semel, 2002). Women express concern that friends could become competitors when men are a regular part of campus life. Qualitative research by Janice Streitmatter (1999) on middle and high school girls attending single-gender schools or taking girls-only classes in coed schools clearly points to the benefits of single-gender formats. For example, girls describe fewer distractions from learning, such as ". . . there are things I do that I probably wouldn't do if there were guys here. . . I can just be myself." They also mention that in coed classes male students receive most of the teacher's attention and get called on more. "In a mixed class . . . you're like off in the background—you're quieter about what you know." In the single-gender format, girls asked and answered questions without the risk of "feeling stupid." Girls did not need to carve out separate space—"the culture was theirs, a place they understood and did not need fear" (Streitmatter, 1999:82,87,105). A powerful message to girls in single-gender environments is that they can aspire to anything males can aspire to.

On the other hand, there are challenges to the assertions about benefits of single-gender education. First, gender appears to be less important than social class in explaining rates of student success. Single-gender schools are more likely to be private schools attended by more affluent students which have better facilities, higher paid teachers, and smaller student–teacher ratios. Private single-gender schools can also expel disruptive students who then retreat to public coeducational schools that must accept them. Second, the negative effects of an already pervasive gender-segregated society are not necessarily challenged by single-gender schools (Hubbard and Datnow, 2002; Salomone, 2003). We have seen that throughout socialization, within-gender solidarity is enhanced through gender segregation, but between-gender understanding is diminished. Educational institutions at all levels are microcosms of the real world, so they need to model that world.

Related to the segregation issue is that single-gender education for boys is likely to be based on an even stronger androcentric pedagogy than that found in either girls' schools or coeducational institutions. The traditional mode of educational performance after elementary school is androcentric. Even the elementary school environment, which on the surface appears to favors girls' passivity rather than boys' activity, is based on a male-centered approach to learning. Classrooms are structured around hierarchy, domination, competition, and win-lose grading and teaching approaches. Throughout school females must adjust to the taken-for-granted androcentric norm that may serve to undermine confidence building. The less preferred model of educational performance in schools is the female preferred model, such as the girls-only physics class described earlier that used teamwork and consensus approaches to learning. Masculinity norms are strongly reinforced in boys' schools by the formal and hidden curriculum. A powerful message to boys in single-gender settings is that they are better than girls. Girls in single-gender settings may believe they cannot succeed if boys are around. Girls in single-gender schools hold less rigid gender stereotypes, but boys hold more. Thus single-gender education may reproduce destructive stereotypes for both genders (Epstein, 1997).

Coeducation can certainly provide a major mechanism for reducing gender segregation and its associated gender stereotyping. If there is a problem of male dominance in the coed classroom that is detrimental to girls, a convincing argument can be made that it is also detrimental to boys. Rather than retreating into gender-segregated schools, the classroom atmosphere can be altered to reflect not only a more gender-sensitive campus or school culture, but also one that is beneficial to both females and males. Feminist pedagogy places a high value on cooperative learning techniques in a supportive environment that can decrease the negative effects of competition, such as disabling fear of failure, as well as increased consensus and teamwork (Maher and Tetreault, 2001; Howie and Tauchert, 2002). Competition is not ignored, but consensus is valued. Skill building for success in a highly competitive workplace is also learned. Regardless of which side of the debate one is on, classroom environments can be modified to capitalize on those successful learning strategies provided by single-gender education.

Sexual Harassment in Schools

Sexual harassment legally includes physical or verbal conduct that is sexual in nature, is unwanted, and creates a hostile environment that interferes with school or work activities (chapter 14). Despite the fact that sexual harassment is illegal, it is so widespread at all levels in schools that it is considered to be a part of everyday life for students (AAUW, 2001). This is especially true in elementary schools where sexual harassment takes the form of bullying behavior of boys to girls—accepted by the boys, tolerated by the girls, and ignored by the teachers. When adults hear comments and do not intervene, both boys and girls believe that the behavior is appropriate (Stein, 1999). Whereas racial comments are swiftly censured, sexually harassing ones are usually dismissed. Surveys of female high school students report that over one-third had observed or experienced it (Sauerwein, 1996). Examples from these students included: "talking about people with large chests," "pinching butts on the bus," and "half of everything said on the Commons." In college, research indicates that between one-third to three-fourths of female faculty and female students experience some form of sexual harassment, ranging from everyday jokes about body or physical contact, demeaning images, negative remarks, and sexist comments, to unwanted advances, demands for sexual favors, and sexual aggression or victimization (Welsh, 1999; Riger, 2000; Wilson, 2000).

When race is added to the picture, some research reports higher rates of sexual harassment for women of color, with African-American women experiencing the highest rates, followed by Latino, white, and Asian/East Indian women (Paludi, 1996). Compared to white women, African-American women may identify their experiences with sexual harassment differently as well. For example, African-American women mention being touched by a professor, comments about racially based physical features, and stereotypes about promiscuity of African Americans as indications of sexual harassment (Mecca and Rubin, 1999). Research on race in sexual harassment is still limited. Other studies report no significant race difference in level or type of sexual harassment. However, because white and African-American women perceive it differently, the race–gender intersection in social constructions of sexual harassment needs to be explored (Kalof et al., 2001). Sexual harassment of males is infrequent, but numbers are growing. Bullying behavior of boys to other boys is common; it decreases with age and is usually ignored unless it involves physical fighting. It can be brutal and humiliating, but it is not considered sexual harassment (Stein, 1999), even when boys bully other boys verbally using sexually derogatory comments that compare them to girls or gay men or boys (pussy, wuss, fag, bitch). Boys do not report bullying from other boys—sexual or otherwise—for the same reason girls do not report sexual harassment—fear of reprisal, especially from peers. The reprisal boys fear takes the form of mocking them for acting like a girl and snitching—not "taking" it like a man. Norms about masculinity make it difficult for males to admit that they may be intimidated by females (Dziech and Hawkins, 1998). Even as college students, although fear of reprisal makes women reluctant to report it, the perceived assault on gender identity begun in elementary school makes it even less likely for men to do so.

Single-Gender Military Schools: Sexual Harassment or Bullying?

Shannon Faulkner became the first female cadet admitted to The Military Citadel of South Carolina (Citadel). She was subjected to death threats, ridicule, and ongoing humiliation by many of her classmates, some school officials, and the public at large. Her car and home were vandalized. To the elation of her classmates, Faulkner dropped out of the Citadel and was portrayed in the media as incapable of withstanding the physical punishment and emotional stress all cadets must endure. In bolstering the legal battles preceding her admittance and following her washing out from the Citadel, stereotypes of women as physically weaker, more emotional, less motivated, and less talented for the ordeals of military college life were offered (Epstein, 1998). Like all women, Shannon Faulkner was "incapable" of doing what men can do because women, of course, are essentially different than men. The two issues discussed here—single-gender schooling and sexual harassment—can be drawn together by considering the legal cases used by The Citadel and Virginia Military Institute (VMI), both historically male-only institutions, to justify their continued exclusion of women, even though both receive public funds. The issues also highlight our continuing discussion about how much males and females are alike and how much they are different.

Disproving stereotypes of women as incapable is fairly easy, given the overwhelming research evidence that women survive and both women and men thrive, side by side with one another in a host of environments—workplace, schools, and the military—from which they (women) had formerly been excluded. Another belief that could not be legally sustained was that sexual tension would distract men (and women) from performance of military duty. Women have been admitted to West Point since 1976, and the ability to wage war, for example, has not been compromised by their presence. The obvious sexism in arguments that rely on notions of one gender being more or less inherently capable, especially in the face of massive evidence to the contrary, makes it difficult for any public figure to support such arguments today. Michael Kimmel (2000) describes the key argument, however, that initially garnered legal support to deny women admittance to VMI. Attorneys presented some of the same evidence discussed earlier that single-gender education benefits females and males:

> Since discrimination is justified on the basis of difference, all VMI had to do was demonstrate those differences. Toward that end they used feminist theorists to buttress their claims, co-opting arguments by Carol Gilligan, Deborah Tannen and others who claim that women responded better to more nurturing and supportive educational methodologies. (Kimmel, 2000:501)

A lower court ruled in favor of VMI. Females, the judge maintained, do not thrive in adversarial settings, and such a setting is a key element to VMI's mission—a mission that could be thwarted if women's "needs" were accommodated. The victory was a brief one. Appeals culminated in a U.S. Supreme Court decision requiring VMI to admit women. The Citadel became coeducational the same week. Today, women make up between 6 and 8 percent of the first-year cadet class in both schools, with a steady increase in applications from women.

Sexual harassment also enters the picture. Cadets at VMI and the Citadel are subjected to grueling hazing "rat lines"—brutal and callous training designed to cement a class and implant unquestioned obedience to military authority (Manegold, 2000). Rat lines are the extreme forms of bullying, but in this case, legitimized and encouraged. Because bullying is not considered sexual harassment, neither is the rat line—cadets of both genders are viewed the "same." Sameness means that both genders adhere to powerful masculinity norms that undoubtedly include derogatory beliefs about women. In adopting these norms, female cadets must walk a fine line of showing support for cadet bonding, which may also mean denigrating other women. Male cadets can be accused of sexual harassment—and expelled—only if bullying becomes sexualized so that the "hidden gender" of the female cadets is revealed and then reviled.

The sameness-difference issue has haunted us throughout this text. Symbolic interactionists maintain that once admitted to "uncontaminated" all-male institutions, such as West Point, the new female cadets are tokens and must constantly negotiate gender differences and similarities—always "doing" gender. "When they stressed sameness they were seen as different; when they stressed difference, they were treated the same." Both male and female cadets believed that equal meant the same, and standards of training should not be lowered, otherwise they would not have enrolled in the first place. But as Michael Kimmel (2000:505,507) suggests, not acknowledging important differences that do exist—treating unlikes alike—is also a form of discrimination. Females and males do not differ in intelligence and capability. However, because educational institutions, like all other social institutions, are gendered, the results of the gendering should be considered in decisions about who gets accepted to highly selective and competitive schools—whether as a female cadet or a male nursing student.

THE LESSONS OF TITLE IX

Title IX of the 1972 Educational Amendment Act addresses many of the educational patterns described in this chapter. This act prohibits sex (gender) discrimination in any school receiving federal assistance, which means that the majority of educational institutions fall under its mandate. At the overt and formal level it can be said that gender discrimination has significantly decreased. Title IX has had a huge impact on athletics and is directly responsible for major increases in the sports participation of female students at all school levels (chapter 14). Title IX forbids sexual harassment of students, and a school may be liable if authorities know it is occurring but fail to act on it. However, we have seen that both males and females are reluctant to report it and if they do, the courts are inconsistent in rulings about specific circumstances that can be used to hold a school liable.

We have seen, however, that discriminatory policies exist throughout the educational process. Title IX has done little to alter gender segregation of academic fields, at either the student or faculty level. This segregation continues throughout all levels of educational institutions. Kindergarten girls play with dolls and boys with trucks. Girls take home economics in middle school. Young men major in mathematics in college. A male Ph.D. teaches Engineering. A female Ph.D. teaches French. He is paid more than her. Even the more liberal world of the university remains gender role oriented and gender separated.

It may be possible to reduce glaring gender discrimination through legal means. This assumes the existence of a favorable political climate that actively initiates and enforces such change. Title IX can serve as a catalyst of change especially when coupled with a major modification in those socialization practices that restrict the educational opportunities for girls and boys, women and men. Gender discrimination may disappear by the time Jane and Dick reach college, but prejudices are likely to linger for their children and grandchildren.

Reflecting on education a century ago, M. Carey Thomas (1857–1935), former president of Bryn Mawr College, stated

> that women, like men, are quickened and inspired by the same love of learning, the same love of science, [and] the same love of abstract truth; that women, like men, are immeasurably benefited, physically, mentally and morally, and are made vastly better mothers, as men made vastly better fathers, by subordinating the distracting instincts of sex to the simple human fellowship of similar education and similar intellectual and social needs. (see Thomas, 1991:338)

Although gender segregation is still the norm, this chapter has documented some encouraging signs that perhaps Thomas's call for "the simple human fellowship of similar education" is within our grasp.

GLOBAL FOCUS: THE DEVELOPING WORLD'S GENDER GAP IN EDUCATION

If similar education between males and females is "within our grasp" in the United States, the picture is far different when looking at the developing world. One of the best ways to make economic development a success is to teach girls to read. Indeed, with only a 10 percent increase in female literacy, family size shrinks 10 percent, child death rates drop 10 percent, and wages rise 20 percent. In the developing world it is estimated that gains in education for women and girls may account for a 40 percent drop in infant mortality. One of the most important global demographic trends is that a woman's education level is the strongest predictor of fertility rate. This is true between countries and among women in the same country (Academy for Educational Development, 2002; World Health Organization, 2003).

More educated children marry later, want fewer children, and have only the number of children they want. Birth rates and child death rates decline fastest where there is access to family planning, health services, and educational opportunities for girls. South Korea, Taiwan, Singapore, Thailand, and Sri Lanka all represent family planning success stories, with most reporting that they have reached the goal of replacement fertility. Compared to other parts of Asia, these countries also have higher levels of female education and literacy (Thomas and Price, 1999). The simple correlation between education and fertility masks its enormous impact, not only on the lives of individual women and their families, but also on the world as a whole, confirming that education is inevitably an agent of social change.

Despite education's many benefits, and although it is no longer reserved for a culture's elite, there is a large and persistent global education gap. The largest gap is between the developed and developing world. In the developing world the largest gap is in Africa. Almost 97 percent of the world's 113 million children not enrolled in primary school are in the developing world. Of these children, 42 million live in sub-Saharan Africa, and another 47 million live in South and West Asia. Most of these children are in poverty, most are in rural areas, and most of them are girls (Pigozzi, 1999; UNICEF, 2003). The adult illiteracy rate in China has been cut by two-thirds since 1949, but the gender gap in illiteracy remains large; less than only 10 percent of men are illiterate compared to one-fourth of women. China reflects the larger global pattern; two-thirds of the illiterate adults in the world are women. The highest female illiteracy rates are in regions with the lowest indicators of human development, specifically in South Asia and sub-Saharan Africa. For example, Pakistan and Nepal have female illiteracy rates of 70 percent and 77 percent, respectively, compared to about 40 percent for men in both countries. For sub-Saharan Africa, the overall adult illiteracy rate is 50 percent for women compared to 34 percent for men. The African country of Niger ranks at the bottom on human development indicators and, predictably, has the world's worst adult illiteracy rates: over three-fourths of all men and an astounding 90 percent of all women are illiterate (UNICEF, 2003; World Bank, 2003; United Nations Development Program, 2004). Children of a literate mother have a better chance of survival than the children living in the same place at the same level of income of a mother who is illiterate.

Investing in women's education brings high returns globally. The elimination of the gender education gap is in the best interest of a thriving global economy, but it is clear that in much of the developing world reducing the gap has not been a priority. As conflict theorists remind us, altering gender role norms to bring about social change brings both benefits and liabilities, depending on how various social groups are affected. The paradox of the globe's gender gap is that women and girls have not amassed the power to challenge these norms in part because of their lack of education.

Summary

1. Historically when women were first granted the right of education, it was to be in line with their wife and mother roles.

2. The process of education is highly gendered and operates through a hidden curriculum. Gender segregation in kindergarten is reinforced by toys and games that provide high levels of activity for boys and quietness for girls.

3. Girls in elementary school have higher achievement levels and receive less criticism but less instructional time than boys. Boys adjust less easy to school but gain more attention from teachers. Children read textbooks that underrepresent girls and cast males and females into stereotyped roles.

4. Boys gain in self-confidence and achievement in high school; girls decline in both, especially Latino girls. Most girls decline in math achievement but gender differences are steadily decreasing. Existing differences are best explained by culture factors due to gender rather than biological factors due to biology. Social class and the race-SES link are better predictors for math performance than is gender.

5. Tracking puts more girls than boys in all vocational courses and in academic courses like English. Textbooks in high school are gender stereotyped, and an andocentric bias exists in standardized achievement tests.

6. Popularity for boys in high school is tied to athletics; for girls it is attractiveness and popularity with boys. Athletics for boys provides powerful gender identity messages; boys who cannot perform in sports can lose self-esteem, and more so if they do co-educational sports. More money and facilities are given to sports for males.

7. Fueled by women over 35 attending part time, women are enrolled in college at higher numbers than men. Women are undermined in college achievement and career orientation by issues related to marriage and motherhood. Men are more consistent with predictions about career in their future plans.

8. Women are distributed in majors that translate to less lucrative jobs. Men are concentrated in science and engineering and dominate fields requiring graduate work. Women in graduate school have fewer mentors of their own gender and spend less time with all faculty.

9. Female college faculty are more likely to be part time, in nontenure tracks, and at lower ranks than males. Compared to faculty men, faculty women are evaluated differently and in line with gender stereotypes by students, colleagues, and administrators.

10. Single-gender education for females is associated with higher self-confidence, leadership, and achievement. Single-gender education for boys is associated with strong androcentric pedagogy. When males and females are schooled separately, understanding between men and women may be further decreased.

11. Sexual harassment by boys to girls in elementary schools is often in the form of bullying. Research on whether women of color are harassed more is unclear. Sexual harassment of males is infrequent but growing. In military schools girls are bullied, but it is not sexual harassment unless sexualized terms are used. Boys use these terms to bully other boys. Female cadets must negotiate how much they are the same and how much they are different from male cadets.

12. Title IX—which prohibits sex discrimination in schools—has dealt with blatant discrimination and has greatly aided sports programs for females. But is has had limited effect in altering gender segregation in academic fields.

13. Education for females is one of the best ways to make economic development a success. When girls are taught to read, family size shrinks, child death rates decrease, and wages increase. A large global gender gap in education persists. Women make up the vast majority of illiterate adults worldwide.

Key Terms

hidden curriculum 296

sexual harassment 311

Title IX of the 1972 Educational Amendment Act 313

Critical Thinking Questions

1. Document the consequences of key gender differences related to behavior, academics, major, and career orientation in the process of education. Based on this evaluation, demonstrate how educators may provide a gender equitable learning process beneficial to both females and males.

2. Applied to your own college setting, demonstrate your understanding of the gendered processes in higher education. How is your college experience consistent or inconsistent with the gender patterns discussed in this chapter? What may account for the level of consistency?

3. As a feminist sociologist, as a functionalist, and as a symbolic interactionist, argue for or against the following statement: single-gender education in elementary school and high school is beneficial to both boys and girls.

RELIGION AND PATRIARCHY

CHAPTER 12

Ethically I am looking for

An absolute endorsement of loving-kindness.

No loopholes except maybe mosquitoes. . . . . .

There will be no concept of infidels;

Consequently the faithful must entertain

Themselves some other way than killing infidels.

—Alice Ostriker, from
Everywoman Her Own Theology (2001)

Something went terribly wrong with Christianity's original gospel of love.

—Riane Eisler, *The Chalice and the Blade*

The transformation of ancient spirituality into modern religion came with a heavy price. Religious imagery has been used to maintain injustice, suffering, and oppression—of nation against nation, men against men, and men against women. Institutionalized religion, whether pagan, Hebrew, Christian, or Islamic, helped maintain hierarchies of domination and oppression but also functioned to alleviate part of the suffering caused by these very hierarchies (Eisler, 1995a:203). In many ancient spiritual and religious traditions and in the societies in which they were practiced, women held influential and esteemed partnership roles with men. As

318

religions became more formal and moved toward institutionalization, the spirituality and the partnership on which many are based receded into the background. Net gains in overall gender equality in all social institutions are recorded across the globe, but organized religion lags behind in the amount of religious authority granted to women compared to men. It is paradoxical that religion is the one institution that should offer the most potential for freedom of expression through liberating spirituality, but the undeniably sexist interpretations and practices—and human rights violations—in the name of religion seriously impede its liberating potential (Eisler, 1995b; Howland, 1999; Nussbaum, 2000). As documented in this chapter, however, revised interpretations provide opportunities to release patriarchy's religious stranglehold and open the doors of churches, temples, and mosques to the empowering messages religions offer to both women and men.

REDISCOVERING THE FEMININE FACE OF GOD

The image of God as a woman is probably quite startling to those who identify with any of the major world religions. The explosion of research on the role and status of women in these religions reveals that these early religions were infused with notions of gender interdependence rather than gender separation. Based on archaeological evidence found in both prehistoric and historic societies, research now offers a view of the first civilizations as exhibiting **gynocentrism**, with an emphasis on female and feminine interests (Sered, 1994; Eisler, 1995a; Gimbutas, 1991, 2001). Whereas androcentrism translated to patriarchy in some ancient societies, gynocentrism did not translate to matriarchy in others. Instead, it translated to partnership. As Riane Eisler (1995b) points out, the terms *patriarchy* and *matriarchy* refer to a ranking of one part of humanity over the other. She asserts that partnership is the third, overlooked alternative that characterized much of early civilization. Unlike patriarchy or matriarchy, partnership is based on the principle of linking and relating rather than domination and separateness. Males and females may be different, but these differences are not associated with either inferiority or superiority. Given the powerful influence of religion in the structure of ancient civilizations, evidence for gynocentric societies offers important messages to contemporary theologians as they struggle with issues related to gender role change in their respective religions.

Goddess Images

The most ancient human image we have of the divine is a figure of a female. When gynocentrism was replaced by androcentrism in partnership oriented societies, the millennia of goddess prehistory and history were relegated to academic oblivion or dismissed by scholars as incidental to the span of humanity (Gimbutas, 2001). From a conflict perspective, when spirituality began the road to institutionalized religion, goddess images were suppressed because their power was threatening to an emerging male-dominated religious status quo. For contemporary women, rediscovering the goddess heritage can affirm their sense of religious wellbeing. Contrary to the conflict perspective, however, a partnership approach does *not* create a new hierarchy of religious images that would serve to empower women but disenfranchise men. From Eisler's partnership viewpoint, both men and women can share in and celebrate the principles rooted in the goddess heritage and use these principles as standards as they work together for religious reform.

The emerging picture, then, demonstrates a religious portrait of ancient civilizations where women played a central role, where female deities were often worshipped, and where religious life was essentially a partnership between men and women, much more than modern institutionalized religion would have us believe. The intent here is to provide a brief chronicle of some images of women as they appear in the mythology and religious heritage of people in the ancient world. Such an account is important for grasping the significance of attitudes toward women in modern world religion that is the focus of the latter part of this chapter.

Women's Religious Roles. Compelling evidence for a continuous, influential goddess heritage and the significance of women's ancient religious roles in this heritage abounds (Roller, 1999; Berger, 2000; Cleary and Aziz, 2000). The cult of the mother-goddess was one of the oldest, most widespread, and longest surviving religions throughout the Paleolithic to Neolithic periods in sites from Western Europe, through the Mediterranean world, and into India. The cult of the mother-goddess provides images of women in roles as leaders, healers, artists, music makers, and food providers. In an early effort to document woman's dominance of prehistoric civilization, Elizabeth Davis's (1971) then-controversial book, *The First Sex*, states that not only is there massive evidence of the matriarchal origins of human society but also that the "further back one traces *man's* history, the larger loomed the figure of woman" (emphasis added) (p. 16). She maintains that in all myth, the goddess is synonymous with gynocracy so when the goddess reigned, women ruled. Although scholars continue to debate the amount of actual power women held in goddess-dominated societies, abundant archaeological evidence on goddess worship does suggest gynocentric (rather than matriarchal) origins of civilization (Eller, 2000; Christ, 2003b).

Archeological evidence attesting to gynocratic religious and artistic traditions has been uncovered in the world's best preserved and oldest Neolithic sites in Catal Huyuk, what is now modern Turkey. These traditions span 800 years, from 6500 to 5700 B.C.E. and are vividly represented by numerous goddess figurines, all emphasizing worship of a female deity. The artifacts of prehistoric European peoples demonstrate representations of the goddess as a symbol of life, fertility, creativity, and regeneration. Although the vast majority of the symbols are associated with life images rather than death images, they all speak to the veneration and powerful sacredness of women (Gimbutas, 2001).

Goddess as Creator. The goddess image is carried through to the idea of the creator when examining accounts from ancient Sumer, Babylon, Assyria, Greece, Egypt, and China. Nammu is the Summerian goddess who gives birth to heaven and earth, Tiamet is the Babylonian "Creator of All," the mother of gods, and in Greek mythology, Metis, loosely translated as the creative power of female intelligence, brings the world into being without a male partner. In the *Tao te ching*, creation is the reproduction of all matter from the womb of the Mother. Paleolithic peoples saw the original source of life on earth not as a divine Father but a divine Mother, and the creative sexual power of women as a miracle of nature, to be revered and blessed. In Chinese Buddhism the goddess of compassion is Kuan Yin, in Hinduism the goddess of destruction is Kali, the consort of Siva who is revered both as a giver and destroyer of life. The twenty-one representations of the female Tibetan deity Tara symbolize compassion, the easing of human suffering, and the guidance to wisdom and salvation. The goddess as the first creator is associated with mythology and religious principles in all corners of the world. It is only in later myth that she is replaced by a god (Engelsman, 1994; King, 1997; Folston, 2002; Lightfoot, 2003).

With the Babylonian empire's dominance in the emerging urban-agricultural world, the warrior-champion Marduk arises as the god of the new city–state. The Marduk-Tiamet story tells of the defeat of Tiamet and her consort, who represent the power of chaos, by the new god Marduk and his followers, who represent the power of order (Ruether, 1983:50). The emergence of the new gods, however, did not initially erase female names and memories. Marduk molded the cosmos out of Tiamet's body, so she retained her place as the creator. Siva in India, Atea in Polynesia, and Ea in Syria are also names of goddesses carried over to the male gods who replaced them. Goddess worship was not eradicated but many practices were driven underground by later religious persecution (Cleary and Aziz, 2000; Lightfoot, 2003). Perhaps the female names given to male gods were, and still are, the vestiges of such practices.

Africa. The oldest record of human habitation is in Africa, and it is there where perhaps the best examples of the goddess as the Mother of All are found. On a continent with an incredible diversity of peoples, customs, and religious symbolism, images of the goddess throughout sub-Saharan Africa vary as well, from Mawu, creator of the world, to Goddess as the Moon, to the goddess as She Who Sends Rain (Stone, 1990). In Ghana, Nigeria, and other parts of west and central Africa, tribal religions recognize a divinity that may be male or female. Other cults have primarily female spirit beings. Even given such diversity, the symbolism that emerges most consistently among African indigenous religions involves the concerns for honesty, courage, sympathy, hope, and humanitarianism, which the goddesses represented and the peoples who worshipped them revered. The roots of this heritage are expressed in the many female-dominated religious cults and secret societies that give meaning to African women's lives and continue today to affirm their power (Sered, 1994; Amadiume, 1997; Nkulu-N'Sengha, 2001).

Asia. The ancient texts of China and India also speak clearly to the goddess image. Taoism, the indigenous religious tradition of China, is illustrated by the *Chuang Tzu*, written in the third century B.C.E. Part of this account is a description of the Era of the Great Purity, a utopian matrilineal society, where life was characterized by happiness, harmony, innocence, and spontaneity and where women held influential and venerated family and extradomestic roles. Most of the symbols in this and other Taoist (Daoist) works are explicitly female and highlight fertility and abundant, unqualified motherly love (Wong, 2002; Despeux and Kohn, 2003). It is interesting that women's spiritual power and social influence found in Taoist societies developed and coexisted in a region dominated by Confucian principles, which were highly patriarchal and hierarchical and viewed women as inferior by nature. Although Confucianism remained the dominant religion, Taoist elements could be discovered within other parts of ancient Chinese culture. Contemporary

Taoism maintains that the "creative principle is symbolically female because the Tao, like an empty womb, is the origin of all things" (Reed, 1987:181).

In India, ancient Buddhist traditions supported women's quest for enlightenment (Shaw, 1997; Gross, 1997, 2002). Taoism shares with Buddhism less restrictive and more positive images of women compared with many other Eastern and Western traditions (Coleman, 2001; Puntarigvivat, 2001; Xiaogan, 2001). In the few Chinese regions where Taoist and Buddhist principles intersected, some evidence suggests that women had such high degrees of power that matriarchal societies were said to exist. Although more research is needed to support this astounding suggestion, contemporary women in these areas hold positions associated with more esteem and power than women in other regions of China (Lindsey, 1999).

The Principle of Gender Complementarity

Beyond the goddess images that dominated many ancient practices and beliefs, some religious systems also incorporated principles of balance where, in principle, neither gender was superior. Most notable among these is the ancient Chinese concept of *Yin* and *Yang*. Although Western interpretation often misrepresents the female principal of Yin as being passive and dominated by the active and aggressive male principal of Yang, this is a distortion of the ancient belief, which emphasized equilibrium, complementarity, and a portion of each principle being incorporated into the other. The Yin-Yang ideal of harmonious balance remains central to the Chinese value system. Much of the original intent of balance was lost as patriarchy extended its influence to all cultural elements, including religion.

Tantric Buddhism in medieval India and Tibet was amenable to both male and female *siddhas*—accomplished ones—whose gender was considered irrelevant to the ultimate Buddhist goal of enlightenment. Buddha's disciples included both men and women, and spiritual paths to enlightenment were open to both men and women. Women could be ordained as nuns just as men could become monks, practices that continue today. In Native American spiritual traditions the complementarity of men and women was evident, with the genders performing unique spiritual practices or sharing others. The matrilineal Iroquois tribes of eastern North America participated in religious ceremonies where both the male and female dimensions were needed, such as rites to encourage the male activity of hunting or the female activity of agriculture (Shimony, 1985). Although it is difficult to generalize about such diverse Native Americans cultures, they were likely to be holistic and organized their worldviews according to the interdependence of natural forces and human forces (Jocks, 2001; Staeger, 2003). With male and female powers balancing each other, social equilibrium was said to be maintained.

Critique. In ancient and contemporary societies, religious traditions incorporating notions of male and female complementarity and balance did not inevitably carry over into other realms. If Tantric Buddhism was a path open to both genders, the Indian and Tibetan cultures made it very difficult for women to pursue such a path, given their restrictions in other institutional settings. Women who wished to follow the path as nuns had to submit to rigid standards of male control established by the monks (Kloppenborg, 1995). For Native Americans, the Iroquois also denied public expression of women in a variety of settings. Gender complementarity does not necessarily translate to gender equity. Complementarity assumes males and females are "designed to make up for one another's deficiencies, rather than inspiring one another to overcome them" (Webster, 1995:194).

Regardless of the inequality that doubtlessly existed in other parts of the society, these accounts of goddess images and male-female complementarity in early religious traditions do provide an alternative and clearly positive view of women. This view can help offset contemporary religious interpretations about women's submissiveness, subordination, and powerlessness that impact three-quarters of the world's 6 billion people who identify with a major world religion.

ISLAM

Islam is the world's second largest and fastest growing religion, representing about one-fifth of the world's population, The word *Islam* translates to *submission*, and Muslims, the adherents of Islam, are ones who have "submitted" to the will of God, or Allah. Founded in the first century, Islam is based on the teachings of Muhammad (570–632), the greatest among God's prophets whose revelations are recorded in the Qur'an (Koran), the holy book of Islam. Islam emerged in response to unique Arab needs and circumstances, including Muhammad's desire to aid the poor and provide economic resources for those who were not under the care and protection of others, including widows, orphans, and unmarried women. Islam introduced changes that were advantageous to women in the areas of marriage, divorce, and inheritance, although other Islamic practices served to disempower women (Brooks, 2002; Hassan, 2002).

Muslims vary considerably in how they interpret the Qur'an in regard to the roles of contemporary women (Khan, 2000; Ruthven, 2000; Moosa, 2003). Much of what is expected of women is based on short narratives about the sayings and deeds of Muhammad's many wives that were passed down orally. These stories are part of the commentaries on the Qur'an that have since become authoritative sources for Islamic teaching. The accuracy of these thousands of narratives is questionable and each period interprets them according to prevailing cultural standards. They have been used to justify a wide range of contradictory attitudes and practices concerning Islamic women. Women are seen as ideal, obedient, and gentle as well as jealous, conspiratorial, and having imperfect minds (Hekmat, 1997; Ahmed, 2002; Hotaling, 2003). In the pre-Islamic Arab world, women had esteemed roles as soothsayers, priestesses, and queens, but it is clear that these images had been swept away once Islam became entrenched in Arab cultures. By the third century, women were more secluded and degraded than anything known in earlier Islamic decades (Mernissi, 1987; Minai, 1991; Shehadeh, 2003). Although contemporary Islam defines men and women as complementary rather than equal, passages from the Qur'an emphasizing inequality over complementarity are favored, such as "men are in charge of women, because God hath made the one of them to excel the other" (*Qur'an, IV*:34). Since men are a step above women and the protectors of women, God gives preference and authority to men over women.

Islamic law is nurtured by a code of ethics that views a woman's key role as providing male heirs. This role may be compromised if women are not restricted in their activities, especially during childbearing years. Muhammad himself was awed by woman's power and what he saw as a mysterious, unlimited sexual drive that, if left unfettered, could wreak social havoc by casting doubt on the legitimacy of the husband's heirs. From a functionalist perspective, the practices involving purdah arose as a response to these attitudes. Women have less freedom outside their homes in Islamic nations where the law is based on interpretations of the Qur'an and where there are high levels of female illiteracy.

Feminist Views of Islam

Female ethnographers are documenting that numerous restrictions on women in the name of the Qur'an are much more likely the result of a nation's history and politics rather than its religion (Scupin, 2000). When women are educated in Islamic history and empowered to interpret the Qur'an, they not only offer more positive messages, but also balance the distorted ones regarding the role and status of Islamic women.

The emergence of a new scholarship on the role of women in Islam written by Muslim women is providing alternative interpretations of the Qur'an and transforming the women of the holy texts into feminist role models (Cooke, 2001). Sufism, the mystical school of Islam, is replete with women saints. Their shrines exist throughout North Africa, India, and the Middle East and are visited by women in search of special needs connected with their family life. Research on Indian Sufism suggests that like men, women from all backgrounds and social classes could follow a religious path and have the potential for sainthood (Bonouvrié, 1995). Another example is in regard to the wives of Muhammad, who hold powerful places as the "Mothers of Believers." These women are venerated for the roles they played in Muhammad's household during the emergence of Islam.

> When we listen here to these women who surrounded the Prophet and whose words and actions held his attention . . . then it is not only a faraway echo that we hear, but rather a very present-day message. . . . Do not these wives, Mothers of Believers, remind us . . . that a society of progress and justice takes place through the restoration of women, to all women, of the dignity and the position which the religion award them? (cited in Ascha, 1995:107)

Islamic Women in the United States

With the global spotlight on the Taliban after 9/11, attention was riveted on Islamic women in the United States, which enlarged the existing dialogue among Muslims regarding women's contribution to the formation of American Islam. Muslim women are altering as well as affirming the traditional values of their religion. Although women are denied the opportunity to be *imams*—religious leaders and administrative officers of mosques—there is strong support for the belief that Islam provides equal rights and responsibilities for women. Most Muslim women earn or expect to earn college degrees, and most work outside the home. But like women of other faiths, there is a debate about how women can successfully reconcile employment and family roles, especially concerning child care. Another debate concerns the proper dress of Muslim women in certain settings (Anway, 1996). Unlike in South Asia and the Middle East, the debate in the United States is often on whether a woman's hair—not her whole body—should be covered (Smith, 1999).

Reflecting the rapid gains in education among Muslim women and the unique, American stamp on Islam, women are actively engaged in these debates and have more influence than their Islamic sisters in the Arab world in resolving them.

HINDUISM

Dating from about 4,500 years ago Hinduism is the oldest of the world's major religions, with almost 800 million followers, most of whom live in India. As Islam is to Arab cultures, Hinduism is incorporated into the cultural fabric in so many ways that it is impossible to visualize what India would be like without it. Because Hinduism is based in one of the most ethnically diverse regions in the world, and its practices have been adapted to suit such a wide variety of cultural circumstances, contradictory images of women may be expected.

The Feminine in Hindu Scripture

The oldest Hindu scriptures, the *Vedas* and *Upanishads* (1800–500 B.C.E.), provide images of women that have been interpreted in many ways. Some condemn women for selfishness, energy, and ambition, especially if they forsake their "higher" level of womanhood and neglect to serve their families (Jacobson and Wadley, 1995; Weisgrau, 2000). An influential work written over a half century ago describes one such woman:

> (They) take pride in proving that they never developed a talent for domesticity . . . (and) society will have to allow for them. Such "masculine" women do not reach the highest of which womanhood is capable. (Radhakrishnan, 1947:142)

These beliefs are fostered by interpretations of the ancient *Ramayana* and *Mahabharata* epics, which describe many Hindu ideals related to the proper role of men and women in their families (Ghosh, 2000). Combined with the Hindu scriptures, these popular epics offer children authoritative messages supporting traditional beliefs about gender roles.

Other interpretations dating to Hinduism's preinstitutionalized era are much more positive. These demonstrate an esteem for femininity and complementarity between spouses.

The Hindu ideal is that male and female are balanced, with man as the creator and woman as the lover, and with a woman's sexual tendencies being as varied and erotic as a man's. Hindus celebrate a number of female goddesses, saints, and deities, the most prominent of whom are linked to symbols of fertility, creation, and hope (Gupta, 2000; Khanna, 2000). Unlike Muslims in India, where males control religious practice and where virtually all significant religious figures are male, Hindus allow women to serve in temples and lead religious rituals (Larson, 1994; Narayanan, 2002). Hinduism has the longest continuing goddess heritage in the world and offers models for men and women to follow and revere.

Despite the variety of religious images offered to Hindu women, it is safe to conclude that they practice rituals congruent with their roles as mothers, wives, and homemakers. These customs exemplify the domestic sphere of life, the only one known to most Hindu women. In many Indian villages, for example, childbirth involves an elaborate series of rituals lasting from pregnancy until the child is introduced to a life outside the home. Many North Indian Hindu women practice rituals expressing their concerns for family and household. Observed only by women, although these ceremonies do not require the services of male priests, they reflect a strong patriarchal society. Some practices involve the direct worship of husbands and brothers for the purpose of obtaining their protection whereas others offer prayers and supplications for the happy marriages of daughters and for the joys of being blessed with male offspring (Younger, 2002; McDaniel, 2003).

Sati

"The greatest misfortune that can befall a (Hindu) wife is to survive her husband" (cited in Jarman, 2002:2). Hindu religious rituals reinforce women's roles as mothers, wives, and homemakers and connections to men for their well-being. When women became "unconnected" to men by widowhood, the widow, referred to as a **sati**, was frequently expected to perform a ritual in which she would be buried alive with her dead husband or, more commonly, self-immolated on his funeral pyre. This section ends with a historical glimpse at this infamous ritual.

The widow-burning ritual originated during the ancient Vedic period, where the widow performed a symbolic self-immolation on her husband's death. In later centuries the symbol became the reality. The practice and veneration of the practice speak to centuries of women's subordinate status in India.

Literally translated to mean "virtuous woman," satis were largely confined to the aristocracy and courts. At time of war, however, widow burning occurred on a massive scale among the widows of soldiers who were spared the humiliation of surrendering to the victors. Becoming a sati was considered the most auspicious moment of her existence, where she is given the "supreme opportunity for self-sacrifice that consummates her life of dedication to her dead husband." A sati brought dignity and honor to her family and her community but a living widow was seen as "not only unfortunate but positively inauspicious, an ogress who ate her husband with karmic jaws" (Young, 1987:83). She would feel guilty the rest of her life that her husband died before her. This sense of guilt was heightened by the Hindu belief that a sin in her previous life was responsible for his earlier death (Bose, 2000).

In principle, this was a voluntary rite on the part of the widow. In practice, her grief was often used by relatives who desired the honor associated with a sati ceremony. Only faithful wives could have the honor of becoming a suttee, so a widow's refusal could be construed as an admission of infidelity (Weitz, 1995; Weinberger-Thomas, 1999). Brought up in a culture where widow remarriages were discouraged, where women were identified only in connection to their husbands, and where widows frequently occupied the lowest rung on the social hierarchy, widowhood magnified a woman's dependence, subservience, and fear of sexual exploitation and abandonment. Given these dire circumstances, a woman consumed with grief and guilt may believe "that the brief agony of sati was better than the long agony of widowhood" (Jarman, 2002:2). When India was ruled by Muslim Mughals, attempts were made to abolish the practice, and the British outlawed it as early as 1829. Yet the British lack of success in eliminating it altogether shows the intransigence of

Hindu religious beliefs tied to personal law and their intimate connection to the social order.

India is rapidly modernizing, though many villages and rural areas are basically untouched by this trend. It speaks to the extraordinary power of socialization that suttee is still associated with the image of virtue for numerous Hindu women. In 1903 over 275 women immolated themselves around Calcutta alone. No longer do dying husbands extract oaths to be a sati from grieving wives, but the practice has not died out. In the last several decades forty recorded cases of the sati ritual are documented, but it is likely that others occur that remain hidden and uncounted. In rural areas of Rajasthan there is some evidence that the practice is symbolically resurging (Pinney, 2001; Sen, 2002). The concern is that the symbol may again become the reality.

JUDAISM

The ancient biblical world of Judaism was a patriarchal world. The two most important documents governing the conduct of Jewish life for both men and women are the *Torah* (law), the first five books of the Hebrew Bible, providing the whole of God's teaching as revealed to the Jewish people, and the *Talmud*, a collection of rabbinic interpretations of scripture transmitted around the middle of the first century. Because the Hebrew Bible and the Old Testament of the Christian Bible contain these five books, the Torah is the shared heritage of both peoples. Interpretation of scripture has been fairly flexible to account for the varying circumstances and cultural challenges faced by the Jewish people, but views of women and their approved roles have remained remarkably stable (Nadell and Sarna, 2001; Raphael, 2002). A strict gendered division of labor dictated family and religious life. Men's duties were to lead, teach, and legislate and women to serve and to follow.

Family Life

Men's family responsibilities included breadwinner and instructing their children in the history and religious obligations demanded by their faith. Women's duties were confined to the household, including overseeing domestic religious rituals, such as preparing Sabbath meals (Fuchs, 2000; Goldberg, 2003). A woman required permission from her husband to engage in any outside activities, and she could divorce him only if he granted it. Ancient customs prescribed daily, rigorous religious duties for men from which women were exempt because they could interfere with domestic roles. If a wife was fulfilling her household responsibilities, including those religious functions centered in the household, then her husband was able to concentrate on his religious obligations, patterns that continue today. Exceptions occur, but throughout Jewish history a woman was described, defined, and judged by her roles as wife and mother (Elper and Handelman, 2000; Taitz et al., 2003). Most of Judaism's 4,000-year heritage is marked by intense prejudice and anti-Semitism, including the Nazi Holocaust. Survival of Judaism itself was dependent on growth in numbers; hence motherhood meant that a woman individually sacrificed for children and family as well as for religious identity (Fine, 2001; Baker, 2002).

Sexuality and Social Control. This concern for stability in family life resulted in excessive control over women's sexuality. The ancient Hebrews severely punished infidelity on the part of a wife, but a husband was punished for infidelity only if he violated another man's rights by consorting with his wife (Daly, 1991:139). The right of a husband to own his wife kept her sexuality under control because she was regarded as a piece of property. An example of this control is found in the following verse:

> I took this woman and when I came near her I did not find the tokens of virginity. . . . The father of the young woman shall say to the elders . . . "he has made shameful charges against her . . . these are the tokens of my daughter's virginity" . . . then the elders . . . shall take the man and whip him . . . But if the thing is true, that the tokens of virginity were not found in the young woman, the . . . the men of the city shall stone her to death. (*Deuteronomy*, 22:14–21)

Women were denied access to the goddess religions that coexisted with Judaism during early biblical times. The goddess religions threatened Jewish monotheism, the religiously based political structure, and the sexual control of women. Patriarchal social order could be assaulted if women took advantage of the freedoms associated with these pagan religions.

The goddess religions are gone but beliefs about controlling women, especially their sexuality, in the name of social order persist (Isaacs, 2000; Riley, 2000; Berquist, 2002). Research on Jewish women in Jerusalem supports the continued dichotomy between women's family and religious lives. Women who conduct their religious lives in the public sphere face conflict with their families over issues of allegiance and time devoted to the various activities in the home and outside the home. Women who have more autonomy in both places are more successful at coping with these conflicts, but only if patriarchal authorities do not view this autonomy as too threatening. As would be expected, women who "suffer the most from the opposition between religion and family are those who choose a religious path very different from the traditional women's way" (Sered, 1991:25). Religious ideology continues to define woman in terms of her domestic life.

The Texts of Terror

The **Texts of Terror**, parts of four books of the Torah that include the Old Testament of the Christian Bible that documented abuse and sexual violence against women, were often used as justifications for restricting women's lives (Trible, 1984; Fischer, 1994). These texts (*Genesis*, 16:1–16 and 21:9–21; II *Samuel*, 13:1–22; *Judges*, 19:1–30, and *Judges*, 11:29–40) testify to rape, murder, human sacrifice, and the widespread abuse of women and girls. In Judges 19:1–30, a concubine flees from her Levite master back to her father's house, where he is entertained by her father, and then prepares to return with her to his own home. Along the way he is invited into the home of a man from Ephraim when the home is besieged. In pleading for the safety of the Levite, the Ephraimite host says:

> Behold, here are my virgin daughter and his concubine; . . . Ravish them and do with them what seems good to you; but against this man do not do such a vile thing. So the man seized his concubine, and put her out to them; and they knew her and abused her all night . . . And as the dawn began to break they

let her go . . . And her master rose up in the morning . . . there was his concubine lying at the door of the house . . . He said to her, "Get up, let us be going." But there was no answer. Then he put her upon the ass . . . and went away to his home. And when he entered his house, he took a knife, and laying hold of his concubine he divided her, limb by limb, into twelve pieces, and sent her throughout all the territory of Israel.

Virgin daughters and concubines are treated as property to be used at will by fathers or masters to entertain male guests.

A number of other biblical references could be included in these texts of terror. They serve as testimony to justify rape of virgins, abandonment of wives, and sexual violence against slave girls and women taken as prisoners of war. Through the use of biblical texts, androcentric law is reinforced by legitimizing the overall oppression of women (Fischer, 1994). This extends to the image of the widow. On the one hand she is a "monument of devotion, wisdom and charity," but she is also vulnerable to religious fanatics, a gossip, and of questionable morals and loose sexual habits. Once a respectful daughter and obedient wife, the independence offered to a widow cast her into a suspicious light. Ancient Israelite texts are more prescriptive than descriptive (Van der Torn, 1995:13). Female independence is checked by poverty and virtue that keeps a widow fettered to others.

Contemporary Images

All branches of Judaism are engaged in making its religious heritage more palatable to contemporary women (Heschel, 2002). Much of this effort is focused on reinterpreting Talmudic legislation and demonstrating the variety of roles Jewish women assumed throughout their religious history. For instance, positive countervoices exist throughout scripture that confirm God's high regard for women. In first century documents Eve is visioned as a woman who may have been naive but certainly not wicked—an unselfish woman whose good character Satan abused. Throughout the Diaspora Jewish women lived their lives as wives and mothers and as earners, organizers, and entrepreneurs. They sought and gained opportunities to climb to prestigious positions and to assume leadership roles in Jewish communities (Van Der Horst, 1995; Diner and Benderly, 2002). As Jewish women confront the misogyny of their own religious traditions, the rediscovered positive images of women are eroding the negative and hostile ones (Berner, 2001; Levine, 2001; Raphael, 2002).

CHRISTIANITY

From its origins 2,000 years ago as a Middle Eastern cult rooted in Judaism, Christianity developed as a result of the life events of its charismatic leader, Jesus of Nazareth, who was born a Jew. Christianity is the largest of the world's religions, representing about one-third of the world's population. Christianity's phenomenal growth rate is in part due to its early focus on class and ethnic inclusiveness (Stark, 1996). Gender inclusiveness highlighted the ministry of Jesus but remained unacknowledged for centuries.

The Bible and Patriarchy

Religious socialization of the young often proceeds from the teaching of biblical stories replete with colorful pictures of David confronting Goliath or Moses parting the sea in the escape from Egypt. These childhood images are nurtured by interpretations that perpetuate gender role stereotypes. The Bible is frequently evoked as the final authority in settling disputes in many areas but in particular those involving women and men.

Because the Bible expresses the attitudes of the patriarchal cultures in which it was written, it is logical that its most popular texts would be representative of those cultures. Historically the androcentric passages have been emphasized. Positive views of women and the partnerships forged between men and women exist throughout the Bible but scripture pointing to the subordination of women is favored, in part because it is more known. When such references are congruent with prevailing sentiment, they continue to legitimize as well as work against altering existing patriarchal power.

The following examples, oft-repeated from the pulpit, demonstrate how androcentric ideology permeates the Bible. It is appropriate to begin with the version of the creation story that is most accepted as representing the traditional view of both Christianity and Judaism.

> And the rib which the Lord God had taken from man, made he woman and brought her unto the man. And Adam said, This is now bone of my bones, and flesh of my flesh; she shall be called Woman, because she was taken out of Man. (Genesis, 2:20–23)

Contrary to all subsequent natural law, woman is made from man. Her status as helpmate and server to man (read "males") is confirmed. The idea that Eve was not only created out of Adam's rib, but also that she was created second, is used to justify the domination of man-husband over woman-wife. The order of creation is not an issue in supremacy when considering that animals were created before humans.

The Writings of Paul. In supporting this perspective, Paul has the dubious honor of formulating views, or having writings attributed to him, that continue to serve as bulwarks for contemporary Christian images of women. On one hand, Paul is closely linked with a "Christianity of female subordination," and his proclamations are used to keep women out of the ministry and confined to religious roles that are home based or if outside the home have a charitable basis. Perhaps Paul was concerned about the scandal and ridicule directed at the fledgling Christian sect if women were encouraged to venture into nontraditional roles that could challenge existing patriarchy. On the other hand, more recent research indicates he accepted the beliefs and practices of earlier inclusive charismatic Christianity, "the theology of equivalence of women." This form of Christianity incorporated women as local leaders, evangelists, and prophets (Ruether, 2001a). Paul acknowledged the idea of equality but insisted on the divinely given quality of sexual differences. Paul's contradictory beliefs about women are evident in the *Pauline* texts, consisting of those biblical passages attributed to Paul that contain striking misogyny as well as more gender egalitarian treatment (Adams, 2000). However, as illustrated by the following passages, it is the former that are the most well known and frequently used to justify the subordination of Christian women.

> But I want you to understand that the head of every man is Christ, the head of every woman is her husband, and the head of Christ is God. (I *Corinthians*, 11:3)

> For a man ought not to cover his head since he is the image and glory of God; but woman is the glory of man. For man was not made from woman, but woman from man. Neither was man created for woman but woman for man. (I *Corinthians*, 11:7–11)

> Let a woman learn in silence with all submissiveness. I permit no woman to teach or have authority over men; she is to keep silent. (I *Timothy*, 2:11–12)

> Wives be subject to your husbands, as to the Lord. For the husband is the head of the wife as Christ is the head of the Church. As the Church is subject to Christ, so let wives also be subject in everything to their husbands. (*Ephesians*, 5:22–24)

Women are repeatedly viewed in terms of their status as possessions of men. The Ten Commandments lists a neighbor's wife, along with his house, fields, manservant, ox, and ass, as property not to be coveted (Exodus, 20:17). Lot offers his daughters to the male guests in his house.

> Behold, I have two daughters who have not known man. Let me bring them out to you and do to them as you please. (*Genesis*, 19:8)

Contemporary compilations of stories about biblical women continue these images. On the surface it would seem that older works like Edith Deen's *Wisdom from Women in the Bible* (1978) are focusing on women's accomplishments at a period of history in which liberating religious interpretation is occurring. Yet Deen presents narratives of women that provide ammunition reinforcing stereotypes about women. For example, Jochebed, the mother of Moses, is praised only for her role in recognizing exceptional promise in their children. The heroic efforts in carrying out this role are ignored. Selfish and possessive women, like the wife of Potiphar, who was responsible for the unfair imprisonment of Joseph, are admonished for their wickedness and deceit. Deen asserts that women are different but not inferior to men, but the images she presents are consistently in line with women's traditional or "acceptable" roles. Those women who either refuse or challenge such roles are chastised, negatively portrayed, or cast into historical oblivion (Lindsey, 1979:793).

Biblical Men. The Christian tradition portrays men as both rational and irrational. They are warriors, leaders, teachers, builders, and cultivators whose minds, talents, and strength are recruited in the service of God. But they are also driven by sexual desires and are irrational in their inability to resist the lure of women. Even in their irrational moments, they are portrayed as multifaceted beings who adapt to and thrive in a variety of roles. In contrast, women are dualistically cast with no room for deviation. Eve may be the mother of humanity, but she is also the temptress responsible for the fall of humanity. Because Eve yielded to the serpent, women thereafter are incapable of leadership (Diehl, 1990:56). Adam succumbs to Eve's feminine wiles but is largely exempt from blame. On the other hand, Mary as the mother of Christ is the idealized image of the perfect woman—a humble, submissive virgin. Joseph is Mary's husband and Jesus' earthly father, but compared to Mary, he is relegated to only a few biblical references. Some biblical scholars may suggest that his "ordinary" roles as carpenter and supporter of the family do not elevate him to the same biblical importance as Christianity's political or religious leaders. In this sense, the Bible tends to neglect unexceptional men—those who for better or worse do not deviate from their roles—but focuses attention on exceptional women—those who for better or worse do deviate from their roles.

Alternative Views of Biblical Women

Numerous biblical alternatives to traditional views are offered by reformists eager to document the abundant stories, images, and metaphors demonstrating a range of interpretive options related to women. Paul's forceful passage (from the Pauline texts) speaks directly to the idea of equality of the genders under God:

> there is neither Jew nor Greek, there is neither slave nor free, there is neither male nor female, for you are all one in Jesus Christ. (*Galatians*, 3:28)

On the heels of the equality issue is the rediscovery of the nontraditional roles women played in biblical times. Mary Magdalene and the women who went to Jesus' tomb hold the credibility of Christianity in their hands. Jesus first appeared to them and they were instructed to gather the disciples. "Mary Magdalene is the first prophet of the new religion and the first of Christ's disciples to see and hear, to believe and to speak. She may be designated as the first Christian" (Hollander, 1994:115; Brock, 2003). Deborah, in the book of *Judges*, is an arbitrator, queen, and commander of the army that she led in the defeat of the Canaanites. In Exodus it is the women who first disobeyed Pharaoh, with his own daughter adopting Moses as her child. Women are wives and mothers as well as leaders, prophetesses, teachers, and tillers of the soil. Even Mary's humility and submissiveness are being taken to task by feminists, who argue that Mary submitted to God alone and not to Joseph or other male authority figures. She was an independent actor when she affirmed the course of her life (Ostling, 1991:64).

It is a rereading of the Gospels with an examination of the life and teachings of Jesus that provides the best message to those interested in recasting biblical imagery concerning women. Jesus' very open attitude toward women is found throughout the Gospels. His acceptance of women was so uncharacteristic of the times that it could not be seen as anything short of scandalous (Magli, 2003). Women were prominent in Jesus' ministry and served vital functions from the beginning. They recognized him early on as the Messiah, they witnessed his death and resurrection, they conversed with him on theological topics, and they were faithful and persistent followers through even the lethal portions of his ministry. Women of biblical times would have been the major beneficiaries of Jesus' ministry. Examples are numerous: He preached that divorce should be forbidden at a time when only husbands had the right of divorce and wives were often abandoned to a life of poverty; he rejected the double standard of sexual morality, helping to absolve women of their temptress image that previously made them solely responsible for sexual misdeeds; and he opened a religious path and monastic life for both men and women. Through his actions he demonstrated that women could join men in spiritual quests and that men and women could relate to one another in radically different ways than the patriarchy of the times ministry (McClelland, 1990; Graetz, 2003).

Gender Roles and American Christians

Religious pluralism is a hallmark of the United States and there are numerous religions, branches of religions, denominations, cults, and new religious movements in various stages of decline and emergence. Of all the groups that comprise the religious salad bowl in the Unites States, the largest in number are under the Christian umbrella. Over three-fourths of the U.S. population identify themselves as Christian, and of these about half are Protestant and one-fourth are Catholic (Adherents, 2002). American Christians share basic theological beliefs, but diverge sharply on key gender related issues.

American Protestants. Protestants are divided into so many denominations and smaller independent churches that is exceedingly difficult to conveniently summarize their attitudes regarding gender roles. However, some generalizations are possible. Mainstream denominations including Methodists, Lutherans of the Evangelical Church in America (ELCA), Presbyterians, and Episcopalians are more inclusive and liberal in their theology, accommodating a variety of interpretations. These denominations are likely to have women in key leadership roles, including ordained ministers and as representatives of their larger denominations. Women take visible, active roles in weekly services and share in church functions with men. Special services spotlighting alternative images of women are conducted. Sunday schools provide children with images of biblical men and women in an array of roles.

Conservative mainstream denominations, including Lutheran Church-Missouri Synod, some Baptist branches, Pentecost's, and small Protestants churches not otherwise affiliated with any specific Protestant groups are more absolutist in their beliefs, viewing the Bible as the literal, unerring word of God. These Protestants are at the core of fundamentalist religious resurgence in the United States. Bolstered by theological interpretations favoring the traditional biblical views noted earlier, male and female adherents hear the message that egalitarian or companionate style families and gender roles are contrary to God's plan for the world. Patriarchal families are godly, wise, desirable, necessary, and in the best interests of family and society. Many support the agenda of the **New Christian Right (NCR),** a fundamentalist political movement composed largely of conservative, Protestants groups that promotes a specific Christian brand of morality based on the Bible and God's will as the ultimate source for political and social life. Issues related to sex and gender are the core of NCR's agenda in its call for restrictions on sex education and opposition to homosexual rights, abortion rights, and the Equal Rights Amendment (Moen, 1994; Jelen, 1999; Johnson, 2000; Williams, 2000).

American Catholics. Probably the most important issues dividing contemporary U.S. Catholics from the authority of the broader Roman Catholic church are attitudes regarding sex and gender. This division shows up among both clergy and laypeople. For example, various orders of nuns have removed themselves from traditional patterns of Catholic hierarchy and worship; they take a distinctly female-centered view of religion, preferring to pray to "Her" rather than "Him." Other parishes stretch church authority to allow altar girls, nuns as campus ministers, and women leading "priestess parishes" in rural areas where there are shortages of male priests (Wallace, 1993; Egan, 1999). Among laypeople, a majority of American Catholics practice birth control other than the rhythm method, support the use of condoms and sex education in schools, believe priests should be allowed to marry, do not believe political candidates should be judged solely on the abortion issue, believe that divorced Catholics need to be welcomed back into the church, and are receptive to women's ordination, all in direct contradiction to Vatican authority (Lippy, 1999; Stange, 2002). Because so many Catholics have beliefs and practices that directly counter Vatican teaching, the church is reluctant to dismiss them from church rosters.

Issues related to women and sexuality have been in the forefront of Catholic controversy for decades. However, a new twist on the sexuality issue recently exploded in the media when widespread sexual abuse by Catholic priests perpetrated on children was revealed. The shock that priests engaged in "serial, predatory and sexual abuse of minors" was magnified when it was learned that Roman Catholic officials who knew of abuse routinely shuffled "problem priests" to other parishes, ignored the problem, or swept it under the rug. These cover-ups were as disturbing to many Catholics as the original abuse, and most people believed that the Church did a poor job in handling the scandal (Roane, 2002). In an unprecedented move, Pope John Paul II convened a meeting of U.S. cardinals at the Vatican to deal with the matter. Along with official apologies, counseling, and monetary compensation for victims, removal from the priesthood and criminal charges for perpetrators are offered as short-term solutions (CNN, 2002; Rice, 2002). Regardless of the success of these solutions, the sex scandal will certainly magnify the existing split in the church and refocus attention on another issue that the Church prefers to ignore— the issue of women's ordination into the Catholic priesthood.

GENDER, RELIGIOSITY, AND LEADERSHIP

Religion is a powerful agent of gender socialization as well as a major source of a person's overall well-being. Degree of religiosity is correlated with lower support on a number of attitudes related to sex and gender including women's ordination, women working outside the home, reproductive choice, contraceptive use, homosexuality, and the Equal Rights Amendment. High levels of religiosity translate to less egalitarianism and more female submission in marriage, a pattern that cuts across all religions (Peek et al., 1991; Balmer, 1994; Kell and Camp, 1999; Franks, 2001; Rogers, 2002). Although measures of religiosity vary, it is safe to conclude that a strong religious commitment in conservative religions, especially fundamentalist Protestantism, predicts a preference for highly traditional gender roles. In turn, this preference discourages many women from seeking major positions of leadership in those very religious organizations to which they derive a sense of well-being.

Gender and Religious Orientation

The issue of women as religious leaders is more significant, with sociological research demonstrating that women have a greater degree of religious orientation than men, a pattern that holds true across the centuries and across the globe (Stark,

2002). Compared to men, women report higher levels of need for a religious dimension in their daily lives and believe that religion is an answer to contemporary problems. Some women report that religion helps guide them in career paths and puts them on equal footing with men outside the home (Witt, 1999). Women pray and read scripture more than men and have higher rates of church and synagogue attendance and practice. This heightened religious orientation is reinforced by women's responsibility for the religious socialization of the children. Women ensure that children receive religious instruction, attend services, and practice the rituals important to their religion.

Sociological Perspectives. All sociological perspectives highlight the link between family and religion in explaining gender differences in level of religious orientation. Functionalists maintain that social cohesion is strengthened when families and communities share the same beliefs derived from the moral communities established by their religion. Traditional gender roles in the home are bolstered by similar messages from the pulpit about the proper place of men and women. Feminists also suggest the church and the family are consistent, but because they both share similar patriarchal structures. For feminists, the social cohesion that functionalists highlight reinforces patriarchy and benefits its male leaders, but does a disservice to women who are excluded from religious leadership by virtue of their gender alone. Because traditional gender roles and patriarchy go hand in hand, inclusiveness and partnership roles sought by men and women congregants are discouraged.

Conflict theorists use classical Marxism to explain women's religion orientation for Christian women. Religion acts as an *opiate*, discouraging people from challenging the religious status quo. Christianity's belief that heavenly rewards come to those who lead humble, pious, and self-sacrificing lives bolsters women's acceptance of an "other worldly" ideology. Marx suggested that religion lulls people into a *false consciousness*, the tendency for oppressed people to accept the ideology of the dominant class, in this sense, the church patriarchy. These beliefs are transmitted via religious socialization in families and go largely unchallenged. The overall result is that oppression, in the name of God, is legitimized. Conflict theorists support biblical interpretations challenging these beliefs and calling for people to use their religions in the active pursuit social justice. Advanced initially by Catholic clergy in Latin America, **liberation theology** calls for redistribution of wealth and economic equality grounded in biblical messages about God's concern for the poor and oppressed. Liberation theology's messages about oppressions of economic inequality and can also be brought to bear on oppressions about gender inequality. Opening up the religious leadership structure to women is a key mechanism challenging gender oppression perpetrated in the name of God and religion.

The Issue of Ordination

Seminaries are being feminized. Over half of all seminary students are women and the numbers are expected to grow. The feminization of divinity schools should lead to a feminization of the pulpit with women's voices offering alternative views and explanations of women from the Bible and the holy texts from other religions (Brinton, 1999). These views are necessary when contemporary women seek equal footing with men as leaders in their religious organizations, whether in churches, synagogues, temples, or mosques.

Confucianism and Islam. In outlining women's roles in the world religions, the religions that stand out as the most restrictive in terms of women's leadership roles are Islam, the second largest religion in the world and on track to become the largest, and Confucianism, the smallest of the world religions. Neither religion can be described as "hierarchal" in leadership structure. In Confucianism a variety of men may organize and lead rituals, although women often ensure that appropriate rituals are conducted in their households. Men are the arbitrators and interpreters of Confucian texts as they pertain to family, business and politics. Confucian ideals consign women to their family and household roles (Woo, 2002). Islam does not have priests but imams are powerful figures, especially in religious states such as Iran and Saudi Arabia, where imams serving large mosques have a great deal of political clout. They have the right to choose and interpret passages from the Qur'an. Muslim women are restricted from becoming imams and as a result are denied an important public opportunity to provide alternative interpretations of the Qur'an.

Judaism. When Jews began to enter modern, Western society in the late nineteenth century, attitudes toward women shifted dramatically. Patriarchy was evident, but the flexible, adaptive quality of Jewish beliefs and practices is again demonstrated in accommodating women's greater independence and higher levels of education. This accommodation is reflected in the increased number of women rabbis in most branches of Judaism. Each of its three main branches, Orthodox, Conservative, and Reform, varies according to the degree to which theology is literally interpreted and acted on in daily life. Orthodox Jews, for example, have the strictest interpretation, viewing the Torah as the absolutely binding word of God. Those who identify as Conservative are less strict, allowing interpretation of the Torah in the context of modern life. Reform Jews, the most liberal and assimilated branch, accept the Torah's ethical guidelines and general religious precepts, but are open to alternative interpretations of the Torah, especially related to gender roles. As the least strict branch, Reform Judaism was the first to make possible rabbinical ordination, with Sally Priesand becoming the first female rabbi in 1972. A year later ordination was open to women in the Conservative branch but the first Conservative rabbi was not ordained until 1985. Among Orthodox Jews, ordination for women is still forbidden. To date, however, there are just over 200 female rabbis, and of these, only a handful are Conservative (Magonet, 2002).

Christianity. Three major Christian faiths do not ordain women: Lutheran Church—Missouri Synod, Eastern Orthodox, and Roman Catholic. In 1972, after a long and bitter struggle that culminated in a controversial ceremony in 1974 in Philadelphia, eleven women were ordained Episcopal priests. Two years later the Episcopal church gave its legal, institutional blessing for the right of women to become priests. Twelve years later, by a margin of two votes, that right to become a priest was extended to women in the Church of England. This came about despite a warning by the Anglican Archbishop of Canterbury that women's ordination would hurt dialogue with the Roman Catholic Church. Episcopalians and Anglicans across the globe show higher levels of acceptance for women priests, but a quarter century later the dust from the first controversial ordinations has not settled (Harris et al., 2000).

Catholicism. Although the Catholic Church may quietly overlook theological principles in accepting the large number of divorced Catholics in its parishes, regarding the issue of women in the priesthood, the church will not budge. The Second Vatican Council (1963 to 1965) monumentally changed the Catholic Church and opened up new roles for men and women to serve the church, but women's ordination was not one of them. A pastoral letter addressing issues raised by Catholic women, including their place in the church, that took nine years to prepare was rejected by U.S. bishops in 1992. This was the first time in history that a pastoral letter proposed for a final vote was defeated (Filteau, 1992). For every proclamation reasserting the Vatican's position that women can never be ordained, a worldwide outcry centered in the United States against the position occurs. Despite the church's acknowledgment that ordaining women could alleviate the serious shortage of priests in many parts of the world, the issue is dealt with by encouraging married men to become priests under certain conditions. The Vatican believes allegiance of Catholics can be maintained without women's ordination. Others take the view that this issue will eventually cause an irrevocable split in the church (Bohlen, 1995; Weaver, 1999).

The priest sex scandal provides more ammunition for ordaining women. Feminists contend that the Church fails to recognize the incredible power held by an all-male priesthood that not only heightens the potential for abuse in all areas, whether related to sex, love, money, or politics, but also covers up the abuse by rallying around the priestly brotherhood to protect its own interests. As noted by one feminist scholar:

> The argument for female priests has never been stronger as a result of this scandal . . . women have no stake in protecting the interests of errant male colleagues. The presence of women (as priests) would inevitably transform the Men's Club of power and privilege the priesthood has become. (Stange, 2002:13A).

Jewish and Lutheran women have the option of shifting to other branches without changing their religion, but for those Catholic women who seek the priesthood, their choices are limited. They can assume leadership roles as lay members of the church, or they can become nuns. This is not to minimize the leadership roles nuns assume or the other vital services they provide. But compared to priests, these roles are much more restrictive and secondary. They are excluded from the position that allows the greatest authority on both doctrinal and parish matters— that of priest. The tradition of nuns as humble helpmates is also impacting their very livelihood. Unlike priests of a diocese, they are not employees of the local bishop; hence they receive no pension. In addition there are far fewer young women entering the convent today, forcing some convents to close. Although nuns are better educated than most women and seldom retire from work unless their health fails, they face grim financial prospects in old age because there are fewer younger nuns to support them.

Protestantism. American Protestantism has fared better in terms of women in positions of authority, with many women preachers emerging from the ranks of Quakers during the colonial era (Dunn, 2001). America's first successful religious commune, the Shakers, was founded by Ann Lee, who preached that God is both male and female. Although the Shakers had no formal ordination process, all adherents, regardless of gender, were permitted complete freedom in teaching and preaching. This is also generally true of other religious sects and churches where women are credited as founders or proved to be the dominant influence in their establishment. Included here are the Seventh Day Adventists, the Spiritualist Church, and the Christian Science Church. By the middle of the twentieth century most mainstream Protestant denominations, including the Methodist and Presbyterian Churches, the United Church of Christ, and the merged ELCA granted full ordination rights to women. Ordination also allows for women to begin the climb to significant positions of administrative leadership offering high levels of decision making within their religious groups.

Clergy Women as Leaders

For those leaders who are clergy, do women differ in their approach to their ministries compared to men? The answer depends on type of minister one has in mind and the type of ministry. In general, male and female ministers differ in their willingness to exercise power over congregations, with women more willing to give the congregation the power over its own affairs. Men and women do not differ in desire for positions of formal authority, approach to preaching, and involvement in social issues beyond the congregation (Lehman, 1993). Gender socialization encourages women to adopt styles of interaction that are relational, open, nonconfrontational, and consensual. These characteristics can serve congregations well when adopted by both male and female clergy. Women and men have different paths to the ministry, but when they arrive and gain acceptance among their parishioners, the differences are muted (Lehman, 2002).

Although women are gradually assuming new roles within the hierarchy of their religions, the battle is far from won. Ordination does not guarantee a call to lead a congregation. Some parishes still refuse to accept female ministers, rabbis, or priests, whether ordained or not, which propels many of them into more peripheral leadership positions. The large majority of ordained women serve as associate pastors, youth ministers, educational directors, or in some other institutional capacity. Women clergy are more likely than their male counterparts to be heads of religious coalitions or leaders of campus churches or temples.

The crux of the clergy issue can be traced back to interpretations of doctrine embodied in a religion's sacred texts. It is the exclusivity of the male image of God in these texts that makes it difficult to see women as representing this image. Although theologians uniformly reject the notion that God is a "male being," centuries of religious patriarchy, institutional sexism, and linguistic convention are barriers to those women and men who support women's ascendance to more authoritative ranks of their respective religions.

TOWARD AN INCLUSIVE THEOLOGY

From this account of religious misogyny, it might seem that feminism and the patriarchal vision of the church cannot be reconciled. Feminists are unwilling to equate religion with oppression. They believe it is not real liberation to sever ties with a religion that is one of the most important elements of their heritage, belief system, and well-being. They choose to work at reform in a number of areas, especially in providing a historical account of women's roles in ancient religions and reevaluating scripture according to that account, whether it be in the Qur'an, Talmud, Vedas, or Bible. Even if religious experience is filtered through misogynous cultural traditions, religion should transcend gender. Every adherent should have the right to fully participate in her or his religion in a manner that best enhances individual well-being and community service. Feminists contend that only when women become aware of the root causes of their contemporary religious status and the sociopolitical nature of religious doctrine can they truly experience their religion. Historical reanalysis of world religions provides meaningful consciousness-raising for women coming to grips with their religious identity.

The Language of Religion

As discussed in chapter 4, language is a powerful force in socialization, and nowhere is this more apparent than in the language of religion. The language of religion can be subdivided into *religious* language, which uses imagery and symbols appealing to emotion and imagination and readily incorporates female imagery, and *theological* language, which uses abstractions evolving out of formal, critical appraisals of religious experience and readily incorporates male imagery. Because theological language is the language of written texts, bestowed with authority, credibility, and importance, female imagery is largely excluded. Theological language is viewed as more legitimate but is a "creation of a male specialist group, whether Brahmans, priests, rabbis, or monks" (King, 1989:44–45).

Male imagery is evoked when conceptualizing God, and in turn such images are used to support the subordination of women. Christians and those from other religions who firmly believe that men and women are equal under God confront a theological language that contradicts this belief. God and god-language is associated with male imagery and masculine traits (Johnson, 2003; Wiley, 2003). Women are portrayed as distracting men from godliness, as Eve did with she tempted Adam. The language is clear: There are "Sons of God" but "Daughters of Eve" (Miller and Swift, 1991a:80). Theologians do agree that the use of the supposed generics *man* and *he* impedes our understanding of God's view of the genders. Yet when congregations begin the arduous task of altering liturgy, hymns, and prayers to conform to nonsexist, inclusive language, resistance runs very high. The old argument reappears: One is not only tampering with tradition but, more importantly, the "language of God."

Supported by trends is *ecumenism*—promoting practices that bring churches together, such as through joint worship and communion—in which mainstream Christian denominations are making headway incorporating inclusive language in the written material used in religious services. For example, the ELCA's *Lutheran Book of Worship*, issued in 1978, contains substantial changes in hymns and prayers allowing for inclusive imagery when compared to the 1958 *Service Book and Hymnal.* Here is a portion of the Nicene Creed which demonstrates that a one-word change suggests a meaningful difference in imagery.

> Who for us men, and for our salvation, came down from heaven. . . . (1958 version)

> For us and for our salvation He came down from heaven. . . . (1978 version)

Though it is inappropriate to remove the word *he* from the second version because it refers directly to Jesus, the word *men* is now deleted. And a hymn titled "Good Christian Men, Rejoice and Sing" in the older hymnal was changed to "Good Christian Friends, Rejoice and Sing." Seemingly subtle changes can have a profound impact on images of men and women.

Reinterpretation of Scripture

Doctrinal reinterpretation of scripture is also viewed as a mode of reform, especially if coupled with changes in linguistic reference. By pointing out alternative translations of key words, introducing nonsexist, inclusive language that minimizes the powerful aspects of male imagery, and highlighting lesser known biblical texts and religious writing that demonstrate both gender equity and nontraditional roles of women, a gradual shift in religious awareness regarding gender roles and relationships is occurring. In Christianity, for example, because theology and preaching are so strongly oriented to masculine images of God, such as *king, father,* and *shepherd,* the feminine corollary of God goes unrecognized. In Matthew 13:31, although it is acknowledged that the man who sowed the mustard seed is God, most miss the parallel image that immediately follows in Matthew 13:33, where God is presented as a woman hiding leaven in meal.

We have already seen that most world religions emerged out of spiritual heritages that were more gender egalitarian that what exists today. But the esoteric and mystical schools of Christian Gnosticism, Islamic Sufism, and the Kabbalah movement of Judaism show a continuous heritage of men and women in equitable partnership (McKechnie, 2001; Buehrens, 2003). This is pointed out by Elaine Pagels (1979) in her classic work recounting the archaeological discovery in Upper Egypt, now referred to as the *Gnostic Gospels,* which offer astonishing evidence that the early Christians viewed women in very different terms than what is implied by the practices of the contemporary church. The texts on which these views are based are providing important alternative perspectives concerning women.

Many biblical writings can be reevaluated with these standards of reform in mind. Consider the lesser quoted of the Judeo-Christian creation stories:

> So God created man in his own image, in the image of God he created him; male and female he created them. (*Genesis,* 1:27)

God is still named as "he," but this version clearly does not have the implication that God's image of people is different depending on gender. Even Paul's most restrictive passages may be reevaluated with the idea that the Gospel liberates people to stand equally before God. Reread Ephesians 5:22–24 with the idea that the words *be subject* were not in the original biblical text. Religious scholars suggest that Paul is calling for mutual submission of the genders within marriage and not the superiority of the husband (Schüssler-Fiorenza, 1984; Groothius, 1997; Perriman, 1998; Carey, 2001). Paul's writings must be scrutinized carefully with an eye toward context, taking into account the historical setting and the gospel of Jesus (Megill-Cobbler, 1993). Given these new directions, Paul's misogyny continues to fade.

Feminist Theology

Religious reform related to the genders is perhaps best expressed by a rapidly growing **feminist theology**, which draws on women's experience as a basic source of content previously shut out of theological reflection. Feminist theology makes theological knowledge visible, understandable, inclusive, and acceptable to all who believe in the liberating power of religion. It may also be viewed as one example of a liberation theology that interprets the Bible from the perspective of an oppressed group. In this sense, female experience is an appropriate metaphor for the divine. Feminist theology is necessary when the female experience is excluded from traditional theology and when women are excluded from institutionalized religious structures (Maynard, 2001; Ruether, 2001b). Feminist theology articulates with the female experience in any of the world's major religions. The following is an account of that experience by a Christian woman.

> The fathers of the church and academy controlled the discourse; when I tried to speak my language they would not hear me. I wanted to talk at gut level where the mercy of God comes from—the bowels of the earth—the language of the Hebrew Bible and not of the Greek philosophers. (Thurston, 1995:4)

Feminist theology is ecumenical from its origins and borrows models from a wide range of disciplines. Although it accepts the idea that a major critique of god-symbolism is called for, there is much disagreement on the solutions to the problems resulting from such a critique, and many theologians remain unwilling to work out the ambiguities of their respective positions (Hogan, 1995). Views of religious tradition advocated by feminist theologians may be grouped in three categories (Christ, 1987:144):

Type 1: Tradition is essentially nonsexist in vision that becomes clear through proper interpretation.

Type 2: Tradition contains both sexist and nonsexist elements; nonsexist elements must be affirmed as revelation and the sexist elements rejected. Nonsexist visions must account for the contemporary experience of all women and embrace their full humanity.

Type 3: Tradition is essentially sexist and must be rejected. New traditions must be created on the basis of both past experience and/or non-biblical religion.

Depending on which viewpoint is subscribed to, god symbolism would be altered. For example, those subscribing to the third position would likely advocate female symbolism for God found both inside and outside of biblical tradition.

Since God is best symbolized by dual male-female imagery, outside sources might include the goddess symbolism of non-Western religions (Pui-Lan, 1988; Christ, 2003a).

The following typology offers a good review of various theological positions that can be incorporated by feminist theologians as they grapple with the problems of patriarchy in religious traditions (Diehl, 1990:38–39). Although the typology is designed with Christian theology in mind, it can be readily applied to other religions.

1. *Strict hierarchalist (traditionalist).* The Bible is the infallible word of God and teaches that man is the leader and woman is his subordinate. The feminist crusade for egalitarianism is unbiblical and a product of modern secular humanism. Patriarchal language in the Bible and in church liturgy should be maintained.

2. *Modern hierarchalist (liberated traditionalist).* The Bible is the infallible word of God and teaches that a woman is subordinate to a man in the religious hierarchy. However, Christianity offers a hierarchy that is less authoritarian and patriarchal than the Jewish tradition from which it emerged. Christ's attitudes toward women, for example, were different than the culture in which he preached. Women's subordination must be viewed in this light.

3. *Biblical feminist (evangelical feminist).* The Bible is the infallible word of God but does not teach that patriarchy is God's ideal. Paul, for example, applied his principles in relation to existing customs. With changed customs, contemporary women should not be subordinate to male church authority.

4. *Mainstream feminist (reformist feminist).* The Bible contains the word of God but is not itself the infallible word of God. When the Bible supports patriarchy, it should not be considered divine revelation. The word of God is found in its redemptive themes or prophetic tradition that criticizes oppression. Christians should work for the full liberation of women in all areas of life.

5. *Radical feminist (revolutionary feminist).* Because patriarchy and androcentrism pervade the Bible, revelation cannot be found in it. Revelation is in the experience of a community of women-affirming Christians seeking liberation from patriarchal oppression. Biblical authority should be rejected. Women must engage in spiritual revolution and rename God based on their own religious experience that is totally free of men.

Feminist theology takes on many forms. Regardless of the position held by any one person, feminist theology has been the major source of new research, scholarship, and critiques on gender as related to religious tradition. Feminist theology serves to infuse institutionalized religion with the inclusive spirituality of its heritage and is the key catalyst reopening religion's liberating potential for both women and men.

Summary

1. When spirituality became institutionalized as religion, women lost prestige and influence. The first civilizations probably had more partnership based spiritual traditions and social institutions. In these gynocratic—female centered—societies, a

goddess heritage provided significant religious roles for women. The goddess as creator and powerful female deities existed throughout Africa and Asia. Many societies exhibited balance and complementarity where in principle neither gender was superior.

2. Muslims vary considerably in interpreting the Qur'an in terms of the role of women. Gender roles are mainly defined as complementary but inequality and women's task to provide male heirs are favored. Feminist Muslims are providing alternative interpretations based on the powerful and esteemed roles of the Prophet's wives. U.S. Muslim women are altering as well as affirming the traditional values of their religion.

3. Interpretations from Hindu scripture are contradictory: Women are idealized as submissive and serving their families and condemned if too ambitious; other views see male and female as balanced and emphasize the continuing goddess heritage of Hinduism. Historically both the low and idealized opinion of women was seen when at widowhood she became a sati and immolated herself on her husband's funeral pyre.

4. In Judaism, scripture has been interpreted to ensure a strict gender division of labor in family and religious life. Contemporary Jewish women must deal with the separation between family and their religious lives outside the home. The Texts of Terror, four books of the Torah and Christian Bible, document sexual violence against women. Today all branches of Judaism are finding positive countervoices in scripture for women.

5. The Christian Bible's images of patriarchy and androcentric ideology have been favored, especially writings of St. Paul. Alternative views are offered by reformists demonstrating nontraditional and vital roles of women, especially Mary Magdalene. American Christians, both Protestants and Catholics, vary considerably in attitudes about women's roles and rights.

6. Women have a greater degree of religious orientation than men. The link between family and religion explains this, specifically related to women's role in the religious socialization of children.

7. Ordination and other leadership roles for women vary by religion and how each religion interprets scripture. Confucianism and Islam are the most restrictive for any public religious roles for women. All branches of Judaism except Orthodox ordain women. Most Christian religions ordain women. The notable exceptions of large groups are Lutheran Church—Missouri Synod and Catholics. The priest shortage and sex scandals in the Catholic Church provide fuel for women's ordination.

8. Female clergy are more willing to share power with congregations and have more consensual interaction styles than male clergy, otherwise there are few differences between them. Ordained women are less likely than men to receive a call to lead a congregation.

9. To make theology more inclusive in all religions, feminists and scholars are providing historical accounts of women in ancient religions, inclusive language is being adopted, ecumenism is encouraged, and scripture is being reinterpreted.

10. Feminist theology is an interdisciplinary field drawing on women's experience previously shut out of theological reflection. A typology of various theological positions on women includes: traditionalist, liberated traditionalist, evangelical feminist, reformist feminist, and revolutionary feminist.

Key Terms

feminist theology 341	liberation theology 335	sati 326
gynocentrism 319	New Christian Right 333	Texts of Terror 328

Critical Thinking Questions

1. Demonstrate how women lost prestige and influence and misogyny increased when spirituality became institutionalized to religion. Specifically reference Hinduism, Judaism, Christianity, and Islam in this discussion. What strategies are used by feminist adherents to deal with the misogyny of their respective religions?

2. Why would functionalism be the dominant theoretical perspective explaining the persistence of gender inequity related to religion? How does feminist theology counter this perspective?

3. Based on your understanding of gender and religious socialization, how can women who are of faiths that restrict ordination and other leadership roles of women work for gender equity in their respective religions?

CHAPTER 13

MEDIA

The noise you hear when the weather and the movies get hot—is the tumbling of actresses, as male stars push them aside into big action films. Out of the way, ladies. Summer is men's work. (Corliss, 2003:57)

The impact of mass media on our lives is profound. This impact is all the more significant because most of it occurs without our conscious awareness. We are bombarded by media sights and sounds daily. We are subjected to music, news, and advertising at our office desks, in elevators, while jogging or driving to and from school or work. Advertisements crop out at virtually every site we encounter daily—from the usual billboards and subway ads to computer pop-ups, to shopping carts in supermarkets. They shout out the newest, best, modern, and most efficient products and services available. Cinema and television offerings allow for almost every conceivable programming taste. With the extraordinary technology available for home entertainment and the advent of video recorders and cable television, we can choose our entertainment specialties without ever leaving home.

As documented in chapter 3, gender socialization occurs via multiple agents. Parents provide the earliest source, but beginning at about age three, television becomes another potent socializer. We rely more and more on the mass media, especially television, to filter the enormous amount of information we receive. This filtering process has a major impact on our ideas about gender. Indeed, one of the most documented, consistent findings is that for both males and females, and in all age and racial categories, heavy television viewing is strongly associated with adherence to traditional and stereotyped views about gender.

Television is strengthened by advertisements, magazines, film, and other media that present the genders in stereotyped ways. It is easy to see why, even at an early age, we form relatively rigid beliefs about what is considered appropriate behavior for boys and girls, women and men. Though media representatives may argue that what is presented merely reflects the reality of gendered beliefs, the question of reinforcing an already sexist society cannot be easily dismissed. After reviewing the media's record on how the genders are portrayed, we will return to this question.

PRINT MEDIA

Of all types of print media, magazines and newspapers are extremely powerful in presenting views about gender roles. Gender stereotypes persist and thrive in print media across the globe, regardless of how media content is adapted to a culture's values and norms (Walker, 1998; Al-Olayan and Karande, 2000; Munshi, 2001). Early research about the impact of print media on attitudes about women and gender came from the source that was also a founding document of the women's movement.

Magazines

The publication of Betty Friedan's *Feminine Mystique* in 1963 challenged notions about contented American women in their homebound roles. Friedan was one of the first to look at the role of the print media, in this case popular women's magazines, in the formation of attitudes about women.

Fiction. Concentrating on the fiction that was the staple of women's magazines until recent decades, Friedan traced the images of women from the emancipated views in the 1930s and 1940s to the "happy housewife" and glorified mother of the 1950s and early 1960s. This beginning led to a great deal of research on gender stereotypes in magazines. Data over the next two decades confirmed the earlier patterns, but with some new twists: The ideal woman of magazine fiction was a housewife with one or two children (homemaker was the less common label). These women may experience psychological difficulties raising a family and attending to their husbands' needs, but they carried out their roles in exemplary manners. Employed women were unfeminine and posed threats to otherwise happy marriages. The baby boom accelerated in the 1950s, and so did the birth rate in magazines. Having a baby was a good bet for saving a floundering marriage. Married women who remained childless and spinsters who remained childless and husbandless were pitied for their wasteful, unhappy lives. Fiction of this period cheered on heroines who, through virtue and passivity, won the hearts of the men they would marry. Widows and divorcees were portrayed as unable to cope without a man. The overall conclusion: The happy housewife was even happier.

Articles. By the 1970s the magazine fiction that had been a key element of women's magazines was being gradually replaced with other material targeted to women. But dramatic changes impacting gender roles were occurring that eventually impacted magazine images as well. The birth rate was leveling off, thousands of women moved into the paid labor force, and the feminist movement was making headlines. Magazines focusing on the challenges of women working outside the home emerged, some with explicitly feminist orientations, such as *Ms.* Older, more traditional magazines such as *Ladies Home Journal* and *McCall's* began to include articles about educational opportunities, employment options, and women' rights. Magazines such as *Savvy, New Woman,* and *Working Woman,* geared to single women or employed married women, also appeared, offering advice to those coping with increased role responsibilities. Nonetheless, compared to the social upheaval in the real world of women, the magazine world of women has been minimally affected. After flirting with themes related to self-development, establishing one's identity, and expanded opportunities, the 1980s witnessed a return to more antiquated images, a situation that remains today (Alexander, 1999). Mothers and homemakers do not fare well in contemporary women's magazines. Magazines promote a traditional motherhood ideology but simultaneously support motherhood myths that undermine women who stay home. Homemakers with children are shown as confused, overwhelmed, and focused only on their households, uninterested and uninvolved in their community or public affairs (Johnston and Swanson, 2003). With a half century of magazines showing a standard of femininity associated with domestic life, appearance, romance, and dating, it is not surprising that in the millennium the dominant theme in magazines like *Cosmopolitan, Glamour,* and *Essence* is how to be more beautiful followed by relationships with men (how to get and keep them). The two are often linked in the same article. Magazine advertisers are happy to oblige women who want both.

Advertising

Images of women in magazines related to beauty, romance, and homemaking are reinforced through advertisements testifying to the power of makeovers and weight loss and the glories of spotless kitchen floors, soft toilet tissue, and antiseptic children. Extensive research has documented the fact that even with some improvement over time, advertising images of women remain based on these traditional gender role norms.

An early major study on gender stereotyping in advertising was done by analyzing magazines according to the number of males and females and the gender of adults, the occupations and activities in which they were presented, and the kinds of products being promoted (Courtney and Lockeretz, 1971). Despite the explosion of women in the labor force, the data showed that women's place is in the home, they do not make important decisions, and they are dependent on men, who in turn regard women as sex objects. Women are only interested in buying cosmetics and cleaning aids. A number of studies quickly followed. Ads were beginning to depict women in more occupational roles, but the vast majority of women were still pictured exclusively in the home. There was a decline in the blatantly sexist ads, but advertisers continued to be insensitive to the real world. Women's concerns centered on appearance, men, and simple decisions revolving around domestic roles (Should I cook turkey or beef for dinner?). Advertisements spanning two decades rarely showed women in nontraditional situations, even in magazines oriented to a wider audience, such as *Newsweek, Look,* and *Sports Illustrated* (Courtney and Whipple, 1983). Since it was first published, the infamous swimsuit issue of *Sports Illustrated* maintains the same content of ideally beautiful and sexy women who are available to men (Davis, 1997).

Advertisements from the 1980s to the present not only maintain these stereotyped images but also in important ways gender stereotyped and biased portrayals of both white and African-American women have increased (Furnham and Bitar, 1993; Plous and Neptune, 1997). With nudity and near-nudity now found in even the more established magazines, it is common to see undressed or scantily dressed women selling all kinds of products. Car and boat ads typically show women in bathing suits provocatively draped over fenders and on cabin decks. Products sold primarily to men, such as machine tools and industrial equipment, use a similar format. In gun magazines women in lingerie or evening gowns clutch men who are holding handguns and rifles. Advertising campaigns for popular brands of clothing and fragrances routinely show near nude women or women and men in sexually provocative scenes—but do not show the items they are selling—only the logo of the company. This content often includes messages related to aggression and violence. Advertisers in magazines such as *Vogue, Harper's, Elle, Glamour, GQ,* and *Esquire* often portray women who are helpless, passive, bound, or are being maimed and abused by men or animals (Wolf, 2002).

It is relatively easy to analyze ads according to general themes and images. But to assess the overall impact, we must recognize that ads sell products and reinforce attitudes in ways that often go unrecognized by the casual reader. Advertisers may embed subliminal messages at a subconscious level to prompt consumers to buy a product. Whether subliminal messages actually increase sales is debatable, but is a standard tool in advertising. The pioneering work of Erving Goffman (1979) concentrated on the subtleties of posture and relative size and positioning of hands, eyes, knees, and other parts of the body in ads. A man is pictured taller than a woman unless he is socially inferior to her. Men and boys are shown instructing women and girls. A woman's eye is averted to the man in the picture with her, but a man's eye is averted only to a superior. Women's hands caress or barely touch. They are rarely shown grasping, manipulating, or creatively shaping. Women have faraway looks in their eyes, especially in the presence of men. Women act like children and are often depicted with children. Replication studies over the past twenty years indicate that these images of women remain fundamentally unchanged (Kang, 1997).

Such depictions are reinforced by how much of the body is shown in an ad. Males represent "face-isms," in that their faces are photographed more often than their bodies. Females represent "body-isms" or "partial-isms," in that their bodies or parts of their bodies are more often shown. Women, for example, appear much more in swimwear than do men (Hall and Crum, 1994). Data continue to confirm these depictions. Face-ism ads still dominate for men as do body-ism ads for women.

They suggest that the face is associated with qualities such as character and intellect whereas the body is associated with qualities such as weight and emotion, thus contributing to beliefs about what is deemed important for men and women (Shields, 2002). Women make desperate efforts to conform to a beauty ideal manipulating their faces and bodies to achieve an impossible standard (Kilbourne, 1995). Adolescent girls and aging women are particularly vulnerable to such advertising and are its prime targets. Ads targeted to young girls play on their insecurities and wishes to be older and more sexually appealing (Willemsen, 1998; Kitch, 2001).

Age and gender stereotypes combine in ads targeted to older women and play on their insecurities and desires to stop the aging clock and maintain their sex appeal. Older women are portrayed much less frequently than men and women in all age groups. Despite the demographic shift favoring longer and healthier lives for women, they are portrayed even less frequently than in the past. Young women advertise products to older women (McConatha et al., 1999; Miller et al., 1999). The fear-of-aging theme has increased cosmetics sales dramatically for the over-50 baby boomers. But there are almost no older models who sell these products. Whereas younger women sell lipstick and hair color to older women, when older women are used in ads at all, it is to tout products signaling body decline, such as for dentures and adult diapers (Jamieson, 1995:153).

Besides beauty products, clothing represents another method to attain the beauty standard by manipulating the body. The most successful models are paid millions to reinforce unnatural images of womanhood, which keep women chained to seasonal, changing, and expensive fashion trends. There is a growing market for seductive clothing designs aimed at little girls.

> When a slinky ensemble for young children, identical to one worn by Madonna on *Saturday Night Live*, received rave reviews . . . buyers and parents instantly snapped them up. . . . People went nuts for those little Madonna outfits . . . women who buy Escada and Chanel for herself flip when she sees something like that for her daughter. (Evans, 1993:117)

Considering the avalanche of physical appearance messages women receive in advertising, symbolic interaction correctly predicts the self-fulfilling prophecies that follow. We have seen that these are demonstrated in everything from self-esteem, cigarette smoking, eating disorders, and mental health, as well as a range of attitudes related to gender. Advertising artificially creates images that become the reality. In addition, as predicted by symbolic interaction's *end-point fallacy*, new labels about attractiveness will produce new behavior in an ongoing process. Beauty standards will continue to change, and consumers will adapt to these standards and change their behavior accordingly in a never-ending cycle.

What is remarkable about such findings is that women—and increasingly men—are very critical of the images. If the people to whom the ads are directed find them distasteful and irritating, how can a double standard continue? From a pure business viewpoint, sexism is disadvantageous in that a product's market potential is not realized. Another problem is that advertisers are the lifeblood of magazines and make concessions to receive their business. Advertisers demand that a "supportive editorial atmosphere" or "complementary copy" appear with their ads. This means that an article about beauty to support or complement an ad about a beauty product must be included on the same page. In this way advertisers literally control the editorial content of the entire magazine (Steinem, 1995:316).

The minimal changes that have occurred are depicting women in more diverse occupational roles and in more general interest magazines. Older women are a huge potential market. While proclaiming that older women are (still) beautiful, advertisers are beginning to use themes suggesting that fitness, vitality, and blazing new trails are associated with aging (Darling, 1994; Krasnow, 1995). These suggest that advertisers may create a new kind of woman. Regardless of age, she is active, involved in an array of projects, and enjoys her home but is not monopolized by it. Some advertisers are only beginning to recognize that women are diverse, lead successful lives, and can balance home and career. The impact of this remains to be seen. The caution here is that another artificial creation emerges along with another set of standards to which women are expected to adhere.

Advertisers must be aware of trends affecting products and services. The moment an improvement is made on a particular product, campaigns begin to sell the public on its virtues. The old is quickly forgotten as the new makes its appearance. To sell means to change. Yet advertising is stubbornly persistent in the manner in which this is done. What is ironic is that ad agencies ignore the research documenting the fact that consumers react negatively to advertising that is sexist and desire campaigns that portray both men and women in nonstereotyped ways. Men have been slower to lobby for these changes than women, but with the rapid increase in print ads and other media showing men as sex objects and portraying perfect male bodies that are as just as unattainable for men, men are joining forces with women to protest sexism in advertising (Nathanson and Young, 2001). Considering this research and the numerous instances of public outrage over certain advertisements, the adage that "sex (and sexism) sells" must be questioned.

FILM

Compared to other media women have enjoyed a more central position in the film industry. Director and producer largely remain the province of men, but women have succeeded as screenwriters, editors, costume designers, critics, and actors. In the early days of film when the studio system was at its height, women dominated the star spotlight. This was reflected in popularity polls and the billings female leads received. Although the contract system allowed studios to literally own actors, women had influence in determining their careers and the parts they received. The female stars of this era were allowed movie roles showing them to be articulate, self-reliant, and independent (Tirohl, 2003). It has only been since the 1940s that female stars have been overshadowed by males. With a few exceptions, this decline has continued to the present (Pomerance, 2001). In contrast to the reality of women's diverse contemporary roles, current film portrayals are sorely lacking in depth and authenticity.

Screen History

Reflected in screen images, World War II encouraged the independence and initiative of women. They were portrayed as efficient homemakers who could make the transition from kitchen to the war industry smoothly, without severely disrupting family life. Or they were shown as nurses serving overseas and at times as combatants who, like men, died for their country. Movies were a critical part of the war effort and emphasized the need for self-sacrifice to ensure victory. Women on the home front were necessary for this effort. The double-duty woman who worked in a defense plant was symbolized by *Rosie the Riveter*, who became the home front heroine.

Although women on the World War II screen possessed self-confidence and strength, a certain ambiguity was also evident. The taken-for-granted functional balance of home and workplace was upset. Both men and women left home to engage in the unlikely occupations of soldier and defense worker. They were fighting to save the American home, and films reassured audiences that after the war women would be as eager as men to return to the natural order of things. True to this message, by the 1950s films reaffirmed the domestic subservience of women.

Good Women and Bad Women. Whereas the war years presented women as multifaceted, after the war they were portrayed as one dimensional, as either good or bad. The "good" woman embodied the feminine mystique. She remained virtuous throughout courtship. Her premarital virginity was never questioned. She might have a successful career, but Mr. Right would change her priorities and definitions of success. After marriage she became the ideal wife and mother. Doris Day and Debbie Reynolds represented this image. The "bad" woman, on the other hand, was the sexpot, who could entice a man away from his faithful wife and loving family. Marilyn Monroe and Ava Gardner represented this image. Regardless of the good–bad dichotomy screen actresses had to endure, these movies were awash with sexual innuendo and hinted broadly at the enticements of immorality. The difference between this era and those to follow, however, was that sexual desires were actualized on the functionalist screen only when it was normative to do so. Just in his fantasies did married Tom Ewell succumb to Marilyn Monroe in the *Seven Year Itch*, and Doris Day would not succumb to Cary Grant in a *Touch of Mink* until they were married.

Although the films of the 1950s display a concern for domestic righteousness, they also reflected the disenchantment women faced in their struggle with narrowly defined gender roles. This period combined both conventional and progressive expressions of the difficulty women faced as they made the transition between domestic roles and newer alternatives. Screen actresses portrayed women torn between desire for security, symbolized by the customary and comfortable lifestyle of home, and desire for adventure and challenge beckoning to them outside home. These conflicts and contradictions of the transitional women helped set the stage for the changes of the next two decades.

If the early days of film romanticized women and put them on a pedestal, the 1960s and 1970s quickly compensated. Blatant sexuality laced with violence became the staple of the era. The new women of this era were loosened from the constraints of family life, but with the breaking of the bonds, an attitude of "they deserve what they get" arose. Women who ventured outside the home were portrayed negatively, suffered, and were usually punished as a result. The favorable images of the war years disintegrated, and women were accorded fewer roles than ever before. Male speaking roles outdistanced female by twelve to one. This period has been referred to as the most disheartening in the screen history for women on the screen and the women they represented off the screen. As the women's liberation movement gained momentum and women were asserting themselves in new realms, a backlash occurred in commercial film (Haskell, 1987, 1997).

James Bond and *His* Girls. By the 1970s sex and sexual violence became explicit enough to create a rating system to determine level of suitability for audiences below a certain age. The system is more concerned with sex than violence so that love scenes are more apt to get the film a restricted rating than rape scenes. The rating system also helps perpetuate the idea that rape is inconsequential. Rapists are often portrayed heroically when their victims love them at the time of the rape or fall in love with them later. In four decades of James Bond films, for example, women are depicted enjoying rape. Bond is the suave, charismatic good guy—the supposed fantasy of every woman and enviable role model of every man. James Bond gets to play out men's fantasies—he drives fast cars, fights ruthless villains, wears a nice suit, and has sex with any "girl" he desires, all who eventually say yes to him. Bond films are a composite of sex, spectacle, and menace (Wilson, 2002). Once raped women are then ignored by the male star, sometimes murdered by him, and often murdered by someone else. Bond must always be free of women. If he inadvertently falls in love with her, she is doomed to die before the end of the picture. Whether Bond pictures or not, rapes and murders are likely alternatives to women in token roles. A "now you see them, now you don't" pattern occurs (Beckman, 2003). As Bond ages, his girls do not. The most enduring Bonds, Sean Connery, Roger Moore, and Pierce Brosnan, were often 30 years older than their leading ladies. The women are as sleek and young as ever, picture after picture.

To maintain a women's audience with a heightened feminist consciousness, the flagrant abuse of women in past Bond films has been acknowledged by producers. The newest Bond, Pierce Brosnan, has been paired with strong, intelligent (always beautiful) lead women in both heroine and villainess roles who, in the later films, match his wit, confidence, and resourcefulness. Partnership rather than submission is touted as the newer thrust of the Bond films, with leading ladies as supposedly sexually liberated as Bond is himself (Chapman, 2000). In an effort at emancipation from Bond, the female leads are publicized as the Bond "women" rather than the "Bond girls" (but still *his* females). Although not as overtly misogynous, the James Bond mystique endures. As late as 1999 *TV Guide* ran a special article on "A Bond Girls Reunion." In a review of Halle Berry's portrayal of Jinx, Pierce Brosnan's Bond girl in *Die Another Day*, resourceful Halle Berry is pictured in an orange bikini with a dagger in a white belt. Pictured above is Ursula Andress wearing nearly the identical outfit in 1962. The caption reads, "Halle Berry is less of a sex symbol than a female equivalent to Bond" (Wilson, 2002:F1).

Pairing Sex and Violence

Despite the occasional spurts of romantic comedies like *You've Got Mail* and *Sleepless in Seattle*, referred to somewhat disdainfully as "chick flicks"—not suitable for male audiences or only if men are coerced by their female partners—film romance has been replaced with sexuality, violence, and their pairing in contemporary mainstream movies. Romantic movies of the past often had bold and capable females (Fred Astaire/Ginger Rogers; Katherine Hepburn/Spencer Tracy). These couples are gone, replaced with prostitutes and girlfriends of questionable morals filling the void. The most typical occupation for women in the last three decades of movies is prostitute or ex-prostitute. Themes of love and adultery are infused with violence and murder.

Mainstream films are often more violent than pornographic films. "Slasher" movies appealing to adolescent males regularly send the message that sexual violence is normal and acceptable. Movies routinely portray scenes of graphic violence against passive female victims. Stalking and its often violent conclusion are associated with comedy and romance in mainstream cinema (Anderson, 1999; Mediascope, 2000). Movies such as *Basic Instinct, Fatal Attraction*, and *What's Love Got to Do with It?* exemplify this trend. Love and violence coincide. Females are victims in movies of horror, murder, and especially rape, in which film directors seem to have a macabre interest. During the past three decades movies with a central rape theme increased dramatically. Although women as rape victims are more sympathetically depicted than in the past, moviegoers are also becoming more desensitized to the issue, reinforcing the notion that the possibility of rape is an inescapable burden women must face.

Aging Females, Ageless Males

Unlike men, women must be young and show high levels of physical strength to be seriously considered for romantic leads and the "kicking butt" roles of sexy heroines (*Crouching Tiger, Hidden Dragon; Miss Congeniality; Charlie's Angels*) in emerging action films appealing to both young men and women (Arons, 2001; Vares, 2001). In Hollywood young translates to under 30. The hottest stars of the 1930s–1960s were women in powerful, multidimensional roles—Bette Davis, Joan Crawford, and Rosalind Russell—and were playing romantic leads well into their 40s and often into their 50s. Today these women would have long before been consigned to obscure roles or relegated to made-for-TV cable movies. After a certain age, women are consigned to play shrews, jealous housewives, lonely executives, or kooky aunts. Only 8 percent of roles for women in the top 250 films go to women over 40 (Waxman, 2002). Younger female faces are sought to replace aging stars. Distinguished female actors such as Faye Dunaway, Shirley MacLaine, and Meryl Streep get old; Mel Gibson, Dustin Hoffman, and Richard Gere get distinguished. Harrison Ford's reprise as *Indiana Jones* is played as an Indie who was older than Sean Connery who played Indie's father in an earlier Jones movie.

These gains may have been short-lived, with even fewer diverse and starring roles offered to females in the 1990s. Over 75 percent of feature-film roles go to men, a figure that increased over the last decade (Lauzen, 2003a). So-called wholesome roles for women, although devoid of the sexual content than may demean women, signals doom in Hollywood. It is a sign she is an aging bygone. By this reasoning, a woman remains marketable only by "shedding her clothes and her dignity" (Anderson, 1994). A rather cynical comment on the paucity of either featured or supporting parts for mature, skilled actresses came in 1993 when the theme for the Academy Awards was "Oscar Celebrates Women in the Movies." Six of the ten nominees for Best Actress and Best Supporting Actress came from Australia, England, and France because Hollywood studios simply did not offer enough meaningful roles for women to even get nominated for the award. In 1996, the public was told that screen actresses had their "meatiest choice of roles in ages," making it difficult to predict Oscar winners (Ciabattari, 1996). This was the "Year of the Backlash," where Hollywood blockbusters were replaced by family friendly and small art films. But most of the "meaty" roles to women in this backlash year were for their portrayals as prostitutes or ex-prostitutes. Within a year Hollywood returned to the blockbusters and greeted the millennium with the gendered Hollywood staples of the previous decades.

There are a few positive signs suggesting a return of women to movies that offer greater role latitude and countering stock Hollywood formulas related to gender. Critically acclaimed, popular films not resting on a male lead, attracting male and female audiences, and highlighting sensitive issues related to friendship and loyalty among women include: *The Joy Luck Club, Turning Point, Steel Magnolias, Waiting to Exhale, Fried Green Tomatoes, Silkwood,* and *Thelma and Louise.* However, the success for some of these was bittersweet. *Fried Green Tomatoes* and *Silkwood* were criticized for lesbian overtones and *Thelma and Louise* for male bashing. While successfully countering masculinist bias in some movies that portray lesbians, other stereotypes persist to make the films more palatable to a wider audience (Kabir, 1994). Filmmakers believe an injection of violence satisfies this criterion. Sharon Stone's portrayal of a bisexual murderer in *Basic Instinct* drew storms of protest from gay men and lesbians. But screenwriter and actress Guinevere Turner, who has done other movies with similar themes, was not bothered. She states, "I'd much rather have killer lesbians than lesbians who kiss once in the beginning and then use a man to get to each other" (Smith, 1994). *Thelma and Louise* was criticized for violence toward men, and the subtext of violence against women was ignored (Welsch, 2001). It is apparent that film critics, too, subscribe to a gender-stereotyped world that is suspicious of loving and cooperative relationships between women. It reveals much about the tenacity of gendered society when decades of movies routinely show females who are mutilated, maimed, murdered, and raped film after film, but when a successful movie reverses the scenario, a charge of man-bashing is leveled against it. The issue society must address is not so much that turnabout is fair play but that violence is viewed as an acceptable mode of conflict resolution.

With limited roles and limited meaty roles going to women, it is not surprising that female stars and superstars far outnumber their female counterparts. A cursory look at current film offerings in the local paper will testify to the scarcity of female stars, strong, multidimensional, or otherwise. Barbra Streisand was the only bankable female lead for a decade. Julia Roberts is the probable frontrunner at the millennium. Sally Field, Meryl Streep, Jessica Lange, Diane Keaton, Susan Sarandon, Demi Moore, Meg Ryan, and Halle Berry occupy star status, but superstardom eludes them and will elude them more as they age. Several of these women have managed to endure the Hollywood roller coaster for women. There is less tolerance for films that are box office bombs starring women. Jack Nicholson, Al Pacino, or Kevin Costner may emerge relatively unscathed from bad reviews and bad movies, but studios are reluctant to offer parts to women who have fallen victim to the critics' ax. Women are almost hidden among the faces of numerous male actors who endure as superstars. Although complaints abound that women are held hostage by Hollywood, the bottom line is male domination of movie marquees.

The film industry offers a number of excuses for portraying women in limited and stereotyped roles that emphasize their sexuality. Male studio executives often maintain that the public disdains "macho" women and that television offers a diverse range of female roles for free. This may suggest that men create inappropriate images for female roles simply because their feedback from women is limited. Roles emerge from male fantasies, the fear men express in dealing with women as allies rather than as adversaries, and the tenacious belief that men must dominate and control women. They cite statistics that the average moviegoer is a young male, and it is his fantasies that are being catered to.

There are challenges to these views. Box office advertising is expected to double by 2007, and much of that advertising is targeted to women. Filmmakers will continue to focus on the key age demographic (young—between 14 and 24), but indications are that male and female will reach parity in the moviegoing public (MacMillan, 2002; Debow, 2003). To make movies that ignore or demean a large portion of the audience does not make good marketing sense. Two decades of Hollywood's service to teenage boys may be matched with offerings geared to teenage girls (*Freaky Friday, Bend It Like Beckham, Whale Rider*) (Schickel, 2003). Because these movies also spotlight rebellious teens who succeed in their challenges to parents, teachers, and the "older" set, they also attract the number of necessary males to ensure box office profitability. It cannot be said that such movies do much to dissuade gender or age stereotypes about teenage girls, but they do offer young women alternatives from the typical female bashing movies they usually see.

The dilemma faced by those in the film industry concerned with the image of women is how to successfully combine the elements of fantasy and realism attracting people to movies in the first place. Mainstream cinema represent women as either "idealized objects of desire or as threatening objects to be tamed" (Pribram, 1993). The limited range of female characters continuously puts them in the same roles: as madonnas, whores, bimbos, psychotics, and bitches (Silvas et al., 1993). On the other hand, should women be portrayed as victims of patriarchy, conquerors against mighty odds, or burnt out employees and soccer moms? Will romance be forever crushed by realism? Movies can still have the requisite fantasy and magic without accepting a narrow range of behavior from female actors. In British actor and Oscar winner Emma Thompson's view, women have to debrief themselves to resist the messages that they have no history or no heroines and to unlearn the stereotypes that chip away at their sense of self-esteem (Italie, 1993).

Filmmakers are only beginning to deal with the struggles facing contemporary women, and few directors are willing to confront the issues. So movies retreat into an unrealistic stereotyped world. Over two-thirds of the public in the United States believe that movies are demeaning to women, but gender stereotypes remain a staple of American cinema (Riordan, 2002). Movies may largely be creations of male fantasies, but women need to invent their own fantasies and portray these as well. Although movies do not have to provide answers for questions concerning gender role change, they can at least offer challenges.

MUSIC

Media cater to a public demanding new sights and sounds to satisfy an unending thirst for entertainment variety. Nowhere is this more apparent than in the world of popular music. Whatever niche is defined—country, rock, pop, rap, hip-hop, alternative, or heavy metal—the quest for musical notoriety, as evidenced by the volume of CD sales, continues unabated. Although the music industry is diverse, it recognizes that a significant portion of the record market is controlled by teens and young adults. With the advent of the rock video, the competition for the teen dollar becomes even stronger. Given the money and time teens spend on it, contemporary music is an important source of socialization.

Music is always at the vanguard of change. Protest movements are fired by songs that unify members against a common foe. Rock musicians take conventional morality to the limits. Such music challenges the traditional and creates the conditions for further change. Because many genres of contemporary music challenge social norms, it would appear to be the one medium where traditional gender roles are also challenged. Evidence counters this assumption. Popular music is the most stereotyped and misogynistic of all media in its gender portrayals.

A half century of popular music sings to the beauty and sex appeal of women, who use them to control men. Through passivity and submissiveness, a woman can manipulate and control him and the relationship. Control, however, may be difficult to assess because she remains dependent on him. Country music in particular stereotypes women in two categories: They are temptresses to men as well as wives who wait patiently for their two-timing husbands to return. No matter what the consequences, "stand by your man" is the response for the long-suffering woman.

Rock Music

Of all popular music, rock claims artistic supremacy and the creative force behind all popular music (Regev, 1994:97). This claim to supremacy serves to legitimize whatever musical representation it offers to its public, including the portrayal of the genders. Popular music may be gender stereotyped, but its rock niche exceeds all others in these portrayals.

Since the 1950s, images of women in rock music have become increasingly associated with sexual violence. The misogyny in "cock rock," heavy metal, and rap lyrics is unconcealed, with little attempt to be subtle. Some images of women in songs contain positive regard, but these exist side by side with blatant misogyny. Women are cast into rigid categories determined by their perceived gender role characteristics. These images are expanded by CD covers depicting women being brutalized by men and animals. Computer images allow these depictions to be acted out. The love–hate dichotomy is featured where men are kissing and killing women at the same time. Boycotts of records showing violent themes against women on their covers have generally failed. But as rock lyrics have become more sexually explicit, some record companies have agreed to put a warning label on their album covers indicating that the words may be unsuitable for audiences below a certain age. Like in the film rating system, it is a significant social comment that sexual themes are considered more offensive than violence against women.

The Women of Rock. Before the advent of rock in the 1950s, female singers occupied one-third of the positions on singles charts, but by 1985 that figure had decreased dramatically to 8 percent (Groce and Cooper, 1990:221). A number of female entertainers, such as Patti Page, Rosemary Clooney, and Doris Day, were popular before World War II and were commercially successful for two decades by combining music and film careers. With the emergence of rock music and its appeal to teenagers, younger male entertainers moved into the spotlight. Only the "girl groups" of the 1960s and 1970s, such as the Supremes, Ronnettes, and Shangri-Las, charted any real successes for female singers during this era.

In the 1960s Janis Joplin broke into the rock culture and emerged as a unique, controversial, and often-contradictory symbol for young women caught in the middle of a confusing period of history. She was viewed as a floozy as well as one who sang of the pains of womanhood, but also a feminist symbol who paved the way for other women destined to enter the sacred realm of the male rock kingdom (Hirshey, 1997). As rock musician Melissa Etheridge attests:

> In 1967, Janis was strange and freakish. Today she would be hip and alternative. Because of her drive to be true to her soul, girls like me in 1976 didn't feel so strange wanting to sing rock 'n' roll. Because she wrote, "either take the love I offer or let me be," I didn't feel so different for wanting power in my life. We didn't have to be secretaries or housewives; we could be rock stars. (Cited in Levins, 1995).

A number of rock bands either led by women or with female and male lead singers and musicians have emerged. Madonna, Gloria Estefan, Shakira, Christina Aguilera, Paula Abdul, and Britney Spears are recognizable as leading women in rock. Many of these women have Latino roots and are hugely successful in the music buying public of the Americas. They have garnered the music industry's most prestigious awards. It cannot be said, however, that their songs substantially differ from, or offer challenges to, stereotyped representations of women. Like pop and country singers they, too, sing mostly of love and pain and chant about vulnerable women being abandoned by men.

Until recently, female rock artists have not produced many popular songs depicting women in a sympathetic light and have had little power in altering the sexist material of their bands and still remaining commercially successful. Resurgent sexism on the rock scene may also counter efforts at change (Powers, 1999). With the rise of the female superstars of rock, however, even if the lyrics do not reflect much change now, it may happen in the near future. Women rock artists are creating new identities that challenge male domination in mainstream rock culture and are gaining control over their own images (Katovich and Makowski, 1999; Schippers, 2001; Grajeda, 2002). A major result of attaining economic independence is that they can seriously challenge rock's misogyny.

Madonna may be the exception to this pattern, but she is also an enigma. Her music frequently counters traditional feminine ideals of dependency and reserve, presenting a postmodern feminist image that shatters all gender barriers. Others condemn her for sending potent messages to teens about the glamour of sex and pregnancy through a fantasy world she creates (cited in Brown and Schulze, 1990:92). She remains an inveterate gender rule breaker but is still judged by different standards than males. Her videos have been banned by MTV and mainstream video networks for sexual and violent content that men would have likely escaped (Gundersen, 2001). But because she has transitioned successfully into film, her multidimensional talents are receiving high marks. Janis Joplin died early in her career. It will be interesting to see if Madonna becomes the feminist role model that may have been Joplin's destiny.

Rock Videos. The misogyny in most rock videos is blatant. In 1981, MTV was introduced to cable subscribers and soon catapulted to become one of the most widely consumed forms of popular culture for adolescents in the United States. Global MTV consumption is also increasing and so is its potential for gendered rock. Rock videos provide a visual extension and support a gender ideology of male power and dominance reinforcing misogyny. Rock videos routinely depict women as emotional, illogical, deceitful, fearful, dependent, and passive and men as adventuresome, domineering, aggressive, and violent. Although over half of rock videos show no women or placed women only in background shots, those videos that do show women usually combine sexual images with acts of violence (Alexander, 1999; Kalof, 1999; Smith and Boyston, 2002). On MTV males appear on the videos twice as often as females. When race is factored in, whites outnumber people of color by almost three to one; women of color are the least represented. However, when they *are* portrayed, African American women tend to have more active roles, such as dancing or playing an instrument. White women are used more for decoration or having no clear purpose in the video.

Heavy metal and rap display the most violent lyrics and images. Women are routinely depicted as sex objects on whom violence is perpetrated, with increasing numbers of rape scenes being enacted. Whereas heavy metal uses more double entendres and symbolic allusions to refer to sexual acts and male domination of women, rap makes these acts more graphic and explicit (McLeod et al., 1997; McLeod et al., 2001). Perhaps the most disheartening statistic with regard to rock videos is that *most* videos combine sexual images with acts of violence. The song titles *Stripped, Raped and Strangled* by Cannibal Corpse and *Smack My Bitch Up* by Prodigy and the following lyrics from *I Want Action* by Poison are typical of the rape themes of best selling albums (Mediascope, 2000): "I want action tonight, If I can't have her, I'll take her and make her."

Research shows that men and women receive these messages differently. Women read the female images in rock videos as either powerful and suggestive of control or as vulnerable and weak. Men read the same images either as teasing and hard to get or as submissive and indecisive (Milburn et al., 2000). There are no significant gender differences in interpretations of male images (Kalof, 1993). Exposure to such images not only desensitizes viewers to erotica but also increases callousness toward women. Consistent with symbolic interaction theory, such research suggests that gender is a social construction shaped by social myths articulated in popular culture (Denzin, 1992). Publicity surrounding the graphic portrayals of sexual themes is exactly what some performers desire. In addition to CD sales, cable subscribers will pay extra for premium channels that show controversial videos that other networks refuse to air.

Women may attempt to break out of the mold in which they are embedded by the rock culture but find themselves in a no-win situation. Indeed, few can act as role models and challenge rock's misogynous lyrics. Madonna may be challenging dependency in women, but her sexual image serves to reinforce the women-as-sex-object orientation already ingrained in rock culture. Her controversial videos maintain this image. With few exceptions such as Tina Turner, who reemerged in rock and catapulted to the superstar category, alternative views of women, demonstrated by female artists themselves, are rarer today than in the 1960s.

TELEVISION

Television is by far the most influential of all media. The power of television is reflected in statistics that in the United States, over 98 percent of households have at least one TV, almost 70 percent have cable, and the average number of sets per home is 2.4, one of which is turned on an average of seven hours per day. These figures translate to about 3,500 hours of viewing time per person per year (U.S. Bureau of the Census, 2004). Although people over age 55 watch the most television, preschoolers and young children may spend up to one-third of the day in front of the set. Children from poor homes watch television more than those from affluent homes, working and lower class children more than those whose parents have higher education and income, and African Americans and Latinos more than European Americans, even when controlling for SES (Kotler et al., 2001; Certain and Kahn, 2002).

Television plays a central role in the lives of most children and is a powerful agent of socialization. TV for children is also much more gender stereotyped than the shows adults watch. Young children are especially vulnerable in believing that television images represent truth and reality, and they may not be able to distinguish fantasy from reality. As we saw in chapter 3, they are still in the formative stages of their identity and use television for role modeling, patterns found for both genders and for children of all races in the United States (Cantor et al., 2001; Murray and Mandara, 2002; Shrum, 2002; Smith et al., 2002).

Gendered Violence

More than 2,000 studies conducted over three decades have documented a clear and consistent correlation between amount of television viewing and aggression. Viewing violence increases the potential for violence and desensitizes the viewer to subsequent violence. The more violent the content, the more aggressive the child or adolescent. Consider the following facts on the aggression–media–television link (American Academy of Pediatrics, 2001; Bushman and Huesmann, 2001; Smailes et al., 2002; Wilson et al., 2002).

- Two out of three TV programs contain violence that threatens or actualizes hurt and killing.
- By sixth grade the average child has witnessed at least 8,000 TV murders and 100,000 other violent acts.
- Nearly 70 percent of children's programs contain physical aggression—an average of 14 violent acts per hour of typical programming.

Other forms of media violence repeat and even exaggerate many of the patterns found on television. Exposure to video game violence is linked to increases in aggressive behavior, particularly in boys (Anderson and Bushman, 2001; Unsworth and Ward, 2001). Because of the ability to manipulate characters, violent video games may have an even stronger connection to aggression in children (Griffiths, 1998; Bensley and Van Eenwyk, 2001).

Television violence is directed toward women. Overall, men kill and women get killed. Men kill more than twice as often as they are killed. White adult males and attractive white boys are more likely to be involved in violence and to get away with it, with girls and women of color, older women, and foreign women the most likely victims (Media Awareness, 2000; Smith et al., 2002). Children learn though gendered media messages that men are aggressive and women are vulnerable. These messages may be altered, but they are not erased in adulthood.

Prime Time

Television prime time revolves around men. Women account for about one-third of all characters, but leading male characters outnumber females about two to one, a consistent trend since the early days of television (Lauzen, 2003a; *Media Report to Women*, 2003). Besides underrepresentation, a great deal of research has focused on the unrealistic, stereotyped portrayals of both television men and women. Men dominate dramatic shows, especially those involving action, adventure, and crime. They play tough and emotionally reserved characters who are unmarried but have beautiful female companions. The profile of prime time men includes the following: He is 30 years old, single, white, handsome, smart, middle class, and sexy. In many of these shows, female characters are simply bystanders who may add sex appeal. Prime time women in lead roles in dramatic shows are the attractive, young lawyers and physicians of *ER* and *The Practice*. Older women, if seen at all, are marginalized, sending powerful messages about what the general population thinks about aging in general and elderly women in particular (Signorielli, 2001).

Most dramas, however, have more women in minor roles. The profile of prime time women includes the following: She is unmarried, employed outside the home, more likely to be in professional occupations than in the past, cares for children if she is a single mother, and is not involved in, but looking for, a romantic relationship (Elasmar, 1999; Schultz, 2001). There are always exceptions to any pattern, and a notable one should be mentioned here. The immense success of *Xena, Warrior Princess* is attributed to the nongender stereotyped traits associated with her character—confidence, strength, and the ability to match any male villain (Minkowitz, 1996; Morreale, 1998). With the action, fantasy, and adventure of the series, young males crossed over to watch what would have been a show directed to an exclusively female audience. On the other hand, when powerful women are shown in partnership with other confident women, Gabrielle, in this instance, overtones of lesbianism are seized on by commentators in attempts to tarnish a show's luster. These attempts failed. Viewers did not retreat from the show and, on the contrary, a new cadre of viewers may have been added (Korte, 1999). As we will see in film, however, when stereotypes related to gender and sexual orientation in media are challenged rather than reinforced, there is often public outcry.

In comedies, women now appear in about the same frequency as men. The completely dependent housewife role in early comedy series like *Leave it to Beaver* and *I Love Lucy* have all but disappeared. The "liberated" women of the 1970s, such as *Maude* and *Rhoda* paved the wave for this trend. The immense popularity of the long-running *Mary Tyler Moore Show* is linked to the fact that this was the only show in which a single career woman was depicted without a steady boyfriend or any major story line revolving around her unmarried and nonmotherhood status. She was Mary, and her boss was always Mr. Grant, but as the show progressed Mary became more confident and admired by her colleagues in the television newsroom where she was employed. This show remains the exception. Some may argue that *Ally McBeal* was the new Mary Richards, but her ditzy character, self-absorption, inappropriate dress and obsession with romance may counter this belief. Homemakers may have disappeared, but there are virtually no comedy or dramas that have the equivalent of a Mary Richards.

Employed Women. The explosion of women in the workplace translated to prime-time television. In the rush to garner the female 20 to 50 age group, television shows depicting employed women mushroomed. By 2000 employed women comprised over three-fourths of prime time female characters, about 15 percent more than those who worked outside the home in real life. Regardless of what they do in their TV workplaces, however, their roles revolve around romantic relationships, marriage, and family. Female characters are more likely to be identified by their marital status; male characters are much more likely to be identified by their occupation. Compared to men, women's occupations are less prestigious and less powerful. The few powerful women in past shows, such as Angela Changing of *Falcon Crest* or Alexis Carrington of *Dynasty*, have also disappeared. When powerful women are shown, they are depicted as ruthless and manipulative, using any means to maintain their positions. Because, unlike men, a woman cannot "have it all"— beauty, power, position, loving family—and still be viewed favorably on television, they have been relegated to perpetual reruns.

Employed women may be married and have children, but virtually none of them, fully 99 percent in one study of network prime time, experience work–family conflicts. Prime time or comedy plots revolve around what happens at work or after work—but not both. This research reflects television's continual lack of attention to the real-world experiences of women (Asher and Lederer, 2000).

In a conclusion very similar to film, the low quality of women's roles is linked to male fantasies of "scantily clad half-wits who need to be rescued" (cited in Atkin et al., 1991:679). Issues related to weight and appearance permeate prime time television. Women and girls are laughed at when they are too heavy—the heavier the woman the more negative the comments about them, especially comments made by men (Fouts & Burggraf, 2000). These images continue despite increases in shows featuring female leads. Younger women are particularly vulnerable to stereotyping and are depicted as empty headed and obsessed with beauty, clothes, shopping, materialism, and dating (Record, 2002). The character of Kelly in the old *Married With Children* is the teenage/young adult caricature of this portrayal. More recent examples of some of these images include Linda of *Becker*, Phoebe of *Friends*, and models Nicole and Paris, in the hugely popular *The Simple Life*, all the more significant because it is a "reality" show.

There are some important exceptions to these trends. The prime time police series *Cagney and Lacey* is a case in point. This series deviated from the prime time television norm and did so successfully for many years. It featured women in lead roles as police officers, bringing them together as partners. The series dealt sensitively and realistically with issues rarely seen on police shows, such as breast cancer, abortion, and child neglect (D'Acci, 1994). Clearly the television audience appreciates these themes and how they are portrayed. The Cagney and Lacey roles were reprised by the original stars in series of popular made-for-television movies. Dealing with issues women face in terms of career and ambition and disappointment and hope at midlife in a realistic, compassionate, yet entertaining way appeals to a large segment of viewers.

It is now common to see more gender related social issues on entertainment-focused dramas and increasingly on comedy series. Despite enduring stereotyped portrayals, women and men are seen pursuing a diversity of nontraditional roles and in real-world living arrangements and occupations far removed from Beaver Cleaver's family. Consider *The Cosby Show, Will & Grace, Medicine Woman, Designing Women, Roc,* and *Diagnosis Murder,* many demonstrating that class, race, age, sexual orientation, and gender diversity can be successfully portrayed. In 1992, the *Murphy Brown* series became a political football when Vice President Dan Quayle argued that it glorified motherhood for unmarried women. The producers countered by using the controversy in the series itself and brought in examples of many families not fitting the supposed traditional family form, a tactic that enhanced the show's popularity.

Yet these changes in prime time network television must be considered in light of overall programming, including cable TV and the market for reruns dating back a half century. Even with the women in lead roles in a few popular series, they still do not typically include major roles, especially for minority women. In terms of their numbers in the population, network TV is overrepresented with African American characters and underrepresented with Latinos, now the largest minority group in the United States. Latino males are almost invisible but unlike the music industry, Latinas are virtually nonexistent. The few background roles they play are as domestics, waitresses, and low level hospital aids. African American women are shown with more frequency and may have more favorable and positive role portrayals than their white counterparts. However, this higher number of characters is still not represented in terms of variety. The dominant characterizations of African American women are narrow and excessive—she is either an asexual mother figure or a sexpot (Goodwin, 1996:185.)

Gender role diversity overall has had minimal impact on the stereotypes embedded within the very programs that are often promoted as representing more realistic gender images. As shows enter the rerun market, *Roseanne* competes with *Charlie's Angels* (Whose angels are they?), making a rerun comeback because of the movie versions, and *Cheers,* the bar owned by womanizer Sam Malone. Regardless of any intent to make programming less gender stereotyped, reruns may counter these efforts.

Soap Operas

Directed at a female audience, soap operas have more female than male lead characters. Soaps are ludicrous in their distortion of reality but are popular because of it. Soaps provide the daytime opportunity for women to escape into a fantasy world of romance and adventure. Soap opera women come to one another for advice on family and sexual matters Soap opera women are likely to be portrayed as schemers, victims, bed-hoppers, and starry-eyed romantics. Family relationships equate women with motherhood, but lust and adultery lurk forever in the background (Benokraitis and Feagin, 1995). The soap opera family is a dominant concern of the women. The family suffers because of affairs that are usually revealed to the children. The forgiving wife holds the family together until her errant husband returns and temporarily makes amends.

Despite these portrayals, however, the women of soaps are also shown as intelligent, self-reliant, and articulate. Soaps appear to both engage and distance their primarily female viewers while keeping them entertained. The strong soap opera women who question the gender status quo and challenge patriarchy show some progressive change regarding gender roles on television. However, with new television niches geared to women who work outside the home, the traditional daytime soap opera may be on the verge of extinction.

Commercials

Television advertising reinforces the hundreds of print images we encounter daily. Nonverbals in print ads can be used effectively, but their use is limited compared to what can be done with television commercials. Television uses hundreds of techniques to create a particular view of a product. Lighting, camera angle, tone of voice, body movement, animation, and color, to name a few, can be infinitely manipulated to provide the ideal sales mix.

Research on thousands of commercials determines the extent and change of gendered content television advertising. The results are similar to print advertisements. As judged by location of the commercial, the single largest occupation for a female is homemaker. She is usually shown at home testifying to the merits of bathroom and kitchen products. Though she is selling products to other women, a man's voice in the background tells her what to do. The large majority of voice-overs are male. She is portrayed in dependent, subordinate, and helping roles to her husband, her children, and her male employer if she works outside the home. If she is African American, this pattern intensifies. Consistent with print ads, television commercials emphasize that women must first and foremost be attractive to be acceptable. About one in every three commercials presents a message about attractiveness to women through a male voice-over. Women now appear with about equal frequency to men in prime time commercials, but they are shown in domestic situations as wife or mother, and when shown with men outside the home, they are portrayed as less assured of themselves and more foolish and immature. These trends have been consistent over time (Furnham and Mak, 1999; Lin, 1999; Bresnahan et al., 2001; Coltrane and Messineo, 2000).

Children's Commercials. Of all forms of television advertising, commercials for children are the most gender stereotyped. Because a child typically views about 20,000 commercials annually, the potential impact on gender attitudes is enormous. Commercials depicting children are strictly gender segregated. Girls are shown in more passive activities and dependent on another person or a doll for entertainment. They learn how to help their mothers, assist in household tasks, serve men and boys—especially where food is concerned—and see how to become beautiful or stay cute. The ads focus on softness and quiet play and use dreamy content, soft music, and fades or dissolves for sequencing. Commercials do not teach independence or autonomy for young girls. The opposite characteristics are depicted in commercials for boys and focus on aggression, action, control, completion, and independence, most in scenes outside the home (Witt, 2000; Kunkel, 2001; Larson, 2003; Palmer and Young, 2003).

Changing these patterns is not encouraging. Females still need males to tell them what to do or buy, even for products like window cleaner, deodorant, or hair color. Gender stereotypes in children's commercials have actually increased. Only a tiny portion of gender possibilities are imaged in children's advertisements. Advertisements picturing children nostalgically "reproduce a world in which girls are girls and boys are boys, and gender works as a simple binary opposition" (Gottfreid, 1994:256). Overall, television advertisers speak in male voices to mostly female consumers.

MEN'S IMAGES IN MEDIA

Given their varied roles in the real world, women have not fared well in media. Men star in more television series, sell more records, make more movies, and are paid more than female media counterparts. But men, too, pay a price for that power and popularity. From the media's standpoint, a man is a breadwinner who cheats on his wife, has no idea how to operate a washing machine or vacuum cleaner, is manipulated by his children, and uses force to solve problems. How have the media contributed to these images?

Advertising

Advertisers divide products according to their emotional appeal; hence, some are seen as masculine and some as feminine. Cars, life insurance, and beer are masculine, so men do the selling to other men. Men also sell women's products, such as cosmetics and pantyhose. In fact, men do most of the selling on television, as evidenced by the use of male voice-overs in both daytime and prime time television. Male voice-overs have decreased slightly over time but in over three-fourths of all commercials the voice of men is heard (Bartsch et al., 2000). Advertising puts men in positions where they direct what all people buy. A man's voice is the voice of authority.

Beer commercials, shown on television usually during sports events, are almost exclusively male oriented. Men respond positively to these ads, but women do not (Slater et al., 1997). Advertisers have chosen to intensify their marketing of beer to males during these events rather than alter content to make beer ads more palatable to women. Themes surrounding beer commercials and other products directed to males are camping, cowboys, competition, and camaraderie. Beer-drinking men are the good old boys who are adventurous, play hard at sports, and have a country spirit. Of all types of advertising geared to men, beer commercials instill the importance of a traditional masculinity image (chapter 9).

For other products and for both print ads and television commercials, although women are increasingly shown in activities outside the home, advertisers do not often show men in family roles. In their nondomestic worlds of workplace and sports bar, men are portrayed as mature, wise, successful, competitive, and powerful. The major exception to this pattern is that when men *are* found in their homes, they are depicted as more foolish than women and as bumbling in the kitchen and inept with their infants and young children (Kaufman, 1999).

Film

Fueled by advertisers, films contribute to the images of men as invulnerable, decisive, and increasingly as sex objects. Films routinely portray men in two thematic ways. The first is the hero theme. Heroes are the hard living and adventurous tough guys engaged in the highly unlikely scenarios of action-adventure plots. Pure fantasy exists in movies where the hero escapes unscathed from the very jaws of death. The twist for some movies is that the hero starts out insisting he is not brave, but is really cowardly at heart. Circumstances prove otherwise as he rescues the maiden, finds the gold, or saves the world from ultimate doom and destruction. John Wayne and Gary Cooper of the past have been replaced by Tom Cruise and Mel Gibson. Often men are linked in "buddy" movies. The plot calls for them to be initially suspicious and competitive on the surface and then gradually move toward genuine—if begrudging—respect and camaraderie. Heroes move in and out of relationships with women. Romance is short-lived, not enough to keep the men from their carefree escapades. They learn to admire one another for traits they see lacking in their own personalities. *The Blues Brothers, Beverly Hills Cop, Batman and Robin*, and *Men in Black* are examples of how heroism and buddies are linked.

Second is the violence theme. Both heroes and villains are violent, and violence is needed to end violence. The kill-and-maim plots of the *Halloween* or *Friday the Thirteenth* movies, the *Star Wars* and *Lord the Rings* epics, and Jackie Chan's movies attest to the acceptability of revenge, killing, and violence in the name of just and honorable causes (Bouzereau, 2000; Crowther, 2000). Male movie characters in these films who do not agree with this formula to resolve the problem are portrayed as cowards and wimps.

The violence theme is increasing rapidly in all genres of movies and most rapidly for movies aimed at younger audiences. The escalation of violence and the graphic display of sexual violence in action-adventure movies is associated with the financial success of movies released to international audiences. In the global economy, films with the highest potential profits are those that have to be minimally edited for non-English speakers or for audiences who cannot read subtitles. The next time you watch a film, note the length of time you are engrossed in a scene that has no dialogue. Chances are it is an action-adventure scene consisting of heroic males in chase scenes, explosions, and nonstop escapades related to violence and destruction.

Television

Television reinforces other images of media masculinity. In prime-time dramas men are portrayed as active, independent, less tied to relationships, and in control. Men acknowledge that power is a double-edged sword, and it may bring adversity as well as rewards, but they are willing to accept the consequences. Shows such as *Law and Order, Nash Bridges,* and *CSI* suggest this pattern. Less favorable portrayals of men are connected to their use of violence and force to deal with ongoing relationships. Whether as heroes or villains, television equates male strength with lack of emotion (other than anger), self-reliance, and the ability to fight out of a difficult spot.

Situation Comedies: Men in Families. The key exception to the image of masculine independence is the situation comedy, where men take on a childlike dependence on their wives in terms of domestic functioning (*King of Queens, The Simpsons, Home Improvement*). It is also rare to find men in loving and nurturing relationships with their television children without a woman hovering in the background. A half century of television refuses to allow men to be shown as competent fathers who are capable of raising young children on their own. In the *Andy Griffith Show,* there was Aunt Bee; in the *Courtship of Eddie's Father,* there was Mrs. Livingston; and in *Family Affair,* there was Mr. French. From the early days of television, only *Rifleman* was shown as a parent who was raising his son alone. Past shows like *Full House* and more recent shows like *Sister, Sister* and *Two-and-a-Half-Men* had single dads in amazingly nontraditional living arrangements where there are other adults always present. Unlike series featuring women as single parents, almost ludicrous circumstances must be invented to accommodate single fathers. The media allow men to display a greater range of roles than women, but stereotypes lurk in most men's imagery as well.

TV's Gender, Race, and Class Link

Like *Mr. Rogers' Neighborhood,* until the mid-1960s, prime-time television was mainly inhabited by white middle-class professional and managerial men of generic northern European background. They were married to women of similar backgrounds who were depicted as full-time homemakers. When male people of color were seen, they usually fell into three categories: African American chauffeurs and bodyguards, Asian cooks and gardeners, and Latino desperadoes and drug lords. However, the next two decades saw a marked shift for people of color in both numbers as well as types of roles, a pattern that continues today. Not only have the number of nonwhite characters jumped to well over 10 percent, a wider range of roles—including more positive portrayals—accompanied the increases. African Americans are the biggest beneficiaries, with a fourteen-fold increase. Asians come in second in both numbers and positive portrayals. Latinos, however, remain a distant third. With the notable exception of *The George Lopez Show,* Latino men are largely supporting players and background figures and are much more likely to be portrayed as poor, deviant, or criminal compared to all other racial and ethnic groups (Lichter and Admundson, 2000).

A gradual but steady blurring of racial differences among men is occurring on prime-time television. However, as racial differences steadily decrease, a corresponding increase in class differences is occurring. Gone are the struggling working class African American families of 1970s television. The laborers, servants, and junk collectors of the Evans family (*Good Times*) and *Sanford and Son* were replaced by the 1980s with business owners, attorneys, and other professionals (*The Jeffersons,*

The Cosby Show). By the 1990s adventure and science fiction shows gave us leading roles for African American secret agents, doctors, lawyers, and police officers (*ER, The Practice, NYPD Blue*). For the white working class, a similar pattern occurred, especially for women. The struggling waitresses of *Alice* and assembly line workers of *Laverne and Shirley* have been supplanted by the professionals of *Ally McBeal, Friends,* and *Sex in the City.*

As men from all races moved up in social class, they left their working class counterparts behind. By the end of the twentieth century, television became a virtual haven for the middle class, and middle class men dominated television in number of series, number of roles and number of starring roles (*Spin City, West Wing, Third Watch*). Many of the middle class men on prime time television are college educated, lead interesting and productive lives, and have disposable income to travel and buy expensive artifacts for their tastefully decorated homes. The desire of advertisers to show a full range of products used by glamorous people is often catered to. The result is television shows built around rather affluent middle class characters (Butsch, 2000). The psychiatrist brothers of *Frasier* represent the middle class standard of prime time television for males. Racial stereotypes are still very apparent, but class stereotypes appear to be on the fast track in overtaking them. Gender stereotypes, however, remain intact.

Working Class Men. In the real world, people in the working class are those who lift, bend, drive, keyboard, clean, load, unload, provide physical care for others, cook, and serve (Ehrenreich, 1998). They are likely to be high school graduates working for a wage rather than a salary and employed in blue collar positions, retail sales, and lower level white collar clerical occupations. Although they represent over two-thirds of employed Americans (chapter 11), the working class of prime time television is mostly unseen. A study of situation comedies over the last half century found working class household heads at only 11 percent of the total. Blue collar families were the most underrepresented at 4 percent. More recent data on situation comedies featuring working class families show slightly fewer upper class than working class families. The majority of sitcom families remain middle class and above, with the working class relegated to the category of "other" (Butsch, 2000; Scharrer, 2001).

Prime time television's construction of men from this small group of working class families is a vastly different reality than that of television's middle class. Blue collar men are depicted as needing supervision, and it is up to middle class professionals to provide it. Working class characters have few starring roles and are usually depicted as friends or relatives of the main characters in situation comedies (*Becker, Everybody Loves Raymond*) or as unsavory characters lurking in the background of police precincts, courtrooms, schools, and hospital waiting rooms in prime time drama (*Judging Amy, Gideon's Crossing, Boston Public*). News media representation of the working class as "irrelevant, outmoded and a dying breed" reinforces these images (Mantsios, 2001:565).

Unlike racial portraits of men, comparable working class portraits have remained virtually the same throughout television's history. Ralph Cramden, Fred Flintstone, and Archie Bunker have been replaced by Homer Simpson and Drew Carey's semiliterate friends. The few shows that portray working class men in lead roles have prototype characters: They are white males depicted as lovable but incompetent, as clowns but losers. They are parochial, inarticulate, and have poor or questionable taste in all things. The men are basically insecure but hide it beneath a thin veil of exaggerated masculinity that is easily unwoven by their ever-suffering wives. Wives hold the family together as their husbands bumble their way through get rich schemes (Lichter et al., 1994; Douglas and Olson, 1995). What is perhaps most revealing, however is that the male household heads of television families in situation comedies over 50 years are not only portrayed more foolishly than in shows featuring middle to upper class families, but the pattern has actually increased over time (Robinson and Skill, 2001; Scharrer, 2001).

The significant holdout to this pattern was *Roseanne,* which for a decade was one of most popular shows on television and is one of the most popular rerun shows. Roseanne's family deviated from the working class norm by showing them in diverse roles dealing sensitively with a range of difficult issues all families face. Comedy was not sacrificed for such diverse portrayals.

Like media created women, men cannot be all that they are meant to be, or all that they are. Men increasingly disdain their sex object and success object media portrayals. They want to be identified as more family oriented, less as sexual exploiters of women, and as attaching less importance to money and status. Tom Hanks and Robert Redford exemplify this; Howard Stern and Donald Trump do not. Until we see men consistently portrayed as loving fathers, compassionate husbands, and household experts, our attitudes about masculinity will not be significantly altered.

GENDER AND MASS MEDIA INDUSTRIES

The lack of women in creative and decision-making positions in media industries helps explain the pervasive gender typing throughout the mass media. Except as secretarial staff, for example, women are numerically underrepresented in all phases of advertising. Because advertising is the medium with the power to quickly alter the pervasive and consistent stereotyping it now supports, an influx of women into managerial positions may provide the industry with more realistic images of women.

Television

The same can be said for television. In 1980 about 30 percent of the employees at network headquarters and network-owned stations were women, but only 10 percent were at the managerial level. Ten years later almost 20 percent of directors of commercial television in news and entertainment shows stations were women. After a decline in the mid-1990s, women now hold about one-fourth of such positions (*Broadcasting,* 1998; *Media Report to Women,* 2003). Although women participate as actors in commercials, soap operas, and prime time television, their representation in production, management, and news is limited.

The major qualifications for entry into these positions are educational background and experience. Although women have very similar educational profiles, their experience is less favorable when compared to male counterparts. Most women managers in television entered the industry within the last decade. Until they move up the hierarchy, in turn creating opportunities for those women who follow, occupational segregation of the genders in the television industry will be the norm.

Broadcast Journalism

Compared to overall television programming, women appear to be making the greatest strides in TV news, at least gaining more on-screen visibility. Joan Lunden, Barbara Walters, Diane Sawyer, and Connie Chung, for example, demonstrate the professionalism and integrity of women broadcasters. Using her popular daytime talk show as a springboard, Oprah Winfrey is moving into broadcast journalism with prime-time specials on topics such as drugs, domestic violence, and child abuse. Until recently the few women who were seen during news programs were billed as "weather girls" and held third-rate positions on the news teams. Today it is common to see female meteorologists responsible for preparing and broadcasting the weather. Metropolitan areas have male-female news teams that vie with one another for ratings. Gradually, inroads have been made by women in the news and weather departments, but it is highly probable that the sports anchor is a man.

But does increased visibility in news and information programs mean that gender barriers are eroding? The answer is both yes and no, and a look at morning television news helps explain why. Each of the three major networks produces a morning show that can be described as combining news with entertainment. Currently, each of these shows is hosted by a male and female team, with commercial ratings indicating that this kind of format is necessary for success. No longer can a man or completely male news team expect to carry the show. Yet the networks insist that audiences favor the male over the female, which justifies more money, more air time, and better stories being given to the male. Women are on the morning news shows, but except for Connie Chung's trek to cable news, there is no permanent female anchor on network evening news.

On the other hand women are increasing their numbers rapidly as foreign/war correspondents. In 1970 only 6 percent of women were foreign correspondents; today over one-third fill this slot. In addition to the high visibility of these positions, they have more control over what they report and how they report war news. They focus more on the human toll of war related to civilian populations and highlight the issues faced by women and children in war torn areas (Gibbons, 2002).

Compared to other areas of broadcast news, the high number of foreign correspondents is startling. The scarcity of women in the other news media is associated with the way feminism is portrayed in television news coverage. Although there is overwhelming support for feminist goals, the news media consistently represent feminism as an unpopular fringe movement and exclude serious feminist comment from the airwaves (Douglas, 1995; Zimmerman, 2003). These war correspondents may change the picture.

Film

The golden days of film coincided with the Depression. Ironically, this period was the golden age for women actors but the dark age for women directors. The position of director is the apex of the film industry. In the silent screen and pre–World War I eras, there were over 30 female directors, more than at any other time in film history. The rise of the studio system and its vertical monopoly model consolidated the production, distribution, and exhibition of films in individual companies and forced many independent filmmakers out of work. Dorothy Arzner was the only woman directing for a studio (1927–1943). During the next two decades Ida Lupino was the only woman directing major feature films, and she established herself even before World War II. The 1970s and 1980s saw actors Elaine May, Penny Marshall, Jodie Foster, and Barbra Streisand emerge as regularly employed directors. In 1991 Barbra Streisand directed the acclaimed multiple Oscar winner *Prince of Tides*. She was notably passed over for receiving what many thought was a certain Oscar nomination for her directorial efforts. For all films released, women comprise about one-fifth of the total number of combined directors, executive producers, writers, and cinematographers. Men continue to direct nine out of ten films in the United States. Women's share of these positions is increasing, but they still hold only a handful of these prized director slots (Lauzen, 2003b). Unlike the United States, Britain, and Australia, which reflect similar patterns of women as directors or high level positions in the film industry, Canada and the European Union have greater numbers of women film executives.

Whereas the position of director remains a male bastion, the number of women producers, editors, and screenwriters is increasing. Although less likely to be established with major studios that produce box office blockbusters, they are responding to opportunities that offer creative work in newer cinematic forms and techniques. Art, documentary, educational, experimental, and the emerging "alternative" cinema are areas in which women are demonstrating their talents. Because women film critics do hold influential positions in the industry, efforts outside mainstream filmmaking are not ignored. This has helped the field of feminist film theory to emerge. In addition, prominent women critics review films from newer perspectives, such as evaluations of how women are portrayed, the quality of the roles women are being offered, and the degree to which films reflect social reality.

These achievements are impressive, but for the most part they account for films outside the mainstream and in lesser known studios. These are not the studios generally producing the movies people will line up outside on a cold Saturday night to see. Significant monetary reward and public recognition of one's creative work are reserved for commercially successful films. Although alternative cinema may provide creative, though not lucrative, outlets for women filmmakers, a male monopoly in the established film industry makes the switch from one system to the other difficult.

Women hold a minimum of influential positions within mass media industries. As women gain positions of power and prestige, gender stereotyped images will be altered. But the media are entrenched in a broader social system that supports the notion of female subordination. Thus, when advertisers are singled out for their blatant sexist portrayals, they defend themselves by saying they are trend followers, not trend setters. They ignore or dismiss the mountains of research indicating that heavy diets of gender stereotypes in all media forms are associated with lower acceptance of gender equality, negative psychological outcomes for both females and males, and increases in risky behavior negatively impacting society as a whole (MacKay and Covell, 1997; Lavine et al., 1999; Wilson et al., 2003). For women in media industries to make a significant impact, their voices need to be heard through decision-making roles (Gallagher, 2001). Social change in the direction of gender equity must continue in other institutions as well.

MEDIA AND SOCIAL CHANGE

Media present views of women and men far removed from the reality of our everyday lives. Men are portrayed as more multidimensional and more positive than women, but still in highly stereotypical ways. Based on their tactics for over three decades, the advertising industry's willingness to reduce gender stereotyping is not very encouraging (Craig, 2003). Advertisers argue that their images reflect society, and these are images the public wants to see. They acknowledge that advertising images may reinforce an already existing sexist society, but they did not create it. From their viewpoint, altering advertising patterns simply to counter sexism risks both public acceptance and monetary returns. Moral responsibility is rarely an issue in deliberations over media images of the genders.

Media are powerful because of our thirst for entertainment and our needs to be moved from the mundane and taken into the a world of fantasy and excitement. Is it possible for media to provide the entertainment, maintain public acceptance, increase profits, and simultaneously provide alternatives to the sexist portrayals of men and women? Because people are uncomfortable with what they see and research indicates that gender role shifts are associated with financial profits, the answer to this question is affirmative. An irony of media and advertising is that they thrive on change, yet are barely beginning to shift away from rigid patterns regarding gender. When convinced that success can be packaged differently, media change will likely accelerate.

Finally there is the issue of moral responsibility. The issue is usually addressed when sexual and violent content of the media consumed by children and teens are examined. Little attention is paid to gender role portrayals. However, by addressing the sexual content of violent media, a latent function regarding gender stereotyping also occurs. Because gender roles are intertwined with this content, changing one will affect change in the other.

The media are formidable socializers and provide images that both reflect (the mirror assumption) and reinforce gender stereotypes. Whether they acknowledge it or not, media do have the power and responsibility to alter stereotypes. Evidence indicates they are slowly moving in this direction. As the public continues to demand entertainment, news, and advertising that offer positive images of their gendered lives in line with social reality, the media will respond accordingly.

Summary

1. Mass media, particularly television, is a major agent of gender socialization. Heavy television viewing is strongly linked to traditional and stereotyped views about gender.

2. Decades of research on magazines show women linked to home and family and interested in beauty and relationships with men. Highly stereotyped advertising showing beautiful women available to men reinforces these images. Symbolic interaction emphasizes sexual subliminals in ads. Age and gender stereotypes in ads play on the insecurities of women as they age. Both men and women are critical of advertising images, but only minimal changes have occurred.

3. In the early days of film women held more powerful and diverse positions. Films during World War II depicted independent, multifaceted women, but after the war women were dichotomized as good (feminine mystique) or bad (sexual and

immoral). Sexual violence in films continues to increase. Mainstream films now routinely pair sex and violence. Females are offered fewer diverse roles and, as they age, fewer roles than males.

4. The film industry claims that stereotypes of gender are what moviegoers want. But female teens and young women represent the newest market, and demeaning this group in film counters this claim.

5. Popular music is highly gender stereotyped, with rock music and its heavy metal segment the most misogynistic. There have been many successful female groups and rock bands led by females, but they have had little power in altering sexist material. Janis Joplin of the past and Madonna may be feminist role models.

6. Rock videos of heavy metal and rap display the most violent lyrics and images related to sexual violence. Men and women receive the messages differently.

7. Gendered violence on television is routine. Amount of television viewing is clearly linked to attitudes and behaviors related to aggression. Television violence is directed toward women.

8. In prime time television drama, leading male characters outnumber females two to one. Prime time women are unmarried, professional, and looking for romance. In comedies men and women are about equal in numbers. In soap operas women leads outnumber male leads. Portrayals of independent, single women without a story line revolving around her relationship with a man are absent from television. Employed women in comedies do not experience work–family conflict. Heavy women and girls obsessed with shopping are laughed at by males and popular characters.

9. The majority of television commercials portray women as homemakers and mothers in helping roles with male voice-overs telling them what to do. One in three commercials has an attractiveness message for women. Children's commercials are the most gender stereotyped: Girls are shown inside their homes in passive, quiet, and dependent roles; boys are shown outside their homes as aggressive, active, in control, and independent. Efforts at changing these portrayals are not encouraging.

10. Men in media are portrayed as competent, wise, and successful breadwinners outside the home but inept in their households. Men do most of the selling on television, to women and to other men. Beer commercials are exclusively male oriented.

11. Men in film are portrayed in two thematic ways: as heroes and in violent scenarios. In prime-time dramas men are powerful and independent; in comedies about families men are portrayed with a childlike dependence on their wives and as incompetent in raising children without other adults present. Racial differences in portrayals of men are decreasing, but class differences are increasing. Working class men have fewer lead roles and are portrayed as laughable or bumblers.

12. Women are underrepresented as mangers in all mass media industries. They are gaining in broadcast journalism, especially as foreign correspondents. Women directors have decreased in numbers; men direct nine of ten films. Women producers, editors, and screenwriters are increasing in number but in less mainstream studios. Female decision-makers in film are necessary to counter gender stereotyped portrayals of women.

13. Although advertisers are reluctant to reduce gender stereotyping, they will do so if they become convinced that success can be packaged differently. Media do have the power and responsibility to alter stereotypes and will respond to a public desiring more positive images of their gendered lives.

Critical Thinking Questions

1. Based on your knowledge of media's influence in gender socialization, why do gender stereotypes persist in advertising when both men and women are critical of the images?

2. Analyze two prime-time television series and two movies that represent stereotypical and nonstereotypical content regarding gender content. What gender features contribute to their success? How can the stereotyped content be altered in ways that still maximize the success of the portrayals?

3. Discuss how the double standard for male and female movie directors, actors, and broadcasters serves to limit opportunities for the advancement of women in mass media industries and also limits the profit of these very industries. How can this double standard be altered in a manner that benefits women and still caters to the programming tastes of the audiences served by mass media?

CHAPTER 14

POWER, POLITICS, AND THE LAW

The Law
Employment
Education and Title IX
Sexual Harassment
Domestic Relations
Reproductive Rights
Crime

We, men and women who hereby constitute ourselves as the National Organization of Women (NOW), believe that the time has come for a new movement toward true equality for all women in America, and toward a fully equal partnership of the sexes, as part of the world-wide revolution of human rights now taking place within and beyond our national borders.

—From NOW's *Statement of Purpose* (1966)

Politics
Women in Office
Barriers to the Female Candidate
The Gender Gap

The Equal Rights Amendment
Ratification's Rocky Path
Issues of Interpretation

Feminism in the Twenty-First Century

The political institution and its legal foundation provide the critical lens through which all gender relations are viewed. In the United States the "equal justice for all" principle around which the law functions is embraced, but people acknowledge that this principle may be compromised. Cultural definitions related to gender, race, social class, religion, age, and sexual orientation often determine how justice will be served. Power is a basic element of the fabric of society and is possessed in varying degrees by people occupying different social categories. Max Weber (1946) defined *power* as the likelihood a person may achieve personal ends despite resistance from others. Because this definition views power as potentially coercive, Weber also considered ways in which power can be achieved through justice. *Authority*, he contended, is power that people determine to be legitimate rather than coercive. When power becomes encoded into law, it is legitimized and translated into the formal structure of society. In Weber's terms, this is known as *rational-legal authority*. As will be demonstrated, women as a group are at a distinct disadvantage when both power and authority are considered.

We have already seen how this is economically true. In virtually all job categories women are rewarded less than men in terms of money and prestige. Interpersonal power is also compromised, even in the family, where women are assumed to have more weight in terms of decision making. To this list can be added the limited political and legal power that women wield. Social stratification is based on differential power, which in turn underlies all inequality. Thus, inequality between the genders persists because the power base women possess is more circumscribed than that of men. Restrictions in terms of political power and legal authority are at the core of inequality.

THE LAW

Key assumptions about the genders permeate the law and provide the basis for how the law is differentially applied.

1. Women are incompetent, childlike, and in need of protection.
2. Men are the protectors and financial caretakers of women.
3. Husband and wife are treated as "one" under the law. The "one" is the husband.
4. Males and females are biologically different, which gives them differing capabilities and differing standards on which to judge their actions (Richardson, 1988:104)

These assumptions are taken for granted and rarely questioned. When formally developed into law, they become sacrosanct.

Law serves to perpetuate yet also alter traditional gender roles. At all governmental levels, laws have been enacted that may offer one or the other gender certain advantages or disadvantages. There is considerable variation on how laws are interpreted and how they are enforced. Even federal legislation is inconsistently applied. What will become clear is that, regardless of the notions of equality and justice, the law cannot be viewed as gender-neutral, much less gender-equal. Although efforts to remedy this situation are ongoing, the following discussion will demonstrate the difficulty of the task ahead. Note that to date legal statutes use the word *sex* rather than *gender* in written law as well as in most discussions concerning it. For consistency, this designation will generally be retained when considering the differential impact of politics and the law on females and males.

Employment

One of the most important pieces of legislation to prohibit discrimination in employment based on sex is the 1964 Civil Rights Act. Title VII of this Act makes it unlawful for an employer to refuse to hire an applicant, to discharge an employee, or to discriminate against any individual with respect to "compensation, terms, conditions, or privileges of employment, because of such individual's race, color, religion, sex, or national origin."

BFOQ. The only way that Title VII can be legally circumvented is through the **bona fide occupational qualification (BFOQ)**, which allows for hiring an employee on the basis of one sex, thereby "discriminating" against the other, if it is deemed critical for carrying out the job. For example, a woman can be hired over a man as an actor for a specific part in a movie to establish "authenticity or genuineness" of the role. Also, if characteristics of one sex are necessary for the job, a person of that sex is hired, such as for the job of wet nurse. The courts have also rejected "customer preference" arguments to hire women over men as flight attendants or "job preference" beliefs that exclude women from positions in which they may be required to work night shifts. With few exceptions, the BFOQ rule is very narrowly interpreted by the courts and is seldom used as a defense for charges of sex discrimination.

Another accomplishment of Title VII has been the elimination of many policies used by employers that may appear to be neutral but can have a "disparate impact" on the gender. When an employer states that all employees have to be within certain height or weight limits, a large proportion of one gender or the other is usually excluded from a particular job. Women, who on the average weigh less than men, have been systematically denied employment opportunities in areas such as law enforcement, security, paramedical fields, mining, and construction by setting such limits. Men, who on the average have larger hands than women, may not be denied factory work where small components must be hand tooled. Employers must now demonstrate that the policy is a business necessity without which the job could not be safely or efficiently carried out. Height and weight designations are often used to assess strength levels, so a direct strength test would be more beneficial to the company and could be accomplished with less disparate impact on women, as well as some men.

Equal Pay Act. Because Title VII mandates the elimination of sex as a basis for hiring, the corollary should be an end to wage discrimination on the same basis. In 1963 the **Equal Pay Act** (EPA), requiring that females and males receive the same pay for the same job, became federal law. However, we have seen that even when controlling for educational level and occupational classification, women earn less on the average than men, an earnings gap that has only slightly improved over the last two decades. How can this obvious disparity in pay continue with the provision of the EPA? The answer is found in the fact that women and men typically hold different jobs, and women's jobs remain undervalued and, hence, underpaid in comparison to those held by men (chapter 10). Occupations are gender segregated and become gender stratified. The question then becomes how to assess jobs on the basis of skill level, effort, and responsibility. By this argument, equal pay should be judged in terms of equal worth.

Comparable Worth. To be interpreted through the provisions of Title VII, *comparable worth* was initiated to deal with a persistent gender gap in pay (Chapter 10). In a suit against the state of Washington, a hospital secretary charged that she was being paid much less than men employed by the state, even though her job was "worth" much more. The same case brought evidence showing that laundry workers, who are mostly female, earned $150 less per month than truck drivers, who are mostly male. In 1983, a federal court ordered the state of Washington to raise the wages of 15,500 employees in predominantly female occupations, which amounted to almost $1 billion in back pay. Two years later a higher court overturned the decision with the argument that market forces created the inequity, and the government has no responsibility to correct them.

Critique. Even if objective measurements for comparable worth can be established, some interpretations suggest that the government should not interfere with supply and demand in a free-market economy. If the pay differential between males and females is a true reflection of market forces, then there must be other reasons that bolster this wage gap. The market-driven pay system is so neutral that if women get paid less, they must either prefer less demanding jobs or are less productive in the jobs they do get (Rhoads, 1993). This justifies the wage gap and offers no room for the possibility that gender discrimination occurs. In this context, comparable worth is seen as a radical departure from traditional economic beliefs and one that would create unnecessary bias in an already fair and neutral system.

On the other hand, the notion of comparable worth issues a challenge to reevaluate all the work that women do, and it can ultimately call into question the existing gender-based hierarchy, particularly when it systematically denies comparable earnings to women. Employers typically use gender to assign people to jobs, which in turn results in wage discrimination. In the public sector, women are assigned to jobs with less pay and shorter career ladders. In the private sector, women are assigned to already overcrowded female-dominated jobs, which in turn creates an oversupply of labor. Again, wage discrimination results (Sorensen, 1994). This trend is confirmed by Canadian data on computer professionals indicating that women make less money and have lower job status than men in the same company. Organizations hiring more women professionals hire those who are less well educated and with less work experience than male employees and thus justify paying them less. Recruitment strategies are aimed at limiting a woman's access to positions of authority (Ranson and Reeves, 1996).

Comparable worth can be used to redress not only the gender wage gap, but also the damage done to overall market productivity. Although it is a departure from the traditional model, functionalism would applaud comparable worth if the system becomes more efficient and productive. Comparable worth has had significant and positive effects on women's wages but negligible effects on employment or employment growth rates. It is a reaction against "an economics discipline that is attached to textbook models of how the world ought to work" (Figart, 1995:780). As such, a powerful economic argument is used to support an institutional theory of wage discrimination. To date, the courts have been inconsistent in decisions regarding comparable worth. Title VII and EPA notwithstanding, the courts subscribe to rigid textbook standards and are reluctant to seriously confront comparable worth if it means "interfering" in economic principles that allow employers to determine salary structures.

Affirmative Action. Another bulwark of federal policy impacting employees is *affirmative action*, the generic term for an employment policy that takes some kind of voluntary or involuntary initiative (under the compulsion of the law) to increase, maintain, or alter the number or position of certain members, usually defined by race or gender (Chapter 10). Affirmative action calls for a fairer distribution of social benefits, a principle that has been constitutionally accepted and applied throughout U.S. history (Johnson, 1993:236). Devised primarily to promote the economic status of African American men, other people of color and ethnic minorities can fall under its scope. In the involuntary situation, the Civil Rights Act allows courts to order employers found guilty of discrimination to devise and implement an affirmative action plan. Public perception and media portrayals notwithstanding, affirmative action policies are *not* the opposite of policies based on merit; neither are they efforts at "reverse" or "inverse" discrimination (Cowan, 2002; Sher, 2002; Thernstrom and Thernstrom, 2002; Pincus, 2003).

The Gender-Race Link. As a program that is beneficial to women, there are mixed results. In compliance reviews, African American males and other minority males have been advanced more than African American females and significantly more than white females. On the other hand, women's overall economic progress is upgraded by affirmative action (Badgett and Lim, 2001). For example, women's employment in male dominated occupations, such as construction and the skilled trades, that are hierarchically organized according to race as well as gender is positively affected by affirmative action (Byrd, 2001; Price, 2002). Because women of color have clearly benefited directly, affirmative action's gender repercussions benefit all women indirectly.

Prompted by partisan politics and polls indicating that people believe there is too much government control in all facets of life and that quotas represent such control, affirmative action is often paraded as a wedge issue prior to elections. Although preferential treatment and affirmative action are not the same, the media have created a full-fledged deception by perpetuating this belief (Jackman, 1995:13). Research suggests that that ideology and perception take precedence over data and experiences in shaping the level of public support for affirmative action. The more the public knows about affirmative action, the more support it receives. Polls indicate that a large majority of people believes that programs should set up objectives, but not rigid quotas, to allow opportunities for women and minorities to get hired. Opposition declines significantly when the scenarios ending affirmative action programs are made clear, such as discouraging women and minority businesses from competing and discouraging programs to help them achieve equal opportunity (Jackman, 1995:12). However, it is also apparent that public opposition increases when affirmative action is associated with quotas and preferential hiring, whether to do with race or gender (Puddington, 1996).

As would be expected, support for affirmative action also varies considerably by demographic category. Although support remains generally dependent on a person's race and gender, age and educational background are becoming key factors. Whites and men are less supportive than people of color and women. Whites are more influenced in their perception by ideology, and people of color are more influenced by experiences (Kleugel and Bobo, 2001). What is interesting, however, is that support appears to be declining for younger people overall, regardless of race. Minority college students, like their white counterparts, generally oppose racial preference, especially on college campuses that have higher numbers of African American but not Asian American enrollments (Rothman et al., 2003). Gender is less of a predictor of level of support for gender-based affirmative action than is race for comparable race-based programs (Baunach, 2002). Overall, gender is a less salient factor than race in perceptions about affirmative action.

The Courts. Given the history of misperception and contentious debate on affirmative action, two decades of Supreme Court cases offer confusing and inconsistent messages about it. In general, rulings did not make a clear distinction between equal opportunity and discrimination, but tougher standards for federal affirmative action programs were enacted. The Clinton administration strongly supported affirmative action and worked on initiatives to further the program; George W. Bush's administration worked on initiatives to dismantle the program. In a high profile case, the Bush White House filed a brief with the Supreme Court against the University of Michigan, opposing their affirmative action policy which used a point system based on a number of admission factors, including test scores, grade point average, and race. The admissions policy was previously upheld by lower courts. The Supreme Court later ruled that race cannot be an overriding factor in admissions but can still be a "less prominent" factor. In the language that fueled misperceptions, the Bush administration cited the ruling as a victory for "diversity without using racial quotas." Opponents cited the narrower use of affirmative action as a retreat from progress related to equalizing opportunity for people of color and by extension, for women (NOW; Law Center, 2003; White House, 2003).

Some women who disagree with affirmative action assert that when women receive special assistance, it reinforces stereotypes about gender roles and stigmatizes those women who gain jobs through it. They are put in a double bind. They may be in a work environment where suspicion and adversity abound because of the belief they got the job over others who were better qualified or that they could not get it through conventional means. When they do succeed in the job, the preferential treatment they received at the outset will tend to devalue their performance. Self-esteem can also be endangered when everyone, including the recipient, believes that being awarded a privilege overrides being given an opportunity to achieve, as one woman recounts at being called a "twofer" after being accepted to a prestigious graduate program in science—a woman of color in a male-dominated field. Despite her outstanding credentials, her status was defined by race and gender (Cruz, 1996). But stigma is a double-edged sword. When former Assistant Attorney General Barbara Babcock was asked how she felt about gaining the position because she was a woman, she answered, "It feels better than being denied the position *because* you're a woman" (emphasis added) (cited in Rhode, 1993:263).

Although it appears that affirmative action is destined to lose political clout, businesses are keenly aware of the benefits and profitability associated with a diverse workforce and with company programs deigned to enhance understanding of diversity among employees (Ryan et al., 2002; Wood, 2003). The irony of a projected decline in affirmative action is that resegregation in higher education and employment will deteriorate the gender and ethnic diversity that businesses seek, but that these very businesses are usually on the vanguard of opposition to affirmative action. It may be that in the long run, businesses will join with supporters of affirmative action to gain back the losses of equality of opportunity.

Equal Employment Opportunity Commission. The viability of law is demonstrated by how earnestly it is enforced. Although the **Equal Employment Opportunity Commission** (EEOC) was created to ensure that Title VII mandates are carried out, enforcement is primarily aimed at protecting minorities, particularly African-American men, rather than women. EEOC often ignores the sex provision because there is fear it would dilute enforcement efforts for minorities. Fortunately, the National Organization for Women was formed in part to protect women's rights and directed its initial efforts at changing EEOC guidelines. These efforts were seriously hampered during the Reagan years, when cases of sex discrimination filed by EEOC dropped by over 70 percent (Kennelly, 1984). This figure would not have changed significantly during the Bush presidency if Anita Hill had not presented a major challenge at the Clarence Thomas confirmation hearings. EEOC's fortunes continue to be buffeted by political agendas and partisan politics. It was revived and strengthened with the Clinton presidency and an administration placing importance on civil rights legislation for minorities in general and women in particular. The subsequent George W. Bush presidency again reduced EEOC's prominence. His administration is accused of "deciding that equalizing the field of opportunity for women and people of color is no longer a priority" (Dervarics, 2003).

Education and Title IX

As mentioned in chapter 11, Title IX of the Educational Amendments Act of 1972 was enacted to prohibit sex discrimination in any school receiving federal assistance. Specifically, the key provision of Title IX states that

> No person in the United States, shall, on the basis of sex, be excluded from participation in, be denied the benefits of, or be subjected to discrimination under any educational program or activity receiving federal financial assistance.

Overall, this legislation is very comprehensive and has at least helped to alter, and in some instances eliminate, blatant discriminatory practices involving the genders in relation to admissions, promotion, and tenure of faculty, health care, dress codes, counseling, housing, sex segregated programs, financial aid, and organizational membership. In each of these areas policies are devised in regard to equitable treatment of both genders that are compatible with the local conditions of the educational institutions involved.

The Courts. The courts allowed for a number of exceptions to the law. Fraternities and sororities may still be gender segregated, as can sex education classes. Housing and living arrangements can also be restricted by gender as long as comparable facilities are available for both men and women. However, the most notable exception concerns the number of educational institutions exempt from Title IX provisions—those that do not receive federal funds as well as public institutions that have historically always been gender segregated. When considering all schools, those that fall under the Title IX mandate include previously integrated public schools and universities and most vocational, professional, and graduate schools. A number of private, religious, and military schools remain excluded. If by choice or legal mandate any single-gender school does begin to admit the other gender, equal admissions requirements must be followed. Issues involving equity for women are at the forefront of Title IX enforcement but in *Mississippi University v. Hogan*, the case related to a violation of men's rights. In this case the U.S. Supreme Court narrowed the scope of gender-based classifications by holding that an all-female state institution that excluded qualified males from its nursing program was in violation of the equal protection clause of the Fourteenth Amendment. It is often overlooked that both men and women have benefited from gender equity legislation originally formulated for women.

Athletics. Beyond the elimination of flagrant sex discrimination policies in schools, Title IX has had a huge impact on athletic programs. Until Title IX, budget allocations to female athletics had been negligible in comparison to monies provided for male athletics. Fearing that an equal redistribution of financial resources would hamper men's programs, the National Collegiate Athletic Association (NCAA) strongly opposed any federal interference that could fall under Title IX mandates. In a compromise to the storm of controversy generated by potential interference in sacrosanct men's sports, the final regulations did not insist on equal spending but instead called for reasonable opportunities for financial assistance for each sex in proportion to the numbers who participated in intercollegiate sports. Big-ticket men's sports were protected from "pesky demands for sex equity," but improvements were made to support women's athletics and opportunities for women to receive athletic scholarships (Stetson, 1997).

Before Title IX, few colleges offered female athletes adequate facilities or training, and no institution of higher education offered females athletic scholarships. Participation in athletics is not benign in its effects. It is associated with better grades, higher gradation rates, and enhanced self-esteem for women (Rishe, 2003). Budgetary allotments for female athletics in schools have steadily increased as well, which may account for the incredible increase from about one in thirty to almost half of high school girls now participating in interscholastic athletics. Before Title IX the 10 to 15 percent of female athletes on campus participated in athletics with poor facilities, funding, and rewards. Today about half of women students participate in college sports, and about 40 percent of scholarship aid goes to female athletes (NCAA, 2002; Eitzen and Sage, 2003). Impressive as these figures are, indicative of the uphill climb is the fact that in 1972 women's athletic programs at 90 percent of all colleges were administered by females, but by 2000 the figure had dramatically dropped to under 20 percent (Acosta and Carpenter, 2002). Title IX may be responsible for eliminating overt discrimination, but beliefs about the place of men and women in athletics and sport organizations prevail. Hegemonic masculinity remains a dominant factor in the control of athletic departments (Whisenant et al., 2002).

The power behind Title IX lies in the potential to cut off federal funding to schools not in compliance. A major setback occurred with the *Grove City College v. Bell* Supreme Court ruling (1984), which states that if an educational institution is proven to be in violation of Title IX, only the specific program involved would have federal funding eliminated, and not the institution as a whole. Many programs that practice some form of gender discrimination, intentional or not, are allowed to continue, although they may directly violate the intent of Title IX. This is particularly true of athletic programs that can exist independent of school budgets because they are often supported by revenue from sports events and contributions from parents of team members and alumni. In overriding a veto by President Reagan, the 1988 Civil Rights Restoration Bill was passed, which in effect nullified the *Grove City College v. Bell* decision and reestablished the earlier broad interpretation of Title IX.

Like affirmative action, however, partisan politics, inconsistent court rulings, and imprecise media accounts about quotas have hampered Title IX enforcement. Any institution receiving federal monies over $50,000 must undergo a self-evaluation on how it measures up to gender equality. If found to be discriminatory, a formal plan must be submitted to rectify the problem. Until recently, most schools ignored this provision. The situation improved during the Clinton administration, and compliance reviews increased fourfold, with Title IX complaints doubling. A return to the conservative political climate during the George W. Bush administration again hampered Title IX enforcement.

Critique. In replaying the affirmative action backlash theme, critics suggest that Title IX hurts women and is discriminatory to men, specifically minority men. In this case, gender equity is seen as robbing racial equity in sports programs, such as when men's opportunities are cut in basketball and football—those programs that have high concentrations of minority participation. Also like affirmative action, these criticisms suggest that race is granted more importance than gender in athletics. Also, although some schools are adding women's teams, such as soccer and tennis, they are eliminating men's teams, such as gymnastics and swimming. Critics of Title IX use the inflammatory "quota" label, associated with levels of public disapproval throughout the spectrum of society, whether in employment, education, or sports. They also assert that in women's sports talents, hard work, and dedication are not rewarded when talent is "shackled" to federal mandate (Gavora, 2003). This latter argument mysteriously suggests that in women are hurt and the women's movement loses ground when Title IX is viewed as responsible for female athletic accomplishments.

Title IX is a major effort in dealing with gender inequity in education. But political maneuvering and charges of reverse sexism are damaging to consensus building. And because Title IX is a formal, legal approach, it must also be assessed in light of the informal biases in education, particularly higher education. Men and women are segregated into different areas of study. High school females are discouraged from taking science and math courses, which are required for certain majors in college, such as engineering or medicine. If discouraged from pursuing athletics in high school, even limited scholarship opportunities for college athletics are unavailable. There are far fewer women than men in the higher ranks in academic institutions. As such, they have limited exposure and influence in serving as role models for aspiring students or for impacting social change. The "presence and availability of female faculty members would serve to broaden women's aspirations, to increase their opportunities for interaction with faculty, and most important, to reduce the male dominance of educational practices and processes" (Fox, 1995:234). Informal processes that continue gender discrimination are powerful. Any legal approach needs to take into account the sources of bias emanating from these informal sources.

Sexual Harassment

Sexual harassment is a form of sex discrimination that is prohibited under Title VII of the 1964 Civil Rights Act (Chapter 11). In 1980 The Equal Employment Opportunity Commission (EEOC) adopted the following definition of sexual harassment:

Unwelcome sexual advances, requests for sexual favors, and other verbal or physical conduct of a sexual nature constitute sexual harassment when:

1. submission to such conduct is made either explicitly or implicitly a term of condition of an individual's employment;
2. submission to or rejection of such conduct by an individual is used as a basis for employment decisions affecting such individuals; or
3. such conduct has the purpose or effect of unreasonably interfering with an individual's work performance or creating an intimidating, hostile, or offensive working environment.

Although sexual harassment is a pervasive problem existing throughout schools, government, and workplaces, until fairly recently it had been an area with a noteworthy lack of interest, reporting, and enforcement.

The Thomas–Hill Controversy. The event that swiftly and dramatically brought the issue to the attention of the public occurred in the 1991 Senate Judiciary hearings on the confirmation of Clarence Thomas for Supreme Court Justice. For three days the nation was riveted to the television during Professor Anita Hill's testimony that Clarence Thomas had engaged in numerous instances of sexual harassment. Hill's testimony centered on Thomas's comments to her regarding sex and sexual matters, her personal appearance, and pressure for dates when she worked as his assistant at the Department of Education and later with the Equal Employment Opportunity Commission. The intensity of this testimony transformed the hearing into a trial where, "regardless of the confirmation, the public decided who was telling the truth." As Hill stated:

> It would have been more comfortable to remain silent . . . I took no initiative to inform anyone. But when I was asked by a representative of this committee to report my experience I felt I had to tell the truth. I could not keep silent. (Cited in Norton and Alexander, 1996b:502)

Impact of Sexual Harassment. The Thomas confirmation hearings allowed a firsthand view of the extent of sexual harassment. A poll conducted immediately after the hearings found that a majority of women in federal jobs, the largest number in the military, experienced sexual harassment (*Parade Magazine*, 1991). Research conducted since confirms that sexual harassment remains pervasive. Gender differences in claims of sexual harassment vary considerably, but it is estimated that in workplaces, between 15 and 20 percent of men claim they have been sexually harassed by women but between 60 and 75 percent of women claim they have been sexually harassed by men. It is safe to conclude that about three-fourths of all women have experienced it in some form at school or work in their lifetimes, a pattern found in the United States, Britain, and Canada (Se'ver, 1999; Wilson, 2000).

Sexual harassment is linked to emotional trauma, compromised work productivity, absenteeism from work and school, a deterioration in morale, and long term depression, all of which can have a serious impact on a person's work and private life. Although its effects are serious, most employees, both men and women alike, do not report sexual harassment, fearing retaliation by employers and coworkers that can amount to career suicide (Dansky and Kilpatrick, 1997; Schneider et al., 1997; Welsh, 1999).

Despite the fear of backlash for reporting, however, the Hill–Thomas confrontation resulted in a massive increase in sexual harassment lawsuits, prompting companies to adopt more rigorous policies to protect employees. The turnabout of the courts has been dramatic. Earlier instances of even blatant abuses of power by supervisors were likely to be disregarded, with the belief that attraction by supervisor to employee was natural and unrelated to the job situation. Employer defenses of sexual harassment continue to erode. For example, a woman does not forfeit her right to be free of sexual harassment when she chooses a work setting that traditionally allowed openly antifemale behavior, vulgar and obscene language, and displays of pornographic material by employees. The courts have challenged the taken-for-granted belief that women in school or workplace roles could expect to be sexually harassed (Martin, 1995; Weitzman, 1999). In a straightforward and unanimous Supreme Court ruling, Justice Sandra Day O'Connor stated that targets of sexual harassment do not need to show they suffered psychological damage to win their suits. The court upheld the notion that sexual harassment violates workplace equality. A feminist perspective suggests that women should be able to enjoy sexual freedom, but sexual harassment is sexism—not sex (Chaucer, 1998). Sexual harassment is offensive, "not because it is sexual per se," but because it does damage to a woman's life (Williams et al., 1999).

The Social Construction of Sexual Harassment. Despite court rulings, confusion still exists about acceptable and unacceptable behavior that has sexual overtones. Men polled about sexual harassment report sympathy, but are often bewildered by sexual harassment claims made by women, suggesting that a communications gap between the genders on the subject may be as wide as the political one. Men and women talk about and construct sexual harassment differently. Women are angry and fearful when they are sexually harassed. Reinforced by *institutional sexism*, both men and women are socialized into powerful beliefs that define women largely in terms of their sexuality (Clason, 2000; MacKinnon, 2000a, 2000b). We have seen how this kind of sexism plays out at school and work, regardless of legal protection. As symbolic interaction theory asserts, sexual harassment will be dislodged through its social reconstruction from an acceptable social condition to an unacceptable social problem. Supporting the symbolic interaction view, the feminist and conflict theorists assert that institutional sexism will stall the process of reconstruction until women increase their sense of empowerment in their schools, workplaces, and families. Sexual harassment is so hard to identify and resolve because of accepted definitions of sexuality that disguise and dismiss sexual domination and exploitation of men over women.

There is a final note on the Hill–Thomas case. In 1991 the public and Congress split on whether they believed Anita Hill lied and perjured herself during the hearings. The fact that Clarence Thomas was confirmed by the narrowest margin ever for a Supreme Court Justice (52–48) clearly indicated this split (Anderson, 2001). By 1997, over 80 percent of the public believed Anita Hill told the truth. In 2001 new information emerged that allegedly confirms her testimony (Brock, 2001). The validity of this new information remains to be determined.

Domestic Relations

Perhaps more than any other area, it is in domestic law where gender inequity is most evident. Legal statutes regarding expected wife–husband marital roles are based on three models (Stetson, 1997).

1. Unity—husband is dominant, and the wife has few rights and responsibilities.
2. Separate but equal—husband is breadwinner and wife is companion and nurturer of children, but they share similar legal rights. Also known as the reciprocity model, this is the functionalist assumption of nonoverlapping, complementary responsibilities.

3. Shared partnership—husband and wife have equal rights and overlapping responsibilities.

Historical circumstances dictate whether one model dominates at any point in time. Because contemporary law is comprised of elements from each theory, with each state having its own pattern, reform in family law is an exceedingly complicated task.

Divorce. Chapter 8 documented the impact of divorce on women and the failure of the law to do much about collecting child support or alimony when it is awarded. The fact that women gain custody of children who are minimally or not supported by their fathers propels many divorced women into poverty (chapter 8).

Property division at the dissolution of the marriage also contributes to women's poverty. Although the trend is to have individual attorneys work out the details of the divorce, these details must be considered in the light of overriding state laws. In a **community property** state, all property acquired during the marriage is jointly owned by the spouses, so in the event of divorce, each partner is entitled to half of the said property. Community property at least implicitly recognizes the value of the housewife role. Residing in a community property state, however, is not a panacea. Equal division of property, which originally was intended to help women, can actually hurt them. A woman is forced to sell her home, often the couple's only "real" property, and she and her children find themselves in less than desirable rental property, often in a new location. They are dislocated from home, friends, school, and neighborhood at the very time these are most needed for psychological support.

The other states are referred to as **common law** states, with property belonging to the spouse in whose name it is held. Any property acquired during the marriage belongs to each spouse individually. Unless a house or car is also in the wife's name, the husband can lay claim to it in a divorce. Because the common law system has severely restricted and penalized women economically, most states have also passed *equitable distribution* laws. Rather than viewing property solely on the basis of whose name it is in, courts are now considering a number of factors, including length of the marriage, amount of time parties spend on child care and household tasks, earnings ability, age, health, and resources available from friends and kin. Most important, this kind of arrangement takes into account the fact that marriage is an economic partnership where both wage earning and homemaking should be considered as contributions, even though the latter is unpaid. This is at least an attempt to redress past abuses where the legal system puts women at a major disadvantage in divorce. But it must be tempered with the fact that regardless of the more recent equitable distribution laws, women still get much less than half of marital property in divorce. Many divorced women who are also single parents were not covered by such laws when their divorces were finalized, and community property is the exception rather than the rule.

Confusion reigns in divorce law. The emergence of punitive and sexually biased legislation results in confusion over such issues as sale of the family home, rights to the ex-spouse's future income, and revising child-support orders to reflect changes in income and inflation. Conflicting interpretations in family law, therefore, increase. More important, gender bias becomes entrenched as a major influence in decisions, contributing to an adversarial relationship to men's and women's positions. Although changes in family form and functioning will worsen this confusion, a positive sign is that there has been at least a shift from lethal patriarchy to partnership.

Family Economics. With regard to Social Security, the housewife role is an economic liability. Women are unpaid for this role and do not contribute to disability or retirement funds for ensuring their future. If a woman is married less than ten years before divorce from or the death of her husband, she is not eligible for his benefits. All the years she put into child rearing and domestic duties are ignored (Hartmann, 1999). Social Security policies were originally based on a division of labor and family life that do not exist today. In 1984, the Retirement Equity Act (REA) was passed to deal with some of these issues and to make pension benefits fairer to women. Under REA, an employer is required to get the spouse's approval before an employee is permitted to waive any spousal benefits offered through the employer, such as pensions or health insurance. Of key importance is that REA allows for pensions to be included as part of property settlements in divorces.

Statistics are dismal in indicating how poverty has become feminized, particularly for elderly and African American women. Inequities related to Social Security, the main source of income for many women, are responsible for this trend. The "separate but equal" theory of the marital relationship establishing that husbands and wives have reciprocal but not equal rights is still strongly evident in domestic law. A husband is required to support his wife and children, and in return a wife must provide services as companion, housewife, and mother. It is left up to the individual couple to determine how these requirements are actualized. In some families the wife controls all household expenses and decides on how one or both salaries are apportioned. In others, husbands provide their wives with allowances and "pin money" to take care of household or personal needs. She may file for divorce if there is evidence of gross financial neglect, or he may do so for unkempt children, a dirty house, or if she refuses to have intercourse. As discussed earlier, until recently spouses have been excluded from charges of rape because sexual intercourse has traditionally been viewed as "his right and her duty." This exemption had also included separated, divorced, and cohabiting couples. Today, there are more provisions for prosecution if the couple is legally divorced or separated, but because of questions concerning consent, most states allow for spousal exemptions.

Domestic Abuse and the Courts. Given the doctrine of reciprocity, it is understandable that the courts have been inconsistent in efforts to prosecute cases of wife abuse. It is ironic that perhaps the most disheartening evidence that the courts continue to be gender biased is in the area of "domestic relations," which is also the most life threatening. We have seen how history reflects the belief that wives are expected to be controlled by their husbands, with the use of physical force as an often acceptable means of control. Feminists have publicized the issue of wife abuse, and awareness of its incidence and lethality has grown. This awareness has led to police training programs in family violence and the establishment of hotlines to provide emergency help and counseling. Judges are increasingly ruling on cases of wife abuse. The problem is that whereas disapproval of wife abuse has grown, judges have not uniformly rejected the traditional viewpoint that wives are expected to be controlled by husbands. Although more judges are ensuring that the rights of abused wives are enforced, a significant number remain unwilling to implement newer legislation protecting battered women.

Justification for this unwillingness is also tied to how a judge determines which laws are the more important ones to enforce. Temporarily barring a husband from his home means the due process rights of the husband may be violated, which some judges see as more important than his wife's right to be protected from assault. The abusive husband is protected over the wishes of the victim. Many judges also accept the stereotype that it is the wife's behavior that caused the battering anyway, the classic "blaming the victim" ideology. Consider, for example, the case of an Ohio judge's comments to a woman who appeared in court to testify against her husband regarding his attacks on her. He told her to study the Bible and "try harder to be a good wife" (Crites, 1987:50). This case is almost two decades old, and the law is gradually changing to allow for more protection of battered wives. But enforcement will be hampered as long as judges maintain a stereotyped, traditional image of the husband–wife relationship.

Reproductive Rights

From the colonial era to the nineteenth century, a woman's right to an abortion could be legally challenged only if there was "quickening"—when she felt the first movements of the fetus. In 1800, not only were there no known statutes concerning abortion, but also drugs to induce abortion were widely advertised in virtually every newspaper. By 1900, every state banned abortion except to save the life of the mother.

A majority of both men and women believe that abortion should be legal and safe, but the percentage for men is higher. Adolescent males have the highest percentage of pro-choice supporters of all age groups of males. Such numbers mask the complexity of the issue. For example, whites are more supportive of abortion rights than African Americans, but there are no significant differences between the races for females of childbearing age. For all races three-fourths approve of abortion when the mother's life is endangered or when pregnancy resulted from rape. Severe fetal deformity is also a major reason for women to elect abortion (Welch et al., 1995; Greenberg, 2001; Roberts et al., 2002). As we will see, religion is the key variable that divides those who do or do not support abortion rights. Catholics, for example, are historically likely to oppose abortion rights, but a significant minority of them remains pro-choice (Dombrowski and Deltete, 2000). It is clear that Americans are deeply ambivalent about abortion. A majority believes that some restrictions should be placed on abortion but few want it outlawed.

Legal History. This changed on January 22, 1973, with two landmark decisions by the Supreme Court. In ***Roe v. Wade*** and *Doe v. Bolton*, the Supreme Court voted seven to two in support of the right to privacy of the women involved in the cases. The states in question, Texas and Georgia, had failed to establish "any compelling interest" that would restrict abortions to the first trimester of pregnancy. Abortion in this instance would be between a woman and her physician. In the second trimester, when an abortion is deemed more dangerous, the state could exert control to protect the health of the mother. Although these cases concluded that women did not have the absolute Constitutional right to abortion on demand, a broadening of the legal right to an abortion was established. The right to an abortion has been challenged ever since.

In 1983 the Supreme Court reaffirmed the 1973 decisions by ruling that second trimester abortions may be performed in places other than hospitals. A city ordinance requiring a physician to inform the woman that "the unborn child is a human life from the moment of conception" was also struck down because *Roe v. Wade* held that a "state may not adopt one theory of when life begins to justify its regulation of abortion." The ordinance was also unacceptable because it intruded on the physician–patient relationship.

Although this can be seen as a victory for reproductive rights, a setback occurred in 1977 with the enactment of the Hyde Amendment, which restricts funding for abortions for women who also receive Medicaid (unless the pregnancy is considered life threatening). Because Medicaid is the health insurance program for the very poor, which is paid out of public monies, some supporters of the Hyde Amendment argued that the government should not be in the business of funding abortions. In 1980, a federal judge in New York ruled that a denial of Medicaid funds for medically necessary abortions was unconstitutional and violated a woman's religious freedom and right to privacy. Although he ordered the state government to resume funding, two weeks later the Supreme Court overturned this ruling, thereby upholding the constitutionality of the Hyde Amendment.

The major test of *Roe v. Wade* came in 1989 with *Webster v. Reproductive Health,* in which the Supreme Court upheld a Missouri law that said life begins at conception and requires physicians to conduct viability tests on fetuses of 20 weeks or more before an abortion could be performed. But *Roe v. Wade* was not overturned. A Reagan Supreme Court appointee, the first woman on the Supreme Court, Sandra Day O'Connor, voted with the majority to retain the constitutionality of legal abortions. Three years later the Supreme Court ruled in *Planned Parenthood v. Casey* that a state cannot place substantial obstacles in the path of a woman's right to choose an abortion prior to fetal viability—the ability of the fetus to survive outside the womb. However, states can still restrict previability abortions as long as the health of the mother and fetus are promoted (Thomson, 1998).

President Clinton was elected to office on a platform that included a pro-choice plank. On the twentieth anniversary of *Roe v. Wade,* less than two weeks after his inauguration he issued an executive order rescinding the so-called gag rule that had prohibited the discussion of abortion as an alternative in clinics receiving public funds. The George W. Bush administration reinstituted the gag rule and reversed many of Clinton's reproductive health and abortion rights initiatives, especially those previously available to poor women. The tactic that taking away a poor woman's right to an abortion would carry over to abortions for other women may be gathering strength. Only eleven states require health insurers to provide coverage for contraceptives, and only fifteen states provide any public funds for abortions (Caiazza, 2002). Until the Bush administration, the political discourse of reproductive health and abortion was not openly framed in religiously oriented language. But allied with the New Christian Right (chapter 12), and despite the separation of church and state cornerstone of the U.S. Constitution, White House documents and speeches routinely blurred the distinction. Although reproductive rights will not be the issue dividing the public into two opposing camps under pro-life and pro-choice banners, it will remain on the political burner in the foreseeable future.

Pro-Life or Pro-Choice. Bolstered by the reaffirmation of divinely ordained sex and gender differences, the New Christian Right has been effective in challenging abortion rights. The association of their moral stance with religion is clear by the term *pro-life*, adopted as a label for their group. Stronger religiosity for the pro-life group is a key element separating these people from the general public. In the United States, Canada, and Europe, a higher degree of religious fundamentalism is strongly associated with lower support for reproductive rights (Wolbrecht, 2000; Kuttner, 2001).

With religion as the factor that distinguishes pro-life activists from others, it is understandable that their antiabortion work is viewed as "God's work." As one pro-life activist said after her arrest for illegally blocking entrance to a clinic that performed abortions, "I know murder is against God's commandments. . . . These children we 'rescue' are the children of God. It's God's will" (cited in Ruth, 2001:272). Antiabortion activists lobby tirelessly against funding for any national or international agencies offering abortion counseling, even if such counseling is only a small part of a broader program of family planning. Tactics to limit or eliminate abortion rights have ranged from gruesome antiabortion films and television commercials, boycotting facilities where abortions are performed, to death threats and bombing of abortion clinics (Press and Cole, 1999). After the murder of physicians in Florida and New York, antiabortion activists were quick to point out that these tactics are neither advocated nor supported, although a small number of extremists in their ranks condoned the killing and publicly stated that it was justifiable homicide (Russo and Horn, 1995; Poppema, 1999; Samuels, 1999). On the other side, and just as tireless, are "pro-choice" activists, who cite public support for abortion rights by the wide spectrum of people noted earlier. Those in this camp argue that abortion rights is actually a referendum on how much women have the right to control their own bodies (Luker, 1984; Cannold, 2000).

Although the abortion issue has been presented to the public as representing two intractable sides, there is agreement that preventing unwanted pregnancy is a desirable option to abortion. People on both sides of the issue are beginning to discuss positive alternatives to abortion, such as sex education, easier access to birth control, and better financial support for parents. Theological debates are also starting to yield common ground (Kelly, 1999; Cannold, 2000; Chesler, 2001). The so-called abortion pill—RU-486—that can terminate a pregnancy within a week of unprotected intercourse is gaining acceptance (Talbot, 1999; Mann, 2000). How these goals are to be achieved relates to the intersection of gender, religion, and politics. Because antiabortion activists argue that life begins at conception, they promote abstinence for the unmarried and only certain types of contraception for the married. The feminist view is that sex education and availability of contraception should be expanded for young people, married or not. However, at least by beginning with the idea that abortion is not in anyone's best interests, there is a glimmer of hope for consensus.

Crime

Crime is a highly gendered activity and the criminal justice system reflects this fact. Statistics from official sources and self-reports indicate that about 90 percent of all serious crimes—murder, assault, violent personal crime, and robbery—and virtually 100 percent of rapes are committed by males, a pattern in the United States and globally. The 10 percent of crime committed by females is mostly in the non-serious/nonviolent category and includes prostitution, shoplifting, forgery, petty larceny, and for juvenile offenders, truancy and alcohol consumption. The male–female arrest ratio is approximately four male offenders to one female offender (see Bureau of Justice Statistics, 2003; NCVS, 2004; UCR, 2004). Both males and females commit substance abuse related crimes but males are much more likely than females to engage in violence to support a drug habit. Because males comprise the criminal rosters, until recently there has been little attention paid to issues of female criminality.

Rising rates of female crime changed this situation. Female crime and arrest rates grew slowly in the 1970s, plateaued in the 1980s, and have grown slowly since. In explanation for the gender patterns of crime, criminologists focus on three general areas differentiated by gender: socialization, economic background, and the manner in which the criminal justice system treats offenders.

Socialization. As detailed in chapter 3, the impact of gendered socialization is profound. In explaining the gender gap in delinquency and crime, social learning and cognitive development theorists focus on early socialization patterns that allow boys to be more autonomous, impulsive, rebellious, and physically aggressive and expect girls to be more "ladylike," nice, protected, monitored, and expressive (Jacobson and Crockett, 2000; Crosnoe et al., 2002; Mason and Windle, 2002). Such traits become part of a gendered core of self-image that are reinforced by peers and other agents of socialization later in life (Laundra et al., 2002; Jensen, 2003). Socialization patterns preparing girls for lives connected to the home and boys for lives outside the home also provide boys more opportunities for criminal activity.

Economics. Augmented by later feminist research highlighting the economic disparity between men and women, landmark works challenged the socialization model (Adler, 1975; Simon, 1975, 2002). These researchers asserted that traditionally lower rates of female crime can be traced to attitudes and behaviors associated with women's lower SES. Women may be engaging in criminal activities because they need to bolster their economic security but also because social change allows them more latitude to engage in nondomestic activities. Because increases in female crime are largely due to property crime, the economic explanation is compelling. In the long run, therefore, the lifestyles and hence the criminality of men and women will be comparable. In addition, the rising subset of "new" female criminals—younger, more violent and with higher rates of recidivism (the return to incarceration)—reflects these changes.

Criminal Justice. The third explanation focuses on crime in relation to patterns favoring the arrest of males over females. The *chivalry hypothesis* suggests that police are reluctant to arrest women and judges are reluctant to incarcerate women precisely because they are female. By virtue of gender, they are treated less harshly and are less severely punished than males in the criminal justice system. This differential treatment serves to mask levels of female criminality. Empirical support for the chivalry hypothesis and its gender disparate effects in arrest, incarceration, and punishment is weak (Kempf-Leonard and Sample, 2000; Atwell, 2002; Harper et al., 2002). Some research suggests that females are treated more—not less—harshly than males for delinquency and crimes related to deviations from gendered behavior. The most common reason that brings a girl to the attention of the courts is referred to as "precocious sexuality," which is seen as more dangerous and immoral for girls compared to boys. Recent increases in arrest and incarceration rates for the subset of females engaged in violent crime and gangs are linked to changes in criminal law that impose stiffer penalties and less latitude ("three strikes you're out") for *all* perpetrators, regardless of gender (Shelden et al., 2001; Atwell, 2002; Chesney-Lind, 2004). In addition, beliefs about equality under the law are slowly making their way into the criminal justice system for both perpetrator and victim.

Prostitution: A Case Study. As a case study, prostitution provides insights on all three explanations. Prostitution, a subset of sex work, is fundamentally a female occupation. Historically, poverty-stricken women turned to prostitution as a means of survival, a pattern that continues today. Some women work occasionally as prostitutes as an aside to their roles as hostesses and adult entertainers. Others derive their total income from prostitution. At the global level children are much more likely to be prostitutes than in the United States. Of the estimated 2 to 3 million children with an average age of 13 to 14 working as prostitutes, between 200,000 and 300,000 are in the United States (Barnitz, 2001; Youth Advocate Program International, 2001). Young girls are recruited, sold, or forced into prostitution by poverty-stricken parents. In parts of the developing world, girls are often abducted from their villages by owners of brothels dotting the sprawling urban slums. A common pattern is that these girls are sold into sexual slavery by impoverished parents (UNICEF, 2003). Although arrest rates of men who engage the services of prostitutes is increasing, sex workers are more likely to be arrested than their clients.

Feminists condemn prostitution when women and girls are exploited as sexual objects for the sexual pleasure of men. Reflected in the explanations noted earlier, there is growing disagreement about the reasons women become sex workers. Do they offer their services because of financial desperation or as a freely chosen occupation? One faction argues that prostitution exists due to male demand, a need to subordinate women to male sexuality. She is vulnerable to rape, sexual violence, and exposure to HIV infection, especially in war-torn areas with a history of human and civil rights abuses (Beyrer, 2001). If a woman chooses prostitution because of economic needs, then it is not a free choice. Therefore, sex traffickers and buyers should be criminalized and prostitution eliminated (Barry, 1979, MacKinnon, 1989). The other faction argues that sex workers are free agents who choose the best job they can of the gendered work available. The sexism in prostitution is no different than sexism in the rest of society. Although the feminization of poverty may be a factor in a woman's choice to become a prostitute, women should not be further impoverished by denying them income from prostitution. Like other service industries, prostitution and its traffickers and buyers can be regulated, but laws against prostitution oppress sex workers the most. Prostitution, therefore, should be decriminalized (Doezema, 1998; Simmons, 1999).

Explanations for criminal activity such as prostitution remain unresolved. We do know, however, that changes in criminal law and the justice system it is supposed to represent have not kept pace with the gender role changes in larger society.

POLITICS

The ability to change the law to reflect equality and justice regarding gender is linked to the presence of women in legislative bodies at all governmental levels. Once the law is changed, interpretation and enforcement must be consistent with gender equality. This also assumes that the women who serve in their political roles view issues related to gender differently than men. Thus, voting behavior should mirror such differences. As we shall see, this assumption has been confirmed. However, women represent only a small minority of the political elites who wield power in the United States. In global rankings between 2000 and 2003, the United States hovers between 52 and 53 out of 179 countries for its percentage of women in national legislatures (WHP, 2003). Women are increasingly being elected to public office, but not in the numbers necessary for achieving parity with men.

Women in Office

It is important for long-term impact that elected women increase their numbers at all levels of government—municipal, state, and federal. In the 100 largest cities in the United States, 14 have women mayors, including four African Americans and one Latina (CAWP, 2003a:2). Since 1971 there has been a fourfold increase in the number of women elected to state legislatures. In the decade between 1974 and 1984, women elected to the fifty state legislatures increased by 100 percent, with six states (California, Florida, Hawaii, Kansas, Maryland, and Rhode Island) averaging 300 percent increases (Riger, 1993). In 2003 Washington had the highest composite index for women in state elected office, followed by Kansas and Colorado; Mississippi had the lowest composite ranking, followed by Kentucky and Louisiana; 20.5 percent of state legislators were women. In 1994 in the state executive branch—which includes governors, lieutenant governors, and attorneys general—women held 21.9 percent of statewide elected offices in the executive branch; by 2003 the percent increased to 25.3 percent (CAWP, 2003b). The early gains were so impressive that two decades ago some political scientists suggested that a 50 percent male–female ratio in state elected officials would occur by the year 2000 (Poole and Zeigler, 1985). As mentioned in the last edition of this text and confirmed by these statistics, that forecast was overly optimistic. It may be several decades before gender parity is reached because the percentage of women in these offices needs to double.

At the Congressional level, except for a decline in the years 1961 through 1969, women have been gradually increasing their numbers. Women held 3 percent of U.S. Congressional seats in 1979 and 13.6 percent in 2003 (14 in the Senate and 59 in the House of Representatives). The 1992 election was heralded as the Year of the Woman, with sharp increases in women being elected officials throughout the United States and again leading to optimistic predictions about women's gains in elected national political slots. Note, too, that women who filled congressional seats in the past were likely to have completed the unexpired terms of their late husbands. Recently elected senators and representatives are definitely a new breed of congressional women who have carved out stellar professional and political careers in their own right. Because of such traditions as the seniority system in Congress, however, it will be some time before this small group gains prominence on important committees and exerts the influence necessary to see goals realized. In examining measures of congressional success by gender as related to when the member first entered Congress, total years served, and reason for leaving, women are less successful than men (Whicker et al., 1993:146). As this study points out, even when women began to be represented in Congress in significant ways, their role in shaping law and public policy was still extremely limited. The current cohorts of women in Congress may significantly alter this pattern.

Women have been appointed to high administrative positions, but the growth pattern is inconsistent, indicating both gains and losses. Reagan was criticized for being the first president in a decade who failed to appoint more women to high level federal posts than his immediate predecessor. However, Reagan can be credited with being the first president to appoint a woman, Sandra Day O'Connor, as a justice to the Supreme Court. Her appointment came long after the public was willing to accept a female in this position. George Bush did appoint more women to Senate-confirmed positions in his first two and a half years in office (20 percent of all appointees) than Reagan did during his eight years as president (12 percent). Even though this percentage decreased as other appointments were made during the Bush administration, it still represents an overall gain for women in higher level public offices. However, these figures must be viewed in light of the fact that many women who did receive political appointments during this period were from the New Right, and usually held positions with inflated titles and no authority (Schroeder, 1993:34).

When considering the previous 12 years, Clinton made auspicious moves in countering the tokenism that was the hallmark of presidential top-level appointees for women. He appointed four women to cabinet-level positions, including Attorney General Janet Reno and Secretary of State Madeline Albright, two of the most powerful posts in the nation. Perhaps more significant is that he soon appointed Ruth Bader Ginsberg, a long time advocate for women's rights, to the Supreme Court. As part of an unprecedented rate of gender and race diversification of the federal judiciary, by 1994 59 percent of judgeships (74 of 126) went to women (38) or minority men (36). Jimmy Carter was the first president to stress diversity on the federal branch, with 34 percent of judicial appointees being women and minority males. Reflecting the belief that the federal judiciary should mirror the life experiences of a wide spectrum of society, Clinton surpassed Carter in such appointments.

During the first year of the George W. Bush administration, of all potential appointees requiring Senate confirmation, 25 percent were women, down sharply from 37 percent in the first year Clinton administration (Tessier, 2002). Bush's most prominent woman appointee was Condoleezza Rice as national security advisor and one his closest aides. Conservative organizations charged Clinton with using a quota system to appoint women. The subsequent Bush administration may have escaped this label in most media accounts of his female appointees, but press releases throughout his years in office indicate Republican satisfaction with the percentage of women appointed to posts. As already noted, the "q-word" is politically inflammatory.

Barriers to the Female Candidate

Public support to elect qualified women to public office at all levels has sky-rocketed. Female elected and appointed officials have proven themselves competent, decisive, and fair in how they conduct their political roles and in the issues they confront in carrying out these roles. The top level elections of women and their appointments by both Republican administrations ensured that women would no longer be relegated to behind-the-scenes positions. Yet women still find themselves hindered from entering the political arena in large numbers.

Many women in public service may still be defined as pioneers in terms of their achievement and leadership in areas traditionally assigned to men. They continue to face different obstacles than those encountered by men in politics. Women must do politics differently, according to former Democratic Governor of Vermont Madeleine Kunin, and endure the experience of intimidation, being demeaned, and being ignored. Using symbolic interactionist language, she suggests that women officeholders must "invent" themselves continuously. Because political structures are not their creations, women must adjust to a male-defined space (Kunin, 1994). This would imply that the space can also be redefined to accommodate a political partnership between the genders.

Socialization Factors. Socialization into gender roles may impede political participation for women. If politics demands a self-serving style and a high degree of competitiveness to be effective, men have the advantage. Women in public office appear to be more public spirited and oriented to principles rather than narrower issues. Although politicians are expected to have higher moral standards than those who elected them to public office, women are expected to be higher than men in this regard. Republicans judge Republican women candidates as more trustworthy than Republican male candidates, but they are also judged as weaker leaders. Democrats hold the opposite view (King, 1999). Although both men and women must run a gauntlet to counter the rumors and smear campaigns now routinely associated with political life, women have a more difficult time overcoming the hurdles. Gender stereotypes may put women at an advantage or disadvantage for public office. Female politicians are often viewed as interlopers in a political realm dominated by men who hold the accepted occupational roles women can aspire to but not attain. Others believe that women will be elected to public office because of anti-incumbent mentality and disillusionment with male politicians, who are seen are morally corrupt and cynical (Schroeder, 1993; Smith and Fox, 2001). Although in the long run it works more to women's political disadvantage, the stereotype of the trustworthy woman who is a political outsider may actually be used to gain political office. It is ironic that to be successful in masculine politics, strategies are called for that are less likely to serve broader public interest.

Beliefs about Women's Roles. Beyond the impact of socialization, a major barrier to women in politics is the constraint imposed by being a mother and a wife. Women must contend with the potential disapproval if the public believes children and husbands are being neglected in the quest for public office. As Senator Dianne Feinstein of California notes, every career woman with a family keeps house, does the wash and cleans the bathrooms; men generally do not—it comes with the gender (Burros, 1993). This is consistent with the weighty research (see chapter 7) that gender equity in the workplace does not translate into gender equity in domestic task sharing. Male candidates begin their ascent in politics sooner in their careers than women. Even high profile activist women often wait until their children are grown to reduce the risk of being labeled neglectful mothers. By earnestly embarking on political careers later in life, women as a group have a difficult time catching up to men and seeking the higher public offices. A woman must also be mindful of the relationship with her husband, who may be unwilling or unprepared to deal with his wife's candidacy. Husbands may play vital, supportive roles in promoting their wives' campaigns, but cultural proscriptions are likely to prevent men from enthusiastically carrying out such activities (Romer, 1990; Whicker and Areson, 1993).

Irrespective of political party, women must face questions about their appearance, marital status, and traditional responsibilities that are rarely asked of men. (Reporters reinforce the notion that women are exceptions: How does she have time for kids and Congress?) The discourse of the media frames women as different beings than men in politics. Press secretaries attempt to counter such discourse by directing the public to websites and materials portraying the women they represent in nonstereotypical manner, highlighting their political clout and diversity of interests (Niven and Zilber, 2001). With ease of access on a 24-hour basis, however, media hold enormous power in fueling the gendered stereotypes of political women. The persistent place of "woman" in headlines indicates that gender is a category of evaluation for women but not for men (Ross, 2002). An example is from a headline reading, "It was a big night for Bay Area women," when Barbara Boxer and Diane Feinstein won Senate seats. Was it not also a big night for Bay Area men who favored these candidates (Jamieson, 1995:167)? As one consultant on women's political issues notes, "If a woman is single, she is either a lesbian or whore; if she's married, she's ignoring her husband and children." Women candidates have been accused of practicing Satanism, being "femi-Nazis," and having abortions, illegitimate children, and affairs with men and women (cited in Schneider, 1992). When newly elected Bill Clinton was attempting to gain support for his first two female candidates for Attorney General, the defining qualification for these women became the manner in which child care and household help was arranged and paid for. Male nominees are not subjected to such questions.

Perhaps these tactics—as appalling as they are—attest to the growing strength of female candidates that opponents must resort to such tactics. Celia Morris suggests that nobody is yet quite sure about what kinds of women can be elected to public office. "Must they be sexless? Must they be ladies? Must they be proper, blameless, and old" (Morris, 1992:101)? The following questions can also be added: Must they be attractive or unattractive? Must they be single or married? Must they have young children? Must they have supportive husbands? In other words, must they be traditional women pursuing a nontraditional path? The questions are contradictory but to date the answers are still yes.

Nations that are highly traditional and socially conservative in attitudes and behavior regarding women have elected women to the highest public office. Women have served as prime ministers and presidents in countries as diverse as Ireland, Norway, Britain, the Philippines, Turkey, Pakistan, Israel, Sri Lanka, and Argentina. Yet American women have been unable to overcome obstacles that prevent them from becoming serious contenders for the presidency. The electorate must be convinced that domestic roles will not hamper women for political office-holding at this highest office. This is a key factor in maintaining the image of the "U.S. presidency as a bastion of maleness" (Whicker and Areson, 1993:165).

Whether differential socialization patterns restrict the supply of female candidates remains debatable. The generation of women that is now seeking office have pioneers behind them who helped pave the way. Marginality can be psychologically debilitating, but activist women have honed their psychological skills in confronting their own professional careers so the jump into the political arena may be less stressful. Socialization into the female gender role may initially be an inhibiting factor for women entering politics, but one that can be adequately dealt with to achieve political success.

Hillary Rodham Clinton was the first First Lady to break the mold of expected roles of women in this position, and continued to do so as senator from New York. Although presidential wives exert a great deal of behind-the-scenes influence, she assumed an unprecedented leadership role in the Bill Clinton administration. She spoke frequently to young women, challenging them to shun gender role stereotypes, aspire to political heights, and become activists (Ciabattari, 1999). She advocated for poor women globally and sought legislation to benefit women in their career and family roles. Her confidence and ability won her high praise but also severe, relentless criticism about the "proper place" of the First Lady. During the media feeding frenzy concerning her husband's affair with Monica Lewinsky, she was accused of keeping too silent (showing her support for him) and speaking too much (showing her lack of support for him). As honorary head of the U.S. delegation to the United Nations Conference on Women, she received high marks for criticizing China's record on human rights on its own turf in Beijing. Her Senate election indicates public reaction much more positive than what would have been predicted by gender role research. While on the one hand, on advice from aides, she accommodated gender role norms by "softening" her image, at the same time she challenged gender stereotypes, in turn forging new definitions of what is acceptable for women in the political sphere. As of this writing, a new gauntlet is before her. She is being criticized for using her position as senator to poise herself for a presidential campaign. Critics ignore the fact that this poising for higher office is the common, acceptable, and expected pattern to forge ahead in public office—apparently for men but not for women.

Structural Barriers. Other limits women may face in politics are barriers imposed by age, social class, education, and occupation. Age is a factor because, as mentioned earlier, women's political careers start later than men's. Compared to men, women are also less likely to have the economic resources needed to run for public office (Clift and Brazaitis, 2003). The lack of resources is linked to important education and backgrounds that realistic and eligible candidates for public office, both women and men, are expected to represent. Celebrities in the fields of sports (Senator Bill Bradley, Governor Jesse Ventura) and entertainment (President Ronald Reagan, Governor Arnold Schwarzenegger, Representative Sonny Bono) have risen to high political offices. Such occupations offer visibility, flexibility, opportunities for developing communication skills, and substantial financial rewards, thus serving as significant training grounds for future politicians. We have already witnessed the financial and social effects of occupational segregation on women. Politically, such segregation hampers women from being recruited as candidates. On the positive side, women have made significant progress in the legal profession, a key source of political eligibility. It is likely that the next decade will witness a rise in women seeking public office who are drawn from these ranks.

The Gender Gap

When women gained the right to vote in 1920 it was widely believed that women's opinions regarding social and political issues differed considerably from those held by men and that such differences would be evident in voting behavior. For over half a century this belief remained unfounded; women, like men, tended to vote along class, ethnic, and regional lines. By the early 1980s, however, a new political trend emerged, first showing up in the shift in party identification of women. By May 1982, 55 percent of women and 49 percent of men identified themselves as Democrats. Only 34 percent of women identified themselves as Republican compared to 37 percent of men (Lynn, 1984:404). Women have shifted to the Democratic side at a faster rate than men. The political "gender gap" was born.

The gender gap phenomenon was so named after the 1980 presidential election, which demonstrated a higher percentage of males voting for Ronald Reagan than females. In this election, Reagan won with eight percentage points less support from women than from men. Within two years of his election, the gap widened. Women were increasingly more opposed to Reagan's policies regarding the economy, foreign relations, environmental protection, and gender equity. In 1988, Bush received 50 percent of women's votes compared to 57 percent of those cast by men, with 8 percent more women than men supporting Dukakis. During the Dukakis–Bush campaign the gender gap narrowed considerably from the beginning to the end of the campaign, and Dukakis was overwhelmingly defeated. In order to diffuse the gender gap it was necessary for the Republican Party to seriously address issues such as parental leave, child care, education, and women's employment. The military bravado that highlighted the Reagan years was substituted for rhetoric that focused on a domestic agenda in a "kinder, gentler" nation. In the 1992 election, the gender gap was formidable, with exit polls showing 47 percent of women voting for Clinton and 36 percent for Bush. For men, the comparable figures were 41 percent and 37 percent. Women cast more votes than men, a statistic that both parties carefully consider in election strategies. Both Democrats and Republicans acknowledge that the gender split encompasses virtually all politics, but Republicans, much more divided on gender-based issues, have been slower to respond to the split. Lack of response, for example, is associated with less fund-raising support for Republican candidates, male or female, challenging Democratic incumbent women and more fund-raising support from women's PACs to nonincumbent female Democratic candidates (Francia, 2001; Stevens, 2003). The perception that the Republican Party is "antiwoman" needs to be addressed to effectively deal with this issue (Mann, 1996; Edsall, 1999; Bruni, 2001). Married, middle-aged white men are a critical force for the Republicans and single women, both white and women of color, are a key constituency of the Democrats. The gender gap phenomenon of the 1980s has emerged as the feminization of politics at the millennium. How each party addresses this feminization is essential to their political success.

If women and men are viewed in terms of those issues, which have a differential impact on women the gap may be wider. Until the 1970s, except for women's higher opposition to capital punishment and military involvement, it would have been difficult to separate the way men and women viewed social and political issues. If there was a gender gap before 1980, it could be summed up with the phrase that men were more likely to be hawks and women more likely to be doves. Whereas this statement largely holds true today, the gender gap has broadened. Research on political attitudes suggests that a significant gap exists in a number of areas, including women's rights (Equal Rights Amendment and reproductive freedom), human compassion (assistance to the poor, support for minority rights, child care, and national health insurance), morally defined choices (substance abuse and alternative lifestyles), and political corruption (opposition to influence peddling). Although women of both parties are more likely to take a liberal position on most of these, they are more conservative on moral issues and antiestablishment on the political corruption issue (Fox, 2000; Stetson, 2000; *Business Week*, 2002).

Whether this indicates that women will vote as a block on any one issue is still debatable. Some research suggests that age, SES, and education may be as important as gender on some issues (Lynn, 1984; Mandel and Dodson, 1992). Although political analysts believe that concerns such as reproductive rights and the Equal Rights Amendment may be more salient for women, younger men and women are equally supportive of them. Women are much more likely to support social programs that can have a direct impact on them, such as funding for day care, and are sympathetic to programs involved with helping the poor and disadvantaged. This support may be related to the economically disadvantageous position in which women find themselves.

Political Party. In addition, men and women are closing ranks on a number of issues that favor feminist attitudes. Although the gender gap is smallest at the municipal level and largest at the state level, women and men in public office and at all levels differ in attitudes both within their own political parties and across ideologies. This is a key point when considering the political party of women who are elected to public office. At the congressional level about two-thirds of women are Democrats; at the state level executive branch, just over half of the women are Democrats; at the state legislative level, Republican women outnumber Democratic women by just about 8 percent (CAWP, 2003b).

At the national level, in the George W. Bush administration, Republican women appointees are highly conservative and match the levels of their male colleagues. But Republican women who hold elected state or national offices express more liberal attitudes—including those related to a feminist agenda on a range of issues than comparable Republican men (Mandel, 1995). With the notable exception of attitudes toward abortion rights, regardless of party, women tend to be more liberal than men. This may suggest that issues that have previously been considered either too feminist oriented or relevant only to women are more mainstream in scope, interest, and priority. It may also be speculated that politically conservative women who are officeholders become more sympathetic to feminist issues as they, too, confront the male stronghold of politics. They may recognize that by virtue of their gender alone, they find themselves hindered in political effectiveness.

If more coalition building occurs, the gender gap may begin to close. Both political parties understand that women have the potential for voting as a bloc if the right mix of issues and circumstances are present. Women are not a homogeneous group, but mobilization around issues of gender may occur. Whether that gap continues to increase will depend on how party leaders respond to the political power women as voters and as elected officials are beginning to wield. Women's presence at the state level is growing and is strongly associated with women-friendly policies (WHP, 2003). In turn, better policies for women should garner more votes for women candidates and the gender related issues they represent. Women have an advantage in these policies. Political strategists cannot afford to ignore existing gender differences and will attempt to leverage them to the benefit of their respective political parties.

THE EQUAL RIGHTS AMENDMENT

Although the Equal Rights Amendment (ERA) to the U.S. Constitution was first introduced in Congress in 1923 and proposed yearly after that, Congress did not pass it until almost half a century later. The House of Representatives passed it with a vote of 354 to 23; the Senate approved it with a vote of 84 to 8. After passage by the Senate on March 22, 1972, the Ninety-Second Congress submitted it to the state legislatures for the three-fourths vote needed for ratification. The original deadline for ratification was in 1979, but ERA proponents managed to muster the support to get this extended until 1982. Despite ratification by 38 states, three additional votes were needed by 1982 when the deadline ran out. Since then, the ERA has been reintroduced yearly into Congress, and Congress has not passed it again. Whereas in this regard history seems to be repeating itself, ERA proponents remain optimistic. The battle for ratification has enhanced their political sophistication and provided a basis of understanding for dealing with the forces that challenge them.

The complexity of issues surrounding the ERA is shrouded by its deceptively simple language. The complete text of the **Equal Rights Amendment** is as follows:

Section 1. Equality of rights under the law shall not be denied or abridged by the United States or by any State on account of sex.

Section 2. The Congress shall have the power to enforce, by appropriate legislation, the provisions of this article.

Section 3. This Amendment shall take effect two years after the date of ratification.

When again passed by Congress, the state legislatures will have another seven years to ratify it. Once ratified, it will become the Twenty-Seventh Amendment to the Constitution.

Support for the ERA is wide, and its passage is favored by a majority of both genders. It has been part of the platform of both political parties and supported by presidents as diverse as Eisenhower, Kennedy, Johnson, and Nixon. Almost 500 major organizations (with well over 50 million members) representing men and women with different interests and philosophies support it. This broad base of support is seen with organizations that include the National Education Association, the International Union of Electrical Radio and Machine Workers, the American Public Health Association, and the United Presbyterian Church. Yet even with this kind of public affirmation, the ERA has yet to be ratified.

Ratification's Rocky Path

During the ten year ratification process, a number of factors combined to defeat the ERA. It is not simply a matter of saying who is in favor of equality and who is not. Few would argue against the principle of equality, but many are suspicious of how equality is to be implemented. The death of the ERA was related to two other key changes occurring in American political attitudes. One had to do with the increased legislative skepticism concerning the U.S. Supreme Court's authority to review legislation (Mansbridge, 1986:4). States feared that the Supreme Court would be harsh in reviewing efforts at implementation and balked at what they assumed would be undue interference in state proceedings.

The New Christian Right. The second change had to do with increased power and organization of the political New Right and its allies in the Christian Coalition. Women's role and status are at the nucleus of the NCR political platform. Adherents of the New Christian Right seek to reverse the tide of gender equity, which they believe has eroded the divinely inspired moral order, and to return the United States to its patriarchal roots (Bendroth, 1999). Similar to fundamentalists worldwide, NCR focuses on the traditional role of women because women's emancipation is seen as a hallmark of modernity and secularization (Armstrong, 2001).

Where the "old" radical right targeted issues of national defense and communism, the ERA became a focus for new attacks. For the first time personal issues related to family, children, sexuality, religion, and women's roles coalesced with a political agenda that resonated with many conservative Americans. Aligned with fundamentalist churches, conservative politicians highlighted the religious and political rhetoric making traditional homemakers sympathetic to the anti-ERA cause. Anxious to retrieve what homemakers believed was a lost status, NCR mounted a massive effort against ratification. With opponents like Phyllis Schlafly fueling "nonissues" like unisex bathrooms and an end to alimony, enough fear and innuendo were generated that minimized viable debate on substantive issues such as the alarming rise in women's poverty. Scare tactics were not only used against ERA ratification but also served to heighten and reinforce conventional suspicion between the genders.

Issues of Interpretation

During the ratification process, much confusion was generated over what ERA would actually change, augment, or accomplish. Whereas anti-ERA groups capitalized on this lack of understanding to help sow the seeds for its defeat, interpretations among its supporters were often inconsistent. Interpretations for what a Constitutional ERA could mean come from some of the 17 states that already have equal rights amendments in their constitutions. For example, although both parents are required in Texas to provide child support, the services of a housewife are counted in kind. In this way Texas recognizes the value of a mother's services not just in terms of financial contributions. Pennsylvania has a similar specification under its own equal rights amendment, which has been interpreted to mean that a divorced mother is not required to work outside the home because her value as a homemaker is recognized. When Medicaid money for abortion was curtailed,

Massachusetts and Connecticut ordered funding on privacy and other grounds. And state equal rights amendments do not protect males for committing sex crimes. These examples give some indication of how equal rights have been carried out in the various states and can serve as a basis for considering the impact of a federal ERA. Organizations such as Common Cause, the National Organization for Women, and the American Civil Liberties Union provide some probable answers to the unsettling questions regarding ERA. These include the following:

1. Women will not be deprived of alimony, child custody, or child support. Men will be eligible for alimony under the same conditions as women, as they are already in most states.
2. Individual circumstances and need will determine domestic relations and community property. ERA does not require both spouses to contribute equal financial support to the marriage. But the law will recognize the homemaker's contribution to the support of the family. Social custom and interpersonal relations in a marriage remain a matter of individual choice.
3. ERA will fit into existing constitutional structures regarding privacy. The sexes will continue to be segregated with regard to public restrooms, sleeping quarters at coeducational colleges, prison dormitories, and military barracks.
4. It will be illegal to enact "protective" labor regulations, such as limiting work hours for one sex or the other.
5. ERA will allow meaningful choices to men and women in terms of family and careers. Those who choose to be homemakers will not be economically deprived for this choice.
6. ERA will nullify state laws that have greater penalties for one sex or the other when committing the same crime.
7. ERA will require that all the benefits of publicly supported education be available to women and men on an equal basis.

A critical issue related to the defeat of ERA had to do with military service and the draft at a time when the United States was barely recovering from the psychological wounds of the Vietnam War. Would ERA require women to register for Selective Service at age 18 as men already must do? Congress already has the power to draft women and historically has been prepared to do so, such as the nurse draft during World War II that was halted when the tide turned in the war. There is now no draft, and military service is voluntary for both men and women. But until Selective Service registration for men is eliminated, then ERA would likely require the same registration for women. Exempting women from the draft also exempts them from equal rights in the Constitution (Kerber, 1998). This issue will be a key point in the new ratification campaign.

For women who do choose military roles there is no evidence that they are incapable of performing in combat. Women served both Gulf Wars in all military occupational specialties except those relating to direct combat. When drawn into combat areas women respond appropriately and often with distinction. Given recent experiences, Congress repealed the law barring women from flying combat aircraft, though it is up to the individual armed services to determine how this option is carried out. ERA would eliminate the barriers to women's full participation in the armed services. Women will no longer be discriminated against in terms of assignment or promotion and would be entitled the same benefits as men, such as in education and health care, when they leave active duty. Like in Israel, the only country in the world to conscript women, this is unlikely to translate to a gender neutral armed forces. Gender differences between men and women in the armed forces can be muted, compensated for, and even exploited to enhance military performance, but they cannot be ignored.

Spearheaded by the National Organization for Women and ERA Campaign Network, a well-founded and growing ERA campaign has been launched. Representing a spectrum of NGO networks, such as the National Council of Women's Organizations made up of 160 member organizations, this campaign is capitalizing on political lessons learned in the first campaign. The campaign is highlighting the wage gap, the issues employed mothers face, and with NOW's slogan "every mother is a working mother," an affirmation of the valuable work all women perform, whether as homemakers or employed outside the home. The new campaigners are acutely aware that their political learning curve may be matched by that of the opposition. ERA supporters, however, represent a much wider spectrum of women and men that is unmatched by opponents. Lessons have to do with the advantages of diversity that can be used to gather support and unify the campaign rather than to divide it.

FEMINISM IN THE TWENTY-FIRST CENTURY

NCR hailed the defeat of the ERA as a defeat for feminism, a morality lesson to women admonishing them about their proper place, and a harbinger of returning women to a pedestal free of the trials and tribulations of the world of men. The inability to garner enough support in the last three states pointed out not only NCR's power but also internal problems hampering the feminist movement. The movement of the 1960s and 1970s focused on the root causes of gender inequality, yet in doing so, issues surrounding motherhood and family were given less priority. Many women of color felt overlooked in the movement's quest for economic parity with men and the inclusion of women in higher level positions. The movement itself was spawned by women who wanted to escape the shackles of the feminine mystique and gain a new sense of independence. To a great extent, this has been accomplished. The challenge ahead is to integrate this newfound independence with continuing concerns related to marriage, motherhood, and parenting.

The tactics that worked 20 years ago may be less effective today. Recognizing that the early movement was most vulnerable on the family issue, and as indicative of the new ERA campaign strategies, the feminists have seriously addressed family issues. As we have seen throughout this text, the key concerns related to employment and family that shape women's experiences and imperatives are at the forefront of the feminist agenda in the twenty-first century. The agenda is also one of inclusiveness and embraces the politics of accommodation, which are starkly different from the old politics of separatism.

The movement is reconciled to the fact that women do not have to be in full agreement with one another to work for feminist goals. The decentralized structure can provide the very catalyst for feminists to work on the array of issues confronting women today. Local feminist groups can target specific concerns that they deem most critical, such as delivering the message to area corporations that maternity leave or adequate day care are necessities. They may lobby for safe homes for abused women or work with other organizations to deal with the problem of violence within families.

The movement today has a more sophisticated understanding the political intricacies and greater knowledge and skill in how to deal with opponents (Freedman, 2002). The last two decades of the twentieth century witnessed a rise in antifeminism that attempted to thwart the problems faced by women by pushing them back into their homes with traditional solutions that cannot possibly work today. In this new century the winds of political change have again shifted toward a more favorable outlook for a feminist agenda. It is perhaps indicative of the success of the women's movement that this agenda has widespread support. People no longer question the right of women to achieve their fullest individual potential, whether inside or outside the home. The earlier movement was characterized by mass mobilization and confrontation. With support from NGOs across the globe allied in working toward common goals and with the technical capacity to garner global awareness for feminist causes, the current movement is less visible but more powerful.

Feminism at the millennium is diverse in programs, tactics, and goals. The United Nations Conference on Women in Beijing was a watershed for women. By encouraging open dialogue, inclusiveness, and consensus building, it attested to the ability of women to work toward goals of sisterhood, female empowerment, and partnering with men. With a heightened degree of political sophistication, that very diversity will contribute to the strength of the movement.

Summary

1. Assumptions about gender in the law include: women need protection, men are protectors, spouses are treated as "one" under the husband, and biological differences between men and women justify different legal standards.

2. Title VII of the 1964 Civil Rights Act can only be circumvented by claiming a BFOQ (bona fide occupational qualification). Regardless of the Equal Pay Act, a gender wage gap exists. Comparable worth strategies to deal with the gap are difficult to measure but call attention to lost market productivity. Originally designed to promote status of African-American men, women have been helped by affirmative action. It is inaccurately portrayed in the media as reverse discrimination, but the more the public understands the policy the more they support it. The Equal Opportunity Employment Commission enforces Title VII, but its strength under Clinton has been reduced under the Bush administration.

3. Title IX prohibits sex discrimination in schools receiving federal funds. It has been most successful for gender equity in athletic programs, such as offering athletic scholarships for females. Backlash, conservative politics, and inconsistent court rulings hurt its enforcement.

4. Sexual harassment is prohibited under Title VII. Anita Hill's testimony of sexual harassment leveled at Clarence Thomas during his confirmation hearings opened the issue to the public and showed the extent and negative effects of it. Symbolic interaction highlights how sexual harassment has been reconstructed from acceptable to unacceptable.

5. Marital roles are based on three legal models: unity—husband is dominant; separate but equal based on breadwinning and nurturing roles; shared partnership—spouses have equal rights and responsibilities.

6. In a divorce, state law determines property divisors: in community property states, spouses jointly own property; in common law states property belongs to spouse in whose name it is held. To deal with inequities other factors such as length of marriage, age, health, and earning abilities are now considered. Social Security rules have hurt homemakers in a divorce. The 1984 Retirement Equity Act was passed to make pensions fairer to women.

7. Many judges do not implement newer legislation designed to protect battered women. Enforcement is hampered because judges maintain a stereotyped traditional image of a husband–wife relationship.

8. Until the nineteenth century, women had a general right to an abortion. In 1973 with *Roe v. Wade* and *Doe v. Dalton* women again obtained this right under certain conditions. Challenges to abortion rights are led by the pro-life groups often under the New Christian Right. As cited by pro-choice activists, a majority of men and women believe abortion should be legal and safe.

9. About 90 percent of serious crimes are committed by men, and four males are arrested for every one female. Socialization allowing more aggression and impulsive behavior for boys and more dependence for girls helps explains the gender gap in crime. Feminist researchers explain the gap according to women's lower SES and need for money. Empirical support for the chivalry hypothesis that police are reluctant to arrest women is weak. Other research suggests females are treated more harshly than males in the criminal justice system. Prostitution reflects all these explanations.

10. Women holding office have increased their numbers, gradually at the congressional level but more rapidly at the state level. Top-level female appointments under Clinton were followed with a sharp decrease under Bush. Support to elect qualified women is strong but is impeded by traditional beliefs about women's roles. Nations in both Europe and Asia have elected women as prime ministers and presidents. Hillary Clinton broke the gender norms about the role of a First Lady and was criticized as well as applauded for it. Age, money, and occupational background serve as limits to women candidates.

11. The gender gap in political attitudes shows women identified more as Democrats than Republicans and showing more support for issues related to women and children and less support for capital punishment and military involvement than men. The gender gap may close when women build coalitions on issues related to gender rather than political party.

12. Support for the Equal Rights Amendment is favored by a majority of men and women. Opposition from the New Christian Right and confusion of its provisions, especially related to drafting women, hampered ratification. A new ERA ratification campaign is building, mounted by its politically astute supporters.

13. Feminism in the twenty-first century capitalizes on consensus building among diverse groups of women, a greater understanding of the family–employment dilemma, and greater political skill.

Key Terms

bona fide occupational
   qualification (BFOQ) 375

common law 385

community property 385

Equal Employment
   Opportunity Commission
   (EEOC) 379

Equal Pay Act 376

Equal Rights
   Amendment 399

Roe v. Wade 387

Critical Thinking Questions

1. Provide evidence for the gender inequity that persists in the legal and criminal justice systems and evaluate the negative differential gender consequences that result. Suggest specific alternatives to make these systems more just related to gender. Can a system be gender-just if it is not gender equitable?

2. Given the increasing number of women officeholders and the concern politicians are expressing related to a gender gap in politics, how do you think public policy will be altered to account for these realities over the next decade?

3. Based on your understanding of gender in the political process, what strategies can feminists use to maximize success in campaigns related to gender equity in employment and education and in garnering support for reproductive rights and ratification of the ERA?

Glossary

agency   the power to adapt and sometimes to thrive in difficult situations

affirmative action   policies of preferential treatment for women and minorities under-represented in certain job categories

agents of socialization   the people, groups, and social institutions that provide information for children to become functioning members of society

androcentrism   male-centered norms operating throughout all social institutions that become the standard to which all persons adhere

androgyny   the integration of traits considered to be feminine with those considered to be masculine

assortive mating   coupling based on similarity

battered women's syndrome   the powerless, dependence, and poor self-image of abused women associated with the belief that they are responsible for the violence against them

blended family   children from remarriages and parents' prior relationships who are brought together in a new family

bona fide occupational qualification (BFOQ)   legally allows for hiring an employee on the basis of one sex under very specific circumstances

civil union   a legal classification entitling same-sex couples to the rights and responsibilities available to married partners

common law   property belongs to the spouse in whose name it is held

community property   all property acquired during the marriage is jointly owned by the spouses

comparable worth   policies designed to upgrade the wages for jobs that employ large numbers of women

compensatory history   chronicles the lives of exceptional women

continuing socialization   learning that provides the basis for the varied roles an individual will fill throughout life

contribution history   chronicles women's contributions to specific social movements

countermodernization   a social movement that either resists modernization or promotes ways to neutralize its effects

culture   a society's total way of life that provides social heritage and guidelines for appropriate behavior

developing nations   countries and regions with poverty level incomes per capita; also referred to as the developing world

developing world   countries and regions with poverty level incomes per capita; also referred to as developing nations

development   programs designed to upgrade the standard of living of the world's poor in ways that allow them to sustain themselves

doing gender   the notion that gender emerges not as an individual attribute but something that is accomplished through interaction with others

dominance model   argues that gendered language is a reflection of women's subordinate status

double standard   the idea that men are allowed to express themselves sexually and women are not

dramaturgical approach   viewing social interaction as if it was an enactment in a theatrical performance

dual-culture model   argues that the interactional styles of males and females are separate but equal

egalitarian marriage   a marriage in which spouses share decision making and assign family roles based on talent and choice rather than on traditional beliefs about gender

empowerment   the ability for women to control their own destinies

end-point fallacy   the negotiation of social reality is an ongoing process where new definitions produce new behavior in a never-ending cycle

Equal Employment Opportunity Commission (EEOC)   a federal agency created to ensure that Title VII of the 1964 Civil Rights Act is carried out

Equal Pay Act   a federal law requiring females and males to receive the same pay for the same job

Equal Rights Amendment   proposed constitutional amendment stating that equality of rights under the law shall not be denied on account of sex

essentialism   the belief that males and females are inherently different because of their biology and genes

expressive role   associated with the expectation that the wife-mother maintains the family through child rearing and nurturing

familism   a Latino cultural value emphasizing the family and its collective needs over personal and individual needs

family of orientation   the family in which one grows up

family of procreation   the family established when one marries or establishes a long term partnership

female genital mutilation (FGM)   a variety of genital operations designed to reduce or eliminate a girl's sexual pleasure and ensure her virginity; also referred to as genital cutting

feminism   an inclusive worldwide movement to end sexism and sexist oppression by empowering women

feminist theology   draws on women's experience as a basic source of content previously shut out of theological reflection

fictive kin   networks among African Americans that absorb friends into kin structures

gender   social, cultural, and psychological traits linked to males and females that define them as masculine or feminine

gender identity   an awareness that there are two sexes who behave differently

gender roles   the expected attitudes and behaviors a society associates with each sex

gender socialization   the process by which individuals learn the cultural behavior of femininity or masculinity that is associated with the biological sex of female or male

gender-typing   expectation for less pay and prestige when the majority of the occupation are those of one gender, usually female

glass ceiling   describes women's failure to rise to senior level positions because of invisible and artificial barriers constructed by male management

globalization   the vision of the world as a single social space where diverse societies borrow, learn, and compete against one another

gynocentrism   an emphasis on female and feminine interests

hegemonic masculinity   asserts that there are a number of competing masculinities that are enacted according to particular places and times

hermaphrodites   infants born with both male and female sex organs or who have ambiguous genitals; also referred to as intersexed

heterosexism   viewing the world only in heterosexual terms, thus denigrating other sexual orientations

hidden curriculum   the informal and unwritten norms that serve to control students, including expectations about gender

homogamy   becoming attracted to and marrying someone similar to yourself

homophobia   the fear and intolerance of homosexuals (gay men and lesbians) and homosexuality

household   a person or group of people occupying a housing unit

human capital model   explains the gender wage gap as due to personal choices in matters of education, childbirth, child rearing, and occupation

informal sector   the usually undocumented economic activities of people who work as subsistence farmers, landless agricultural laborers, street vendors, or day workers

instrumental role   associated with the expectation that the husband-father maintains the family through earning income

intersexed   infants born with both male and female sex organs or who have ambiguous genitals; also referred to as hermaphrodites

Islamization   a religious fundamentalist movement seeking a return to an idealized version of Islam as a remedy against corrupt Western values

Knights of Labor   first major union opened for women and African Americans calling for equal pay for equal work

liberation theology   calls for redistribution of wealth and economic equality grounded in biblical messages about God's concern for the poor and oppressed

life course   the roles people play over a lifetime and the ages associated with those roles

machismo   among Latinos, associating the male role with virility, sexual prowess, and the physical and ideological control of women

marianismo   among Latinos, associating the female role with female over male spiritual and moral superiority and glorification of motherhood

marriage gradient   a pattern in which women tend to marry men of higher socioeconomic status

marriage squeeze   an unbalanced ratio of marriage-age women to marriage-age men that limits the pool of potential marriage partners

microcredit   a system providing small loans to a group of very poor borrowers to start small businesses and open their first savings accounts; also called microenterprise lending

microenterprise programs   provides for income-earning manufacturing or agricultural activities located in or around the households of very poor people

morbidity rate   the amount of disease or illness in a population in a given time period

mortality rate   the total number of deaths in a population in a given time period

motherhood mandate   the belief that motherhood demands selfless devotion to children and a subordination of a mother's life to the needs of children and family

misogyny   the disdain and hatred of women

National American Women's Suffrage Association   organization working for women's political rights formed in 1890 with the merger of two suffrage groups

National Organization for Women   organization formed in 1966 heralding the return of feminism in the United States

National Organization of Men Against Sexism   a male liberation group working to reduce the negative effects of power and unyielding masculinity

New Christian Right (NCR)   a fundamentalist political movement of conservative, Protestant groups that promotes morality based on the Bible and God's will as the ultimate source for political and social life

nongovernmental organizations (NGOs)   privately funded nonprofit groups concerned with relief and development and advocacy for the poor

nonverbal communication   using bodily and situational features in communication, such as posture, eye contact, touching, and personal space

norm   a shared rule that guides people's behavior in specific situations

nuclear family   consists of wife, husband, and their dependent children who live apart from other relatives in their own residence

pater familias   the absolute power over all family members granted to the eldest man in the family in ancient Rome

patriarchy   male-dominated social structures leading to the oppression of women

primary socialization   begins in the family and allows the child to acquire necessary skills to fit into society, especially language learning and acceptable behavior to function effectively in a variety of social situations

registers   sociolinguistic term for a variety of language defined by its use in social situations

Roe v. Wade   Landmark 1973 Supreme Court case establishing the legal right to an abortion

role   the expected behavior associated with a status

rule of thumb   an English Common Law provision once allowing a husband to beat his wife with a stick no bigger than his thumb

sandwich generation   women caught between caring for the older and younger generations at the same time

sati   a Hindu widow who until the twentieth century was frequently expected to be buried alive or self-immolated with her dead husband on his funeral pyre

schema   a cognitive structure used to understand the world, interpret perception, and process new information

second shift   the shift of unpaid work in the home for women who are also employed full time for pay

self   the unique and highly valued sense of identity that distinguishes each individual from all other individuals

Seneca Falls Convention   1848 convention held in Seneca Falls, New York, hailed as the birth of the women's movement in the United States

serial monogamy   a pattern of marriage–divorce–remarriage

sex   the biological characteristics distinguishing male and female

sexism   the belief that the status of female is inferior to the status of male

sexual dimorphism   the separation of the sexes into two distinct groups

sexual harassment   legally includes physical or verbal conduct that is sexual in nature, is unwanted, and creates a hostile environment that interferes with school or work activities

sexual orientation   a preference for sexual partners of one gender (sex) or the other

sexual scripts   shared beliefs concerning what society defines as acceptable sexual thoughts, feelings, and behaviors for each gender

social construction of reality   the shaping of perception of reality by the subjective meanings brought to any experience or social interaction

social control   measures a society uses to ensure that people generally conform to norms, including those related to gender

social institutions   organizational structures that ensure the basic needs of society are met in established, predictable ways

social stratification   the way a society divides people into ranked categories or statuses

socialization   the lifelong process by which we learn culture, develop a sense of self, and become functioning members of society

sociobiology   a field using evolutionary theory to examine the biological roots of social behavior

status   a category or position a person occupies, such as gender, that is a significant determinant of how she or he will be defined and treated

status set   statuses that are occupied simultaneously

stereotype   an oversimplified conception that people who occupy the same status share certain traits in common

subculture   segments of a culture that share characteristics distinguishing it from the broader culture

Texts of Terror   parts of four books of the Torah that include the Old Testament of the Christian Bible documenting abuse and sexual violence against women often used as justifications for restricting women

theory   an explanation that guides the research process and provide a means for interpreting the data

Title VII of the 1964 Civil Rights Act makes job discrimination and occupational segregation of women illegal

Title IX of the 1972 Educational Amendment Act prohibits sex (gender) discrimination in any school receiving federal assistance

transgender describes people who do not conform to culturally defined traditional gender roles associated with their sex

transsexuals genetic males or females who psychologically believe they are members of the other gender

True Womanhood the Victorian standard for women to subscribe to the virtues of piety, purity, submissiveness, and domesticity

References

AARP (American Association of Retired Persons). 2003. "Women get more bad news about hormone therapy." *AARP Bulletin* July–August:19.

AAUW (American Association of University Women). 1999. *Gender Gaps: Where Schools Still Fail Our Children*. New York: Marlowe.

———. 2001. *Hostile Hallways: Bullying, Teasing, and Sexual Harassment in Schools*. Washington, DC: Association of University Women Educational Foundation.

Abel, Emily K. 2001. "Historical perspectives on caregiving: Documenting women's experiences." In Alexis J. Walker et al. (eds.), *Families in Later Life: Connections and Transitions*. Thousand Oaks, CA: Pine Forge.

Abbey, Antonia, Frank M. Andres, and L. Jill Halman. 1994. "Psychosocial predictors of life quality: How are they affected by infertility, gender and parenthood." *Journal of Family Issues* 15(2):253–71.

Abbey, Antonia, Pam Mcauslan, and Lisa Thomson Ross. 1998. "Sexual assault perception by college men: The role of alcohol, misperception of sexual intent and sexual beliefs and experiences." *Journal of Social and Clinical Psychology* 17(2):167–95.

ABC News. 2001. "A boy or a girl? Fertility clinic says parents can choose. *Good Morning America*, October 2. Available online at: http://abcnews.go.com/sections/GMA/GoodMorning America/GMA011001

Abouchedid, Kamal, and Ramzi Nasser. 2000. "External and internal social barriers in stereotyping university majors." *Current Research in Social Psychology* April: 151–69.

Abowitz, Deborah A. 2002. "On the road to 'happily ever after:' A survey of attitudes toward romance and marriage among college students." Paper presented at the Southern Sociological Society, New Orleans, LA.

Abselson, Reed. 1999. "A push from the top shatters a glass ceiling." *New York Times* August 22:1, 23.

Academy for Educational Development. 2002. "Support for increasing investment in education is growing." *AED Focus Issue: Basic Education*. Available online at: http://www.aed.org/edu_basic.html

Acosta, R.V. and L. J. Carpenter. 2002. *Women in Intercollegiate Sport: A Twenty-Five Year Update: A Longitudinal Study, 1977–2002*. Brooklyn, NY: Brooklyn College, Department of Physical Education.

Adams, Abigail. 1776/1996. "Remember the ladies letters." In Mary Beth Norton and Ruth M. Alexander (eds.), *Major Problems in American Women's History*. Lexington, MA: D. C. Heath.

Adams, Edward. 2000. *Constructing the World: A Study in Paul's Cosmological Language*. Edinburgh, Scotland: T & T Clark.

Adams, Karen L., and Norma C. Ware. 1995. "Sexism and the English language: The linguistic implications of being a woman." In Jo Freeman (ed.), *Women: A Feminist Perspective*. Mountain View, CA: Mayfield.

Adherents. 2002. "Largest religious groups in the United States of America." Available online at: http://www.adherents.com/rel_USA

Adler, Freda. 1975. *Sisters in Crime: The Rise of the New Female Criminal*. New York: McGraw-Hill.

Adler, Jerry. 1991. "Drums, sweat and tears." *Newsweek* (June 24):48–51.

Afifi, Walid A., and Sandra L. Fulkner. 2000. "On being 'just friends': The frequency and impact of sexual activity in cross-sex friendships." *Journal of Personal and Social Relationships* 17(2):205–22.

Aguinis, Herman and Christine A. Henle. 2001. "Effects of nonverbal behavior on perceptions of a female employee's power bases." *Journal of Social Psychology* 141(4):537–49.

Ahmed, Akbar S. 2002. "Muhammad." In John Miller and Aaron Kenedi (eds.), *Inside Islam: The Faith, the People, and the Conflicts of the World's Fastest-Growing Religion*. (pp. 11–26). New York: Marlowe.

Akita, Kimiko. 2000. "Japanese feminism: Women being mothers to men." *Women & Language* 5(2):63.

Albrecht, Steven F. 2001. "Stalking, stalkers, and domestic violence: Relentless fear and obsessive intimacy." In Joseph A. Davis (ed.), *Stalking Crimes and Victim Protection: Prevention, Intervention, Threat Assessment, and Case Management*. (pp. 81–96). Boca Raton, FL: CRC Press.

Alderman-Swain, Wanda, and Juan Battle. 2000. "The invisible gender: Educational outcomes for African American females in father-only versus mother-only households." *Race and Society* 3(2):165–82.

Aldous, Joan, and Gail M. Mulligan. 2002. "Fathers' child care and children's behavior problems: A longitudinal study." *Journal of Family Issues* 23(5):624–47.

Alexander, Susan H. 1999. "Messages to women on love and marriage from women's magazines." In Marian Meyers (eds.), *Mediated Women: Representations in Popular Culture*. (pp. 25–38). Cresskill, NJ: Hampton.

Algoe, Sara B., Brenda N. Buswell, and John D. DeLamater. 2000. "Gender and job status as contextual cues for the interpretation of facial expression of emotion." *Sex Roles* 42(3–4):183–208.

Allen, Paula Gunn. 1995. "When women throw down bundles: Strong women make strong nations." In Sheila Ruth, *Issues in Feminism: An Introduction to Women's Studies*. Mountain View, CA: Mayfield.

Allgower, Annette, Jane Wardle, and Andrew Steptoe. 2001. "Depressive symptoms, social support, and personal health behaviors in young men and women." *Health Psychology* 20(3):233–7.

Allyn, David. 2000. *Make Love Not War: The Sexual Revolution: An Unfettered History.* Boston: Little, Brown.

Al-Olayan, Fahad S., and Kiran Karande. 2000. "A content analysis of magazine advertisements from the United States and the Arab world." *Journal of Advertising* 29(3):69–82.

Amadiume, Ifi. 1997. *Reinventing Africa: Matriarchy, Religion and Culture.* New York: Zed.

Amato, Paul R. 2001. "Children of divorce in the 1990s: An update of the Amato and Keith (1991) meta-analysis." *Journal of Family Psychology* 15(3): 355–70.

Amato, Paul R., David R. Johnson, Alan Booth, and Stacy J. Rogers. 2003. "Continuity and change in marital quality between 1980 and 2000." *Journal of Marriage and the Family* 65(1)1–22.

Amato, Paul R., and Denise Previti. 2003. "People's reasons for divorcing: Gender, social class, the life course, and adjustment." *Journal of Family Issues* 24(5):602–26.

Amba, Joyce C., and Freya L. Sonenstein. 2002. "Sexual activity and contraceptive practices among teenagers in the United States, 1988 and 1995." *Vital and Health Statistics.* Series 23(21): May. Centers for Disease Control and National Center for Health Statistics.

American Academy of Pediatrics. 2001. "Media violence." *Pediatrics* 108(5):1222–26.

ANAD. 2003. "Facts about eating disorders." National Association of Anorexia Nervosa and Associated Disorders. Available online at: http://www.altrue.net/site/anadweb/content

Anastaskos, Kiki. 2002. "Structural adjustment policies in Mexico and Costa Rica." In Rekha Datta and Judith Kornberg (eds.), *Women in Developing Countries: Assessing Strategies for Empowerment.* (pp. 113–27). Boulder, CO: Lynne Rienner.

Andereycken, Walter V. 2003. "Prognosis of anorexia nervosa." *American Journal of Psychiatry* 160:1535.

Andersen, Arnold, Leigh Cohen, and Thomas Holbrook. 2000. *Making Weight: Men's Conflicts with Food, Weight, Shape and Appearance.* Carlsbad, CA: Gurze.

Anderson, C. A., and Brad J. Bushman. 2001. "Effects of violent video games on aggressive behavior, aggressive cognition, aggressive affect, physiological arousal, and prosocial behavior: A meta-analytic review of the scientific literature." *Psychological Science* 12(5):353–9.

Anderson, C. Leigh, Laura Locker, and Rachel Nugent. 2002. "Microcredit, social capital, and common pool resources." *World Development* 30(1):95–105.

Anderson, Irina, and Victoria Swainson. 2001. "Perceived motivations for rape: Gender differences in beliefs about female and male rape." *Current Research in Social Psychology* 6(8):np.

Anderson, John, 1994. "Held hostage in Hollywood: Female stars buy into bad roles, big time." *St. Louis Post-Dispatch* December 4:3C.

Anderson, Kristin J. Accomando, 1999. "Madcap misogyny and romanticized victim-blaming: Discourses of stalking in 'There's Something about Mary.'" *Women & Language* 22(1):24–28.

Anderson, Margaret. 2001. "A nation's downward spiral into cynicism: Revisiting Clarence Thomas and Anita Hill. *SWS Network News* 28(4):20–21.

Anderson, Robert N. 2001. "Deaths: Leading causes for 1999." *National Vital Statistics Report* 49(11): October 12.

Andryszewski, Tricia. 2000. *Gay Rights.* Brookfield, CT: Twenty-First Century Books.

Angier, Natalie. 2001. "Researchers piecing together autoimmune disease puzzle." *New York Times* June 19. D1,D8.

Anjum, Mohini. 2000. "Nation and gender-historical perspective." *Sociological Bulletin* 49(1):111–16.

Ankarloo, Bengt, Stuart Clark and William Monter. 2002. *Witchcraft and Magic in Europe: The Period of the Witch Trials.* Philadelphia: University of Pennsylvania.

Antilla, Susan. 1995. "Young white men only, please: Women accuse a broker of blatant discrimination." *New York Times* April 26:C1, D7

Antoniuk, Tricia. 1999. "Policy alternatives for a diverse community: Lesbians and family law." In T. Richard Sullivan (ed.), *Queer Families, Common Agendas: Gay People, Lesbians, and Family Values.* (pp. 47–60). Binghamton, NY: Harrington Park.

Antonucci, Toni C., Jennifer E. Lansford, and Hiroko Akiyama. 2002. "Differences between men and women in social relations, resource deficits, and depressive symptomatology during later life in four nations." *Journal of Social Issues* 58(4):767–83.

Anway, Carol L. 1996. *Daughters of Another Path: Experiences of American Women Choosing Islam.* Lee's Summit, MO: Yawna.

Anzaldua, Gloria E. 1995. "The strength of my rebellion." In Sheila Ruth, *Issues in Feminism: An Introduction to Women's Studies.* Mountain View, CA: Mayfield.

Apostoleris, Nicholas H. 1998. "Girl's assertiveness in the presence of boys." *Small Group Research* 29(2): 198–211.

Applebaum, Herbert A. 1998. "Colonial women." In *The American Work Ethic and the Changing Work Force* (chapter 5). Westport, CT: Greenwood.

Archer, John. 1991. "The influence of testosterone on human aggression." *British Journal of Psychology* 82:1–28.

———. 1994. "Violence between men." In John Archer (ed.), *Male Violence* (pp. 121–40). London: Routledge.

Archer, John, R. Holloway, and K. McLaughlin. 1995. Self-reported physical aggression among young men." *Aggressive Behavior* 21:325–42.

Archer, John, and Barbara Lloyd. 2002. *Sex and Gender.* Cambridge, UK: Cambridge University.

Arendell, Terry. 1992. "After divorce: Investigations into father absence." *Gender & Society* 6(4): 562–86.

Arias, Elizabeth, Robert N. Anderson, Hsiang-Ching Kung, Sherry L. Murphy, and Kenneth D.

Krochanek. 2003. "Deaths: Final data for 2001." *National Vital Statistics Report* 52(3):September 18.

Arias, Ileana, and Karen T. Pape. 2001. "Psychological abuse: Implications for adjustment and commitment to leave violent partners." In K. Daniel O'Leary and Roland D. Maiuro (eds.), *Psychological Abuse in Violent Domestic Relations.* (pp. 137–52). New York: Springer.

Armstrong, Karen. 2001. "Cries of rage and frustration." *New Statesman* Sept. 24:17–18.

Arnold, F., M. K. Chloe, and T. K. Roy. 1998. "Son preference, the family-building process and child mortality in India." *Population Studies* 52:301–15.

Arnot, Madeleine, Miriam David, and Gaby Weiner. 1999. *Closing the Gender Gap: Postwar Education and Social Change.* Cambridge, UK: Polity.

Arnup, Katherine. 1999. "Out in this world: The social and legal context of gay and lesbian families." In T. Richard Sullivan (ed.), *Queer Families, Common Agendas: Gay people, Lesbians, and Family Values.* (pp. 1–26). Binghamton, NY: Harrington Park.

Arons, Wendy. 2001. "If her stunning beauty doesn't bring you to your knees, her deadly drop kick will: Violent women in the Hong Kong kung fu film." In Martha McCaughey and Neal King (eds.), *Reel Knockouts: Violent Women in the Movies.* (pp. 27–51). Austin, TX: University of Texas.

Aronson, P. 1999. "The balancing act: Young women's exercitations and experiences of work and family." *Research in the Sociology of Work* 7:55–83.

Ascha, Ghassan. 1995. "The 'Mothers of the Believers': Stereotypes of the Prophet Muhammad's wives." In Ria Kloppenborg and Wouter J. Hanegraaff (eds.), *Female Stereotypes in Religious Traditions.* Leiden, Netherlands: Brill.

Asher, Lauren, and Lisa Lederer. 2000. "Work/family conflicts still largely absent from entertainment." Common Dreams Progressive Newswire February 9. Available online at: http://www.commondreams/.org/news2000/0209-o1

Asia-Pacific Population and Policy. 1994. "After the demographic transition: Policy responses to low fertility in four Asian countries." *East-West Center Program on Population* No. 30:1–4.

Association of American Colleges & Universities. 1995. "Valuable lessons from women's colleges." *On Campus with Women* 24(5):3.

———. 1999. "The chilly climate: Quantifying its impact." *On Campus with Women* 28(4):Summer:5.

Atkin, David J., Jay Moorman, and Carolyn A. Lin. 1991. "Ready for prime time: Network series devoted to working women in the 1980s." *Sex Roles* 25(11–12):677–85.

Atkins, David C., Sona Dimidjian, and Neil Jacobson. 2001. "Why do people have affairs? Recent research and future directions about attributions for extramarital involvement." In Valerie Manusov and John H. Harvey (eds.), *Attribution, Communication Behavior, and Close Relationships.* (pp. 305–19). Cambridge, UK: Cambridge University.

Atkins, David C., and Neil S. Jacobson. 2001. "Understanding infidelity: Correlates in a national random sample." *Journal of Family Psychology* 15(4):735–49.

Atwater, Lynn. 1982. *The Extramarital Connection: Sex, Intimacy, Identity.* New York: Irvington.

Atwell, Mark Welek. 2002. *Equal Protection of the Law? Gender and Justice in the United States.* New York: P. Lang.

Audi, Robert. 2000. *Religious Commitment and Secular Reason.* Cambridge, UK: Cambridge University.

Baca Zinn, Maxine. 2000. "Feminism and family studies for a new century." *Annals of the American Academy of Political and Social Science* 571(September):42–56.

Badgett, M., V. Lee, and Jeanette Lim. 2001. "Promoting women's economic progress through Affirmative Action." In Mary C. King (ed.), *Squaring Up: Policy Strategies to Raise Women's Incomes in the United States.* (pp. 179–99). Ann Arbor: University of Michigan.

Badinter, Elisabeth. 1995. *XY: On Masculine Identity.* New York: Columbia University.

Bagilhole, Barbara. 2002. *Women in Non-Traditional Occupations: Challenging Men.* Houndmiils, Basingstoke, Hampshire, UK: Palgrave Macmillan.

Baker, Christina. 2000. "Telling our stories: Feminist mothers and daughters." In Andrea O'Reilly and Sharon Abbey (eds.), *Mothers and Daughters: Connection, Empowerment and Transformation.* (pp. 203–12). Lanham, MD: Rowman & Littlefield.

Baker, Cynthia M. 2002. *Rebuilding the House of Israel: Architectures of Gender in Jewish Antiquity.* Stanford, CA: Stanford University.

Baker, Kathleen, Carol Ann Beck, et al. 2003. "The relationship between maternal employment and perceptions of child, spouse, and self." ERIC, *Resources in Education* Accession No.: ED472514.

Balanoff, Elizabeth. 1990. "The American woman and the labor movement: Bitter fruit in the economy of profit." In Frances Richardson Keller (ed.), *Views of Women's Lives in Western Tradition.* Lewiston, NY: Edwin Mellen.

Baldwin, Bruce A. 1995. "The family circle." In Kathleen R. Gilbert (ed.), *Marriage and Family 95/96* (Annual Editions). Guilford, CT: Dushkin/Brown & Benchmark.

Ball, Richard E. 1993. "Children and marital happiness of black Americans." *Journal of Comparative Family Studies* 24(2):203–18.

Balmer, Randall. 1994. "American fundamentalism: The ideal of femininity." In John Stratton Hawley (ed.), *Fundamentalism and Gender.* New York: Oxford University.

Bandura, Albert, and Richard H. Walters. 1963. *Social Learning and Personality Development.* New York: Holt, Rinehart & Winston.

Banerjee, Neela. 2001. "Some bullies seek ways to soften up: Toughness has risks for women executives." *New York Times* August 10, C1, C2.

Bank, Barbara J. 1999. "Some dangers of binary thinking: Comment on 'Why smart people believe that schools shortchange girls.'" *Gender Issues* 17(2):83–6.

Banner, Lois W. 1984. *Women in Modern America: A Brief History.* San Diego, CA: Harcourt Brace Jovanovich.

Barer, Barbara M. 2002. "Men and women aging differently." In Harold Cox (ed.), *Aging* (Annual Editions). Guilford, CT: McGraw-Hill/Dushkin.

Barile, Crystal Ann. 2001. "The never-married Caucasian American woman in mid-life as a departure from the stereotypes of the old maid spinster." *Dissertation Abstracts International: Section B: The Sciences and Engineering* 61(9-B): 4969.

Barnett, Rosalind C. 1997. "Gender, employment, and psychological well-being: Historical and life-course perspectives." In Margie E. Lachman and Jacquelyn Boone James (eds.), *Multiple Paths of Midlife Development.* (pp. 323–44). Chicago: University of Chicago.

Barnitz, Laura. 2001. "Effectively responding to the commercial exploitation of children: A comprehensive approach to prevention, protection, and reintegration services." *Child Welfare* 80(5): 597–610.

Barrett, Susan E. 2001. "Children of lesbian parents: The what, when and how of talking about donor identity." In Jennifer M. Lehmann (ed.), *The Gay and Lesbian Marriage and Family Reader: Analyses of Problems and Prospects for the 21st Century.* (pp. 195–208). New York: Gordian Knot.

Barry, Herbert, III, and Aylene S. Harper. 2000. "The last three letters identify most female last names." *Psychological Reports* 87(1):48–54.

Barry, Kathleen. 1979. *Female Sexual Slavery.* New York: Basic Books.

Barstow, Anne Llewellyn. 1994. *Witchcraze: A New History of the European Witch Hunts.* London: Pandora.

Bartfield, Judi. 2003. "Falling through the cracks: Gaps in child support among welfare recipients." *Journal of Marriage and the Family* 65(1):72–89.

Bartholet, Elizabeth, and Elaine Draper. 1994. "Rethinking the choice to have children." *American Behavioral Scientist* 37(8):1058–73.

Barton, Edward Read. 2000. "Parallels between mythopoetic men's work/men's peer emotional support groups and selected feminist theories." In Edward Read Barton (ed.), *Mythopoetic Perspectives of Men's Healing Work: An Anthology of Therapists and Others.* (pp. 3–20). Westport, CT: Bergin & Garvey.

Bartsch, Robert A., Teresa Burnett, and Tommye Diller. 2000. "Gender representation in television commercials: Updating and update." *Sex Roles* 43(9–10):735–43.

Basile, Kathleen C. 2002. "Prevalence of wife rape and other intimate partner sexual coercion in a nationally representative sample of women." *Violence and Victims* 17(5):511–24.

Basow, Susan A., and Kelly Johnson. 2000. "Predictors of homophobia in female college students." *Sex Roles* 42(4/6):391–404.

Bassani, Cherylynn. 2003. "A look at changing parental ideologies and behaviors in Japan."

Sociological Research Online http://www.socresonline.org.uk

Batalova, Jeanne A., and Philip N. Cohen. 2002. "Premarital cohabitation and housework: Couples in cross-national perspective." *Journal of Marriage and the Family* 64(3):743–55.

Batten, Mary. 1992. *Sexual Strategies.* New York: Jeremy P. Tarcher/Putnam.

Bauman, Kurt. 1999. "Shifting family definitions: The effect of cohabitation and other nonfamily household relationships on measures of poverty." *Demography* 36(3):315–25.

Baunach, Dawn Michelle. 2001. "Gender inequality in childhood: Toward a life course perspective." *Gender Issues* 19(3):61–86.

———. 2002. "Progress, opportunity, and backlash: Explaining attitudes toward gender-based affirmative action." *Sociological Focus* 35(4):345–62.

Bauserman, Robert. 2002. "Child adjustment in joint-custody versus sole-custody arrangements: A meta-analytic review." *Journal of Family Psychology* 16(1):91–102.

Baxandall, Rosalyn, and Linda Gordon (eds.). 1999. *America's Working Women: A Documentary History, 1600 to the Present.* New York: Norton.

Baxter, Janeen. 2000. "The joys and justice of housework." *Sociology* 34(4):609–31.

Baxter, Leslie A., Tim Dun, and Erin Sahlstein. 2001. "Rules for relating communicated among social network members." *Journal of Personal and Social Relationships* 18(2):173–99.

Beal, Carole R. 1994. *Boys and Girls: The Development of Gender Roles.* New York: McGraw-Hill.

Becker, Gary S. 1994. "Working women's staunchest allies: Supply and demand." In Susan F. Feiner (ed.), *Race and Gender in the American Economy: Views from Across the Spectrum.* Englewood Cliffs, NJ: Prentice Hall.

Beckman, Karen Redrobe. 2003. *Vanishing Women: Magic, Film, and Feminism.* Durham, NC: Duke University.

Beddoe, Deirdre. 1989. *Back to Home and Duty: Women Between the Wars, 1918–1939.* London: Pandora.

Behling, Laura. 2001. *The Masculine Woman in America, 1890–1935.* Urbana: University of Illinois.

Beier, Margaret E., and Philip L. Ackerman. 2003. "Determinants of health knowledge: An investigation of age, gender, abilities, personality and interests." *Journal of Personality and Social Psychology* 84(2):439–48.

Beitel, Ashley H., and Ross D. Parke. 1998. "Parental involvement in infancy: The role of maternal and paternal attitudes." *Journal of Family Psychology* 12(2):268–88.

Belanger, Daniele. 2002. "Son preference in a rural village in North Viet Nam." *Studies in Family Planning* 33(4):321–34.

Belkin, Lisa. 2003. "The opt-out revolution." *New York Times Magazine* October 26:42–47, 58, 85–86.

Beller, Michal, and Naomi Gafni. 2000. "Can item format (multiple choice vs. open-ended) account for gender differences in mathematics achievement?" *Sex Roles* 42(1–2):1–21.

Belsky, Jay, and John Kelly. 1994. *The Transition to Parenthood: How a First Child Changes a Marriage: Why Some Couples Grow Closer and Others Apart.* New York: Delacorte.

Bem, Sandra Lipsitz. 1981. "Gender schema theory: A cognitive account of sex-typing." *Psychological Review* 88:354–64.

———. 1983. "Gender schema theory and its implications for child development: Raising gender-aschematic children in a gender-schematic society." *Signs* 8:598–616.

———. 1985. "Androgyny and gender-schema theory: A conceptual and empirical integration." In T. B. Sonderegger (ed.), *Nebraska Symposium on Motivation 1984: Psychology and Gender* 32:179–226. Lincoln: University of Nebraska.

———. 1993. *The Lenses of Gender: Transforming the Debate on Sexual Inequality.* New Haven, CT: Yale University.

———. 1996. "Transforming the debate on sexual inequality: From biological difference to institutionalized androcentrism." In Joan C. Chrisler, Carla Golden, and Patricia D. Rozee (eds.), *Lectures on the Psychology of Women.* New York: McGraw-Hill.

Bem, Sandra Lipsitz, and Daryl J. Bem. 1970. "Case study of a nonconscious ideology: Training the woman to know her place." In Daryl J. Bem (ed.), *Beliefs, Attitudes and Human Affairs.* Belmont, CA: Brooks and Cole.

Bendroth, M. L. 1999. "Fundamentalism and the family: Gender, culture, and the American profamily movement." *Journal of Women's History* 10(4):35–53.

Beneke, Tim. 2004. "Men on rape." In Michael S. Kimmel and Michael A. Messner (eds.), *Men's Lives.* (pp. 195–208). Boston: Allyn & Bacon.

Beneria, Lourdes. 1998. "Accounting for women's work: The progress of two decades." In Frank Ackerman et al. (eds.), *The Changing Nature of Work.* (pp. 319–22). Washington, DC: Island Press.

———. 2001. "The enduring debate over unpaid labour." In Martha Fetherolf Loutfi (ed.), *Women, Gender and Work: What is Equality and How Do We Get There?* (pp. 85–110). Geneva: International Labour Office.

Benjamin, Jessica. 1988. *The Bonds of Love: Psychoanalysis, Feminism and the Problem of Domination.* New York: Pantheon.

Benjet, Corina, and Laura Hernandez-Guzman, 2001. "Gender differences in psychological well-being of Mexican early adolescents." *Adolescence.* 36(Spring):47–65.

Benokraitis, Nijole, and Joe Feagin. 1995. *Modern Sexism: Blatant, Subtle, and Covert Discrimination.* Englewood Cliffs, NJ: Prentice Hall.

Bensley, Lillian, and Juliet Van Eenwyk. 2001. "Video games and real-life aggression: Review of the literature." *Journal of Adolescent Health* 29(4):244–57.

Bergen, Raquel Kennedy. 1996. *Wife Rape: Understanding the Response of Survivors and Service Providers.* Thousand Oaks, CA: Sage.

Bergen, Raquel Kennedy, and Kathleen A. Boyle. 2000. "Exploring the connection between pornography and sexual violence." *Violence and Victims* 15(3):227–34.

Berger, Helen A. 2000. "High priestess: Mother, leader, teacher." In Wendy Griffin (ed.), *Daughters of the Goddess: Studies of Healing, Identity, and Empowerment.* (pp. 103–18). Walnut Creek, CA: AltaMira.

Bergqvist, Christina, and Anita Nyberg, 2002. "Welfare state restructuring and child care in Sweden." In Sonya Michel and Rianne Mahon (eds.), *Child Care Policy at the Crossroads: Gender and Welfare State Restructuring.* (pp. 287–308). New York: Routledge.

Bernard, Neal D. 2003. "Nutritional factors in menstrual pain and premenstrual syndrome." *PCRM Clinical Research.* Physician's Committee for Responsible Medicine. Available online at: http://www.perm.org/research/mentrual.html

Berner, Leila Gal. 2001. "Hearing Hannah's voice: The Jewish feminist challenge and ritual innovation. In Yvonne Yazbeck and John L. Esposito (eds.), *Daughters of Abraham: Feminist Thought in Judaism, Christianity, and Islam.* (pp. 35–49). Gainesville: University Press of Florida.

Berquist, Jon L. 2002. *Controlling Corporeality: The Body and the Household in Ancient Israel.* New Brunswick, NJ: Rutgers University.

Bevan, Robin. 2001. "Boys, girls and mathematics: Beginning to learn from the gender debate." *Mathematics in School* 30(4):2–6.

Beyer, Sylvia. 1999. "The accuracy of academic gender stereotypes." *Sex Roles* 40(9–10):787–813.

Beynon, John. 2002. *Masculinities and Culture.* Buckingham, UK: Open University Press.

Beyrer, Chris. 2001. "Shan women and girls in the sex industry in Southeast Asia: Political causes and human rights implications." *Social Science and Medicine* 53(4):543–50.

Bianchi, Suzanne M. 1999. "Feminization and juvenilization of poverty: Trends, risks, causes, and consequences." *Annual Review of Sociology* 25:307–33.

Bianchi, Suzanne M., and Lynne M. Casper, 2001. "American families resilient after 50 years of change." Washington DC: Population Reference Bureau (News Release, January 5).

Bianchi, Suzanne M., Melissa A. Milkie, Liana C. Sayer, and John P. Robinson. 2000. "Is anyone doing the housework? Trends in the gender division of household labor." *Social Forces* 79 (1):191–229.

Biggins, J. Veronica. 1999. "Making board diversity work: Shaping a diverse board into a strategic asset." *The Corporate Board* July/August.

Bigner, Jerry J. 1999. "Raising our sons: Gay men as fathers." In T. Richard Sullivan (ed.), *Queer families, Common Agendas: Gay People, Lesbians, and Family Values.* (pp. 61–78). Binghamton, NY: Harrington Park.

Binder, Ron. 2001. "Changing a culture: Sexual assault prevention in the fraternity and sorority community." In Allen J. Ottens and Kathy

Hotellling (eds.), *Sexual Violence on Campus: Policies, Programs and Perspectives.* (pp. 120–40). New York: Springer.

Bing, Janet. 1999. "Brain sex: How the media report and distort brain research." *Women & Language* 22(2):4–13.

Bird, Chloe E. 1999. "Gender, household labor, and psychological distress: The impact of the amount and division of housework." *Journal of Health and Social Behavior* 40(1):32–45.

Bird, S. Elizabeth. 2000. "Growing up pink or blue: Using children's television commercials to analyze gender enculturation." In Patricia C. Rice and David W. McCurdy (eds.), *Strategies in Teaching Anthropology.* (pp. 141–44). Upper Saddle River, NJ: Prentice Hall.

Bischoping, Katherine. 1993. "Gender differences in conversation topics." *Sex Roles.* 28(1–2):1–18.

Bishop, Beverley. 2000. "The diversification of employment and women's work in contemporary Japan." In J. S. Eades, Tom Gill, and Harumi Befu (eds.), *Globalization and Social Justice in Contemporary Japan.* (pp. 93–109). Melbourne, AS: Trans Pacific.

Björkqvist, Kaj. 1994. "Sex differences in physical, verbal and indirect aggression: A review of recent research." *Sex Roles* 30:177–88.

Björkqvist, Kaj, and Pirkko Niemelä. 1992. "New trends in the study of female aggression." In Kaj Björkqvist and Pirkko Niemelä (eds.), *Of Mice and Women: Aspects of Female Aggression.* San Diego, CA: Academic Press.

Blackwell, Debra, and Danile T. Lichter. 2000. "Mate selection among married and cohabiting couples." *Journal of Family Issues* 21(3):275–302.

Blackwell, Judith C., Murray E. G. Smith, and John S. Sorenson (eds.). 2003 . "Feminism and the women's movement." Part 6 in *Culture of Prejudice: Arguments in Critical Social Science.* Peterborough, Ontario, CA: Broadview.

Blair-Loy, Mary. 2003. *Competing Devotions: Career and Family Among Women Executives.* Cambridge, MA: Harvard University.

Bleakley, Alan. 2002. "Teaching as hospitality: The gendered 'gift' and teaching style." In Gillian Howie and Ashley Tauchert (eds.), *Gender, Teaching and Research in Higher Education: Challenges for the 21st Century* (pp. 73–85). Aldershot, UK: Ashgate.

Bleske, April L., and David M. Buss. 2000. "Can men and women be just friends?" *Personal Relationships* 7(2):131–51.

Bleske, April L., and Todd K. Shackelford. 2001. "Poaching, promiscuity, and deceit: Combating mating rivalry in same-sex relationships." *Personal Relationships* 8(4):407–24.

Block, Jeanne H. 1984. *Sex Role Identity and Ego Development.* San Francisco: Jossey-Bass.

Blood, Robert O., Jr., and Donald M. Wolfe. 1960. *Husbands and Wives: The Dynamics of Married Living.* New York: Free Press.

Blumen, Orna. 2002. "Criss-crossing boundaries: Ultraorthodox women go to work." *Gender, Peace and Culture* (2):133–51.

Blumer, Herbert. 1969. *Symbolic Interactionism: Perspective and Method.* Englewood Cliffs, NJ: Prentice Hall.

Blumstein, Philip, and Pepper Schwartz. 1983. *American Couples.* New York: Pocket Books.

Bly, Robert. 1990. *Iron John.* Reading, MA: Addison-Wesley.

Bock, Gisela. 2002. "The French Revolution: The dispute is resumed." Part 2 in *Women in European History.* Oxford, UK: Blackwell.

———. 2003. "Challenging dichotomies in women's history." In Mary Beth Norton and Ruth M. Alexander (eds.), *Major Problems in American Women's History.* Boston: Houghton Mifflin.

Bodrova, V. V. 2002. "Reproductive behavior as a factor of depopulation in Russia." *Sotsiologicheskie Issledovaniya* (abstract) 28(6):96–102.

Boekhout, Brock, Susan S. Hendrick, and Clyde Hendrick. 2000. "The loss of loved ones: The impact of relationship infidelity." In John H. Harvey and Eric D. Miller (eds.), *Loss and Trauma: General and Close Relationship Perspectives.* (pp. 358–74). New York: Brunner-Routledge.

Bohlen, Celestine. 1995. "Catholics defying an infallible church." *New York Times,* November 26:E3.

Bold, Mary. 2001. "Blended Families: Building block 2." Center for Parent Education, University of North Texas. http://www.unt.edu/cpe/module1blk2blend

Bolego, C., A. Polli, and R. Paoletti. 2002. "Smoking and gender." *Cardiovascular Research* 53(3): 568–76.

Bond, James T. 2003. *Highlights of the National Study of the Changing Workforce.* New York: Families and Work Institute.

Bonouvrié, Netty. 1995. "Female Sufi saints on the Indian subcontinent." In Ria Kloppenborg and Wouter J. Hanegraaff (eds.), *Female Stereotypes in Religious Traditions.* Leiden, Netherlands: Brill.

Bose, Mandakranta. 2000. "Sati: The event and the ideology." In Mandakranta Bose (ed.), *Faces of the Feminine in Ancient, Medieval, and Modern India* (pp. 21–32). New York: Oxford University

Boserup, Ester. 1970. *Women's Role in Economic Development.* London: Allen and Unwin.

Bosmajian, Haig. 1995. "The language of sexism." In Paula S. Rothenberg (ed.), *Race, Class and Gender in the United States: An Integrated Study.* New York: St. Martin's.

Bould, Sally. 2001. "Women and caregivers for the elderly." In Jean M. Coyle (ed.), *Handbook on Women and Aging.* Westport, CT: Praeger.

Boushey, Heather. 2001. "Closing the wage gap." *Charleston Sunday Gazette,* April 8.

Boustany, Nora. 1994. "Saudi women try new ways to overcome bars to advancement." *Washington Post* August 31:31.

———. 2002. "Up from the underground, Russia's feminists speak out." *Washington Post* November 1:A28.

Bouzereau, Laurent. 2000. *Ultraviolent Movies: From Sam Peckinpah to Quentin Tarantino.* New York: Citadel.

Bowerbank, Sylvia. "Of mice and women: Early modern roots of ecological feminism." *Women and Environments International Magazine* 52/53 (Fall):27–9.

Bowling, Stephanie Weiland, and Ronald J. Werner-Wilson. 2000. "Father-daughter relationships and adolescent female sexuality: Paternal qualities association with responsible sexual behavior." *Journal of HIV/AIDS Prevention and Education for Adolescents and Children* 3(4):5–28.

Boyatzis, Chris J., and Julie Eades. 1999. "Gender differences in preschoolers' and kindergartner's artistic production and preference." *Sex Roles* 41(7–8):627–38.

Boyko, Olga V. 2002. "How social issues were represented in the Russian press in the 1990s." *Sotsiologicheskie Issledovaniya* (abstract) 28(6): 120–28.

Bozett, Frederick W. 1987. *Gay and Lesbian Parents.* New York: Praeger.

Brainerd, Elizabeth. 2000. "Women in transition: Changes in gender wage differentials in Eastern Europe and the former Soviet Union. *Industrial and Labor Relations Review* 54(1):138–62.

Bramlett, Matthew D., and William D. Mosher. 2001. "First marriage dissolution, divorce, and remarriage: United States." *Advance Data (CDC)* No. 323, May 31. Centers for Disease Control & National Center for Health Statistics

Brannon, Robert. 1976. "The male sex role: Our culture's blueprint of manhood and what it's done for us lately." In D. David and Robert Brannon (eds.), *The 49% Majority.* Reading, MA: Addison-Wesley.

Branson, Susan. 2001. "Women and the family economy in the early Republic: The case of Elizabeth Meredith." In Joseph M. Hawes and Elizabeth I. Nybakken (eds.), *Family and Society in American History.* (pp. 72–94). Urbana: University of Illinois.

Braudy, Leo. 2003. *From Chivalry to Terrorism: War and the Changing Nature of Masculinity.* New York: Alfred A. Knopf.

Bregar, Louis. 2000. *Freud: Darkness in the Midst of Vision.* New York: John Wiley.

Bresnahan, Mary Jiang, Yasuhiro Inoue, and Wen Ying Liu. 2000. "Changing gender roles in prime-time commercials in Malaysia, Japan, Taiwan, and the United States. *Sex Roles* 45(1–2):117–31.

Briggs, Robin. 2002. *Witches and neighbours: The Social and Cultural Context of European Witchcraft.* Oxford, UK: Blackwell.

Brinton, Henry G. 1999. "Taking the church to uncharted waters." *Washington Post* April 4:A1, B5.

Broadbent, Kaye. 2001. "Shortchanged? Part-time workers in Japan." *Japanese Studies* 21(3): 293–304.

———. 2002a. "Flexibility at work: The feminisation of part-time work in Japan." *Journal of Industrial Relations* 44(1):3–18.

———. 2002b. "Gender and part-time work in Japan." *Equal Opportunities International* 21(3): 57–74.

Broadcasting. 1998. "Cover story: Women's work still excludes top jobs." 128(32):22.

Brock, Ann Graham. 2003. *Mary Magdalene, the First Apostle: The Struggle for Authority.* Cambridge, MA: Harvard University.

Brock, David. 2001. *Blinded by the Right: The Conscience of an Ex-Conservative.* New York: Crown.

Brockmann, Hilke. 2001. "Girls preferred? Changing patterns of sex preferences in the two German states." *European Sociological Review* 17(2):189–202.

Brod, Harry. 2003. "Scholarly studies on men: The new field is an essential complement to women's studies." In Estelle Disch (ed.), *Reconstructing Gender: A Multicultural Anthology.* (pp. 411–14). New York: McGraw-Hill.

Broder, Sheri. 2002. *Tramps, Unfit Mothers, and Neglected Children: Negotiating the Family in Nineteenth Century Philadelphia.* Philadelphia: University of Pennsylvania.

Brody, Jane E. 1996. "Sex and the survival of the fittest: Calamities are a disaster for men." *New York Times* April 24.

Brody, Leslie R. 2000. "The socialization of gender differences in emotional expression: Display rules, infant temperament and differentiation." In Agneta H. Fisher (ed.), *Gender and Emotion: Social Psychological Perspectives.* Cambridge, UK: Cambridge University.

Brooks, Fred. 2002. "Impacts of child care subsidies on family and child well-being." *Early Childhood Research Quarterly* 17(4):498–511.

Brooks, Geraldine. 2002. "Women in Islam." In John Miller and Aaron Kenedi (eds.), *Inside Islam: The Faith, the People, and the Conflicts of the World's Fastest-Growing Religion.* (pp. 213–34). New York: Marlowe.

Brown, Dorothy M. 1987. *Setting a Course: American Women in the 1920s.* Boston: Twayne.

Brown, Ian. 1994. *Man Medium Rare: Sex, Guns and Other Perversions of Masculinity.* New York: Dutton.

Brown, Jane D., and Laurie Schulze. 1990. "The effects of race, gender and fandom on audience interpretations of Madonna's music videos." *Journal of Communication* 40(2):88–102.

Brown, Lyn Mikel, and Carol Gilligan. 1992. *Meeting at the Crossroads: Women's Psychology and Girls' Development.* Cambridge, MA: Harvard University.

Brown, Norman M., and Ellen S. Amatea. 2000. *Love and Intimate Relationships: Journeys of the Heart.* Philadelphia: Brunner/Mazel.

Brown, Susan L. and Alan Booth. 1997. "Cohabitation versus marriage: A comparison of relationship quality." *Journal of Marriage and the Family* 58(3): 668–78.

Brown, Ursula M. 2000. *The Interracial Experience: Growing up Black/White in the United States.* Westport, CT: Praeger.

Browne, Kingsley R. 2002. *Biology at Work: Rethinking Sexual Equality.* New Brunswick, NJ: Rutgers University.

Bruni, Frank. 2001. "G.O.P. tries to counter lack of support among women." *New York Times* August 1:A14.

Buehrens, John A. 2003. *Understanding the Bible: An Introduction for Skeptics, Seekers, and Religious Liberals.* Boston: Beacon.

Bueno, Eva P. 2002. "One step at a time: Japanese women walking." *Journal of Mundane Behavior* 3(1).

Buijzen, Moniek, and Patti M. Valkenberg. 2000. "The impact of television advertising on children's Christmas wishes." *Journal of Broadcasting & Electronic Media* 44(3):456–70.

Buist, Kirsten, Maja Dekovic, Wim Meeus, and Marcel Van Aken. 2002. "Developmental patterns in adolescent attachment to mother, father and sibling." *Journal of Youth and Adolescence* 31(3):167–76.

Bullers, Susan. 2000. "The mediating role of perceived control in the relationship between social ties and depressive symptoms." *Women & Health* 31(2/3):97–116.

Bumiller, Elisabeth. 1995. The Secrets of Mariko. New York: Times Books.

Bumpus, Matthew F., Ann C. Crouter, and Susan M. McHale. 2001. "Parental autonomy granting during adolescence: Exploring gender differences in context." *Development Psychology* 37(2):163–73.

Bunch, Charlotte. 1993. "Prospects for global feminism." In Alison M. Jaggar and Paula S. Rothenberg (eds.), *Feminist Frameworks: Alternative Theoretical Accounts of the Relations Between Women and Men.* (pp. 249–52.) New York: McGraw-Hill.

Bunker, Barbara B., Josephine M. Zubek, Virginia J. Vanderslice, and Robert W. Rice. 1992. "Quality of life in dual-career families: Commuting versus single-residence couples." *Journal of Marriage and the Family* 54:399–407.

Bunster-Bunalto, Ximena. 1993. "Surviving beyond fear: Women and torture in Latin America." In Alison M. Jaggar and Paula S. Rothenberg (eds.), *Feminist Frameworks: Alternative Theoretical Accounts of the Relations Between Women and Men.* New York: McGraw-Hill.

Burchinal, Margaret R., Frank Porter Graham, and Lauren Nelson. 2000. "Family selection and child care experience: Implications for studies of child outcomes." *Early Childhood Research Quarterly* 15(3):385–411.

Bureau of Justice Statistics. 2002. "Rape and sexual assault: Reporting to police and medical attention, 1992–2000. Washington, DC: U.S. Department of Justice, Office of Justice Programs. Available online at: http://www.ojp.usdoj.gov/bjs/abstract/rsarp00

———. 2003a. "Intimate partner violence, 1993–2001." Washington, DC: U.S. Department of Justice, Office of Justice Programs. Available online at: http://www.ojp.usdoj.gov/bjs/abstract/ipv01

———. 2003b. *Sourcebook of Criminal Justice.* Washington DC: U.S. Department of Justice.

Burleson, Brent R, and Wayne H. Denton. 1997. "The relationship between communication skill and marital satisfaction: Some moderating effects." *Journal of Marriage and the Family* 59(4):884–902.

Burn, Shawn Meghan. 1996. *The Social Psychology of Gender.* New York: McGraw-Hill.

Burn, Shawn Meghan. 2000. "Heterosexuals' use of 'fag' and 'queer' to deride one another: A contributor to heterosexism and stigma." *Journal of Homosexuality* 50(2):1–11.

Burnett, Paul C. 2002. "Teacher praise and feedback and student's perceptions of the classroom environment." *Educational Psychology* 22(1):1–16.

Burns, Angie. 2000. "Looking for love in intimate heterosexual relationships." *Feminism & Psychology* 10(4):481–85.

———. 2002. "Women in love and men at work: The evolving heterosexual couple?" *Psychology, Evolution and Gender* 4(2):149–72.

Burris, Beverly H. 1991. "Employed mothers: The impact of social class and marital status on the prioritizing of family and work." *Social Science Quarterly* 72:50–66.

Burros, Marian. 1993. "Even women at top still have floors to do." *New York Times* May 31:1,11.

Burt, R. S. 1998. "The gender of social capital." *Rationality & Society* 10(1):5–46.

Bushman, Brad J., and L. Rowell Huesmann. 2001. "Effects of televised violence on aggression." In Dorothy G. Singer and Jerome L. Singer (eds.), *Handbook of Children and the Media.* Thousand Oaks, CA: Sage.

Buss, David M., Todd K. Shackelford, Lee A. Kirkpatrick, and Randy J. Larson. 2001. "A half century of mate preferences: The cultural evolution of values." *Journal of Marriage and the Family* 63(2):491–503.

Bussey, K., and Albert Bandura. 1992. "Self-regulatory mechanisms governing gender development." *Child Development* 63:1236–50.

Butler, Amy E. 2002. *Two Paths to Equality: Alice Paul and Ethel M. Smith in the ERA Debate, 1920–1929.* Albany: State University of New York.

Butsch, Richard. 2000. "Ralph, Fred, Archie, and Homer: Why television keeps recreating the white, male, working-class buffoon." In Tracey E. Ore (ed.), *The Social Construction of Difference and Inequality: Race, Class, Gender, and Sexuality.* (pp. 361–70). Mountain View, CA: Mayfield.

Butt, Peter. 2001. *Modern Legal Drafting: A Guide to Using Clearer Language.* Cambridge, NY: Cambridge University.

Buzawa, Eve S., and Carl G. Buzawa. 2003. *Domestic Violence: The Criminal Justice Response.* Thousand Oaks, CA: Sage.

Byrd, Barbara. 2001. "Great work if you can get it: Women in the skilled trades." In Mary C. King (ed.), *Squaring Up: Policy Strategies to Raise Women's Incomes in the United States.* (pp. 200–25). Ann Arbor: University of Michigan.

Cabrera, Natasha J., Catherine S. Tamis-LaMonda, and Robert H. Bradley. 2000. "Fatherhood in the twenty-first century." *Child Development* 71(1): 127–86.

Cagatay, Nilufer. 2001. *Gender, Poverty and Trade.* United Nations Development Program. New York: United Nations. Available online at: http://www.undp.org/rbap/Trade/Gender

Cagatay, Nilufer, Caren Grown, and Aida Santiago. 1989. "The Nairobi Women's Conference: Toward a global feminism." In Laurel Richardson and Verta Taylor (eds.), *Feminist Frontiers II: Rethinking Sex, Gender and Society.* New York: Random House.

Caiazza, Amy. 2002. "Does women's representation in elected office lead to women-friendly policy?" Research-in-Brief, May. IWPR Publication #1910 Institute for Women's Policy Research.

Campbell, D'Ann. 1984. *Women at War with America: Private Lives in a Patriotic Era.* Cambridge, MA: Harvard University.

Campbell, Patricia B., and Jo Sanders. 2002. "Challenging the system: Assumptions and data behind the push for single-sex schooling." In Amanda Datnow and Lea Hubbard (eds.), *Gender in Policy and Practice: Perspectives on Single-Sex and Coeducational Schooling.* New York: Routledge/ Falmer.

Canary, Daniel J., and Marianne Dainton (eds.). 2003. *Maintaining Relationships Through Communication: Relational, Contextual and Cultural Variations.* Mahwah, NJ: Lawrence Erlbaum.

Canedy, Dana. 2001. "Troubling label for Hispanics: 'Girls most likely to drop out.'" *New York Times* March 25:1, 20.

Canican, Francesca. 2003. "The feminization of love." In Michael S. Kimmel (ed.), *The Gendered Society Reader.* New York: Oxford University.

Cannold, Leslie. 2000. *The Abortion Myth: Feminism, Morality, and the Hard Choices Women Make.* Hanover, NH: Wesleyan University.

Cantor, Joanne L., L. Rowell Huesmann, Jo Groebel, Neil M. Malamuth, Emily A. Impett, Edward Donnerstein, Stacy Smith, and Brad J. Bushman. 2001. "Some hazards of television viewing: Fears, aggression and sexual attitudes." In Dorothy G. Singer and Jerome L. Singer (eds.), *Handbook of Children and the Media.* (pp. 207–307). Thousand Oaks, CA: Sage.

Cantor, Muriel G. 1993. Book review of *Women and Print Culture: The Construction of Femininity in the Early Periodical,* by Kathryn Shevelow. *Gender & Society* 7(2):301–2.

Caplow, Theodore, Louis Hicks, and Ben J. Wattenberg. 2001. *The First Measured Century.* Washington, DC: AEI Press

Carey, Philip. 2001. "One role model for all: The biblical meaning of submission." In Rita Halteman and Kari Finger Sandhaas (eds.), *The Wisdom of Daughters; Two Decades of the Voice of Christian Feminism.* Philadelphia: Innisfree Press.

Carllson, Ingvar. 1995. "Why?" Foreward to *Men on Men: Eight Swedish Men's Personal Views on Equality, Masculinity and Parenthood.* Stockholm, Sweden: Equality Affairs Division of the Ministry of Health and Social Affairs.

Carlson, Douglas W. 1990. "Discovering their heritage: Women and the American past." In June Steffensen Hagen (ed.), *Gender Matters: Women's Studies in the Christian Community.* Grand Rapids, MI: Zondervan.

Carlson, Mary. 1994. "A Trojan horse of worldliness? Maidservants in the burgher household in Rotterdam at the end of the seventeenth century." In Els Kloek, Nicole Teeuwen, and Marijke Huisman (eds.), *Women of the Golden Age: An International Debate on Women in Seventeenth-Century Holland, England and Italy.* Amsterdam: Hilversum Verloren.

Carpenter, Siri. 2001. "Does estrogen protect memory?" *Monitor on Psychology* 32(1):January. American Psychological Association. Available online at: http://www.apa.org/monitor/jan01/estrogen/html

Carr, Deborah. 2001. "Widowhood: Research dispels some common myths." Paper presented at the Population Association of America, March. http://www.umich.edu/~newsinfo/Releases/2001/Mar01

Carrington, Christopher. 1999. *No Place Like Home: Relationships and Family Life Among Lesbians and Gay Men.* Chicago: University of Chicago.

Cartier, Carolyn L. 2001. *Globalizing South China.* Oxford, UK: Blackwell.

Cartledge, Paul. 2003. *The Spartans: The World of Warrior-Heroes of Ancient Greece, From Utopia to Crisis and Collapse.* Woodstock, NY: Overlook.

Casey, M. B., E. Pezaris, and R. L. Nuttall. 1992. "Spatial ability as a predictor of math achievement: The importance of sex and handedness patterns." *Neuropsycholgia* 30:35–45.

Casper, Lynne M., and Philip N. Cohen. 2000. "How does POSSLQ measure up? National estimates of cohabitation." *Demography* 37(2):237–45.

Catalyst. 2002. *Women in law: Making the Case.* New York: Catalyst. Available online at: http://www.catalystwomen.org

Catanzarite, Lisa, and Vilma Ortiz. 1995. "Racial/ethnic differences in the impact of work and family on women's poverty." *Research in Politics and Society* 5:217–37.

Cate, Rodney M., Lauren A. Levin, and Lucinda S. Richmond. 2002. "Premarital relationship stability." *Journal of Personal and Social Relationships* 19(2):261–84.

Cauley, Jane A. et al. 2003. "Effects of estrogen plus progestin on risk of fracture and bone mineral density." *Journal of the American Medical Association* 290(13):1729–38.

CAWP. 2003a. "Women in elected office 2003: Fact Sheet Summaries." Center for American Women and Politics. Available online at: http://www.cawp.rutgers.edu

CAWP. 2003b. "Women in elected office 2003." Fact Sheet. Center for American Women and Politics. Available online at: http://www.cawp.rutgers.edu

Caygill, Lisa, Anne Campbell, and Louisa Shirley. 2002. "Sex-typed preferences in three domains: Do two-year olds need cognitive variables?" *British Journal of Psychology* 93(2):203–17.

CDC. 2002. *HIV/AIDS surveillance report.* Centers for Disease Control. Available online at: http://www.cdc.gov/hiv/stats.htm

————. 2003. "HIV/AIDS among U.S. women: Minority and young women at continuing risk." Centers for Disease Control. Available online at: http://www.cdc.gov/hiv/pubs/facts/women/htm

Center for Policy Alternatives. 2002. "Equal pay." *2002 Policy Summary.* Washington, DC: Center for Policy Alternatives. http://www.stateaction.org

Center on Budget and Policy Priorities. 2001. "Declining share of children lived with single parents in the late 1990s." June 15. http://www.cbpp.org/6-15-01wel2

Certain, Laura K., and Robert S. Kahn. 2002. "Prevalence, correlates, and trajectory of television viewing among infants and toddlers." *Pediatrics* 109(4):634–42.

Cervantes, Christi A., and Maureen A. Callanan. 1998. "Labels and explanations in mother-child emotion talk: Age and gender differentiation." *Developmental Psychology* 34(Jan.):88–98.

Chafetz, Janet Saltzman. 1988. *Feminist sociology: An Overview of Contemporary Theories.* Itasca, IL: F. E. Peacock.

Chamberlin, Marilyn S., and JoAnn S. Hickey. 2000. "Gender-based attribution of faculty performance by students: A cross-disciplinary case of stereotypes or reality?" Paper presented at the Southern Sociological Society, New Orleans, LA., April.

Chan, Patricia Meyer. 2000. Am I smart enough? Bright high school girls in advanced mathematics." *Dissertation Abstracts International Section A: Humanities & Social Sciences* 61(4-A):1305.

Chapman, James. 2000. *License to Thrill: A Cultural History of James Bond Films.* New York: Columbia University.

Chatty, Dawn. 2000. "Women and working in Oman: Individual choice and cultural constraints." *International Journal of Middle East Studies* 32(2):241-54.

Chaucer, L. S. 1998. *Reconcilable Differences: Confronting Beauty, Pornography and the Future of Feminism.* Berkeley: University of California.

Chen, Chuansheng, Kari Edwards, and Brandy Young. 2001. "Close relationships between Asian American and American college students." *Journal of Social Psychology* 141(1):85–100.

Cherlin, Andrew J. 1999. "Going to extremes: Family structure, children's well-being, and social science." *Demography* 36(4):421–8.

Cheshire, Tamara. 2001. "Cultural transmission in urban American Indian families." *American Behavioral Scientist* 44(9):1528–35.

Chesler, Ellen. 2001. "New options, new politics." *American Prospect* Fall:A12–A14.

Chesney-Lind, Meda. 2004. *The Female Offender: Girls, Women and Crime.* 2nd ed. Thousand Oaks, CA: Sage.

Chick, Kay A., Rose Ann Heilman-Houser, and Maxwell W. Hunter. 2002. "The impact of child care on gender role development and gender stereotypes." *Early Childhood Education Journal* 29(3):149–54.

Chilman, Catherine Street. 1995. "Hispanic families in the United States: Research perspectives." In Mark Robert Rank and Edward T. Kain (eds.), *Diversity and Change in Families: Patterns, Prospects, and Policies.* Englewood Cliffs, NJ: Prentice Hall.

Chira, Susan. 1998. *A Mother's Place: Taking the Debate About Working Mothers Beyond Guilt and Blame.* New York: HarperCollins.

Chodorow, Nancy. 1993. "Family structure and feminine personality." In Stevi Jackson et al. (eds.), *Women's Studies Essential Readings.* New York: New York University.

————. 2001. "The sexual sociology of adult life." In Roberta Satow (ed.), *Gender and Social Life.* (pp. 4–25). Needham Heights, MA: Allyn & Bacon.

Choi, Namkee G. 2001. "Relationship between life satisfaction and postretirement employment among older women." *International Journal of Aging & Human Development* 52(1):45–70.

Christ, Carol P. 1987. *Laughter of Aphrodite: Reflections on a Journey to the Goddess.* San Francisco: Harper & Row.

————. 2003a. *She Who Changes: Re-imagining the Divine in the World.* New York: Palgrave Macmillan.

————. 2003b. "Why women need the goddess: Phenomenological, psychological, and political reflections." In Philip E. Divine and Celia Wolf-Devine (eds.), *Sex and Gender: A Spectrum of Views.* (pp. 358–62). Belmont, CA: Wadsworth/Thompson.

Christensen, Bryce. 2001. "The strange politics of child support." *Society* 39(1):63–70.

Chung, Man Cheung, Steven Farmer et al. 2002. "Gender differences in love styles and post traumatic reactions following relationship dissolution." *European Journal of Psychiatry* 16(4): 210–20.

Ciabattari, Jane. 1996. "Oscar picks in the year of the backlash." *Parade Magazine* March 17:26.

————. 1999. "Women who could be President." *Parade Magazine* February 7:6–7.

Ciabattari, Teresa. 2002. "Are cohabiters sharing the housework? Mixed evidence from the NSFH." Paper at the Southern Sociological Society, New Orleans, LA. April.

Cicerello, Antoinette, and Eugene P. Sheehan. 1995. "Personal advertisements: A content analysis." *Journal of Social Behavior and Personality* 10:751–56.

Clark, Catherine L., Phillip R. Shaver, and Matthew F. Abrahams. 1999. "Strategic behaviors in romantic relationship initiation." *Personality and Social Psychology Bulletin* 25(6):707–20.

Clark, Ruth Anne. 1998. "A comparison of topics and objectives in a cross section of young men's and women's everyday conversations." In Daniel J. Canary and Kathryn Dindia (eds.), *Sex Differences and Similarities in Communication: Critical Essays and Empirical Investigations of Sex and Gender in Interaction.* (pp. 303–21). Mahwah, NJ: Lawrence Erlbaum.

Clark, Shelley. 2000. "Son preference and sex composition of children: Evidence from India." *Demography* 37(1):95–108.

Clark, Victoria. 2002. "Resistance and normalization in the construction of lesbian and gay families: A discursive analysis." In Adrian Coyle and Celia Kitzinger (eds.), *Lesbian and Gay Psychology: New Perspectives.* (pp. 98–116). Oxford, UK: BPS Blackwell.

Clarke, Simon. 2002. "Budgetary management in Russian households." *Sociology* 36(3):539–57.

Clason, Marmy. 2000. "The social construction of sexual harassment." *Women & Language* 23(2):56.

Claussen, Dane S. 2000. "'So far, news coverage of Promise Keepers has been more like advertising': The strange case of Christian men and the print mass media." In Dane S. Claussen (ed.), *The Promise Keepers: Essays on Masculinity and Christianity.* (pp. 281–307). Jefferson, NC: McFarland.

Cleary, Thomas, and Sartaz Aziz. 2000. *Twilight Goddess: Spiritual Feminism and Feminine Spirituality.* Boston: Shambhala.

Clements, Barbara Evans. 1994. *Daughters of Revolution: A History of Women in the USSR.* Arlington Heights, IL: Harlan Davidson.

Clements, Barbara Evans, Rebecca Friedman, and Dan Healey (eds.). 2002. *Russian Masculinities in History and Culture.* Houndmills, Hampshire, UK: Palgrave.

Clements, M. 1998. *The Impoverished Woman: Single Women Reinventing Single Life.* New York: W. W. Norton.

Clendinen, Dudley, and Adam Nagourney. 1999. *Out for good: The Struggle to Build a Gay Rights Movement in America.* New York: Simon & Schuster.

Clift, Eleanor. 2003. *Founding Sisters and the Nineteenth Amendment.* Boston: Wiley.

Clift, Eleanor, and Tom Brazaitis. 2003. *Madame President: Women Blazing the Leadership Trail.* New York: Routledge.

Clum, John M. 2002. *He's all Man: Learning Masculinity, Gayness and Love from American Movies.* New York: Palgrave.

CNN. 2002. "Pope responds to sex abuse cases." March 22. Available online at: http://www.cnn.com/2002/WORLD/europe/03/21/vatican.sex.abuse

Coates, Jennifer. 1998. "Gossip revisited: Language in all-female groups." In Jennifer Coates (ed.), *Language and Gender: A Reader.* Malden, MA: Blackwell.

———. 2003. *Men Talk: Stories in the Making of Masculinities.* Malden, MA: Blackwell.

Cobb, Nathan P., Jeffry H. Larson, and Wendy L. Watson. 2003. "The development of the attitudes about romance and mate selection scale." *Family Relations: Interdisciplinary Journal of Applied Family Studies.* 52(3):222–31.

Cofer, Judith Ortiz. 1995. "The myth of the Latin woman: I just met a girl named Maria." In Paula S. Rothenberg (ed.), *Race, Class, and Gender in the United States: An Integrated Study.* New York: St. Martin's.

Cohen, Carol. 2003. "Wars, wimps, and women: Talking gender and thinking war." In Michael S. Kimmel (ed.), *The Gendered Society Reader.* New York: Oxford University.

Cohen, Susan, and Mary F. Katzenstein. 1991. "The war over the family is not over the family." In Mark Hutter (ed.), *The Family Experience: A Reader in Cultural Diversity.* New York: Macmillan.

Cohen, Theodore F. 1993. "What do fathers provide? Reconsidering the economic and nurturant dimensions of men as parents." In Jane C. Hood (ed.), *Men, Work, and Family.* Newbury Park, CA: Sage.

Cohler, Bertram J., and Galatzer-Levy, Robert M. 2000. *The Course of Gay and Lesbian Lives: Social and Psychological Perspectives.* Chicago: University of Chicago.

Colapinto, John. 2000. *As Nature Made Him: The Boy Who was Raised as a Girl.* New York: HarperCollins.

Cole, Marcy Leslie. 2000. "The experience of never-married women in their thirties who desire marriage and children." *Dissertation Abstracts International, A: The Humanities and Social Sciences* 60(9):3526-A

Coleman, James William. 2001. *The New Buddhism: The Western Transformation of an Ancient Tradition.* Oxford, NY: Oxford University.

Coleman, Marilyn, Lawrence H. Ganong, and Mark A. Fine. 2000. "Reinvestigating remarriage: Another decade of progress." *Journal of Marriage and the Family* 62(4):1288–1307.

Colley, Ann, and Todd Zazie. 2002. "Gender-linked differences in the style and content of e-mails to friends." *Journal of Language and Social Psychology* 21(4):380–92.

Collins, Patricia Hill. 1993. "The meaning of motherhood in black culture and black mother/daughter relationships." In Jodi Wetzel, Maro Linn Espenlaub, Monys A. Hagen, Annette Bennington McElhiney, and Carmen Braun Williams (eds.), *Women's Studies Thinking Women.* Dubuque, IA: Kendall/Hunt.

———. 1996. "Toward a new vision: Race, class and gender as categories of analysis and connection." In Karen E. Rosenblum and Toni-Michelle Travis (eds.), *The Meaning of Difference: American Constructions of Race, Sex and Gender, Social Class and Sexual Orientation.* New York: McGraw-Hill.

Collins, Randall. 1975. *Conflict Sociology.* New York: Academic Press.

———. 1979. *The Credential Society: An Historical Sociology of Education and Stratification.* New York: Academic Press.

Coltrane, Scott. 1996. *Family Man: Fatherhood, Housework and Gender Equity.* New York: Oxford University.

———. 1997. "Scientific half-truths and postmodern parody in the family values debate." *Contemporary Sociology* 26(1):7–10.

———. 2003. "Household labor and the routine production of gender." In Michael S. Kimmel (ed.), *The Gendered Society Reader.* New York: Oxford University.

Coltrane, Scott, and Melinda Messineo. 2000. "The perpetuation of subtle prejudice: Race and gender imagery in 1990s television advertising." *Sex Roles* 42(5–6):363–89.

Colwell, Malinda J., Gregory S. Pettit, Darrell Meece, John E. Bates, and Kenneth A. Dodge. 2001. "Cumulative risk and continuity in nonparental care from infancy to early adolescence." *Merrill-Palmer Quarterly* 47(2):207–34.

Committee on Adolescence. 2003. "Identify and treating eating disorders." *Pediatrics* 111(1):204–11.

Comstock, George, and Haejung Paik. 1991. *Television and the American Child.* San Diego, CA: Academic Press.

Conkright, Lea, Dorothy Flannagan, and James Dykes. 2000. "Effects of pronoun type and gender role consistency on children's recall and interpretation of stories." *Sex Roles* 43(7–8):481–97.

Conlin, Michael. 1999. "Peer group micro-lending programs in Canada and the United States." *Journal of Development Economics* 60(1):249–69.

Connor, Daniel F. 2002. *Aggression and Antisocial Behavior in Children and Adolescents: Research and Treatment.* New York: Guilford.

Connor, Jane, Fiona Byrne, Jodi Mindell, Donna Cohen, and Elizabeth Nixon. 1986. "Use of the titles Ms., Miss, or Mrs.: Does it make a difference?" *Sex Roles* 14(9/10):545–49.

Conrad, Peter, and Joseph W. Schneider. 1990. "Professionalization, monopoly and the structure of medical practice." In Peter Conrad and Rochelle Kern (eds.), *The Sociology of Health and Illness: Critical Perspectives.* New York: St. Martin's.

Conroy, Carol A. 1998. "Influence of gender and program of enrollment on adolescents' and teens' occupational and educational aspirations." *Journal of Vocational and Technical Education* 14(2):18–28.

Constantine-Simms, Delroy. 2001. *The Greatest Taboo: Homosexuality in Black Communities.* Los Angeles: Alyson.

Conze, Susanne. 2001. "Women's work and emancipation in the Soviet Union, 1941–50." In Melani Ilic (ed.), *Women in the Stalin Era.* (pp. 216–35). Houndmills, Hampshire, UK: Palgrave.

Cooke, Miriam. 2001. *Women Claim Islam: Creating Islamic Feminism through Literature.* New York: Routledge.

Coolidge, Shelley Donald. 1997. "Honey, will I see you on Labor Day?" *Christian Science Monitor* August 26. Available online at: http://csmonitor.com/durable/1998/08/26/econ/econ.l.html

Coontz, Stephanie. 1992. *The Way We Never Were: American Families and the Nostalgia Trap.* New York: Basic Books.

———. 1997. *The Way We Really Are: Coming to Terms with America's Changing Families.* New York: Basic Books.

Cooper, Marianne. 2004. "Being the 'go-to guy': Fatherhood, masculinity, and the organization of work in Silicon Valley." In Michael S. Kimmel and Michael A. Messner (eds.), *Men's Lives.* (pp. 268–88). Boston: Allyn & Bacon

Corey, Shana. 2003. *Players in Pigtails.* New York: Scholastic.

Corliss, Richard. 2003. "Movies have the same old reliable guys and a crop of brand-new gals. It must be summer." *Time* July 14:57–58, 61.

Cornwall, A., and N. Lindisfarne. 1994. *Dislocating Masculinity: Comparative Ethnographies.* London: Routledge.

Correll, Shelley J. 2001. "Gender and the career choice process: The role of biased self-assessments." *American Journal of Sociology* 106(6): 1691–730.

Cose, Ellis. 1995. *A Man's World: How Real is Male Privilege and How High is its Price?* New York: HarperCollins.

Costello, Cynthia B., and Anne J. Stone. 2002. *The American Woman: 2001–2002: Getting to the Top.* New York: Women's Research & Education Institute.

Cote, Linda R., and Sandra T. Azar. 1997. "Child age, parent and child gender, and domain differences in parents' attributions and responses to children's outcomes." *Sex Roles* 36(1–2):23–51.

Countdown 2005. 1997. "USAID takes initiative." *Newsletter of the Microcredit Summit Campaign* 1(2):10–11.

Courtenay, Will H. 2000. "Behavioral factors associated with disease, injury and death among men: Evidence and implications for prevention." *Journal of Men's Studies* 9(1):81–142.

Courtney, Alice E., and Sarah Wernick Lockeretz. 1971. "A woman's place: An analysis of the roles portrayed by women in magazine advertisements." *Journal of Marketing Research* 8:92.

Courtney, Alice E., and Thomas W. Whipple. 1983. *Sex Stereotyping in Advertising.* Lexington, MA: Lexington Books.

Cowan, Gloria. 2000a. "Beliefs about causes of four types of rape." *Sex Roles* 42(9–10):807–23.

———. 2000b. "Women's hostility toward women and rape and sexual harassment myths." *Violence Against Women* 6(3):238–46.

Cowan, J. L. 2002. "Inverse discrimination." In Stephen Cahn (ed.), *The Affirmative Action Debate* (pp. 5–7). London: Routledge.

Cowley, Geoffrey, and Karen Springen. 2002. "The end of the age of estrogen?" *Newsweek* June 22: 38–41.

Cox, Deborah L., Sally D. Stabb, and Joseph F. Hulgus. 2000. "Anger and depression in girls and boys: A study of gender differences." *Psychology of Women Quarterly* 24(1):110–12.

Cox, Martha C., Blair Paley, and C. Chris Payne. 1999. "The transition to parenthood: Marital conflict and withdrawal and parent-infant interactions." in Martha J. Cox and Jeanne Brooks-Gunn (eds.), *Conflict and Cohesion in Families: Causes and Consequences.* (pp. 87–104). Mahwah, NJ: Lawrence Erlbaum.

Coyle, Adrian, and Celia Kitzinger (eds.). 2002. *Lesbian and Gay Psychology: New Perspectives.* Oxford, UK: BPS Blackwell.

CPS. 2001. "Highlights of women's earnings in 2000." *Current Population Survey*, August.

Washington, DC: U.S. Census Bureau/Bureau of Labor Statistics.

Craig, Steve. 2003. "Madison Avenue versus the feminine mystique: The advertising industry's response to the women's movement." In Sherrie A. Inness (ed.), *Disco Divas: Women and Popular Culture in the 1970s.* (pp. 24–38). Philadelphia: University of Pennsylvania.

Crawford, Mary. 1995. *Talking Difference: On Gender and Language.* London: Sage.

Crawford, Mary, Amy C. Stark, and Catherine Hackett Renner. 1998. "The meaning of Ms.: Social assimilation of a gender concept." *Psychology of Women's Quarterly* 22(2):197–208.

Crean, Susan. 1993. "Anna Karenina, Scarlett O'Hara, and Gail Bezaire: Child custody and family law reform." In Anne Minas (ed.), *Gender Basics: Feminist Perspectives on Women and Men.* Belmont, CA: Wadsworth.

Crimmins, Eileen M., and Yasuhiko Saito. 2001. "Trends in healthy life expectancy in the United States, 1970–1990: Gender, race and educational differences." *Social Science & Medicine* 52(11): 1629–41.

Crites, Laura L. 1987. "Wife abuse: The judicial record." In Laura L. Crites and Winifred L. Hepperle (eds.), *Women, the Courts and Equality.* Beverly Hills, CA: Sage.

Crittenden, Ann. 2001. *The Price of Motherhood: Why the Most Important Job in the World is the Least Valuable.* New York: Metropolitan/Owl.

Croll, Elisabeth J. 2000. *Endangered Daughters: Discrimination and Development in Asia.* London: Routledge.

Crosnoe, Robert, Kristan G. Erickson, and Sanford M. Dornbusch. 2000. "Protective functions of family relationships and school factors on the deviant behavior of adolescent boys and girls: Reducing the impact of risky relationships." *Youth and Society* 33(4):515–44.

Cross, Susan E., and Hazel Rose Markus. 1993. "Gender in thought, belief and action: A cognitive approach." In Anne E. Beall and Robert J. Sternberg (eds.), *The Psychology of Gender.* New York: Guilford.

Crouter, Ann C., Melissa R. Head, Matthew F. Bumpass, and Susan M. McHale. 2001. "Household chores: Under what conditions do mothers lean on daughters?" In Andrew J. Fuligni (ed.), *Family Obligation and Assistance During Adolescence: Contextual Variations and Developmental Implications.* (pp. 23–41). San Francisco: Jossey-Bass.

Crowder, Kyle D., and Stewart E. Tolnay. 2000. "A new marriage squeeze for black women: The role of racial intermarriage by black men." *Journal of Marriage and the Family* 62(3): 792–807.

Crowley, Donna Annyce. 2001. "Gender-linked differences in the use of references to location in written language: A gender schema approach." *Dissertation Abstracts International: Section B: Sciences and Engineering* 62(2-B):1107.

Crowther, Bosley. 2000. "Movies to kill people by." In Stephen Prince (ed.), *Screening Violence.* (pp. 51–53). New Brunswick, NJ: Rutgers University.

Cruz, Yolanda. 1996. "A twofer's lament." In Harold A. Widdison (ed.), *Social Problems 96/97* (Annual Editions). Guilford, CT: Dushkin/Brown & Benchmark.

Cullen, Lisa Takeucki. 2003. "I want your job, lady!" *Time* May 12:52–56.

Cunningham, Mick. 2001a. "The influence of parental behaviors on children's attitudes toward gender and household labor in early adulthood." *Journal of Marriage and the Family* 63(1):111–22.

Cunningham, Mick. 2001b. "Parental influences on the gendered division of housework." *American Sociological Review* 66(2):184–203.

Curran, Laura, and Laura S. Abrams. 2000. "Making men into dads: Fatherhood, the state, and welfare reform. *Gender & Society* 14(5):662–78.

Curry, Timothy Jon. 2004. "Fraternal bonding in the locker room: A profeminist analysis of talk about competition and women." In Michael S. Kimmel and Michael A. Messner (eds.), *Men's Lives.* (pp. 204–17). Boston: Allyn & Bacon.

Curtis, Kristen Taylor, and Christopher F. Ellison. 2002. "Religious heterogamy and marital conflict." *Journal of Family Issues* 62(3):792–807.

Curzan, Anne. 2003. *Gender Shifts in the History of English.* Cambridge, UK: Cambridge University.

Cussins, Charis M. Thompson. 2000. "Primate suspect: Some varieties of science studies." In Shirley C. Strum and Linda M. Fedigan (eds.), *Primate Encounters: Models of Science, Gender and Society.* (pp. 329–57). Chicago: University of Chicago.

D'Acci, Julie. 1994. *Defining Women: Television and the Case of Cagney and Lacey.* Chapel Hill, NC: University of North Carolina.

Dade, Lennell R., and Lloyd R. Sloan. 2000. "An investigation of sex-role stereotypes in African Americans." *Journal of Black Studies* 30(5):676–90.

Dahan-Kalev, Henriette. 2001. "Tensions in Israeli feminism: The Mizrahi Ashkenazi Rift." *Women's Studies International Forum* 24(6):669–84.

———. 2003. "Mizrahi feminism: The unheard voice." In Kalpana Mira and S. Rich (eds.), *Jewish Feminism in Israel: Some Contemporary Perspectives.* (pp. 96–112). Hanover, NH: University Press of New England.

Dahrendorf, Ralf. 1959. *Class and Class Conflict in Industrial Society.* Stanford, CA: Stanford University.

Dalton, Claire and Elizabeth M. Schneider. 2000. *Battered Women and the Law.* New York: Foundation Press.

Daly, Frederica Y. 1994. "Perspectives of Native American women on race and gender." In Ethel Tobach and Betty Rosoff (eds.), *Challenging Racism and Sexism: Alternatives to Genetic Explanations.* New York: The Feminist Press.

Daly, Mary. 1991. "I thank thee, Lord, that thou has not created me a woman." In Evelyn Ashton-Jones and Gary Olson (eds.), *The Gender Reader.* Boston: Allyn & Bacon.

Daniel, Jessica Henderson. 1999. "Adolescent girls of color: Declaring their place and 'voice.'" In Norine G. Johnson, Michael C. Roberts, and Judith Worrell (eds.), *Beyond Appearance: A New Look at Adolescent Girls.* Washington, DC: American Psychological Association.

Daniels, Cynthia. 1993. "There's no place like home." In Alison M. Jaggar and Paula S. Rothenberg (eds.), *Feminist Frameworks: Alternative Theoretical Accounts of the Relations between Women and Men.* New York: McGraw-Hill.

Dansky, B. S., and D. G. Kilpatrick. 1997. "Effects of sexual harassment." In W. O'Donahue (ed.), *Sexual Harassment: Theory, Research and Treatment.* (pp. 152–74). New York: Allyn & Bacon.

Darling, Lynn. 1994. "Age, beauty and truth." *New York Times* January 23 (Section 9):1, 5.

Das Gupta, Monica. 2002. *Why is Son Preference so Persistent in East and South Asia?* Washington, DC: World Bank.

Daswani, Kavita. 1999. "Second wives club." *South China Morning Post Magazine,* November 28:7–14

Daulaire, Nils, Pat Leidl, Laurel Mackin, Colleen Murphy, and Laura Stark. 2002. *Promises to Keep: The Toll of Unintended Pregnancies on Women's Lives in the Developing World.* Washington, DC: Global Health Council

David, Grainger. 2003. "Alpha romeos." *Fortune,* August 11:48, 50.

Davidson, Sara. 1988. "Having it all." In J. Gipson Wells (ed.), *Current Issues in Marriage and the Family.* New York: Macmillan.

Davies, Bronwyn. 1989. *Frogs and Snails and Feminist Tales: Preschool Children and Gender.* Sydney: Allen & Unwin.

Davies, Lorraine, William R. Avison, and Donna D. McAlpine. 1997. "Significant life experiences and depression among single and married mothers." *Journal of Marriage and the Family* 59(2):294–308.

Davis, Elizabeth Gould. 1971. *The First Sex.* New York: Penguin.

Davis, Laurel R. 1997. *The Swimsuit Issue and Sport: Hegemonic Masculinity in Sports Illustrated.* Albany: State University of New York.

Dawson, Jane. 2002. "Egalitarian responses in postcommunist Russia." In Craig N. Murphy (ed.), *Egalitarian Politics in the Age of Globalization.* (pp. 96–123). Houndmills, Hampshire, UK: Palgrave.

DeBeauvoir, Simone. 1953. *The Second Sex.* H. M. Parshey (tr.). New York: Knopf.

Debow, Larry. 2003. "Veronis' advertising '03: Steady as she goes." August 11. Outdoor Advertising Association of America. Available online at: http://www.oaaa.org/news/release.asp? RELEASE_ID=1370

De Brauw, Alan, Jikun Huang, and Scott Rozelle. 2002. "The evolution of China's rural labor markets during the reforms." *Journal of Comparative Economics* 30(2):329–53.

Deckard, Barbara Sinclair. 1983. *The Women's Movement: Political, Socioeconomic and Psychological Issues.* New York: Harper & Row.

Deen, Edith. 1978. *Wisdom from Women in the Bible.* San Francisco: Harper & Row.

DeFrancisco, Victoria Leto. 1998. "The sounds of silence: How men silence women in marital relations." In Jennifer Coates (ed.): *Language and Gender: A Reader.* Malden, MA: Blackwell.

DeGenova, Mary Kay. 1997. *Families in Cultural Context: Strengths and Challenges in Diversity.* Mountain View, CA: Mayfield.

De Hart, Jane Sherron, and Linda K. Kerber. 2003. "Introduction: Gender and the new women's history." In Linda K. Kerber and Jane Sherron De Hart (eds.), *Women's America: Refocusing the Past.* New York: Oxford University.

DeKeserdy, Walter S., and Martin D. Schwartz. 1998. *Woman Abuse on Campus: Results from the Canadian National Survey.* Thousand Oaks, CA: Sage.

Delaney, Janice, Mary Jane Lupton, and Emily Toth. 1988. *The Curse: A Cultural History of Menstruation.* Urbana: University of Illinois.

DeLeon, B. 1993. "Sex role identity among college students: A cross-cultural analysis. *Hispanic Journal of Behavioral Sciences* 15:476–89.

Dement'eva, I. F. 2001. "Negative factors of childrearing in a single-parent family." *Sotsiologicheskie Issledovaniya* (abstract) 27(11):108–13.

Demos, John Putnam. 1996. "The poor and powerless witch." In Mary Beth Norton and Ruth M. Alexander (eds.), *Major Problems in American Women's History.* Lexington, MA: D. C. Heath.

Dempsey, Kenneth C. 2001. "Feelings about housework: Understanding gender differences." *Australian Journal of Marriage and the Family* 7(2): 141–59.

De Munck, Victor C., and Andrey Korotayev. 1999. "Sexual equality and romantic love: A reanalysis of Rosenblatt's study on the function of romantic love." *Cross-Cultural Research* 33(3):265–77.

Dennerstein, L., E. Dudley, and J. Guthrie. 2002. "Empty nest or revolving door? A prospective of women's quality of life in midlife during the phase of children leaving and reentering home." *Psychological Medicine* 32:545–50.

Denzin, Norman. 1992. *Symbolic Interactionism and Cultural Studies: The Politics of Interpretation.* Cambridge, MA: Blackwell.

———. 1993. "Sexuality and gender: An interactionist/poststructural reading." In Paula England (ed.), *Theory on Gender/Feminism on Theory.* New York: Aldine De Gruyter.

Dervanics, Charles. 2003. "Educators, activists criticize Bush's position on affirmative action." *Black Issues in Higher Education* February 13.

Desai, Manisha. 2001. "India: Women's movement from nationalism to sustainable development." In Ly Walter (ed.), *Women's Rights: A Global View.* (pp. 99–112). Westport, CT: Greenwood.

De St. Croix, Geoffrey. 1993. "The class struggle in the ancient Greek world." In Stevi Jackson et al. (eds.), *Women's Studies Essential Readings.* New York: New York University.

DeSantis, Mark, and Nathan Sierra. 2000. "Women smiled more often and openly than men when photographed for a pleasant, public occasion in

20-super(th) century United States Society." *Psychology: A Journal of Human Behavior* 37(3–4): 21–31.

Despeaux, Catherine, and Livia Kohn. 2003. *Women in Daoism.* Cambridge, MA: Three Pines.

Deutsch, Francine. 1999. *Having it All: How Equally Shared Parenting Works.* Cambridge, MA: Harvard University.

———. 2004. "Strategies men use to resist." In Michael S. Kimmel and Michael A. Messner (eds.), *Men's Lives.* (pp. 469–74). Boston: Allyn & Bacon.

Deutscher, Irwin. (with Linda Lindsey). 2005. *Preventing Ethnic Conflict: Successful Cross-National Social Strategies.* Lanham, MD: Rowman & Littlefield.

Devens, Carol. 1996. "Resistance to Christianity by the native women of New France." In Mary Beth Norton and Ruth M. Alexander (eds.), *Major Problems in American Women's History.* Lexington, MA: D.C. Heath.

De Waal, Frans B. M, and Peter L. Tyack (eds.). 2003. *Animal Social Complexity: Intelligence, Culture, and Individualized Societies.* Cambridge, MA: Harvard University.

Diamond, Milton. 1982. "Sexual identity, mono-zygotic twins reared in discordant sex roles and a BBC follow-up." *Archives of Sexual Behavior* 11:181–86.

Diamond, Milton, and H. K. Sigmundson. 1997. "Management of intersexuality: Guidelines for dealing with people with ambiguous genitalia." *Archives of Pediatric and Adolescent Medicine* 151:1046–50.

Diaz, Rafael M., George Ayala, and Edward Bein. 2001. "The impact of homophobia, poverty, and racism on the mental health of gay and bisexual Latino men: Findings from three U.S. cities." *American Journal of Public Health* 91(6):927–32.

Diehl, David. 1990. "Theology and feminism." In June S. Hagen (ed.), *Gender Matters: Women's Studies for the Christian Community.* Grand Rapids, MI: Zondervan.

Dietrich, Lisa C. 1998. *Chicana Adolescents: Bitches, 'Ho's, and Schoolgirls.* Westport, CT: Praeger.

Dietz, Tracy L. 1995. "Patterns of intergenerational assistance within the Mexican American family: Is the family taking care of the older generation's needs?" *Journal of Family Issues* 16(3):344–56.

Diner, Hasia, and Beryl Lieff Benderly. 2002. *Her Works Praise Her: A History of Jewish Women in America from Colonial Times to the Present.* New York: Basic Books.

Ditsworth, Dahlia. 2001. "The portrayal of gender in the children's television program Sesame Street and its effects on the unintended audience." *New Jersey Journal of Communication* 9(2):214–26.

Dittman, Ralf W. 1998. "Ambiguous genitalia, gen-der-identity problems, and sex reassignment." *Journal of Sex & Marital Therapy* 24(4):255–71.

Divorce. 2002. "World divorce statistics." *Divorce Magazine.* Available online at: http://www.divorcemag.com/statistics/statsWorld

Dobash, Russell P., R. Emerson Dobash, Margo Wilson, and Martin Daly. 2004. "The myth of sexual symmetry in marital violence." In Michael S. Kimmel (ed.), *The Gendered Society Reader.* Oxford, NY: Oxford University.

Dodd, Elizabeth, Traci A. Giuliano, and Jori M. Boutell. 2001. "Respected or rejected: Perceptions of women who confront sexist remarks." *Sex Roles* 45(7–8):567–77.

Dodd, David K., Brenda L. Russell, and Cynthia Jenkins. 1999. "Smiling in school yearbook photos: Gender differences from kindergarten to adulthood." *The Psychological Record* 49(4): 543–54.

Dodge, Norton D., and Murray Feshbach. 1992. "The role of women in Soviet agriculture." In Beatrice Farnsworth and Lynnes Viola (eds.), *Russian Peasant Women.* New York: Oxford University.

Doezema, Jo. 1998. "Forced to choose: Beyond the voluntary v. forced prostitution dichotomy." In Kamala Kempadoo and Jo Doezema (eds.), *Global Sex Workers: Rights, Resistance, and Redefinition* (pp. 34–50). New York: Routledge.

Doka, Kenneth A., and Terry Martin. 2001. "Take it like a man: Masculine response to loss." In Dale A. Lund (ed.), *Men Coping with Grief.* Amityville, NY: Baywood.

Dombrowski, Daniel A., and Robert Deltete. 2000. *A Brief, Liberal, Catholic Defense of Abortion.* Urbana: University of Illinois.

Donovan, Josephine. 1985. *Feminist Theory: The Intellectual Traditions of American Feminism.* New York: Frederick Ungar.

Dorfman, Daba C. 2001. "The impact of mother's work on the life choices and sense of self of the young adult daughter during motherhood." *Dissertation Abstracts International, A: The Humanities and Social Sciences* 62(1):327-A.

Douglas, Susan J. 1995. "Missing voices: Women and the U.S. news media." In Sheila Ruth (ed.), *Issues in Feminism: An Introduction to Women's Studies.* Mountain View, CA: Mayfield.

Douglas, William, and Beth M. Olson. 1995. "Beyond family structure: The family in domestic comedy." *Journal of Broadcasting & Electronic Media* 39:236–61.

Dowling, Colette. 2000. *The Frailty Myth: Women Approaching Physical Equality.* New York: Random House.

Doyal, Lesley. 2000. "Gender equity in health: Debates and dilemmas" *Social Science & Medicine* 51(6):931–9.

Doyle, James A. 1995. *The Male Experience.* Dubuque, IA: Brown & Benchmark.

Drake, Christopher R., and Marita P. McCabe. 2000. "Extrarelationship involvement among heterosexual males: An explanation based on the theory of planned behavior, relationship quality, and past behavior." *Journal of Applied Social Psychology* 30(7):1421–39.

Drucker, Jane. 2001. *Lesbian and Gay Families Speak Out: Understanding The Joys and Challenges of Diverse Family Life.* Reading, MA: Perseus.

D'Souza, Neila, and Ramini Natarajan. 1986. "Women in India: The reality." In Lynn B. Iglitzin and Ruth Ross (eds.), *Women in the World, 1975–1985: The Women's Decade.* Santa Barbara, CA: ABC-Clio.

Dublin, Thomas. 1996. "Women workers in the Lowell mills." In Mary Beth Norton and Ruth M. Alexander (eds.), *Major Problems in American Women's History.* Lexington, MA: D. C. Heath.

Duck, Steve, and P. H. Wright. 1993. "Re-examining gender differences in same-gender friendships." *Sex Roles* 32(5–6):375–91.

Dugger, Karen. 1991. "Social location and gender-role attitudes: A comparison of black and white women." In Judith Lorber and S. A. Farrell (eds.), *The Social Construction of Gender.* Newbury Park, CA: Sage.

Duncan, Karen A. et al. 1999. "Balancing employment and household work activities: The role of workplace location." *Canadian Home Economics Journal* 49(1):17–23.

Dunn, Mary Maples. 2001. "Saints and sisters: Congregational and Quaker women in the early colonial period." In Robert R. Mathisen (ed.), *Critical Issues in American History: A Reader.* Waco, TX: Baylor University.

Duran-Aydintug, Candan, and Kelly A. Causey. 2001. "Child custody determination: Implications for lesbian mothers." In Jennifer M. Lehmann (ed.), *The Gay and Lesbian Marriage and Family Reader: Analyses of Problems and Prospects for the 21st Century.* (pp. 47–64). New York: Gordian Knot.

Duxbury, Linda, and Christopher Higgins. 1994. "Interference between work and family: A status report on dual-career and dual-earner mothers and fathers." *Employee Assistance Quarterly* 9(3–4):55–80.

Dziech, Billie Wright, and Michael W. Hawkins. 1998. *Sexual Harassment in Higher Education: Reflections and New Perspectives.* New York: Garland.

Eagly, A. H., R. D. Ashmore, M. G. Makhijani, and L. C. Longo. 1991. "What is beautiful is good, but . . . : A meta-analytic review of research on the physical attractiveness stereotype." *Psychological Bulletin* 110:109–28.

Eccles, Jacquelynne S., Carol Freedman-Doan, Pam From, Janis Jacobs, and Yoon Kwang Suk. 2000. "Gender-role socialization in the family: A longitudinal approach." In Thomas Eckes and Hanns M. Trautner (eds.), *The Developmental Social Psychology of Gender.* Mahwah, NJ: Lawrence Erlbaum.

Eckert, Penelope, and Sally McConnell-Ginet. 2003. *Language and Gender.* Cambridge, UK: Cambridge University.

Economist. 2001. "Third person singular: Finding substitutes for 'he' and 'his.'" April 14:20.

Eder, Donna, and David A. Kinney. 1995. "The effect of middle school extracurricular activities on adolescent's popularity and peer status." *Youth and Society* 26(3):298–324.

Edin, Kathryn. 2000a. "What do low-income single mothers say about marriage?" *Social Problems* 47(1):112–33.

———. 2000b. "Few good men: Why poor mothers don't marry or remarry." *American Prospect* 11(4):26–31.

Edsall, Thomas B. 1999. "Women's political muscle is shaping the 2000 race." *Washington Post* March 11:A1, A18–19.

Edwards, June. 2002. *Women in American Education, 1820–1955: The Female Force and Educational Reform.* Westport, CT: Greenwood.

Edwards, Tamala. 2000. "Flying solo." *Time* August 28: 47–53.

Egan, Jennifer. 1999, "Why a priest?" *The New York Times Magazine* April 4:28–33.

Egan, Susan K., and David G. Perry. 2001. "Gender identity: A multidimensional analysis for psychological adjustment." *Developmental Psychology* 37(4):451–63.

Eggebeen, David J., and Chris Knoester. 2001. "Does fatherhood matter for men?" *Journal of Marriage and the Family* 63(2):381–93.

Ehlers, Tracy Bachrach. 1993. "Debunking marianismo: Economic vulnerability and survival struggles among Guatemalan wives." In Mari Womack and Judith Marti (eds.) *The Other Fifty Percent: Multicultural Perspectives on Gender Relations.* Prospect Heights, IL: Waveland.

Ehrenreich, Barbara. 1998. "The silenced majority: Why the average working person has disappeared from American media and culture." In Margaret L. Andersen and Patricia Hill Collins (eds.), *Race, Class and Gender: An Anthology* (pp. 147–49). Belmont, CA: Wadsworth.

Ehrlich, Susan, and Ruth King. 1993. "Gender-based language reform and the social construction of meaning." In Stevi Jackson et al. (eds.), *Women's Studies Essential Readings.* New York: New York University.

Eichstedt, Julie A., Lisa A. Serbin, Diane Poulin-Dubois, and Maya G. Sen. 2002. "Of bears and men: Infants' knowledge of conventional and metaphorical gender stereotypes." *Infant Behavior & Development* 25(3):296–310.

Eisler, Riane Tennenhaus. 1995a. *The Chalice and the Blade: Our History, Our Future.* San Francisco: HarperSanFrancisco.

———. 1995b. *Sacred Pleasure: Sex, Myth, and the Politics of the Body.* San Francisco: HarperSanFrancisco.

Eisler, Riane, and David Loye. 1990. *The Partnership Way.* New York: HarperSanFrancisco.

Eisold, Barbara K. 2001. "Recreating mother: The consolidation of 'heterosexual' gender identification in the young sons of homosexual men." In Jennifer M. Lehmann (ed.), *The Gay and Lesbian Marriage and Family Reader: Analyses of Problems and Prospects for the 21st Century* (pp. 221–38). New York: Gordian Knot.

Eitzen Stanley, and George H. Sage. 2003. *Sociology of North American Sport.* New York: McGraw-Hill.

El Guindi, Fadwa 1999. *Veil: Modesty, Privacy and Resistance.* Oxford, UK: Berg.

Elasmar, Michael, Kazumi Hasegawa, and Mary Brain. 1999. "The portrayal of women in U.S. prime time television." *Journal of Broadcasting & Electronic Media* 43(1):20–34.

Elizabeth, Vivienne. 2000. "Cohabitation, marriage, and the unruly consequences of difference." *Gender & Society* 14(1):87–110.

Eller, Cynthia. 2000. *The Myth of Matriarchal Prehistory: Why an Invented Past Won't give Women a Future.* Boston: Beacon.

Elliot, Leland, and Cynthia Brantley. 1997. *Sex on Campus: The Naked Truth about the Real Lives of College Students.* New York: Random House.

Elliott, Brian, 1994. "Biography, family history and the analysis of social change." In Michael Drake (ed.), *Time, Family and Community: Perspectives on Family and Community History.* Oxford, UK: Open University.

Elliott, Marta. 2001. "Gender differences in causes of depression." *Women & Health* 33(3/4):163–77.

Ellis, L. 1986. "Evidence of neuroandrogenic etiology of sex roles from a combined analysis of human, nonhuman primate and nonprimate, mammalian studies." *Personality and Individual Differences* 7:519–52.

Ellison, Christopher, and John P. Bartkowski. 2002. "Conservative Protestantism and the division of household labor among married couples." *Journal of Family Issues* 23(8):950–85.

Elliston, Deborah. 1999. "Negotiating transnational sexual economies: Female and same-sex sexuality in 'Tahiti and Her Islands.'" In Evelyn Blackwood and Saskia Wieringa (eds.), *Female Desires: Same-Sex Relations and Transgender Practices across Cultures.* New York: Columbia University.

Ellyson, S. L., J. F. Dovidio, and C. E. Brown. 1992. "The look of power: Gender differences and similarities." In Cecilia Ridgeway (ed.), *Gender Interaction and Inequality.* New York: Springer-Verlag.

Elper, Ora Wiskind, and Susan Handelman (eds.). 2000. *Torah of the Mothers: Contemporary Jewish Women Read Classical Texts.* New York: Urim.

Engel, Gina, Kenneth R. Olson, and Carol Patrick. 2002. "The personality of love: Fundamental motives and traits related to components of love." *Personality and Individual Differences* 32(5):839–53.

Engels, Friedrich. 1942 (original 1884). *The Origin of the Family, Private Property, and the State.* New York: International.

Engelsman, Joan Chamberlain. 1994. *The Feminine Dimension of the Divine.* Wilmette, IL: Chiron.

England, Paula, Joan A. Hermson, and David A. Cotter. 2000. "The devaluation of women's work: A comment on Tam." *American Journal of Sociology* 105(6):1741–51.

Epstein, Cynthia Fuchs. 1997. "The myths and justifications of sex segregation in higher education: VMI and the Citadel." *Duke Journal of Gender Law and Policy* 4:185–210.

———. 1998. "Great divides: Deceptive distinctions and rhetorical strategies in the VMI and Citadel cases." *Gender Issues* 16(1–2):34–46.

Erdwins, Carol J., Louis C. Buffardi, Wendy J. Casper, and Alison O'Brien. 2001. "The relationship of women's role strain to social support, role satisfaction, and self-efficacy." *Family Relations* 50(3):230–38.

Erera, Pauline I., and Karen Fredriksen. 2001. "Lesbian stepfamilies: A unique family structure." In Jennifer M. Lehmann (ed.), *The Gay and Lesbian Marriage and Family Reader: Analyses of Problems and Prospects for the 21st Century.* (pp. 80–94). Lincoln, NE: Gordian Knot.

Eskridge, William N., and Nan D. Hunter. 2001. *Sexuality, Gender and the Law.* New York: Foundation Press.

Esterberg, Kristin, Phyllis Moen, and Donna Demster McClain. 1994. "Transition to divorce: A life course approach to women's marital duration and dissolution." *Sociological Quarterly* 35(2):289–307.

Etaugh, Claire. 2001. "Attitudes of employed women towards parents who choose full-time or part-time employment following their child's birth. *Sex Roles* 44(9/10):611–19.

Evans, Debra. 1993. *Beauty and the Best.* Colorado Springs, CO: Focus on the Family Publishing.

Evans, Lorraine, and Kimberley, Davies. 2000. "No sissy boys here: A content analysis of the representation of masculinity in elementary school reading textbooks." *Sex Roles* 42(3–4):255–70.

Evans, Sara. 2000. "The first American women." In Linda K. Kerber and Jane Sherron De Hart (eds.), *Women's America: Refocusing the Past.* (pp. 30–38). New York: Oxford University.

Ezawa, Aya Elise. 2003. "Motherhood, family and inequality in contemporary Japan." *Dissertation Abstract International, A: The Humanities and Social Sciences* 63,11:4113–4114-A

Fagot, Beverly I., and Mary D. Leinbach. 1995. "Gender knowledge in egalitarian and traditional families." *Sex Roles* 32(7–8):513–26.

Fagot, Beverly I., and Leslie Leve. 1998. "Gender identity and play." In Doris Pronin Fromberg and Doris Bergen (eds.), *Play from Birth to Twelve and Beyond: Contexts, Perspectives, and Meanings.* New York: Garland.

Faludi, Susan. 1996. "Backlash." In Karen E. Rosenblum and Toni-Michelle Travis (eds.), *The Meaning of Difference: American Constructions of Race, Sex and Gender, Social Class and Sexual Orientation.* New York: McGraw-Hill.

———. 2000. *Stiffed: The Betrayal of the American Man.* San Francisco: HarperCollins.

Fan, Cindy, and Youqin Huang. 1998. "Waves of rural brides: Female marriage migration in China." *Annals of the Association of American Geographers* 88(2):227–51.

Fan, Cindy C., and Ling Li. 2002. "Marriage and migration in transitional China: A field study of Gaozhou, Western Guangdong." *Environment and Planning* A 34:619–38.

Fan, Pi-Ling, and Margaret Mooney Marini. 2000. "Influences on gender-role attitudes during the transition to adulthood." *Social Science Research* 29(2):258–83.

Faragher, John Mack. 1996. "The separate worlds of men and women on the Overland Trail." In Mary Beth Norton and Ruth M. Alexander (eds.), *Major Problems in American Women's History.* Lexington, MA: D. C. Heath.

Farhi, Farideh. 2001. "Religious intellectuals, the 'woman question,' and the struggle for the creation of a democratic sphere in Iran."

International Journal of Politics, Culture, and Society 15(2):315–39.

Farley, Reynolds, and Richard Alba. 2002. "The new second generation in the United States." *International Migration Review* 36(3):669–701.

Fasteau, Marc F. 1974. *The Male Machine.* New York: McGraw-Hill.

Fausto-Sterling, Anne. 1992. *Myths of Gender: Biological Theories about Women and Men.* New York: Basic Books.

———. 1993. "Hormonal hurricanes: Menstruation, menopause and female behavior." In Laurel Richardson and Verta Taylor (eds.), *Feminist Frontiers III: Rethinking Sex, Gender and Society.* New York: McGraw-Hill.

———. 2000. *Sexing the Body: Gender Politics and the Construction of Sexuality.* New York: Basic Books.

Feeney, Judith A. 2001. *Becoming Parents: Exploring the Bond between Mothers, Fathers, and their Infants.* Cambridge, UK: Cambridge University.

Fehr, Beverley, and Ross Broughton. 2001. "Gender and personality differences in conceptions of love: An interpersonal theory analysis." *Personal Relationships* 8(2):115–36.

Feminist Research Center. 2000. "Empowering women in business." Feminist Majority Foundation. Available online at: http://www. feministorg/research/ewb_toc.html

Fenstermaker, Sarah, and Candace West (eds.). 2002. *Doing Gender, Doing Difference: Inequality, Power and Institutional Change.* New York: Routledge.

Ferguson, Dianne L., Audrey Desjarlais, and Gwen Meyer. 2000. *Improving Education: The Promise of Inclusive Learning.* Education Development Center. Newton, MA: National Institute for Urban School Improvement.

Fermlee, Diana H. 1995. "Causes and consequences of women's employment discontinuity, 1967–1973." *Work and Occupations* 22(2):167–87.

Fernea, Elizabeth Warnock. 1998. *In Search of Islamic Feminism.* New York: Doubleday.

Fetto, John. 2000. "Be mine." *American Demographics* 22(2):11–12.

Fields, Jason, and Lynne M. Casper. 2001. "America's families and living arrangements." *Current Population Reports* (June). U.S. Census Bureau.

Fiese, Barbara H., and Gemma Skillman. 2000. "Gender differences in family stories: Moderating influence of parent gender role and child gender." *Sex Roles* 43(4–6):267–83.

Figart, Deborah M. 1995. Book review of Elaine Sorensen's *Comparable worth: Is it a worthy policy? Gender & Society* 9(6):779–81.

Figert, Anne E. 1996. *Women and the Ownership of PMS: The Structuring of a Psychiatric Disorder.* Hawthorne, NY: Aldine de Gruyter.

Filteau, Jerry. 1992. "Bishops reject proposed pastoral on women." *St. Louis Review* 51(November 20):1, 10.

Fine, Lawrence. 2001. *Judaism in Practice: From the Middle Ages through the Early Modern Period.* Princeton, NJ: Princeton University.

Fingerson, Laura. 2000. "Do parents' opinions matter? Family processes and adolescent sexual behavior." Paper presented at the American Sociological Association, Washington, DC, August.

Fischer, Irmgard. 1994. "'Go and suffer oppression' said God's messenger to Hagar." In Elisabeth Schüssler Fiorenza and M. Shawn Copeland (eds.), *Violence Against Women.* London: Stichtin Concillium/SCM Press.

Fischer, Kirsten. 2002. "The imperial gaze: Native American, African American and colonial women in European eyes." In Nancy A. Hewitt (ed.), *A Companion to American Women's History.* Oxford, UK: Blackwell.

Fischman, Josh. 2001. "Do men experience menopause?" *U.S. News & World Report* 141(July 30):47.

Fishel, Elizabeth. 2000. *Reunion: The Girls We Used to Be, The Women We Became.* New York: Random House.

Fitzpatrick, Tony. 2002. "Analyses offer new perspective on human origin." *The Record* 26(4):1, 6. Washington University in St. Louis.

Fivush, Robyn, Melissa A. Brotman, Janine P. Buckner, and Sherryl H. Goodman. 2000. "Gender differences in parent-child emotion narratives." *Sex Roles* 42(3–4):233–53.

Flaherty, Mary. 2001. "How a language gender system creeps into perception." *Journal of Cross-Cultural Psychology* 32(1):18–31.

Flanigan, C. 2001. *What's Behind the Good News: The Decline in Teen Pregnancy Rates during the 1990s.* Washington, DC: The National Campaign to Prevent Teen Pregnancy.

Fletcher, Michael A. 2002. "Degrees of separation: Gender gap among college graduates has educators wondering where the men are." *Washington Post,* June 25, A1, A10.

Flowers, Ronald B. 2001. *Sex Crimes, Predators, Perpetrators, Prostitutes and Victims: An Examination of Sexual Criminality and Victimization.* Springfield, IL: Charles C. Thomas.

Foley, Sallie, and Dennis P. Sugrue. 2002. *Sex Matters for Women: A Complete Guide for Taking Care of Your Sexual Self.* New York: Guilford.

Forbes, Gordon B., and Leah E. Adams-Curtis. 2000. "Gender role typing and attachment to parents and peers." *Journal of Social Psychology* 140(2):258–60.

Forbes, Gordon B., Leah E. Adams-Curtis, Kay B. White, and Nicole R. Hamm. 2002. "Perceptions of married women and married men with hyphenated surnames." *Sex Roles* 46(5–6):167–75.

Forrester, David Anthony. 2000. "Revisiting men's health curriculum." In Mary Lebreck Kelley and Virginia Macken Fitzsimons (eds.), *Understanding Cultural Diversity: Culture, Curriculum, and Community in Nursing.* (pp. 169–76). Sudbury, MA: Jones and Bartlett.

Foschi, Martha. 2000. "Double standards for competence: Theory and research." *Annual Review of Sociology* 26:21–42.

Foucault, Michael. 1990. "The uses of pleasure," Volume II of Robert Hurley (trans.), *The History of Sexuality.* New York: Vintage.

Foulston, Lynn. 2002. *At the Feet of the Goddess: The Divine Feminine in Local Hindu Religion*. Brighton, UK: Sussex Academic.

Fouts, Gregory, and Kimberley Burggraf. 2000. "Television situation comedies: Female weight, male negative comments. And audience reactions." *Sex Roles* 42(9–10):925–32.

Fox, Mary F. 1995. "Women and higher education: Gender differences in the status of students and scholars." In Jo Freeman (ed.), *Women: A Feminist Perspective*. Mountain View, CA: Mayfield.

Fox, Mem. 1993. "Men who weep, boys who dance: The gender agenda between the lines in children's literature." *Language Arts* 70(2):84–88.

Fox, Richard. 2000. "Gender and Congressional elections." In Sue Tolleson-Rinehart and Jyl L. Josephson (eds.), *Gender and American Politics: Women, Men and the Political Process*. Armonk, NY: M.E. Sharpe.

Fox-Genovese, Elizabeth. 1995. "For women only." *Washington Post* March 26.

Francia, Peter L., 2001. "Early fundraising by nonincumbent female Congressional candidates: The importance of women's PACs." *Women & Politics* 23(1–2):7–20.

Frankfort-Nachmias, Chava. 2001. "Israel: The myth of gender equality." In Lynn Walter (ed.), *Women's Rights: A Global View*. (pp. 127–40). London: Greenwood.

Franklin, M., and J. Ramage. 1999. "Till long-distance do us part." *Kiplinger's Personal Finance Magazine* 53(1):56.

Franks, Myfanwy. 2001. *Women and Revivalism in the West: Choosing Fundamentalism in a Liberal Democracy*. Houndsmills, Hampshire, UK: Palgrave.

Frayser, Suzanne G. 1999. "Human sexuality: The whole is more than the sum of its parts." In David N. Suggs and Andrew W. Miracle (eds.), *Culture, Biology and Sexuality*. Athens: University of Georgia.

Fredricks, Jennifer L., and Jacquelynne S. Eccles. 2002. "Children's competence and value beliefs from childhood through adolescence: Growth trajectories in two male-sex-typed domains." *Developmental Psychology* 38(4):519–33.

Freedman, Estelle. 2002. *No Turning Back: The History of Feminism and the Future of Women*. New York: Ballantine.

Freedman, Marcia. 2003. "Theorizing Israeli Feminism, 1970–2000." In Kalpana Misra and Melanie S. Rich (eds.), *Jewish Feminism in Israel: Contemporary Perspectives*. (pp. 1–16). Hanover, NH: Brandeis University.

Freedman, Rita. 2001. "Myth America grows up." In Sheila Ruth (ed.), *Issues in Feminism: An Introduction to Women's Studies*. (pp. 138–47). Mountain View, CA: Mayfield.

Freeman, Jo. 1995. "From suffrage to women's liberation: Feminism in twentieth-century America." In Jo Freeman (ed.), *Women: A Feminist Perspective*. Mountain View, CA: Mayfield.

French Howard. 2001a. "Diploma at hand, Japanese women find glass ceiling reinforced with iron." *New York Times* January 1.

———. 2001b. "Japanese date clubs take the muss out of mating." *New York Times International* February 13.

Freud, Sigmund. 1962. *Three Contributions to the Theory of Sex* (A. A. Brill, trans.). New York: E. P. Dutton.

Frey, Kurt, and Mahzad Hojjat. 1998. "Are love styles related to sexual styles?" *Journal of Sex Research* 35(3):265–71.

Frey, Sylvia R., and Marion J. Morton. 1986. *New World, New Roles: A Documentary History of Women in Pre-industrial America*. Westport, CT: Greenwood.

Friedan, Betty. 1963. *The Feminine Mystique*. New York: W. W. Norton.

Friedman, Elisabeth. 2002. "Getting rights for those without representation: The success of conjunctural coalition-building in Venezuela." In Nikke Craske and Maxine Molyneux (eds.), *Gender and the Politics of Rights and Democracy in Latin America*. (pp. 57–78). Houndmills, Hampshire, UK: Palgrave.

Frisco, Michelle L., and Kristi Williams. 2003. "Perceived housework equity, marital happiness, and divorce in dual-earner households." *Journal of Family Issues* 24(1):51–73.

Frodi, Ann, Jacqueline Macaulay, and Pauline Ropert Thome. 1977. "Are women always less aggressive than men? A review of the experimental literature." *Psychological Bulletin* 84(4):634–60.

Fu, Xuanning, and Tim B. Heaton. 2000. "Status exchange in intermarriage among Hawaiians, Japanese, Filipinos and Caucasians in Hawaii: 1983–1994." *Journal of Comparative Family Studies* 31(1):45–61.

Fuchs, Lawrence H. 2000. *Beyond Patriarchy: Jewish Fathers and Families*. Hanover, NH: University Press of New England.

Fulghum, Robert. 1997. *True Love*. New York: HarperCollins.

Fuligni, Andrew J., Vivian Tseng, and May Lam. 1999. "Attitudes toward family obligations among adolescents with Asian, Latin American, and European backgrounds." *Child Development* 70(4):1030–44.

Fuller, Patricia Anne. 2001. "Living single: A phenomenological study of the lived experiences of never-married professional African American women." *Dissertation Abstracts International, A: The Humanities and Social Sciences* 62(4):1592–93-A.

Fur, Gunlog. 2002. "Some women are wiser than some men: Gender and native American history." In Nancy Shoemaker (ed.), *Clearing a Path: Theorizing the Past in Native American Studies*. (pp. 75–106). New York: Routledge.

Furnham, Adrian, and Nadine Bitar. 1993. "The stereotyped portrayal of men and women in British television advertisements." *Sex Roles* 29(3–4):297–310.

Furnham, Adrian, and Twiggy Mak. 1999. "Sex-role stereotyping in television commercials: A review and comparison of fourteen studies done on five continents over 25 years." *Sex Roles* 41(4–6):413–37.

Gabbidon, Shaun L. 2001. "African American male college students after the million man march: An exploratory study." *Journal of African American Men* 15–26.

Gabe, Thomas. 2003. *Trends in Welfare, Work and the Economic Well-Being of Female-Headed Families with Children.* New York: Novinka.

Gagen, Elizabeth A. 2000. "An example to us all: Child development and identity construction in early 20th century playgrounds." *Environment and Planning A* 32(4):599–616. Gagnon, John H. 1990. "The explicit and implicit of the scripting perspectives in sex research." *Annual Review of Sex Research* 1:1–43.

Gallagher, Margaret. 2001. *Gender Setting: New Agenda for Media Monitoring and Advocacy.* London: Zed.

Gallagher, Ann. M., Richard DeLisi, and Patricia C. Holst. 2000. "Gender differences in advanced mathematical problem solving." *Journal of Experimental Child Psychology* 75(3):165–90.

Gallant, Mary J., and Jay E. Cross. 1993. "Wayward Puritans in the ivory tower: Collective aspects of gender discrimination in academia." *Sociological Quarterly* 34(2):237–56.

Gallivan, Joanne. 1999. "Gender and humor: What makes the difference." *North American Journal of Psychology* 1(2):307–18.

Gambone, Kirsten, Jordan Arena et al. 2002. "Change in attitudes toward maternal employment during the past decade." *ERIC Resources in Education*, CG031648.

Ganatra, Bela, Siddhi Hirve, and V. N. Rao. 2001. "Sex-selective abortion: Evidence from a community-based study in Western India." *Asia-Pacific Population Journal* 16(2):109–24.

Ganley, Anne L. 1988. "Feminist therapy with male clients." In Mary Ann Dutton-Douglas and Leonore E. A. Walker (eds.), *Feminist Psychotherapies: Integration of Therapeutic and Feminist Systems.* Norwood, NJ: Ablex.

Garcia, A. M. 1991. "The development of Chicana feminist discourse." In Judith Lorber and S. A. Farrell (eds.), *The Social Construction of Gender.* Newbury Park, CA: Sage.

Gardiner, Judith Kegan. 2002. *Masculinity Studies and Feminist Theory.* New York: Columbia University.

Garey, Anita Ilta, and Terry Arendell. 2001. "Children, work and family: Some thought on 'mother-blame.'" In Rosanna Hertz and Nancy Marshall (eds.), *Working Families: The Transformation of the American Home.* (pp. 293–303). Berkeley: University of California.

Garfinkel, Perry. 1985. *In a Man's World: Father, Son, Brother, Friend and Other Roles Men Play.* New York: New American Library.

Garnets, Linda D. 1996. "Life as a lesbian: What does gender have to do with it?" In Joan C. Chrisler, Carla Golden, and Patricia D. Rozce (eds.), *Lectures on the Psychology of Women.* New York: McGraw-Hill.

Garside, Rula Bayrakdar, and Bonnie Klimes-Dougan. 2002. "Socialization of discrete negative emotions: Gender differences and links with psychological distress." *Sex Roles* 47(3–4):115–28.

Gavora, Jessica. 2003. *Tilting the Playing Field: Schools, Sports, Sex, and Title IX.* San Francisco: Encounter Books.

Gavron, Daniel. 2000. *The Kibbutz: Awakening from Utopia.* Lanham, MD: Rowman and Littlefield.

Gearing, Robin, Nilco Zand, and Georgie Colvin. 2001. "Engaging fathers: A point of entry in promoting a culture of peace." *Journal of the Association for Research on Mothering* 3(2):57–73.

Geerkin, Michael, and Walter Gove. 1983. *At Home and at Work: The Family's Allocation of Labor.* Beverly Hills, CA: Sage.

Geis, Florence L. 1993. "Self-fulfilling prophecies: A social psychological view of gender." In Anne E. Beall and Robert J. Sternberg (eds.), *The Psychology of Gender.* New York: Guilford.

Gelb, Joyce. 2000. "The Equal Opportunity Law: A decade of change for Japanese women?" *Law & Policy* 22(3–4):385–407.

Gelernter, David. 1996. "Why mothers should stay home." *Commentary.* February.

Gelles, Richard J., and Murray A. Straus. 1995. "Profiling violent families." In Mark Robert Rank and Edward L. Kain (eds.), *Diversity and Change in Families: Patterns, Prospects, and Policies.* Englewood Cliffs, NJ: Prentice Hall.

Gender Equality Bureau. 2003. *Women in Japan Today.* Tokyo: Cabinet Office. Available online at: http://www.gender.go.jp/english_contents/women2003/index

Gerdes, Eugenia Proctor. 2003. "Have we come a long way? Changes for academic women since 1970." *SWS Network News* 20(3)11–13.

Gerschick, Thomas J., and Adam Stephen Miller. 2004. "Coming to terms: Masculinity and physical disability." In Michael S. Kimmel and Michael A. Messner (eds.), *Men's Lives.* (pp. 349–62). Boston: Allyn & Bacon.

Gerson, Kathleen. 1993. *No Man's Land: Men's Changing Commitments to Family and Work.* New York: Basic Books.

Gerstel, Naomi. 2000. "The third shift: Gender and care work outside the home." *Qualitative Sociology* 23(4):467–83.

Gerstel, Naomi, and McGonagle K. 1999. "Job leaves and the limits of the Family and Medical Leave Act." *Work & Occupations* 26:510–34.

Gerstmann, Evan. 2003. *Same-Sex Marriage and the Constitution.* Cambridge, UK: Cambridge University.

Gheytanchi, Elham. 2001. "Civil society in Iran: Politics of motherhood and the public sphere." *International Sociology* 16(4):557–76.

Ghosh, Jayatri. 2000. "Satyavati: The matriarch of the Mahabharata." In Mandakranta Bose (ed.), *Faces of the Feminine in Ancient, Medieval, and Modern India.* (pp. 33–47). New York: Oxford University

Ghosh, Jayati, and Georg M. Pomeroy. 2003. "Sex ratios in China and India: A comparative approach." Paper presented at the Association of American Geographers, New Orleans, LA. March 5.

Gibbons, Sheila. 2002. "Female war correspondents changing war coverage." *Women's Enews*, September 10. Available online at: http://www.womensenews.org/article.cfm?aid=1074

Giddings, Paula. 1993. "Strong women and strutting men: The Moynihan Report." In Virginia Cyrus (ed.), *Experiencing Race, Class, and Gender in the United States*. Mountain View, CA: Mayfield.

Gilbert, Lucia Albino, and Jill Rader. 2001. "Current perspectives on women's adult roles: Work, family and life." In Rhoda K. Unger (ed.), *Handbook of the Psychology of Women and Gender.* (pp. 156–69). New York: Wiley.

Gilbert, Lucia Albino, and Sarah J. Walker. 2001. "Contemporary marriage: Challenges for clients and therapists." In Gary R. Brooks and Glenn E. Good (eds.), *The New Handbook of Psychotherapy with Men: A Comprehensive Guide to Settings, Problems, and Treatment Approaches.* (pp. 387–402). San Francisco: Jossey-Bass/Pfeiffer.

Gilbert, Melissa. 1996. "Attributional patterns and perceptions of math and science among fifth-grade through seventh-grade girls and boys." *Sex Roles* 35:489–506.

Gilder, George. 1974. "In defense of monogamy." *Commentary* 58 (November):31–36.

Gillespie, Rosemary. 2000. "When no means no: Disbelief, disregard and deviance as discourses of voluntary childlessness." *Women's Studies International Forum* 23(2):223–34.

Gilligan, Carol. 1982a. *In a Different Voice.* Cambridge, MA: Harvard University.

———. 1982b. "Adult development and women's development: Arrangements for a marriage." In J. Giele (ed.), *Women in the Middle Years.* New York: Wiley.

Gilligan, Carol, J. M. Taylor, and A. Sullivan. 1995. *Between Voice and Silence: Women and Girls, Race and Relationship.* Cambridge, MA: Harvard University.

Gimbutas, Marija. 1991. *The Civilization of the Goddess: The World of Old Europe.* San Francisco: HarperSanFrancisco.

———. 2001. *The Language of the Goddess: Unearthing the Hidden Symbols of Western Civilization.* London: Thames & Hudson.

Gimenez, Martha E. 2001. "Marxism, and class, gender, and race: Rethinking the trilogy." *Race, Gender & Class* 8(2):23–33.

Gittings, John. 2000. "China to outlaw 'second wives.'" *The Guardian* October 27. Available online at: http://www.guardian.co.uk

Giuliano, Traci A., Kathryn E. Popp, and Jennifer L. Knight. 2000. "Football versus Barbies: Childhood play activities as predictors of sport participation by women." *Sex Roles* 42(3–4):159–81.

Glazer, Deborah J., and Jack Drescher (eds.). 2001. *Gay and Lesbian Parenting.* New York: Haworth.

Glazer-Raymo, Judith. 1999. *Shattering the Myths: Women in Academe.* Baltimore: Johns Hopkins University.

Gleason, Jean Berko, and Richard Ely. 2002. "Gender differences in language development." In Ann McGillicuddy-De Lisi and Richard De Lisi (eds.), *Biology, Society and Behavior: The Development of Sex Differences in Cognition.* Westport, CT: Ablex.

Glenn, Evelyn N., and Roslyn L. Feldberg. 1995. "Clerical work: The female occupation." In Jo Freeman (ed.), *Women: A Feminist Perspective.* Mountain View, CA: Mayfield.

Glenn, Norval. 1997. "A reconsideration of the effect of no-fault divorce on divorce rates." *Journal of Marriage and the Family* 59(4):1023–30.

Global Health Council. 2003. "HIV/AIDS." Available online at: http://www.globalhealth.org/ view_top.php?id=227

Goffman, Erving. 1963. *Behavior in Public Places.* New York: Free Press.

———. 1971. *Relations in Public.* New York: Basic Books.

———. 1979. *Gender Advertisements.* New York: Harper & Row.

Goldberg, Harvey E. 2003. *Jewish Passages: Cycles of Jewish Life.* Berkeley: University of California.

Goldin, Claudia. 2000. "The changing economic role of women: A quantitative approach." In Robert J. Rotberg (ed.), *Social Mobility and Modernization: A Journal of Interdisciplinary History Reader.* (pp. 315–42). Cambridge, MA: MIT.

Goldman, Debra. 2000. "Consumer republic: Boys' names have become the province of girls." *AdWeek Midwest* 61(47):22.

Goldman, Wendy Z. 2002. *Women at the Gates: Gender and Industry in Stalin's Russia.* Cambridge, UK: Cambridge University.

Goldscheider, Frances K. 2000. "Men, children and the future of the family in the third millennium." *Futures* 32(6):525–38.

Goldstein, Joshua R. 1999. "Kinship networks that cross racial lines: The exception or the rule?" *Demography* 36(3):399–407.

Golosov, Grigorii V. 2001. "Political parties, electoral systems and women's representation in the Regional Legislative assemblies of Russia, 1995–998." *Party Politics* 7(1):45–68.

Good, Glenn E., Nancy B. Sherrod, and Mark G. Dillon. 2000. "Masculine gender role stressors and men's health." In Richard M. Eisler and Michel Hersen (eds.), *Handbook of Gender, Culture and Health.* (pp. 63–84). Mahwah, NJ: Lawrence Erlbaum.

Goodman, Ellen. 1999. "TV gives Fiji new look at self." *St. Louis Post-Dispatch* June 1.

Goodman, Ellen, and Patricia O'Brien. 2000. *I Know Just What You Mean: The Power of Friendship in Women's Lives.* New York: Simon & Schuster.

Goodwin, Beverly J. 1996. "The impact of popular culture on images of African American women." In Joan C. Chrisler, Carla Golden, and Patricia D. Rozee (eds.), *Lectures on the Psychology of Women.* New York: McGraw-Hill.

Goodwin, Robin, and Tatiana Emelyanova. 1995. "The perestroika of the family: Gender and occupational differences in family values in modern day Russia." *Sex Roles* 32(5–6):337–51.

Gordon, R. 1998. "The limits of limits on divorce." *Yale Law Review* 107(5):1435–65.

Gottfried, Barbara. 1994. "The reproduction of gendering: Imaging kids in ads for adults." In Harry Eiss (ed.), *Images of the Child*. Bowling Green, OH: Bowling Green State University Popular Press.

Gottlieb, Andrew R. 2003. *Sons Talk about Their Gay Fathers: Life Curves*. Binghamton, NY: Harrington Park.

Gow, Kathryn N. 2000. "Banking on women: Achieving healthy economies through microfinance." *WE International* 48/49:11–13.

Graetz, Naomi. 2003a. *S/he Created Them: Feminist Retellings of Bible Stories*. Piscataway, NJ: Gorgias.

———. 2003b. "Women and religion in Israel." In Kalpana Misra and Melanie S. Rich (eds.), *Jewish Feminism in Israel: Contemporary Perspectives* (pp. 17–56). Hanover, NH: Brandeis University.

Graham, Fiona. 2003. *Inside the Japanese Company*. London: Routledge/Curzon.

Grajeda, Tony. 2002. "The 'feminization' of rock." In Roger Beebe, Denise Fulbrook, and Ben Saunders. *Rock Over the Edge: Transformations in Popular Music Culture* (pp. 233–54). Durham, NC: Duke University.

Grameen Dialogue. 1999. Dhaka. No. 37 (January).

Granger, Dorothy. 2002. "Friendships between black and white women." *American Behavioral Scientist* 45(8):1208–13.

Gray, Francine du Plessix. 1991. "Sex roles in the Soviet Union." In Carol J. Verburg (ed.), *Ourselves Among Others: Cross-Cultural Readings for Writers*. Boston: Bedford.

Gray, J. Glenn. 1992. "The enduring appeals of battle." In Larry May and Robert Strikwerda (eds.), *Rethinking Masculinity: Philosophical Explorations in Light of Feminism*. Lanham, MD: Rowman & Littlefield.

Greard, Octavia. 1893. *L'Education des Femmes par les Femmes*. Paris: Librairie Hachette.

Green, Karen. 1995. *The Woman of Reason: Feminism, Humanism and Political Thought*. New York: Continuum.

Greenberg, Anna. 2001. "Will choice be aborted?" *American Prospect* Fall:A25–A28.

Greenberg, Sarah. 2001. "Spousal caregiving: In sickness and in health." *Journal of Gerontological Social Work* 35(4)69–82.

Greenglass, Esther R. 2002. "Work stress, coping, and social support: Implications for women's occupational well-being." In Debra L. Nelson and Ronald J. Burke (eds.), *Gender, Work Stress, and Health*. Washington, DC: American Psychological Association.

Greenhalgh, Susan. 2001. "Fresh winds in Beijing: Chinese feminists speak out on the one-child policy and women's lives." *Signs* 26(3):847–886.

Greenwood, Dara, and Linda M. Isbell. 2002. "Ambivalent sexism and the dumb blonde: Men's and women's reactions to sexist jokes." *Psychology of Women Quarterly* 26(4):341–50.

Greif, Geoffrey L. 1995. "Single fathers with custody following separation and divorce." *Marriage and Family Review* 20(1–2): 213–32.

Grieco, Elizabeth M., and Rachel C. Cassidy. 2001. "Overview of race and Hispanic origin." *Census 2000 Brief*, March. U.S. Census Bureau.

Griffin, Joan M., Rebecca Fuhrer, Stephen Stansfeld, and Michael Marmot. 2002. "The importance of low control at work and home on depression and anxiety: Do these effects vary by gender and social class?" *Social Science & Medicine* 54(5):783–98.

Griffiths, M. 1998. "Violent video games and aggression: A review of the literature." *Aggression and Violent Behavior* 4:203–12.

Groce, Stephen B. 2000. "Blending teaching, research and learning through examination of gender and sexual scripts: An analysis of male and female college students' perception of sexual attitudes and behaviors." Paper presented at the Southern Sociological Society, New Orleans, LA. April.

Groce, Stephen B., and Margaret Cooper. 1990. "Just me and the boys? Women in local-level rock and roll." *Gender & Society* 2(4):220–28.

Grogan, Sarah, and Helen Richards. 2002. "Body image: Focus groups with boys and men." *Men & Masculinities* 4(3):219–32.

Groothuis, Rebecca Merrill. 1997. *Good News for Women: A Biblical Picture of Gender Equality*. Grand Rapids, MI: Baker Books.

Gross, Alan F. 1992. "The male role and heterosexual behavior." In Michael S. Kimmel and Michael A. Messner (eds.), *Men's Lives*. New York: Macmillan.

Gross, Rita. 1997. "Some Buddhist perspectives on the goddess." In Karen L. King (ed.), *Women and Goddess Traditions: In Antiquity and Today*. (pp. 406–25). Minneapolis, MN: Fortress.

———. 2002. "Buddhism." In Arvind Sharma and Katherine K. Young (eds.), *Her Voice, Her Faith: Women Speak on World Religions*. (pp. 11–58). Boulder, CO: Westview.

Grossman, Herbert, and Suzanne H. Grossman. 1994. *Gender Issues in Education*. Boston: Allyn & Bacon.

Grote, Nancy K., Kristen E. Naylor, and Margaret S. Clark. 2002. "Perceiving the division of family work to be unfair: Do comparisons, enjoyment, and competence matter?" *Journal of Family Psychology* 16(4):510–22.

Guerrero, Laura K., and Renee L. Reiter, 1998. "Expressing emotion: Sex differences in social skills and communicative responses to anger, sadness, and jealousy." In Daniel J. Canary and Kathryn Dindia (eds.), *Sex Differences and Similarities in Communication: Critical Essays and Empirical Investigations of Sex and Gender in Interaction*. (pp. 321–50). Mahwah, NJ: Lawrence Erlbaum.

Guilbert, Douglas E., Nicholas A. Vacc, and Kay Pasley. 2000. "The relationship of gender role beliefs, negativity, distancing, and marital instability." *Journal of Counseling and Therapy for Couples & Families*. 8(2):124–32.

Guinn, Bobby, and Vern Vincent. 2002. "Determinants of coping responses among Mexican American adolescents." *Journal of School Health* 72(4):152–6.

Gumbiner, Jann. 1998. "Professors as models and mentors: Does gender matter?" *Psychological Reports* 82(1):94.

Gundersen, Edna. 2001. "Madonna hits an MTV/VH1 wall." *USA Today* March 22:2D.

Gupta, Samjukta Gombrich. 2000. "The goddess, women, and their rituals in Hinduism." In Mandakranta Bose (ed.), *Faces of the Feminine in Ancient, Medieval, and Modern India.* (pp. 87–108). New York: Oxford University.

Gutner, Toddi. 2002. "A balancing act for Gen X women." *Business Week,* January 21:83.

Hacker, Andrew. 2003. *Mismatch: The Growing Gulf Between Women and Men.* New York: Scribner.

Hackstaff, Karla B. 1999. *Marriage in a Culture of Divorce.* Philadelphia: Temple University.

Hader, Shannon L., Dawn K. Smith, Janet S. Moore, and Scott D. Holmberg. 2001. "HIV infection in women in the United States." *Journal of the American Medical Association* 285(9):1186–92.

Hagewen, Rachel E. 2002. "Division of household labor in same-sex families." Paper presented at the Southern Sociological Society, New Orleans, LA, March.

Haines, Michelle. 2001. "Gender and gender role in relation to anger and anger expression." *Dissertation Abstracts International Section B: The Sciences & Engineering* 61(9-B)5017.

Halberstam, David. 1994. "Popular, pretty, polite, not too smart." *New York Times Book Review* September 11:15–17.

Hall, Cathy W., Nichelle B. Davis, Larry M. Bolen, and Rosina Chia. 1999. "Gender and racial differences in mathematical performance." *Journal of Social Psychology* 139(6):677–89.

Hall, Christine C., and Matthew J. Crum. 1994. "Women and 'bodyisms' in television beer commercials." *Sex Roles* 31(5–6):329–37.

Hall, Edward T. 1966. *The Hidden Dimension.* Garden City, NY: Doubleday.

Hall, Judith A., Jason D. Carter, and Terrence G. Horgan. 2000. "Gender differences in nonverbal communication of emotions." In Agneta H. Fischer (ed.), *Gender and Emotion: Social Psychological Perspectives.* New York: Cambridge University.

Hall, Judith A., and Gregory B. Friedman. 1999. "Status, gender, and nonverbal behavior: A study of structured interactions between employees of a company." *Personality and Social Psychology Bulletin* 25(9):1082–91.

Hall, Judith A., Terrence G. Horgan, and Jason D. Carter. 2002. "Assigned and felt status in relation to observe-coded and participant-reported smiling." *Journal of Nonverbal Behavior* 26(2):63–81.

Hall, Judith A., Lavonia Smith LeBeau, Jeanette Gordon Reinoso, and Frank Thayer. 2001. "Status, gender, and nonverbal behavior in candid and posed photographs: A study of conversations between university employees." *Sex Roles* 44(11–12):677–92.

Halpern, Diane F. 2000. *Sex Differences in Cognitive Ability.* Mahwah, NJ: Lawrence Erlbaum.

Halpern, Carolyn Tucker, J. Richard Udry, Benjamin Campbell, Chirayath Suchindran et al. 1994. "Testosterone and religiosity as predictors of sexual attitudes and activity among adolescent males: A biosocial model." *Journal of Biological Science* 26(2): 217–34.

Halstead, Mark J. 2001. "Living in different worlds: Gender differences in the developing sexual values and attitudes of primary school children." *Sex Education* 1(1):59–76.

Han, Shin-Kap, and Phyllis Moen. 2001. "Coupled careers: Pathways through work and marriage in the United States. In Hans-Peter Blossfeld and Sonja Drobnic (eds.), *Careers of Couples in Contemporary Societies: From Male Breadwinner to Dual Earner Families.* (pp. 201–31). Oxford, UK: Oxford University.

Hank, Karsten, and Gunnar Andersson. 2002. "Parental gender indifference or persistent sex preferences for children at the turn of the 21st century?" *Max Planck Institute for Demographic Research Working Paper* WP 2002-049. October. Rostock, Germany.

Harden, Jeni. 2001. "'Mother Russia' at work: Gender divisions in the medical profession." *European Journal of Women's Studies* 8(2):181–99.

Hardesty, Constance, Deeann Wenk, and Carolyn Stout Morgan. 1995. "Paternal involvement and the development of gender expectations in sons and daughters." *Youth and Society* 267(3): 283–97.

Harjo, Suzan Shown. 1993. "The American Indian experience." In Harriette Pipes McAdoo (ed.), *Family Ethnicity: Strength in Diversity.* Newbury Park, CA: Sage.

Harper, Rosalyn L., Gemma C. Harper, and Janet E. Stockdale. 2002. "The role and sentencing of women in drug trafficking crime." *Legal and Criminological Psychology* 7(1):101–14.

Harragan, Betty Lehan. 1977. *Games Mother Never Taught You.* New York: Rawson.

Harris, Barbara Clementine, Suzanne R. Hiatt, Rose Wu, and Mabel Kathahweire. 2000. *Women's Ordination in the Episcopal Church: Twenty-Five Years Later.* Cambridge, MA: Episcopal Divinity School.

Harris, Christine R. 2002. "Sexual and romantic jealousy in heterosexual and homosexual adults." *Psychological Science* 13(1):7–12.

Harris, Ian, Jose B. Torres, and Dale Allender. 1994. "The responses of African American men to dominant norms of masculinity within the United States." *Sex Roles* 31(11–12):703–19.

Harris, Sandy, Sandra Lowery, and Michael Arnold. 2002. "When women educators are commuters in commuter marriages." *Advancing Women in Leadership* Winter. Available online at: http://www.advancingwomen.com/awl/winter2002/harris.html

Harris, Shanette M. 2002. "Father absence in the African American community: Towards a new paradigm." *Race, Gender & Class* 9(4):111–33.

Harrison, G. Pope, Jr., Katharine A. Phillips, and Roberto Olivardia. 2000. *The Adonis Complex: The Secret Crisis of Male Body Obsession.* Carlsbad, CA: Gurze.

Hartmann, Heidi. 1993. "The unhappy marriage of Marxism and feminism." In Stevi Jackson et al. (eds.), *Women's Studies Essential Readings*. New York: New York University.

———. 1999. "Strengthening Social Security for women." *Report from the Working Conference on Women and Social Security*. Washington, DC: Institute for Women's Policy Research.

Harvey, Elizabeth. 1999. "Short-term and long-term effects of early parental employment on children of the National Longitudinal Survey of Youth." *Developmental Psychology* 35(2):445–59.

Hasell, Mary Joyce, and John Scanzoni. 2000. "Cohousing in HUD housing: Problems and prospects." *Journal of Architectural and Planning Research* 17(2):133–45.

Hashmi, Taj ul-Islam. 2000. *Women and Islam in Bangladesh: Beyond Subjection and Tyranny*. Houndmills, Hampshire, UK: Palgrave.

Haskell, Molly. 1987. *From Reverence to Rape: The Treatment of Women in the Movies*. New York: Holt, Rinehart and Winston.

———. 1997. *Holding My Own in No Man's Land: Women and Men and Film about Feminists*. New York: Oxford University.

Hassan, Riffat. 2002. "Islam." In Arvind Sharma and Katherine K. Young (eds.), *Her Voice, Her Faith: Women Speak on World Religions*. (pp. 215–242). Boulder, CO: Westview.

Hatch, Holly, and Deborah Kirby Forgays. 2001. "A comparison of older adolescent and adult females' responses to anger-provoking situations." *Adolescence* 36(143):557–70.

Hattery, Angela J. 2001a. "Tag-team parenting: Costs and benefits of utilizing nonoverlapping shift work in families with young children." *Families in Society* 82(4):419–27.

———. 2001b. *Women, Work and Family: Balancing and Weaving*. Thousand Oaks, CA: Sage.

Hattiangadi, Anita U. 2000. *A Closer Look at Comparable Worth*. Washington DC: Employment Policy Foundation.

Hayashi, Hiroko. 2003. "Parasite singles." Freeman Foundation Institute on Japan presentation of Social Issues in Japanese Society. Tokai University, Honolulu, May 29.

Hayes, Christopher G. 2000. "A brief writing assignment introducing non-sexist pronoun usage." *Teaching English in the Two-Year College* 28(1): 74–77.

Haynes, Gladys Verneal Oosting. 2001. "Playmate selections of preschool children." *Dissertation Abstracts International Section A: Humanities & Social Sciences* 62(3-A): September, 907.

Hays-Mitchell, M. 1999. "From survivor to entrepreneur: Gendered dimensions of microenterprise development in Peru." *Environment and Planning A* 31(2):251–71.

Healey, Kevin. 2000. "The irresolvable tension: Agape and masculinity in the Promise Keepers movement." In Dane S. Claussen (ed.), *The Promise Keepers: Essays on Masculinity and Christianity*. (pp. 215–25). Jefferson, NC: McFarland.

Heaton, Tim B., and Cardell K. Jacobson. 2000. "Intergroup marriage: An examination of opportunity structures." *Sociological Inquiry* 70(1): 30–41.

Heaven, Catherine P., and Kathleen McCluskey-Fawcett. 2001. "Intergenerational attitudes toward maternal employment." Paper presented at the Society for Research in Child Development, Minneapolis, April.

Hegarty, Peter. 2002. " 'It's not a choice, it's the way we're built': Symbolic beliefs about sexual orientation in the U.S. and Britain." *Journal of Community & Applied Social Psychology* 23(3): 153–66.

Heine, Katherine. 2003. "AIDS moves beyond 'high risk' groups in India. AlterNet: Reuters Foundation: December 13. Available online at: http://www.alternet.org/thefacts

Hekmat, Anwar. 1997. *Women and the Koran: The status of Women in Islam*. Amherst, NY: Prometheus.

Helgesen, Sally. 1990. *The Female Advantage: Women's Ways of Leadership*. New York: Doubleday.

Helms-Erikson, Heather. 2001. "Marital quality ten years after the transition to parenthood: Implications of the timing of parenthood and the division of housework." *Journal of Marriage and the Family* 63(4):1089–110.

Helweg, Robert, Lisbeth Anderson, and Gerald Tindal. 2001. "Influence of elementary student gender on teachers' perceptions of mathematics achievement." *Journal of Educational Research* 95(2):93–102.

Henderson, Dianne L. 2001. Prevalence of gender DIF in mixed format high school exist examination." Paper presented at the American Educational Research Association, April, Seattle.

Hendrick, Susan S., and Clyde Hendrick. 1992. *Romantic Love*. Newbury Park, CA: Sage.

Hendry, Joy. 1993. "The role of the professional housewife." In Janice Hunter (ed.), *Japanese Women Working*. London: Routledge.

Heng, Li. 2002. "Men outnumber women, population structure worries China." *People's Daily Sept. 27*.

Henley, Nancy M. 1977. *Body Politics: Power, Sex and Nonverbal Communication*. Englewood Cliffs, NJ: Prentice Hall.

———. 1989. "Molehill or mountain: What we know and don't know about sex bias in language." In Mary Crawford and Margaret Gentry (eds.), *Gender and Thought: Psychological Perspectives*. New York: Springer-Verlag.

———. 2002. "Body politics and beyond." *Feminism & Psychology* 12(3):295–310.

Henly, Julia R., and Sandra Lyons. 2000. "The negotiation of child care and employment demands among low income parents." *Journal of Social Issues* 56(4):683–706.

Hepler, Juanita B. 2000. "Joining the 'in crowd': The social interactions and peer relations of preadolescent youth." *Journal of School Social Work* 11(1):67–84.

Hequembourg, Amy L., and Michael P. Farrell. 2001. "Lesbian motherhood: Negotiating marginal-mainstream identities." In Jennifer M. Lehmann (ed.), *The Gay and Lesbian Marriage and Family Reader: Analyses of Problems and Prospects for the 21st Century.* (pp. 126–48). New York: Gordian Knot.

Herbert, T. Walter. 2002. *Sexual Violence and American Manhood.* Cambridge, MA: Harvard University.

Hertz, Frederick. 1998. *Legal Affairs: Essential Advice for Same-Sex Couples.* New York: Henry Holt.

Heschel, Susannah. 2002. "Judaism." In Arvind Sharma and Katherine K. Young (eds.), *Her Voice, Her Faith: Women Speak on World Religions.* (pp. 145–68). Boulder, CO: Westview.

Hesli, Vicki L., Ha-Lyong Jung, William M. Reisinger, and Arthur H. Miller. 2001. "The gender divide in Russian politics: Attitudinal and behavioral considerations." *Women & Politics* 22(2):41–80.

Hess, Ursula, Sylvie Blairy, and Robert E. Kleck. 2000. "The influence of facial emotion displays, gender, and ethnicity on judgments of dominance and affiliation." *Journal of Nonverbal Behavior* 24(4):265–83.

Hesse-Biber, and Gregg Lee Carter. 2000. *Working Women in America: Split Dreams.* New York: Oxford University.

Hewlett, Sylvia. 2002. *Creating a Life: Professional Women and the Quest for Children.* New York: Talk Miramax.

Hibbard, David R., and Duane Buhrmester.1998. "The role of peers in the socialization of gender-related social interaction styles." *Sex Roles* 39(3–4):185–202.

Hicks, Jennifer. 2002. "The economics of race and gender." February 6 *Women's Village.* Available online at: http://www.imdiversity.com/villages/women

Hiedemann, B., O. Suhomlinova, and A. M. O'Rand. 1998. "Economic independence, economic status, and empty nest in midlife marital disruption." *Journal of Marriage and the Family* 60:219–31.

Higginbotham, Elizabeth. 2000. "Women and employment: Obstacles and prospects." Women's History Month Presentation at Maryville University of St. Louis, March 16.

———. 2002. "Black professional women: Job ceilings and employment sectors." In Roberta Satow (ed.), *Gender and Social Life.* Needham Heights, MA: Allyn & Bacon.

Higginbotham, Evelyn Brooks. 2003. African American women in history." In Mary Beth Norton and Ruth M. Alexander (eds.), *Major Problems in American Women's History.* Boston: Houghton Mifflin.

Hill, Fanny Christina. 1997. "Rosie the Riveter." In Susan Ware (ed.), *Modern American Women: A Documentary History.* (pp. 215–19). New York: McGraw-Hill.

Hill, Frances. 2000. *The Salem Witch Trials Reader.* Cambridge, MA: Da Capo.

Hill, Shirley A. 2001. "Class, race and gender dimensions of child rearing in African American families." *Journal of Black Studies* 31(4):494–508.

———. 2002. "Teaching and doing gender in African American families." *Sex Roles* 47(11–12): 493–506.

Hillman, Jennifer L. 2000. *Clinical Perspectives on Elderly Sexuality.* New York: Academic/Plenum.

Hindu. 2003. (*The Hindu Magazine*) August 31. Available online at: http://www.hindu.com/thehindu/mag/2003/08/31/

Hirao, Keiko. 2001. "Mothers as the best teachers: Japanese motherhood and early childhood education." In Mary C. Brinton (ed.), *Women's Working Lives in East Asia.* (pp. 180–203). Stanford, CA: Stanford University.

Hird, Myra, and Kimberly Abshoff. 2000. "Women without children: A contradiction in terms? Voluntary childless women." *Journal of Comparative Family Studies* 31(3):347–66.

Hirschmann, Nancy J. 2003. *The Subject of Liberty: Toward a Feminist Theory of Freedom.* Princeton, NJ: Princeton University.

Hirshey, Geri. 1997. "Women of rock." *Rolling Stone* 773:November 13.ber 13.

Hitchcock, Amanda. 2001. "Rising number of dowry deaths in India." July 4. *World Socialist Web Site.* Available online at: http://www.wsws.org/articles/2001/jul2001/ind-j04/shtml

Hite, Shere. 1994. "Women as Revolutionary Agents of Change: The Hite Reports and Beyond." Madison: University of Wisconsin.

Hochschild, Arlie Russell. 2003. *The Second Shift* (with new introduction). New York: Penguin.

Hoelter, Lynette Faye. 2002. "Fair is fair—or is it? Perceptions of fairness in the household division of labor." *Dissertation Abstracts International, A: Humanities and Social Sciences* 62(7):2587-A.

Hoff, Joan. 2003. "The negative impact of the American Revolution on white women." In Mary Beth Norton and Ruth M. Alexander (eds.), *Major Problems in American Women's History.* Boston: Houghton Mifflin.

Hofferth, Sandra L., 2003. "Race/ethnic differences in father involvement in two-parent families: Culture, context, or economy?" *Journal of Family Issues* 24(2):185–216.

Hoffman, Lois W. 2000. "Maternal employment: Effects of social context." In Ronald D. Taylor and Margaret C. Wang (eds.). *Resilience across Contexts: Family, Work, Culture, and Community.* (pp. 147–76). Mahwah, NJ: Lawrence Erlbaum.

Hoffman, Lois W., and Deborah D. Kloska. 1995. "Parents' gender-based attitudes toward marital roles and child rearing: Development and validation of new measures." *Sex Roles* 32:273–95.

Hoffman, Lois W., and Lise M. Youngblade. 1999. *Mothers at Work: Effects on Children's Well-Being.* Cambridge, UK: Cambridge University.

Hoffmann, Melissa L., and Kimberly K. Powlishta. 2001. "Gender segregation in childhood: A test of the interaction style theory." *Journal of Genetic Psychology* 162(3):298–313.

Hoffnung, Michele. 1995. "Motherhood: Contemporary conflict for women." In Jo Freeman (ed.), *Women: A Feminist Perspective.* Mountain View, CA: Mayfield.

Hogan, Linda. 1995. *From Women's Experience to Feminist Theology*. Sheffield, UK: Sheffield Academic Press.

Holland, Dorothy, and Margaret A. Eisenhart. 1990. *Educated in Romance: Women, Achievement and College Culture*. Chicago: University of Chicago.

Hollander, Anne. 1994. "A woman of extremes." Book review of Susan Haskins' *Mary Magdalene: Myth and Metaphor. New Yorker* (October) 3:112–17.

Hollingworth, Leta S. 2000. "Leta S. Hollingworth on coercive pronatalism. Reprint from the June 1916 edition of *American Journal of Sociology* titled 'Social devices for impelling women to bear and rear children.'" *Population and Development Review* 26(2):353–63.

Holmes, Janet, and Miriam Meyerhoff (eds.). 2003. *The Handbook of Language and Gender*. Malden, MA: Blackwell.

Holmes, Ronald M., and Stephen T. Holmes. 2002. *Profiling Violent Crimes: An Investigative Tool*. Thousand Oaks, CA: Sage.

Hong, Lawrence K. 1987. "Potential effects of the one-child policy on gender equality in the People's Republic of China." *Gender & Society* 1(3):317–26.

Honig, A. S. 2002. "Choosing childcare for young children." In Marc H. Borstein (ed.), *Handbook of Parenting; Volume 5 – Practical Issues in Parenting*. Mahwah, NJ: Lawrence Erlbaum.

Hopkins, Patrick D. 1992. "Gender treachery: Homophobia, masculinity, and threatened identities." In Larry May and Robert Strikwerda (eds.), *Rethinking Masculinity: Philosophical Explorations in Light of Feminism*. Lantham, MD: Rowan & Littlefield.

Hossain, Ziarat, and Jaipaul L. Roopnarine. 1993. "Division of household labor and child care in dual-earner African-American families with infants." *Sex Roles* 39:571–83.

Hossain, Ziarat. 2001. "Division of household labor and family functioning in off-reservation Navajo Indian families." *Family Relations* 50(3):255–61.

Hotaling, Edward. 2003. *Islam without Illusions: Its Past, its Present, and its Challenge for the Future*. Syracuse, NY: Syracuse University.

Houseknecht, Sharon K., and Jaya Sastry. 1996. "Family 'decline' and child well-being: A comparative assessment." *Journal of Marriage and the Family* 58(3):726–39.

Howie, Gillian and Ashley Tauchert. 2002. "Part III: Feminist pedagogies." In Gillian Howie and Ashley Tauchert (eds.), *Gender, Teaching and Research in Higher Education: Challenges for the 21st Century*. Aldershot, UK: Ashgate.

Howitz, Jeannine O. 2001. "Reflections of a feminist mom." In Susan E. Chase and Mary F. Rogers (eds.), *Mothers and Children: Feminist Analyses and Personal Narratives*. (pp. 81–85). New Brunswick, NJ: Rutgers University.

Howland, Courtney W. (ed.). 1999. *Religious Fundamentalism and the Human Rights of Women*. New York: St. Martin's.

Hrdy, Sarah Blaffer. 1999. *The Woman that Never Evolved*. Cambridge, MA: Harvard University.

———. 2000. *Mother Nature: A History of Mothers, Infants, and Natural Selection*. New York: Ballantine.

Hubbard, Julie A. 2001. "Emotion expression processes in children's peer interaction: The role of peer rejection, aggression, and gender." *Child Development* 72(5):1426–38.

Hubbard, Lee, and Amanda Datnow. 2002. "Are single-sex schools sustainable in the public sector?" In Amanda Datnow and Lea Hubbard (eds.), *Gender in Policy and Practice: Perspectives on Single-Sex and Coeducational Schooling*. New York: Routledge/Falmer.

Hudson, Repps. 2003. "Fed researchers find that timing is everything for women who want to have it all." *St. Louis Post-Dispatch* April 15:C1, C3.

Huesmann, L. Rowell (ed). 1994. *Aggressive Behavior: Current Perspectives*. New York: Plenum.

Hungerford, T. L. 2001. "The economic consequences of widowhood on elderly women in the United States and Germany." *Gerontologist* 41(1):103–11.

Hunt, M. 1974. *Sexual Behavior in the 1970s*. Chicago: Playboy.

Hunter, Andrea G., and James Earl Davis. 1994. "Hidden voices of black men: The meaning, structure and complexity of manhood." *Journal of Black Studies* 25(1):20–40.

Hussain, R., F. F. Fikree, and H. W. Berendes. 2000. "The role of son preference in reproductive behavior in Pakistan." *Bulletin of the World Health Organization* 78(3):379–88.

Huston, Michelle, and Pepper Schwartz. 1996. "Gendered dynamics in the romantic relationships of lesbians and gay men." In Julie T. Wood (ed.), *Gendered Relationships*. Mountain View, CA: Mayfield.

Hyde, Janet S., and K. C. Kling. 2001. "Women, motivation and achievement." *Psychology of Women Quarterly* 25(4):364–78.

Iarskaia, Valentina, and Elena R. Iarskaia-Smirnova, 2002. "Ain't men's business: Gender analysis of employment in social work." *Sotsiologicheskie Issledovaniya* (abstract) 28(6):74–82.

Ibhawoh, Bonny. 2000. "Between culture and constitution: Evaluating the cultural legitimacy of human rights in the African state." *Human Rights Quarterly* 22(3):838–60.

Ide, Sachiko, and Naomi Hanaoka McGloin (eds.). 1990. *Aspects of Japanese Women's Language*. Tokyo: Kurosio.

Ilic, Melanie. 1999. *Women Workers in the Soviet Interwar Economy: From "Protection" to "Equality."* Houndmills, Hampshire, UK: Macmillan.

IMSA. 1995. *Statement: 1993–94 Calculus-based Physics/mechanics Study*. Aurora: Illinois Mathematics and Academy.

India News. 2001. "Empowering women." Special Edition, Spring:7–8 Washington, DC: Embassy of India.

Inoue, Miyako. 2002. "Gender, language, and modernity: Toward an effective history of Japanese women's language." *American Ethnologist* 29(2): 392–422.

Intons-Peterson, Margaret Jean. 1988. *Children's Concepts of Gender.* Norwood, NJ: Ablex.

Isaacs, Ronald H. 2000. *Every Person's Guide to Jewish Sexuality.* Northvale, NJ: Jason Aronson.

Ishii-Kuntz, M. 1997. "Intergenerational relationships among Chinese, Japanese, and Korean Americans. *Family Relations* 46:23–32.

ISR. 2002. "U.S. husbands are doing more housework while wives are doing less." *Institute of Social Research.* University of Michigan. Available online at: http://www.umich.edu/newsinfo/Releases/2002/Mar02

Italie, Hillel. 1993. "Emma Thompson: Fame, feminist, forster." *St. Louis Post-Dispatch* (January 3):6C.

Iwao, Sumiko. 1993. *The Japanese Woman: Traditional Image and Changing Reality.* Cambridge, MA: Harvard University.

Jabusch, Willard E. 2000. "The myth of cohabitation: Research by L. Waite." *America* 183(10): 14–16.

Jackman, Jennifer. 1995. "1995 women's equality poll released." *Feminist Majority Report* 7(2):1, 12–13.

Jackson, Anita P., Ronald P. Brown, and Karen E. Patterson-Stewart. 2000. "African Americans in dual-career commuter marriages: An investigation of their experiences." *Family Journal-Counseling and Therapy for Couples and Families* 8(1):22–36.

Jackson, Aurora P. 1994b. "Psychological distress among single, employed, black mothers and their perceptions of their young children." *Journal of Social Service Research* 19(3–4):87–101.

Jackson, Kathy Merlock. 1994a. "Targeting baby-boom children as consumers: Mattel uses television to sell talking dolls." In Harry Eiss (ed.), *Images of the Child.* Bowling Green, OH: Bowling Green State University Popular Press.

Jackson, Keith. 2003. *The Changing Face of Japanese Management.* New York: Routledge.

Jacobs, Deborah L. 1994. "Back from the mommy track." *New York Times* October 9(Section 3):1, 6.

Jacobs, Janie E., Stephanie Lanza, and D. Wayne Osgood. 2002. "Changes in children's self-competence and values: Gender and domain differences across grades one through twelve." *Child Development* 73(2):509–27.

Jacobson, Doranne, and Susan S. Wadley. 1995. *Women in India: Two Perspectives.* New Delhi, India: Manohar.

Jacobson, Kristen C., and Lisa J. Crockett. 2000. "Parental monitoring and adolescent adjustment: An ecological perspective." *Journal of Research on Adolescence* 10(1):65–97.

Jain, A., and J. Belsky. 1997. "Fathering and acculturation: Immigrant Indian families with young children." *Journal of Marriage and the Family* 59:873–83.

Jalilvand, Mahshid. 2000. "Married women, work, and values." *Monthly Labor Review* 123(8):26–31.

James, Jeffrey D. 2001. "The role of cognitive development and socialization in the initial development of team loyalty." *Leisure Sciences* 23(4):233–61.

Jamieson, Kathleen Hall. 1995. *Beyond the Double Bind: Women and Leadership.* New York: Oxford University.

Jarman, Francis. 2002. "Sati: From exotic custom to relativist controversy." *CultureScan* 2(5): December.

Jeffrey, Julie Roy. 1998. *Frontier women: "Civilizing the West? 1840–1880.* New York: Hill and Wang.

Jelen, Ted G. 1999. "On the hegemony of liberal individualism: A reply to Williams." *Sociology of Religion* 60(1):35–40.

Jensen, Alice. 2004. "The language of menopause." Unpublished manuscript for the School of Health Professions, Maryville University of St. Louis.

Jensen, Gary F. 2003. "Gender variation in delinquency: Self-images, beliefs, and peers as mediating mechanisms." In Ronald L. Akers and Gary F. Jensen (eds.), *Social Learning Theory and the Explanation of Crime.* (pp. 151–78). New Brunswick, NJ: Transaction.

Jensen, Joan M. 1994. "Native American women and agriculture: A Seneca case study." In Vicki L. Ruiz and Ellen Carol DuBois (eds.), *Unequal Sisters: A Multicultural Reader in U.S. Women's History.* New York: Routledge.

Jepsen, Lisa K., and Christopher A. Jepsen. 2002. "An empirical analysis of the matching patterns of same-sex and opposite-sex couples." *Demography* 39(3):435–53.

Jimenez-Vasquez, R. 1995. "Hispanics: Cubans." *Encyclopedia of Social Work.* Washington, DC: National Association of Social Work.

Jocks, Christopher Ronwaniente. 2001. "A Native American perspective: To protect the ground we walk on." In John C. Raines and Daniel C. Maguire (eds.), *What Men Owe to Women: Men's Voices from World Religions.* (pp. 259–80). Albany: State University of New York.

Joe, Jennie R., and Dorothy Lonewolf Miller. 1994. "Cultural survival and contemporary American Indian women in the city." In Maxine Baca Zinn and Bonnie Thornton Dill (eds.), *Women of Color in U.S. Society.* Philadelphia: Temple University.

John, Daphne, and Beth Anne Shelton. 1997. "The production of gender among black and white women and men: The case of household labor." *Sex Roles* 36:171–93.

John, Daphne, Beth Anne Shelton, and Kristen Luschen. 1995. "Race, ethnicity, gender, and perceptions of fairness." *Journal of Family Issues* 16(3):357–79.

John, Mary E. 2001. "Gender, development and the women's movement: Problems for a history of the present." In Rajeswari S. Rajan (ed.), *Signposts: Gender Issues in Post-Independence India.* (pp. 100–24). New Brunswick, NJ: Rutgers University.

Johnson, Colleen L. 1999. "Fictive kin among oldest African Americans in the San Francisco Bay area." *Journal of Gerontology, Series B: Psychological Sciences and Social Sciences* 54B(6):S368–S375.

Johnson, David R., and Laurie K. Scheuble. 2002. "What should we call our kids? Choosing children's surnames when parents' last names differ." *Social Science Journal* 39(3):419–29.

Johnson, Elizabeth. 2003. "Basic linguistic options: God, women, and equivalence." in Philip E. Divine and Celia Wolf-Devine (eds.), *Sex and Gender: A Spectrum of Views.* (pp. 363–68). Belmont, CA: Wadsworth/Thompson.

Johnson, Fern L. 1996. "Friendships among women: Closeness in dialogue." In Julia T. Wood (ed.), *Gendered Relationships.* Mountain View, CA: Mayfield.

Johnson, Fern L., and Elizabeth J. Aries. 1998. "The talk of women friends." In Jennifer Coates (ed.), *Language and Gender: A Reader.* (pp. 215–225). Malden, MA: Blackwell.

Johnson, Fern L., and Karren Young. 2002. "Gendered voices in children's television advertising." *Critical Studies in Media Communication* 19(4):461–80.

Johnson, Hortense. 1943/1996. "Hortense Johnson on black women and the war effort, 1943." In Mary Beth Norton and Ruth M. Alexander (eds.), *Major Problems in American Women's History.* Lexington, MA: D.C. Heath.

Johnson, Ida M., and Robert T. Sigler. 2000. "Forced sexual intercourse among intimates." *Journal of Family Violence* 15(1):95–108.

Johnson, Pamela, and Jennifer A. Johnson. 2001. "The oppression of women in India." *Violence Against Women* 7(9):1051–68.

Johnson, Richard W., Usha Sambamoorthi, and Stephen Crystal. 1999. "Gender differences in pension wealth: Estimates using provider data." *Gerontologist* 39(3):320–33.

Johnson, Roberta Ann. 1993. "Affirmative action as a woman's issue." In Lois Lovelace Duke (ed.), *Women in Politics: Outsiders or Insiders?* Englewood Cliffs, NJ: Prentice Hall.

Johnson, Stephen D. 2000. "Who supports the Promise Keepers?" *Sociology of Religion* 61(1): 93–104.

Johnson, Tony W., and Ronald F. Reed (eds.). 2002. "The moral superiority of women as teachers, 1846" and "The one best system and the feminization of the teaching profession: Horace Mann's twelfth annual report, 1848." In *Historical Documents in American Education.* Boston: Allyn & Bacon.

Johnston, Deidre D., and Debra H. Swanson. 2003. "Invisible mothers: A content analysis of motherhood mythologies and myths in magazines." *Sex Roles* 49(1–2):21–33.

Jolivet, Muriel. 1997. *Japan: The Childless Society.* New York: Routledge.

Jones, Katina. 2000. *150 Most Profitable Home Businesses for Women.* Holbrook, MA: Adams Media.

Jones, Lisa A. 2000. "Women making sense of sex: Romantic love, power, and agency." Paper presented at the American Sociological Association, August, Washington, DC.

Joos, Kristin E. 2003. "LGBT parents and their children." *SWS Network News* 20(4):9–14.

Jordan, Ellen, and Angela Cowan. 1995. "Warrior narratives in the kindergarten classroom: Renegotiating the social contract?" *Gender & Society* 9(6):727–43.

Joseph, Miriam. 2001. *Perceived Cultural Influences on Generativity Identified by Childless Women.* Dissertation, St. Louis University.

Josephson, Jyl J. 1997. *Gender, Families and State: Child Support Policies in the United States.* New York: Rowman & Littlefield.

Joyner, Kara, and Richard J. Udry. 2000. "You don't bring me anything but down: Adolescent romance and depression." *Journal of Health and Social Behavior* 41(4):369–91.

Judd, Elizabeth. 1990. "The myths of the golden age and the fall: From matriarchy to patriarchy." In Frances Richardson Keller (ed.), *Views of Women's Lives in Western Tradition.* Lewiston, NY: Edwin Mellen.

Jung, John. 2001. *Psychology of Alcohol and other Drugs: A Research Perspective.* Thousand Oaks, CA: Sage.

Kabir, Shameem. 1994. "Lesbian desire on the screen: The hunger." In Liz Gibbs (ed.), *Daring to Dissent: Lesbian Culture from Margin to Mainstream.* London: Cassell.

Kaledin, Eugenia. 1984. *Mothers and More: American Women in the 1950s.* Boston: Twayne.

Kalmijn, Matthijs. 1998. "Intermarriage and homogamy." *Annual Review of Sociology* 24(1): 395–421.

Kalmijn, Matthijs, and Henk Flap. 2001. "Assortive meeting and mating: Unintended consequences of organized settings for partner choices." *Social Forces* 79(4):1289–312.

Kalof, Linda. 1993. "Dilemmas of femininity: Gender and the social construction of sexual imagery." *Sociological Quarterly* 34(4):639–51.

———. 1999. The effects of gender and music video imagery on sexual attitudes." *Journal of Social Psychology* 139(3):378–85.

Kalof, Linda, Kimberly K. Eby, Jennifer L. Matheson, and Rob J. Kroska. 2001. "The influence of race and gender on student self-reports of sexual harassment by college professors." *Gender & Society* 15(2):282-302.

Kamen, Paula. 2003. *Her Way: Young Women Remake the Sexual Revolution.* New York: New York University.

Kandiyoti, Deniz. 1991. *Women, Islam and the State* (Edited volume). Philadelphia: Temple University.

Kang, Mee-Eun. 1997. "The portrayal of women's images in magazine advertisements: Goffman's gender analysis revisited." *Sex Roles* 37(11–12): 979–96.

Kantor, Martin. 1998. *Homophobia.* Westport, CT: Praeger.

Kaplan, Gisela T. 2003. *Gene Worship: Moving beyond the Nature/Nurture Debate over Genes, Brain, and Gender.* New York: Other Press.

Karakhanova, T. M. 2003, "Working women's value orientations and paid work time use." *Sotsiologicheskie Issledovaniya* (abstract) 29(3): 74–81.

Karant-Nunn, Susan C., and Merry E. Weisner-Hanks. 2003. *Luther on Women: A Source Book.* Cambridge, UK: Cambridge University.

Karlsen, Carol F. 2004. "The devil in the shape of a woman: The economic basis of witchcraft." In Linda K. Kerber and Jane Sherron De Hart (eds.), *Women's America: Refocusing the Past.* New York: Oxford University.

Karniol, Rachel, and Amir Aida. 1997. "Judging toy breakers: Gender stereotypes have dubious effects on children." *Sex Roles* 36(3–4):195–205.

Karon, John M., Patricia L. Fleming, Richard W. Steketee, and Kevin M. De Cock. 2001. "HIV in the United States at the turn of the century: An epidemic in transition." *American Journal of Public Health* 91(7):1060–68.

Kashiwagi, Keiko, and Sono Hasuka. 2000. "Attitude and emotion toward mother-child separation (sending a child to day-care center) in working mothers and non-working mothers." *Japanese Journal Family Psychology* 14(1):61–74.

Katovich, Michael A., and Marya S. Makowski. 1999. "Music periods in the rock and post rock eras: The rise of female performers on a provocative stage." *Studies in Symbolic Interaction* 23:141–66.

Kaufman, Debra R. 1995. "Professional women: How real are the recent gains?" In Jo Freeman (ed.) *Women: A Feminist Perspective.* Mountain View, CA: Mayfield.

Kaufman, Gayle. 1999. "The portrayal of men's family roles in television commercials." *Sex Roles* 38:469–79.

Kaufman, Gayle, and Peter Uhlenberg. 2000. "The influence of parenthood on the work effort of married men and women." *Social Forces* 78(3):931–49.

Kaufman, Michael T. 1999. "Bessie Cohen, 107, survivor of 1911 Shirtwaist fire, dies," *New York Times Obituaries,* February 24:C22.

Kazemzadeh, Masoud. 2002. *Islamic Fundamentalism, Feminism, and Gender Inequality in Iran under Khomeini.* Lanham, MD: University Press of America.

Keel, Pamela K., and Kelly L. Klump. 2003. "Are eating disorders culture-bound syndromes? Implications for conceptualizing their etiology." *Psychological Bulletin* 129(5):747–69.

Keenan, JoAnne Wilson, Judith Solsken, and Jerri Willett. 1999. "Only boys can jump high: Reconstructing gender relations in a first/second-grade classroom." In Barbara Kamler (ed.), *Constructing Gender and Difference: Critical Research Perspectives on Early Childhood.* (pp. 33–70). Cresskill, NJ: Hampton.

Keiliz, Susan. 2002. "Improving judicial system responses to domestic violence: The promises and risks of integrated case management and technology solutions." In Albert R. Roberts (ed.), *Handbook of Domestic Violence Intervention Strategies: Policies, Programs, and Legal Remedies.* (pp. 147–72). New York: Oxford University.

Kell, Carl L., and L. Raymond Camp. 1999. *In the Name of the Father: The Rhetoric of the New Southern Baptist Convention.* Carbondale: Southern Illinois University.

Kelle, Helga. 2000. "Gender and territoriality in games played by nine- to twelve-year old schoolchildren." *Journal of Contemporary Ethnography* 29(2):164–97.

Keller, Evelyn Fox. 2000. "Women, gender, and science: Some parallels between primatology and developmental biology." In Shirley C. Strum and Linda M. Fedigan (eds.), *Primate Encounters: Models of Science, Gender and Society* (pp. 382–97). Chicago: University of Chicago.

Keller, James R. 2002. *Queer (Un)friendly Film and Television.* Jefferson, NC: McFarland.

Kelly, E. L. 1999. "Theorizing corporate family policies: How advocates built 'the business case' for 'family-friendly' programs." *Research in the Sociology of Work* 7:169–202.

Kemp, Alice Abel. 1994. *Women's Work: Degraded and Devalued.* Englewood Cliffs, NJ: Prentice Hall.

Kempf-Leonard, K., and Lisa L. Sample. 2000. "Disparity based on sex: Is gender specific treatment warranted?" *Justice Quarterly* 17(1):89–128.

Kennelly, E. 1984. "Republicans in fear of a gender gap, feature women at convention." *National NOW Times* (September–October):3.

Kennison, Sheila M., and Jessie L. Trofe. 2003. "Comprehending pronouns: A role for word-specific gender stereotype information." *Journal of Psycholinguistic Research* 32(3):355–78.

Kenway, Jane, and Elizabeth Bullen. 2001. *Consuming Children: Education, Entertainment, and Advertising.* Buckingham, UK: Open University.

Kerber, Linda K. 1988. "Why should girls be learn'd and wise?: Two centuries of higher education for women as seen through the unfinished work of Mary Baldwin." In John Mack and Florence Howe (eds.), *Women and Higher Education in American History.* New York: W.W. Norton.

Kerber, Linda K. 1998. *No Constitutional Right to be Ladies: Women and the Obligations of Citizenship.* New York: Hill and Wang.

Kerr, Mary Margaret, and C. Michael Nelson. 2002. *Strategies for Addressing Behavior Problems in the Classroom.* Upper Saddle River, NJ: Merrill/Prentice Hall.

Kesner, I. F. 1988. "Director's characteristics and committee membership: An investigation of type, occupation, tenures, and gender." *Academy of Management Journal* 31:66–84.

Kessler-Harris, Alice. 1991. "Where are the organized women workers?" In Linda K. Kerber and Jane Sherron De Hart (eds.), *Women's America: Refocusing the Past.* New York: Oxford University.

Keuls, Eva. 1993. *The Reign of the Phallus: Sexual Politics in Ancient Athens.* Berkeley: University of California.

Keville, Terri D. 1993. "The invisible woman: Gender bias in medical research." *Women's Rights Law Reporter* 15(2–3):123–42.

Khan, Sayyid Ahmad. 2000. "The rights of women." In Mansoor Moaddel and Kamran Talattof (eds.), *Contemporary Debates in Islam: An Anthology of Modernist and Fundamentalist Thought.* (pp. 159–62). New York: St. Martin's.

Khandker, Shahidur. 1998. *Fighting Poverty with Microcredit: Experience in Bangladesh.* New York: Oxford University.

Khanna, Madhu. 2000. "The goddess woman equation in Sakta Tantras." In Mandakranta Bose (ed.), *Faces of the Feminine in Ancient, Medieval, and Modern India* (pp. 109–23). New York: Oxford University

Khasbulatova, O. A., and L. S. Egorova. 2002. "Social feeling among women and men in medium sized Russian cities." *Sotsiologicheskie Issledovaniya* (abstract) 28(11):48–54.

Khotkina, Zoya. 1994. "Women in the labour market: Yesterday, today and tomorrow." In Anastasia Posadskaya and the Moscow Gender Centre (eds.), *Women in Russia: A New Era in Russian Feminism.* London: Verso.

Kilbourne, Jean. 1995. "Beauty and the beast of advertising." In Paula S. Rothenberg (ed.), *Race, Class, and Gender in the United States: An Integrated Study.* New York: St. Martin's.

Kim, Jungmeen E., and Phyllis Moen. 2002. "Retirement transitions, gender and psychological well-being: A life-course ecological model." *Journal of Gerontology* 57B(3):212–22.

Kim, Walter, and Wendy Cole. 2000. "Twice as nice: Expensive second weddings." *Time* 155(25):53–4.

Kimmel, Michael S. 1996. "Men and women's studies: Premises, perils and promise." In Nancy Hewitt, Jean O'Barr, and Nancy Rosebaugh (eds.), *Talking Gender: Public Images, Personal Journeys, and Political Critiques.* (pp. 153–66). Chapel Hill: University of North Carolina.

———. 2000. "Saving the males: The sociological implications of the Virginia Military Institute and the Citadel." *Gender & Society* 14(4):494–16.

———. 2004. "Clarence, William, Iron Mike, Tailhook, Senator Packwood, Spur Posse, Magic . . . and Us: A second look." In Michael S. Kimmel and Michael A. Messner (eds.), *Men's Lives.* (pp. 565–85). Boston: Allyn & Bacon

Kincheloe, Joe L. 1999. *How Do We Tell the Workers? The Socioeconomic Foundations of Work and Vocational Education.* Boulder, CO: Westview.

Kinelski, Kristin, Jessie Markowitz, and Catherine Chambliss. 2002. "The effects of maternal employment on the attitudes, work expectations, and self-esteem of urban and suburban middle school parents." ERIC: *Resources in Education,* CG031601.

King, David. C. 1999. "The trouble with (Republican) women." *JFK Bulletin* May. Harvard University.

King, Karen L. (ed.). 1997. *Women and Goddess Traditions: In Antiquity and Today.* Minneapolis, MN: Fortress.

King, Ursula. 1989. *Women and Spirituality.* New York: New Amsterdam.

Kinsella, Kevin, and Victoria Velkoff. 2001. "An aging world: 2001." *International Population Reports* November. U.S. Census Bureau.

Kinsey, Alfred E., Wardell B. Pomeroy, and Clyde E. Martin. 1948. *Sexual Behavior in the Human Male.* Philadelphia: Saunders.

Kinsey, Alfred E., Wardell B. Pomeroy, Clyde E. Martin, and H. Gephard. 1953. *Sexual Behavior in the Human Female.* Philadelphia: Saunders.

Kitano, Harry H. L., and Roger Daniels. 1995. *Asian Americans: Emerging Minorities,* Englewood Cliffs, NJ: Prentice Hall.

Kitch, Carolyn. 2001. *The Girl on the Magazine Cover: The Origins of Visual Stereotypes in American Mass Media.* Chapel Hill: University of North Carolina.

Klaus, Marshall H., and J. H. Kennell. 1983. *Bonding: The Beginnings of Parent-Infant Attachment.* New York: Mosby.

Klein, Hugh, Kenneth S. Shiffman, and Denise A. Welka. 2000. "Gender-related content of animated cartoons, 1930 to the present." *Advances in Gender Research* 4:291–317.

Klein, Uta. 2002. "The gender perspective of civil-military relations in Israeli society." *Current Sociology* 50(5):669–86.

Kleinbaum, Abby Wettan. 1990. "Amazon legends and misogynists: The women and civilization question." In Frances Richardson Keller (ed.), *Views of Women's Lives in Western Tradition.* Lewiston, NY: Edwin Mellen.

Kleinfeld, Judith. 1998. "Why smart people believe that schools shortchange girls: What you see when you live in a tail: The shortchanged group is really African-American males." *Gender Issues* 16(1–2):47–63.

Kleinplatz, Peggy J. 2000. "On the outside looking in: In search of women's sexual experience." *Women & Therapy* 24(1–2):123–32.

Kleugel, James R., and Lawrence D. Bobo. 2001. "Perceived group discrimination and policy attitudes: The sources and consequences of the race and gender gaps." In Alice O'Connor, Chris Tilly, and Lawrence D. Bobo (eds.), *Urban Inequality: Evidence from Four Cities* (pp. 163–213). New York: Russell Sage.

Kling, Kristen C., Janet Shibley Hyde, and Carolin J. Showers. 1999, "Gender differences in self-esteem: A meta-analysis." *Psychological Bulletin* 125(4):470–500.

Kloek, Els, Nicole Teeuwen, and Marijke Huisman (eds.). 1994. *Women of the Golden Age: An International Debate on Women in Seventeenth-Century Holland, England and Italy.* Amsterdam: Hilversum Verloren.

Kloppenborg, Ria. 1995. "Female stereotypes in early Buddhism: The women of the Therigatha." In Ria Kloppenborg and Wouter J. Hanegraaff (eds.), *Female Stereotypes in Religious Traditions.* Leiden, Netherlands: Brill.

Klugman, Karen. 1999. "A bad hair day for G.I. Joe." In Beverly Lyon Clark and Margaret R. Higonnet (eds.), *Girls, Boys, Books, Toys: Gender in Children's Literature and Culture.* (pp. 69–82). Baltimore: Johns Hopkins University.

Knapp, Kiyoko Kamio. 1999. "Don't awaken the sleeping child: Japan's gender equality law and the rhetoric of gradualism." *Columbia Journal of Gender & Law* 8(2):178–83.

Knickmeyer, Nicole, Kim Sexton, and Nancy Nishimura. 2002. "The impact of same-sex friendships on the well-being of women: A review of the literature." *Women & Therapy* 25(1):37–59.

Knudson-Martin, Carmen, and Anne Rankin Mahoney. 1998. "Language and processes in the construction of equality in new marriages." *Family Relations* 47(1):81–91.

Kohlberg, Lawrence. 1966. "A cognitive-developmental analysis of children's sex role concepts and attitudes." In Eleanor Maccoby (ed.), *The Development of Sex Differences*. Stanford, CA: Stanford University.

Kolaric, Giselle C., and Nancy L. Galambos. 1995. "Face-to-face interactions in unacquainted female-male adolescent dyads: How do girls and boys behave?" *Journal of Early Adolescence* 15(3):363–82.

Korn/Ferry International. 2002. *What Women Want in Business: A Survey of Executives and Entrepreneurs.* Los Angeles: Korn/Ferry International. Available online: http://www.kornferry/Library

Korte, Michele. 1999. "Xena: Cyberprincess." *Advocate* March:24–33.

Kosberg, Robert L., and Andrew S. Rancer. 1999. "Enhancing argumentativeness and argumentative behavior: The influence of gender and training." In Linda Longmire and Lisa Merrill (eds.), *Untying the Tongue: Gender, Power, and the Word.* Westport, CT: Praeger/Greenwood.

Kotler, Jennifer A., Aletha C. Huston, and John C. Wright. 2001. "Television use in families with children." In Jennings Bryant and J. Alison Bryant (eds.), *Television and the American Family.* (pp. 33–48). Mahwah, NJ: Lawrence Erlbaum.

Kozik-Rosabal, Genet. 2000. "'Well we haven't noticed anything bad going on, said the principle: Parents speak out about their gay families and schools." *Education and Urban Society* 32(3):368–89.

Krahe, Barbara. 2000. "Sexual scripts and heterosexual aggression." In Thomas Eckes and Hanns M. Trautner (eds.), *The Developmental Social Psychology of Gender.* (pp. 273–94). Mahwah, NJ: Lawrence Erlbaum.

Kramer, Heinrich, and Jacob Sprenger. 2000. "Methods of the devil." In Elaine G. Breslaw (ed.), *Witches of the Atlantic World: A Historical Reader and Primary Sourcebook.* (pp. 21–27). New York: New York University.

Krasnow, Iris. 1995. "Women at 50: Fit, fulfilled and blazing." *Washington Post,* July 10:D5.

Kraus, Vered. 2002. *Secondary Breadwinners: Israeli Women in the Labor Force.* Westport, CT: Praeger.

Krauss, Daniel A., and Bruce D. Sales. 2000. "Legal standards, expertise, and experts in the resolution of contested child custody cases." *Psychology, Public Policy and Law* 6(4):843–79.

Kroska, Amy. 2000. "Time for theoretical bargaining: Re-examining theories of household labor." Paper presented at the American Sociological Association, Washington, DC, August.

———. 2003. "Investigating gender differences in the meaning of household chores and child care." *Journal of Marriage and the Family* 65(2):456–73.

Kuhlmann, Annette. 1996. "Indian country in the 1990s: Changing roles of American Indian women." Paper presented at the Midwest Sociological Society, Chicago. April.

Kulik, Liat. 2000. "The impact of education and family attributes on attitudes and responses to unemployment among men and women. *Journal of Sociology and Social Welfare* 27(2):161–83.

Kunin, Madeleine. 1994. *Living a Political Life: One of America's First Woman Governors Tells Her Story.* New York: Alfred A. Knopf.

Kunkel, D. 2001. "Children and television advertising." In Dorothy Singer and Jerome L. Singer (eds.), *Handbook of Children and the Media.* Thousand oaks, CA: Sage.

Kurdek, Lawrence A. 1998. "Relationship outcomes and their predictors: Longitudinal evidence from heterosexual married, gay, gay cohabiting, and lesbian cohabiting couples." *Journal of Marriage and the Family* 60:553–68.

Kurdek, Lawrence A., and Chad Kennedy. 2001. "Differences between couples who end their marriage by fault or no-fault legal procedures." *Journal of Family Psychology* 15(2):241–53.

Kurian, Priya A. 2000. *Engendering the Environment: Gender in the World Bank's Environmental Policies.* Aldershot, UK: Ashgate.

Kurtz, Demie. 1995. *For Richer, For Poorer: Mothers Confront Divorce.* New York: Routledge.

———. 2002. "Caring for teenage children." *Journal of Family Issues* 23(6):748–67.

Kuttner, Robert. 2001. "Body politics." *American Prospect* Fall:A1.

Kuznets, Lois R. 1999. "Taking over the doll's house: Domestic desire and nostalgia in toy narratives." In Beverly Lyon Clark and Margaret R. Higonnet (eds.), *Girls, Boys, Books, Toys: Gender in Children's Literature and Culture.* (pp. 142–53). Baltimore: Johns Hopkins.

Kyratzis, Amy. 2001a. "Children's gender indexing in language: From the separate world's hypothesis to considerations of culture, context and power." *Research on Language and Social Interaction* 34(1):1–13.

———. 2001b. "Emotion talk in preschool same-sex friendship groups: Fluidity over time and context." *Early Education & Development* 12(3):359–92.

LaFrance, Marianne. 2002. "Smile boycotts and other body politics." *Feminism & Psychology* 12(3):319–23.

LaFrance, Marianne, and Marvin A. Hecht. 2000. "Gender and smiling: A meta-analysis. In Agneta H. Fischer (ed.), *Gender and Emotion: Social Psychological Perspectives.* New York: Cambridge University.

LaFrance, Marianne, Marvin A. Hecht, and Elizabeth Levy Paluck. 2003. "The contingent smile: A meta-analysis of sex differences in smiling." *Psychological Bulletin* 129(2):305–34.

Lakhani, Sadaf. 2002. "Gender and poverty, women, land and labour." *Development in Action* (Student Action). Available online at: http://www.studentactionindia.org.uk/newspages/dia_articles/ 28.php

Lakoff, Robin. 1975. *Language and Woman's Place.* New York: Colsphon.

Lamb, Michael. 2002a. "Infant-father attachments and their impact on child development." In Catherine S. Tamis-LeMonda and Natasha Cabrera (eds.), *Handbook of Father Involvement: Multidisciplinary Perspectives.* Mahwah, NJ: Lawrence Erlbaum.

———. 2002b. "Nonresidential fathers and their children." In Catherine S. Tamis-LeMonda and Natasha Cabrera (eds.), *Handbook of Father Involvement: Multidisciplinary Perspectives.* Mahwah, NJ: Lawrence Erlbaum.

Lambdin, Jennifer R., Kristen M. Greer, and Kari Selby Jibotian. 2003. "The animal=male hypothesis: Children's and adults' beliefs about the sex of non-specific stuffed animals." *Sex Roles* 48(11–12):471–82

Landen, M., O. Bodlund, L. Ekselius, G. Hambert, and B. Lundstrom. 1998. *Lakartidningen* 98(July 25):3322–6.

Landry, Bart. 2000. *Black Working Wives: Pioneers of the American Family Revolution.* Berkeley: University of California.

Lane, Richard, and Jay Wurts. 1998. *In Search of the Woman Warrior: Four Mythical Archetypes for Modern Women.* Boson: Element.

Lang, Sabine. 1998. *Men as Women, Women as Men: Changing Gender in Native American Cultures.* Austin: University of Texas.

Langley, Merlin R. 1994. "The cool pose: An Africentric analysis." In Richard G. Majors and Jacob U. Gordon (eds.), *The American Black Male: His Present Status and His Future.* Chicago: Nelson-Hall.

Langley, Winston E., and Vivian C. Fox (eds.). 1998. "Employed mothers and child care during the Depression and World War II." Document 93: 255–57. In *Women's Rights in the United States: A Documentary History.* Westport, CT: Praeger.

Lansford, Jennifer E., and Jeffrey G. Parker. 1999. "Children's interaction in triads: Behavioral profiles and effects of gender and patterns of friendships among members." *Developmental Psychology* 35(1):80–93.

Lareau, Annette. 2002. "Invisible inequality: Social class and childrearing in black families and white families." *American Sociological Review* 67(5):747–76.

LaRossa, Ralph, Betty Anne Gordon, Ronald Jay Wilson, Annette Bairan, and Charles Jaret. 1991. "The fluctuating image of the 20th century American father." *Journal of Marriage and the Family* 53:531–44.

Larson, Gerald James. 1994. "Hinduism in India and in America." In Jacob Neusner (ed.), *World Religions in America: An Introduction.* (pp. 177–202). Louisville, KY: Westminster/John Knox.

Larson, Mary Strom. 2001. "Interactions, activities and gender in children's television commercials: A content analysis." *Journal of Broadcasting & Electronic Media* 45(1):41–56.

———. 2003. "Gender, race and aggression in television commercials that feature children." *Sex Roles* 48(1–2):67–75.

Lasswell, Marcia. 2002. "Marriage and family." In Susan G. Kornstein and Anita H. Clayton (eds.), *Women's Mental Health: A Comprehensive Textbook* (pp. 515–26). New York: Guilford.

Laumann, Edward O., and Jenna Mahay. 2002. "The social organization of women's sexuality." In Gina M. Wingood and Ralph J. DiClemente (eds.), *Handbook of Women's Sexual and Reproductive Health: Issues in Women's Health.* (pp. 43–70). New York: Kluwer Academic/Plenum.

Laundra, Kenneth H., Gary Kiger, and Stephen J. Bahr. 2002. "A social development model of serious delinquency: Examining gender differences." *Journal of Primary Prevention* 22(4):389–407.

Lauzen, Martha M. 2003a. *Boxed In: Women on Screen and Behind the Scenes in the 2002–2003 Prime-Time Season.* San Diego, CA: School of Communication, San Diego State University.

Lauzen, Martha M. 2003b. *The Celluloid Ceiling: Behind-the-Scenes and On-Screen Employment of Women in the Top 250 Films of 2002.* San Diego, CA: School of Communication, San Diego State University.

Lavine, Howard, Donna Sweeney, and Stephen H. Wagner. 1999 "Depicting women as sex objects in television advertising: Effects on bodily dissatisfaction." *Personality and Social Psychology Bulletin* 25(6):1049–58.

Law Center. 2003. "Narrow use of affirmative action preserved in college admissions." *CNN.* December 25. Available online at: http://www.cnn.com.2003/LAW/06/23/scotus.affirmativeaction

Laws, Judith Long, and Pepper Schwartz. 1981. *Sexual Scripts: The Social Construction of Female Sexuality.* Washington, DC: University Press.

Lawson, Erma Jean, and Aaron Thompson. 1999. *Black Men and Divorce.* Thousand Oaks, CA: Sage.

Leaper, Campbell. 1994. "Exploring the consequences of gender segregation on social relationships." In Campbell Leaper (ed.), *Childhood Gender Segregation: Causes and Consequences.* (pp. 67–86). San Francisco: Jossey-Bass.

———. 2000. "Gender, affiliation, assertion, and the interactive context of parent-child play." *Developmental Psychology* 36(3):381–93.

———. 2002. "Parenting boys and girls." In Marc H. Bornstein (ed.), *Handbook of Parenting: Volume I: Children and Parenting.* (pp. 189–25). Mahwah, NJ: Lawrence Erlbaum.

Leaper, Campbell, Lisa Breed, and Laurie Hoffman. 2002. "Variations in the gender-stereotyped content of children's television cartoons across genres." *Journal of Applied Social Psychology* 32(8): 1653–62.

Lebra, Takie Sugiyama. 1984. *Japanese Women: Constraint and Fulfillment.* Honolulu: University of Hawaii.

Lebsock, Suzanne. 1990. "'No obey': Indian, European, and African women in seventeenth-century Virginia." In Nancy A. Hewitt (ed.), *Women, Families, and Communities: Readings in American History, Volume One: to 1877.* Glenview, IL: Scott, Foresman.

Lee, Christina. 1998. *Women's Health: Psychological and Social Perspectives.* Thousand Oaks, CA: Sage.

Lee, Grace O.M. 2002. "The challenges of global capitalism: Unemployment and state workers' reactions and responses in post-reform China." *International Journal of Human Resources Management* 13(3):399–415.

Lee, Richard M., and Tina Hsin-tine Liu. 2001. "Coping with intergenerational family conflict: Comparison of Asian Americans, Hispanic and European American college students." *Journal of Counseling Psychology* 48(4):410–19.

Lee, Valerie E., and H. M. Marks. 1990. "Sustained effects of the single-sex secondary school experience on attitudes, behaviors, and values in college." *Journal of Educational Psychology* 82(3): 578–92.

Leeb, Rebecca Toby. 2001. "Here's Looking at You, Kid! Sex Differences, Sex-typing, and Mutual Gaze Behavior in Young Infants." *Dissertation Abstracts International: Section B: The Sciences and Engineering* 61(12-B):6692.

Lehman, Edward C., Jr. 1993. *Gender and Work: The Case of the Clergy.* Albany: State University of New York.

————. *Women's Path into Ministry: Six Major Studies.* Durham, NC: Duke Divinity School.

Lehman, Peter. 2004. "In an imperfect world, men with small penises are unforgiven: The presentation of the penis/phallus in American films of the 1990s." In Michael S. Kimmel and Michael A. Messner (eds.), *Men's Lives.* (pp. 522–32). Boston: Allyn & Bacon.

Lehne, Gregory K. 1992. "Homophobia among men: Supporting and defining the male role." In Michael S. Kimmel and Michael A. Messner (eds.), *Men's Lives.* New York: Macmillan.

Leiblum, Sandra R. 2002. "Reconsidering gender differences in sexual desire: An update." *Journal of Sexual & Relationship Therapy* 17(1):57–68.

Leonard, Elizabeth Dermody. 2002. *Convicted Survivors: The Imprisonment of Battered Women who Kill.* Albany: State University of New York.

Leppänen, Jukka M., and Jari K. Hietanen. 2001. "Emotion recognition and social adjustment in school-aged girls and boys." *Scandinavian Journal of Psychology* 42(5):429–35.

Lerner, Gerda. 1995. "A new angle of vision." In Sheila Ruth (ed.), *Issues in Feminism: An Introduction to Women's Studies.* Mountain View, CA: Mayfield.

Lerner, Gerda. 1996. "Placing women in history." In Mary Beth Norton and Ruth M. Alexander (eds.), *Major Problems in American Women's History.* Lexington, MA: D. C. Heath.

Letherby, Gayle. 2002. "Childless and bereft? Stereotypes and realities in relation to 'voluntary' and 'involuntary' childlessness and womanhood." *Sociological Inquiry* 72(1):7–20.

Letich, Larry. 1991. "Do you know who your friends are?: Why most men over 30 don't have friends and what they can do about it." *Utne Reader* (May–June): 85–87.

Levine, A., and J. Cureton (eds.). 1998. *When Hope and Fear Collide: A Portrait of Today's College Student.* San Francisco: Jossey-Bass.

Levine, Amy-Jill. 2001. "Settling at Beer-lahai-roi." In Yvonne Yazbeck and John L. Esposito (eds.), *Daughters of Abraham: Feminist Thought in Judaism, Christianity, and Islam.* (pp. 12–34). Gainesville: University Press of Florida.

LeVine, Robert A. 1990. "Gender differences: Interpreting anthropological data." In Malkah T. Notman and Carol C. Nadelson (eds.), *Women and Men: New Perspectives on Gender Differences.* Washington, DC: American Psychiatric Press.

Levine, Stephen B. 1998. *Sexuality in Mid-Life.* New York: Plenum.

Levins, Harry. 1995. "People" column. *St. Louis Post-Dispatch* March 19:2A.

Levstik, Linda S. 2001. "Daily acts of ordinary courage: Gender-equitable practice in the social studies classroom." In Patricia O'Reilly and Elizabeth M. Penn (eds.), *Educating Young Adolescent Girls.* (pp. 189–211). Mahwah, NJ: Lawrence Erlbaum.

Lev-Wiesel, Rachel. 2000. "The effect of children's sleeping arrangements (communal vs. familial) on fatherhood among men in an Israeli kibbutz." *Journal of Social Psychology* 140(5):580–8.

Lewis, Jan E. 2002. "A revolution for whom? Women in the era of the American Revolution." In Nancy A. Hewitt (ed.), *A Companion to American Women's History.* Oxford, UK: Blackwell.

Lewis, Karen Gail. 2001. *With or Without a Man: Single Women Taking Control of Their Lives.* Boulder, CO: Bull.

Li, Jianghong, and William Lavely. 2003. "Village context, women's status, and son preference among rural Chinese women." *Rural Sociology* 68(1)87–106.

Liben Lynn S., Rebecca S. Bigler, and Holleen R. Krogh. 2002. *Child Development* 73(3):810–28.

Liben Lynn S., Holleen R. Krogh, and Rebecca S. Bigler. 2001. "Pink and blue collar jobs: Children's judgments of job status and job aspirations in relation to sex of worker." *Journal of Experimental Child Psychology* 79(4):346–63.

Lichtenstein, Bronwen. 2000. "Secret encounters: Black men, bisexuality, and AIDS in Alabama." *Medical Anthropology Quarterly* 14(3):374–93.

Lichter, Daniel T., and Nancy C. Landale, 1995. "Parental work, family structure, and poverty among Latino children." *Journal of Marriage and the Family* 57:346–54.

Lichter, Daniel T., and D. R. Graefe. 2001. "Finding a mate? The marital and cohabitation histories of unwed mothers." In L. Wu and B. Wolfe (eds.), *Out of Wedlock: Causes and Consequences of Nonmarital Fertility.* (pp. 317–43). New York: Russell Sage Foundation.

Lichter, S. Robert, and Daniel R. Amundson. 2000. "Distorted reality: Hispanic characters in TV entertainment." In Clara Rodriquez (ed.), *Latin Looks.* (pp. 57–92). Boulder, CO: Westview.

Lichter, S. Robert, L.S. Lichter and S. Rothman. 1994. *Prime Time: How TV Portrays American Culture.* Washington, DC: Regency.

Liddle, Joanna, and Sachiko Nakajima. 2000. *Rising Suns, Rising Daughters: Gender, Class and Power in Japan*. London: Zed.

Lienemann, Wolfgang. 1998. "Churches and homosexuality: An overview of recent official church statements on sexual orientation." *Ecumenical Review*. January.

Liff, Sonia, and Kate Ward. 2001. "Distorted views through the glass ceiling: The construction of women's understandings of promotion and senior management positions." *Gender, Work & Organization* 8(1):19–36.

Lightfoot, J. L. (trans.). 2003. *On the Syrian Goddess*. New York: Oxford University.

Ligos, Melinda. 2001. "Escape route from sexist attitudes on Wall Street." *New York Times* May 30:C10.

Lin, Carolyn. 1999. "The portrayal of women in television advertising." In Marian Meyers (ed.), *Mediated Women: Representations in Popular Culture*. (pp. 253–70). Creskill, NJ: Hampton.

Linden, Wolfgang, et al. 2003. "There is more to anger coping than 'in' or 'out.'" *Emotion* 3(1):12–29.

Lindgren, Elaine H. 1996. *Land in her Own Name: Women as Homesteaders in North Dakota*. Norman: University of Oklahoma.

Lindsey, Linda L. 1979. Book review of *Wisdom from Women in the Bible* by Edith Deen. *Review for Religious* 38(5):792–93.

———. 1984. "Career paths in pharmacy: An exploration of male and female differences." Paper presented at the Midwest Sociological Society, Chicago.

———. 1988. "The health status of women in Pakistan: The impact of Islamization." Paper presented at the Midwest Sociological Society, Minneapolis.

———. 1992. "Gender and the workplace: Some lessons from Japan." Paper presented at the Midwest Sociological Society, Kansas City.

———. 1995. "Toward a model of women in development." Paper presented at the Midwest Sociological Society, Chicago.

———. 1996a. "Women and agriculture in the developing world." In Paula J. Dubeck and Kathryn Borman (eds.), *Women and Work: A Handbook*. New York: Garland.

———. 1996b. "Gender equity and development: A perspective on the U.N. Conference on Women." Paper presented at the Midwest Sociological Society, Chicago.

———. 1996c. "Full-time homemaker as unpaid laborer." In Paula J. Dubeck and Kathryn Borman (eds.), *Women and Work: A Handbook*. New York: Garland.

———. 1997. "Smoking out the gender connection." *Chicago Tribune*, March 28:Sect. 1(11).

———. 1998. "Gender issues in Japanese style management: Implications for American corporations." Paper presented at the Asian Studies Development Program National Conference, Baltimore.

———. 1999. "The politics of cultural identity and minority women in China." Paper presented at the Mid-Atlantic Region for Asian Studies, Gettysburg, PA.

———. 2002a. "Gender segregation in a global context: Focus on Afghan women." Paper presented at the Midwest Sociological Society, Milwaukee.

———. 2002b. "Globalization and human rights: Focus on Afghan women." In *September 11 and Beyond*. (pp. 62–67). Upper Saddle River, NJ: Prentice Hall.

———. 2004. "The paradox of women and economic development in China." Paper presented at the Midwest Sociological Society, Kansas City.

Lindsey, Linda L., and Stephen Beach. 2004. *Sociology*. Upper Saddle River, NJ: Prentice Hall.

Lipke, David. 2000. "The state of matrimony." *American Demographics* 22(11):14, 16.

Lipovskaya, Olga. 1994. "The mythology of womanhood in contemporary 'Soviet' culture." In Anastasia Posadskaya and the Moscow Gender Centre (eds.), *Women in Russia: A New Era in Russian Feminism*. London: Verso.

Lippa, Richard A., and Francisco D. Tan. 2001. "Does culture moderate the relationship between sexual orientation and gender-related personality traits?" *Cross-cultural Research: The Journal of Comparative Social Science* 35(1):65–87.

Lippy, Charles H. 1999. "Pluralism and American religious life in the later twentieth century." In Peter W. Williams (ed.), *Perspectives on American Religion and Culture*. (pp. 48–60). Malden, MA: Blackwell.

Lips, Hilary M. 2001. *Sex & Gender: An Introduction*. Mountain View, CA: Mayfield.

Lloyd, Kim M., and Scott J. South. 1996. "Contextual influences on young men's transition to first marriage." *Social Forces* 74:1097–119.

Lockhart, William. H. 2000. "'We are one in life,' but not of one gender ideology: Unity, ambiguity and the Promise Keepers." *Sociology of Religion* 61(1):73–92.

Loraux, Nicole. 1998. *Mother in Mourning: With the Essay of Amnesty and its Opposite* (Corinne Pache, Trans.). Ithaca, NY: Cornell University.

Louie, Miriam Ching Yoon, and Nguyen Louie. 1998. In Gwyn Kirk and Margo Ozawa-Rey (eds.), *Women's Lives: Multicultural Perspectives*. (pp. 145–51). Mountain View, CA: Mayfield.

Low, Alaine, and Soraya Tremayne (eds.). 2001. *Sacred Custodians of the Earth: Women, Spirituality and the Environment*. New York: Berghahn.

Low, Bobbi S. 2000. *Why Sex Matters: A Darwinian Look at Human Behavior*. Princeton, NJ: Princeton University.

Low, Jason, and Peter Sherrard. 1999. "Portrayal of women in sexuality and marriage and family textbooks: A content analysis of photographs from the 1970s to the 1990s." *Sex Roles* 40(3–4):309–18.

Luciak, Ilja A. 2001. *After the Revolution: Gender and Democracy in El Salvador, Nicaragua, and Guatemala*. Baltimore: Johns Hopkins University.

Luciano, Lynne. 2001. *Looking Good: Male Body Image in Modern America*. New York: Hill and Wang.

Luck, Mike, Margaret Bamford, and Peter Williamson. 2000. *Men's Health: Perspectives, Diversity and Paradox*. Oxford, UK: Blackwell Science.

Lueptow, Lloyd B., Lori Garovich-Szabo, and Margaret B. Lueptow. 2001. "Social change and the persistence of sex-typing." *Social Forces* 80(1):1–36.

Luker, Kristin. 1984. *Abortion and the Politics of Motherhood.* Berkeley, CA: University of California.

Lundskow, George N. 2002. *Awakening to an Uncertain Future: A Case Study of the Promise Keepers.* New York: Peter Lang.

Lynch, Jean M., and Kim Murray. 2000. "For the love of the children: The coming out process for lesbian and gay parents and stepparents." *Journal of Homosexuality* 39(1):1–24.

Lynn, David B. 1969. *Parental and Sex Role Identification: A Theoretical Formulation.* Berkeley, CA: McCutchan.

Lynn, Naomi B. 1984. "Women and politics: The real majority." In Jo Freeman (ed.), *Women: A Feminist Perspective.* Palo Alto, CA: Mayfield.

Lystra, Karen. 1989. *Searching the Heart: Women, Men and Romantic Love in Nineteenth Century America.* New York: Oxford University.

Macauley, Marcia. 2001. "Tough talk: Indirectness and gender in requests for information." *Journal of Pragmatics* 33(2):293–16.

Maccoby, Eleanor E. 1998. *The Two Sexes: Growing up Apart, Coming Together.* Cambridge, MA: Belknap/Harvard University.

———. 2000. "Perspective on gender development." *International Journal of Behavioral Development* 24(4):398–406.

Maccoby, Eleanor Emmons, and Carol Nagy Jacklin. 1974. *The Psychology of Sex Differences.* Stanford, CA: Stanford University.

MacDermid, Shelley M., Gabriela Heilburn, and Laura Gillespie DeHaan. 1997. "The generativity of employed mothers in multiple roles: 1979 and 1991." In Margie E. Lachman and Jacquelyn Boone James (eds.), *Multiple Paths of Midlife Development.* (pp. 207–40). Chicago: University of Chicago.

MacKay, Judith. 2001. "Global sex: Sexuality and sexual practices around the world." *Sexual & Relational Therapy* 16(1):71–82.

MacKay, Natalie J., and Katherine Covell. 1997. "The impact of women in advertisements on attitudes toward women." *Sex Roles* 36:573–83.

MacKellar, Landis, and David Horlacher. 2000. "Population ageing in Japan." *Innovation* 13(4):413–30.

MacKinnon, Catharine A. 1989. *Toward a Feminist Theory of the State.* Cambridge, MA: Harvard University.

———. 2000a. "The social causes of sexual harassment." In Edmund Wall (ed.), *Sexual Harassment, Confrontation and Decisions.* (pp. 141–56). Amherst, NY: Prometheus.

———. 2000b. "Sexual harassment as sex discrimination." In Edmund Wall (ed.), *Sexual Harassment, Confrontation and Decisions.* (pp. 157–66). Amherst, NY: Prometheus.

———. 2003. *Sex Equality: Lesbian and Gay Rights.* New York: Foundation Press.

Macklin, Eleanor D. 1988. "Cohabitation in the United States." In J. Gipson Wells (ed.), *Current Issues in Marriage and the Family.* New York: Macmillan.

MacLean, Ian. 1980. *The Renaissance Notion of Woman: A Study in the Fortunes of Scholasticism and Medical Science in European Intellectual Life.* Cambridge, UK: Cambridge University.

MacMillan, Carrie. 2002. "Making the movie." *Promo Magazine* Dec. 1.

Madson, Laura, and Robert M. Hessling. 2001. "Readers' perceptions of four alternatives to masculine generic pronouns." *Journal of Social Psychology* 141(1):156–8.

Maestripieri, Dario. 2001. "Is there mother-infant binding in primates?" *Developmental Review* 21(1):93–120.

Magana, Sandra M. 1999. "Puerto Rican families caring for an adult with mental retardation: Role of familism." *American Journal on Mental Retardation* 104(5):466–82.

Magli, Ida. 2003. *Women and Self Sacrifice in the Christian Church: A Cultural History from the First to the Nineteenth Century* (Janet Sethre, trans.). Jefferson, NC: McFarland.

Magonet, Jonathan. 2002. "Judaism." In John Bowker (ed.), *The Cambridge Illustrated History of Religions.* (pp. 180–213). Cambridge, UK: Cambridge University.

Mahal, Montarin, and Elaine Lindgren. 2002. "Microfinance and women's empowerment in rural Bangladesh." Paper presented at the Midwest Sociological Society, Milwaukee.

Maher, Frances A., and Mary Kay Thompson Tetreault. 2001. *The Feminist Classroom: Dynamics of Gender, Race and Privilege.* Lanham, MD: Rowan & Littlefield.

Maiese, D. R. 2002. "Healthy people 2010—leading health indicators for women." *Women's Health Issues* 12(4):155–64.

Mainstreaming. 1995. *Mainstreaming of Gender Equality in Norway: Introducing the Gender Perspective into Norwegian Public Administration.* Oslo: Royal Ministry of Children and Family Affairs.

Majors, Richard G., and J. Billson. 1992. *Cool Pose: The Dilemmas of Black Manhood in America.* New York: Lexington.

Majors, Richard G., Richard Tyler, Blaine Peden, and Ron Hall. 1994. "Cool pose: A symbolic mechanism for masculine role enactment and coping by black males." In Richard G. Majors and Jacob U. Gordon (eds.), *The American Black Male: His Present Status and his Future.* Chicago: Nelson-Hall.

Makita, Tetsuo, and Mieko Idae. 2001. "Highlights of value change in Japan." *International Journal of Public Opinion Research* 13(4):426–32.

Malley, Maeve, and Damian McCann. 2002. "Family therapy with lesbian and gay clients." In Adrian Coyle and Celia Kitzinger (eds.), *Lesbian and Gay Psychology: New Perspectives.* (pp. 198–218). Oxford, UK: BPS Blackwell.

Mamonova, Tatyana (ed.). 1994. *Women's Glasnost vs. Naglost: Stopping Russian Backlash.* Westport, CT: Bergin and Garvey.

Mandel, Ruth B., and Debra L. Dodson. 1992. "Do women officeholders make a difference?" In

Paula Ries and Anne J. Stone (eds.), *The American Woman, 1992–93: A Status Report.* New York: W. W. Norton.

Manegold, Catherine S. 2000. *In Glory's Shadow: Shannon Faulkner, The Citadel and a Changing America.* New York: Alfred A. Knopf.

Manley, Joan E. 1995. "Sex-segregated work in the system of professions: The development and stratification of nursing." *Sociological Quarterly* 36(2):297–314.

Mann, Judy. 1996. "A report on the GOP's war against women." *Washington Post* January 17:E15.

———. 2000. "We need the abortion pill now." *Washington Post* June 23:C9.

Manning, Wendy D. 2001. "Childbearing in cohabitating unions: Racial and ethnic differences." *Family Planning Perspectives* 33(5):217–23.

Manning, Wendy D., and Nancy S. Landale, 1996. "Racial and ethnic differences in premarital childbearing." *Journal of Marriage and the Family* 58(1):63–77.

Mansbridge, Jane J. 1986. *Why We Lost the ERA.* Chicago: University of Chicago.

Manson, JoAnn E. et al. 2003. "Estrogen plus progestin and the risk of coronary heart disease." *New England Journal of Medicine* 349(6):523–34.

Mantsios, Gregory. 2001. "Media magic: Making class invisible." In Paula S. Rothenberg (ed.), *Race, Class and Gender in the United States: An Integrated Study.* (pp. 563–71). New York: Worth.

Marelich, William D., Dale E. Berger, and Robert B. McKenna. 2000. "Gender differences in the control of alcohol-impaired driving in California." *Journal of Studies on Alcohol* 61(3):396.

Marks, Jonathan. 2000. "98% alike? What our similarity to apes tells us about our understanding of genetics." *Chronicle of Higher Education* May 12:B7.

Marks, Stephen R., Ted L. Huston, Elizabeth M. Johnson, and Shelley M. MacDermid. 2001. "Role balance among white married couples." *Journal of Marriage and the Family* 63(4):1083–98.

Markus, Hazel Rose, M. Crane, S. Bernstein, and M. Siladi. 1982. "Self schemas and gender." *Journal of Personality and Social Psychology* 42:38–50.

Marleau, Jacques D., and Jean-Francois Saucier. 2002. "Preference for a first-born boy in Western societies." *Journal of Biosocial Science* 34(1):13–27.

Marshall, Amy D., and Amy Holtzworth-Munroe. 2002. "Varying forms of husband sexual aggression: Predictors and subgroup differences." *Journal of Family Psychology* 16(3):286–96.

Marshall, Barbara L., 2000. *Reconfiguring Gender: Explorations in Gender and Politics.* Peterborough, Ontario, CN: Broadview.

Marshall, Nancy L., Wendy Wagner Robeson, and Nancy Keefe. 1999. "Gender equity in early childhood education." *Young Children* 54(4):9–13.

Martin, Carol Lynn. 1994b. "Cognitive influences on the development and maintenance of gender segregation." In Campbell Leaper (ed.), *Childhood Gender Segregation: Causes and Consequences.* San Francisco: Jossey-Bass.

———. 2000. "Cognitive theories of gender development." In Thomas Eckes and Hanns M. Trautner (eds.), *The Developmental Social Psychology of Gender.* Mahwah, NJ: Lawrence Erlbaum.

Martin, Carol Lynn, and Lisa M. Dinella. 2002. "Children's gender cognitions, the social environment, and sex differences in cognitive domains." In Ann V. McGillicuddy-De Lisi & Richard De Lisi (Eds.), *Biology, Society, and Behavior: The Development of Gender Differences in Cognition.* (pp. 207–239). Westport, CT: Ablex.

Martin, Carol Lynn, and C. F. Halverson. 1983. "Gender constancy: A methodological and theoretical analysis." *Sex Roles* 9:775–90.

Martin, Carol Lynn, and Jane K. Little. 1990. "The relation of gender understanding to children's sex-typed preferences and gender stereotypes." *Child Development* 61:1427–39.

Martin, Carol Lynn, Diane N. Ruble, and Joel Szkrybalo. 2002. "Cognitive theories of early gender development." *Psychological Bulletin* 128(6):903–33.

Martin, Emily. 1994a. "Medical metaphors of women's bodies: Menstruation and menopause." In Elizabeth Fee and Nancy Krieger (eds.), *Women's Health, Politics and Power: Essays on Sex/Gender, Medicine, and Public Health.* Amityville, NY: Baywood.

Martin, Karin A., 1998. "Becoming a gendered body: Practices of preschools." *American Sociological Review* 63(4):494–511.

Martin, Susan Erlich. 1995. "Sexual harassment: The link joining gender stratification, sexuality and women's economic status." In Jo Freeman (ed.), *Women: A Feminist Perspective.* Mountain View, CA: Mayfield.

Marx, Karl. 1967 (original, 1867–95). *Das Capital.* New York: International.

Mason, Gail. 2002. *The Spectacle of Violence: Homophobia, Gender and Knowledge.* London: Routledge.

Mason, W. Alex, and Michael Windle. 2002. "Gender, self-control, and informal social control in adolescence: A test of three models of the continuity of delinquent behavior." *Youth and Society* 33(4):479–514.

Massey, Douglas S., and Garvey Lundy. 2001. "Use of Black English and racial discrimination in urban housing markets: New methods and findings." *Urban Affairs Review* 36(4):452–69.

Masters, William H., and Virginia Johnson. 1970. *Human Sexual Inadequacy.* Boston: Little, Brown.

Mathis, Susan. 1994. "Propaganda to mobilize women for World War II." *Social Education* 58(2):94–96.

Mattei, Laura R. Winsky. 1998. "Gender and power in American legislative discourse." *Journal of Politics* 60(2):440–61.

Matthews, Janie R. 2000. *Successful Scientific Writing: A Step-by-Step Guide for the Biological and Medical Sciences.* Cambridge, NY: Cambridge University.

Matthews, Rebecca, and Victor Nee. 2000. "Gender inequality and economic growth in rural China." *Social Science Research* 29(4):606–32.

Matthews, Sharon, and Chris Powers. 2002. "Socio-economic gradients in psychological distress: A focus on women, social roles and work-home characteristics." *Social Science & Medicine* 54(5):799–810.

Mattis, Mary C. 2001. "Advancing women in business organizations: Key leadership roles and behaviors of senior leaders and middle managers." *Journal of Management Development* 20(4):371–88.

Mattox, Mickey Leland. 2003. *Defender of the Most Holy Matriarchs: Martin Luther's Interpretation of the Women of Genesis in the Enarrationes in Genesis, 1535–45.* Leiden, Netherlands: Brill.

Maushart, Susan. 1999. *The Mask of Motherhood: How Becoming a Mother Changes Everything and Why We Pretend it Doesn't.* New York: New Press (W. W. Norton)

Maynard, Mary. 2001. "Beyond the 'big three': The development of feminist theory into the 1990s." In Darlene M. Juschka (ed.), *Feminism in the Study of Religion: A Reader.* (pp. 292–313). London: Continuum.

Mayo Clinic. 2002. "Premenstrual syndrome." Women's Health Center. Available online at: http://www.mayoclinic.com

McAdoo, Harriette Pipes. 1990. "A portrait of African-American families in the United States." In S. E. Rix (ed.), *The American Woman, 1990–91: A Status Report.* New York: W. W. Norton.

McBride, James. 1995. *War, Battering, and Other Sports: The Gulf between American Men and Women.* Atlantic Highlands, NJ: Humanities Press.

McCarthy, Barry. 2001. "Male sexuality after fifty." *Journal of Family Psychotherapy* 12(1):29–37.

McClelland, Scott E. 1990. "The new reality in Christ: Perspectives from biblical studies." In June S. Hagen (ed.), *Gender Matters: Women's Studies for the Christian Community.* Grand Rapids, MI: Zondervan.

McConatha, Jasmin T., Frauke Schnell, and Amy McKenna. 1999. "Description of older adults in magazine advertisements." *Psychological Reports* 85(3):1051–6.

McDaniel, June. 2003. *Making Virtuous Daughters and Wives: An Introduction to Brata Rituals in Bengali Folk Religion.* New York: State University of New York.

McDaniel, Susan A. 1996. "Toward a synthesis of feminist and demographic perspectives on fertility." *Sociological Quarterly* 37(1):83–104.

McDevitt, Thomas. 1999. "Population trends: Peru." *International Brief* IB/99-1:March. U.S. Census Bureau.

McDonough, Peggy, David R. Williams, and James S. House. 1999. "Gender and the socioeconomic gradient in mortality." *Journal of Health and Social Behavior* 40(1):17–31.

McElhinny, Bonnie. 2003. "Theorizing gender in sociolinguistics and linguistic anthropology." In Janet Holmes and Miriam Meyerhoff (eds.), *The Handbook of Language and Gender.* Malden, MA: Blackwell.

McEwen, Bruce S. 1990. "Sex differences in the brain: What they are and how they arise." In Malkah T. Notman and Carol C. Nadelson (eds.), *Women and Men: New Perspectives on Gender Differences.* Washington, DC: American Psychiatric Press.

McFalls, Joseph A. 2003. "What's a household? What's a family?" In *Population Bulletin (November)* Population Reference Bureau.

McGarry, K. J. 2003. *Fatherhood for Gay Men: An Emotional and Practical Guide to Becoming a Gay Dad.* New York: Harrington Park.

McGinn, Susan Killenberg. 2002. "Friend or foe? Aggressiveness in primates rare; most social behavior affiliated. *The Record* 26(3):1,6. Washington University in St. Louis.

McHale, Susan M., Ann C. Crouter, and Corinna J. Tucker. 1999. "Family context and gender role socialization in middle childhood: Comparing girls to boys and sisters to brothers." *Child Development* 70(4):990–1004.

McKechnie. 2001. *The First Christian Centuries: Perspectives on the Early Church.* Downers Grove, IL: InterVaristy.

McKeever, Matthew, and Nicholas H. Wolfinger. 2001. "Reexamining the economic costs of marital disruption for women." *Social Science Quarterly* 82(1):202–17.

McKelvey, Mary W., and Patrick C. McKenry. 2000. "The psychological well-being of black and white mothers following marital dissolution." *Psychology of Women's Quarterly* 24(1):4–14.

McLeod, Douglas M., Benjamin H. Detenber, and William P. Eveland, Jr. 2001. "Behind the third-person effect: Differentiating perceptual processes for self and other." *Journal of Communication* 51(4):678–95.

McLeod, Douglas M., William P. Eveland, Jr., and Amy L. Nathanson. 1997. "Support for censorship of violent and misogynic rap lyrics: An analysis of the third-person effect." *Communication Research* 24:153–74.

McLeod, Glenda. 1991. *Virtue and Venom: Catalogues of Women from Antiquity to the Renaissance.* Ann Arbor: University of Michigan.

McLloyd, Vonnie C., Ana Mari Cauce, and David Takeuchi. 2000. "Marital processes and parental socialization in families of color: A decade review of research." *Journal of Marriage and the Family* 62(4):1070–93.

McLoughlin, Merrill. 1988. "Men versus women: The new debate over sex differences." *U.S. News & World Report* August 8:48, 51–56.

McManus, Patricia A., and Thomas A. DiPrete. 2001. "Losers and winners: The financial consequences of separation and divorce for men." *American Sociological Review* 66(2):246–68.

McWilliams, Susan, and Judith A. Howard. 1993. "Solidarity and hierarchy in cross-sex friendships." *Journal of Social Issues* 49(3):191–202.

Mead, Margaret. 2001 (orig. 1935). *Growing up in New Guinea.* New York: HarperCollins.

Mealey, L. 2000. *Sex Differences: Developmental and Evolutionary Strategies.* San Diego: Academic Press.

Mecca, Susan J., and Linda J. Rubin. 1999. "Definitional research on African American students and sexual harassment." *Psychology of Women Quarterly* 23(4):813–17.

Mechanic, Mindy B., Mary H. Uhlmansiek, and Terri L. Weaver. 2002. "The impact of severe stalking experienced by acutely battered women." In Keith E. Davis, Irene Hanson, and Roland D. Maiuro (eds.), *Stalking: Perspectives on Victims and Perpetrators.* (pp. 89–111). New York: Springer.

Media Awareness Network. 2000. "The media and masculinity." Oakland, CA: Children Now. Media Awareness Network. http://www.media-awareness. ca/eng/issues/stats

———. 2003. "Masculinity and sports media." Available online at: http://www.media-awaness. ca/english/issues/stereotyping/men_and_ masculinity

Media Report to Women. 2003. "Industry statistics." Communication Research Associates. Available online: http://www.mediareporttowomen.com/ statistics

Mediascope. 2000. "Violence, women and the media." *Issue Brief Series.* Studio City, CA: Mediascope Press.

Medora, Nilufer P., Jeffry H. Larson, Nuran Hortacsu, and Dave Parul. 2002. "Perceived attitudes towards romanticism: A cross-cultural study of American, Asian-Indian and Turkish young adults." *Journal of Comparative Family Studies* 33(2):155–78.

Megill-Cobbler, Thelma. 1993. "Reading Paul on women." *Lutheran Women Today* 6(January):12–15.

Mehler, Philip S. 2001. "Diagnosis and care of patients with anorexia nervosa in primary care settings." *Annals of Internal Medicine* 134(11):1048–59.

Mehrotra, Nilika. 2002. "Perceiving feminism: Some local responses." *Sociological Bulletin* 51(1): 58–79.

Mellen, Henry S. 2002. "Rough-and-tumble between parents and children and children's social competence." *Dissertation Abstracts International: Section B: Sciences and Engineering* 63(3-B):1588.

Melton, Willie, and Linda L. Lindsey. 1987. "Instrumental and expressive values in mate selection among college students revisited: Feminism, love and economic necessity." Paper presented at the Midwest Sociological Society, Chicago. April.

Mena, Jennifer. 2000. "Men's groups delve into the concept of 'machismo'." *St. Louis Post-Dispatch* December 31:EV8.

Mennino, Sue Falter, and April Brayfield. 2002. "Job-family trade-offs: The multidimensional effects of gender." *Work & Occupations* 29(2): 226–56.

Merli, M. Giovanna, and Herbert L. Smith. 2002. "Has the Chinese family planning policy been successful in changing fertility preferences?" *Demography* 39(3):557–72.

Mernissi, Fatima. 1987. *Beyond the Veil: Male-Female Dynamics in Modern Muslim Society.* Bloomington: Indiana University.

Messman, Susan J., Daniel J. Canary, and Kimberley S. Hause. 2000. "Motive to remain platonic, equity, and the use of maintenance strategies in opposite-sex friendships." *Journal of Social and Personal Relationships* 17(1):67–94.

Messner, Michael A. 1995. "Masculinities and athletic careers." In Margaret L. Andersen and Patricia Hill Collins (ed.), *Race, Class, and Gender: An Anthology.* Belmont, CA: Wadsworth.

Metz, Isabel, and Phyllis Tharenou. 2001. "Women's career advancement: The relative contribution of human and social capital." *Group & Organization Management* 26(3):312–42.

Meyerowitz, Joanne. 1990. "The roaring teens and twenties reexamined: Sexuality in the furnished room districts of Chicago." In Nancy A. Hewitt (ed.), *Women, Families and Communities: Readings in American History, Volume Two: From 1865.* Glenview, IL: Scott, Foresman.

Meyers, Diana T. 2002. *Gender in the Mirror: Cultural Imagery and Women's Agency.* Oxford, UK: Oxford University.

Meyerson, D. E., and J. K. Fletcher. 2000. "A modest manifesto for shattering the glass ceiling." *Harvard Business Review* 127–36.

Mickelson, Roslyn Arlin. 1990. "The attitude-achievement paradox among black adolescents." *Sociology of Education* 63:44–61.

Migliaccio, Todd Anthony. 2003. "Doing gender, doing friendship: How gendered expectations influence friendships." *Dissertation Abstracts International, A: the Humanities and Social Sciences* 63(8):February, 3010-A.

Milburn, Michael A., Roxanne Mather, and Sheree D. Conrad. 2000. "The effects of viewing R-rated movie scenes that objectify women in perceptions of date rape." *Sex Roles* 43(9–10): 645–64.

Miles, Rosalind. 1989. *The Women's History of the World.* Topsfield, MA: Salem House.

Milkman, Ruth. 2003. "Gender at work: The sexual division of labor during World War II." In Linda K. Kerber and Jane Sherron De Hart (eds.), *Women's America: Refocusing the Past.* New York: Oxford University.

Mill, John Stuart. 1869/2002. *The Basic Writings of John Stuart Mill: On Liberty, The Subjection of Women and Utilitarianism.* New York: Modern Library.

Miller, Brent C., Cynthia R. Christopherson, and Pamela K. King. 1993. "Sexual behavior in adolescence." In Thomas P. Gullota, Gerald R. Adams, and Raymond Montemayor (eds.), *Adolescent Sexuality.* Newbury Park, CA: Sage.

Miller, Brian. 1992. "Life-styles of gay husbands and fathers." In Michael S. Kimmel and Michael A. Messner (eds.), *Men's Lives.* New York: Macmillan.

Miller, Casey, and Kate Swift. 1991a. *Words and Women Updated: New Language in New Times.* New York: HarperCollins.

———. 1993. "Who is man?" In Anne Minas (ed.), *Gender Basics: Feminist Perspectives on Women and men.* Belmont, CA: Wadsworth.

Miller, Cristanne. 1994. "Who says what to whom." In Camille Roman, Suzanne Juhasz, and Cristanne Miller (eds.), *The Women and Language Debate: A Sourcebook.* New Brunswick, NJ: Rutgers University.

Miller, Gwen A. 2002. "Contact and conquest in colonial North America." In Nancy A. Hewitt (ed.), *A Companion to American Women's History*. Oxford, UK: Blackwell.

Miller, Merry N., James H. Quillen, and Andres J. Pumariega. 2001. "Culture and eating disorders: A historical and cross-cultural review." *Psychiatry: Interpersonal & Biological Processes* 64(2):93–110.

Miller, Patricia N., Darryl W. Miller, and Eithne M. McKibbin. 1999. "Stereotypes of the elderly in magazine advertisements, 1956–1996." *International Journal of Aging and Human Development* 49(4):319–37.

Miller-Bernal, Leslie. 1991. "Single-sex education: An anachronism or a beneficial structure?" In Laura Kramer (ed.), *The Sociology of Gender: A Textreader*. New York: St. Martin's.

Millett, Kate. 1995. "Sexual politics." In Stevi Jackson et al. (eds.), *Women's Studies Essential Readings*. New York: New York University.

Million, Joelle. 2003. *Woman's Voice, Woman's Place: Lucy Stone and the Birth of the Woman's Rights Movement*. Westport, CT: Praeger.

Minai, Naila. 1991. "Women in early Islam." In Carol J. Verburg (ed.), *Ourselves among Others: Cross-Cultural Readings for Writers*. Boston: Bedford Books.

Minkowitz, Donna. 1996. "Xena: She's big, tall, strong—and popular." *Ms. Magazine* July–August: 74–77.

Minton, Camille, and Kay Pasley. 1996. "Fathers' parenting role identity involvement: A comparison of nondivorced and divorced, nonresident fathers." *Journal of Family Issues* 17(1) (January):26–45.

Minton, Lynn. 1997. "What do you look for in a girl?" *Parade Magazine* June 8:17.

Miracle, Tina S., Andrew W. Miracle, and Roy F. Baumeister. 2003. *Human Sexuality: Meeting Your Basic Needs*. Upper Saddle River, NJ: Prentice Hall.

Mirande, Alfredo. 1997. *Hombres y Machos: Masculinity and Latino Culture*. Boulder, CO: Westview.

Mir-Hosseini, Ziba. 2001. "Iran: Emerging feminist voices." In Lynn Walter (ed.), *Women's Rights: A Global View*. (pp. 113–25). Westport, CT: Greenwood.

Mirowsky, John, and Catherine E. Ross. 2003. *Social Causes of Psychological Distress*. Hawthorne, NY: Aldine de Gruyter.

Mirowsky, John, Catherine E. Ross, and John Reynolds. 2000. "Links between social status and health status." In Chloe E. Bird, Peter Conrad, and Allen M. Fremont (eds.), *Handbook of Medical Sociology*. (pp. 47–67). Upper Saddle River, NJ: Prentice Hall.

Mischel, W. A. 1966. "A social learning view of sex differences in behavior." In E. E. Maccoby (ed.), *The Development of Sex Differences*. Stanford, CA: Stanford University Misra, Joya. 2002. "Class, race, and gender and theorizing welfare states." *Research in Political Sociology* 11:19–52.

Mishra, Vinod, T.K. Roy, and Robert D. Retherford. 2004. "Sex differentials in childhood feeding, health care, and nutritional status in India." Population and Development Review 30(2): 269-95.

Mitchell, Juliet. 2000. *Psychoanalysis and Feminism*. New York: Basic Books.

Mitter, Sara S. 1991. *Dharma's Daughters: Contemporary Indian Women and Hindu Culture*. New Brunswick, NJ: Rutgers University.

Moen, Matthew. 1994. "From revolution to evolution: The changing nature of the Christian right." *Sociology of Religion* 3:345–57.

Moen, Phyliss. 2003. *It's about Time: Couples and Careers*. Ithaca, NY: ILR Press.

Moen, Phyllis, Julie Robison, and Donna Dempster-McClain. 1995. "Caregiving and women's well-being: A life course approach." *Journal of Health and Social Behavior* 36(3):213–301.

Moffatt, Michael. 1989. *Coming of Age in New Jersey: College and American Culture*. New Brunswick, NJ: Rutgers University.

Moghadam, Valentine M. 1999. "Gender and the global economy." In Myra Marx Feree, Judith Lorber and Beth B. Hess (eds.). *Revisioning Gender*. (pp.128–60). Thousand Oaks, CA: Sage.

———. 2002. "Islamic feminism and its discontents: Toward a resolution of the debate." *Signs* 27(4):1135–71.

Mojab, Shahrzad. 1998. "Muslim women and Western feminists: The debate on particulars and fundamentals." *Monthly Review-New York* 50(7): 19–30.

Molina, Olga. 2000. "African American women's unique divorce experiences." *Journal of Divorce & Remarriage* 32(3/4):93–9.

Money, John. 1995. *Gendermaps: Social Constructionism, Feminism and Sexosophical History*. New York: Continuum.

Money, John, and Anke A. Ehrhardt. 1972. *Man and Woman, Boy and Girl*. Baltimore: Johns Hopkins University.

Money, John, and P. Tucker. 1975. *Sexual Signatures*. Boston: Little, Brown.

Mongeau, Paul A., Melody Yeazell, and Jerold L. Hale. 1994. "Sex differences in relational message interpretations on male- and female-initiated first dates: A research note." *Journal of Social Behavior and Personality* 9(4):731–42.

Monsour, Michael. 2002. *Women and Men as Friends: Relationships across the Life Span in the 21st Century*. Mahwah, NJ: Lawrence Erlbaum.

Monsour, Michael, Bridgid Harris, Nancy Kurzweil, and Chris Beard. 1994. "Challenges confronting cross-sex friendships: 'Much ado about nothing'?" *Sex Roles* 31(1/2):55–77.

Montagu, Ashley. 1999. *The Natural Superiority of Women*. Lanham. MD: Altamira.

Moore, Alinde J., and Dorothy C. Stratton. 2002. *Resilient Widowers: Older Men Speak for Themselves*. New York Springer.

Moore, Valerie Ann. 2000. "Comparing kids' constructions of race and gender." Paper presented at the American Sociological Association, San Francisco.

Moosa, Ebrahim. 2003. "The debts and burdens of critical Islam. In Omid Safi (ed.), *Progressive Muslims: On Justice, Gender and Pluralism*. Oxford, NY: Oneworld.

Morgan, S. Philip, Antonio McDaniel, Andrew T. Miller, and Samuel H. Preston. 1993. "Racial differences in household and family structure at the turn of the century." *American Journal of Sociology* 98(4):799–828.

Morreale, Joanne. 1998. "Xena: Warrior princess as feminist camp." *Journal of Popular Culture* 32(2):79-86.

Morris, Celia. 1992. "Changing the rules and the roles: Five women in public office." In Paula Ries and Anne J. Stone (eds.), *The American Woman, 1992–93: A Status Report*. New York: W. W. Norton.

Morris, Lois B. 2001. "She feels sick. The doctor can't find anything wrong." *New York Times* June 24. Sect. 15:4

Morris, Melanie H., and Chuck West. 2001. "Post-divorce conflict and avoidance of intimacy." *Journal of Divorce and Remarriage* 35(3–4): 93–105.

Morry, Marian M., and Erica Winkler. 2001. "Student acceptance and expectation of sexual assault." *Canadian Journal of Behavioural Science* 33(3):188–92.

Mort, Jo-Ann, and Gary Brenner. 2000. Kibbutzim: Will they survive the new Israel?" *Dissent* 47(3):64–70.

Morton, Joel. 200. "Silencing the men's movement: Gender, ideology, and popular discourse." In Edward Read Barton (ed.), *Mythopoetic Perspectives of Men's Healing Work: An Anthology of Therapists and Others*. (pp. 87-99). Westport, CT: Bergin & Garvey.

Mott, Frank, L. 1994. "Sons, daughters and fathers' absence: Differentials in father-leaving probabilities and in home environments." *Journal of Family Issues* 15(1):97–128.

Motzafi-Haller, Pnina. 2000. "Reading Arab feminist discourses: A postcolonial challenge to Israeli feminism." *Hagar: International Social Science Review* 1(2):63–89.

———. 2001. "Scholarship, identity, and power: Mizrahi women in Israel." *Signs* 26(3):697–734.

Moya, Miguel, Francisca Exposito, and Josefa Ruiz. 2000. "Close relationships, gender and career salience. *Sex Roles* 4(9–10):825–46.

Moynihan, Daniel P. 1965. *The Negro Family: The Case for National Action*. Office of Policy Planning and Research, U.S. Department of Labor. Washington, DC: U.S. Government Printing Office.

Mulac, Anthony, James J. Bradac, and Pamela Gibbons. 2001. *Human Communication Research* 27(1):121–52.

Mullen, Mary K. 1990. "Children's classifications of nature and artifact pictures into female and male categories." *Sex Roles* 23:577–87.

Munshi, Shoma (ed.). 2001. *Images of the Modern Woman in Asia: Global Media, Local Meanings*. Richmond, Surrey: Curzon Press.

Murnen, Sarah K. 2000. "Gender and the use of sexually degrading language." *Psychology of Women Quarterly* 24(4):319–27.

Murphy, Caryle. 1993. "Lowering the veil: Muslim women struggle for careers in a society ruled by men and religion." *Washington Post*, February 17:A1, A24–25.

Murphy, Suzanne, and Dorothy Faulkner. 2000. "Learning to collaborate: Can young children develop better communication strategies through collaboration with a more popular peer?" *European Journal of Psychology and Education* 15(4):389–404.

Murray, Carolyn Bennett, and Jelani Mandara. 2002. "Racial identity development in African American children: Cognitive and experiential antecedents." In Harriette Pipes McAdoo (ed.), *Black Children: Social, Educational, and Parental Environments*. (pp. 73–96). Thousand Oaks, CA: Sage.

Murray, Stephen O. 2000. *Homosexualities*. Chicago: University of Chicago.

Muse, Dahabo Ali. 2000. "Feminine pain." Cited in "Female genital mutilation also known as female circumcision" by Comfort Momoh. Pamphlet from the African Well Women's Clinic of the Guy's & St. Thomas Hospital Trust. London.

Mutchler, Matt G. 2000. "Seeking sexual lives: Gay youth and masculinity tension." In Peter Nardi (ed.), *Gay Masculinities*. Thousand Oaks, CA: Sage.

Myers, Scott M., and Alan Booth. 2002. "Forerunners of change in nontraditional gender ideology." *Social Psychology Quarterly* 65(1): 18–37.

Nadell, Pamela S., and Jonathan D. Sarna (eds.). 2001. *Women and American Judaism: Historical Perspectives*. Hanover, NH: University Press of New England.

Nagao, Noriko. 1993. "Marriage partner selection in Japan." Paper presented to Gender Roles class, Maryville University, December 16.

Najafizadeh, Mehrangiz. 2003. "Women's empowering carework in Post-Soviet Azerbaijan." *Gender & Society* 17(2):293–304.

Najmabadi, Afsaneh. 2000. "(Un)veiling feminism." *Social Text* 18,3(64):29–45.

Nakosteen, R. A., and M. A. Zimmer. 1997. "Men, money and marriage: Are high earners more prone than low earners to marry?" *Social Science Quarterly* 78:66–82.

Nanda, Serena. 1997. "The hijras of India." In Martin B. Duberman (ed.), *A Queer World: The Center for Lesbian and Gay Studies Reader*. New York: Center for Lesbian and Gay Studies, City University.

Narasimhan, Sakuntala. 2000. "Special report: A married women's right to live." *Ms.* 10(6): 76–81.

Narayanan, Vasudha. 2002. "Hinduism." In Arvind Sharma and Katherine K. Young (eds.), *Her Voice, Her Faith: Women Speak on World Religions*. (pp. 11–58). Boulder, CO: Westview.

Nathanson, Amy I., Jocelyn McGee, and Barbara J. Wilson. 2002. "Counteracting the effects of female stereotypes on television via active mediation." *Journal of Communication* 52(4):922–37.

Nathanson, Paul, and Katherine K. Young. 2001. *Spreading Misandry: The Teaching of Contempt for Men in Popular Culture.* Montreal: McGill Queens University.

National Center for Children in Poverty. 2000. *Child poverty fact sheet* (July). Washington, DC.

National Center for Education Statistics. 2003. *Digest of Education Statistics.* Office of Educational Research and Improvement. Washington, DC: U.S. Department of Education.

National Center for Health Statistics. 2002. "Cohabitation, marriage, divorce, and remarriage in the United States." *Series Report* 23(2).

———. 2004. *Health, United States, 2003.* Hyattsvile, MD: NCHS.

National Center for Victims of Crime. 1997. "Male rape." Available online at: http://www.ncvc.org/gethelp/malerape

National Institute on Alcohol Abuse and Alcoholism. 1999. "Are women more vulnerable to alcohol's effects." *Alcohol Alert* No.26: December.

National Institute on Drug Abuse. 2002. "Trends in prescription drug abuse." *Research Report Series—Prescription Drugs: Abuse and Addiction.* Available online at: http://www.drugabuse.gov/ResearchReports/Prescription/prescription5.html

National Strategy for Suicide Prevention. 2001. "At a glance—suicide among the elderly." U.S. Department of Health and Human Services. http://www.mentalhealth.org/suicideprevention/ elderly

Navajas, Setgio et al. 2000. "Microcredit and the poorest of the poor: Theory and evidence from Bolivia." *World Development* 28(2):333–46.

NCAA. 2002. *Gender Equality Report, 1999-00.* Indianapolis, IN: National Collegiate Athletic Association.

NCVS. 2003. *National Crime Victimization Survey.* Bureau of Justice Statistics. Washington, DC: U.S. Department of Justice.

Neff, James Alan, Bruce Holamon, and Tracy Davis Schluter. 1995. "Spousal violence among Anglos, blacks and Mexican Americans: The role of demographic variables, psycho-social predictors, and alcohol consumption." *Journal of Family Violence* 10(1):1–21.

Nelson, Adia. 2000. "The pink dragon is female: Halloween costumes and gender markers." *Psychology of Women Quarterly* 24(2):137–44.

Nelson, Debra L., and Ronald J. Burke. 2002. "A framework for examining gender, work stress and health." In Debra L. Nelson and Ronald J. Burke (eds.), *Gender, Work Stress, and Health.* Washington, DC: American Psychological Association,

Nelson, E. D. 1993. "Sugar daddies: 'Keeping' a mistress and the gentleman's code." *Qualitative Sociology* 16(1):43–68.

Nelson, Fiona. 1999. "Lesbian families: Achieving motherhood." In T. Richard Sullivan (ed.), *Queer Families, Common Agendas: Gay People, Lesbians, and Family Values* (pp. 27–46). New York: Harrington Park.

Nelson, Randy J. 1995. *An Introduction to Behavioral Endocrinology.* Sunderland, MA: Sinauer.

Neppl, Tricia K., and Ann D. Murray. 1997. "Social dominance and play patterns among preschoolers: Gender comparisons." *Sex Roles* 36(5–6): 381–93.

Neumark-Sztainer, Dianne, and Peter J. Hannan. 2000. "Weight-related behavior among adolescent girls and boys: Results from a national survey." *Archives of Pediatrics & Adolescent Medicine* 154(6):569–77.

Newberger, Eli H. 1999. *The Men They Will Become: The Nature and Nurture of Male Character.* Reading, MA: Perseus.

NICHD (National Institute of Child Health and Human Development). 2002. Early Childcare Research Network. "Parenting and family influences when children are in child care: Results from the NICHD study of early child care." In John G. Borkowski, Sharon Landesman Ramey, and Marie Bristol-Power (eds.), *Parenting and the Child's World: Influences on Academic, Intellectual, and Social-Emotional Development.* Mahwah, NJ: Lawrence Erlbaum.

Nielsen, Francois. 1994. "Sociobiology and sociology." *Annual Review of Sociology* 20:267–303.

Nilsen, Alice Pace. 1993. "Sexism is English: A 1990s update." In Virginia Cyrus (ed.), *Experiencing Race, Class, and Gender in the United States.* Mountain View, CA: Mayfield.

Nishimuri, Junko. 2001. "The uneasiness of housewives and the housewife as an institution: From the analysis of life stories of midlife women in contemporary Japan." *Japanese Journal of Family Sociology* 12(2):223–35.

Niven, David, and Jeremy Zilber. 2001. "How does she have time for the kids and Congress? Views on gender and media coverage." *Women & Politics* 23(1–2):147–65.

Nkulu-N'Sengha, Mutombo. 2001. "Bumuntu paradigm and gender justice: Sexist and antisexist trends in African traditional religions." In John C. Raines and Daniel C. Maguire (eds.), *What Men Owe to Women: Men's Voices from World Religions.* (pp. 69–108). Albany: State University of New York.

NOMAS. 2000. *"A brief history of NOMAS and the M&Ms."* http://www.nomas.org/history

NORC. 2000. *General Social Survey Cumulative Codebook.* Chicago, IL: National Opinion Research Center.

———. 2002. *General Social Survey Cumulative Codebook.* Chicago: National Opinion Research Center.

Norman, Michael. 1998. "Getting serious about adultery." *New York Times* July 4:A15, A17.

Norris, Mary E. 1992. "The impact of development on women: A specific-factors analysis." *Journal of Development Economics* 38(1):183–201.

Norsigian, Judy. 1996. "The women's health movement." In Kary L. Moss (ed.), *Man-Made*

Medicine: Women's Health, Public Policy, and Reform. (pp. 79–98). Durham, NC: Duke University.

Norton, Mary Beth. 2003. "The positive impact of the American Revolution on white women." In Mary Beth Norton and Ruth M. Alexander (eds.), *Major Problems in American Women's History.* Boston: Houghton Mifflin.

Norton, Mary Beth, and Ruth M. Alexander (eds.). 1996a. *Major Problems in American Women's History.* Lexington, MA: D. C. Heath.

———. 1996b. "Anita Hill's testimony before the Senate Judiciary Committee, 1991." In Mary Beth Norton and Ruth M. Alexander (eds.), *Major Problems in American Women's History.* Lexington, MA: D. C. Heath.

Notter, David. 2002. "Towards a cultural analysis of the modern family: Beyond the revisionist paradigm in Japanese family studies." *International Journal of Japanese Sociology* 11:88–101.

NOW. 2003. "NOW blasts White House opposition to U. Michigan policy, points out Bush benefited from affirmative action." January 16:National Organization for Women. Available online at: http://www.now.org/press/01-03/01-16

———. 2004. "NOW history." National Organization for Women. Available online at: http://www.now.org/history/history

Nussbaum, Karen. 2002. *Working Women.* Washington, DC: AFL-CIO. ussbaum, Martha Craven. 1999. *Sex and Social Justice.* Oxford, NY: Oxford University.

Nussbaum, Martha Craven. 2000. *Women and Human Development: The Capabilities Approach.* Cambridge, UK: Cambridge University.

NWHIC. 2003. "The health of minority women." July. National Women's Health Information Center. U.S. Department of Health and Human Services. Available online at: http://www.4women.gov

O'Connell, Martin T. 1997. "Children with single parents; How they fare." *CENBR/97-1*:September. Washington, DC: U.S. Census Bureau.

O'Keefe, Abigail Tuttle. 2002. "It's not what mothers do but the reasons they do it: Mothers' reasons for their employment decisions and mothers' well-being." *Dissertation Abstracts International: Section B: The Sciences & Engineering* 63(1-B):568.

O'Neil, Robert Paul. 2002. "Sexual profanity and interpersonal judgment." *Dissertation Abstracts International: Section A: The Humanities and Social Sciences* 63(2):781-A.

O'Neill, William L. 1989. *Feminism in American history.* New Brunswick, NJ: Transaction.

O'Reilly, Andrea. 2000. "Feminist thought on motherhood, the motherline, and the mother-daughter relationship." In Andrea O'Reilly and Sharon Abbey (eds.), *Mothers and Daughters: Connection, Empowerment and Transformation.* (pp. 143–60). Lanham, MD: Rowman & Littlefield.

O'Reilly, Patricia. 2001. "Learning to be a girl." In Patricia O'Reilly and Elizabeth M. Penn (eds.), *Educating Young Adolescent Girls* (pp. 11–27). Mahwah, NJ: Lawrence Erlbaum.

Oakley, Ann. 1993. "Becoming a mother." In Stevi Jackson et al. (eds.), *Women's Studies Essential Readings.* New York: New York University.

Odeon, K. 1997. *Great Books for Girls.* New York: Ballantine.

Off-Centre. 2001. "Matchmakers have their work cut out." *Financial Times* May 5/6.

Office of Child Support Enforcement. 2000. "Getting to know the future customers of the office of child support." U.S. Department of Health and Human Services. http://www.acf.dhhs.gov/programs/cse/pubs/ reports/projections

Ogawa, Naohiro, Robert D. Retherford, and Yasuhiko Saito. 2003. "Caring for the elderly and holding down a job: How are women coping in Japan?" *Asia-Pacific Population & Policy* April: No. 65.

Ohara, Yumiko. 2000. *A Critical Discourse Analysis: Ideology of Language and Gender in Japanese.* Ph.D. Dissertation. University of Hawaii at Manoa.

———. 2001. "Finding one's voice in Japanese: A study of the pitch levels of L2 users." In Aneta Pavlenko, Adrian Black-ledge, Ingrid Piller, and Marya Teutsch-Dwyer (eds.), *Multilingualism, Second Language Learning, and Gender.* (pp. 231–54). Berlin: Mouton de Gruyter.

Ohara, Yumiko, and Scott Saft. 2003. "Using conversation analysis to track gender ideologies in social interaction: Toward a feminist analysis of a Japanese phone-in consultation TV program." *Discourse & Society* 14(2):153–72.

Ohtsu, Makoto. 2002. *Inside Japanese Business: A Narrative History, 1960–2000.* Armonk, NY: M. E. Sharpe.

Okamoto, Dina G., and Lynn Smith-Lovin. 2001. "Changing the subject: Gender, status, and the dynamics of topic change." *American Sociological Review* 66(6):852–73.

Ollenburger, Jane C., and Helen A. Moore. 1992. *A Sociology of Women: The Intersection of Patriarchy, Capitalism and Colonization.* Englewood Cliffs, NJ: Prentice Hall.

Olson, Laura Olson. 2003. "Whatever happened to June Cleaver? The fifties mom turns eighty." *Race, Gender and Class.* 10(1):129–43.

OneWorld. 2003. "AIDS pandemic set to explode for India's millions." Available online at: http://www.oneworld.net/article/view/74050/1/

Oquendo, Maria A., Steven P. Ellis, and Steven Greenwald. 2001. "Ethnic and sex differences in suicide rates relative to major depression in the United States." *American Journal of Psychiatry* 158(10):1652–58.

Orenstein, Peggy. 1994. *School Girls: Young Women, Self-Esteem, and the Confidence Gap.* New York: Doubleday.

———. 1997. "Shortchanging girls: Gender socialization in schools." In Dana Dunn (ed.), *Workplace/Women's Place: An Anthology.* (pp. 43–52). Los Angeles: Roxbury.

———. 1998. "Almost equal." *New York Times Magazine* April 5: 42–46.

———. 2001. "Unbalanced Equations: Girls, Math, and the Confidence Gap." In Roberta Satow (ed.), *Gender and Social Life.* Needham Heights, MA: Allyn & Bacon.

Osawa, Mari. 2000. "Government approaches to gender equality in the mid-1990s." *Social Science Japan Journal* 3(1):3–19.

Osborne, Jason W. 2001. "Testing stereotype threat: Does anxiety explain race and sex difference in achievement." *Contemporary Educational Psychology* 26(3):291–310.

Osman, Susanne L. 2003. "Predicting men's rape perceptions based on the belief that 'no' really means 'yes.'" *Journal of Applied Social Psychology* 33(4):683–92.

Ostling, Richard N. 1991. "The search for Mary: Handmaid or feminist?" *Time* (December 30):62–66.

Ostriker, Alicia. 2001. "Everywoman her own theology." In Susan M. Shaw and Janet Lee (eds.), *Women's Voices, Feminist Visions.* (p. 511). Mountain View, CA: Mayfield.

Ostrowiak, Noya. 2001. *Motherhood is Not a Rehearsal: Bottom-Line Mentoring for Parents.* Hampton, GA: Southern Charm Press.

Ottens, Allen J. 2001. "The scope of sexual violence on campus." In Allen J. Ottens and Kathy Hotellling (eds.), *Sexual Violence on Campus: Policies, Programs and Perspectives.* (pp. 1–29). New York: Springer.

Oygard, Lisbet, and Stein Hardeng. 2001. "Divorce support groups: How do group characteristics influence adjustment to divorce?" *Social Work with Groups* 24(1):69–87.

Pagels, Elaine. 1979. *The Gnostic Gospels.* New York: Random House.

Palczewski, Catherine Helen. 1998. "Take the helm, man the ship…and I forgot my bikini! Unraveling why woman is not considered a verb: Part 2 of 2." *Women & Language* 21(2):4–8.

Paley, Judith. 2003. "Estrogen and Memory." Available online at: http://www.womenof.com/Articles/hc11402a.asp

Palgi, Michal. 2003. "Gender equality in the kibbutz—From ideology to reality." In Kalpana Misra and Melanie S. Rich (eds.), *Jewish Feminism in Israel: Contemporary Perspectives.* (pp. 76–95). Hanover, NH: Brandeis University.

Palkovitz, R. 2002. "Involved fathering and child development: Advancing our understanding of good fathering." In Catherine S. Tamis-LeMonda and Natasha Cabrera (eds.), *Handbook of Father Involvement: Multidisciplinary Perspectives.* Mahwah, NJ: Lawrence Erlbaum.

Palmer, Craig T. 2001. "Twelve reasons why rape is not sexually motivated: A skeptical examination." In Roy F. Baumeister (ed.), *Social Psychology and Human Sexuality: Essential Readings.* (pp. 225–35). Philadelphia: Psychology Press.

Palmer, Edward L., and Brian M. Young (eds.). 2003. *The Faces of Televisual Media: Teaching, Violence, Selling to Children.* Mahwah, NJ: Lawrence Erlbaum.

Paludi, Michele A. 1996. *Sexual Harassment on College Campuses: Abusing the Ivory Power.* Albany: State University of New York.

Pappas-Deluca, Katina. 1999. "Transcending gendered boundaries: Migration for domestic labour in Chile." In Janet H. Momsen (ed.), *Gender, Migration, and Domestic Service.* (pp. 98–114). London: Routledge.

Parade Magazine. 1991. "Sexual harassment: Gender gap on Capitol Hill." November 17:10.

Parke, Ross D. 2002. "Parenting in the new millennium: Prospects, promises, and pitfalls." In James P. McHale and Wendy S. Grolnick (eds.), *Retrospect and Prospect in the Psychological Study of Families.* (pp. 65–93). Mahwah, NJ: Lawrence Erlbaum.

Parke, Ross D., D. J. McDowell, M. Kim, C. Killian, J. Dennis, M. L. Flyr, and M. N. Wild. 2002. "Fathers' contributions to children's peer relationships." In Catherine S. Tamis-LeMonda and Natasha Cabrera (eds.), *Handbook of Father Involvement: Multidisciplinary Perspectives.* Mahwah, NJ: Lawrence Erlbaum.

Parsons, Talcott. 1966. *Societies: Evolutionary and Comparative Perspectives.* Englewood Cliffs, NJ: Prentice Hall.

Parsons, Talcott, and Robert F. Bales (eds.). 1955. *Family, Socialization, and Interaction Process.* Glencoe, IL: Free Press.

Pasley, Kay, and Carmelle Minton. 2001. "Generative fathering: After divorce and remarriage: Beyond the 'disappearing dad.'" In Theodore F. Cohn (ed.), *Men and Masculinity: A Text Reader.* (pp. 239–48). Belmont, CA: Wadsworth.

Passet, Joanne Ellen. 2003. *Sex Radicals and the Quest for Women's Equality.* Urbana: University of Illinois.

Patford, Janet L. 2000. "Partners and cross-sex friends: A preliminary study of the way marital and de facto partnerships affect verbal intimacy with cross-sex friends." *Journal of Family Studies* 6(1):106–19.

Pavelka, Mary S. McDonald. 1998. "The nonhuman primate perspective: Old age, kinship, and social partners in a monkey society." In Jeanette Dickerson-Putman and Judith K. Brown (eds.), *Women among Women: Anthropological Perspectives on Female Age Hierarchies.* (pp. 89–99). Urbana: University of Illinois.

Payne, Kaye E. 2001. *Different but Equal: Communication between the Sexes.* Westport, CT: Praeger/Greenwood.

Peek, Charles W., George D. Lowe, and L. Susan Williams. 1991. "Gender and God's work: Another look at religious fundamentalism and sexism." *Social Forces* 69(4):1205–25.

People's Daily. 2002. "China sees a high gender ratio of newborns." May 9. Available online at: http://www.china.org.cn/english/2002/May/32360.htm

Perdue, Theda. 1994. "Cherokee women and the trail of tears." In Vicki L. Ruiz and Ellen Carol DuBois (eds.), *Unequal Sisters: A Multicultural Reader in U.S. Women's History.* New York: Routledge.

Perkins, Daniel F., and Richard M. Lerner. 1995. "Single and multiple indicators of physical attractiveness and psychosocial behavior among young adolescents." *Journal of Early Adolescence* 15(3):269–98.

Perriman, Andrew. 1998. *Speaking of Women: Interpreting Paul.* Leicester, UK: Apollos.

Perry, Alex. 2001. "Crossing the line." *Time* May 7:18–21.

Perry-Jenkins, Maureen, Rena L. Repetti, and Ann C. Crouter. 2000. "Work and family in the 1990s." *Journal of Marriage and the Family* 62(4):981–98.

Peters, Christine. 2003. *Patterns of Piety: Women, Gender and Religion in Late Medieval and Reformation England.* Cambridge, UK: Cambridge University.

Peters, Joan K. 1997. *When Mothers Work: Loving our Children without Sacrificing Our Selves.* Reading, MA: Addison-Wesley.

Philaretou, Andreas G., and Katrherine R. Allen. 2001. "Reconstructing masculinity and sexuality." *Journal of Men's Studies* 9(3):301–21.

Phillips, L. E. 1999. "Love, American style." *American Demographics* 21:56–57.

Philpot, Carol L. 2001. "Someday my prince will come." In Susan H. McDaniel and Don-David Lusterman et al. (eds.), *Casebook for Integrating Family Therapy: An Ecosystem Approach.* (pp. 253–63). Washington, DC: American Psychological Association.

Phipps, Shelley, Peter Burton, and Lars Osberg. 2001. "Time as a source of inequality within marriage: Are husbands more satisfied with time for themselves than wives?" *Feminist Economics* 7(2):1–21.

Piaget, Jean. 1950. *The Psychology of Intelligence.* London: Routledge.

———. 1954. *The Construction of Reality in the Child.* New York: Basic Books.

Pierce, Dean. 2001. "Language, science and queer people: Social and cultural change strategies." In Mary E. Swigonski and Robin S. Mama (eds.), *From Hate Crimes to Human Rights: A Tribute to Matthew Shepard.* New York: Haworth.

Pigozzi, Mary Joy. 1999. "Educating the girl child: Best foot forward?" *UN Chronicle* 36(2):39–41.

Pilkington, Jane. 1998. "Don't try and make out I'm not nice: The different strategies men and women use when gossiping." In Jennifer Coates (ed): *Language and Gender: A Reader.* Malden, MA: Blackwell.

Pincus, Fred. 2003. *Reverse Discrimination: Dismantling the Myth.* Boulder, CO: Lynne Rienner.

Pinney, Christopher. 2001. "Fueling the fire of the sati debate." *Times Higher Educational Supplement.* August 10:30.

Pittman, Joe F., Jennifer L. Kerpelman, and Catherine A. Solheim. 2001. "Stress and performance standards: A dynamic approach to time spent in housework." *Journal of Marriage and the Family* 63(4):1111–21.

Plant, E. Ashby, Janet Shibley Hyde, Dacher Keltner, and Patricia G. Devine. 2000. "The gender stereotyping of emotions." *Psychology of Women Quarterly* 4(1):81–92.

Plante, Ellen M. 1997. *Women at Home in Victorian America: A Social History.* New York: Facts on File.

Platts, Georgia. 2000. "Voices of loss: Motherhood and the social construction of identity." *Dissertation Abstracts International, A: The Humanities and Social Sciences.* 60(8):3154-A.

Plous, S., and Dominique Neptune. 1997. "Racial and gender biases in magazine advertising." *Psychology of Women Quarterly* 21(4):627–44.

Plummer, David. 1999. *One of the Boys: Masculinity, Homophobia, and Modern Manhood.* Binghamton, NY: Harrington Park.

Plummer, Gillian. 2000. *Failing Working-Class Girls.* London: Trentham.

Poire, B.A., J. K. Burgoon, and R. Parrott. 1992. "Status and privacy restoring communication in the workplace." *Journal of Applied Communication Research* 4:419–36.

Pollak, Jane. 2001. *Soul Proprietor: 101 Lessons from a Lifestyle Entrepreneur.* Freedom, CA: Crossing Press.

Pomerance, Murray. 2001. "Introduction: Gender in film at the end of the twentieth century." In M. Pomerance (ed.), *Ladies and Gentlemen, Boys and Girls: Gender in Film at the End of the Twentieth Century.* Albany: State University of New York.

Pomerantz, Eva M., and Diane N. Ruble. 1998. "The role of maternal control in the development of sex differences in child self-evaluation factors." *Child Development* 69(2):458–78.

Pomfret, John. 2001. "In China's countryside, 'It's a boy!' too often." *Washington Post,* May 29:A1.

———. 2002. "In China, the rich seek to become the 'big rich.'" *Washington Post Foreign Service* March 17: A01.

Poole, Keith T., and L. Harmon Zeigler. 1985. *Women, Public Opinion and Politics: The Changing Political Attitudes of American Women.* New York: Longman.

Pooler, William S. 1991. "Sex of child preferences among college students." *Sex Roles* 25(9–10): 569–576.

Pope, Mark, and Matt Englar-Carlson. 2001. "Fathers and sons: The relationship between violence and masculinity." *Family Journal* 9(4): 367–73.

Popenoe, David. 2003. "Modern marriage: Revising the cultural script." In Michael S. Kimmel (ed.), *The Gendered Society Reader.* New York: Oxford University.

Popp, Danielle, Roxanne A. Donovan, and Mary Crawford. 2003. "Gender, race, and speech style stereotypes." *Sex Roles* 48(7–8):317–25.

Poppema, Suzanne. 1999. "The future of *Roe v. Wade:* Medical." In Patricia Ojea and Barbara Quigley (eds.), *Women's Studies* (Annual Editions). (pp. 117–18). Guilford, CT: Dushkin/ McGraw-Hill.

Population Reference Bureau. 2002. *Ameristat* (2000 Census, Marriage/Family; Race/Ethnicity). http://www.ameristat.org

Porter, Elisabeth. 2001. "Interdependence, parenting and responsible citizenship." *Journal of Gender Studies* 10(1):5–15.

Porter, Rhonda C. 1999. "Gender differences in mathematics performance." Paper presented at the Holmes Partnership annual meeting, Boston, January.

Povey, Elaheh Rostami. 2001. "Feminist contestations of institutional domains in Iran." *Feminist Review* 69:44–72.

Powell, Gary N., and Laura M. Graves. 2003. *Women and Men in Management.* 3rd ed. Thousand Oaks, CA: Sage.

Powell, Kimberley A., and Lori Abels. 2002. "Sex-role stereotypes in TV programs aimed at the preschool audience: An analysis of Teletubbies and Barney & Friends." *Women & Language* 25(1):14–22.

Powers, Ann. 1999. "A surge of sexism on the music scene." *New York Times* August 2: B1, B3.

Powers, Bill. 2001. "Quiet! Dad is dusting his G.I. Joes." *New York Times* December 30:Section 9:1.

Press, Andrea L., and Elizabeth R. Cole. 1999. *Speaking of Abortion: Television and Authority in the Lives of Women.* Chicago: University of Chicago.

Press, Julie E., and Eleanor Townsley. 1998. "Wives' and husbands' housework reporting: Gender, class, and social desirability." *Gender & Society* 12(2):188–218.

Prettyman, Sandra Spikard. 1998. "Discourses on adolescence, gender, and schooling: An overview." *Educational Studies: A Journal in the Foundations of Education* 29(4):329–40.

Pribram, E. Deidre. 1993. "Female spectators." In Stevi Jackson et al. (eds.), *Women's Studies Essential Readings.* New York: New York University.

Price, Vivian. 2002. "Race, Affirmative action, and women's employment in U.S. highway construction." *Feminist Economics* 8(2):87–113.

Prior, Mary. 1994. "Freedom and autonomy in England and the Netherlands: Women's lives and experience in the seventeenth century." In Els Kloek, Nicole Teeuwen, and Marijke Huisman (eds.), *Women of the Golden Age: An International Debate on Women in Seventeenth-Century Holland, England and Italy.* Amsterdam: Hilversum Verloren.

Puddington, Arch. 1996. "What to do about affirmative action." In Harold A. Widdison (ed.), *Social Problems 96/97* (Annual Editions). Guilford, CT: Dushkin/Brown & Benchmark.

Pugliesi, Karen. 1995. "Work and well-being: Gender differences in the psychological consequences of employment." *Journal of Health and Social Behavior* 36(1):57–71.

Pui-Lan, Kwok. 1988. "Mothers and daughters, writers and fighters." In Letty M. Russell et al. (eds.), *Inheriting our Mother's Garden: Feminist Theology in Third World Perspective.* Philadelphia: Westminster.

Puntarigvivat, Tavivat. 2001. "A Thai Buddhist perspective." In John C. Raines and Daniel C. Maguire (eds.), *What Men Owe to Women: Men's Voices from World Religions.* (pp. 211–38). Albany: State University of New York.

Quaiser-Pohl, Claudia, and Wolfgang Lehmann. 2002. "Girls' spatial abilities: Charting the contributions of experiences and attitudes in different academic groups." *British Journal of Educational Psychology* 72(2):245–60.

Queenan, Patrick Lydon. 2000. "Gender differences in the socialization of social and emotional competence in preschool-aged children." *Dissertation Abstracts International: Section B: The Sciences and Engineering* 61(2-B):1094.

Quicke, Andrew, and Karen Robinson (ed.). 2000. "Keeping the promise of a moral majority: A historical/critical comparison of the Promise Keepers and the Christian Coalition, 1989–98." In Dane S. Claussen (ed.), *The Promise Keepers: Essays on Masculinity and Christianity.* (pp. 7–19). Jefferson, NC: McFarland.

Quinn, Beth A. 2002. "Sexual harassment and masculinity: The power and meaning of 'girl watching.'" *Gender & Society* 16(3):386–402.

Raag, Tarja. 1999. "Influences of social expectations of gender, gender stereotypes, and situational constraints on children's toy choices." *Sex Roles* 41(11–12):809–31.

Rabinowitz, Frederic E., and Sam V. Cochran. 1994. *Man Alive: A Primer of Men's Issues.* Pacific Grove, CA: Brooks/Cole.

Rachlin, Katherine. 2002. "Transgender individuals' experiences of psychotherapy." *International Journal of Transgenderism* 6(1):January-March:np.

Radcliffe, Sarah A. 1999. "Race and domestic service: Migration and identity in Ecuador." In Janet H. Momsen (ed.), *Gender, Migration, and Domestic Service.* (pp. 83–97). London: Routledge.

Radford, M. J., and V. Vaccarino et al. 2001. "Sex differences in cardiac catheterization: The role of physician gender." *Journal of the American Medical Association* 286:2849–56.

Radhakrishnan, Sarvepalli. 1947. *Religion and Society.* London: Allen and Unwin.

Rahman, Aminur. 1999. "Micro-credit initiatives for equitable and sustainable development: Who pays?" *World Development* 27(1):67–82.

Rai, Shirin. 2002. *Gender and the Political Economy of Development: From Nationalism to Globalization.* Cambridge, UK: Polity.

Rainer, Goldfrad et al. 2002. "Influence of patient gender on admission to intensive care." *Journal of Epidemiology and Community Health* 56(4):418–23.

Rank, Mark R. 2000. "Poverty and economic hardship in families." In David H. Demo, Katherine R. Allen, and Mark A. Fine (eds.), *Handbook of Family Diversity.* Oxford, UK: Oxford University.

Ranson, Gillian. 1998. "Education, work and family decision making: Finding the 'right time' to have a baby." *Canadian Review of Sociology and Anthropology* 35(4):517–33.

Ranson, Gillian, and William Joseph Reeves. 1996. "Gender earnings, and proportions of women: Lessons from a high-tech occupation." *Gender & Society* 10(2):168–84.

Raphael, Marc Lee. 2002. *Gendering the Jewish Past.* Williamsburg, VA: College of William and Mary.

Rapoport, Tamar, Yoni Garb, and Anat Penso. 1995. "Religious socialization and female subjectivity: Religious-Zionist adolescent girls in Israel." *Sociology of Education* 68(1):48–61.

Rastogi, Mudita, and Karen S. Wampler. 1999. "Adult daughters' perceptions of the mother-daughter relationship: A cross-cultural comparison." *Family Relations* 48(3):327–36.

Ratcliff, Kathryn Strother. 2002. *Women and Health: Power, Technology, Inequality, and Conflict in a Gendered World.* Boston: Allyn & Bacon.

Raymo, James M., Jr. 2003. "Educational attainment and the transition to first marriage among Japanese women." *Demography* 40(1):83–103.

Record, Angela R. 2002. "Born to shop: Teenage women and the marketplace in the postwar United States." In Eileen R. Meehan and Ellen Riordan (eds.), *Sex and Money: Feminism and the Political Economy in the Media.* (pp. 181–95). Minneapolis: University of Minnesota.

Reed, Barbara. 1987. "Taoism." In Arvind Sharma (ed.), *Women in World Religions.* Albany: State University of New York.

Reeves, Martha E. 2000. *Suppressed, Forced Out and Fired: How Successful Women Lose Their Jobs.* Westport, CT: Quorum.

Regan, Pamela C. 2000. "Love relationships." In Lenore Szuchman and Frank Muscarella (eds.), *Psychological Perspectives on Human Sexuality.* (pp. 232–82). New York: Wiley.

Regev, Motti. 1994. "Producing artistic value: The case of rock music." *Sociological Quarterly* 35(1):85–102.

Reid, JoAnne. 1999. "Little women/little men: Gender, violence and embodiment in an early childhood classroom." In Barbara Kamler (ed.), *Constructing Gender and Difference: Critical Perspectives on Early Childhood.* (pp. 167–90). Cresskill, NJ: Hampton.

Reid, Scott A., Natasha Keerie, and Nicholas A. Palomares. 2003. "Language, gender salience, and social influence." *Journal of Language and Social Psychology* 22(2):210–33.

Reineke, Martha J. 1995. "Out of order: A critical perspective on women in religion." In Jo Freeman (ed.), *Women: A Feminist Perspective.* Mountain View, CA: Mayfield.

Rendon, Laura I., and Richard O. Hope. 1995. "An educational system in crisis." In L. I. Rendon and R. O. Hope (eds.), *Educating a New Majority: Transforming America's Educational System for Diversity.* (pp. 1–32). San Francisco: Jossey-Bass.

Renk, Kimberley, Rex Roberts et al. 2003. "Mothers, fathers, gender role and time parents spend with their children." *Sex Roles* 48(7–8):305–15.

Rennison, C. M. 2001. "National Crime Victimization Survey, Criminal victimization 2000: Change 1999–2000 with Trends 1993–2000." Washington, DC: U.S. Department of Justice, Bureau of Justice Statistics.

Retherford, Robert D., Naohiro Ogawa, and Rikiya Matsukura. 2001. "Late marriage and less marriage in Japan." *Population and Development Review* 27(1):65–102.

Reynolds, J. Lynn, and Rodney A. Reynolds. 2000. "Ecumenical Promise Keepers: Oxymoron or fidelity?" In Dane S. Claussen (ed.), *The Promise Keepers: Essays on Masculinity and Christianity.* (pp. 175–81). Jefferson, NC: McFarland.

Reynolds, Katsue Akiba. 1998. "Female speakers of Japanese in transition." In Jennifer Coates (ed.), *Language and Gender: A Reader.* Malden, MA: Blackwell.

Rhoades, Helen. 2002. "The 'no-contact mother': Reconstructions of motherhood in the era of the 'new father.'" *International Journal of Law, Policy and the Family* 16(1):71–94.

Rhoads, Steven E. 1993. *Incomparable Worth: Pay Equity Meets the Market.* New York: Cambridge University.

Rhode, Deborah L. 1993. "Gender equality and employment policy." In Sherri Matteo (ed.), *American Women in the Nineties: Today's Critical Issues.* Boston: Northeastern University.

Rhodes, Angel R. 2002. "Long-distance relationships in dual-career commuter couples: A review of counseling issues." *Family Journal-Counseling and Therapy for Couples and Families* 10(4):398–404.

Rhonda, James P. 1996. "The attractions of Christianity for the native women of Martha's Vineyard." In Mary Beth Norton and Ruth M. Alexander (eds.), *Major Problems in American Women's History.* Lexington, MA: D. C. Heath.

Rice, Patricia. 2002. "Sexual abuse by priests." *St. Louis Post-Dispatch* April 28:B1, B4.

Rice, Susan. 2001. "Sexuality and intimacy for aging women." In J. Dianne Garner and Susan O. Mercer (eds.), *Women as They Age.* New York: Haworth.

Richardson, Laurel. 1986. "Another world." *Psychology Today* (February):23–27.

———. 1988. *The Dynamics of Sex and Gender: A Sociological Perspective.* New York: Harper & Row.

———. 1996. "Gender stereotyping in the English language." In Karen E. Rosenblum and Toni-Michelle C. Travis (eds.), *The Meaning of Difference: American Constructions of Race, Sex and Gender and Sexual Orientation.* New York: McGraw-Hill.

Richie, B. E., and V. Kanuha. 2000. "Battered women of color in public health care systems." In Anne Minas (ed.), *Gender Basics: Feminist Perspectives on Women and Men.* Belmont, CA: Wadsworth/Thompson Learning.

Ridgeway, Cecilia L., and Lynn Smith-Lovin. 1999. "The gender system and interaction." *Annual Review of Sociology* 25:191–216.

Rieker, Patricia P., and Chloe E. Bird. 2000. "Sociological explanations of gender differences in mental and physical health." In Chloe E. Bird, Peter Conrad, and Allen M. Fremont (eds.), *Handbook of Medical Sociology.* (pp. 98–113). Upper Saddle River, NJ: Prentice Hall.

Riger, Stephanie. 1993. "Gender dilemmas in sexual harassment: Policies and procedures." In Sherri Matteo (ed.), *American Women in the Nineties: Today's Critical Issues.* Boston: Northeastern University.

———. 2000. *Transforming Psychology: Gender in Theory and Practice.* New York: Oxford University.

Riley, Glenda. 1995. Part 1: "Women in early America to 1763." And Part 2: "Women on the frontier." In *Inventing the American Woman: An*

Inclusive History, Volume I. Wheeling, IL: Harlan Davidson.

Riley, Lisa A., and Jennifer L. Glass. 2002. "You can't always get what you want: Infant care preferences and use among employed mothers." *Journal of Marriage and the Family* 64(1):2–15.

Riley, Pamela, and Gary Kiger. 1999. "Moral discourse on domestic labor: Gender, power and identity in families." *Social Science Journal* 36(3):541–48.

Riley, Patrick. 2000. *Civilizing Sex: On Chastity and the Public Good.* Edinburgh, Scotland: T & T Clark.

Riordan, Cornelius. 1994. "Single-gender schools: Outcomes for African and Hispanic Americans." *Research in Sociology of Education and Socialization* 10:177–205.

———. 2002. "What do we know about the effects of single-sex schools in the private sector? Implications for public schools." In Amanda Datnow and Lea Hubbard (eds.), *Gender in Policy and Practice: Perspectives on Single-Sex and Coeducational Schooling.* New York: Routledge/Falmer.

Riordan, Ellen. 2002. "Intersections and new directions: On feminism and political economy." In Eileen R. Meehan and Ellen Riordan (eds.), *Sex and Money: Feminism and Political Economy in the Media.* (pp. 3-15). Minneapolis: University of Minnesota.

Rishe, Patrick James. 2003. "A reexamination of how athletic success impacts graduation rates: Comparing student-athletes to all other undergraduates." *American Journal of Economics and Sociology* 62(2):407–27.

Riska, Elianne. 2001. *Medical Careers and Feminist Agendas: American, Scandinavian, and Russian Women Physicians.* Hawthorne, NY: Aldine de Gruyter.

Risman, Barbara J. 2001. "Necessity and the invention of mothering." In Roberta Satow (ed.), *Gender and Social Life.* (pp. 26–31). Needham Heights, MA: Allyn & Bacon.

Risman, Barbara J., and Danette Johnson-Summerfield, 2001. "Doing it fairly: A study of postgender marriages." In Theodore F. Cohen (ed.), *Men and Masculinity: A Text Reader.* Belmont, CA: Wadsworth.

Risman, Barbara J., and Pepper Schwartz. 2002. "After the sexual revolution: Gender politics in teen dating." *Contexts* 1(1):Spring:16–24.

Ritchie, and Ronald. 2001. In Joy Ritchie and Kate Ronald (eds.), *Available Means: An Anthology of Women's Rhetorics.* (pp. 138–142). Pittsburgh: University of Pittsburgh.

Roane, Kit R. 2002. "The long arm of abuse: Problem priests cross not just states but oceans as well." *U.S. News & World Report* May 6:26–29.

Roberts, Albert R., and Karel Kurst-Swanger, 2002. "Police responses to battered women: Past, present, and future." In Albert R. Roberts (ed.), *Handbook of Domestic Violence Intervention Strategies: Policies, Programs, and Legal Remedies.* (pp. 101–26). New York: Oxford University.

Roberts, Christy D., Laura M. Stough, and Linda H. Parrish. 2002. "The role of genetic counseling in the elective termination of pregnancies involving fetuses with disabilities." *Journal of Special Education* 36(1):48–55.

Robinson, David L., Jaafar Behbehani, and Mumtaz Shukkur. 1999. "Sex, temperament, and language-related differences in examination performance: A study of multiple-choice and written-answer tests." *Psychological Reports* 85(3):1123–34.

Robinson, James D., and Thomas Skill. 2001. "Five decades of families on television: From the 1950s through the 1990s." In Jennings Bryant and J. Alison Bryant (eds.), *Television and the American Family.* (pp. 139–62). Mahwah, NJ: Lawrence Erlbaum.

Rodgers, Joseph Lee, Paul A. Nakonezny, and Robert D. Shull. 1999. "Did no-fault divorce legislation matter? Definitely yes and sometimes no: Reply to N.D. Glenn." *Journal of Marriage and the Family* 61(3):803–9.

Rodman, Aronson, Kimberley M. Bucholz, and Ester Schaeler. 2001. "The post-feminist era: Still striving for equality in relationships." *American Journal of Family Therapy* 29(2):109–24.

Roehling, Patricia V., and Marta Bultman. 2002. "Does absence make the heart grow fonder? Work-related travel and marital satisfaction." *Sex Roles* 46(9/10):279–93.

Roen, Katrina. 2002. "'Either/or and 'both/neither': Discursive tensions in transgender studies." *Signs* 27(2)501–22.

Rogers, Mary F. 1999. *Barbie Culture.* London: Sage.

Rogers, Stacy J., and Paul R. Amato. 2000. "Have changes in gender relations affected marital quality?" *Social Forces* 79(2):731–53.

Rogers, Stacy J., and Danelle D. DeBoer. 2001. "Changes in wives' income: Effects on marital satisfaction, psychological well-being, and the risk of divorce." *Journal of Marriage and the Family* 63(2):458–72.

Rogers, Wyatt M. 2002. *Christianity and Womanhood: Evolving Roles and Responsibilities.* Westport, CT: Praeger.

Roller, Lynn E. 1999. *In Search of God the Mother: The Cult of Anatolian Cybele.* Berkeley: University of California.

Romer, Nancy. 1990. "Is political activism still a masculine endeavor?" *Psychology of Women Quarterly* 14(2):229–43.

Romo, Harriett D. 1998. "Latina high school leaving: Some practical solutions." *ERIC Digest* Report No.: EDO-RC-97-8.

Roof, Judith. 1997. "The girl I never wanted to be: Identity, identification, and narrative." In Martin B. Duberman (ed.), *A Queer World: The Center for Lesbian and Gay Studies Reader.* New York: Center for Lesbian and Gay Studies, City University.

Root, Maria P. P. 2001. *Love's Revolution: Interracial Marriage.* Philadelphia: Temple University.

Roscoe, Will. 1998. *Changing Ones: Third and Fourth Genders in Native North America.* New York: St. Martin's.

Rose, A., and S. R. Asher. 1999. "Children's goals and strategies in response to conflicts with a friend." *Developmental Psychology* 35:69–79.

Rosener, Judy B. 1995. *America's Competitive Secret: Utilizing Women as a Management Strategy.* New York: Oxford University.

Rosenfeld, Isodore. 2001. "PMS update." *Parade Magazine,* June 3:7.

Rosenfeld, Sarah, Jean Vertefuille, and Donna D. McAlpine. 2000. "Gender stratification and mental health: An exploration of dimensions of the self." *Social Psychology Quarterly* 63(3): 208–23.

Rosin, Hazel M., and Karen Korabik. 2002. "Do family-friendly policies fulfill their promise? An investigation of their impact on work, family conflict and work and personal outcomes." In Debra L. Nelson and Ronald J. Burke (eds.), *Gender, Work Stress, and Health.* Washington, DC: American Psychological Association.

Ross, Hildy, and Heather Taylor. 1989. "Do boys prefer daddy or his physical style of play?" *Sex Roles* 20(1–2):23–31.

Ross, Karen. 2002. *Women, politics, media: Uneasy relations in comparative perspective.* Creskill, NJ: Hampton.

Rossi, Alice S. 1977. "Biosocial aspects of parenting." *Daedalus* 106:1–32.

———. 1984. "Gender and parenthood: An evolutionary perspective." *American Sociological Review* 49:1–19.

———. 2001. "The impact of family problems on social responsibility." In Alice S. Rossi (ed.), *Caring and Doing for Others: Social Responsibility in the Domains of Family, Work and Community.* (pp. 321–47). Chicago: University of Chicago.

Rothman, Barbara Katz, and Mary Beth Caschetta. 1995. "Treating health: Women and medicine." In Jo Freeman (ed.), *Women: A Feminist Perspective.* Mountain View, CA: Mayfield.

Rothman, Stanley, Seymour Martin Lipset, and Neil Nevitte. 2003. "Racial diversity reconsidered." *The Public Interest* 151:25–38.

Rouse, Linda P. 2002. *Marital and Sexual Lifestyles in the United States: Attitudes, Behaviors and Relationships in Social Context.* Binghamton. NY: Haworth Clinical Practice Press.

Rouxel, Geraldine. 2000. "Cognitive-affective determinants of performance in mathematics and verbal domains: Gender differences." *Learning and Individual Differences* 12(3):287–310.

Roy, Shreeparna. 2000. "The impact of structuraladjuectment and the changing nature of women's work in the People's Republic of China." *Indian Journal of Gender Studies* 7(1):1–16.

Roy, Ranjan. 1994. "AIDS explosion feared in India's prostitute towns." *St. Louis Post-Dispatch* March 27:67G.

Rozelle, Scott, Xiao-Yuan Dong, Linxiu Zhang, and Andrew Mason. 2002. *Gender Wage Gaps in Post-reform Rural China.* Development Research Group/Poverty Reduction and Economic Management Network. World Bank, May.

Rudd, Jane. 2001. "Dowry-murder: An example of violence against women." *Women's Studies International Forum* 24(5):513–22.

Ruether, Rosemary Radford. 1983. *Sexism and God-talk: Toward a Feminist Theology.* Boston: Beacon.

———. 2001a. "Christian feminist theology: History and future." In Yvonne Yazbeck and John L. Esposito (eds.), *Daughters of Abraham: Feminist Thought in Judaism, Christianity, and Islam.* (pp. 65–80). Gainesville: University Press of Florida.

———. 2001b. "Feminist theology in a global context." In Rita Halteman and Kari Finger Sandhaas (eds.), *The Wisdom of Daughters; Two Decades of the Voice of Christian Feminism.* Philadelphia: Innisfree Press.

Ruiz, Vicki L., and Ellen Carol DuBois (eds.). 1994. *Unequal Sisters: A Multicultural Reader in U.S. Women's History.* New York: Routledge.

Rupp, Leila J. 1999. *A Desired Past: A Short History of Same-Sex Love in America.* Chicago: University of Chicago.

Ruscher, Janet B. 2001. *Prejudiced Communication: A Social Psychological Perspective.* New York: Guildford.

Russell, Diana E. H. 1998. *Dangerous Relationships: Pornography, Misogyny and Rape.* London: Sage.

Russo, Nancy Felipe, and Jody H. Horn. 1995. "Unwanted pregnancy and its resolution: Options, implications." In Jo Freeman (ed.), *Women: A Feminist Perspective.* Mountain View, CA: Mayfield.

Ruth, Sheila. 2001. *Issues in Feminism: An Introduction to Women's Studies.* Mountain View, CA: Mayfield.

Ruthven, Malise. 2000. *Islam in the World.* Oxford, NY: Oxford University.

Ryan, John, James Hawden, and Allison Branick. 2002. "The political economy of diversity: Diversity programs in Fortune 500 companies." *Sociological Research Online* 7(1):May. Available online at: http://www.socresonline.org.uk

Ryan, Scott D. 2000. "Examining social workers' placement recommendations of children with gay and lesbian adoptive parents." *Families in Society* 81(5):517–28.

Sabo, Donald F. 2004. "Masculinities and men's health: Moving toward post-superman era prevention." In Michael S. Kimmel and Michael A. Messner (eds.), *Men's Lives.* (pp. 321–34). Boston: Allyn & Bacon.

Sabo, Donald F., and Joe Panepinto. 2001. "Football ritual and the social reproduction of masculinity." In Theodore F. Cohen (ed.), *Men and Masculinity: A Text Reader.* (pp. 78–86). Belmont, CA: Wadsworth.

Sachs-Ericsson, Natalie, and James A. Ciarlo. 2000. "Gender, social roles, and mental health: An epidemiological perspective." *Sex Roles* 43(9/10): 605–28.

Sadker, David, and Myra Sadker. 2002. "The miseducation of boys." In Susan M. Bailey (ed.), *The Jossey-Bass Reader on Gender and Education.* (pp. 182–203). San Francisco: Jossey-Bass.

Sadker, Myra, and David Sadker. 2004. "Missing in interaction." In Amanda Konradi and Martha Schmidt (eds.), *Reading Between the Lines: Toward an Understanding of Current Social Problems.* (pp. 445–55). New York: McGraw-Hill.

————. 1994. *Failing at Fairness: How America's Schools Cheat Girls.* New York: Charles Scribner's.

Sadovnik, Alan R., and Susan F. Semel. 2002. "Transition to coeducation at Wheaton College: Conscious coeducation and gender equity in higher education." In Amanda Datnow and Lea Hubbard (eds.), *Gender in Policy and Practice: Perspectives on Single-Sex and Coeducational Schooling.* New York: Routledge/Falmer.

Salmelo-Aro, Katariina, Jari-Erik Nurmi, and Terhi Saisto. 2000. "Women's and men's personal goals during the transition to parenthood." *Journal of Family Psychology* 14(2):171–86.

Salomone, Rosemary. 2003. *Same, Different, Equal: Rethinking Single-Sex Schooling.* New Haven, CT: Yale University.

SAMHSA. 2002. "Alcohol use among girls." Substance Abuse and Mental Health Services Administration, U.S. Department of Health and Human Services. Available online at: http://www.health.org/govpubs/rpo993

Samuels, David. 1999. "The making of a fugitive." (Anti-abortion odyssey). *New York Times* March 21:47–53, 62.

Samuels, Patrice D. 1999. "Back at work but never far from family." *New York Times* October 10:10.

Sanasarian, Eliz (ed.). 1982. *The Women's Rights Movement in Iran: Mutiny, Appeasement and Repression from 1900 to Khomeni.* Westport, CT: Greenwood.

Sanday, Peggy Reeves. 2000. "The socio-cultural context of rape: A cross-cultural study." In Michael S. Kimmel (ed.), *The Gendered Society Reader.* (pp. 55–72). New York: Oxford University.

Sanderson, Susan, and Vetta L. Sanders Thompson. 2002. "Factors associated with perceived parental involvement in childrearing." *Sex Roles* 46(3–4):99–111.

Sandler, Bernice R. 2004. "The chilly climate: Subtle ways in which women are often treated differently at work and in classrooms." In Joan Z. Spade and Catherine G. Valentine (eds.), *The Kaleidoscope of Gender: Prisms, Patterns and Possibilities.* (pp. 187–190). Belmont CA: Wadsworth.

Sarkar, Tanika. 2001. *Hindu Wife, Hindu Nation: Community, Religion, and Cultural Nationalism.* London: Hurst.

Sarlo, Chris. 2000. "Single-parent families: Then and now—what are the consequences for the children." *Fraser Forum* (July). Available online at: http//www.theinvoledfather.com

Sassler, Sharon, and Robert Schoen. 1999. "The effect of attitudes and economic activity on marriage." *Journal of Marriage and the Family* 61: 147–59.

Sato, Barbara Hamill. 2003. *The New Japanese Woman: Modernity, Media, and Women in Interwar Japan.* Durham, NC: Duke University.

Sauerwein, Kristina. 1996. "Survey of students: Sexual harassment an issue for many." *St. Louis Post-Dispatch Metro Post* January 17:2W.

SBA. 2001. "Women in business, 2001." October. Washington, DC: U.S. Small Business Administration Office of Advocacy.

Scharrer, Erica. 2001. "From wise to foolish: The portrayal of the sitcom father, 1950s–1990s." *Journal of Broadcasting and Electronic Media* 45(1): 23–40.

Scharrer, Erica. 2001. "Men, muscles, and machismo: The relationship between television exposure and aggression and hostility in the presence of hypermasculinity." *Media Psychology* 3(2): 159–88.

Schickel, Richard. 2003. "Going crazy over girls." *Time* August 18:62.

Schieman, Scott. 2003. "Socioeconomic status, job conditions, and well-being: Self-concept explanations for gender-contingent effects." *Sociological Quarterly* 627–46.

Schifter, Jacobo, and Johnny Madrigal. 2000. *The Sexual Construction of Latino Youth: Implications for the Spread of HIV/AIDS.* New York: Haworth.

Schippers, Mimi. 2002. *Rockin' Out of the Box: Gender Maneuvering in Alternative Hard Rock.* New Brunswick, NJ: Rutgers University.

Schlafy, Phyllis. 2003. *Feminist Fantasies.* Dallas, TX: Spence.

Schmid-Mast, Marianne. 2001. "Gender differences and similarities in dominance hierarchies in same-gender groups based on speaking time." *Sex Roles* 44(9–10):537–56.

Schmitt, David P. 2002. "A meta-analysis of sex differences in romantic attraction: Do rating contexts moderate tactic effectiveness judgments?" *British Journal of Social Psychology* 41(3):387–402.

Schmitt, David P. Todd K. Shackelford, and David M. Buss. 2001. "Are men really more 'oriented' toward short-term mating than women? A critical review of theory and research." *Psychology, Evolution & Gender* 3(3):211–39.

Schneider, Karen. 1992. "Women run political gauntlet: Candidates struggle to counteract rumors, while boys will be boys." *St. Louis Post-Dispatch* September 19:B1.

Schneider, Kimberly, S. Swan, and L. F. Fitzgerald. 1997. "Job related psychological effects of sexual harassment in the workplace: Empirical studies from two organizations." *Journal of Applied Psychology* 82:401–15.

Schnittker, Jason, Jeremy Freese, and Brian Powell. 2002. "Who's a feminist and what do they believe? Age ideology and feminist self-identification." Paper presented at the Southern Sociological Society, New Orleans, LA. April.

Schroeder, Debra S., and Clifford R. Mynatt. 1999. "Graduate students' relationships with their male and female professors." *Sex Roles* 40(5–6): 393–420.

Schroeder, Patricia. 1993. "Women and politics." In Jodi Wetzel, Margo Linn Espenlaub, Monys A. Hagen, Annette Bennington McElhiney, and Carmen Braun Williams (eds.), *Women's Studies/ Thinking Women.* Dubuque, IA: Kendall/ Hunt.

Schuette, Christine Turner. 2000. "Children's evaluations of gender roles in a home context." *Dissertation Abstracts International: Section B: Sciences and Engineering* 61 (1-B):566.

Schultz, Susy. 2001. "Prime-time family hour is least diverse." *Women's ENews* May 8. Available online at: http://www.womensenews.org/article.cfm?aid=5 42&content=archive

Schüssler-Fiorenza, Elizabeth. 1984. *The Challenge of Feminist Biblical Interpretation.* Boston: Beacon.

Schwartz, Pepper. 1994. *Peer Marriage: How Love between Equals Really Works.* New York: Free Press.

———. 2002. "Maintaining relationships at the millennium." In John H. Harvey and Amy Wenzel (eds.), *A Clinician's Guide to Maintaining and Enhancing Close Relationships.* (pp. 303–12). Mahwah, NJ: Lawrence Erlbaum.

Schwartz, Pepper, and Virginia Rutter. 1998. *The Gender of Sexuality.* Thousand Oaks, CA: Pine Forge.

Scott, Christopher F., and Susan Sprecher. 2000. "Sexuality in marriage, dating and other relationships: A decade review." *Journal of Marriage and the Family* 62(4):999–1017.

Scott, Kimberly A. 2000. "Selfhood developed: Verbal and nonverbal expressiveness in first-grade African-American girls' play." Paper presented at the American Sociological Association, San Francisco.

Scully, Diana. 1993. "Understanding sexual violence." In Stevi Jackson et al. (eds.), *Women's Studies Essential Readings.* New York: New York University.

Scully, Diana, and Pauline Bart. 2003. "A funny thing happened on the way to the office: Women in gynecology textbooks." *Feminism & Psychology* 13(1):11–16.

Scully, Diana, and Joseph Marolla. 1990. "Riding the bull at Gilley's: Convicted rapists describe the rewards of rape." In James M. Henslin (ed.), *Social Problems Today: Coping with the Challenges of a Changing Society.* Englewood Cliffs, NJ: Prentice Hall.

Scupin, Raymond. 2000. "Islam." In R. Scupin (ed.), *Religion and Culture: An Anthropological Focus.* (pp. 395–420). Upper Saddle River, NJ: Prentice Hall.

Se'ver, Aysan. 1999. "Sexual harassment: Where we were, where we are and prospects for the new millennium: Introduction to the special issue." *The Canadian Review of Sociology and Anthropology* 36(4):469–97.

Seal, David Wyatt, Gina Agostinbelli, and Charlotte A. Hannett. 1994. "Extradyadic romantic involvement: Moderating effects of sociosexuality and gender." *Sex Roles* 31(1–2):1–22.

Sefton, Dru. 2001. "Increasing number of breadwinner wives changes home dynamics." *St. Louis Post-Dispatch* September 21:E1E7.

Segura, Denise A. 1998. "Working at motherhood: Chicana and Mexican immigrant mothers and employment." In Karen V. Hansen and Anita Ilta Garey (eds.), *Families in the U.S.: Kinship and Domestic Politics.* (pp. 727–44). Philadelphia: Temple University.

———. 1994. "Inside the work worlds of Chicana and Mexican immigrant women." In Maxine Baca Zinn and Bonnie Thornton Dill (eds.), *Women of Color in U.S. Society.* Philadelphia: Temple University.

Seifert, E. 2000. "Strategies for a successful long-distance marriage: The story of two administrators." In A. Pankake, G. Schroth, and C. Funk (eds.), *Women as School Executives: The Complete Picture.* (pp. 214–18). Austin, TX: Texas Council of School Executives.

Sen, Mala. 2002. *Death by Fire: Sati, Dowry Death, and Female Infanticide in Modern India.* New Brunswick, NJ: Rutgers University.

Serbin, Lisa A. Diane Poulin-Dubois, Karen A. Colburne, Maya G. Sen, and Julie A. Eichstedt. 2001. "Gender stereotyping in infancy: Visual preferences for and knowledge of stereotyped toys in the second year." *International Journal of Behavioral Development* 25(1):7–15.

Sered, Susan Starr. 1991. "Conflict, complement and control: Family and religion among Middle Eastern Jewish women in Jerusalem." *Gender & Society* 5(1):10–29.

———. 1994. *Priestess, Mother, Sacred Sister: Religions Dominated by Women.* New York: Oxford University.

Seymour, John A. 2000. *Childbirth and the Law.* New York: Oxford University.

Shanghai Star. 2002. "China's missing girls." October 24.

Shannon, Brennfleck. 2001. *Caregiving Sourcebook.* Detroit, MI: Omnigraphics.

Sharp, Edlaine B., and Mark Joslyn. 2001. "Individual and contextual effects on attributions about pornography." *Journal of Politics* 63(2):501–19.

Shaw, Miranda. 1997. "Worship of women in Tantric Buddhism: Male is to female as devotee is to goddess." In Karen L. King (ed.). *Women and Goddess Traditions: In Antiquity and Today.* (pp. 111–36). Minneapolis, MN: Fortress.

Sheffield, Carole E. 1995. "Sexual terrorism." In Jo Freeman (ed.), *Women: A Feminist Perspective.* Mountain View, CA: Mayfield.

Shehadeh, Lamia Rustum. 2003. *The Idea of Women in Fundamentalist Islam.* Gainesville: University Press of Florida.

Shelden, Randall G., Sharon K. Tracy, and William B. Brown. 2001. *Youth Gangs in American Society.* Belmont, CA: Wadsworth/Thomson.

Shelton, Beth Anne. 2000. "Understanding the distribution of housework between husbands and wives." In Linda J. Waite and Christine Bachrach et al (eds.), *The Ties that Bind: Perspectives on Marriage and Cohabitation.* (pp. 343–55). New York: Aldine de Gruyter.

Shelton, Beth Anne, and Ben Agger. 1993. "Shotgun wedding, unhappy marriage, non-fault divorce? Rethinking the feminism-marxism relationship." In Paula England (ed.), *Theory on Gender/Feminism on Theory.* New York: Aldine De Gruyter.

Shelton, Beth Anne, and Juanita Firestone. 1989. "Household labor time and the gender gap in earnings." *Gender & Society* 3(1):105–12.

Shen, Fern. 1995. "For the battered spouse, insurers' bias worsens pain." *Washington Post* March 9:A1, A16.

Sher, George. 2002. "Justifying reverse discrimination in employment." In Stephen Cahn (ed.), *The Affirmative Action Debate.* (pp. 58–67). London: Routledge.

Sherwood, Jessica Holden, and Barbara J. Risman. 2000. "Children and gender: The case of feminist kids." *Advances in Gender Research* 4:319–353.

Shibamoto, Janet S. 1985. *Japanese Women's Language.* Orlando, FL: Academic Press.

Shidlo, Ariel. 1994. "Internalized homophobia: Conceptual and empirical issues in measurement." In Beverly Greene and Gregory M. Herek (eds.), *Lesbian and Gay Psychology: Theory, Research, and Clinical Applications.* Thousand Oaks, CA: Sage.

Shields, Vickie Rutledge. 2002. *Measuring Up: How Advertising Affects Self-Image.* Philadelphia: University of Pennsylvania.

Shikakura, Hisayo, and Gavin W. Hougham. 2000. "High school education for girls in Japan: Do traditional gender-role values still matter?" Paper presented at the American Sociological Association, August, Washington DC.

Shimony, Annemarie. 1985. "Iroquois religion and women in historical perspective." In Y. Y. Haddad and E. B. Findly (eds.), *Women, Religion and Social Change.* Albany: SUNY.

Shinberg, Diane S. 2001. "Sex and sickness: Gender and socioeconomic inequalities in adult health." *Dissertation Abstracts International, A: The Humanities and Social Sciences* 62(4), October:1591-A.

Shook, Nancy J., Deborah A. Gerrity, Joan Jurich, and Allen E. Segrist. 2000. "Courtship violence among college students: A comparison of verbally and physically abuse couples." *Journal of Family Violence* 15(1):1–22.

Shostock, Albert L., 2001. *Shelters for Women and Their Children: A Comprehensive Guide to Planning and Operating Safe and Caring Residential Programs.* Springfield, IL: Charles C. Thomas.

Shrier, Diane K. 2002. "Career and workplace issues." In Susan G. Kornstein and Anita H. Clayton (eds.), *Women's Mental Health: A Comprehensive Textbook.* (pp. 527–41). New York: Guilford.

Shrum, L. J. 2002. "Media consumption and perceptions of social reality: Effects and underlying processes." In Jennings Bryant and Dolf Zillmann (eds.), *Media Effects: Advance in Theory and Research.* Mahwah, NJ: Lawrence Erlbaum.

Shumaker, Sally A. 2003. "Estrogen plus progestin and the incidence of dementia and mild cognitive impairment in postmenopausal women." *Journal of the American Medical Association* 289(20):2673–84.

Sichel, Deborah. 2003. "Neurohormonal aspects of postpartum depression and psychosis." In Margaret G. Spinelli (ed.), *Infanticide: Psychosocial and Legal Perspectives on Mothers Who Kill* (pp. 61–69). Washington, DC: American Psychiatric Publishing.

SIDA. 1995. *Gender Equality in Development Cooperation: Taking the Next Step.* Stockholm: Swedish International Development Cooperation Agency.

Sidanius, Jim, and Yesilernis Pena. 2003. "The gendered nature of family structure and group-based anti-egalitarianism: A cross-national analysis." *Journal of Social Psychology* 143(2):243–51.

Sify. 2003. "India no longer shying away from AIDS." *Sify News*: December 31. Available online at: http://sify.com/news/fullstory

SIGI. 2001. "Statistics." Sisterhood is Global Institute. Available online: http://www. sigi.org. Resources/stats

Signorielli, Nancy. 2001. "Aging on television." *Generations* 25(3):34–38.

Silvas, Sharon, Barbara Jenkins, and Polly Grant. 1993. "The overvoice: Images of women in the media." In Jodi Wetzel, Margo Linn Espenlaub, Monys A. Hagen, Annette Bennington McElhiney, and Carmen Braun Williams (eds.), *Women's Studies Thinking Women.* Dubuque, IA: Kendall/Hunt.

Simmons, Melanie. 1999. "Theorizing prostitution: The question of agency." In *Sex Work and Sex Workers* (Sexuality and Culture Series, Volume 2). New Brunswick, NJ: Transaction.

Simmons, Tavia, and Grace O'Neill. 2001. "Households and families: 2000." *Census 2000 Brief:* U.S. Census Bureau.

Simon, Rita James. 1975. *The Contemporary Woman and Crime.* Washington, DC: U.S. Government Printing Office.

———. 2002. "Women and violent crime." In Wendy McElroy (ed.), *Liberty for Women: Freedom and Feminism in the Twenty-First Century.* (pp. 231–38). Chicago: Ivan R. Dee.

Simon, Robin W. 2000. "The importance of culture in sociological theory and research on stress and mental health: A missing link?" In Chloe E. Bird, Peter Conrad, and Allen M. Fremont (eds.), *Handbook of Medical Sociology.* (pp. 68–78). Upper Saddle River, NJ: Prentice Hall.

———. 2002. "Revisiting the relationships among gender, marital status, and mental health." *American Journal of Sociology* 107(4):1065–96.

Simon, Robin W., and Kristen Marcussen. 1999. "Marital transitions, marital beliefs, and mental health." *Journal of Health and Social Behavior.* 40:111–25.

Simpson, Jeffry A., W. Stevens Rholes, and Lorne Campbell. 2003. "Changes in attachment orientations across the transition to parenthood." *Journal of Experimental Social Psychology* 39(4):317–31.

Siwatu, Mxolisi S. 2003. "Platonic same-sex friendship intimacy: The effects of sex and gender." Paper presented at the Southern Sociological Society, New Orleans, LA.

Skinner, Patricia. 2001. *Women in Medieval Italian Society, 500–1200.* Harlow, UK: Pearson Education.

Slater, Michael D. et al. 1997. "Adolescent responses to TV beer ads and sports content." *Journalism and Mass Communications Quarterly* 74(1):108–22.

Smailes, Elizabeth M., Stephanie Kasen, Judith S. Brook, Jeffrey G. Johnson, and Patricia Cohen. 2002. "Television viewing and aggressive behavior during adolescence and adulthood." *Science* 295(5564):2468–71.

Smith, Barbara. 1995. "Myths to divert black women from freedom." In Sheila Ruth, *Issues in Feminism: An Introduction to Women's Studies.* Mountain View, CA: Mayfield.

Smith, Dorothy. 2000. "Schooling for inequality." *Signs* 25(4):1147–51.

———. 2003. "Women's perspectives as radical critique of sociology." In Sharlene Nagy Hesse-Biber and Michelle L. Yaiser (eds.), *Feminist Perspectives on Social Research.* New York: Oxford University.

Smith, Eric R. A. N. and Richard L. Fox. 2001. "The electoral fortunes of women candidates for Congress." *Political Science Quarterly* 54(1):205–21.

Smith, James P., and F. R. Welch. 1986. *Closing the Gap: Forty Years of Economic Progress for Blacks.* Santa Monica, CA: Rand.

Smith, Jane I. 1999. *Islam in America.* New York: Columbia University.

Smith, Janet S. 1992. "Women in charge: Politeness and directives in the speech of Japanese women." *Language in Society* 21:59–82.

Smith, Russell. 1994. "Invisible women: Hollywood puts on blinders when it comes to lesbians." *St. Louis Post-Dispatch* July 17:3C, 6C.

Smith, Stacy L., and Aaron R. Boyston. 2002. "Violence in music videos: Examining the prevalence and context of physical aggression." *Journal of Communication* 52(1):61–83.

Smith, Stacy L., and Barbara J. Wilson. 2002. "Children's consumption of and fear reactions to television news." *Media Psychology* 4(1):1–26.

Smith, Stacy L., Barbara J. Wilson, and Carolyn M. Colvin. 2002. "Engaging in violence on American television: A comparison of child, teen, and adult perpetrators." *Journal of Communication* 52(1): 36–60.

Smith, Yolanda L. S., L. Cohen, and Peggy T. Cohen-Kettenis. 2002. "Postoperative psychological functioning of adolescent transsexuals: A Rorschach study." *Archives of Sexual Behavior* 31(3):255–61.

Smith-Lovin, Lynn, and Charles Brody. 1989. "Interruptions in group discussions: The effects of gender and group composition." *American Sociological Review* 54:424–35.

Smith-Rosenberg, Carroll. 1996. "The female world of love and ritual." In Mary Beth Norton and Ruth M. Alexander (eds.), *Major Problems in American Women's History.* Lexington, MA: D. C. Heath.

Smock, Pamela. J. 2000. "Cohabitation in the United States: An appraisal of research themes, findings and interpretations." *Annual Review of Sociology* 26:1–20.

Smock, Pamela J., Wendy D. Manning, and Sanjiv Gupta. 1999. "The effect of marriage and divorce on women's economic well-being." *American Sociological Review* 64(6):794–812.

Snarey, J. 1993. *How Fathers Care for the Next Generation.* Cambridge, MA: Harvard University.

Snodgrass, S.E. 1992. "Further effects of role versus gender on interpersonal sensitivity." *Journal of Perosnality and Social Psychology* 62:154–58.

So, Alvin Y. 2001. "Social relations between Pearl River Delta and Hong Kong." Presentation to the Pearl River Delta seminar, Asian Studies Development Program. Robert Black College, University of Hong Kong, May 29.

Sobol, Jeffrey, Barbara Rauschenbach, and Edward A. Frongillo. 2003. "Marital status and body weight changes: A U.S. longitudinal analysis." *Social Science & Medicine* 56(7):1543–55.

Solomon, Richard, and Cynthia Pierce Liefeld, 1998. "Effectiveness of a family support center approach to adolescent mothers: Repeat pregnancy and school drop-out rates." *Family Relations* 47(2):139–44.

Sommers, Christa Hoff. 2000. *The War Against Boys: How Misguided Feminism is Harming our Young Men.* New York: Simon & Schuster.

Sorber, Ann Verbeck. 2001. "The role of peer socialization in the development of emotion display rules: Effects of age, gender, and emotion." *Dissertation Abstracts International Section B: Sciences and Engineering* 62(2-B):1119.

Sorensen, Elaine. 1994. *Comparable Worth: Is it a Worthy Policy?* Princeton, NJ: Princeton University.

Sorenson, Elaine, and C. Zibman. 2000. *Child support offers some protection against poverty.* Washington, DC: Urban Institute. http://www.newfederalism. org

South, Scott J., and Kim M. Lloyd. 1995. "Spousal alternatives and marital dissolution." *American Sociological Review* 60(1):21–25.

Spender, Dale. 1989. *The Writing or the Sex: Or Why You Don't have to Read Women's Writing to Know it's No Good.* New York: Teacher's College Press.

———. 1993. "Language and reality: Who made the world?" In Stevi Jackson et al. (eds.), *Women's Studies Essential Readings.* New York: New York University.

Sperling, Valerie. 1999. *Organizing Women in Contemporary Russia: Engendering Transition.* Cambridge, UK: Cambridge University.

Sperling, Valerie, Myra Marx Ferree, and Barbara Risman. 2001. "Constructing global feminism: Transnational advocacy networks and Russian women's activism." *Signs* 26(4):1155–86.

Spiller, Katherine. 1993. "The Feminist Majority Report: Corporate women and the mommy track." In Alison M. Jaggar and Paula S. Rothenberg (eds.), *Feminist Frameworks: Alternative Theoretical Accounts of the Relations between Women and Men.* New York: McGraw-Hill.

Spinelli, Margaret G. (ed.). 2003. *Infanticide: Psychosocial and Legal Perspectives on Mothers Who Kill.* Washington, DC: American Psychiatric Publishing.

Spongberg, Mary. 2002. *Writing Women's History Since the Renaissance.* New York: Palgrave Macmillan.

Spraggins, Renee E. 2001. "U.S. Census Bureau releases profile of nation's women." March 15. http://www.census.gov/Press-Release/www2001

———. 2003. "Women and men in the United States: March 2002. Population Characteristics." *Current Population Reports.* March. U.S. Census Bureau.

Sprecher, Susan, and Pamela C. Regan. 2002. "Liking some things (in some people) more than others: Partner preferences in romantic relationships and friendships." *Journal of Social and Personal Relationships* 19(4):463–81.

Sprecher, Susan, and Maura Toro-Morn. 2002. "A study of men and women from different sides of earth to determine if men are from Mars and women are from Venus in their beliefs about love and romantic relationships." *Sex Roles* 46(5/6):131–47.

St. Louis University. 1999. "National study finds heart attacks in women are under-detected and under-treated." February 10. Available online at: http://www.slu.edu/publications/nb/new/02199.shtml

Stack, Carol. 1994. "Different voices, different visions: Gender, culture and moral reasoning." In Maxine Baca Zinn and Bonnie Thornton Dill (eds.), *Women of Color in U.S. Society.* Philadelphia: Temple University.

Staeger, Rob. 3003. *Native American Religion.* Philadelphia: Mason Crest.

Stahly, Geraldine B. 2004. "Battered women: Why don't they just leave?" In Joan C. Chrisler, Carla Golden and Patricia D. Rozee (eds.), *Lectures on the Psychology of Women.* (pp. 310–331). New York: McGraw-Hill.

Stamps, Leighton. 2002. "Maternal preference in child custody decisions." *Journal of Divorce and Remarriage* 37(1–2):1–11.

Stange, Mary Zeiss. 2002. "Female priests provide answer." *USA Today* April 4:13A.

Stanley, David. 2000. *Moon Handbooks: Tahiti.* Emeryville, CA: Avalon.

Staples, Brent. 1995. "Learning to batter women: Wife-beating as inherited behavior." (Editorial-Notebook). *New York Times* February 12.

Staples, Robert. 1997. "An overview of race and marital status." In Harriette Pipes McAdoo (ed.), *Black Families.* (pp. 269–72). Thousand Oaks, CA: Sage.

Stark, Rodney. 1996. *The Rise of Christianity: A Sociologist Reconsiders History.* Princeton, NJ: Princeton University.

2002. "Physiology and faith: Addressing the 'universal' gender differences in religious commitment." *Journal for the Scientific Study of Religion* 41(3):495–507.

Starrels, Marjorie, and Kristin E. Holm. 2000. "Adolescents' plans for family formation: Is parental socialization important." *Journal of Marriage and the Family* 62(2):416–29.

Stasio, Marilyn. 2001. "It's not just a 'women's issue' anymore." *Parade Magazine.* January 21:14, 16.

Statham, Anne, Laurel Richardson, and Judith A. Cook. 1991. *Gender and University Teaching: A Negotiated Difference.* Albany: State University of New York.

Staudt, Kathleen. 1998. *Policy, Politics & Gender: Women Gaining Ground.* West Hartford, CT: Kumarian.

Stearns, Peter N. 2002. *Fat History: Bodies and Beauty in the Modern West.* New York: New York University.

Steering Committee of the Physicians Health Study Research Group. 1989. "Final report of the aspirin component of the ongoing physician's health study." *New England Journal of Medicine* 321(3):129–35.

Steil, Janice. 1995. "Supermoms and second shifts: Marital inequality in the 1990s." In Jo Freeman (ed.), *Women: A Feminist Perspective.* Mountain View, CA: Mayfield.

Stein, Harry. 1987. "The case for staying home." In Ollie Pocs and Robert H. Walsh (eds.), *Marriage and Family* (Annual Editions). Guilford, CT: Dushkin.

Stein, Leon. 2001. *The Triangle Fire.* Ithaca, NY: Cornell University.

Stein, Nan. 1999. *Classrooms and Courtrooms: Facing Sexual Harassment in K-12 Schools.* New York: Teachers College Press.

Steinem, Gloria. 1995. "Sex, lies and advertising." In Jo Freeman (ed.), *Women: a Feminist Perspective.* Mountain View, CA: Mayfield.

Steinpreis, Rhea A., Katie A. Anders, and Dawn Ritzke. 1999. "The impact of gender on the review of the curricula vitae of job applicants and tenure candidates: A national empirical study." *Sex Roles* 41(7/8):509–28.

Stepenoff, Bonnie. 1999. *Their Fathers' Daughters: Silk Mill Workers in Northeastern Pennsylvania, 1880–1960.* Selinsgrove, PA: Susquehanna University.

Stephens, Mary Ann Parris, Lynn M. Martire, and Jennifer Ann Druley. 2001. "Balancing parent care with other roles: Interrole conflict of adult daughter caregivers." *Journals of Gerontology: Series B: Psychological Sciences and Social Sciences* 56B(1):24–34.

Stephens, Walter. 2002. *Demon Lovers: Witchcraft, Sex, and the Crisis of Belief.* Chicago: University of Chicago.

Stern, M., and K. H. Karraker. 1989. "Sex stereotyping of infants: A review of gender labeling studies." *Sex Roles* 20(3):501–22.

Sternberg, Robert J. 1988. *The Triangle of Love.* New York: Basic Books.

Stets, Jan E., and Stacy A. Hammons. 2002. "Gender, control, and marital commitment." *Journal of Family Issues* 23(1):3–25.

Stetson, Dorothy McBride. 1997. *Women's Rights in the U.S.A.: Policy Debates and Gender Roles.* New York: Garland.

———. 2000. "Gendering policy debates: Job training and abortion regulation." In Sue Tolleson-Rinehart and Jyl L. Josephson (eds.), *Gender and American Politics: Women, Men and the Political Process.* Armonk, New York: M. E. Sharpe.

Stevens, Allison. 2003. "The strength of these women shows in their numbers." *CQ Weekly* October 25:2625–7.

Stevens, Evelyn P. 2000. "Marianismo: The other face of machismo in Latin America." In Anne Minas (ed.), *Gender Basics: Feminist Perspectives on Women and Men.* (pp. 456–63). Belmont, CA: Wadsworth.

Stewart, Karen. 1998. "Women in business: The experiences of women in the U.S. workforce." In

Donna Musialowski Ashcraft (ed.), *Women's Work: A Survey of Scholarship by and about Women.* New York: Haworth.

Stewart, Stephanie, Heather Stinnett, and Lawrence B. Rosenfeld. 2000. "Sex differences in desired characteristics of short-term and long-term relationship partners." *Journal of Social and Personal Relationships* 17(6):843–53.

Stiers, Gretchen A. 2000. *From this Day Forward: Commitment, Marriage, and Family in Lesbian and Gay Relationships.* New York: St. Martin's.

Stikker, Allerd. 2002. *Closing the Gap: Exploring the History of Gender Relations.* Amsterdam: Amsterdam University.

Stohs, Joanne Hoven. 2000. "Multicultural women's experience of household labor, conflicts, and equity." *Sex Roles* 42(5–6):339–61.

Stoltenberg, John. 1995. "How men have (a) sex." In Sheila Ruth, *Issues in Feminism: An Introduction to Women's Studies.* Mountain View, CA: Mayfield.

Stone, Linda, and Nancy P. McKee. 2000. "Gendered futures: Student visions of career and family on a college campus. *Anthropology & Education Quarterly* 31(1):67–89.

Stone, Merlin. 1990. *When God was a Woman.* New York: Dorset.

Stratton, Jo Anna L. 1981. *Pioneer Women: Voices from the Kansas frontier.* New York: Simon & Schuster.

Strauss, Valerie. 2000. "Equal opportunity learning." *Washington Post* Feb. 22:A09.

Street, Sue, Jeffrey Kromrey, and Ellen Kimmel. 1995. "University faculty gender roles perceptions." *Sex Roles* 32(5–6):407–22.

Streitmatter, Janice L. 1999. *For Girls Only: Making a Case for Single-Sex Schooling.* Albany: State University of New York.

Streitmatter, Rodger. 1997. "Creating Rosie the Riveter: Propelling women in the workforce." *In Mightier than the Sword: How the News Media have Shaped American History.* Boulder, CO: Westview.

Strikwerda, Robert A., and Larry May. 2000. "Male friendship and intimacy." In Anne Minas (ed.), *Gender Basics: Feminist Perspectives on Women and Men.* Belmont, CA: Wadsworth/Thompson Learning.

Strough, JoNell, and Cynthia A. Berg. 2000. "Goals as a mediator of gender differences in high-affiliation dyadic conversations." *Developmental Psychology* 36(1):117–25.

Strum, Shirley C., and Linda M. Fedigan. 2000. "Changing views of primate society: A situated North American perspective." In Shirley C. Strum and Linda M. Fedigan (eds.), *Primate Encounters: Models of Science, Gender and Society.* (pp. 3-56). Chicago: University of Chicago.

Stuart, Peggy. 1992. "What does the glass ceiling cost you?" *Personnel Journal* 71(11):70–9.

Sturt, Patrick. 2003. The time-course of the application of binding constraints in reference resolution." *Journal of Memory and Language* 48(3): 542–62.

Sudha, S., and S. Irudaya Rajan. 2000. "Female demographic disadvantage in India 1981–1991: Sex selective abortion and female infanticide." In Shahra Razavi (ed.), *Gendered Poverty and Well-Being.* (pp. 171–204) Oxford, UK: Blackwell.

Suitor, J. Jill, and Rebecca S. Carter. 1999. "Jocks, nerds, babes and thugs: Research notes on regional differences in adolescent gender norms." *Gender Issues* 17(3):87–101.

Sullivan, Maureen Elizabeth. 2000. "Conscious kinship: Lesbian coparent families and the undoing of gender." *Dissertation Abstracts International, A: The Humanities and Social Sciences* 60(10):3807-A.

Sutton, Linda. 1999. *Love Matters: A Book of Lesbian Romance and Relationships.* Binghamton, NY: Harrington Park.

Suzuki, Atusko. 1991. "Egalitarian sex role attitudes: Scale development and comparison of American and Japanese women." *Sex Roles* 24(5–6):245–59.

Swann, Joan. 2003. "Schooled language: Language and gender in educational settings." In Janet Holmes and Miriam Meyerhoff (eds.), *The Handbook of Language and Gender.* Malden, MA: Blackwell.

Sweeney, Diana Michelle. 2001. "Applying gender schema theory: Measuring the effects of an androgynous appearance." *Dissertation Abstracts International: Section B: Sciences and Engineering* 61(9-B):5061.

Sweeney, Megan M. 2002a. "Remarriage and the nature of divorce: Does it matter which spouse chose to leave?" *Journal of Family Issues* 23(3):410–40.

———. 2002b. "Two decades of family change: The shifting economic foundations of marriage." *American Sociological Review* 67(1):132–47.

Sweeting, Helen, and Patrick West. 2003. "Sex differences in health at ages 11, 13, and 15." *Social Science & Medicine* 56(1):31–39.

Swetkis, Doreen, Faith D. Gilroy, and Roberta Steinbacher. 2002. "Firstborn preference and attitudes toward using sex selection technology." *Journal of Genetic Psychology* 163(2): 228–38.

Swirski, Barbara, and Marilyn P. Safir (eds.). 1991. *Calling the Equality Bluff: Women in Israel.* New York: New York Teacher's College, Columbia University Teacher's College.

Sylvester, Christine. 1995. "African and Western feminisms: World-traveling the tendencies and possibilities." *Signs* 20(4):941–69.

Taitz, Emily, Sondra Henry, and Cheryl Tallan. 2003. *JPS Guide to Jewish Women, 600 B.C.E.–1900 C.E.* Philadelphia: Jewish Publication Society.

Takahara, Kumiko. 1991. "Female speech patterns in Japanese." *International Journal of the Sociology of Language* 92:61–85.

Talbot, Margaret. 1999. "The little white bombshell." *New York Times Magazine* June 11:39–43, 61–63.

Takano, Deborah-Foreman. "Hit or myth: The perpetuation of popular Japanese stereotypes in Japan-published English textbooks" in M.J. Hardman and Anita Taylor (eds.), *Hearing Many Voices.* (pp. 119-32). Cresskill, NJ: Hampton.

Tam, Tony. 1997. "Sex segregations and occupational gender inequality in the United States." *American Journal of Sociology* 102:320–92.

Tanifuji, Etsushi. 1995. "Feminism." *Japan Update* (March) 42.

Tannen, Deborah. 1994. *Gender and discourse*. New York: Oxford University.

———. 2001a. *Talking from 9 to 5: Women and Men at Work*. New York: Quill.

———. 2001b. *You Just Don't Understand: Women and Men in Conversation*. New York: Quill.

Tasker, Fiona. 2002. "Lesbian and gay parenting." In Adrian Coyle and Celia Kitzinger (eds.), *Lesbian and Gay Psychology: New Perspectives*. (pp. 81–97). Oxford, UK: BPS Blackwell.

Tavernise, Sabrina. 2003. "Women redefine their roles in new Russia." *New York Times International* March 9:4.

Tavris, Carol. 1996. "The mismeasure of woman." In Karen E. Rosenblum and Toni-Michelle C. Travis (eds.), *The Meaning of Difference: American Constructions of Race, Sex and Gender, Social Class, and Sexual Orientation*. New York: McGraw-Hill.

Taylor, Alison. 2002. *The Handbook of Family Dispute Resolution: Mediation Therapy and Practice*. San Francisco: Jossey-Bass.

Temple, Charles. 1993. "What if Beauty had been ugly? Reading against the grain of gender bias in children's books." *Language Arts* 70(2):89–93.

Tenenbaum, Harriet R., and Campbell Leaper. 2002. "Are parents' gender schemas related to their children's gender-related cognitions? A meta-analysis." *Developmental Psychology* 38(4): 615–30.

Tepper, Clary A., and Kimberly Wright Cassidy. 1999. "Gender differences in emotional language in children's picture books." *Sex Roles* 40(3–4):265–80.

Terborg-Penn, Rosalyn. 1991. "Discontented black feminists: Prelude and postscript to the passage of the Nineteenth Amendment." In Kathryn Kish Sklar and Thomas Dublin (eds.), *Women and Power in American History: A Reader, Volume II from 1870*. Englewood Cliffs, NJ: Prentice Hall.

Tescione, Susan M. 1998. "A women's name: Implications for publication, citation, and tenure." *Educational Researcher* 27(8):38–42.

Tessier, Marie. 2002. "Bush appointees include fewer women." *Women's ENews* February 11. Available online: http://www.womensenews.org/org/article.cfm/dyn/aid/812

Thayer, Julian F., and Bjorn Helge Johnsen. 2000. "Sex differences in judgment of facial affect: A multivariate analysis of recognition errors." *Scandinavian Journal of Psychology* 41(3):243–46.

Theorell, Tores. 2001. "Stress and health from a work perspective." In Jack Dunham (ed.), *Stress in the Workplace: Past, Present, and Future*. (pp. 34-51). London: Whurr.

Thernstrom. Stephan, and Abigail Thernstrom. 2002. "Does your 'merit' depend on your race? A rejoinder to Bowen and Bok." In Stephen Cahn (ed.), *The Affirmative Action Debate*. London: Routledge.

Thomas, M. Carey. 1991. "Educated woman." In Evelyn Ashton-Jones and Gary A. Olson (eds.), *The Gender Reader*. Boston: Allyn & Bacon.

Thomas, Neil, and Neil Price. 1999. "The role of development in global fertility decline." *Futures* 31(8):779–802.

Thompson, Nicola Diane (ed.). 1999. *Victorian Women Writers and the Woman Question*. Cambridge, UK: Cambridge University.

Thomson, Michael. 1998. *Reproducing Narrative: Gender, Reproduction and Law*. Aldershot, UK: Ashgate.

Thorne, Barrie. 1993. *Gender Play: Girls and Boys in School*. New Brunswick, NJ: Rutgers University.

———. 2002. "Do boys and girls have different cultures?" In Susan M. Bailey (ed.), *The Jossey-Bass Reader on Gender and Education*. (pp. 125–52). San Francisco: Jossey-Bass.

Thornton, Arland. 1988. "Cohabitation and marriage in the 1980s." *Demography* 25:497–508.

Thornton, Arland, and Linda Young-DeMarco. 2001. "Four decades in attitudes toward family issues in the United States: The 1960s through the 1990s." *Journal of Marriage and the Family* 63(4):1009–37.

Thornton, J., and M. Lasswell. 1997. *Chore Wars: How Households Can Share the Work and Keep the Peace*. Berkeley, CA: Conari.

Thurlow, Crispin. 2001. "Naming the 'outside within': Homophobic pejoratives and the verbal abuse of lesbian, gay and bisexual high-school students." *Journal of Adolescence* 24(1):25–38.

Thurston, Anne. 1995. *Because of Her Testimony: The Word in Female Experience*. Dublin: Gill and MacMillan.

Tirohl, Blu. 2003. "Fast talking dames." *Journal of Gender Studies* 12(2):145–6.

Toro-Morn, Maura I. 1995. "Gender, class, family, and migration: Puerto Rican women in Chicago." *Gender & Society* 9(6):712–26.

Treas, Judith, and Deidre Giesen. 2000. "Sexual infidelity among married and co-habiting Americans." *Journal of Marriage and the Family* 62:48–60.

Trible, Phyllis. 1984. *The Texts of Terror*. Philadelphia: Fortress.

Trigger, Bruce G. 2001. "Early Native North American responses to European contact." In Albert L. Hurtado and Peter Iverson (eds.), *Major Problems in American Indian History*. Boston: Houghton Mifflin.

Trudel, Gilles. 2002. "Sexuality and marital life: Results of a survey." *Journal of Sex & Marital Therapy* 28(3):229–49.

Tuch, Richard. 2000. *The Single Woman-Married Man Syndrome*. Northvale, NJ: Jason Aronson.

Tuck, Bryan, Jan Rolfe, and Vivienne Adair. 1994. "Adolescents' attitudes toward gender roles within work and its relationship to gender, personality type and parental occupation." *Sex Roles* 31(9–10):547–58.

Tucker, Corinna Jenkins, Susan M. McHale, and Ann C. Crouter. 2003. "Dimensions of mothers' and fathers' differential treatment of siblings: Links with adolescents' sex-typed personal qualities." *Family Relations* 52(1):82–89.

Turestsky, V. 1999. "Child support trends." Center for Law and Social Policy. Available online at: http://www.clasp.org/pubs/childassurance

Turkat, Ira Daniel. 2002. "Shared parenting dysfunction." *American Journal of Family Therapy* 30(5):385–93.

Turnbull, William, and Jenny I. M. Cerpendale. 2002. "Talk and the development of social understanding." *Early Education & Development* 12(3):455–77.

Turner, Sarah E., and William G. Brown. 1999. "Choice of major: The changing (unchanging) gender gap." *Industrial and Labor Relations Review* 52(2):289–313.

U.S. Bureau of the Census. 2001. *Statistical Abstract of the United States.* Washington, DC: U.S. Department of Commerce.

U.S. Bureau of the Census. 2004. *Statistical Abstract of the United States.* Washington, DC: U.S. Department of Commerce.

U.S. Commission on Human Rights. 2000. "Indian tribes: A continuing quest for human survival." In Anne Minas (ed.), *Gender Basics: Feminist Perspectives on Women and Men.* (pp. 50–43). Belmont, CA: Wadsworth.

UCR. 2004. "Crime in the United States (annual)." *Uniform Crime Reports.* Washington, DC: U.S. Government Printing Office.

Ulrich, Miriam, and Ann Weatherhall. 2000. "Motherhood and infertility: Viewing motherhood through the lens of infertility." *Feminism & Psychology* (Special Issue: Reproduction) 10(3):323–36.

Umberson, Debra, Kristin Anderson, Jennifer Glick, and Adam Shapiro. 1998. "Domestic violence, personal control, and gender." *Journal of Marriage and the Family* 60(2)442–52.

UNDP. 2003. United Nations Development Program. *Human Development Indicators, 2003.* Human Development Index (HDI) value. Available online: http://www.undp.org/hdr2003/indicator/

UNFPA. 2004. United Nations Population Fund. *The State of the World Population, 2003.* New York: United Nations.

UNICEF. 2003. *The State of the World's Children.* United Nations Children's Fund. London: Oxford University.

Uniform Crime Reports. 2002. *Crime in the United States.* Washington, DC: Federal Bureau of Investigation, U.S. Department of Justice.

United Nations Development Program. 2004. *Human Development Report, 2003.* New York: Oxford University.

Unsworth, Gabrielle, and Tony Ward. 2001. "Video games and aggressive behavior." *Australian Psychologist* 36(3):184–92.

Udry, J.R. 2000. "The biological limits of gender construction." *American Sociological Review* 65:443–57.

Urla, Jacqueline, and Alan C. Swedlund. 2000. "The anthropometry of Barbie: Unsettling ideals of the feminine body in popular culture." In Londa Schiebinger (ed.), *Feminism & the Body.* Oxford, UK: Oxford University.

USAID. 2002. "Life expectancy will drop worldwide due to AIDS." U.S. Agency for International Development Press Release. July 8. Available online: http://www.usaid.gov/press/release/2002/pr020708.html

————. 2003. "India-Program briefing." October 8. United States Agency for International Development. Available online: http://www.usaid.gov/locations/asia_near_east/counties/india/india_brief

Vallone, Lynne. 1999. "Grrrls and dolls: Feminism and female youth culture." In Beverly Lyon Clark and Margaret R. Higonnet (eds.), *Girls, Boys, Books, Toys: Gender in Children's Literature and Culture.* (pp. 196-209). Baltimore: Johns Hopkins.

Van Bezooijen, Renee. 1996. "Pitch and gender related personality traits." In Natasha Warner et al (eds.), *Gender and Belief Systems: Proceedings of the Fourth Berkeley Women and Language Conference.* (pp. 755–65). Berkeley, CA: Berkeley Women and Language Group.

Van Der Horst, Pieter W. 1995. "Images of women in ancient Judaism." In Ria Kloppenborg and Wouter J. Hanegraaff (eds.), *Female Stereotypes in Religious Traditions.* Leiden, Netherlands: Brill.

Van Der Torn, Karel. 1995. "Torn between vice and virtue: Stereotypes of the widow in Israel and Mesopotamia." In Ria Kloppenborg and Wouter J. Hanegraaff (eds.), *Female Stereotypes in Religious Traditions.* Leiden, Netherlands: Brill.

Vandewater, Elizabeth A., and Abigail J. Stewart. 1997. "Women's career commitment patterns and personality development." In Margie E. Lachman and Jacquelyn Boone James (eds.), *Multiple Paths of Midlife Development.* (pp. 375–410). Chicago: University of Chicago.

Van Kirk, Sylvia. 2001. "The role of Native American women in the fur trade society of Western Canada, 1670–1830." In Albert L. Hurtado and Peter Iverson (eds.), *Major Problems in American Indian History.* Boston: Houghton Mifflin.

Van Wie, Victoria E, and Alan M. Gross. 2001. "The role of woman's explanations for refusal on men's ability to discriminate unwanted sexual behavior in a date rape scenario." *Journal of Family Violence* 16(4):331–44.

Vares, Tina. 2001. "Action heroines and female viewers: What women have to stay." In Martha McCaughey and Neal King (eds.), *Reel Knockouts: Violent Women in the Movies.* (pp. 219–43). Austin: University of Texas.

Vargas, Virginia. 2002. "The struggle by Latin American feminists for rights and autonomy." In Nikke Craske and Maxine Molyneux (eds.), *Gender and the Politics of Rights and Democracy in Latin America.* (pp. 199–222). Houndmills, Hampshire, UK: Palgrave.

Vartanian, Thomas P., and Justine M. McNamara. 2002. "Older women in poverty: The impact of midlife factors." *Journal of Marriage and the Family* 64(2)532–48.

Ventura, Stephanie J., and Christine A. Bachrach. 2000. "Nonmarital childbearing in the United States, 1940–99. *National Vital Statistics Reports* 48(16):October 18 (Centers for Disease Control and Prevention).

Vindhya, U. 2000. "'Dowry deaths' in Andhra Pradesh, India." *Violence Against Women* 6(10): 1085–108.

Vingerhoets, Ad, and Jan Scheirs. 2000. "Sex differences in crying: Empirical findings and possible explanations." In Agneta H. Fischer (ed.), *Gender and Emotion: Social Psychological Perspectives.* New York: Cambridge University.

Vinovskis, Maris A. 1986. "Young fathers and their children: Some historical and policy perspectives." In Arthur B. Elster and Michael E. Lamb (eds.), *Adolescent Fatherhood.* Hillsdale, NJ: Lawrence Erlbaum.

Vissing, Yvonne Marie. 2002. *Women Without Children: Nurturing Lives.* New Brunswick, NJ: Rutgers University.

Von Drehle, Dave. 2003. *Triangle: The Fire that Changed America.* New York: Atlantic Monthly Press.

Von Hassell, Malve. 1993. "Issei women: Silences and fields of power." *Feminist Studies* 19(3):549–69.

Wade, Terrence J., John Cairney, and David J. Pevalin. 2002. "Emergence of gender differences in depression during adolescence: National panel results from three countries." *Journal of the American Academy of Child and Adolescent Psychiatry* 41(2):190–98.

Waite, Linda J., Christine Bachrach, Michelle Hindin, Elizabeth Thomson, and Arland Thornton (eds.). 2000. *The Ties that Bind: Perspectives on Marriage and Cohabitation.* New York: Aldine de Gruyter.

Waite, Linda J., and Maggie Gallagher. 2000. *The Case for Marriage: Why People are Happier, Healthier and Better Off Financially.* New York: Doubleday.

Walker, Nancy A. (ed.). 1998. *Women's Magazines 1940–1960: Gender Roles and the Popular Press.* Boston: Bedford/St. Martin's.

Wallace, Ruth. 1993. "The social construction of a new leadership role: Catholic women pastors." *Sociology of Religion* 54(1):31–42.

Walsh, Mary Williams. 2001. "So where are the corporate husbands?" *New York Times* June 24:3,13.

Walzer, S. 2001. "Thinking about the baby: Gender and the division of infant care." In Theodore F. Cohen (ed.), *Men and Masculinity: A Text Reader.* (pp. 192–206). Belmont, CA: Wadsworth.

Wang, Danyu. 2000. "Stepping on two boats: Urban strategies of Chinese peasants and their children." *International Review of Social History* 45(Suppl. 8):179–96.

Wang, Wen C. 1998. "The consequences of gender preference in China." Paper presented at the International Sociological Association, Montreal.

Ward, Martha C. 1999. *A World Full of Women.* Boston: Allyn & Bacon.

Waring, Marilyn. 1988. *If Women Counted: A New Feminist Economics.* San Francisco: Harper-SanFrancisco.

Warner, Rebecca L., and Brent S. Steel. 1999. "Child rearing as a mechanism for social change: The relationship of child gender to parents' commitment to child equity." *Gender & Society* 13(4): 503–17.

Warren, Karen J. 1997. *Ecofeminism: Women, Culture, Nature.* Bloomington: Indiana University.

Warren, Roland C. 2001. "Securing the home front: A father's role." *Our Children* 27(3):7.

Warwick, Ian, and Peter Aggleton. 2002. "Gay men's physical and emotional well-being: Re-orienting research and health promotion." In Adrian Coyle and Celia Kitzinger (eds.), *Lesbian and Gay Psychology: New Perspectives.* (pp. 135–53). Oxford, UK: BPS Blackwell.

Wasserman, J., R. W. Whitmer, T. L. Bazzarre, S. T. Kennedy, N. Merrick, R. Z. Goetzel, R. L. Dunn, and R. J. Ozminkowski. 2000. "Gender-specific effects of modifiable health risk factors on coronary heart disease and related expenditures." *Journal of Occupational and Environmental Medicine* 42(11):1060–9.

Watson, Jonathan. 2000. *Male Bodies: Health, Culture, and Identity.* Buckingham, UK: Open University.

Watson, Rubie S. 1993. "The named and the nameless: Gender and person in Chinese society." In Caroline B. Brettell and Carolyn F. Sargent (eds.), *Gender in Cross-Cultural Perspective.* Englewood Cliffs, NJ: Prentice Hall.

Waxman, Sharon. 2002. "75 percent of roles are still male." *Washington Post* November 29.

Weatherall, Ann. 2002. *Gender, Language and Discourse.* Hove, UK: Routledge.

Weathers, Charles. 2001. "Changing white-collar workplaces and female temporary workers in Japan." *Social Science Japan Journal* 4(2):201–18.

Weaver, Mary Jo. 1999. "American Catholics in the twentieth century." In Peter W. Williams (ed.), *Perspectives on American Religion and Culture.* (pp. 154–67). Malden, MA: Blackwell.

Weber, Max. 1946. *From Max Weber: Essays in Sociology* (H. H. Gerth and C. W. Mills, eds. & trans.). New York: Oxford University Press.

Webster, Alison R. 1995. *Found Wanting: Women, Christianity and Sexuality.* London: Cassell.

Weiler, Jeanne Drysdale. 2000. *Codes and Contradictions: Race, Gender Identity, and Schooling.* Albany: State University of New York.

Weinberger-Thomas, Catherine. 1999. *Ashes of Immortality: Widow-Burning in India* (Jeffrey Mehlman and David Gordon White, trans.). Chicago: University of Chicago.

Weisgrau, Maxine K. 2000. "Vedic and Hindu traditions." In R. Scupin (ed.), *Religion and Culture: An Anthropological Focus.* (pp. 225–48). Upper Saddle River, NJ: Prentice Hall.

Weitz, Rose. 1995. "What price independence? Social reactions to lesbians, spinsters, widows and nuns." In Jo Freeman (ed.), *Women: A Feminist Perspective.* Mountain View, CA: Mayfield.

Weitzman, Allan. 1999. "Employer defenses to sexual harassment." *Duke Journal of Gender Law and Policy* 6(1):53–55.

Weitzman, Lenore J., and Mavis Maclean. 1992. *Economic Consequences of Divorce: The International Perspective*. Oxford, UK: Clarendon.

Welch, Michael R., David C. Leege, and James C. Cavendish. 1995. "Attitudes toward abortion among U.S. Catholics: Another case of symbolic politics?" *Social Science Quarterly* 76(1):142–97.

Welsch, Janice R. 2001. "On the road with Louise and Thelma." In Murray Pomerance (ed.), *Ladies and Gentlemen, Boys and Girls: Gender in Film at the End of the Twentieth Century*. (pp. 249–66). Albany: State University of New York.

Welsh, Patrick. 2001. "Unlearning machismo: Men changing men in post-revolutionary Nicaragua." In Bob Pease and Keith Pringle (eds.) *A Man's World? Changing Men's Practices in a Globalized World*. (pp. 177–90). London: Zed.

Welsh, Sandy. 1999. "Gender and sexual harassment." *Annual Review of Sociology* 25:169–90.

Welter, Barbara. 1996. "The cult of true womanhood, 1820–1860." In Mary Beth Norton and Ruth M. Alexander (eds.), *Major Problems in American Women's History*. Lexington, MA: D. C. Heath.

Wennemo, Irene. 2001. "The transformation of family life." Seminar: The Nordic Alternative (March 12) Stockholm. Available online at: http://www.nnn.se/seminar

Wertz, Richard W., and Dorothy C. Wertz. 1990. "Notes on the decline of midwives and the rise of medical obstetricians." In Peter Conrad and Rochelle Kern (eds.), *The Sociology of Health and Illness: Critical Perspectives*. New York: St. Martin's.

West, Bonnie. 2000. "Freedom!" *Woman's Day* 63(September 1):164.

West, Candace. 1994. "Rethinking 'sex differences' in conversational topics." In Camille Roman, Suzanne Juhasz, and Cristanne Miller (eds.), *The Women and Language Debate: A Sourcebook*. New Brunswick, NJ: Rutgers University.

West, Lee, Jennifer Anderson, and Steve Duck. 1996. "Crossing the barriers to friendships between men and women." In Julia T. Wood (ed.), *Gendered Relationships*. Mountain View, CA: Mayfield.

West, Michael O. 1999. "Like a river: The Million Man March and the black nationalist tradition in the United States." *Journal of Historical Sociology* 12(1):81–100.

Wexler, Barbara. 2003. *Violent Relationships: Battering and Abuse among Adults*. Detroit, MI: Gale.

Whaley, Rachel Bridges. 2001. "The paradoxical relationship between gender inequality and rape: Toward a refined theory. *Gender & Society* 15(4):531–55.

Wharton, Amy S., and Rebecca J. Erickson. 1995. "The consequences of caring: Exploring the links between women's job and family emotion work." *Sociological Quarterly* 36(2):273–96.

Wharton, Carol S. 1994. "Finding time for the 'second shift': The impact of flexible work schedules on women's double days." *Gender & Society* 8(2):189–205.

Whicker, Marcia Lynn, and Todd W. Areson. 1993. "The maleness of the American presidency." In Lois Lovelace Duke (ed.), *Women in Politics: Outsiders or Insiders?* Englewood Cliffs, NJ: Prentice Hall.

Whicker, Marcia Lynn, Malcolm Jewell, and Lois Lovelace Duke. 1993. "Women in Congress." In Lois Lovelace Duke (ed.), *Women in Politics: Outsiders or Insiders?* Englewood Cliffs, NJ: Prentice Hall.

Whisenant, Warren A., Paul M. Pedersen, and Bill L. Obenour. 2002. "Success and gender: Determining the rate of advancement for intercollegiate athletic directors." *Sex Roles* November.

White House. 2003. "President applauds Supreme Court for recognizing value of diversity." June. Available online at: http://www.whitehouse.gov/mews/releases/2003/06/20030623

White, Linda. 2001. "Democracy in a Confucian-based society." In Lynn Walter (ed.), *Women's Rights: A Global View*. (pp. 141–54). Westport, CT: Greenwood.

White, Merry. 1991. *Challenging Tradition: Women in Japan*. New York: Japan Society.

WHP. 2003. "Run, women, run: Encouraging women to seek elected office." *American Scene* Fall. The White House Project.

Wiederman, Michael W. 2001. "Gender differences in sexuality: Perceptions, myths and realities." *Family Journal of Counseling and Therapy for Couples and Families*. 9(4):468–71.

Wiesner-Hanks, Merry E. 2001. *Gender in History*. Malden, MA: Blackwell.

Wiley, Juli Loesch. 2003. On the fatherhood of God. Is 'God the Mother' just as good?" In Philip E. Divine and Celia Wolf-Devine (eds.), *Sex and Gender: A Spectrum of Views*. (pp. 369–74). Belmont, CA: Wadsworth/Thompson.

Wilkinson, Sue. 2002. "Lesbian health." In Adrian Coyle and Celia Kitzinger (eds.), *Lesbian and Gay Psychology: New Perspectives*. (pp. 117–34). Oxford, UK: BPS Blackwell.

Willemsen, Tineke M. 1998. "Widening the gender gap" Teenage magazines for girls and boys." *Sex Roles* 38(9–10):851–61.

Willer, Lynda R. 2001. "Warning: Welcome to your world baby, gender message enclosed: An analysis of gender messages in birth congratulation cards." *Women & Language* 24(1):16–23.

Williams, Christine. 2003. "The glass escalator: Hidden advantages for men in the 'female' professions." In Michael S, Kimmel (ed.), *The Gendered Society Reader*. New York: Oxford University.

Williams Christine L., Patti A. Giuffre, and Kirsten Dellinger. 1999. "Sexuality in the workplace: Organizational control, sexual harassment, and the pursuit of pleasure." *Annual Review of Sociology*. 25:73–93.

Williams, Jean Calterone. 2003. *A Roof over My Head: Homeless Women and the Shelter Industry*. Boulder, CO: University Press of Colorado.

Williams, Rhys H. 2000. "Introduction—Promise Keepers: A comment on religion and social movements." *Sociology of Religion* 61(1):1–10.

Williams, Walter L. 1996. "The berdache tradition." In Karen E. Rosenblum and Toni-Michelle C. Travis (eds.), *The Meaning of Difference: American Constructions of Race, Sex and Gender, Social Class and Sexual Orientation*. New York: McGraw-Hill.

Williams, Walter L., and John Doyle. 1994. "Rethinking choice for men and polarization among women." *American Behavioral Scientist* 37(8):1104–21.

Williamson, N. E. 1976. *Sons or Daughters: A Cross-Cultural Survey of Parental Preferences*. Beverly Hills, CA: Sage.

Willmott, Ceri. 2002. "Constructing citizenship in the *Poblaciones* of Santiago, Chile: The Role of Reproductive and Sexual Rights." In Nikke Craske and Maxine Molyneux (eds.), *Gender and the Politics of Rights and Democracy in Latin America*. (pp. 124–48). Houndmills, Hampshire, UK: Palgrave.

Wilson, Andrea E., and Melissa A. Hardy. 2002. "Racial disparities in come security for a cohort of aging American women." *Social Forces* 80(2):1283–1306.

Wilson, BarbaMra J., Stacy L. Smith, W. James Potter, Dale Kunkel, Daniel Linz, Carolyn M. Colvin, and Edward Donnerstein. 2002. "Violence in children's programming: Assessing the risks." *Journal of Communication* 52(1):5–35.

Wilson, Calvin. 2002. "A Bond with 007." *St. Louis Post-Dispatch* November 22:F1–F4.

Wilson, Clint C., Felix Gutierrez, and Lena M. Chao. 2003. *Racism, Sexism, and the Media: The Rise of Class Communications in Multicultural America*. Thousand Oaks, CA: Sage.

Wilson, Edward O. 1975. *Sociobiology: The New Synthesis*. Princeton, NJ: Princeton University.

———. 1978. *On Human Nature*. Cambridge, MA: Harvard University.

Wilson, Fiona. 2000. "The social construction of sexual harassment and assault on university students." *Journal of Gender Studies* 9(2):171–87.

Wilson, Robert A. 1966. *Feminine Forever*. New York: M. Evans.

Wilson, Steve R., and Eric S. Mankowski. 2000. "Beyond the drum: An exploratory study of group processes in a mythopoetic men's group." In Edward Read Barton (ed.). *Mythopoetic Perspectives of Men's Healing Work: An Anthology of Therapists and Others*. (pp. 21–45). Westport, CT: Bergin & Garvey.

Winkler, Ann E. 1993. "The living arrangements of single mothers with dependent children: An added perspective." *The American Journal of Economics and Sociology* 52(1):1–18.

Winkvist, Anna, and Humaira Zareen Akhtar. 2000. "God should give daughters to rich families only: Attitudes toward childbearing among low-income women in Punjab, Pakistan." *Social Science and Medicine* 51(1):73–81.

Wirth, Linda. 2001. "Women in management: Closer to breaking through the glass ceiling?" In Martha Fetherolf Loutfi (ed.), *Women, Gender and Work: What is Equality and How do We Get There?* (pp. 239–50). Geneva: International Labour Office.

Witt, G. Evans. 1999. "Women show their spiritual side." *American Demographics* 21(4):23.

Witt, Susan D. 2000. "The influence of television on children's gender role socialization." *Childhood Education* 76(5):322–24.

Wolbrecht, Christina. 2000. *The Politics of Women's Rights: Parties, Positions and Change*. Princeton, NJ: Princeton University.

Woldow, Norman. 1996. "Explaining male/female biological differences: Social science, culture and sociobiology." Unpublished manuscript from the Biology Department, Maryville University, St. Louis.

Wolensky, Kenneth C., Nicole H. Wolensky, and Robert P. Wolensky. 2002. *Fighting for the Union Label: The Women's Garment Industry and ILGWU in Pennsylvania*. University Park: Pennsylvania State University.

Wolf, Margery. 1993. "The birth limitation program: Family versus state." In Stevi Jackson et al. (eds.), *Women's Studies Essential Readings*. New York: New York University.

Wolf-Devine, Celia. 2002. "Proportional representation of women and minorities." In Stephan Cahn (ed.), *The Affirmative Action Debate*. (pp. 168–75). London: Routledge.

Wolfe, Leanna. 1993. *Women Who May Never Marry*. Atlanta, GA: Longstreet.

Wolf, Naomi. 1993 *Fire with Fire: The New Female Power and How it Will Change the Twenty-First Century*. New York: Random House.

———2002. *The Beauty Myth: How Images of Beauty are Used Against Women*. New York: Perennial.

Woloch, Nancy. 1994. *Women and the American Experience*. New York: McGraw-Hill.

Wollstonecraft, Mary. 1792/1970. *The Vindication of the Rights of Woman*. Farnborough, UK: Gregg.

Women's Health Initiative. 2003. "WHI findings." Available online at: http://www.whi.org/findings/default.asp

Wong, Eva. 2002. "Taoism." In Arvind Sharma and Katherine K. Young (eds.), *Her Voice, Her Faith: Women Speak on World Religions*. (pp. 119–144). Boulder, CO: Westview.

Woo, Terry. 2002. "Confucianism." In Arvind Sharma and Katherine K. Young (eds.), *Her Voice, Her Faith: Women Speak on World Religions*. (pp. 99–118). Boulder, CO: Westview.

Wood, Eileen, Serge Desmarais, and Sara Gugula. 2002. "The impact of parenting experience on gender stereotyped toy play of children." *Sex Roles* 47(1–2):39–49.

Wood, Julia T. 2003. *Gendered Lives: Communication, Gender and Culture*. Belmont, CA:

Wood, Peter. 2003. "Diversity in America." *Society* 40,4(264):60–67.

Wood, Wendy, F. Y. Wong, and J. G. Cachere. 1991. "Effects of media violence on viewers' aggression in unconstrained social interaction." *Psychological Bulletin* 109:371–83.

Woollet, Anne, and Ann Phoenix. 1993. "Issues related to motherhood." In Stevi Jackson et al. (eds.), *Women's Studies Essential Readings*. New York: New York University.

Worell, Judith. 1996. "Feminist identity in a gendered world." In Joan C. Chrisler, Carla Golden, and Patricia D. Rozee (eds.), *Lectures on the Psychology of Women*. New York: McGraw-Hill.

World Bank. 2003. *World Development Indicators*. Washington, DC: World Bank.

World Health Organization. 2003. *World Health Report, 2003: Shaping the Future*. Geneva: WHO.

Worobey, J. 2001. "Associations between temperament and love attitudes in a college sample." *Personality and Individual Differences* 31(3):461–69.

Wu, Zheng. 1995. "Premarital cohabitation and postmarital cohabiting union formation." *Journal of Family Issues* 16(2):212–32.

Xiao, Hong. 2000. "Class, gender, and parental values in the 1990s." *Gender & Society* 14(6): 785–803.

Xiaogan, Liu. 2001. "A Taoist perspective: Appreciating and applying the principle of femininity." In John C. Raines and Daniel C. Maguire (eds.), *What Men Owe to Women: Men's Voices from World Religions*. (pp. 239–58). Albany: State University of New York.

Xu, Feng. 2000. *Women Migrant Workers in China's Economic Reform*. Houndmills, Basingstoke, Hampshire, UK: Macmillan.

Yaish, Meir, and Vered Kraus. 2003. "The consequences of economic restructuring for the gender earning gap in Israel, 1972–1995." *Work, Employment and Society* 17(1):5–28.

Yamaguchi, Kazuo. 2000. "Married women's gender-role attitudes and social stratification: Communities and differences between Japan and the United States." *International Journal of Sociology* 30(2):52–89.

Yancey, George. 2002. "Who interracially dates: An examination of the characteristics of those who have interracially dated." *Journal of Comparative Family Studies* 33(2):179–190.

Yeung, W. Jean, John F. Sandberg, and Pamela E. Davis-Kean. 2001. "Children's time with fathers in intact families." *Journal of Marriage and the Family* 63(1):136–54.

Yongping. Li. and P. Xizhe. 2000. "Age and sex structures." In Peng Xizhe and Zhigang Guo (eds.), *The Changing Population of China*. (pp. 64–76). Oxford, UK: Blackwell.

Young, Katherine K. 1987. "Introduction." In Arvind Sharma (ed.), *Women in World Religions*. Albany: State University of New York.

Young, Kevin, Philip White, and William McTeer. 1994. "Body talk: Male athletes reflect on sport, injury, and pain." *Sociology of Sport Journal* 11(2):175–94.

Young, Michael, George Denny, Tamera Young, and Raffy Luquis. 2000. "Sexual satisfaction among married women." *American Journal of Health Studies* 16(2):73–84.

Younger, Paul. 2002. *Playing Host to Deity: Festival Religion in South Indian Tradition*. New York: Oxford University.

Youth Advocate Program International. 2001. *Report on the Commercial Sexual Exploitation of Children in the United States*. November. Washington, DC. Available online at: http://www.yapi.org

Ypeij, Johanna Louisa. 2000. *Producing Against Poverty: Female and Male Micro-Entrepreneurs in Lima, Peru*. Amsterdam: Amsterdam University.

Yu, Wei-hsin. 2002. Jobs for mothers: Married women's labor force reentry and part-time, temporary employment." *Sociological Forum* 17(3): 493–52.

Yunus, Muhammad, and Alan Jolis. 1999. *Banker to the Poor: Micro-Lending and the Battle Against World Poverty*. New York: Public Affairs.

Zahl, Paul F. M. 2001. *Five Women of the English Reformation*. Grand Rapids, MI: William B. Eerdmans.

Zambrana, Ruth E. 1994. "Puerto Rican families and social well-being." In Maxine Baca Zinn and Bonnie Thornton Dill (eds.), *Women of Color in U.S. Society*. Philadelphia: Temple University.

Zdravomyslova, Elena. 2002. "Overview of the feminist movement in contemporary Russia." *Diogenes* 49,2(194):35–39.

Zeichner, Amos, Dominic J. Parrott, and Henry E. Adams. 2002. "Homophobia: Personality and attitudinal correlates." *Personality & Individual Differences* 32(7):1269–78.

Zenie-Ziegler, Wedad. 1988. *In Search of Shadows: Conversations with Egyptian Women*. London: Zed.

Zhang, Heather Xiaoquan. 1999. "Understanding changes in women's status in the context of the recent rural reform." In Jackie West, Zhao Minghua, Chang Xiangun, and Cheng Yuan (eds.), *Women of China: Economic and Social Transformation*. (pp. 45–66). London: Macmillan.

Zhang, Liru, and Jon Manon. 2000. "Gender and achievement: Understanding gender differences and similarities in mathematics assessment." Paper presented at the American Educational Research Association, New Orleans, LA, April.

Zhou, Xueguang, and Phyllis Moen. 2001. "Job-shift patterns of husbands and wives in urban China." In Hans-Peter Blossfeld and Sonja Drobnic (eds.), *Careers of Couples in Contemporary Societies: From Male Breadwinner to Dual Earner Families* (pp. 332–37). New York: Oxford University.

Zick, Cathleen D., W. Keith Bryant, and Eva Oesterbacka. 2001. "Mothers' employment, parental involvement and the implications for intermediate child outcomes." *Social Science Research* 30(1):25–49.

Zimmer, Michael. 2001. "Explaining marital dissolution: The role of spouses' traits." *Social Science Quarterly* 82(3):464–77.

Zimmerman, Laura. 2003. "Where are the women? The strange case of the missing feminists: When was the last time you saw one on TV?" *Women's Review of Books*.

Zimmerman, Toni Schindler, Shelley A. Haddock, Lisa R. Current, and Scott Ziemba. 2003.

"Intimate partnership: Foundation to the successful balance of family and work." *American Journal of Family Therapy* 31(2):107–24.

Znamensky, Vladimir, Keith T. Adams, Bruce S. McEwen, and Teresa A. Milner. 2003. "Estrogen levels regulate the subcellular distribution of phosphorylated akt in hippocampal CA1 dendrites." *Journal of Neuroscience* 23(March): 2340–47.

Zorza, Joan. 2001. "Alcohol and sexual violence among college students." In Allen J. Ottens and Kathy Hotellling (eds.), *Sexual Violence on Campus: Policies, Programs and Perspectives.* New York: Springer.

Name Index

Subject Index